D0439463

Jordan

Jenny Walker, Matthew D Firestone

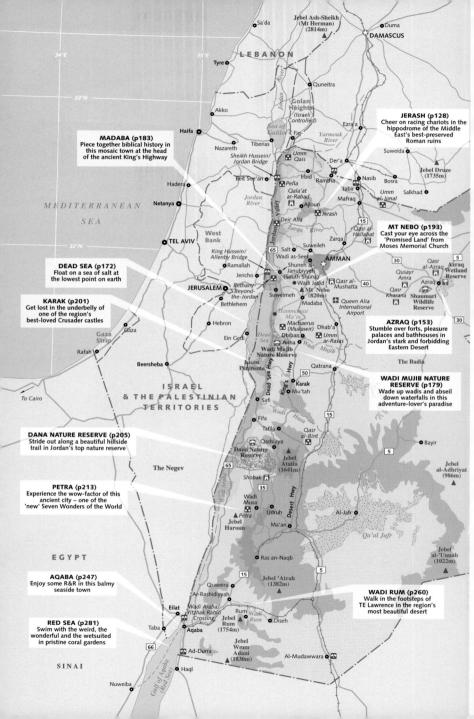

MADABA (p183)
Piece together biblical history in this mosaic town at the head of the ancient King's Highway

JERASH (p128)
Cheer on racing chariots in the hippodrome of the Middle East's best-preserved Roman ruins

MT NEBO (p193)
Cast your eye across the 'Promised Land' from Moses Memorial Church

DEAD SEA (p172)
Float on a sea of salt at the lowest point on earth

KARAK (p201)
Get lost in the underbelly of one of the region's best-loved Crusader castles

AZRAQ (p153)
Stumble over forts, pleasure palaces and bathhouses in Jordan's stark and forbidding Eastern Desert

WADI MUJIB NATURE RESERVE (p179)
Wade up wadis and abseil down waterfalls in this adventure-lover's paradise

DANA NATURE RESERVE (p205)
Stride out along a beautiful hillside trail in Jordan's top nature reserve

PETRA (p213)
Experience the wow-factor of this ancient city – one of the 'new' Seven Wonders of the World

AQABA (p247)
Enjoy some R&R in this balmy seaside town

WADI RUM (p260)
Walk in the footsteps of TE Lawrence in the region's most beautiful desert

RED SEA (p281)
Swim with the weird, the wonderful and the wetsuited in pristine coral gardens

Jebel Ash-Sheikh
(Mt Herman)
(2814m)

Sa'da

Duma

DAMASCUS

Tyre

LEBANON

Akko

Quneitra

Golan
Heights
(Israeli
Controlled)

Ezra'a

Suweida

Jebel Druze
(1735m)

Haifa

Tiberias

Sea of Galilee

Yarmouk River

Umm
Qais

Fiq

Der'a

Nasib

Bosra

Salkhad

Nazareth

Sheikh Hussein/
Jordan Bridge

Irbid

Ramtha

Jabir

Umm
al-Jimal

Hadera

Beit She'an

Pella

Qala'at
ar-Rabad

Ajloun

Mafraq

Netanya

Jordan River

Jerash

Qasr al-
Hallabat

Azraq
Wetland
Reserve

MEDITERRANEAN
SEA

Deir Alla

Zarqa River

Tel Aviv

West
Bank

King Hussein/
Allenby Bridge

Salt

Suweileh

Wadi as-Seer

AMMAN

Zarqa

Qusayr
Amra

Qasr
al-Azraq

Azraq

Jerusalem

Ramallah

Jericho

Shuneh al-
Janubiyyeh
(South Shuna)

Wadi Jadid

Qasr al-
Mushatta

Qasr
Kharana

Shaumari
Wildlife
Reserve

Bethany-
Beyond-
the-Jordan

Suweimeh

Mt Nebo
(820m)

Madaba

Queen Alia
International
Airport

Bethlehem

Hebron

Hammamat
Ma'in

Dhab'a

Ein Gedi

Macherus
(Mukawir)

Umm
ar-Rasas

Dhiban

Dead
Sea

Ariha

Wadi Mujib
Nature Reserve

Wadi Mujib

Gaza
Strip

Gaza

Lisan
Peninsula

Qatrana

The Badia

Rafah

Beersheba

ISRAEL
& THE PALESTINIAN
TERRITORIES

Karak

Mu'tah

Safi

King's Hwy

Dead Sea Hwy

To Cairo

Fifa

Wadi Hasa

Tafila

Qasr
al-Bint

Bayir

Jebel
al-Adhriyat
(986m)

Qadsiyya

The Negev

Dana Nature
Reserve

Jebel
Atatia
(1641m)

Shobak

Wadi Araba

Wadi
Musa

Udruh

Desert Hwy

Al-Jafr

Qa'al Jafr

EGYPT

Petra

Jebel
Haroun

Ma'an

Jebel
al-'Unnab
(1022m)

Ras an-Naqb

Quweira

Jebel 'Atrah
(1382m)

Eilat

Ay-Rashidiyyah

Wadi Araba/
Yitzhak Rabin
Crossing

Rum

Wadi
Rum

Diseh

Taba

Aqaba

Jebel
Rum
(1754m)

Ad-Durra

Jebel
Wmm
Adani
(1830m)

Al-Mudawwara

SINAI

Haql

Gulf of Aqaba (Red Sea)

Nuweiba

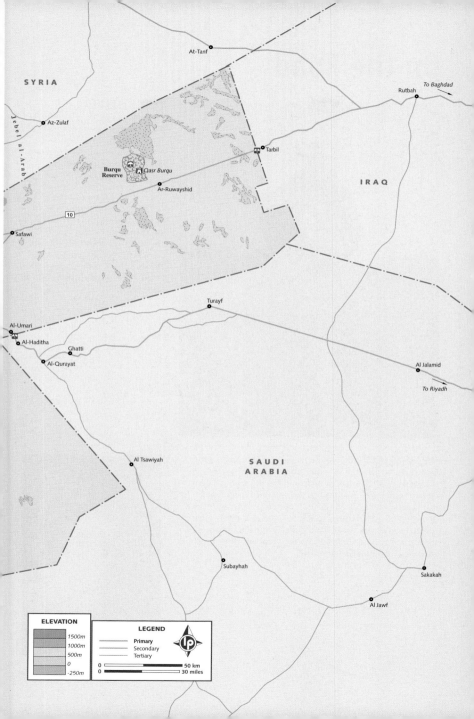

On the Road

JENNY WALKER
Coordinating Author

If a picture tells a thousand words, this shot ought to be censored. The horse and I are poised on the edge of a precipice and instructions to 'step this way' are not going down too well. We're on a short cut to Petra's Treasury (p223), but this cliff edge is as close as I dare get to that iconic building while on four legs. Despite the terror of the moment, I'll never forget galloping across the roof of the world that day, and thank Mahmoud for sharing his 'top spot' with me.

MATTHEW D FIRESTONE Jordan is a pretty far-flung and off-the-beaten-path destination, though I discovered just how true this statement could be while on assignment in the country's Eastern Desert. For roughly one long and lonely week, I spent hours and hours each day driving across barren gravel plains in search of the remote desert castles (p158). Most times, the only other person I laid eyes on was my own reflection in the mirror, though there is a certain calm and serenity that one finds when they're all alone in the middle of the desert.

For full author biographies see p340.

Jordan Highlights

Travellers are unfailingly enthusiastic about Jordan. 'It may be small in size,' said one traveller on the King's Highway, 'but it's big in heart'. While on the road, we asked travellers in Jordan to join the authors in commenting on their 'big-heart moments' in this magically diverse and historical country.

PATRICK SYDER

1 **BLOOMING BEAUTIFUL**

Carpets of scarlet poppies strewn across the desert near Siq al-Barid (Little Petra, p244), ribbons of pink oleander in the wadis at Dana (p205), the surprise flutter of velvet petals on a black iris along the King's Highway…Jordan is home to some of the region's most magnificent floral displays. For a truly sublime show, visit the remote ruins of Umm Qais (p141) in the far north of the country on a sunny afternoon in April: armfuls of knee-high daisies and nascent thistles, pale yellow hollyhocks and cerise-petalled mallow compete for a sliver of warmth between fallen masonry.

Jenny Walker, Lonely Planet Author, England

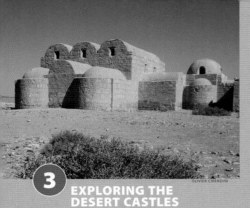

OLIVIER CIRENDINI

RUINS OF EMPIRE

If you thought Roman ruins were boring, think again. Jordan has some of the best ruins I've ever seen. The Roman Theatre (p98) and Citadel (p97) in Amman were highlights of my trip, and wandering along the colonnaded street of Jerash (p124) was awesome. With its baths, temples, theatres and hippodrome, I could really begin to imagine this Roman city in full swing. It must have been bustling with market traders, guards and gladiators – and you can still see the grooves worn into the limestone floor by chariot wheels. I loved the bagpipers and guys dressed as Roman gladiators (p128) too. This is history at its best.

Debbie Martin, Traveller, England

③ EXPLORING THE DESERT CASTLES

The gravel plains of eastern Jordan are home to the iconic desert castles (p158), a collection of early Umayyad structures that are remarkably incongruous with their barren surroundings. While visiting Jordan's far-flung eastern frontier requires a bit of advanced planning, the region is extremely rewarding for independent travellers in search of the less-beaten path. The desert castles are surreal sights that represent the furthest fringes of tourism in Jordan.

Matthew D Firestone, Lonely Planet Author, USA

MARK DAFFEY

MARK DAFFEY

④ THE HAND OF HOSPITALITY

Azraq (p153) is special for us. Here we saw the workings of the Royal Society for the Conservation of Nature (RSCN) firsthand – the wetlands being returned to life and craft industries being nurtured. Chechen mothers prepared wonderful food at Azraq Lodge (p155), working with their sons to make it special for us. This was the hand of hospitality that one would normally expect in someone's home rather than in a hotel.

Sibylle Hertig & Andreas Rüetschi, Travellers, Switzerland

HOW LOW CAN YOU GO?

The Dead Sea (p172), with its healing mud packs and salty, flat-calm, viscous water, was definitely my highlight. It's amazing to sit by the shore and think that all the mackerel and all the sticklebacks in the world are swimming around 1000ft above your head – and that's without getting your feet wet!

Sam Owen, Traveller, England

5

JANE SWEENEY

LAND OF MILK & HONEY

I came to Jordan looking for the biblical land of 'milk and honey' to feel, rather than just know, that it existed. What struck me most were the mountains. They are really different – smooth-capped, bright and colourful, especially in Petra (p213). They look so lovely early in the morning – not just lumps of rock but almost animate. Each rock, wherever we went in Jordan, seemed to be waiting to tell us something frightening but important – almost like talismans from the past.

Agnes Quadros, Traveller, India

6

JOHN ELK III

MARK DAFFEY

HANDMADE HISTORY

For centuries, Madaba (p183) has been a crossroad for caravans moving goods for sale, legions of armies pushing the borders of their empires, and pilgrims driven by their own faiths in search of the Promised Land. I loved it because to this day it retains the marks of those cultural exchanges – in its old buildings, churches, museums and its people. Perhaps the best visual representation of this rich past is in the town's magnificent collection of mosaics. It fascinates me how this tradition of mosaic-making continues today, not least in the town's unique mosaic school (p188).

Fernando Perego, Traveller, Peru

8 TEA & TALK

I had an extraordinary time at Mukawir (p195). It is a beautiful place and I was the only visitor. People in the village handed me from one person to another – for tea and a chat, and more tea and more chat! Even the bus driver waited for me as he explained that his was the last bus back to Madaba. I didn't see much of the ruins that day, but I learnt more about Jordanian life than I expected.

Nathalie Ollier, Traveller, Belgium

HANAN ISACHA

9 A PATH WELL-TRODDEN

DAMIEN SIMONE

You may not be walking in the path of literal kings, but in traversing the King's Highway (p182) you are most certainly following in some pretty big footsteps. These include those of the Nabataeans (their fabled city of Petra lies at the end of the King's Highway), the Romans (whose military outpost at Umm ar-Rasas is a Unesco World Heritage Site) and the Crusaders (the castles of which, at Karak and Shobak, are highlights in their own right).

Jenny Walker, Lonely Planet Author, England

ON THE EDGE AT DANA

If you want an authentic taste of the variety of wildlife, spectacular scenery and history of the Dana Nature Reserve (p205), you can't do better than to take the Steppe Trail from the campsite at Rummana to the 6000-year-old hilltop village of Dana. You walk along the hoodoo-haunted rim of Wadi Shagg al Kelbe, and then contour around the steep, rocky slopes of Jebel Rummana with the depths of Wadi Dana yawning below. On the way you might be lucky enough to see the vivid blue flash of a Sinai Agama lizard scampering across the rocks, while secretive ibex graze in the sheltered gullies.

Roly Smith, Traveller, England

ANDERS BLOMQVIST

PETRA COOL

Visit Petra (p213) during the cooler months! This allows for an amazing experience free from the throngs of peak-season visitors. We were able to walk down the Siq with the only sound being the echo of a horse carriage and to have parts of Petra absolutely to ourselves. You can take 'tourist-free' photos of beautiful Petra and its Bedouin environment, camels and donkeys. More practical advantages include not having to carry so much water and enjoying a comfortable temperature for walks to the Monastery (p230) and High Place of Sacrifice (p225).

**Sharon Stark, Traveller,
New Zealand**

CLINT LUCAS

GETTING IN TOUCH WITH THE SOUL

What a delight for our family visiting Jordan, garden of the Holy Land. When you look at the mosaic map in Madaba (p184) depicting Bethlehem and neighbouring holy sites, it has more significance than just reading books. The stunning Bethany-Beyond-the-Jordan (p169), where John baptised Jesus Christ, inspires meditation. But paramount to our visit was Mt Nebo (p193): atop the mountain, it makes you feel as if you are back in ancient times contemplating the Jordan Valley, Dead Sea, Jericho and Jerusalem as Moses did. Go to the Serpentine Cross at sunset and the Promised Land will get in touch with your soul.

Xavier Hay, Traveller, France

JEAN ROBERT

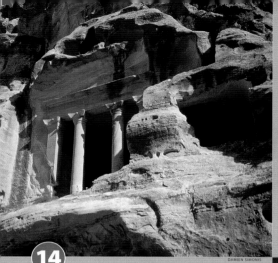

TEA IN A TENT

Wadi Rum (p260) was a highlight of our Jordan trip. A nice young Jordanian man drove us through the desert – very remote, and mountains with a great variety of colours. Take the Wadi Rum 1 circuit, which is highly recommended and less tourist-oriented. Wadi Rum 2 is also interesting though there are more people visiting it. You can share Bedouin tea in a tent but please, do not take a photo of a Bedouin person before asking permission – they are human beings, not photo opportunities.

Irene & Gerardo Gerson, Travellers, Argentina

14 TRAVELLING THROUGH TIME

There's this wonderful site on the road out of Siq al-Barid (Little Petra, p244); you must go there. Archaeologists go crazy about this place – it's a pre-pottery Neolithic (PPN) site. It's better preserved than Al-Beidha (p245), which is also a good site. In fact, there are so many fascinating sites you could spend a lifetime here and not see them all. Like Khirbet Feinan (p205): we walked around the old copper workings and it was like going back in time. Nothing has been touched – it's as if the workers have just stepped out for a break.

Francesca Balossi, Traveller, Italy

13

15 FOODSCAPES OF AMMAN

While Amman (p86) lacks the monumental Islamic architecture typical of other Middle Eastern capitals, you don't have to look very hard to find reminders of where you are in the world. Indeed, the streets of Amman are overflowing with typical Arabic-style restaurants (p108), offering up regional specialties such as shish kebab, hummus, felafel and some seriously syrupy sweets. After you've indulged in your fill, settle the stomach with a steaming glass of *shai* (tea) and the occasional puff from an apple-scented nargileh (water pipe).

Matthew D Firestone, Lonely Planet Author, USA

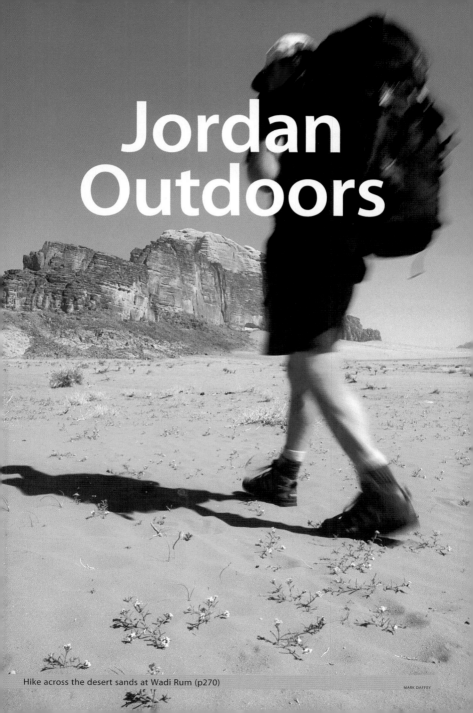

Jordan
Outdoors

Hike across the desert sands at Wadi Rum (p270)

MARK DAFFEY

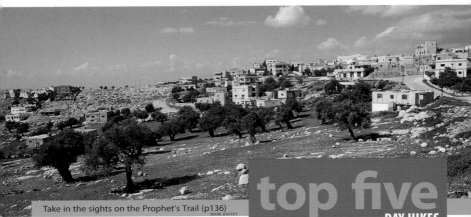

Take in the sights on the Prophet's Trail (p136)
MARK DAFFEY

top five
DAY HIKES

While Jordan may not be the first place that comes to mind when planning an outdoor adventure, this tiny speck of a country is incredibly underrated. One of the world's great travel secrets, Jordan is more accessible than the Amazon, warmer than Nepal, cheaper than the USA, and less touristy than Morocco. And while much of the Middle East is embroiled in conflict and strife, Jordan remains an oasis of relative peace and tranquillity.

Looking for some good day hikes? Here are a few of our favourites:

Ajloun Nature Reserve (p135) Follow the Prophet's Trail through fruit orchards and oak forests to the birthplace of the prophet Elijah

Dana Nature Reserve (p205) The hike from Wadi Dana to Feinan goes through breathtaking rock escarpments and sandstone cliffs

Petra (p230) Jordan's most famous archaeological site is criss-crossed by dozens of trails that were laid down by the ancient Nabataean traders

Wadi Mujib Nature Reserve (p179) The reserve's signature Malaqi Trail combines slot canyon hiking and waterfall rappelling

Wadi Rum (p260) Home to the country's best hiking, Wadi Rum is regarded as one of the most captivating deserts on the planet

What Jordan lacks in size, it more than makes up for in beauty, especially if you're a fan of dramatic deserts. It's home to Wadi Rum, where the epic *Lawrence of Arabia* was filmed. It's also home to some of the region's best rock-climbing spots, and provides ample opportunities for wild camping amid rugged landscapes. The country can be explored on foot, by cycle and on camelback.

When you're ready to swap the sand for the sea, head south to the coast, where you can grab some diving gear and take a plunge into the Red Sea. While Egypt garners most of the international spotlight, Jordan also boasts world-class diving, yet attracts only a fraction of the crowds. Indeed, Jordan is ripe for adventure travel, both on land and in the sea.

While your friends and family may question your choice of destination, ignore the temptation to explore more hyped-up countries, and embrace the pleasures of off-the-beaten-path travel. But, do us a favour and don't tell too many people – after all, we certainly don't want to be the ones who let the secret out…

HIKING

According to an ancient Arab proverb, 'the deeper you go into the desert, the closer you come to God'. Regardless of your religious or spiritual convictions, Jordan's deserts have a magnetic draw that is irresistible to hikers and trekkers. Jordan has been traversed over the ages by countless groups including early hunters and gatherers, Greek soldiers and Roman legions, Christian and Islamic missions, Ottoman and Mamluk marauders and nomadic Bedouin. In fact, many of the country's most famed hiking trails have been laid down over the course of several millennia, yet have changed little since the dawn of antiquity. With the help of a local guide and with a desire to leave behind the trappings of civilisation, you can penetrate the heart of Jordan's hauntingly barren yet dramatic desert landscapes.

For more information, see p289.

DIVING

Divers do it deeper – or so the saying goes – though there's plenty to see in the shallows off the coast of Aqaba. Whether you're an old salty dog or still wet behind the ears, the Red Sea impresses veteran and rookie divers alike. From crumbling wrecks and towering reefs to circling sharks and cruising turtles, Jordan's underwater world never fails to impress. And, while the vast majority of Middle East–bound divers head to neighbouring Egypt, Jordan's obscurity as a diving destination is partially responsible for the pristine nature of its reefs. So, strap on your fins, take the plunge and best of luck in finding Nemo!

For more information, see p277.

Explore the reefs of Aqaba (p281)

JOHN ELK III

top five
REASONS TO DIVE

Though few people need convincing, here are a few reasons why you should get your feet wet:

- A bad day's diving is better than a good day's work
- Deep diving gets you higher than smoking a narguileh (water pipe)
- Everything looks bigger underwater
- People look sexy in skin-tight neoprene rubber
- Because the mile-high club is for amateurs

A home in the desert at Wadi Rum (p272)
BRIAN CRUICKSHANK

CAMPING

Sleeping beneath the stars takes on a whole new meaning in Jordan. Deep in the desert, far from any contaminating sources of light pollution, the night skies shine with celestial brilliance. However, back-country camping is not for the casual outdoorsman (or outdoorswoman) as getting lost – or worse – is a very real possibility. Fortunately, aspiring campers can employ the services of Bedouin – nomadic people who have inhabited the deserts of the Middle East for generations on end. With the help of a reliable guide, and perhaps a few camels to carry your gear, the vast nothingness of the desert is yours to explore.

For more information, see p285.

CYCLING

There is no more rewarding means of transport than cycling, though cycling in Jordan isn't easy. You are going to need strength, determination and nerves of steel to pedal your way across lonely desert highways and wide-open vistas – not to mention a few spare tyres here and there. Dehydration can kill, so heed our simple advice – pack lots and lots of water, and go heavy on the sunscreen.

For more information, see p315.

A hot and dusty cycle to the Dead Sea (p315) 1APIX

top five
HELL (AND HEAVEN) ON WHEELS

Think you've got what it takes to cycle Jordan? Be prepared for the following:

- Blazing heat – the mercury boils out in the desert, so drink plenty of fluids
- Psycho drivers – Jordanians are a polite people, at least until they get behind the wheel of a car
- Crazy kids – children get their kicks by hurling rocks at passing bikers – wear your helmet
- Random potholes – Jordan's roads aren't in the best of shape, so carry lots of spare parts
- Blood, sweat and glory – you're going to bleed and sweat and bleed some more, but it'll all be worth it in the end

CLIMBING BOOKS, CLUBS & WEBSITES

Before you hit the rocks, check out the following:

- *Treks & Climbs in Wadi Rum, Jordan* and *Walks & Scrambles in Wadi Rum* by Tony Howard and Di Taylor.
- *Trekking & Canyoning in the Jordanian Dead Sea Rift* by Itai Haviv.
- Adventure Peaks (www.adventurepeaks.com) organises climbing trips to Wadi Rum.
- Wadi Rum Rock Page (www.wadirum.net) is an online guide to climbing routes at Wadi Rum.

CLIMBING

Being stuck between a rock and a hard place isn't so bad, assuming you're strapped into a sturdy harness and tied to a taut rope. If this sounds like your kind of thrill ride, then you'll be happy to hear that Jordan has some of the best crags in the Middle East. As if this isn't enough of an incentive to grab your cams and hexes, you'll also be happy to hear that rainfall is rare in the desert, which means that you'll almost never have to worry about losing your grip.

For more information, see p271 and p291.

CAMEL TREKKING

There are few Middle Eastern experiences more quintessential than camel trekking. While these ill-tempered and foul-smelling beasts of burden aren't always the most cooperative of creatures, they do provide a memorable way of crossing the desert plains, and riding camelback is certainly preferable to walking. And, while there is a bit of a learning curve (to say the least!), all you really need to do is grab the reins, find your balance and give a loud 'Yallah! Yallah!'.

For more information, see p269 and p289.

top five
CAMEL CRED

Camels may be the ships of the desert, but they're also 100% eco-friendly. Here's why:

- Camels are powered by grass and shrubs, not precious fossil fuels
- Cars leak harmful fluids: camels only take a leak when necessary
- Camel poop burns hotter and brighter than you'd imagine
- Camel exhaust smells bad, but doesn't contribute to global warming
- Camels are recyclable, mainly in the form of shish kebab

Alternative transport, Jordan style   ANDERS BLOMQVIST

Contents

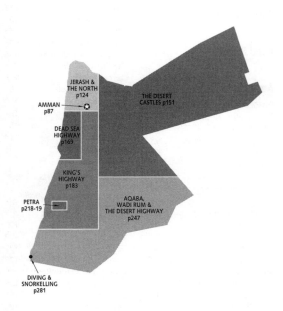

Destination Jordan

So it's official. Petra, jewel in the crown of Jordan's antiquities, has been declared by popular ballot as one of the 'new' Seven Wonders of the World. Jordan's authorities, together with tour operators, hoteliers and even the Bedouin of Petra themselves, have been quick to understand the commercial value of this marketing coup, and prices have risen accordingly. The magnificent rock-hewn city of the Nabataeans hardly needed further billing. Since Johann Ludwig Burckhardt rediscovered it in the 19th century, it has been a favourite destination for Europeans – and at sunset on a winter's day, when the rose-pink city catches alight, it's easy to see why it has charmed a new generation of visitors.

Not to be outdone by Petra's success, Wadi Rum – that epic landscape of TE Lawrence and David Lean's *Lawrence of Arabia* – is a contender as one of the Seven *Natural* Wonders of the World. Surely two such accolades would be entirely disproportionate to the minimal size of Jordan.

But Jordan, straddling the ancient Holy Land of the world's three great monotheistic religions, and once an important trading centre of the Roman Empire, is no stranger to punching above its weight. Stand on Mt Nebo, newly consecrated by Pope John II, and survey the land promised to Moses; unfurl a veil at Mukawir, where Salome cast a spell over men in perpetuity; float in the Dead Sea, beside a pillar of salt, reputed to be Lot's disobedient wife. Go just about anywhere in Jordan and you'll find every stone bears a tale.

With so much history wrapped up in this tiny desert kingdom, it's easy to overlook the modern face of Jordan – something the government is trying to address in ambitious tourist developments at Aqaba and along the Dead Sea. And 'ambitious' is an appropriate word. In a country of minimal resources – where water is in critically short supply, arable land accounts for less than 5% of the landmass, and unemployment and inflation are hovering around 15% – the disproportionate investment in Jordan's coastal pleasure domes appears to border on the reckless.

This is especially so when you consider the neighbourhood it shares. Wedged between Iraq and Israel and the Palestinian Territories, Jordan has had to shelter millions of refugees in recent decades, straining health care and education systems and changing the demography of the country forever. Palestinians now account for the majority of the population involved in all aspects of government and trade. The Bedouin population, meanwhile, contends with a minimum wage of $155 a month.

If the Seven Wonders of the World ballot showed anything, however, it was the extent to which, despite the mixed origins of its people, the current economic difficulties and the insecurity of life in a volatile region, Jordanians are united in their pride for their country. And there's a lot to be proud of. The monarchy under King Abdullah continues the acclaimed role of peacemaker between Arab and Western interests, Jordan is a regional leader in protecting the environment and promoting sustainable tourism, and its capital city is enjoying a modern renaissance.

In common with many Arab countries, Jordan is at a crossroads as it shapes up to integration within the modern, global community. Unlike many of its neighbours, however, Jordan has recognised that the past is part of its future, and while the politicians plan a way to maximise on the country's unique legacy, the Bedouin still herd their sheep across an unchanged landscape in effortless continuity with the ancient past.

FAST FACTS

Population: 6.2 million

Population growth rate: 2.3%

Inflation: 15.5%

GDP: US$31.01

Main exports: clothing, pharmaceuticals, potash, phosphates, fertilisers, vegetables

Average annual income: US$5000

Average male life expectancy: 76 years

Average female life expectancy: 81 years

Male literacy rate: 95%

Female literacy rate: 85%

Getting Started

Jordan is an easy and enjoyable country to visit. The logistics of travel, from obtaining visas on arrival to accessing the liberally-sprinkled ATMs, are a breeze. Best of all, as Jordan is a compact country and travel times are short, you can enjoy a range of world-class sights within a relatively short period of time. You can even combine a visit with other Middle Eastern top spots from Jerusalem to Damascus, both just a few hours by road. Jordan is one country where it pays to have a little more cash at your disposal. Enjoying a dive in the spectacular Red Sea, taking a 4WD excursion in Wadi Rum, hiking with a guide in Dana Nature Reserve or staying at a luxury spa on the Dead Sea are highlights well worth saving for.

WHEN TO GO

See Climate Charts (p292) for more information.

For a small country, Jordan has an extraordinary range of climates. The best time to visit is in spring (March to May), when wildflowers put on a spectacular display, and autumn (September to November), when the daytime temperatures are not too extreme.

Winter can be surprisingly cold. Snow in Amman is not unheard of (even Petra gets the occasional fall) and the deserts can be freezing, especially at night. Aqaba is the exception, with average daytime maximum temperatures of around 20°C in January.

A FAMILY AFFAIR

Eid al-Fitr, the great celebration at the end of Ramadan, is primarily a family occasion. At this time, public transport is heavily booked and hotel rooms are hard to find, especially in Aqaba.

In high summer (July and August) the weather in the humid Jordan Valley is oppressive, with suffocating daytime highs exceeding 35°C. It's also fiercely hot in desert areas, though the dry heat is easier to tolerate. Festivals are welcome summer distractions.

It's best to avoid the month of Ramadan as visitors are obliged to refrain from eating, drinking or smoking in public during the day and many restaurants close for the whole period. See p296 for more on Ramadan.

Note also that many of the excellent trails operated in Jordan's Dana, Wadi Mujib and Ajloun nature reserves only operate between April and October.

COSTS & MONEY

By neighbouring standards, Jordan is not a cheap country, and the rising price of oil is fuelling inflation to such an extent that prices in this

---

DON'T LEAVE HOME WITHOUT...

- Your driver's licence (p317) and Professional Association of Diving Instructors (PADI) diving card
- A Syrian visa if you are heading north (see p303)
- A Jordanian visa if heading from Israel and the Palestinian Territories across King Hussein/ Allenby Bridge (see p310)
- A sleeping sheet if you're staying overnight in Wadi Rum
- A torch (flashlight) for exploring archaeological sites
- Mosquito repellent and net if you intend to hike and camp through wadis or sleep on hotel roofs (as permitted, for example, at some smaller hotels in Petra)
- A hat, sunscreen, sunglasses, long sleeves and covering for your neck if you're planning a summer visit. A water carrier that fits a 1.5L bottle is also useful.

book, especially for accommodation and transport, may have increased by the time you read this. That said, you can still find value for money, especially if you can afford a few extra dinars for a midrange hotel, or for a purchase from a quality craft shop. If you're on a tight budget, there are plenty of cheap sleeps and eats in major towns if you don't mind stripping back to basics (JD4 for a rooftop mattress, for example, or JD8 for a bed in a dorm).

More liveable budget hotels charge about JD15/20/25 for a single/double/triple. A good midrange single/double costs from JD25/35 up to JD65/75, while top-end doubles start at JD80.

Street snacks such as a felafel or shwarma sandwich cost just a few fils and you can get a decent budget meal for JD1 to JD3. In mid-range restaurants, main courses start from around JD4. Jordan's top restaurants offer excellent value for money (especially in comparison with Western prices), with main courses starting from JD8, sumptuous buffets from JD15 and quality dining experiences from JD35 (usually including wine).

Public transport costs about JD2 per hour in a comfortable, long-distance private bus, or less than JD1 per hour of travel in a public bus or minibus. Public buses and minibuses can be exasperatingly slow however, as most towns are linked by sporadic services that only leave when full. Car hire is reasonable and recommended, especially for exploring the King's Highway, the Dead Sea Highway and remote Eastern desert.

The entrance fee to Petra (JD31 for three days) hasn't increased for a number of years. If you're on a tight budget it may seem steep but it's worth every dinar! Entry to other popular sights such as Jerash costs JD8, but most places are free or cost just a dinar or two.

TRAVELLING RESPONSIBLY

In a region only recently concerned with conservation, it's refreshing to find that Jordan is ahead of the game. Not only are the authorities – especially through the work of the Royal Society for the Conservation of Nature (RSCN) – keen to promote sustainable tourism with regard to Jordan's natural heritage, they are also keen to maintain the country's cultural heritage by preserving Islamic values, supporting arts and craft initiatives (such as soap-making at Ajloun, see p136) and supporting traditional lifestyles (as with the employment of Bedouin drivers in Wadi Rum).

Of course it's not easy balancing the need for increased tourism against the environmental cost of more visitors. While tourism revenue at Wadi Rum, for example, is needed for the upkeep of the protected area, it's hard to minimise the impact of more feet and wheels upon a fragile desert ecosystem. A balance can be achieved, however, with the cooperation of visitors.

If you'd like to know how to minimise the negative impact of your visit, or contribute positively through your travel experience in Jordan, then you may like to use the following checklist to inform the choices you make on the road.

- **Save water** Jordan has a critical water shortage (see p73 and p154 for the consequences of excessive water use).
- **Use local guides and services** Not only is interacting with local people, such as the Bedouin in Wadi Rum and Petra (see p55), an opportunity to learn about a unique way of life, it's also a way of helping preserve local traditions.

HOW MUCH?

Souvenir keffiyah (scarf) from JD5

Postcard 200 fils

Cup of tea 500 fils

Cup of Western coffee JD2

See also Lonely Planet Index, *inside front cover.*

COSTS PER DAY

The minimum cost per day for budget travel is between JD15 to JD30. Upgrade to midrange hotels and chartered taxis for JD60. For JD100, you can throw in the cost of some car hire.

RSCN & SUSTAINABLE TOURISM

The Royal Society for the Conservation of Nature (RSCN) is a byword in Jordan for sustainable tourism. See www.rscn .org.jo for details.

- **Buy wisely** Shop at craft centres where profits are returned to local communities (see p197 for an idea of how this helps).
- **Use our GreenDex** The list of sustainable travel options on p358 will help in planning destination-friendly travel. Also see below for a review of Jordan's top sustainable tourism initiatives.
- **Dress and behave respectfully** Many Jordanians see the liberalisation of customs and manners as a bad habit caught from the West and an erosion of their cultural and Islamic heritage (see p56).
- **Spend money...** A few travellers think it's clever to avoid entrance fees and survive on muesli they brought from home. If you're one of them, try to make your visit count more positively by spending a little!
- **...but don't give it away** Give tips only for services rendered (such as buying a souvenir from kids at Petra) to discourage the counterproductive activity of begging.

THE COMMUNITY-BASED TRAVEL TRAIL   *Ethan Gelber*

In this age of eco-awareness, responsible tourism plays an important part in community development. Interest in Jordan's nature reserves has, for example, demonstrated how their appeal can economically benefit neighbouring communities. This is certainly true of protected lands in which the Royal Society for the Conservation of Nature (RSCN) has a hand, especially around Ajloun, Dibeen, Azraq, Shaumari, the Dead Sea, Mujib, Dana and Wadi Rum. But more and more local communities, large and small, are also uniting behind other tourism endeavours that return profits directly to the community.

Feeling the Local Motion

- **Abraham Path Initiative** (p52; www.abrahampath.org; ☎ 02-647 5766, 077-7072212) has waymarked a one-day Al Ayoun Trail through villages in the Ajloun area. Call ahead for a descriptive brochure.
- **JARA** (Jebel Amman Residents Association; www.jara-jordan.com) is a village initiative within a city. It spearheaded the now-famous Souk Jara street market (Fawzi al-Malouf Street, open 10am to 10pm Friday, May to August) and other projects that enhance the historic centre of Amman.
- The nonprofit **Jordan Living History Association** (JLHA) develops and promotes accurate historical re-enactments and supports 65 people in Jerash alone, including many army veterans – a chronically underemployed group. JLHA's most spectacular undertaking is the **Roman Army Chariot Experience of Jerash** (p128; www.jerashchariots.com). It also operates at Petra (Nabataean Court), the Ajloun and Karak castles (Salahadin warriors) and the Roman Theatre (orators).
- **Madaba Tourism Development Association** (www.visitmadaba.org) is a voluntary community-based organisation developing tourism products in and around Madaba that use local skills and resources.
- **Neighbours Paths** (www.foeme.org) are four community-based tours in off-the-beaten-track Dead Sea Basin areas along the Jordan River. It focuses on cross-border issues like water and peace-building.
- **Zikra Initiative** (www.zikrajordan.org) is a fast-developing, homespun program that connects urbanites (Jordanians and internationals) to people living in rural areas. A modest participation fee helps fund activities and provision microloans for local village 'entrepreneurs'.

Getting Crafty

Some Jordan craft shops display quality wares fashioned as part of community-based income-generating programs:

- **Jordan Handicraft Producers Association** (Map p90; ☎ 4626295; 34 Khirfan Street, Jebel Amman; ⏱ 8am-4pm Sat-Thu), with 500 members working from home and small workshops, has inaugurated a new showroom in a 120-year-old stone building.

TRAVEL LITERATURE

Johann Ludwig (also known as Jean Louis) Burckhardt spent many years in the early-19th century travelling extensively through Jordan, Syria and the Holy Land, disguised as a pilgrim and compiling a unique and scholarly travelogue detailing every facet of the culture and society he encountered along the way. The result is *Travels in Syria and the Holy Land*, which documents his 'rediscovery' of Petra (see p215).

The redoubtable Englishwoman Gertrude Bell wrote a few memoirs about her travels in the region in the early 20th century, including the somewhat dated and light-hearted *The Desert and the Sown*, though it's mostly concerned with Syria.

TE Lawrence's classic *Seven Pillars of Wisdom* is one of those books that most people have heard of but few people have read. That's not altogether surprising given its long-winded accounts of skirmishes on

- **Jordan River Foundation** (p114; www.jordanriver.jo) has its primary showroom in Jebel Amman, displaying works from its three major projects – Bani Hamida Women's Weaving Project (p197), Al-Karma Centre Jordan River Designs Project (embroidery) and Wadi Al-Rayan Handicraft Project (woven cattail-reed and banana-leaf products).

- Jordanian Hashemite Fund for Human Development's **Beit al-Bawadi** (p114; www.beitalbawadi .com) in Abdoun hosts a ceramics showroom, weekly **farmers market** (Souq al-Ard; ⏰ 10am-2pm Sat Oct-Jul) and community-development partners tackling recycling, poverty reduction and hunger alleviation.

- **Made in Jordan** (p242; www.madeinjordan.com), in Wadi Musa, sells crafts from various local enterprises. Products include olive oil, soap, paper, ceramics, table runners, embroidery, camel-hair shawls and bags.

- **Nature shops** figure prominently at the Wild Jordan Centre (p114) in Amman and RSCN visitor centres in Ajloun, Azraq, Mujib, Dana and Wadi Rum.

- **Noor Al-Hussein Foundation** (www.nooralhusseinfoundation.org) maintains a showroom in Aqaba (p259) as well as links to now-independent projects selling NHF-labelled products in Iraq Al-Amir (p119), Salt (p121) and Wadi Musa (Nabataean Women's Cooperative).

Dwelling on Dwellings

There are a few sustainably run accommodation options in Jordan.

- **Ammarin Bedouin Camp** (p245; www.bedouincamp.net) near Little Petra.

- **Dana Hotel** (p209; dana.hotel@yahoo.com) overlooking the Dana Biosphere Reserve.

- **Ibbin Apartments** (Map p126; ☎ 0795636154; r JD20-40) are 24 community cooperative-owned, fully equipped, two-bedroom lodgings. Experience rural life in Jordan just 15km northwest of Jerash.

- **RSCN** (www.rscn.org.jo) runs ethical and sustainable accommodation with nature and community sensibilities in mind.

- **Bedouin cooperative campgrounds** at Wadi Rum (p272) and Diseh (p275).

Finding Fair Services

- The **Jordan Inbound Tour Operators Association** (www.jitoa.org), a voluntary umbrella organisation, is a good place to research tour operators.

- **Fair Trade Jordan** (www.fairtradejordan.org) has an online database that reviews all tourism-related products and services according to responsible criteria.

TOP 10

JORDAN

DRIVES

Jordan is a wonderful place to hire a car and go exploring, as the landscape changes dramatically from desert to temperate within a remarkably short distance. For details of some of the most spectacular drives linking the King's Highway and Dead Sea Highway, see the boxed text, p170.

1 Umm Qais (p141) to Al-Himma (p145): Along the border of three nations

2 Mt Nebo (p193) to Suweimeh: Panoramic views over the Promised Land

3 Dead Sea Panorama (p177) to Dead Sea Highway: Views of the salt sea

4 Dead Sea Highway, south of Safi (p180): Fields red with tomatoes

5 Madaba (p183) to Hammamat Ma'in (p177): Hell's cauldron of sulphurous springs

6 Across Wadi Mujib (p198) and Wadi Hasa (p204): The 'Grand Canyons' of Jordan

7 Qadsiyya to Dana Guest House (p209): Unravelling views of Wadi Dana

8 Around Wadi Rum (p269): Driving in the dunes in a 4WD

9 Little Petra (p244) to Feinan (p205): A superb journey through time

10 Aqaba (p247) to Azraq (p153): Across the inauspicious *Badia*

ECO-EXPERIENCES

There are heaps of opportunities to support Jordan's conservation efforts while enjoying some of the best hospitality and wilderness areas. Here are 10 'must-dos' if you're keen to travel green.

1 Hike to see Ajloun's soapmakers at work (p136).

2 Savour a wild-berry smoothie in Amman's Wild Jordan Centre (p95).

3 Learn about Azraq's Chechens over a home-cooked feast at Azraq Lodge (p155).

4 Buy a hand-loomed rug from the Bani Hamida workshop (p197)

5 Wake up to birdsong at beautiful Rummana campground (p210)

6 Enjoy a vegetarian supper in candlelit Feinan Lodge (p210)

7 Give your sunglasses an embroidered treat from Dana craft shop (p207)

8 Buy a handmade string of cloves in Petra (p213)

9 Take a camel trip in the company of a Bedouin guide (p289)

10 Overnight with the Bedouin at a camp in Wadi Rum (p272)

RUINS

Almost every stone in Jordan has a history, and the stone piles listed here have more history than most.

1 Jerash (p124): Superb Roman ruins

2 Karak Castle (p199): Biggest Crusader castle in Jordan

3 Khirbet Tannour (p204): Minimal Nabataean site in spectacular landscape

4 Madaba (p195): Remote Bronze Age dolmens

5 Petra (p217): Unparalleled Nabataean capital

6 Qusayr Amra (p161): Saucy frescoes in a 'desert castle'

7 Shobak Castle (p211): Remote Crusader castle

8 Umm al-Jimal (p151): Abandoned basalt village in Eastern desert

9 Umm Qais (p141): Roman and Byzantine city

10 Umm ar-Rasas (p197): World Heritage site of churches and mosaics

---

UNESCO WORLD HERITAGE SITES IN JORDAN

- Petra (listed 1985; p213)
- Qusayr Amra (listed 1985; p161)
- Dana Nature Reserve (Biosphere Reserve, listed 1998; p205)
- Umm ar-Rasas (listed 2004; p197)

---

horseback. Nevertheless, Lawrence documents the Arab Revolt of 1919 in 'colour and flair' if not without partiality; he is at his most inspired when describing the desert scenery of Wadi Rum.

Annie Caulfield's *Kingdom of the Film Stars: Journey into Jordan* is an entertaining, personal account of the author's relationship with a Bedouin man in Jordan. Similarly, Marguerite van Geldermalsen's *Married to a Bedouin* is a sympathetic account of bringing up a family in the ancient city of Petra. *Walking the Bible* by Bruce Feiler is an engaging travelogue that follows Feiler's travels through Egypt, Israel and the Palestinian Territories and Jordan, searching for the physical roots of the Bible. Feiler shows considerably more empathy for people and places in Israel and the Palestinian Territories than those of the Arab world, but writes well on the archaeology of the Holy Land.

For books on Petra, see p218.

FILMS

Don't miss David Lean's epic *Lawrence of Arabia* (1962), starring Peter O'Toole as Lawrence and filmed partly in Wadi Rum. The lesser-known *A Dangerous Man: Lawrence After Arabia* (1991) stars Ralph Fiennes in one of his earliest film roles.

Petra's Siq and Treasury landed a starring role as the hiding place of the Holy Grail in the closing scenes of Stephen Spielberg's *Indiana Jones and the Last Crusade* (1989), starring Harrison Ford and Sean Connery. The film plays nightly in the budget guesthouses of Wadi Musa.

INTERNET RESOURCES

Bible Places (www.bibleplaces.com) Interesting rundown on biblical sights in Jordan and Israel and the Palestinian Territories.

Jordan Jubilee (www.jordanjubilee.com) The best website about Jordan, loaded with practical tips; offers a wonderful window onto Jordanian society.

Jordan Tourism Board (www.visitjordan.com) Good official website.

Lonely Planet (www.lonelyplanet.com). The Thorn Tree has an active range of Jordan experts who offer good advice if you post a question.

Madaba (www.madaba.freeservers.com) Excellent description of Madaba's attractions and other nearby sites.

Ministry of Tourism and Antiquities (www.tourism.jo) Online brochures, maps and more

RSCN (www.rscn.org.jo) Accessible information about Jordan's environmental and ecotourism projects. The 'Adventures' and 'Wild Jordan' sections are particularly recommended.

A CLASSIC THAT NEARLY WASN'T

Lawrence left the manuscript of his masterpiece at 'Reading Station', while changing trains' in 1919. He rewrote a second draft from memory but burned 'all but one page' of it. The third version, partially written in Amman, has endured.

Itineraries

CLASSIC ROUTES

IN THE FOOTSTEPS OF KINGS
One Week / Amman to Aqaba

Get a taste for Jordan's Roman history at the **citadel** (p97) in Amman on day one, before cheering on the racing chariots at the spectacular Roman ruins of **Jerash** (p124) on day two. On day three, piece together a biblical history in the mosaic town of **Madaba** (p183) and, like Moses, survey the Promised Land from neighbouring **Mt Nebo** (p193).

Spend day four following the caravans of history by travelling the ancient King's Highway to Petra, crossing the mighty Wadi Mujib gorge. Visit the Crusader castles in **Karak** (p201) and **Shobak** (p211) and listen for hooves clattering through cobbled corridors.

Make an early start on day five to see the **Siq** (p223) at Petra at its best. Climb the High Place of Sacrifice and picnic under an oleander bush. On day six, slither through narrow **Wadi Muthlim** (p231) and end your visit to the rose-red city at the iconic **Monastery** (Al-Deir; p230).

Finish the week at **Wadi Rum** (p260), pacing through the beautiful desert by camel. From here, the lively seaside town of **Aqaba** (p247) is only an hour away.

Unravel a path through Jordan's most famous sites, brushing sides (real and imagined) with Roman legionnaires, Christian craftsmen, Islamic warriors and Bedouin nomads. Hire a car or charter a taxi for the King's Highway and overnight in Amman, Wadi Musa and Aqaba.

GET PHYSICAL IN JORDAN'S GREAT OUTDOORS
Two Weeks / Amman to Madaba

In the first three days, get a taste for the cedar-lands of the north by visiting **Amman** (p86), **Jerash** (p123) and the oak woodlands of **Ajloun Nature Reserve** (p135). Spend day four descending to the Jordan Valley, pausing at the point where Jesus was baptised in **Bethany-Beyond-the-Jordan** (p169).

Follow the river to the **Dead Sea** (p172) and treat yourself to a spa and a night of luxury in one of the **Dead Sea resorts** (p176 and an early morning float on day five at the world's lowest point. Survey the West Bank from a higher vantage point at the **Dead Sea Panorama** (p177) en route for **Wadi Mujib Nature Reserve** (p179). Splash, swim and struggle through 'Petra with water' on the unguided **Siq Trail** (p180). Dry out along the Dead Sea Highway to **Lot's Cave** (p181) and swap stories about the adventure at candlelit **Feinan Lodge** (p210).

Enjoy days six and seven at Aqaba, sparing time for a **dive or snorkel** (p277) in the fabled Red Sea. With batteries recharged, tackle a hike in **Wadi Rum** (p260) on day eight and overnight in a **Bedouin camp** (p272). On days nine and 10 in Petra, join **Petra by Night** (p238) for a magical view of the Siq.

Follow the ancient King's Highway from Petra to Madaba on day 11, calling in at **Siq al-Barid** (Little Petra, p244) and **Shobak** (p211), then staying overnight at **Dana Nature Reserve** (p209). Relax on day 12 taking village walks, or a longer hike with a guide.

Spend day 13 making the most of the King's Highway to Madaba, pausing at **Herod's Castle** (p196) in Mukawir en route. Allow time on the last day for some **souvenir shopping** (p191) in Madaba, the closest town to the international airport, or at craft shops in nearby **Mt Nebo** (p193).

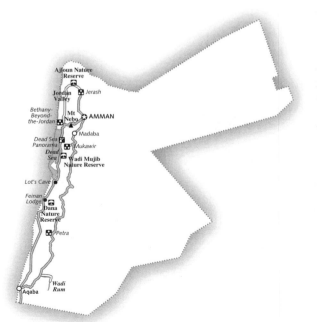

Store up some energy for this ambitious route around Jordan's most magical places, combining some physical effort with the extreme sport of spa-going. Hire a car or charter a taxi from the Dead Sea resorts to Aqaba, and to traverse the King's Highway.

ROADS LESS TRAVELLED

DESOLATELY INSPIRING   Three Weeks / Jerash to Umm al-Jimal

Collect a car from the airport or Amman and head north to **Jerash** (p123), your base for three days. Visit Ajloun and the Islamic castle of **Qala'at ar-Rabad** (p134). Amble on to **Umm Qais** (p141) and edge round the top of the country through numerous checkpoints along the border between three nations. Follow the signs to **Pella** (p146), then return to Jerash.

From **Salt** (p120) take the **descent** (p170) to Bethany-Beyond-the-Jordan. Follow signs for **Mt Nebo** (p193) through Bedouin grazing grounds. Stay the next three days in **Madaba** (p183), using one day to explore the town, one for visiting **Hesban** (p195) and another to go to **Mukawir** (p195) and the **Wadi Mujib lookout** (p198). Take an escort to the dolmens of **Wadi Jadid** (p195) continuing on an unmapped road to the Dead Sea Highway. Aiming for **Feinan Lodge** (p210), note an unmapped road to the right sign-posted 'Bayder'. This **drive** (p170) leads from the desert of Wadi Araba into **Siq Al-Barid** (Little Petra, p244).

After three days in **Petra** (p213) and three in **Wadi Rum** (p260), brave the Hwy 5 from Ma'an across the featureless and forbidding Badin, noting the white boulders that litter the endless plain. After crossing such barren lands, even the shrunken waters of **Azraq** (p153) seem like a miracle.

Use Azraq as a base to explore the desert castles of **Qasr Karama** (p163) and **Qusayr Amra** (p161) before taking Hwy 10 to the brooding basalt ruins of **Umm al-Jimal** (p151), a fitting end to a desolate but inspiring tour.

Want to get away from it all? Then this wild route, zigzagging from high ground to low ground along some of the most spectacular and remote roads in the region, could be the trip for you. Expect only sheep and goats for company.

JORDAN'S NATURE RESERVES   Two Weeks / Amman to Wadi Mujib

Follow 'a road less travelled' in spring when hiking paths will be knee-deep in wildflowers. Fuel up on organic fare at the **Wild Jordan Centre** (p95) in Amman before beginning this energetic itinerary, and book accommodation and guides for Jordan's reserves at the same time.

Hike through pistachio and oak hillsides in **Ajloun Nature Reserve** (p135) to meet local soapmakers, remembering to buy a bar from the shop before you leave. Enquire about **Abraham's Path** (p52) if you want your hike to take on more epic dimensions in the footsteps of the prophet. The nearby **Dibeen Nature Reserve** (p137) is peaceful for a picnic under the peeling barks of strawberry trees, in the company of Jordanian families fleeing the fumes of Amman.

For a complete contrast, head next for the rarely visited **Azraq Wetland Reserve** (p156) and **Shaumari Wildlife Reserve** (p156), for your best chance of spotting oryx. In addition, there's the pleasure of meeting the Chechen locals. Ask at **Azraq Lodge** (p155) for a tour of its cottage industries.

Next, sample the grazing lands around **Madaba** (p183). Strike out for the **Spring of Moses** (p195) and follow any goat track wrapped around the contours: you're bound to find a glass of mint tea with local Bedouin at the end of it. Camp at **Rummana** (p210) and thread your way along the escarpment of **Dana Nature Reserve** (p205) to the terraced gardens of Dana Village. Hike through three bio-zones to **Feinan Lodge** (p210) on the floor of **Wadi Araba** (p181).

Travel along the Desert Highway to wet and wild **Wadi Mujib Nature Reserve** (p179) where you may cross a party of schoolchildren squealing their way up the **Siq Trail** (p180) as you're sliding down.

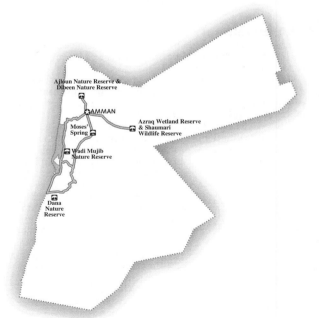

Ajloun Nature Reserve & Dibeen Nature Reserve

AMMAN

Azraq Wetland Reserve & Shaumari Wildlife Reserve

Moses' Spring

Wadi Mujib Nature Reserve

Dana Nature Reserve

Although this itinerary through Jordan's nature reserves takes you off-road, it doesn't consign you to a fortnight of your own company. Appreciate the wisdom of the Royal Society for the Conservation of Nature's policy of local involvement as you meet the people of Jordan (see p74 for details).

TAILORED TRIPS

BIBLICAL JORDAN

The east bank of the Jordan has been repeatedly touched by the prophets, and modern-day pilgrims can follow in the footsteps of such illustrious company as Abraham, Jacob, Moses, Joshua, Elijah, John the Baptist and Jesus. Over 100 sites in Jordan are mentioned in the Bible alone.

The single most important site is **Bethany-Beyond-the-Jordan** (p169), where Jesus is said to have been baptised and where Elijah ascended to heaven on a fiery chariot. Just north of here Joshua led the tribes of Israel across the Jordan River into the Promised Land.

From here, it's a short climb along the old pilgrim road to **Mt Nebo** (p193), where Moses finally saw the Promised Land before dying.

A day trip south of Madaba's famous **mosaic map** (p186) are the ruins of **Herod's castle** (p195) at Mukawir, where John the Baptist was imprisoned and beheaded at the behest of Salome.

At the southern end of the Dead Sea is **Lot's Cave** (p181) where Lot's wife turned to salt and Lot's daughters seduced their father, after they all fled the destruction of **Sodom and Gomorrah** (p181).

Back up north, Jesus performed one of his lesser-known miracles at Gadara (modern **Umm Qais**, p141), turning a band of brigands into a pack of swine.

LOCATING LAWRENCE

Jordan is **'El-Lawrence'** (p250) country, the land the eccentric, camel-riding, dagger-wielding Englishman made his own during the Arab Revolt of 1917–19.

'Rumm the Magnificent' is the natural place to look for Lawrence's ghost. Stride past 'crags like gigantic buildings', now named **Seven Pillars of Wisdom** (p265) in his honour, and go in search of springs where this officer of the British army once took a naked dip.

Advance through Wadi Umran by **camel** (see Tours, p274), the words 'to Aqaba' floating in the wind. You won't meet the Ottomans there: their empire ended as the Arab Revolt swept north. You may pass a goods train though, rattling by on mended tracks that Lawrence once helped blast with dynamite.

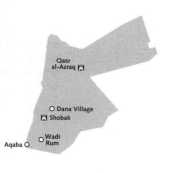

Turn north as winter sets in, and pad 'among the walls and snowy roofs' of **Shobak** (p211). Follow the hillcrest to the 'chess-board houses of **Dana village'** (p205), and stare into sunny Araba, 'fresh and green, thousands of feet below'.

Lawrence was proud of riding between Aqaba and **'Azraq the Remote'** (Qasr al-Azraq; p159) in three days. In only one, you can be sitting in Lawrence's room. He and his Arab companions left Azraq 'riding into a glowing west, while…schools of cranes flew into the sunset like the out-drawn barbs of arrows' – a good place to let Lawrence's memory rest.

History

Climbing off his donkey, a shepherd in a terraced field near Madaba tethers the animal to a giant thistle and seeks refuge from the heat of the day under a dolmen. Stretched full length under the cold stone roof of this ancient burial chamber, he almost blends into the landscape – until his mobile phone erupts in a rendition of 'We wish you a merry Christmas'.

History is not something that happened 'before' in Jordan. It's a living, breathing part of everyday life, witnessed not just in the pragmatic treatment of ancient artefacts but also in the way people live. Jordanians value their heritage and are in no hurry to eschew ways of life that have proved successful for centuries. The familiar lineal approach to history, therefore, where one event succeeds another in an expectation of so-called 'progress', is almost irrelevant in a country where past and present merge together so seamlessly.

The very entity of Jordan is a case in point. The political state within its current borders is a modern creation, but it encompasses territory (east of the Jordan River) that has hosted the world's oldest civilisations. The Egyptians, Assyrians, Babylonians, Greeks, Nabataeans, Romans, Crusaders and Turks all traded, built cities and fought their wars here, leaving behind rich cultural influences – leaning posts upon which the modern Jordanian has built a proud identity.

> The well-respected scholar Bernard Lewis has written several books on the Middle East that encompass Jordan, including *The Middle East: A Brief History of the Last 2000 Years*. Philip Hitti's *History of the Arabs* is also recommended.

LIFE IN THE 'FERTILE CRESCENT' (10,000–4000 BC)

Stand on top of the knoll at Shkarat Msaiad, on the seldom-used road from Little Petra to Wadi Araba (see the boxed text, p170), and survey the minimal mounds of stone and you could be forgiven for wondering what all the fuss is about. Despite the isolated beauty of the place, there isn't much to see but some stone walling. Yet this is the kind of place that archaeologists rave about because what you are looking at, they will solemnly tell you, is a 'PPN'.

A PPN, for the uninitiated, stands for Pre-Pottery Neolithic and it is significant because such sites indicate a high degree of organisation among early communities. In fact, at this sheltered spot in the hills, you are looking at the very dawn of civilisation. If nothing else, the traces of shelter, water collection and farming demonstrate the basic immutability of life.

Jordan has a remarkable number of early settlements, largely thanks to its location within the 'fertile crescent' – the rich arc of lands that included Mesopotamia, Syria and Palestine. The fecundity of the soil in this

TIMELINE

c 250,000 BC	c 100,000 BC	c 20,000 BC
With the aid of hand axes made of flint, early humans hunt elephants across the plains in the mild, wet climate of the Jordan Valley.	The Red Sea, lying in a branch of the great Rift Valley, retreats from Wadi Araba leaving the Dead Sea and Lake Galilee as two separate lakes.	Hunters and gatherers live in seasonal camps and rear their own livestock, with goats forming a substantial part of the diet in the early communities at Wadi Madamagh, near Petra.

RIFT VALLEY & THE BIOGRAPHY OF A SEA

You can't think about history in Jordan without factoring in its geographic position on the edge of the ancient Rift Valley. It's hard to imagine, standing beside the apologetic trickle of water that runs through Bethany-Beyond-the-Jordan today, that some 100,000 years ago the entire Jordan Valley was under the fertile waters of the Red Sea. When the sea retreated it left two landlocked stretches of water – the Sea of Galilee (known in Jordan as Lake Tiberius) and the Dead Sea.

The Dead Sea has been called many names in its time, including the logical 'Salt Sea' and the less flattering 'Stinking Sea' (slap a little Dead Sea mud on your face and you'll soon see why). A Greek traveller, Pausanius, first gave it the current name, noticing that the extreme brackishness of the water made it unsupportive of life. The high salinity is due to the fact that the sea has no outlet and the high summer temperatures evaporate the fresh water more quickly than it is replenished. Pick any desiccating day in June and stand at the point where the River Jordan flows into the Dead Sea: at 400m below sea level, this is the lowest point on earth and it's surprising any fresh water manages to flow in these conditions. Each year, due to intensive irrigation in the Jordan Valley, less and less water flows. This, together with the potash industry on the southern shore, has caused many environmentalists to lament the death of this extraordinary stretch of water (see the boxed text, p173).

But if it is a Dead Sea, who would care if it vanished? Well, for one thing, the mineral elements of the Dead Sea have long been associated with health-giving properties. Book into an extravagant spa by the Dead Sea's edge, and you will be part of a tradition that extends back to biblical times. Herod visited the spa at Callirhöe near Herodus Spring to treat his itching skin, and Byzantine Christians followed suit along pilgrim roads to Bethany-Beyond-the-Jordan, Mt Nebo and Lot's Cave.

Useful in extending life, the Dead Sea has been useful in death, too. Study the haunting eyes of the Ain Ghazal statues in the National Archaeological Museum in Amman (dated from around 6000 BC, they're reputedly the oldest sculptures in the world) and you'll see that they are blackened with bitumen. The Greeks and Romans named the Dead Sea the 'Sea of Pitch' on account of the bitumen that used to float to the surface. This substance was harvested by the Nabataeans who sold it to the Egyptians, who in turn used it for waterproofing funeral boats and for mummification. Ships laden with bitumen regularly crossed the sea in ancient times, as illustrated in a section of the 6th-century Madaba mosaic map (see p184). The last piece of bitumen surfaced from the Dead Sea in 1936.

It's little surprise, then, that city states sprung up around this trade, including in all probability Sodom and Gomorrah (see the boxed text, p181). The cities grew rich on indigo, sulphur, sugar (which was introduced into Europe from the Dead Sea area) and copper from the world's earliest copper mines.

Today the Dead Sea and its environs continue to contribute to human health and wealth with important revenue generated through tourism and potash industries. Part of the sea's western shore belonged to Jordan when the famous Dead Sea scrolls were discovered by a Bedouin shepherd at Qumran in 1947. Israel took control of the entire western shore in 1967 after the Six Day War, giving the term 'Rift Valley' a particularly modern resonance.

c 10,000 BC	c 8000 BC	c 6000 BC
Casual shelters are replaced with round huts of stone and wood. The collection of wild grains leads to the cultivation of crops with early tools such as sickles, pestles and mortars.	Some of the world's earliest settlements are established at Ain Ghazal and al-Beidha and neighbouring Jericho. Inhabitants tame, breed and cook domestic animals.	The fertility sculptures from Ain Ghazal (some of the world's oldest sculptures) and the wall paintings at Teleilat Ghassul in the Jordan Valley show that the early inhabitants of the region valued cultural activity.

region allowed early humans to move from a hunter-gatherer existence to settlement in the world's earliest villages, dating between 10,000 and 8500 BC. One such village in Jordan is Al-Beidha, near Petra. It's tempting to think of our ancient forebears as simple people living simple lives, but the inhabitants of villages like Al-Beidha built houses of stone and wood; they tamed, bred and cooked domestic animals; they planted wild seeds, grew crops, crushed grains and kept food in mud vessels hardened under the sun; and they began wearing and forming decorative items – like the astonishing fertility sculptures from Ain Ghazal dated around 6000 BC. These early settlers even left a record of their existence through wall paintings, such as those at Teleilat Ghassul in the Jordan Valley.

If you have lingering doubts about the sophistication of the ancients, ponder then the fields of dolmens that are scattered throughout the country, and were constructed between 5000 and 3000 BC. Come across the local shepherds and they may well ask you: 'Why are you here? Is anything good here?' That would be a great question to pose to the ancients who carefully aligned their last resting places along the shoulders rather than the ridges of the semi-arid hills. As for us moderns, these highly charged sites force a reconsideration of these early people: how did they lever the monumental bridging stones into place and what power of belief prompted such laborious, collaborative effort? Many of Jordan's archaeological treasures provoke more questions than they answer in our human quest to understand more about our origins.

FROM METALS TO MASSACRES (4000–1200 BC)

Invest enough importance in an object, and someone else will inevitably want one as well. There's evidence that Jordan's first farmers swapped desirable items among themselves well before 4000 BC, perhaps triggering the rivalry to make and trade more accurate tools and more beautiful adornments. One commodity useful for both tools and adornments was copper – of which Jordan has plenty. Visit Khirbet Feinan in present-day Dana Nature Reserve and the vast areas of black copper slag illustrate the importance of copper mining for the ancient people of the region.

Within a thousand years, experimentation with metalwork led to the mixing of copper and tin to create bronze, a hardier material that allowed for the rapid development of tools and, of course, weapons.

It's no coincidence that during the Bronze Age (3200–1200 BC) the region's settlements showed both greater signs of accumulated luxury items and a preoccupation with security, with defensive walls built around towns such as Pella. Early invaders included the Amorites, whose arrival in the area is often associated with the violent destruction of the five Cities of the Plain (near the southern end of the Dead Sea), including the settlements of Sodom and Gomorrah (see the boxed text, p181).

From the earliest settlements, some people devoted themselves to animal husbandry, sustained by the meat, milk and wool of their livestock, while others planted olives, wheat and barley and farmed the land. This distinction between the 'desert and the sown' is apparent to this day.

According to a German survey, 15,000–20,000 tons of copper was produced from Feinan's copper-smelting sites – some of the oldest such sites in the region. This has left 150,000–200,000 tons of slag dotting the arid landscape.

---

c 5000 BC	c 4000 BC	c 2900 BC
Monumental stone dolmen near Ar-Rawdah indicate that burials are now linked with the notion of an afterlife. The ingenious skill in engineering the bridging stones into place is a wonder – and a mystery.	Permanent settlements are established in modern-day Amman and in the southern desert regions, while copper is mined at Khirbet Feinan. Arts, such as pottery, illustrate the influence of more powerful neighbours in Egypt.	City-states emerge across the Middle East. Towns at Amman, Pella, Deir Alla and Tell Irbid are fortified and trade develops with neighbouring powers in Syria, Palestine and Egypt.

DIGGING UP THE PAST *Matthew D Firestone*

What is Archaeology?

Few disciplines are as widely misunderstood by the general public as archaeology. On the one hand, there is the romanticised image of Dr Indiana Jones, the swashbuckling adventurer who battles the forces of evil in search of lost treasure. On the other hand, there is the stale image of lofty academics digging around in the dirt for the trash of the ancients. If the truth be told, archaeology probably lies somewhere in the middle of these two extremes.

Archaeology is defined as the scientific study of human cultures through the discovery and analysis of material remains. While it is highly unlikely that present-day archaeologists will stumble upon lost cities such as Machu Picchu and Angkor Wat, their techniques for determining when and how events happened have become increasingly more sophisticated. However, modern archaeology is still reliant on three fundamental methods: surveying, excavation and analysis.

In the early days, archaeologists placed more emphasis on local knowledge than detailed surveys, though surveys have become essential as prospective sites have become more difficult to locate. Survey work is generally performed as a precursor to excavation, since it's cost effective in both time and money. Although surveying can be as simple as combing the surface of an area, it's becoming increasingly sophisticated through the use of magnetometers, metal detectors and sonar.

The stereotypical image of an archaeological expedition is that of the excavation, whereby the vast majority of data is uncovered from the ground. To the untrained eye an excavation appears as little more than a glorified construction site, but the process is both precise and highly refined. Operating from a detailed site plan, excavations seek to remove and preserve physical artefacts while obtaining information regarding stratigraphy, soil composition and artefact association.

Perhaps the most time-consuming and difficult part of any archaeological project is the analysis stage, which can sometimes stretch for several years beyond the actual excavation. Analysis begins by cleaning and cataloguing artefacts so they can be compared with existing collections and classified typologically. It's also possible to determine the precise date and material composition of an artefact through carbon dating and chemical analyses.

Invasion was not confined to the boundaries of modern-day Jordan. By the late Bronze Age (1500–1200 BC) the whole of the Middle East appeared to be at war. Wealthy city states in Syria collapsed, Egyptians retreated within their own borders from outposts in the Jordan Valley, and marauding foreigners ('Peoples of the Sea') reshaped the political landscape of the Eastern Mediterranean. The latter also brought the Philistines, who settled on the west bank of the Jordan and gave the land its current name of Palestine.

UNITY IN ADVERSITY (1200–333 BC)

Throughout the country's history it is difficult to talk about Jordan as a single entity. That's because, at least until the latter part of the 20th century AD, its borders have expanded and retreated and its peoples have

c 2300 BC	c 1500 BC	c 1200 BC
Sodom and Gomorrah, among the five so-called Cities of the Plain, are destroyed in a cataclysmic disaster on the southeast corner of the Dead Sea.	The Middle East enters a period of turmoil in which the influence of Egypt declines. The Philistines arrive in the area west of the Jordan, giving the land its current name of Palestine.	Ammon, Moab and Edom – based at Rabbath Ammon (Amman), Dhiban and Bozrah (Buseira) respectively – emerge as the dominant kingdoms to the east of the Jordan. Moses and the Israelites are refused access to Edom.

The History of Archaeology in Jordan

The history of archaeology is quite literally the history of the Middle East itself. In the first half of the 19th century a strong desire emerged to know how the recorded traditions of the Bible related to the archaeological remains discovered in the holy lands. While questions of this nature ultimately lead to ambiguous results, they did prompt the formation and propagation of the modern archaeological movement.

From 1860 to 1920 Jordan and the Levant were explored by a collection of British, American, French and German surveyors, including a young archaeology student from Oxford by the name of TE Lawrence (of Arabia). The peak of the era's discovery was in 1868 when an expedition unearthed the now-famous Mesha Stele, which was raised by King Mesha of Moab in honour of his victories over the Israelite kings. However, there was little additional progress as the Ottoman hold over the territory was unsteady at best, and the locals were not terribly partial to foreigners poking around.

Following the British mandate of Jordan in 1920, modest excavation projects aimed at consolidating the main standing monuments began throughout the country. In 1930s, however, archaeological efforts in Jordan were given a big boost following the discovery of remarkable mosaics at Madaba, which are regarded today as some of the finest in the Levant. But the outbreak of WWII, and the subsequent Arab-Israeli wars, ushered in a 30-year hiatus.

Since the 1970s there has been an exponential increase in archaeological activity, which has yielded some of the country's most important discoveries. Excavations at prehistoric Ain Ghazal in Amman produced 8500-year-old, life-size plaster statues, while a project at the nearby Citadel unearthed remains of the Temple of Hercules. Other recent finds include the Greek manuscript library at Petra, ancient temple complexes in the Jordan Valley, early mining sites west of Kerak and the baptism site of Jesus Christ: Bethany-Beyond-the-Jordan. Today, as more and more Jordanians take a greater interest in their heritage, archaeologists are hoping to receive the support and funding that they require in order continue unlocking the country's history and material culture.

come and gone, largely driven by the political ambitions and expediencies of more powerful regional neighbours.

Around 1200 BC, however, something akin to a recognisable 'Jordan' emerged from the regional mayhem in the form of three important kingdoms: Edomites in the south, whose capital was at Bozrah (modern Buseira, near Dana); the Moabites near Wadi Mujib; and the Ammonites on the edge of the Arabian Desert with a capital at Rabbath Ammon (present-day Amman). It is unlikely that any of the three kingdoms had much to do with each other until the foundation of the new neighbouring city-state of Israel (see the boxed text, p36).

Israel quickly became a military power to be reckoned with, dominating the area of Syria and Palestine and coming into inevitable conflict with the neighbours. Under King David the Israelites wrought a terrible

850 BC	582 BC	c 539 BC
The divided Israelite empire is defeated by Mesha, king of Moab, who recorded his victories on the famous Mesha Stele in the Moabite capital of Dhiban.	Ammon, Moab and Edom enjoy brief unity after near annihilation by the Israelites under King David and King Solomon. The union is short-lived and soon they are reduced to Babylonian provinces under King Nebuchadnezzar II.	The Babylonians fall to the Persians, and Trans-Jordan becomes part of a vast Persian satrapy.

THE CITY-STATE OF ISRAEL

The kingdoms of Edom, Moab and Ammon are mentioned in the Bible, especially in connection with the wandering Jews of the Exodus. According to the Old Testament, Moses and his brother, Aaron, led their people through Sinai in Egypt looking for a permanent territory to inhabit. They were forbidden entry to southern Jordan by the Edomites, but managed to wind their way north, roughly along the route of the modern King's Highway, towards the Jordan River. Moses died on Mt Nebo, in sight of the Promised Land, and it was left to his son Joshua to lead the Israelites across the river to the West Bank where they conquered the city of Canaan and established the city-state of Israel.

---

revenge on Edom, massacring almost the entire male population; Moab also succumbed to Israelite control and the people of Ammon were subject to forced labour under the new Jewish masters. However, Israelite might proved short-lived and, after King Solomon's brief but illustrious reign, the kingdom split into Israel and Judah.

By the middle of the first millennia BC – perhaps in response to Israelite aggression – Ammon, Moab and Edom became a unified entity, linked by a trade route known today as the King's Highway (see the boxed text, p44). The fledgling amalgam of lands, however, was not strong enough to withstand the might of bullying neighbours, and it was soon overwhelmed by a series of new masters: the Assyrians, Babylonians and Persians. It would be centuries before Jordan achieved a similar distinct identity within its current borders.

THE MIDDLE MEN OF THE MIDDLE EAST (333 BC–AD 324)

War and invasion was not the utter disaster for the people of the region that it may have been. Located at the centre of the land bridge between Africa and Asia, the cities surrounding the King's Highway were particularly well placed to service the needs of passing foreign armies. They also profited from the caravan routes that crossed the deserts from Arabia to the Euphrates, bringing shipments of African gold and South Arabian frankincense via the Red Sea ports in present-day Aqaba and Eilat. The Greeks, the Nabataeans and the Romans each capitalised on this passing bounty, leaving a legacy of imported culture and learning in return.

The Greeks

By the fourth century BC the growing wealth of Arab lands attracted the attention of a young military genius from the West known as Alexander of Macedon. Better known today as Alexander the Great, the precocious 21-year-old stormed through the region in 334 BC, winning territories from Turkey to Palestine.

At his death in 323 BC in Babylon, Alexander ruled a vast empire from the Nile to the Indus, with similarly vast dimensions of commerce.

c 500 BC	333 BC	c 323 BC
The innovation of the camel saddle transforms the lives of Arab nomads and eventually brings new caravans to Jordan's southern deserts en route to Damascus.	Alexander the Great wins the Battle of Issus, defeating Persian King Darius III. This entices the great general south to Syria and Palestine, which in due course comes under the expansive empire of Greece.	Alexander dies in Babylon but Greek influence remains, particularly through the language which gives access to the treasures of classical learning. The cities of Philadelphia (Amman), Gadara, Pella and Jerash blossom under Hellenistic rule.

Over the coming centuries, Greek became the lingua franca of Jordan (at least of the written word), giving access to the great intellectual treasures of the classical era. The cities of Philadelphia (Amman), Gadara, Pella and Jerash blossomed under Hellenistic rule, and prospered through growing trade, particularly with Egypt, which fell under the same Greek governance.

The Nabataeans

Trade was the key to Jordan's most charismatic period of history, thanks to the growing importance of a nomadic Arab tribe from the south, known as the Nabataeans. The Nabataeans produced only copper and bitumen (for waterproofing boat hulls – see the boxed text, p32) but they knew how to trade in the commodities of neighbouring nations. Consummate middlemen, they used their exclusive knowledge of desert strongholds and water supplies to amass wealth from the caravan trade, first by plundering and then by levying tolls on the merchandise that traversed the areas under their control.

The most lucrative trade involved the transportation, by camel, of frankincense and myrrh along the Incense Route from southern Arabia to outposts farther north. The Nabataeans were also sole handlers of spices shipped to Arabia by boat from Somalia, Ethiopia and India. Suburbs at the four corners of their capital, Petra, received the caravans and handled the logistics, processing products and offering banking services and fresh animals before moving the goods west across the Sinai to the ports of Gaza and Alexandria, for shipment to Greece and Rome.

The Nabataeans never possessed an 'empire' in the common military and administrative sense of the word; instead, from about 200 BC, they established a 'zone of influence' that stretched from Syria to Rome. As the Nabataean territory expanded under King Aretas III (84–62 BC), they controlled and taxed trade throughout the Hejaz (northern Arabia), the Negev, the Sinai, and the Hauran of southern Syria. Nabataean communities were influential as far away as Rome, and Nabataean tombs still stand at the impressive site of Madain Saleh in Saudi Arabia.

The Nabataean sphere of influence spread from Arabia to Syria, peaking around the time of Christ. The Nabataeans transformed themselves from desert traders into masterful architects, hydraulic engineers and craftsmen, whose influence connected Arabia to the Mediterranean.

The Romans

You only have to visit Jerash for five minutes, trip over a fallen column and notice the legions of other columns beside, to gain an immediate understanding of the importance of the Romans in Jordan – and the importance of Jordan to the Romans. This magnificent set of ruins is grand on a scale that is seldom seen in modern building enterprises and indicates the amount of wealth the Romans invested in this outpost of their empire. Jerash was clearly worth its salt and, indeed, it was the lucrative trade associated with the Nabataeans that attracted the Romans in the first place. It's perhaps a fitting legacy of their

c 100 BC	30 BC	9 BC–AD 40
While Greek generals squabble over who rules which parts of the Trans-Jordan, a tribe of nomadic Arabs quietly makes money from passing caravans. They establish their capital at Petra, the heart of the old Edomite kingdom.	Herod the Great expands the castle at Mukawir, which will in a few years' time set the stage for Salome's dance and the beheading of John the Baptist.	Aretas IV, the greatest of the Nabataean kings, presides over a city of wealth and beauty. The craftsmen of this hidden cluster of tombs, temples and houses adapt their knowledge of Greek and Roman architecture.

SALUTE THE TROOPS *Jenny Walker*

Have you ever considered how and why Rome managed to conquer the lands of the Middle East so easily? Pay a visit to the spectacular ruins at Jerash, and you may just find the answer.

The answer doesn't lie in the ruins of empire scattered around the site but in the novel re-enactment, held twice daily at the Hippodrome. Visitors to this event will have a chuckle at the lively repartee of the master of ceremonies, one Adam Al-Samadi, otherwise known as Gaius Victor, on duty at the Hippodrome. Dressed as a Roman legionnaire with a feather pluming from his helmet, he stands erect like a true centurion. 'Salute the troops,' he demands in a cockney English accent as he hitches his tunic and raises a spear to the amassed veterans of the Jordan army – in their new uniform of the Sixth Roman Legion.

'These men,' Gaius says imperiously to the huddled audience on the bleachers, 'they didn't want to die in some godforsaken battlefield. They wanted to go home to their wives and mistresses in civilised Rome and draw their pensions.' That's why, he argues, the Roman soldiers were the best in the world: 'Get in, get out, stop messing about – eight minutes of fighting, then fresh men for the next eight minutes of fighting.'

A trundle of soldiers shuffles into formation and slams down gleaming shields; they advance across the arena like a gleaming, metal-plated, human tank, impervious to the lances of the leather-clad natives – if rather more vulnerable to the giggles from spectators. 'So Gaius Victor,' I ask after the show. 'What is that makes such an erudite fellow like you do a job like this?' 'Call it bread and circuses,' he says. 'That's what kept people happy under the Romans and I guess that's what keeps us happy today.'

That sounds like a logical enough answer, but then his eyes mist over and he adds: 'You know, there's the moment in the performance when you say "Salute the troops" and watch them salute you back. To this day, it gives me a thrill that I can't explain.' Forget the disciplined armies; forget the orderly organisation of labour and provisions – local people fell under the magic of Rome. As a spare soldier blasts the horn from atop Jerash's triumphal arch, his scarlet cloak furling behind him and the flag of Jordan blowing in the wind, it's easy to see how.

rule that the Jordanian currency, the dinar, derives its name from the Latin *denarius*.

The Romans brought many benefits to the region, constructing two new roads through Jordan – the Nova Via Traiana (AD 111–14) linking Bosra with the Red Sea, and the Strata Diocletian (AD 284–305) linking Azraq with Damascus and the Euphrates. A string of forts in the Eastern Desert at Qasr al-Hallabat, Azraq and Umm al-Jimal was also built to shore up the eastern rim of the empire.

The 2nd and 3rd centuries were marked by a feverish expansion of trade as the Via Traiana became the main thoroughfare for Arabian caravans, armies and supplies. The wealth benefited the cities of Jerash, Umm Qais and Pella, members of the Decapolis (see p125), a league of provincial cities that accepted Roman cultural influence but retained their independence.

After the Roman conquest of Syria in 64 BC, Emperor Trajan set his sights on the Nabataean empire in AD 106 and quickly absorbed it into the new Roman province of Arabia Petraea. The capital was later transferred to Bosra (in modern Syria).

AD 26	c 33	106
Jesus Christ is baptised in Bethany-Beyond-the-Jordan by John the Baptist. The first church is built a few years later at Rihab, 40km from Amman, where 70 of Jesus' disciples take shelter from persecution in Jerusalem.	The oldest church in the world, dating from AD 33 to AD 70 (and only recently discovered) shelters the '70 beloved by God and Divine' – the disciples of Jesus Christ who fled persecution.	Roman Emperor Trajan absorbs the Nabataean empire into the province of Arabia Petraea, signalling the end of Petra's heyday.

GATEWAY TO THE AFTERLIFE: THE NABATAEAN RELIGION *Jenny Walker*

A friend, her husband and young daughter recently visited Petra on the Petra Night Tour. Arriving there at prayer time in the evening, there was no one on the gate. Some local workers, who had just finished laying the path of candles to the Treasury, waved through the family of three and off they set off along the candlelit Siq, completely alone. About a quarter of the way down, they began to realise there was something amiss. By halfway along, the young daughter, overwhelmed by the towering shadows of this sacred way, begged her parents to turn back. A few moments later, all three were hastily beating a retreat. Only those who have ever been in Petra's Siq alone will understand the power this extraordinary passage has on the soul. It was chosen surely for exactly this reason for it was no ordinary passage: it was a gateway to the afterlife.

Surprisingly little is known about Nabataean religion, considering that their preoccupation with the afterlife dominates much of their capital at Petra. It is known, however, that the early desert polytheistic religion of the original Arabian tribe absorbed Egyptian, Greek and Roman, and even Edomite and Assyrian beliefs, to create a unique faith.

The main Nabataean god was Dushara, the mountain god, who governed the natural world. Over the years he came to be associated with the Egyptian god Osiris, Greek god Dionysus and the Roman god Zeus.

For fertility, the Nabataeans prayed to the goddess Al-'Uzza (the Very Strong), who became associated with Aphrodite and Isis. Al-Kutba was the god of divination and writing, linked to Hermes and Mercury. Allat (literally 'Goddess') was associated with Athene.

Early representations of the Nabataean gods were non-figurative. Divine stones known as *baetyls* marked important wadis, junctions, canyons and mountaintops, representing the presence of the divine. Religious processions to Petra's spiritual 'High Places' were an important part of the community's religious life, culminating in a sacrifice (perhaps human) and ritual purification.

Though the secrets of Nabataean religious ceremonies are hidden in history, there is a strong sense of what one might call 'spiritual presence' enveloping Petra's high places of sacrifice: the god blocks, carved niches, altars and sacrificial basins all indicate that the hilltops were holy ground, used by the priests for mediating between heaven and earth.

With the eventual demise of the Roman Empire, and the fracturing of trade routes over the subsequent centuries, Jordan's entrepreneurial leadership of the region never quite regained the same status.

SPIRIT OF THE AGE (AD 324–1516)

For one and a half thousand years after the birth of Jesus, the history of Jordan was characterised by the expression of organised faith in one form or another. Under the influence of Rome, Christianity replaced the local gods of the Nabataeans, and several hundred years later Islam took its place – but not before a struggle that left a long-term legacy, and a string of Crusader forts.

111–14	c 200–300	c 284–305
The Romans build the Nova Via Taiana, following the path of the ancient King's Highway between Bosra and the Red Sea, bringing new life to an ancient thoroughfare.	This golden age for Roman Arabia is marked by the building of grand monuments in the cities of the Decapolis. Emperor Hadrian even honours Jerash with a visit on his journey to Palestine.	The Romans build the Strata Diocletian linking Azraq with Damascus and the Euphrates. A string of forts in the Eastern Desert at Qasr al-Hallabat, Azraq and Umm al-Jimal are also built to shore up the eastern rim of the empire.

BIBLICAL SITES OF JORDAN *Matthew D Firestone*

The eastern banks of the Jordan River are home to no fewer than 100 sites of biblical importance. From Abraham and Moses to John the Baptist and Jesus Christ, the founding fathers of the three Western monotheistic traditions are all intimately tied to the Jordanian landscape. Along with Israel and the Palestinian Territories, Jordan has been the destination of religious pilgrimages for centuries.

Regardless of whether or not you take the biblical word for fact, there is a strong body of archaeological evidence to suggest that many of the places depicted in the Good Book once existed. In fact, the roots of modern archaeology in the Middle East stem from the desire to place a historical context on the canon of scripture. Even if you're not a religious person by nature, visiting sites of biblical significance can be an incredibly moving and even spiritual experience.

The following list presents a brief overview of the most famous biblical sites in Jordan:

'Ain Musa or Ayoun ('Ain) Musa
Biblical reference: *Then Moses raised his arm and struck the rock twice with his staff. Water gushed out, and the community and their livestock drank* (Numbers 20:11)
Historical record: the exact location of where Moses struck the rock is open to debate – it's either 'Ain Musa, which is north of Wadi Musa near Petra (see p237), or Ayoun ('Ain) Musa, near Mt Nebo (see p195).

Dead Sea
Biblical reference: *...while the water flowing down to the Sea of Arabah was completely cut off...* (Joshua 3:16)
Historical record: the Sea of Arabah (the Dead Sea), also known as the Salt Sea, is mentioned several times in the Bible (see p172).

Jebel Haroun
Biblical reference: *Remove Aaron's garments and put them on his son Eleazar, for Aaron will be gathered to his people: he will die there. Moses did as the Lord commanded: they went up to Mount Hor in the sight of the whole community* (Numbers 10:26–27)
Historical record: Mount Hor is believed to be Jebel Haroun in Petra, which is also revered by Muslims as a holy place (see p233).

Jebel Umm al-Biyara
Biblical reference: *He [the Judean King, Amaziah] was the one who defeated ten thousand Edomites in the Valley of the Salt and captured Sela in battle...* (2 Kings 14:7)
Historical record: the village on top of Umm al-Biyara mountain in Petra is believed to be the ancient settlement of Sela (see p233).

Lot's Cave
Biblical reference: *Now Lot went up out of Zo'ar, and dwelt in the hills with his two daughters, for he was afraid to dwell in Zo'ar; so he dwelt in a cave with his two daughters* (Genesis 19:30)
Historical record: the cave where Lot and his daughters lived for years after Lot's wife turned into a pillar of salt is thought to be just off the Dead Sea Highway, not far from Safi (see p181).

324	614	629
Emperor Constantine converts to Christianity. On his death Christianity becomes the dominant religion of the Byzantine Empire and many churches are built. East of the Jordan, Madaba is the focus of pilgrim trails to Jerusalem.	Emperor Heraclius forces the invading Persians into a peace agreement, but despite this victory Byzantine Christian rule in the Trans-Jordan is soon to end: a storm is brewing in Arabia, bringing Islam in its wake.	Muslim forces lose the Battle of Mu'tah against the Christian Byzantines. After the death of Prophet Mohammed (632), they win the decisive Battle of Yarmouk in 636 and Islam becomes the region's dominant religion.

Machaerus

Biblical reference: *The King was sad, but because of his oaths and his dinner guests, he gave orders that her request be granted, and had John beheaded in the prison* (Matthew 14:9–12)

Historical record: John the Baptist had claimed that Herod Antipas' marriage to his brother's wife, Herodias, was unlawful. So, at the request of Salome, Herodias' daughter, John was killed (see p195).

Mt Nebo

Biblical reference: *Go up into...Mount Nebo in Moab, across from Jericho, and view Canaan, the land I am giving the Israelites as their own possession. There on the mountain that you have climbed you will die* (Deuteronomy 32:49–50)

Historical record: Mt Nebo is revered as a holy place because it is where Moses is reported to have died, although his tomb has never been found (see p193).

Tell al-Kharrar

Biblical reference: *Then Jesus came from the Galilee to the Jordan to be baptised by John* (Matthew 3:13)

Historical record: Tell al-Kharrar is regarded as Bethany-Beyond-the-Jordan where Jesus was baptised by John the Baptist (see p169).

Umm Qais

Biblical reference: *When he [Jesus] arrived at the other side in the region of Gadarenes, two demon-possessed men coming from the tombs met him* (Matthew 8:28–34)

Historical record: Umm Qais is known as Gadara in the Bible, as well as in other ancient scriptures (see p141).

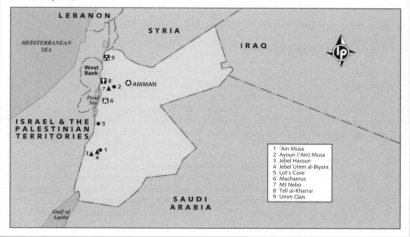

1	'Ain Musa
2	Ayoun ('Ain) Musa
3	Jebel Haroun
4	Jebel Umm al-Biyara
5	Lot's Cave
6	Machaerus
7	Mt Nebo
8	Tell al-Kharrar
9	Umm Qais

c 700	**747**	**c 1000**
The Umayyads from Syria overtake the region and build some extraordinary bathhouses, hunting lodges and fortified meeting places (known today as the Desert Castles) in the arid desert east of Amman.	An earthquake shatters northern Jordan and Syria, weakening the Umayyads' hold on power. They're replaced by the Abbasids, signalling a period of Persian cultural dominance and less tolerance towards Christianity.	The Fatimids, a Shiite dynasty from Cairo, take control of Palestine, Jordan and southern Syria. They rule for less than a century, replaced by the Seljuk Turks – themselves under pressure from Asian invaders.

Conversion to Christianity

Think of the history of the Christian religion, and most people understandably focus on the 'Holy Land' to the west of the River Jordan. And yet, if recent evidence is to be believed, the Christian church may never have evolved (at least not in the way we know it today) if it hadn't been for the shelter afforded the early proponents of the faith on the *east* bank of the Jordan.

In 2008, 40km northeast of Amman, archaeologists uncovered what they believe to be the first church in the world. Dating from AD 33 to AD 70, the church, which was buried under St Georgeous Church in Rihab, appears to have sheltered the 70 disciples of Jesus Christ. Described in the mosaic inscriptions on the floor of the old church as the '70 beloved by God and Divine', these first Christians fled persecution in Jerusalem and lived in secrecy, practising their rituals in the underground church. Pottery dating from the 3rd to the 7th century shows that these disciples and their families lived in the area until late Roman rule.

The conversion by Emperor Constantine to Christianity in AD 324 eventually legitimised the practice of Christianity across the region. East of the Jordan, churches were constructed (often from the building blocks of former Greek and Roman temples) and embellished with the elaborate mosaics that are still visible today at Madaba, Umm ar-Rasas and Petra. Christian pilgrims began to search for relics of the Holy Land, building churches en route at biblical sites such as Bethany, Mt Nebo and Lot's Cave. It was the archaeological rediscovery of these churches 1400 years later that confirmed the lost location of these biblical sites to a forgetful modern world (see the boxed text, p40).

The Rise of Islam

Reminders of Christianity are scattered across Jordan today, not least in the observance of the faith in towns such as Madaba. But listen to the bells peal on a weekend, and moments later they will be replaced by the Muezzin's call to prayer from the neighbouring mosque. Islam is present not just in Jordan's mosques but in the law, in social etiquette and at the very heart of the way people live their lives – in Bedouin camps as well as in modern city centres. So how did Islam reach here and how did it replace Christianity as the dominant religion?

From 622 (10 years before the death of the prophet Mohammed) the armies of Islam travelled northwards, quickly and easily spreading the message of submission (Islam) well beyond the Arabian Peninsula. Although they lost their first battle against the Christian Byzantines at Mu'tah (near Karak) in 629, they returned seven years later to win the Battle of Yarmouk. Jerusalem fell in 638 and Syria was taken in 640. Islam, under the Sunni dynasty of the Umayyads, became the dominant religion of the region, headquartered in the city of Damascus, and Arabic replaced

---

The discovery in 2008 of the world's oldest church was described by senior Orthodox clerics as an 'important milestone for Christians all around the world'. Jordanian authorities are now hoping to develop the site as a tourist attraction.

Prophet Mohammed's son-in-law, the caliph Ali, was assassinated in 660. He was succeeded by Mu'awiya, who established the Umayyad dynasty (661-750). The bitter dispute over this succession split Islam into two factions, the Sunnis and the Shiites (see p59).

1095	1115–87	1193
Pope Urban II sparks a 'holy war' in revenge for the destruction of churches by the Seljuks and to protect pilgrim routes to the Holy Land. Within five years, Crusaders capture Jerusalem, slaughtering countless inhabitants.	Crusader King Baldwin I builds Montreal, the castle in Shobak, and follows it with Karak Castle in 1142. Despite these superb defences, Saladin beats the Crusader armies in the decisive Battle of Hittin in 1187.	Saladin dies and the ensuing family in-fighting enables the Crusaders to recapture much of their former territory.

Greek as the lingua franca. Within 100 years Muslim armies controlled a vast empire that spread from Spain to India.

The Umayyads' rich architectural legacy included the Umayyad Mosque in Damascus and the Dome of the Rock in Jerusalem. In eastern Jordan, the Umayyads' close attachment to the desert led to the construction of a string of opulent 'desert castles' (p158), including the brooding Qasr Kharana (built in 710) and Qusayr Amra (711).

Despite the blossoming of Islamic scholarship in medicine, biology, philosophy, architecture and agriculture over the next three centuries, the area wedged between Jerusalem and Baghdad remained isolated from the sophisticated Arab mainstream. This is one reason why Jordan possesses relatively few demonstrations of Islamic cultural exuberance.

The Crusades & Holy War

The armies of Islam and Christianity have clashed many times throughout history and the consequences (and language of religious conflict) resonate to this day both within the Middle East and across the world at large.

The Crusades of the 12th and 13th centuries are among the most famous of the early conflicts between Muslims and Christians. Survey the mighty walls of the great Crusader castles at Karak and Shobak and it's easy to see that both sides meant business: these were holy wars (albeit attracting mercenary elements) in which people willingly sacrificed their comfort and even lives for their faith in the hope of gaining glory in the hereafter – ironically, according to Islam at least, a hereafter shared by all people of the book, Christians, Jews and Muslims.

Built by King Baldwin I in the 12th century, the castles were part of a string of fortifications designed to control the roads from Damascus to Cairo. They seemed inviolable, and they may have remained so but for Nureddin and Saladin, who between them occupied most of the Crusader strongholds in the region, including those of Oultrejordain (meaning 'across the Jordan'). The Damascus-based Ayyubids, members of Saladin's family, squabbled over his empire on his death in 1193, enabling the Crusaders to recapture much of their former territory along the coast.

The Ayyubids were replaced by the Mamluks who seized control of the area east of the Jordan and rebuilt the castles at Karak, Shobak and Ajloun. They used these strongholds as lookouts and as a series of staging posts for message-carrying pigeons. Indeed, thanks to the superior communications that this unique strategy afforded, you could argue that the Crusaders were defeated not by the military might of Islam but on the wings of their peace-loving doves.

WESTERN LOVE AFFAIR WITH THE MIDDLE EAST (1516–1914)

The Ottoman Turks took Constantinople in 1453 and created one of the world's largest empires. They defeated the Mamluks in present-day

Maalouf's lively *The Crusades Through Arab Eyes* recasts the West's image of knights in shining armour as ruthless barbarians who pillaged the Middle East, the horrors of which still reside in the collective Arab consciousness.

Nureddin (literally 'Light of the Faith') was the son of a Turkish tribal ruler. He united the Arab world and defeated the Crusaders in Egypt. His campaign against the Crusaders was completed by Saladin (Restorer of the Faith), a Kurdish scholar and military leader.

1258	1400–01	1453
The Mongols storm Baghdad and the armies of Genghis Khan's son reach as far as Ajloun and Salt. They are repelled by the Mamluks who rebuild the castles at Karak, Shobak and Ajloun.	The brutal Central Asian invader Tamerlane destroys much of the Mamluk Empire, the final ripple of a wave of invasions from Central Asia that changes the face of the Middle East.	Ottoman rule is established in Constantinople (modern-day Istanbul), creating one of the world's largest empires that extends throughout the Middle East

HISTORY OF A HIGHWAY

When pondering the King's Highway, a fair question is to ask: 'Which king?' In fact, the highway was never the personal project of royalty: it gained its name through the sense of major thoroughfare, often referred to in the Arabian Orient as 'royal road'.

The highway runs for 297km between Madaba and Petra; for a thousand years before Christ it linked the kingdoms of Ammon, Moab and Edom. One of the earliest mentions of the highway is in the biblical episode where Moses was refused passage along the highway by the King of Edom. The Nabataeans used the route to transport frankincense, originating in southern Arabia, and other exotic commodities to the important trading posts of Syria. In later times, the highway received a suitably Roman makeover under Emperor Trajan, who widened and rerouted part of the highway to facilitate the passage of troops.

The highway has great religious significance for both Christians and Muslims. Attracted by the holy sites of Mt Nebo and protected by the Crusader forces, Christians used the route for pilgrimage, building and embellishing many shrines along the way, such as the Church of St Stephen at Umm Ar-Rasas. The Muslims used the route on pilgrimage to Mecca until the Ottomans developed the Tariq al-Bint in the 16th century – the approximate path of the Hejaz Railway, built in 1900, and the modern Desert Highway.

Inevitably, the importance of the King's Highway declined and it was only in the 1950s and 1960s that it was upgraded to a tarmac road. Today it's a rural, often pot-holed route, which despite ambling through some of the loveliest and most striking landscape in Jordan betrays little of its former status as a road fit for kings. For a more information on the highway see www.ancientroute.com.

Jordan in 1516, but concentrated their efforts on the lucrative cities of the region, such as the holy city of Jerusalem and the commercial centre of Damascus. The area east of the Jordan once again became a forgotten backwater. Forgotten, that is, by the Ottoman Empire, but not entirely ignored by Western interests. Indeed, the period of gradually weakening Ottoman occupation over the next few centuries also marked an increasingly intense scrutiny by the Europeans – the British and the French in particular.

In the preface to *Les Orientales* (1829) Victor Hugo wrote that the whole of the European continent appeared to be 'leaning towards the East'. This was no new phenomenon. Trade between the West and the East was long established and stories of the 'barbaric pearl and gold' of Arabia soon aroused the interests of a wider public. By the late 18th century people were making pleasure trips to the Syrian desert, adopting articles of Albanian and Turkish dress, carrying pocket editions of Persian tales and penning their own travelogues.

Burckhardt's monumental rediscovery of Petra in 1812 led to a further explosion of interest in the region. Societies were founded for the purpose of promoting Middle East exploration and scholars began translating

The Qala'at ar-Rabad at Ajloun (p134) was built by the Ayyubids. In 1250 they were ousted by the Mamluks, a group of foreign, adolescent warriors serving as a soldier-slave caste for the Ayyubids, and the Mamluks ruled for the next 300 years.

c 1516–1916	1798	1812
The Ottomans lavish their attentions on Jerusalem and Damascus while the area east of the Jordan becomes a cultural and political backwater.	Napoleon Bonaparte invades Egypt, bringing the Middle East within the sphere of Western political rivalry – a rivalry which influences the political landscape of Trans-Jordan over the next century and a half.	Burckhardt rediscovers Petra for the Western world, sparking off an enduring fascination with the fabled Pink City, and the region in general, among Western travellers, archaeologists, writers and artists.

Persian, Arabic and Sanskrit texts. Many aspects of the Orient were explored in Western fiction, much of which attracted a wide and enthusiastic readership. Indeed, by the end of the 19th century the fascination with the Arabian East was no 'airy fantasy' but a highly complex relationship defined by scientists, scholars, travellers and fiction writers.

This is the cultural backdrop upon which the political manoeuvrings of the 20th century were played out.

FIGHTING FOR AN ARAB LAND (1914–46)

Writing of the Arab Revolt that passed through the heart of Jordan in the early 20th century, TE Lawrence described the phenomenon as 'an Arab war waged and led by Arabs for an Arab aim in Arabia'. This is a significant statement as it identifies a growing sense of political identity among Arab people throughout the last half of the 19th century and beginning of the 20th century. This pan-Arab consciousness grew almost in proportion (or at least coincidentally) to the territorial interest of Western powers in Arab lands. Slowly, in place of loose tribal interests Arabs came to define themselves as a single, unified entity – an Islamic 'other' perhaps to the Christian European threat pulsing around the Suez.

Arabs were prepared to fight for this new Arab nationalism, as Lawrence describes in the *Seven Pillars of Wisdom,* his account of the Arab Revolt:

> As time went by our need to fight for the ideal increased to an unquestioning possession, riding with spur and rein over our doubts. Willy-nilly it became a faith.

What Lawrence could not have known at the time was just how prophetic of the coming jihad in the later part of the 20th century those words would be.

The Arab Revolt

Ironically, the new Arab nationalist movement cut its teeth not on a Western Christian enemy but on the Ottomans, the apathetic Muslim rulers who dominated most of the Middle East, including the area either side of the Jordan. The revolt was fought by Arab warriors on horseback, loosely formed into armies under Emir Faisal, the ruler of Mecca and guardian of the Muslim holy places, who had taken up the reins of the Arab nationalist movement in 1914. He was joined by his brother Abdullah and the enigmatic British colonel TE Lawrence, known as Lawrence of Arabia (see the boxed text, p250). Lawrence helped with coordination and securing supplies from the Allies in a campaign that swept across the desert from Arabia, wrested Aqaba from the Ottomans and eventually ousted them from Damascus. By 1918 the Arabs controlled modern Saudi

Between 1775 and 1825, 87 volumes on aspects of the Near East were published in Britain alone and 46 reviews of the same books appeared in leading journals between 1805 and 1825.

The betrayal of the Arab cause by Western allies was underlined by the secret Sykes-Picot Agreement of 1916 in which 'Syria' (modern-day Syria &Lebanon) was intended for the French and 'Palestine' (an area including modern Israel, the Palestinian Territories and Jordan) for the British.

1908	**1914–18**	**1916**
The Ottoman Empire, by now 'the sick man of Europe', builds the Hejaz Railway linking Damascus with the holy city of Medina, via Amman, in an effort to reassert influence in the region.	During WWI Jordan sees fierce fighting between the Ottoman Turks (allied with the Germans) and the British, based in Suez (Egypt). By 1917 British troops occupy Jerusalem and, a year later, the rest of Syria.	The Arab Revolt, led by Faisal and backed by the British with the famous assistance of TE Lawrence, storms Aqaba, disrupts the Hejaz Railway and marches on Damascus.

THE HEJAZ RAILWAY

The Hejaz Railway was built between 1900 and 1908 to transport pilgrims from Damascus to the holy city of Medina, reducing the two-month journey by camel and on foot to as little as three days. For Jordan, and Amman in particular, this meant a boom in trade. The 1462km line was completely funded by donations from Muslims – but functioned for less than 10 years. The trains and railway line were partially destroyed in the Arab Revolt of 1917 during WWI. The line was rebuilt as far south as Ma'an, but is now only used for cargo. There is occasional talk of introducing a tourist passenger service between Aqaba and Wadi Rum.

Arabia, Jordan and parts of southern Syria. Faisal set up government in Damascus and dreamed of an independent Arab realm.

Glad of the help in weakening the Ottoman Empire (allies of Germany during WW1), the British promised to help Faisal. The promise was severely undermined, however, by the 1917 Balfour Declaration:

> His Majesty's Government view with favour the establishment in Palestine of a National Home for the Jewish people, and will use their best endeavours to facilitate the achievement of this object.

This contradictory acceptance of both a Jewish homeland in Palestine and the preservation of the rights of the original Palestinian community lies at the heart of the seemingly irreconcilable Arab-Israeli conflict.

The Creation of Jordan

The Arab Revolt may not have immediately achieved its goal during peace negotiations, but it did lead directly (albeit after over two decades of wrangling with the British) to the birth of the modern state of Jordan.

At the 1919 Paris Peace Conference the British came to an agreement with Faisal, who was given Iraq, while his elder brother Abdullah was proclaimed ruler of Trans-Jordan, the land lying between Iraq and the east bank. A young Winston Churchill drew up the borders in 1921 (see the boxed text, p165). Abdullah made Amman his capital. Britain recognised the territory as an independent state under its protection in 1923, and a small defence force, the Arab Legion, was set up under British officers. A series of treaties after 1928 led to full independence in 1946, when Abdullah was proclaimed king.

TROUBLES WITH PALESTINE (1946–94)

If there is one element that defines the modern history of Jordan, it's the relationship with the peoples on the other side of the river – not just the Jews but also (and perhaps more especially) the Palestinians, whose numbers today make up the majority of the population of Jordan.

1917	1923	1930s
The Balfour Declaration giving Jews a home in Palestine is not the reward the Arabs are promised. In a reluctant compromise, Faisal's brother, Abdullah, becomes ruler of Trans-Jordan.	Britain recognises the territory as an independent emirate under its protection in 1923, and a small defence force, the Arab Legion, is set up under British officers and the nominal control of Emir Abdullah.	The persecution of Jews under the Nazis accelerates the rate of Jewish immigration to Palestine, fuelling more violence between Jews and Arabs. A 1939 proposal to create a bi-national state is rejected by both sides.

Much of the conflict stems from the attempts to create a Jewish national homeland in Palestine, where Arab Muslims accounted for about 90% of the population. Their resentment was understood by Arabs across the region and informed the dialogue of Arab-Israeli relations for the rest of the 20th century.

New Hashemite Kingdom of Jordan

In 1948 resentment escalated into conflict between Arab and Israeli forces, with the result that Jordan won control of East Jerusalem and the West Bank. King Abdullah, reneging on assurances regarding Palestinian independence, annexed the territory and proclaimed the new Hashemite Kingdom of Jordan (HKJ). The new state won immediate recognition from Britain and the USA, but regional powers disapproved of the annexation, added to which the unprecedented immigration of Palestinian refugees placed a strain on limited domestic resources.

In July 1951 King Abdullah was assassinated outside Al-Aqsa Mosque in Jerusalem. The throne eventually passed to his beloved 17-year-old grandson, Hussein, in May 1953. Hussein offered a form of citizenship to all Palestinian Arab refugees in 1960, but refused to relinquish Palestinian territory. Partly in response, the Palestine Liberation Organization (PLO) was formed in 1964.

> When it was founded, the PLO had the blessing of the Arab League to represent the Palestinian people and train guerrilla fighters. The Palestine National Council (PNC) became the executive body of the PLO, with a remit to govern Palestine.

The Six Day War

After a period of relative peace and prosperity, conflict between Arab and Israeli forces broke out again in the 1960s, culminating in the Six Day War, provoked by Palestinian guerrilla raids into Israel from Syria. When the Syrians announced that Israel was amassing troops in preparation for an assault, Egypt responded by asking the UN to withdraw its Emergency Force from the Egypt–Israel border. Nasser then closed the Straits of Tiran (the entrance to the Red Sea), effectively sealing the port of Eilat. Five days later Jordan and Egypt signed a mutual defence pact, dragging Jordan into the oncoming hostilities.

On 5 June 1967 the Israelis dispatched a predawn raid that wiped out the Egyptian Air Force on the ground. In the following days they decimated Egyptian troops in Sinai and Jordanian troops on the West Bank, and overran the Golan Heights in Syria.

The outcome for Jordan was disastrous: it lost the whole of the West Bank and its part of Jerusalem, which together had supplied Jordan with its two principal sources of income – agriculture and tourism. It also resulted in yet another huge wave of Palestinian refugees.

Black September

After the 1967 defeat, the frustrated Palestinians within Jordan became increasingly militant, and by 1968 Palestinian *fedayeen* (guerrilla)

1946	**1948**	**1950**
Jordan gains full independence from the British, and Emir Abdullah is crowned king. In 1947, the UN votes for partition of Palestine but the proposal is rejected by the Arab League.	The State of Israel is proclaimed, the British withdraw immediately and renewed hostilities break out between Arabs and Jews. Half a million Palestinians flood into the area now known as the West Bank.	King Abdullah annexes the West Bank and east Jerusalem, despite paying lip service to Arab declarations backing Palestinian independence and expressly ruling out territorial annexations.

fighters were effectively acting as a state within a state, openly defying Jordanian soldiers.

In 1970 Palestinian militants fired on King Hussein's motorcade and held 68 foreigners hostage in an Amman hotel, while the rogue Popular Front for the Liberation of Palestine hijacked and destroyed three Western planes in front of horrified TV crews. Martial law and bloody fighting (which claimed 3000 lives) followed. Yasser Arafat was spirited out of Amman disguised as a Kuwaiti sheikh in order to attend an Arab League summit in Cairo. A fragile ceasefire was signed, but it was not until midway through 1971 that the final resistance (around Ajloun) was defeated. The guerrillas were forced to recognise Hussein's authority and the Palestinians had to choose between exile and submission. Most chose exile in Lebanon.

Relinquishing Claims to Palestinian Leadership

In 1974 King Hussein reluctantly relinquished Jordan's claims to the West Bank by recognising the PLO as the sole representative of Palestinians with the right to set up a government in any liberated territory. By 1988 the King had severed all Jordan's administrative and legal ties with the West Bank.

In the meantime profound demographic changes, including a sharp rise in population, particularly of young people, had reshaped Jordan. Economic migration, both from the countryside to the city and from Jordan to the increasingly wealthy Gulf States, together with improved education changed social and family structures. Most significantly, Palestinians no longer formed an edgy minority of refugees but instead took their place as the majority of Jordan's population.

A PLO-Israeli declaration of principles in September 1993 set in motion the process of establishing an autonomous Palestinian authority in the Occupied Territories. With this declaration, the territorial question was virtually removed as an obstacle to peace between Jordan and Israel.

The complete integration of Palestinian refugees into all aspects of mainstream Jordanian life is due in no small part to the skilful diplomacy of King Hussein. The numerous assassination attempts (there were at least 12) that dogged the early years of his reign were replaced with a growing respect for his genuine, deep-rooted concern for the Palestinians' plight – which is significant in a region where few other countries were willing to shoulder the burden.

Peace with Israel

On 26 October 1994 Jordan and Israel and the Palestinian Territories signed a momentous peace treaty that provided for the removal of all economic barriers between the two countries and closer cooperation on security, water and other issues.

But there is a twist to the final chapter of relations between Jordan and Palestine in the 20th century. There was a clause in the treaty recognising the 'special role of the Hashemite Kingdom of Jordan in the Muslim holy shrines in Jerusalem'. This inclusion aroused the suspicions of some

1951	1953	1960
King Abdullah is assassinated at Al-Aqsa Mosque in Jerusalem, ending his dream of a single Arab state encompassing Syria, Lebanon, Jordan, Israel and Palestine – a dream which has antagonised Abdullah's Arab neighbours.	Hussein becomes king of Jordan, after his brother is diagnosed with schizophrenia. Despite being British educated, Hussein makes his mark by ousting remaining British troops. They return after Hussein's failed 1958 union with Iraq.	Jordan offers a form of citizenship to all Palestinian Arab refugees but refuses to relinquish Palestinian territory. In response, the Palestine National Liberation Organisation is formed in 1964 with the backing of the Arab League.

KING HUSSEIN

Since his death, King Hussein has become a legend of a leader. On succeeding to the throne on 2 May 1953 at the age of 18, the youthful, British-educated Hussein was known more for his love of pretty women and fast cars. Forty-five years later he was fêted as one of the Middle East's great political survivors, king against all the odds and the de facto creator of the modern state of Jordan.

King Hussein's loyalty to his people was well known. In a role emulated by his son decades later, Hussein would disguise himself as a taxi driver and ask passengers what they really thought of the king.

Hussein's lasting legacy, however, extends well beyond his successful domestic policy. Throughout his reign he maintained close and friendly ties with Britain and courted trade with the West. From his sustained efforts at diplomacy to avert the 1991 Gulf War to his peace agreement with Israel in 1994, the urbane and articulate king of a country in one of the world's toughest neighbourhoods came to be seen as a beacon of moderateness and stability in a region known for neither attribute. This reputation was secured in 1997 when a Jordanian soldier shot and killed seven Israeli schoolgirls in northern Jordan. King Hussein personally attended the funeral in a public display of grief and solidarity with the Israeli families.

Hussein married four times (see the boxed text, p61) and fathered 11 children. He was a highly popular man with many interests and was an accomplished pilot. After a long battle with cancer, during which time he continued his role as peace negotiator between Israel and Palestine, he died in Jordan in February 1999. He was greatly mourned not just by those who knew him but by Jordan and the region at large.

He has come to be regarded as a man who firmly steered the nascent country of Jordan through potentially devastating crises, balancing the demands of Arab nationalism against the political expedience of cooperation with Western interests. In so doing, he helped pave the way for Jordan's modern role in the world as a bridge between two ideologies.

Palestinians regarding the intentions of King Hussein, who at the outset of his long career had enjoyed more than just a 'special role' on the west bank of the Jordan. The treaty made Jordan unpopular within the region at the time, but in the longer term barely cast a shadow over the illustrious reign of one of the Middle East's most beloved rulers.

Relations with Israel & the Palestinian Territories Today

It has been over a decade since the historic 1994 peace treaty and the long-term effect of peace with Israel is still being assessed. While the treaty was branded by some Palestinians as a betrayal, the world at large regarded it as a highly significant step towards vital East-West ties. Flash points between the two nations continue to occur, not just over the fate of the Palestinian people but also over issues such as water supply (see p73), which many predict will replace oil as the conflict zone of the next few decades.

1967	**1970**	**1988**
Israel wins the Six Day War, gaining Jerusalem and the West Bank and resulting in another huge influx of Palestinian refugees. Al-Fatah dominates the PLO under Yasser Arafat and trains guerrillas for raids on Israel.	Black September results in thousands being injured in clashes between the Jordanian government and Palestinian guerrillas. Three hijacked aircraft are blown up by the PLO.	King Hussein relinquishes all remaining ties with the West Bank. The focus turns to home and in 1989 women are allowed to vote for the first time and the legalisation of political parties soon follows.

THE IRAQI DILEMMA (1990–2008)

For the past two decades Jordan has been preoccupied with its neighbours to the east rather than the west – a shift in focus necessitated firstly by the Gulf War and subsequently by the US-led invasion of Iraq.

Given that the founding fathers of the modern states of Iraq and Jordan were brothers, it is not surprising that the two countries have enjoyed periods of close collaboration over the years. In 1958 King Hussein tried to capitalise on this dynastic dimension by establishing the Arab Federation, a short-lived alliance between Jordan and Iraq that was intended to counterbalance the formation of the United Arab Republic between Egypt and Syria. Although the alliance did not last long, the connection between the neighbours remained strong, especially in terms of trade.

The Gulf War

When Saddam Hussein invaded Kuwait in 1990, Jordan found itself in a no-win situation. On the one hand, the Palestinian majority in Jordan backed Saddam's invasion, having been given assurances by Saddam that the showdown would result in a solution to the Palestinian question on the West Bank. On the other hand, King Hussein recognised that siding with Iraq would antagonise Western allies and risk Jordan's dependence on US trade and aid. As a solution, he sided publicly with Baghdad while complying, officially at least, with the UN embargo on trade with Iraq. As a result, although US and Saudi aid was temporarily suspended, loans and help were forthcoming from other quarters, particularly Japan and Europe.

Despite these new streams of income, the Gulf War exacted a heavy financial penalty on the small and relatively poor, oil-less state of Jordan. Ironically, however, Jordan's third wave of refugees in 45 years brought some relief as 500,000 Jordanians and Palestinians returned from the Gulf States. They brought with them a US$500 million windfall that stimulated the economy throughout the 1990s and helped turn Amman, in particular, into a cosmopolitan, modern city.

Current War in Iraq

The current war in Iraq, following the US-led invasion of the country after the events of 9/11, scuppered Jordan's access to cheap oil while compromising its main market for exports. It has also brought another influx of refugees (see the boxed text, p58) – this time Iraqi in origin.

The need to house these refugees has led to an increase in house prices in Amman, putting home ownership beyond the reach of many Jordanians. This, together with an overall escalation in prices has driven up inflation: it topped 5.4% in 2007 and is now a major issue for the government. Tolerance with Iraqi refugees is wearing thin, particularly as most state their intention to return home after the conflict, adding to the sense that Jordanians see little benefit from their role as temporary safe haven.

UN assessments put the total cost to Jordan of the Gulf War (mid-1990 to mid-1991) at over US$8 billion. The UN naval blockade of Aqaba alone, aimed at enforcing UN sanctions against Iraq, cost Jordan US$300 million a year in lost revenue between 1991 and 1994.

A History of Jordan, by Philip Robbins, details the modern history of Jordan from the 1920s to the present day and is one of very few specific books to focus on the Hashemite Kingdom. The other main available work is Kamal Salibi's The Modern History of Jordan.

1990	1994	1999
Saddam Hussein's invasion of Kuwait, supported by the Palestinians, requires careful diplomacy by King Hussein, who publicly supports Baghdad while suing for peace. Palestinian Gulf workers flood into Jordan.	A historic peace treaty between Israel and Jordan is signed, ending 46 years of war. A clause within the treaty regarding Jordan's 'special role' over Muslim holy shrines in Jerusalem strains relations with Arab neighbours.	King Hussein dies on 7 February. His funeral is attended by former and current presidents of Israel, USA, UK, Russia, Germany and France, among others, indicating his valued role as mediator for peace. His son, Abdullah, becomes king.

JORDAN TODAY

For much of the Middle East, 'democracy' – which is perceived as promoting the interests of the individual over those of the community – is an alien concept. Islamic societies in Arab countries tend to place much more emphasis on the community rather than the individual. Respect for the community, together with a tribal tradition of respect for elders, leads to the favouring of strong, centralised government under an autocratic leader – what might be called, in other words, benign dictatorship. Of course, such a system is only as good as the leader.

Benign Dictatorship

When it comes to good leaders, they don't come much better than King Hussein, regarded now as one of the great peacemakers of modern history (see the boxed text, p49) and deeply caring of his people.

Towards the end of his reign, King Hussein presided over a form of authoritarian government, tempered by parliamentary intervention, familiar to tribal desert monarchies across the Arab world. In November 1989 the first full parliamentary elections since 1967 were held in Jordan, and women were allowed to vote for the first time. Four years later most political parties were legalised and allowed to participate in parliamentary and municipal elections.

Jordan now has multiple registered parties, including a communist party and the main opposition Islamic Action Front (IAF), which is connected with the fundamentalist Muslim Brotherhood. Criticising the king, however, remains against the law.

Hussein's son, Abdullah, who studied in the USA and attended Sandhurst in the UK, came to the throne on 9 June 1999, ushering in a modernising monarchy in touch with the sensibilities of a globalised world.

The king has thus far demonstrated his father's diplomatic acumen in placating regional neighbours (especially the Syrians and Palestinians who are critical of Jordan's relations with Israel) while finding ways of integrating with the rest of the world. His efforts in this regard have already won him Western support, especially in his promotion of a peaceful resolution to the current Palestinian *intifada* (uprising), and helped him to secure billions of dollars of US aid and a prestigious free-trade agreement.

Jordan Circa 2008

King Abdullah belongs to the new generation of Arab leaders in favour of social and economic reform, and this, together with his drive to stamp out corruption, has helped win public favour.

Parliamentary elections last took place in November 2007 when independent, pro-government candidates won the majority of seats. Prime Minister Nader al-Dahabi has strong backing in parliament, but has

King Abdullah is a keen pilot, scuba diver and rally driver; he enjoys Western food and speaks better English than Arabic. Married to Queen Rania (see the boxed text, p61), he has three children: Crown Prince Hussein, Princess Iman and Princess Salma.

King Abdullah backs the promotion of women's rights and supports freedom of the press, albeit tempered by local sensibilities: Jordan Media City, the country's state-of-the-art media hub, transmits 120 channels.

2000	**2001**	**c 2004**
Jordan accedes to the World Trade Organisation, and the European Free Trade Association in 2001. Trade significantly increases under the free-trade accord with the USA and Jordanian Qualifying Industrial Zones (QIZ).	The US invasion of Iraq is strenuously protested by Arab countries in the region. King Hussein sides publicly with Baghdad while complying, officially at least, with the UN embargo on trade with Iraq.	Water supply becomes a major issue in the region. Jordan considers a pipeline between the Red Sea and the shrinking Dead Sea and begins negotiations for transporting water from ancient aquifers in Diseh to Amman.

A NEW PATH THROUGH JORDAN'S HISTORY

Sitting around the conference table at Ajloun Nature Reserve, with Post-it notes covering the whiteboard, the gathering looks like a modern corporate training session. In fact, this is a planning meeting with an agenda much less worldly – and much more ancient – in origin.

The assembled company is discussing the course of Abraham's Path, which winds not just through the neighbouring woodlands of Ajloun but also through history itself. Someone unfurls a map with a list of GPS coordinates that indicate the 45km of the route already open to the public. The rest of the 1000km path, which begins in Turkey and ends in Israel, taking 10 weeks to hike, exists only as yet on paper. 'We're not in a hurry,' Tyler Norris, the executive director of the project explains. 'The path is 4000 years old.' Planning its resurrection can take a day or two.

Building a new path, or unravelling an old one, isn't an overnight activity. Apart from the obvious difficulties of cutting and mapping a viable route, there are also negotiations to be made – not just with landowners but with whole communities who need to be convinced that they stand to benefit from the passing traffic of a new pilgrim route. Then there are the border crossings. This is no ordinary path, but one that traverses contemporary conflict zones: how do you persuade Syrians, for example, to let people walk along a path that is connected with Israel?

But the project staff are not phased. Abraham's Path is more than just a trail through history: it's a path of connection and healing. 'Abraham was chosen,' says one of the route-planners, 'because he was the first monotheist and is therefore a figure common to the three billion people who believe in Judaism, Christianity and Islam.'

The point of the path is neither political nor religious, however. It is first and foremost a magnificent hike through some of the most historically significant lands known to humanity. The organisers (who have large-scale international backing) hope that by walking the trail, people will gain a greater understanding of this ancient and troubled region and go home with more tolerance and respect for the people who live either side of divisive borders. 'Great conflicts are complex,' says Norris. 'Sometimes only a story can heal them.' This particular story is certainly one worth following. For more information see www.abrahampath.org.

Jordan is ranked 86th out of 177 countries in the Human Development Index. Tourism contributes 11% of GDP and over US$800 million annually to the economy. In Jordan 80% of people have a mobile phone, compared with 25% in Egypt.

yet to convince the electorate of his abilities, especially in the light of continuing unemployment problems (the official rate for 2007 was 13.5%), which have forced many Jordanian to move abroad – a trend the government is trying to reverse. The government is currently developing health-care and housing safety nets and is focused on improving education.

To help improve productivity and make Jordan a more attractive country for foreign investment, the government has reduced the debt-to-GDP ratio and promoted Jordan as a hi-tech service centre. A major challenge now facing Jordan is reducing dependence on foreign grants. The current resurgence of tourism (after a setback due to the war in Iraq) is helping in this regard, and the bitter experiences of the suicide bombings of three hotels in Amman in 2005 and a random shooting in 2007 (see p95) are thankfully becoming distant memories.

2005

Three hotels in Amman are blown up in coordinated suicide attacks in Amman, masterminded by the Iraqi wing of Al-Qaeda. Tourism, which had been booming since the 1994 peace treaty, takes an immediate hit.

2007

As one of many steps in the modernisation of the country's political, economic and social structure, 20% of seats in municipal councils are reserved for women.

2008

Iraq contributes to the maintenance of the 500,000 Iraqi refugees currently residing in Jordan. The arrival of the Iraqis is the fourth such influx of refugees in the modern history of this geographically small country.

The Culture

THE NATIONAL PSYCHE

Ahlan wa sahlan! It's one of the most common greetings in Arabic and one that defines the way Jordanians relate to the people around them, especially guests. The root words mean 'people' or 'family' *(ahl)* and 'ease' *(sahl),* so translated loosely the expression means 'be as one of the family and at your ease'. It's a gracious thought, and one that ends up in English simply as 'welcome' or (more commonly to tourists) 'welcome to Jordan'. Among Arabs it's used to mean anything from 'hello' to 'you're welcome' (after thanks).

Arab traditions of hospitality and kindness are deeply ingrained in the psyches of most Jordanians, especially the Bedouin. Rooted in the harsh realities of life in the desert, these traditions have been virtually codified into all social behaviour. Century-old notions of hospitality mix with an easy modernity and wonderful sense of humour that make Jordanians easy to get along with.

Writers over the centuries have commented on the dignity, pride and courtesy of the Bedouin in particular, characterising them as courageous and fierce fighters but also loyal friends. Yet there is an increasing polarisation in Jordanian society, and in many ways the modern Western-looking outlook of Amman's young middle and upper classes contrasts starkly with the conservative Bedouin morality of the countryside.

Bedouin concepts of honour *(ird)* run deep but sit uneasily with the freedoms many affluent Jordanian women have come to expect. Rapid social change connected with the rise of tourism has also led to a clash of social values in places like Petra and Wadi Musa. The effect of tourism on traditional Bedouin hospitality and lifestyle has yet to be studied.

However, Jordanians still share many values, including a deep pride in their country and respect for the Jordanian royal family, which itself stems in part from the ingrained tribal respect for local elders, or sheikhs. Islam dominates the Jordanian view of the world, of course, as does the Palestinian experience, which is hardly surprising when you consider that 65% of Jordanians are Palestinian.

A belief in and surrender to God's will (Islam literally means 'submission') is fundamental to the Jordanian psyche. Ask Jordanians, *kaif halak?* (how are you?) and they will reply, *al-hamdu lillah* (fine, thanks be to God). Ask if peace will come soon to the Middle East, or even if the bus to Jerash will leave on time, and the reply will doubtless be *in sha' Allah* (God willing). Say your goodbyes with *ma'a salama* and you will be told *Allah ysmalakh* (God keep you safe).

Sharing deep ethnic and cultural ties with both Palestine and Iraq, many Jordanians are frustrated and at times even angered by American and European policies towards the Middle East, but Jordanians are always able to differentiate a government and its policies from its people. Regardless of your nationality, you'll never be greeted with animosity in Jordan, but rather with courtesy and hospitality that is deeply impressive and often quite humbling.

DAILY LIFE

Like much of the Middle East, Jordan is a country that has deep sentimental attachments to the desert (the historical source of Arab tradition), but with an increasingly urban society the gap between rural and city

The checked keffiyah headdress is an important national symbol in Jordan – red and white for the Bedouin; black and white for the Palestinians – held in place by the black rope-like *agal*.

Jordan has a regionally renowned education system; about 87% of Jordanians are literate and about 97% of children attend primary school. School is compulsory for children from the ages of five to 14.

'AHLAN WA SAHLAN' – WELCOME TO JORDAN

Jordan has been entertaining travellers for centuries, so perhaps it is natural that these words of welcome are so frequently uttered. People say 'welcome' to foreigners in many countries, but in Jordan this is not just a stock phrase or a preliminary for hard sell – it is a genuine invitation to be 'at ease'. Here are a few snapshots collected from travellers, Jordanians and visitors that illustrate some of the many ways in which a traveller is made to feel welcome.

■ 'After making it clear to a porter at the airport that we didn't want help, we were surprised when he shook our hands, told us his name, said "welcome" and walked away!'

■ 'A congregation of lads at Jerash assembled to show us the way. Inevitably we thought they all wanted pens or money, but in fact, they just wanted to show us the way.'

■ 'We're always a bit uncomfortable about being British in places like this – you know, given the past and that – but we wish we had a pound for every time someone's said to us: "Ah British! Good friends with Jordan." It's touching really. All considered.'

■ 'The past is the past. People are people. Your God, my God the same. So where's the problem. *Mafi mushkala* (no problem). Come, have tea! Now politicians, that's another story…'

■ 'I got used to giving a lift to anyone who asked for one. Well, the transport's not up to much in some places. I thought it a bloody nuisance at first but nothing made me feel more at home in the end. The biggest problem was trying to find a way of politely refusing to go home for lunch afterwards.'

■ 'He only had a bunch of spring onions in his bag – the work of the morning in the field. He gave us half, and a sprig of coriander. As a gardener, that's what I call real generosity.'

■ 'My wife cooks very well. Come home. Eat at us. We'll take you to the airport in the morning.'

communities is growing ever wider. There is also increasing economic polarisation, especially in Amman – just compare gritty downtown with affluent Abdoun.

The well-educated middle and upper classes of Amman shop in malls, drink lattes in mixed-sex Starbucks and obsess over the latest fashions. Mobile phones dominate life in Jordan as they do abroad. Yet in other districts of the same city, urban unemployment is high and entire neighbourhoods of Amman are made up of Palestinian and Iraqi refugees.

At the other end of the spectrum is traditional Bedouin life, deeply rooted in the desert, semi-nomadic and centred on herding. For more on the Bedouin, see the boxed text, opposite.

Due to high unemployment, economic migration is common in Jordan and most families have at least one male who is temporarily working away from home, whether in Amman, the Gulf States or further abroad. The remittances sent home by these absent workers are increasingly important to family budgets. Each economically active person has to support, on average, four other people.

The Bedouin are known for their sense of humour, which they list – alongside courage, alertness and religious faith – as one of the four secrets of life, encouraging tolerance and humility.

Family ties are all-important to both modern and traditional Jordanians. Most Jordanian women only socialise with other women, and often only inside the family group, while Jordanian men chat with other men in male-only coffeehouses. Attitudes towards women remain quite traditional.

Marriages are often arranged and matches are commonly made between cousins. The marriage ceremony usually takes place in either the mosque or the home of the bride or groom. After the marriage the men of the family drive around the streets in a long convoy, sounding their horns, blasting out music and making as much ballyhoo as possible. After that the partying goes on until the early hours of the morning – often until sunrise.

Many families, especially in smaller towns and rural areas, remain traditional in terms of divisions within the house. As a rule, various parts of the house are reserved for men and others for women. This becomes particularly apparent when guests are present.

Meals are generally eaten on the floor, with everyone gathered around several trays of food shared by all. More traditional families are often quite hierarchical at meal times. The grandparents and male head of the house may eat in one circle, the latter's wife and the older children and other women in the family in another, and the small children in yet another.

THE MODERN CARETAKERS OF THE DESERT *Jenny Walker*

Pulling up outside a small enclosure on the edge of Diseh near Wadi Rum, Mr Zawaedh, President of the Diseh Villages Touristic Cooperative, proudly calls us over to inspect the arrival of the newest member of the community. The small bundle of pale fur and oversized legs belongs to a two-day-old camel, shivering in the winter winds. 'I call him Ibn Jinny, son of Jenny,' he said. I took this to be a compliment and mused that this man belonged to roughly the same tribe of people whom TE Lawrence less than a century ago had described as 'uncompromising, hard-headed' and 'unsentimental'. Settling down to a glass of tea in time-honoured fashion, I recognise the characteristics 'kind and hospitable' used to describe the tribespeople of Wadi Rum in 1879 by the great English explorer and Arabist, Richard Burton.

As we pass through the village, and eventually cross the sands from one Diseh camp to another, you can't help but notice the same tribal name cropping up. 'This is our territory,' explains Mr Zawaedh, surveying the invisible line in the seamless desert. 'Over there is Wadi Rum protected area – the territory of the Zalabia.' At last the unfathomable distinction between Operator 1 and Operator 2 routes at the Visitors Centre falls into place.

Whether Zawaedha or Zalabia and whether from Wadi Rum, Wadi Musa or the great *Badia* beyond, the Bedouin are universally proud of 'their Jordan' and welcome guests who visit them in their ancient tribal lands. It's not surprising, then, that many of the country's Bedouin now make a living from tourism. 'This is the Bedouin life,' enthuses one camp owner near Wadi Musa. 'This is our art, our craft, to reveal the wonders of our country.' For centuries the Bedouin have been doing the same, albeit for slightly different purposes, offering bread and salt to those in need on the understanding that the same courtesy will be offered them in return. The currency today is usually money, but the principle of easing the passage of strangers through traditional tribal territories remains unchanged. Unchanged, too, is the principle of 'word of mouth' in advertising friendly encampments, though today the internet has replaced the camel caravan as the modus operandi.

Of course, the changes have required sacrifices. As we sit on the edge of the great arena of sand in the heart of Wadi Rum, a host from the Zalabia tribe casts a wistful eye over the spectacle of night creeping up over the land of his forefathers. 'Life before was simple and free,' he says, fidgeting with a mobile phone and a possible booking for the family camp. 'We managed goats and sheep and looked for water. Now there's education and working with tourists, even tribal conferences in New York – there's more money, but it's hard.' For most people, including most Jordanians, hard means a goat-hair bed and scorpions, insufferable heat and freezing nights, not enough to eat and being forever thirsty. But for those who were (and the few who still are) brought up that way, this is the life where, in the words of a Bedouin ranger, the 'herdsmen sing', where the desert is as familiar 'as the palms of one's own hand' and where the mind can rest in the cradle of the sands.

We watch a camel drift across the horizon. 'Where is he going?' I ask. 'Probably south, across the border to Saudi Arabia – he knows no borders.' 'How will you get him back?' 'He comes back when he's ready – in one month, or in six months, we'll find him or he'll find us.' A white-crowned black wheatear hops onto the rock and sings to the sunset. Our host takes it as a cue to perform ablutions for prayer. Clearly and thankfully, it's going to take more than a computer and a tribal conference in New York to take the nomad out of the Bedouin: like the camel that returns when ready, the Bedouin know where home is.

SOCIAL GRACES *Jenny Walker*

Standing wedged between the door and a table and with no room to back out politely, my Jordanian companion looked in horror as a foreign man proffered a large, hairy hand in her direction and gushed a greeting. 'Can you believe it,' Maryam said, 'and in Ramadan too!' I asked why she didn't simply refuse to shake hands: 'I didn't want to embarrass him,' she said. The scenario is a common enough one and it highlights both the desirability of learning a few courtesies as a traveller and also of the Jordanian good-natured tolerance of social faux pas.

Handshaking is an important part of the ritual of greeting in Jordan but usually only between members of the same sex. If you witness an accident, for example, the first few moments will probably be taken up with copious handshaking, greeting and asking after each man's family … before a slanging match erupts about who is to blame. When the police turn up, the whole ritual will be repeated again. It may even be accompanied by kisses on the cheek if the police are friends with the injured parties.

Don't think that seeing two men kissing gives you the right to do the same, mind you. All signs of affection, except between members of the same sex (and of the strictly platonic kind), is frowned upon in public. Not that you'd guess that these days from the relaxed attitudes of trendsetters in the city who openly walk arm in arm with a loved one.

Hands and arms are one thing: you can get away with a bit of blundering with those limbs (like using your left hand to give something, forgetting to touch your heart when refusing something – or, for that matter, forgetting to refuse something you intend eventually to accept). Feet, however, are entirely another matter. 'He sat there,' sighed Eiad, 'waving his feet at us right through supper – it really put me off eating. And why do foreign men have such big feet? And why don't they wash them?' This is a hard one to answer, but here is a bit of quick advice for anyone contemplating a visit to a home or a mosque: wash them, unsock them and tuck them under you when sitting on the floor.

Of course, learning the subtleties of 'custom and manner' is difficult in one's own culture and doubly so in someone else's. But that said, making the effort to fit in is invariably appreciated. And there's not much harm that can't be undone with a smile, a box of baklava and a compliment about the lovable children. Perhaps social 'differences' between nations are not so different after all.

In the evenings locals in the cities may window-shop, stroll around the streets, enjoy a leisurely meal, go to the cinema or watch TV. Men may pass the time in a local coffeehouse, playing cards, smoking a nargileh (water pipe) or perhaps watching European football on the TV, while the kids play the real thing on the streets outside.

POPULATION

The population of Jordan stood at about 6.2 million in 2008, a substantial increase from just 586,000 in 1958. Some 953,000 of these are registered as refugees (primarily from the wars of 1948 and 1967, and the more recent conflicts in Iraq) with the UN Relief & Works Agency (UNRWA). In an effort to reduce the expected population of eight million in 2024, the Jordanian National Population Commission is hoping to dramatically reduce the birth rate, through the promotion of family planning, to 2.1 children per family. In 2008 the fertility rate stood at 2.4 children, well on the way to meeting this target.

Approximately 2.2 million people live in the capital, Amman, and a further 850,000 live in neighbouring Zarqa and suburbs. The majority (98%) of Jordanians are Arab (which includes Bedouin); over 60% are Palestinian Arabs. There are also small communities of Circassians, Chechens, Armenians and Western expatriates. According to UNHCR, there are now between 450,000 and 500,000 exiled Iraqis living in Jordan.

There are numerous Bedouin tribes (or subclans) from the influential Beni Sakr and Huweitat to the smaller but very visible Bdoul and Ammareen of Petra.

The Bedouin are the original desert dwellers of Arabia, perceived by many as the representatives and guardians of the very essence of 'Arab-ness'. They form the majority of the indigenous population, although today not more than 40,000 Bedouin can be considered truly nomadic.

Arabs

Over 98% of Jordanians are Arab, descended from various tribes that migrated to the area from all directions over the centuries.

PALESTINIANS

About one half of Jordan's population, according to **Minorities at Risk** (www.cidcn .umd.edu/mar), is made up of Palestinians who fled, mostly from the West Bank, during the wars of 1948 and 1967 and after the Gulf War in 1990–91.

Palestinians have been granted the right to Jordanian citizenship, and many have exercised that option. Palestinians play an important part in the political, cultural and economic life of Jordan, and although many occupy high positions in government and business, many continue to dream of a return to an independent Palestine. This is partly why so many have resisted integration and continue to live in difficult condi-tions in the 10 official refugee camps that dot the landscape (see the boxed text, p58).

Circassians & Chechens

The Circassians (Turkic Muslims from the Caucasus) fled persecution in Russia in the late 19th century to settle in the Jordan Valley, becom-ing prosperous farmers. There are now about 40,000 Circassians (living mainly in Wadi as-Seer and Na'ur, both near Amman) but intermarriage has made them virtually indistinguishable from Arabs.

Historically and ethnically related to the Circassians is the small (about 4000) Shiite community of Chechens, the only other recognised ethnic minority in Jordan.

RELIGION

Although the population is overwhelmingly Islamic, Jordan is officially secular, and freedom of religion is a statutory right of the Jordanian constitution.

Islam

Islam is the predominant religion in Jordan. Muslims are called to prayer five times a day. The midday prayers on Friday, when the sheikh of the mosque delivers his weekly *khutba* (sermon), are considered the most important.

Islam shares a common heritage with two other great monotheistic faiths, Judaism and Christianity, although it was founded seven centuries after the latter. The holy book of Islam is the Quran, meaning literally 'reading' or 'recitation'. The Quran is believed to be the word of God, communicated to the Prophet Mohammed directly in a series of revela-tions in the early 7th century. For Muslims, Islam is the apogee of the monotheistic faiths from which it derives so much. Muslims tradition-ally attribute a place of great respect to Christians and Jews, whom they consider *Ahl al-kitab* (the People of the Book).

EARLY YEARS OF ISLAM

Born into a trading family of the Arabian city of Mecca (in present-day Saudi Arabia) in AD 570, Mohammed began receiving revelations in

Islam, Judaism and Christ-ianity share many of the same prophets: Abraham (Ibrahim), Noah (Nuh), Moses (Musa), Jesus (Isa), John the Baptist (Yahya), Job (Ayyub), Joshua (Yosha), Lot (Lut) and Noah (Nuh). Mohammed is not considered divine, but rather the last of these prophets.

For a sensitive, accessible and compact account of Islamic belief and practice, try *Islam: A Short History* by Karen Armstrong. It also tackles the modern dilemmas facing Islam.

REFUGEES IN JORDAN

Occupying the calm eye of the storm in the Middle East, Jordan has a long tradition of absorbing the displaced peoples of its troubled neighbours – so much so, in fact, that the majority of its population is made up of people who are non-Jordanian in origin.

By far the largest proportion of this non-Jordanian contingent is Palestinian, and no country has absorbed more Palestinian refugees than Jordan. As of 2006, official estimates put the total number of Palestinian refugees in Jordan at 1.5 million; unofficial figures, according to the UN Office for the Coordination of Humanitarian Affairs, are closer to 3.5 million.

Most of the refugees have become an integral part of Jordanian life, with many succeeding in business, politics and cultural pursuits. In the aftermath of the 1990 Iraqi invasion of Kuwait, as many as 500,000 Iraqi refugees entered Jordan. Although they placed a huge strain upon already creaking infrastructure, they also brought with them an estimated US$500 million, sparking a boom in the economy.

Nonetheless, around 329,150 refugees (16% of the total refugee population in Jordan) are housed in 10 camps administered by the UN Relief & Works Agency (UNRWA), which remains responsible for all health, education and relief programs. The first four camps were set up after 1948, with the remaining six established after the 1967 war. As at December 2006, the largest camps were those at Baqa'a (with 90,575 inhabitants), the Amman New Camp (50,609), Marqa (44,198) and Jebel al-Hussein (29,520), with large camps also at Zarqa, Jerash and Irbid. The original tent shelters have long since been replaced with more permanent structures and often more resemble suburbs than refugee camps.

In contrast to the periodic assimilation of Palestinians, whose arrival is usually accompanied by much sympathy on the part of Jordanians, the influx of Iraqi refugees over the past five years has become the subject of considerable local resentment. This is partly due to the economic spending power of the newcomers, which has led to an astronomical hike in property prices in and around Amman. This in turn has helped fuel inflation throughout Jordan.

Jordan has repeatedly appealed for international aid to cope with the 500,000 Iraqi refugees (UNHCR estimate) currently residing in Jordan. Over 50,000 Iraqi pupils alone have enrolled in the country's overcrowded state schools. In 2008 Iraq gave $8 million to the UN refugee agency intended to help its smaller and poorer neighbour provide education and health services for its nationals, but this doesn't scratch the surface of the estimated economic burden on the Jordanian economy of over $2 billion.

Unlike the Palestinians, almost all (95%) Iraqi refugees have registered their intent to return home when the security situation improves. As relations stand, many Jordanians think this can't come a day too soon.

Contact the Jordanian **Department of Palestinian Affairs** (☎ 06-5666172; www.un.org/unrwa /refugees/jordan.html) for information. See www.unhcr.org for more on the Iraqi refugee situation.

AD 610, and after a time began imparting the content of Allah's message to the inhabitants of Mecca. Mohammed's call to submit to God's will was not universally well received, making more of an impact among the poor than among the wealthy families of the city, who feared his interference in the status quo.

> Among Muslims it is customary to follow a mention of the Prophet Mohammed's name with the phrase *Salla Allahu Wa Salam* (Peace Be Upon Him). In all written references to him, this phrase is shortened to an acronym (PBUH).

By AD 622 Mohammed was forced to flee with his followers to Medina, an oasis town some 300km to the north and now Islam's second holy city. This migration (the Hejira) marks the beginning of the Islamic calendar: year 1 AH or AD 622.

In Medina, Mohammed continued to preach. Soon he and his followers clashed with the rulers of Mecca, led by the powerful Quraysh tribe. By 630 his followers returned to take Mecca. In the two years before his death, many of the surrounding tribes swore allegiance to him and the new faith.

Mecca, as home of the sacred Kaaba – a cube-shaped building allegedly built by Ibrahim (Abraham) and his son Ismail and housing a black stone of ancient spiritual focus – became Islam's holiest city. Muslims ('those who submit') are enjoined to this day to face Mecca when praying.

After Mohammed's death in 632, Arab tribes conquered the Middle East, Egypt and North Africa, Spain and eventually France, taking Islam with them. The Arabic language and Islamic faith remained long after the military conquests faded into history, uniting large parts of Europe, Africa and Asia in a shared cultural and religious ideology. For more on the historical spread of Islam, see p42.

SUNNIS & SHIITES

Islam split into different sects soon after its foundation, based not so much on theological interpretation but on an historical event. When the Prophet died in 632, he left no instructions as to who should be his successor, nor the manner in which the future Islamic leaders (known as caliphs) should be chosen.

In the ensuing power struggle, *shi'a* (partisans) supported the claim of Ali bin Abi Taleb, Mohammed's cousin and son-in-law, to become leader of the Muslims, while others supported the claim of the Umayyads, the dynasty established by Caliph Mu'awiyah. From that point the Muslim community split into two competing factions: the Shiites, who are loyal to the descendants of Mohammed, and the Sunnis, the orthodox bedrock of Islam.

Within Jordan most Muslims are Sunnis belonging to the Hanafi school of thought. A minority of around 15,000 Druze in Northeast Jordan (including the town of Azraq) follow a form of Shiite Islam.

The spread of Islam in the 7th century has been described by historian Bernard Lewis as 'one of the swiftest and most dramatic changes in the whole of history'.

ISLAMIC CUSTOMS

The first words a newborn baby hears are the call to prayer. A week later this is followed by a ceremony in which the baby's head is shaved and an animal is sacrificed. The major event of a boy's childhood is circumcision, which normally takes place sometime between the ages of seven and 12.

Before praying, Muslims follow certain rituals. They must wash their hands, mouth, ears, arms, feet, head and neck in running water. All mosques have a small area set aside for this purpose. If no mosque is nearby and there is no water available, scouring with sand suffices; where there is no sand, the motions of washing must still be enacted.

Muslims must cover their head, face Mecca (all mosques are oriented so that the mihrab, or prayer niche, faces the correct way – south-southeast in Jordan) and follow a set pattern of gestures and genuflections. Muslims do not require a mosque to pray and you'll often see Jordanians praying by the side of the road or at the back of their shop; many keep a small prayer rug handy for such times.

In everyday life Muslims are prohibited from drinking alcohol and eating pork (as the pig is considered unclean), and must refrain from fraud, usury, slander and gambling. Followers of Islam believe in angels, the infallibility of the Quran (and parts of the Bible), a day of judgment, predestination of worldly affairs and life after death.

Bismillah, literally 'In the name of God, the Merciful, the Compassionate', is the opening phrase of all suras (verses) in the Quran and is used in general conversation as an expression of sincerity or to commend something to God.

Christianity

Statistics on the number of Christians in Jordan are wildly contradictory. Christians are believed to account for 5% to 6% of Jordan's population. Most live in Karak, Madaba, Salt, Fuheis, Ajlun and Amman where churches abound representing the three major branches of Christianity in Jordan: Orthodox, Catholic (known in Jordan as Latin) and (to a far lesser extent) Protestant.

About two-thirds of Christians in Jordan are Greek Orthodox. This church has an Arabic liturgy, and is the mother church of the Jacobites (Syrian Orthodox), who broke away in the 6th century. Coptic Orthodox and Armenian Orthodox Christians are also represented in Jordan.

Most of the other third of Christians are Greek Catholics, or Melchites, under the authority of the patriarch who resides in Damascus. This church observes a Byzantine tradition of married clergy being in charge of rural parishes, while diocesan clergy are celibate.

WOMEN IN JORDAN

Women in Jordan have access to a full education (in 2002 the number of girls in primary and secondary schools was almost identical to the number of boys); they are entitled to vote (Jordanian women got the vote in 1967 but didn't have a chance to use it for the first time until 1989); many work in male-dominated industries and businesses; and they are permitted to drive cars. In 2001 the legal age of marriage was lifted from 15 years old for women and 16 for men to 18 for both, although Islamic judges are still permitted to sanction underage marriages.

In recent years Jordanian women have made great progress in male-dominated professions. Jordan's first female MP (Toujan Faisal) was elected in the early 1990s (a minimum of six women MPs is guaranteed by royal decree), the first female taxi driver appeared in 1997, first mayor (in Ajlun) in 1995, first judge in 1996 and first ambassador to the European Union in 2001. But the rise of a few women to senior positions has

THE FIVE PILLARS OF ISLAM

In order to live a devout life, a Muslim is expected to carry out at least the Five Pillars of Islam:

■ Haj – the pinnacle of a devout Muslim's life is the pilgrimage to the holy sites in and around Mecca. The haj takes place in the last month of the year, Zuul-Hijja, and Muslims from all over the world travel to Saudi Arabia for the pilgrimage and subsequent feast of Eid al-Adha. The returned pilgrim earns the right to be addressed as Haji. Women may perform the haj with a male chaperon.

■ Salat – this is the obligation of prayer, ideally expressed five times a day when the muezzins call upon the faithful to pray: before sunrise, noon, mid-afternoon, sunset and before mid-night. Communal prayers are only obligatory on Friday, although the strong sense of community makes joining together in a *masjid* ('place of prostration', ie mosque) preferable to most.

■ Shahada – this is the profession of the faith and the basic tenet of Islam: 'There is no God but Allah and Mohammed is his prophet' *(La il-laha illa Allah Mohammed rasul Allah)*. This is commonly heard as part of the call to prayer, and at other events such as births and deaths. People can often be heard muttering the first half of the sentence to themselves, as if seeking a little strength to get through the trials of the day.

■ Sawm – Ramadan, the ninth month of the Muslim calendar, commemorates the revelation of the Quran to Mohammed. In a demonstration of the Muslims' renewal of faith, they are urged to abstain from sex and from letting anything (including cigarettes) pass their lips from dawn to dusk every day of the month. For more on Ramadan, see Holidays (p296) and Celebrations (p79).

■ Zakat – giving alms to the poor has always been an essential part of Islamic social teaching and, in some parts of the Muslim world, has been developed into various forms of tax as a way of redistributing funds to the needy. The moral obligation towards one's poorer neighbours continues to be emphasised at a personal and community level, and many Islamic groups run large charitable institutions, including Amman's Islamic Hospital.

THE ROYAL WOMEN OF JORDAN

Claiming unbroken descent from Prophet Mohammed, Jordan's Hashemite royal family is a nationally beloved and regionally respected institution. Of course, all monarchies have their critics from time to time, not least for seeming arcane in their function, but Jordan's modern royal family has helped to redefine the royal image through benign and diplomatic governance (especially with regard to Middle East peace issues), as well as through a history of charitable works.

In a region where men are more commonly the public face of royal initiatives, Jordan has been unusual for the high profile of its royal women. Visit many of the small women's cooperatives like Bani Hamida in Mukawir, and you will likely find some mention of either Queen Noor or Queen Rania in the patronage or even funding of the project.

So who are these two influential women? Queen Noor (www.noor.gov.jo) was the late King Hussein's fourth wife. She was born as Lisa Halaby, an architect and urban planner from Washington DC who studied at Princeton. Born into a distinguished Arab-American family (her father served under the administration of John F Kennedy and was head of Pan-Am for a while), she met King Hussein while working on a project for Royal Jordanian Airlines. After a much-scrutinised whirlwind romance they married in a traditional Islamic ceremony in 1978.

Adopting the name Queen Noor upon her conversion to Islam, Jordan's new queen signalled the beginning of a new era. Throughout her tenure she campaigned for women's rights, children's welfare and community improvement, setting up the Noor Foundation. Queen Noor took an important role in explaining Jordan's stand against the 1990 Gulf War to American audiences. Since her husband's death, Queen Noor has scaled back her public presence but still supports many worthy causes.

Queen Rania (www.queenrania.jo) is the wife of the present king. Since King Abdullah's accession to the throne in 2004 she has assumed a prominent position on a number of issues. Born in Kuwait to a notable Jordanian family of Palestinian origin, and educated at the American University of Cairo, she married King Abdullah in 1993. As Jordan's new first lady, she has followed Queen Noor's example in establishing her own charity, the Jordan River Foundation, supporting local women's initiatives. Not afraid of a public profile, she can be seen in activities as diverse as campaigning for the rights of women to running the Dead Sea Marathon.

---

yet to be matched by across-the-board equality. The majority of women work in health and education; the highest levels of inequality remain in the media and the political arena. Less than 1% of judges are women. In 1991 14% of the labour force was made up of women; by 2007, according to UN data, this had risen to 25.5%.

Compared with neighbouring Muslim countries, polygamy (by men) is rare although legal; segregation is uncommon (except in some homes, restaurants and mosques); there are no official restrictions about dress codes; and female infanticide and female circumcision are extremely rare. Very few women wear the *hejab* veil and almost none wear full-body chador, though many women wear a headscarf.

Amendments to the law in 2002 made it possible for women to file for divorce if they repay the dowry given by their husband, though the social stigma regarding divorce remains strong. The legal changes also require men who marry more than once (Islam allows four wives if each wife is assured equal treatment) to inform both their first and their new wives.

Arranged marriages and dowries are still common, but parents do not often enforce a wedding against their daughter's wish. A woman's 'honour' is still valued in traditional societies, and sex before marriage can still be dealt with harshly by other members of a woman's family (see the boxed text, p62).

Women in more traditional societies are starting to gain some financial independence through a number of Jordanian organisations that encourage small-scale craft production (see p65) and local tourism projects.

Queen Noor is not the mother of the present king. That distinction belongs to King Hussein's second wife, Princess Muna, who was from England. They were married for 10 years (1961–71), having met on the film set of *Lawrence of Arabia*.

CRIMES OF HONOUR

In 2004 a book entitled *Forbidden Love*, written by Norma Khouri, arrived on the bookshelves. Within weeks, the author (to the delight of her publisher, Random House) found she had a bestseller on her hands. Better and bigger than that, she had overnight become the convenient voice the West wanted to hear: an Arab woman speaking out against the supposed 'tyranny of Islam'. Soon she was feted on chat shows and courted by newspaper journalists, and her tale assumed the quality of moral crusade taken up with indignation by worthy people around the world.

Her story was a harrowing one that described the death in Jordan of her childhood friend, the legendary Dalia: a killing carried out by the girl's Islamic knife-wielding father for a harmless flirtation with a Christian soldier. This event, together with the author's description of it, apparently led to Khouri's flight to the USA from the benighted country of her birth and a fatwa being placed on her head. Comparisons with author Salman Rushdie begin to form…except that Rashdie never claimed that his works of fiction were fact.

A 2008 documentary, *Forbidden Lies,* charts Khouri's exposure as a conartist of extraordinarily compromised integrity and her book as a pack of lies. The very existence of Dalia is called into question and with it a pall of uncertainty covers the issue of 'honour killings', which is the book's central theme.

And this, of course, is the real tragedy behind one of the biggest literary hoaxes of the 21st century. Honour killings – where a woman is killed by male members of the family to protect familial honour – do occur in Jordan.

On average (according to government statistics) 15 women are murdered each year for bringing shame on their families by having sex out of wedlock, refusing an arranged marriage, leaving their husbands, or simply being the victim of rape or sexual assault. Women in the family are often complicit in the murder.

Articles 340 and 98 of Jordan's legal code exempt a husband or close male relative for killing a wife caught in an act of adultery and offer leniency for murders committed in a 'fit of rage'. Most perpetrators are given short prison sentences, sending the message that the state in part condones these actions. King Abdullah has tried to impose tougher sanctions against honour killings, but little progress has thus far been made. Besides, as *Forbidden Lies* points out, the problem will not be solved by a change of law – only a change of attitude.

Jordanian journalist Rana Husseini is one among several high-profile Jordanians who are committed not just to bringing these killings to the Jordanian public's attention but also to spreading a more widespread intolerance towards the practice. Effecting radical change of deep-rooted cultural values is not something that can be accomplished overnight. Sensationalist accounts that capitalise on the practice only serve to undermine this work. Indeed, Khouri's book, for example, forced a suspension of work by Husseini and others, fearing that their efforts would appear to be unpatriotic at a time when Jordan was being unfairly demonised by the Western media.

The dust is settling and the painstaking case-by-case documentation of each crime has resumed, but it will take more than the global humiliation of the biggest conartist of the decade for Jordanians to talk about this subject openly again.

For more information, look out for the documentary *Crimes of Honour* by Shelley Saywell, filmed in Jordan and the West Bank.

ARTS

As Jordan has been at the crossroads of so many international 'caravans' of art and culture over the centuries, it's quite hard to define an essentially Jordanian aesthetic. The modern arts, especially popular literature, fine arts and music, are dominated by the Egyptian and Lebanese and show a strong Western influence. That said, there are a few local names to look out for and Jordanians will be gratified if you are able to identify them.

LITERATURE ON WOMEN IN JORDAN

■ One of the better books in a genre dominated by sensationalist writing is *Nine Parts of Desire: The Hidden World of Islamic Women* by Geraldine Brooks, a former *Wall St Journal* correspondent, who includes an account of her encounter with Queen Noor.

■ *Price of Honour: Muslim Women Lift the Veil of Silence on the Islamic World,* by Jan Goodwin, also has a chapter on Jordan, though it dates from the mid-1990s.

■ Two scholarly investigations into the position of women in Islam include *The Veil and the Male Elite: A Feminist Interpretation of Women's Rights in Islam* by Fatima Mernissi, with a specific focus on Morocco, and the more historical *Women and Gender in Islam* by Leila Ahmed, written from a feminist viewpoint and with particular emphasis on Egypt.

■ *Into the Wadi* by Michele Drouart is a readable account of an Australian woman's marriage to a Jordanian man and her attempts to gain a greater understanding of Jordanian society. Marguerite van Geldermalsen's *Married to a Bedouin* explores similar territory.

Literature

For a country with such a rich history, it is somewhat surprising that few classical writers have emerged from this region. One Jordanian poet, however, who stands out from the crowd is Mustafa Wahbi al-Tal, also known as Irar. Born in Irbid in 1899, he was renowned for his incisive and humorous poems about Arab nationalism and anticolonialism.

In the last few decades, several renowned writers have emerged in Jordan. Mounis al-Razzaz, who died in 2002, was regarded by many as the driving force behind contemporary Jordanian literature. His works speak of the transition of Amman from a small village to a modern metropolis and the turmoil in the wider Arab world (most notably in his satirical final work *Sweetest Night*).

Some other writers attracting international interest include Ramadan al-Rawashdeh, whose novel *Al-Hamrawi* won the Naguib Mahfouz Arabic Novel Prize. Look out also for his *The Shepherds' Songs*. Rifka Doudeen is one of an emerging number of female authors, and is renowned for her short stories called *Justifiable Agony* and *The Outcast*.

Other writers to watch out for: young short-story writer Basma Nsour; Hashim Gharaybeh; novelist and playwright Mefleh al-Adwan, who won the coveted Unesco prize for creative writing in France in 2001; Raga Abu Gazaleh; Jamal Naji; Abdel Raouf Shamoun; and Abdullah Mansour.

Many Palestinian Jordanian writers graphically relate firsthand experiences of the Arab-Israeli conflict and the national struggle for a homeland. Taher al-Edwan's *The Fact of Time,* telling the story of a Palestinian family fleeing to Amman in 1948, is regarded as an important Jordanian novel. One of the few Jordanian titles translated into English is the complex novel *Prairies of Fever,* written by Jordanian-based Palestinian poet Ibrahim Naserallah.

More widely available from abroad are the following works by Jordanian authors. Diana Abu-Jaber is a celebrated Jordanian-American author who draws on her family's memories of Jordanian cultural identity and father's love of Jordanian food. Her first novel, *Arabian Jazz,* is a hit-or-miss tale of a Jordanian-American family in upstate New York. Her second novel, *Crescent,* is an eloquent story of Iraqi emigrant life in Los Angeles, a haunting and luscious tale of exile, love and food.

East of the Jordan, by Laila Halaby, also deals with the issues of migration and the clash of modernity and tradition among four young Jordanian

The veneration for the written word in Arab culture is reflected in the treatment of the calligrapher, who until recent times was the most sought-after and highly paid artist in a community.

If you thought only hard-up Western tourists stayed in budget hotels, read *A Beggar at Damascus Gate* by Palestinian writer Yasmin Zahra, told in flashbacks from a budget hotel in Petra.

cousins living in Jordan and the USA. *Story of a City: A Childhood in Amman* by Abd al-Rahman Munif eloquently describes life in 1940s Amman from a child's perspective. Munif's other major work, *Cities of Salt,* follows the development of a village in an unspecified country in Arabia in the 1930s, when oil is discovered. Unusually, the main character is the city, and its transformation under the influence of the West, rather than its inhabitants. The novel was translated by Peter Theroux (brother of travel writer Paul) and banned in Saudi Arabia. In 1992 Munif was awarded the Sultan al-Uways award, the Arab equivalent of a Nobel Prize for Literature.

In 2003 the internationally renowned Jordanian journalist Rana Husseini won the coveted Ida B Wells award for Bravery in Journalism.

Jordan has produced several famous journalists in recent years. Rana Husseini is a human-rights activist dedicated to exposing the problem of crimes of honour through her writing (see the boxed text, p62). Fouad Hussein is another high-profile journalist, investigating the so-called 'Grand Strategy' of Al-Qaeda: in his work, Hussein explores the possibility that Al-Qaeda is not a random group of disaffected Islamic extremists but a highly organised body with a rational, intellectual core. Their manifesto, his work similarly suggests, is not random violence but carefully orchestrated phases of a master plan intended to lead to the cultural annihilation of the West. It makes for an uncomfortably plausible read.

If you are beginning to think that Jordanian literature is lacking a fun element, then buy a comic in Jordan and think again. Suleiman Bakhit, a young Jordanian self-taught artist, is on a mission to bring superheros of a distinctly Arab nature to the Middle East (see the boxed text, below).

Painting

The 7th-century Umayyad frescoes at the desert castle, Qusayr Amra (p161), in Jordan's eastern *Badia* (basalt desert) and the Byzantine

---

WALT DISNEY OF THE ARAB WORLD

Anyone who has been to Jordan, or the Middle East in general, will quickly realise that superheroes who wear their underpants over (rather than under) their clothes are not going to cut the mustard with the public. Suleiman Bakhit, aspiring Walt Disney of the Arab world, is an entrepreneurial cartoonist from Jordan who realised just that when he started to create cartoon characters that Arab people could identify with. Out with the men in tights, then, and in with a cast of Arab superheroes that include a fighter pilot (modelled on a Jordanian hero from a battle with the Israeli air force), kids from the block c 2050 (in a world where adults and oil have met their demise), mounted Arab warriors and many more.

Bakhit's own life story could have been co-opted from one of his own storyboards. Brutally assaulted after 9/11 by four white men in the US, he turned his anger into something positive by joining an outreach programme in schools. His message was a simple one: Muslim Arabs are not cartoon villains; they are real people with ordinary human aspirations and sensitivities. In that case, one of the American kids wanted to know, which comic books do Arab children read? Realising that the cartoon figures he had loved as a child (Superman, Batman) were all borrowed from the West, Bakhit decided it was high time someone came up with an Arab superman; a homespun hero who would express local aspirations in the Arabic language – and knew where to wear his underpants.

Returning to Jordan, Bakhit taught himself to draw and eventually set up Jordan's first comics company called Aranim (from the words Arab and animation) Media Factory, with a grant from the King Abdullah Development Fund. With cartoonists polishing his images from Brazil to Britain, and Jordanian illustrators training up to join him – not to mention merchandising in the pipeline, and TV shows and computer games already in production – Bakhit has opened an Aladdin's cave of opportunity that he hopes will eventually catch the imagination of the whole region. It would seem that Aladdin, after half a century at Disney, is finally going home.

mosaics of the Madaba region (p183) are high points of Jordan's historical visual arts. For more about mosaics, see p187.

Jordan's contemporary-art scene, which is very much influenced by Western concepts of abstraction, postmodernism and conceptualism, is best explored through a visit to Darat al-Funun (p101) and the Jordan National Gallery of Fine Arts (p101) in Amman.

While you are there, you may come across Mohammed al-Saifi, a young Jordanian painter from Amman renowned for employing industrial tools like aerosol sprays in work more usually expressed through a paintbrush. Another contemporary artist gaining local recognition is Hani Alqam, who has enjoyed success at a number of recent exhibitions in Amman.

Music & Dance

Traditional Jordanian music is largely derived from the Bedouin influence. The sound of men chanting at a distant wedding, drifting across the desert on a still night, is haunting. Up close, the musical aspects of the festivities are clearly rooted in ancient traditions. A row of men, arm in arm, gently sways backwards and forwards engaged in what appears to be an almost trance-like chant. Songs deal with romantic concepts of honour and chivalry and draw their inspiration from the oral histories – part poetry, part folk song and part story – that have been handed down for generations by elders assembled around desert campfires.

Like modern literature, contemporary Arab music reflects a synthesis of indigenous and Western influences. Instrumentalists generally accompany a vocalist rather than perform in their own right, but there are a couple of instrumentalists who are currently stealing the show from the singers: Sakher Hattar (born 1963 in Amman) is renowned as the finest oud player in the region, winning many awards such as first place in the International Competition for Oud in Cairo in 1993. He has performed in Germany, the USA, France and Tunisia.

Hani Naser is known as the 'Hand Drum Wizard' of Jordan, specialising in hand percussion instruments like the goblet drum and *djembe*. He has made recordings with the Rolling Stones, Ry Cooder, Santana, Lou Reed and many other famous international artists.

Popular music differs little from that of neighbouring Arab countries, with Egyptian and Lebanese superstars such as Amr Diab and Fairouz dominating the airwaves. Many travellers eventually get caught up in the particular magic of Arabic pop, which is probably a good thing because you'll be hearing it in one form or another wherever you go. The most common style of pop music focuses on a star performer backed by anything from a small quartet to a full-blown orchestra. The resulting sliding strings are more Bollywood than Beethoven, while the singers' voices slip and slide around the notes rather than lingering on them. The highly produced mix is then given a pounding percussive drive that gets the heads nodding.

Popular Jordanian singers include Qamar Badwan, the Bedouin singer Omar Abdullat and the female performer Rania Kurdi, who is part of a younger generation of modern Jordanian pop stars.

Craft Industries

Several NGOs such as the **Noor Al-Hussein Foundation** (www.noor.gov.jo/nhf.htm) and **Jordan River Foundation** (www.jordanriver.jo) have recently spurred a revival of locally produced crafts, as part of a program to raise rural living standards and the status of rural women. For more information on these local cottage industries and the impact they have on local communities, see the boxed texts on p22 and p197.

The most popular Bedouin instruments are the *ruababa*, a melancholy one-stringed violin, and the lute-like oud. If you take the Petra by Night Tour (see p238), you may be treated to a performance of these instruments in front of Petra's Treasury.

Fine examples of Bedouin jewellery, Jordanian crafts and traditional costumes are on display at the Folklore Museum and Museum of Popular Traditions at the Roman Theatre in Amman (p98).

For a list of shops selling fair-trade craft products, see the GreenDex, p358.

WEAVING

Jordan has a long-established rug-making industry dating back to the country's pre-Islamic, Christian communities. *Mafrash* (rugs) are usually of the flat, woven kind, compared with carpets that have a pile. To this day, especially in the largely Christian town of Madaba and in the Bedouin village of Mukawir, it's possible to watch kilims based on early Byzantine designs being made in the backrooms of a colourful kilim showroom. Even if you hadn't intended to buy one of these woven, woollen rugs, you'll find it impossible not to get carried away by the enthusiasm of the carpet vendors, who will good-naturedly unfurl all their rugs for you without much prospect of a sale.

The cost of a kilim (anywhere between JD50 and JD500) depends on whether natural vegetable dyes are used, the length, thickness of thread, intricacy of pattern and age of the rug – the older the better.

EMBROIDERY

Embroidery is an important skill among Jordanian women and most learn the craft at a young age. Teenagers traditionally embroider the clothes they will need as married women. Embroidery provides an occasion for women to socialise, often with a pot of tea and spiced up with a pinch of local gossip. Palestinian embroidery is famed throughout the region and you'll see the characteristic red embroidery cross-stitch on traditional dresses, known as *roza*, in shops across Jordan. Purses featuring intricate flower designs in silk thread make a more portable memento.

COPPERWARE

Copper has a special place in Jordan and some of the oldest copper mines in the world date from the region (especially near Feinan, now in the Dana Nature Reserve). Copper is used in everyday utensils, as well as for heirlooms such as the family serving dish, copper tray or coffee pot. For many years these pieces have been replicated for the tourist industry, but with a bit of careful looking you can find gems that with a bit of spit and polish will light up the corner of a room back home. The best places to look for quality pieces are in the antique stores in Amman, many of which are attached to the top-end hotels. You are unlikely to find an antique older than about 50 years (and it's illegal to import anything older than 100 years), but that doesn't mean to say the items haven't been much loved by the families who once used them.

Treasures from an Ancient Land: The Art of Jordan, by the renowned Arabist Pitr Bienkowski, gives an excellent overview of Jordanian culture, particularly pottery, sculpture and jewellery.

JEWELLERY

A bride traditionally receives a gift of jewellery on her wedding day as her dowry, and this remains her personal property throughout (and after) the marriage. The most common designs are protective silver amulets, such as the 'hand of Fatima' (Fatima was the daughter-in-law of the Prophet Mohammed), which are used as protection from evil spirits known as djinn (from which we get the word 'genie'). Antique items such as silver headdresses decorated with Ottoman coins and ornately decorated Bedouin daggers (straight, rather than the famously curved Yemeni and Omani versions) are becoming harder to find. Many of the most beautiful antique pieces were produced by Circassian, Armenian and Yemeni silversmiths in the early 20th century.

Heather Colyer Ross looks into popular art forms in *The Art of Bedouin Jewellery,* a useful asset for those contemplating purchasing some pieces.

See the boxed text, p258, for an idea of the cultural significance of jewellery in Jordan.

MEDIA

By regional standards Jordan maintains a reasonably free media, although it's tempered by local sensibilities, and the government maintains tighter control over local radio and TV than it over the newspapers.

The English-language *Jordan Times* has good coverage of domestic and international events. The *Star,* subtitled 'Jordan's Political, Economic and Cultural Weekly', is similar but published only every Tuesday. It also has a double-page supplement in French called *Le Jourdain.*

Of the many local Arabic daily and weekly newspapers printed in Amman, *Ad-Dustour, Al-Ra'i* and *Al-Aswaq* are among the more popular.

SPORT

It may not count for much in the international arena, but Jordan is proud of its regional commitment to sport. Children are brought up playing a variety of different games including basketball, squash and swimming, and the country sent a small but highly dedicated team of seven to the Beijing Olympics in 2008.

In common with other Arab countries, the most popular sport in the country is football (soccer). There is barely a patch of ground in and around towns that hasn't been smoothed for an ad hoc game by avid youth clubs members aspiring to play in Jordan's national team. The Premier League Championship plays mostly on Friday during winter (from about September to March), and features teams from Amman and most major towns. Fans take the game very seriously, with large attendance at all league matches.

Other sports that Jordanians enjoy watching, participating in locally and competing in internationally include judo, table tennis, kite flying, volleyball and horse racing. The latter includes long-distance endurance races (see the boxed text, below, as well as www.enduranceworldonline .com and www.endurance.net). An assorted group of athletes and amateurs participates in an endurance race of another kind in the popular,

---

TO FINISH IS TO WIN

Befitting of an Arab nation of horse lovers, one interesting event to look out for is the Endurance Race that takes place annually in Wadi Rum. Around 100 horses begin the race, but on average only around one-third finish. Both horses and riders must have pre-qualified (ie finished special 80km rides throughout the year) in order to be allowed to start the Rum Ride. One of the very few women regularly to take part in this supreme test of endurance is Suzie Shinaco of Bait Ali in Wadi Rum. Here is her firsthand account of the race:

'The Endurance Race is a one-horse, one-rider FEI event (ie official international race) covering 120km in a day. The winners usually finish at an average speed of 20km an hour – a steady canter. It is run in five loops (roughly three by 30km plus two by 15km) with very strict vet checks in between. The best place to observe all the goings on is the vet checks (think Formula One pit stops). Each team has a specific time to meet very strict vet parameters before being either allowed to continue (after a specific time of enforced rest) or being pulled by the vet committee as being 'unfit to continue'. Once you develop an 'eye' it becomes fascinating to watch how the teams work to get the horses vetted as quickly as possible – thereby 'stopping the clock' until it is time to start the next loop. Believe me, Formula One has nothing on this! Even though a horse finishes the distance, he must still pass a final vet check to 'prove' he is in theory still 'fit to continue' in order to be placed at all or be 'pulled' even at the finish – this is the part they call character building. Endurance has the adage 'to finish is to win'. Many people use a multitude of different types of horse, not all of which are specifically designed to excel at endurance or perhaps not trained as a superathlete in the way top-class horses are; so endurance riding, especially at grassroots level, can become a personal challenge to pace you and your horse to reach the end over distances of anything from 40km to 160km – or even multiday rides covering 400km and more. The major objective is to finish; to win, or to get into the top 10, is just the icing on the cake.'

In April 2008, according to the rally website (www.jordanrally.com), Jordan became 'the first Arab country to host a round of the FIA World Rally Championship'. Taking place in a 40km radius of the Dead Sea resorts, half of this annual rally takes place below sea level.

50km **Amman-Dead Sea Ultra Marathon** (www.deadseamarathon.com) held every April (see p291 for details).

One sport that's hitting the bull's eye in Jordan is darts. With its traditional association with Western drinking establishments, darts may seem like an unlikely game to gain popularity in an Arab country, but for some reason it has a huge number of fans in Jordan. This may have something to do with the recent televising of professional darts and partly to do with the emergence of 'The Jordanian Dragon'. The Dragon is a young darts-playing phenomenon called Ramzi Qattan. No stranger to international sport (his father was a handball professional and his cousin is an international rugby player), he already throws his fair share of 180s and has an average of 102.8. He now has his sights set on being the first Jordanian to appear in the BDO world championship. With King Abdullah said to be a fan, this is one sport that is helping bridge the sporting divide between West and East.

Major sporting events are held at the massive Sports City, in northern Amman, and at Al-Hasan Sports City in Irbid. Prince Feisal (King Abdullah's younger brother) is closely involved in Jordan's sporting infrastructure and is in charge of the country's Olympic committee.

Environment

The true servants of the most gracious are those who tread gently on the earth.

Quran (sura 25, verse 63)

With some application, you can have breakfast in the desert, lunch under a hilltop pine and dinner eating fresh bananas from the subtropical Jordan Valley. There are not many places in the world where the land exhibits such extraordinary diversity within such compact area. For the naturalist, this is what makes Jordan a dream. Thankfully Jordanian authorities have been quick to recognise the country's appeal in this regard and have put in place several ecotourism projects aimed at encouraging nature-loving visitors. Whether you're a raptor enthusiast, wish to witness the seasonal bird migrations, or are just a casual fan of flowers, there is sure to be something to please you in Jordan's modest acreage.

THE LAND

At 91,860 sq km, Jordan is slightly smaller than Portugal or the US state of Virginia. Distances are short – it's only 430km from Ramtha, on the Syrian border in the north, to Aqaba in the south. TE Lawrence was

---

FORBIDDEN FRUIT IN THE JORDAN VALLEY *Jenny Walker*

It's a Tuesday in July 2008. We have just passed our eighth road block in as many miles, following the thin, reed-covered ribbon of the Jordan River from Umm Qais to a dusty town in the middle of the Jordan Valley. This is border country, historically disputed land, where the names alone (Golan Heights, West Bank) cast a long shadow over the fields of onions and tomatoes. And it is onion and tomatoes that bring us here, on this day of palpably increased border tension, to interview a farmer about the water crisis in a year of very little rain.

Mr Abu Eiad casts an eye up to the cloudless sky and pronounces with profound stoicism, 'It's God's will'. He is happy, he says. With two wives, four sons and two daughters, why shouldn't he be happy? It also transpires that he has something else to smile about hidden between the limes and lemons of his farm. We go to take a look, weaving between the vast plastic-sheeted fields of corporate neighbours: some dry-baked like old leather, others artificially green under their polythene coating. We creep ever closer to the river, and the border with Israel and the Palestinian Territories.

Suddenly, the giant neighbours drop away, and a beautiful vale of emerald green orchards and small, neatly trimmed fields comes into view. 'This,' explains Abu Eiad, 'is the land of my father. We have farmed this area in the same way forever.' There is no plastic in sight: 'The fruits and vegetables taste better that way,' he says, leading us to the source of all this natural bounty. In the hillside, firmly within the family plot, gushes a clear, potent spring of water. It trickles through the gently sloping farmland, diverted by stones onto the citrus trees one day and the potato fields the next, the excess siphoned off to help the neighbours. According to Abu Eiad's wife, they want help for new technologies to develop their enterprise. Casting a look at the Garden of Eden in front of us, with its plump, organic fruit and glossy aubergines, it's hard to imagine that anything could improve on their winning formula.

'Take a picture!' Abu Eiad insists, waving to us from the watercourse about 3ft from the Jordan River – waving distance, in fact, from the tin-helmeted border guard who thankfully is looking the other way. But it isn't the border that's the focus of the shot: on this 60th anniversary of Israel's independence (as we discover later), the focus is on two farmers, either side of the thin ribbon of reeds, plucking weeds from their onion beds, just as other *falaheen* have been doing in the Jordan Valley for centuries.

pleased that he could cover Azraq to Amman in a hard, three-day camel ride. Today you can travel by car from tip to toe in around six hours. If you want to see anything, though, there's a lot to be said for the camel.

Jordan can be divided into three major regions: the Jordan Valley, the east bank plateau and the desert, each of which is examined below.

Jordan Valley Ecosystem

Jordan edges the Great Rift Valley that stretches from East Africa's lakes to southern Syria. The rift was created as the Arabian plate pulled away from the African plate, a geological event that gave rise to the Red Sea. Jordan's Wadi Araba, the Dead Sea and the Jordan Valley lie right on this fault line. Sit under the thermal water that springs from the effervescent mountainside at Hammamat Ma'in and it's easy to see that this process of tectonic separation isn't yet complete.

Flowing through the northern part of the valley is the lowest-lying river on earth, the River Jordan, fed from the Sea of Galilee (Lake Tiberias), the Yarmouk River and hillside streams. The permanent fresh water has given rise to a humid, subtropical valley, highly fertile and intensively farmed, wedged between the Syrian border and the Dead Sea.

Walk under the flame and tamarisk trees in the Jordan Valley and you may see warblers and buntings, sunbirds and the occasional kingfisher feeding on the abundant flies. You may see the odd rodent or an endangered otter, heading for the reed beds beside the narrowed river. What you won't see is the lion that once prowled the valley, nor the bear, elephant, rhino and herds of wild ass that Palaeolithic remains prove were once resident here.

Not everything in the region has changed, however. The fish in Madaba's famous mosaic, twisting back from certain death at the mouth of the River Jordan, show that the Dead Sea was as insupportable of life in Byzantine times as it is today. The sea might be virtually barren, but the surrounding cliffs are not: small oases of date palm and hanging gardens of fern give shelter for partridge and the noisy Tristam's grackle, and the sandstone bluffs (particularly around Wadi Mujib) are the habitat of elusive Nubian ibex.

East Bank Plateau Ecosystem

High above the Jordan Valley – cut by a series of epic gorges carved out in slow motion by the wadis of Zarqa, Mujib and Hasa – is the hilly and mostly temperate East Bank Plateau. Much of this high ground rises between 600m and 900m above sea level. The plateau ends at Ras an-Naqb, from where the Desert Highway drops down to the desert floor near Aqaba. This Red Sea port is on the Gulf of Aqaba, a sea that sustains 230 species of coral and 1000 types of fish.

The forested and sparsely inhabited hills of northern Jordan (less than 1% of Jordan is covered by woodland) are comprised of Aleppo pines, evergreen oak and the red-barked strawberry tree. By day fan-tailed ravens hover for picnic scraps, but at dusk tawny owls sound the alarm. This is home to ill-tempered wild boar, marbled polecats, stone martens and crested porcupines, none of which you'd want to meet on a dark night.

In spring (particularly March and April), the area explodes with colour as wildflowers, including pink hollyhocks, poppies and yellow daisies, bloom in magnificent abundance. This is a good time, too, to try and spot the black iris (actually a deep purple), the national flower of Jordan (see the boxed text, p321).

Jordan's location on the edge of the Great Rift Valley makes it an important migration route for birds. Over half a million birds fly by during spring, in transit between Russia, Central Europe and Africa.

The Birds of the Hashemite Kingdom of Jordan by Ian J Andrews is the definitive ornithological guide to the region.

A successful breeding program of the Nubian ibex by the RSCN began in the Wadi Mujib Nature Reserve in 1989. Some have now been reintroduced into the wild and the herds are increasing.

LOVING THE LAND

It's easy to spot a guide at one of the six flagship nature reserves run by the Royal Society for the Conservation of Nature (RSCN) – they exude such a passion for their place of work. This is hardly surprising when you consider that, as part of the RSCN's far-sighted policy to involve local people, the rangers are almost all born and raised nearby.

Take Majid, a ranger at Ajloun. He loves the evergreen oak forests because he played in them when he was young; he remembers village grandfathers harvesting the strong strawberry-tree timber to build houses and local grandmothers using the fruit to settle stomach ailments. There were also hunts for roe deer and wild boar – the same species Majid is now helping to reintroduce and protect today.

Hunting may be banned within the parks, but locals communities are still given a vested interest in the land they call their own. At Ajloun, six of the surrounding villages are involved in the maintenance of the reserve: 'Our families want to protect their sons' employment,' says Majid, 'so they are keen to support the reserve and make it work for the benefit of the whole community.'

Naturally, not everyone is equally committed and the reserve faces problems such as illegal cutting of firewood for valuable oils and the odd attempt at poaching. The clever part of the RSCN philosophy, however, is that villagers are not banned from exploiting their birthright resources without being offered an alternative income. At Ajloun, for example, a guided trail offers visitors a chance to meet with the area's soap makers: these enterprising women make their eco-friendly products from natural resources in low-impact cottage industries and sell them at fair prices in the Ajloun Reserve shop.

At each of the reserves, the challenges may be slightly different (extraction of water in Mujib and Azraq, overgrazing in Dana – see the boxed text, p206, for another warden's tale), but the story of culturally sensitive and sustainable development is the same. To quote Chris Johnson, Director of Wild Jordan (the marketing arm of the RSCN), it is this 'amazing relationship between landscape and people' that is securing of Jordan's ancient wild lands for future generations – indeed, saving them for the sons of Majid.

The East Bank plateau contains the main centres of population (Amman, Irbid, Zarqa and Karak) and has been crossed by Christian and Islamic caravans for centuries. The plateau landscape of fig and olive groves, occasional vineyards and closely cropped pasturelands reflects this human interaction. Hike anywhere around Madaba in the hot summer months and you'll see the Bedouin still grazing their sheep and goats on the hillside; they descend to lower ground in the cooler months to escape the bitter winds. Since the time of Moses, their husbandry has shaped the lie of the land.

Pockets of pristine plateau wilderness remain, however, especially towards the southern end of the plateau around Dana Nature Reserve. This rocky wilderness of outstanding biodiversity is the habitat of the beautiful but elusive caracal (Persian lynx), a feline with outrageous tufts of black hair on the tips of its outsized ears.

Desert Ecosystem

On its southern and eastern flanks, the East Bank plateau glides gradually into the desert. Most of Jordan, indeed over 90% of the land, can be classified as desert, which is home to only 5% of the population. The forbidding volcanic basalt rock of the northeast (known as the Hauran in Syria) gives way to the soft-whittled sandstone and granite of the south and the famously photogenic *jebels* (mountains) of Wadi Rum. In between, the stony wasteland known as the *Badia* slides into 1000km of nothingness, interrupted only by the occasional succulent or vetch, a wandering camel and camouflaged lizards, skinks and snakes.

Jordan boasts over 2500 species of wild plants and flowers, including about 20 species of orchid. *Wildflowers of Jordan & Neighbouring Countries* by Dawud MH Al-Eisawi has useful photographs that will help you identify some of them.

When you travel along Route 5, or across empty Route 10, it's impossible to imagine that anything could survive such desolation. But then, miraculously, you reach Azraq Wetland Reserve or the lake at Burqu. All at once it's easy to see why these desert oases attract epic numbers of migrating birds. Crouched over the fishing rights of their small patches of water, herons and egrets wait patiently among the croaking toads; marsh harriers wheel in the air, and larks and grouse keep close to the ground. Where there are birds, there are mammals: predators like the desert fox, rare wolf and Asiatic jackal lurk beyond the fringes of oases waiting for a careless rodent, like the long-legged jerboa, or desert hare, to run out of luck.

Some desert species ran out of luck a long time ago, hunted to extinction before conservation became part of the modern sensibility. In Shaumari Wildlife Reserve there's a chance to see the magnificent animals that once roamed these plains – ostrich, gazelle, onager (wild donkey) and oryx – before they are reintroduced to the wild.

PROTECTED AREAS

Established in 1966, the **Royal Society for the Conservation of Nature (RSCN)** (www.rscn.org.jo) is an unusual non-governmental organisation (NGO) in that it has a national mandate to run biodiversity projects on behalf of the nation. Indeed, it is Jordan's main environmental agency.

The RSCN has been successful in its founding remit: to help save animal, plant and bird species from extinction and to reintroduce several locally extinct species, such as the Arabian oryx (p157). Over the past two decades, however, the RSCN has developed a much wider focus, recognising that tourism has an important role to play (see the boxed text, p74). The result has been a modern and highly successful program of ecotourism projects, centred on RSCN reserves. The RSCN also conducts public awareness programs among Jordanians, especially children; sponsors environmental clubs throughout the country; trains guides; combats poaching and hunting, and lobbies against mining.

The RSCN maintains six of the reserves listed (not the Wadi Rum protected area). These should not be confused with Jordan's 'national parks', which are unstructured, recreational areas, eg Aqaba Marine Park (p279).

Ajloun Nature Reserve (13 sq km, established 1988) This pretty reserve has pistachio and oak forest, spring flowers, wild boar and martens, and a program to reintroduce the roe deer. Easy trails and attractive facilities make it a winner. See p135.

Azraq Wetland Reserve (12 sq km, 1977) This environmentally damaged marshland attracts hundreds of species of migratory birds, which visit in spring and autumn. A boardwalk leads around the reserve, via a bird hide. The nearby lodge is in itself a piece of fine conservation. See p156.

Dana Nature Reserve (320 sq km, 1989) This spectacular Unesco Biosphere Reserve is home to a diverse Rift Valley ecosystem, encompassing rugged mountains and desert with 600 species of plants, 200 species of bird and over 40 species of mammal. There are walking trails, tented and hotel accommodation, and several archaeological sites. See p205.

Dibeen Nature Reserve (8 sq km, 2005) One of the last Aleppo Pine forests left in Jordan, Dibeen protects endangered species such as the Persian squirrel. See p137.

Shaumari Wildlife Reserve (22 sq km, 1975) This small reserve, established to reintroduce the locally extinct Arabian oryx, blue-necked and red-necked ostrich, gazelle and onager, is currently undergoing major redevelopment to upgrade tourist facilities. See p156 for details.

Wadi Mujib Nature Reserve (212 sq km, 1988) This reserve, with chalets on the Dead Sea, is used for the captive breeding of Nubian ibexes. It has an impressive ecotourism program, with canyon walks and waterfall rappelling. See p179.

Wadi Rum Protected Area (540 sq km, 1998) This outrageously beautiful piece of desert, under the control of ASEZA (the Aqaba government), is in the heartland of the Bedouin. Camping, camel treks and 4WD excursions are easy to organise. See p260.

Jebel is the Arabic word for (usually arid) mountain. Jebel Umm Adaani (1832m), the highest peak in Jordan, lives up to that description. 'Wadi' is the word for (usually dry) watercourse or flood channel. Wadi Mujib belies that description with its permanently flowing water.

A must for any amateur wildlife-watcher is *Field Guide to Jordan* by Jarir Maani.

NATIONAL PARKS & RESERVES

Ajloun Nature Reserve	1 A1
Azraq Wetland Reserve	2 B2
Dana Nature Reserve	3 A2
Dibeen Nature Reserve	4 A1
Shaumari Wildlife Reserve	5 B2
Wadi Mujib Nature Reserve	6 A2
Wadi Rum Protected Area	7 A3

PROPOSED NATIONAL RESERVES

Abu Rukbeh Reserve	8 A2
Aqaba Reserve	9 A3
Bayer Reserve	10 B2
Burqu Reserve	11 B1
Fifa Reserve	12 A2
Jebel Masuda Reserve	13 A3
Qatar Reserve	14 A3
Rajel Reserve	15 B1
Yarmouk River Reserve	16 A1

In addition to the above reserves, the RSCN, together with the Jordanian government, hopes to create nine new protected areas (see Map p73) in regions of special scientific interest where indigenous wildlife in under threat. These include the following:

Burqu Reserve (400 sq km) After the debacle in the Azraq wetlands (see the boxed text, p154), the desert lake at Burqu needs urgent protection.

Fifa Reserve (27 sq km) This area alongside the Dead Sea has rare subtropical vegetation, and is home to migratory water birds.

Rajel Reserve (908 sq km) In the middle of the Eastern Desert, this represents the only source of water in an otherwise desolate region and contains several threatened desert animals and plants.

Yarmouk River Reserve (30 sq km) Because of its close proximity to the border of Israel and the Palestinian Territories, this area has remained undeveloped and is home to many natural features including water birds, endangered gazelles and otters.

ENVIRONMENTAL ISSUES

In 1995 the Jordanian Parliament passed the Law of the Protection of the Environment as part of an impressive commitment to environmental protection. Jordan is not, however, without environmental problems, the chief of which is the chronic shortage of water.

Water

Relying mainly on rainwater and subterranean aquifers that are already in many cases overexploited (see the boxed text, p154), Jordan is the 10th most water-impoverished country in the world. With 90% of Jordan's rivers already being diverted, a population increasing by almost

The killifish, unique to the Azraq Wetlands, has recently been saved from extinction but its situation remains precarious. For more about the wetlands, see the boxed text, p154.

3.5% annually and persistent droughts, this situation is likely to worsen rather than improve. Currently, about 60% more water is used than is replenished from natural sources and, by some estimates, the country is due to run out of water within 20 years.

Jordan is not alone in this problem. Water is a hot political issue across the region, contributing to several skirmishes over the years and continuing to spike relations between Jordan and its neighbours. Since the 1960s, for example, Israel and the Palestinian Territories has drawn around one-third of its water from the Jordan River; this river has now been reduced to a trickle, half of which is 50% raw sewage and effluent from fish farms. After the 1994 peace treaty, Israel and the Palestinian Territories permitted Jordan to extract 50 million cu metres per year from Lake Tiberias, but disputes rumble on over whether Jordan is getting its fair share. On a more positive note, the joint Syrian–Jordanian Wahdah Dam on the Yarmouk River now gives power to Syria and water to Jordan (mainly for Amman and Irbid).

Jordan is addressing the water crisis in a number of domestic projects too, targeting the country's outmoded agricultural practices and crumbling infrastructure. Jordan's farmers (around 5% of the population) use 75% of the water (quite often inefficiently), so modernising farming practices and plugging leaks in city pipelines to prevent half of Amman's water being lost are crucial elements of the country's strategic plan.

In 2008 Jordan signed a contract with GAMA Energy, a Turkish company, to extract 100 million cu metres of water a year from the 300,000-year-old aquifer in Diseh near Wadi Rum. The near-billion-dollar project is expected to take four years to complete and involves drilling 55 wells and building a 325km pipeline from Diseh to Amman.

Jordan's nature reserves represent about 1% of Jordan's total land area – a small percentage compared with land allocated in Saudi Arabia (9%) and USA (11%). When measured as a ratio of habitable land versus size of population, however, the figure is considerably more generous.

RSCN: A BYWORD FOR SUSTAINABLE TOURISM

One might expect that the man responsible for setting up one of the most enlightened environmental programs in the Middle East would be strapped behind a desk somewhere impossible to reach. On the contrary, Chris Johnson is found mid-breakfast (a feast of homemade eggs, beans and local cheese brought in by his staff) sharing quality time with his team. As the director of Wild Jordan (the marketing arm of the RSCN) since 1994, this modest man is the first to point out that the successes to date are shared ones.

In fact, teamwork is a good way of describing what the RSCN's policy of environmental management is all about. As Mr Johnson explains, teamwork begins at the RSCN, which employs 330 Jordanian people; it includes getting corporate business involved to back eco-ventures (such as the chic Wild Jordan Café within the RSCN headquarters building in Amman); and crucially it involves local communities through income-generating projects that complement rather than threaten traditional lifestyles. Thanks to the combined interests of all these 'stakeholders', the RSCN's work is surprisingly high-profile in Jordan, with Jordanian nationals comprising 50% to 60% of the annual 60,000 visitors to the country's nature reserves.

Despite being clearly passionate about what he describes as the 'golden triangle of ecotourism' (Dana, Petra and the Rift-edge landscape of Jebel Masuda), Mr Johnson is no tree-hugging eco-warrior. On the contrary, he has his feet firmly on the ground: 'You can't protect wildlife without thinking of economic development,' he explains. 'Tourism is the main tool being used to sustain our reserves; by visiting us, tourists make a direct contribution to preserving Jordan's natural heritage.'

With fantastic accommodation (see GreenDex p358) serving wonderful food in beautiful places; walking, hiking and scrambling trails to suit all legs; and a series of shops that make you wish you'd packed a bigger suitcase, the RSCN's flagship reserves are a highlight of a 'sustainable visit' to Jordan.

The extraction of non-renewable fossil water inevitably has its critics and others are looking to the even more radical plan to construct a series of desalination plants, hydroelectric power stations and canals linking the Red Sea with the Dead Sea (see the boxed text, p173), thereby raising the level of the Dead Sea and creating a fresh water supply.

Hunting, Overgrazing & Desertification

About 20 species of mammal have become extinct in Jordan in the past 100 years. Some were hunted and poached (especially after WWII, when weapons flooded the region), spelling the end for Jordan's lion, cheetah, bear, gazelle and wild ass. The last leopard was killed near Dana in 1986, although there have been unsubstantiated sightings since.

The continuing threats to bird and animal species (24 out of Jordan's remaining 77 species of mammals are globally threatened) include poor land management, such as deforestation; the pumping of water from vital areas such as the Jordan River, Dead Sea and the Azraq Wetlands; urban sprawl; unremitting use of pesticides, especially near water sources in the Jordan Valley; air and water pollution; and overgrazing.

Overgrazing, together with erosion and drought, has led to widespread desertification (the seemingly unstoppable spread of the desert to previously fertile, inhabited and environmentally sensitive areas). According to the RSCN, millions of hectares of fertile land have become infertile and uninhabitable. This means there are now fewer pastures for livestock and crops, and reduced land for native animals and plants. Jordan is home to about three million sheep and goats, but there is no longer enough pasture to feed them.

Measures to help combat these threats include the restriction of grazing, banning of hunting and employment of local rangers to protect endangered species. At Dana Nature Reserve, for example, grazing within the protected area is restricted to certain times of the year.

Jordan has just 140 cu metres of renewable water per capita per year, compared to the UK's 1500, Israel's 340 and the Palestine Authority's 70. Jordan's figure is expected to fall to 90 cu metres by 2025. Anything under 500 cu metres is considered to be a scarcity of water.

Effects of Tourism

The impact on the environment of mass tourism is an issue under constant review. Tourism has caused a rapid increase in pollution from cars and industries, and has exacerbated the demand for precious water.

RESPONSIBLE TOURISM

Responsible tourism is a concept that is just beginning to catch on in Jordan. Travellers can help lead the way by observing the following:

- **Leave as found** For as long as outsiders have been searching for, and stumbling over, the ancient monuments of Jordan, they have also been chipping bits off, hauling items home or leaving their contributions engraved on the stones. Please don't be one of their number.

- **Bag it and bin it** When asked why Jordanian people litter, an official at the Royal Society for the Conservation of Nature (RSCN) said that it didn't trouble their experience of the wilderness because people simply didn't notice it. Education is the key, and visitors (who by and large prefer to sit in the wilds without the decoration of drifting plastic bags and tin cans) have a role to play in setting a good example in taking their rubbish home.

- **Follow the rules** As tempting as it may be to reach out for a starfish in the Red Sea, light a fire for an ad hoc campground, take a photo without someone's permission, or skinny dip in a water hole, these are acts that erode the natural and cultural heritage of this country.

- **Pay your dues** Pay the entrance fees – they are the lifeline that helps to maintain Jordan's reserves.

AN 'ENVIRONMENTAL MAN' *Jenny Walker*

Taheen Shinaco, owner of Bait Ali, walks into the open-air dining area at the heart of his idyllic camp, and immediately his pet, captive-bred African grey squawks with pleasure. 'A gift,' Taheen explains, 'and now a friend' as the parrot hops onboard his shoulder for the duration of the interview. Taheen has run Bait Ali with his British wife and horse-riding enthusiast, Susie, for the past eight years, during which time they've created from scratch one of the best-run, environmentally aware camps in Wadi Rum. I ask Taheen, now that guests are becoming more eco-savvy, what it means to be green in the tourism industry.

What compromises do you have to make running a modern, eco-friendly camp? I'm an environmental man. I like nature and I don't like plastic. That's why you won't see anything but natural materials on my camp – like these tables from old railway sleepers. That said, we have to live with the times. That's why we spent lots of money to install new electricity cable and it's also why we have bought some quad bikes. I'm against loud music and I won't allow it on the camp, but I can't isolate myself from the rest of the tourist industry: our guests want light when they go to the bathroom and they want to get out into the desert on their own.

What do you do about water and firewood? Water is a big problem and we find people have no respect for it – they leave the tap running and have several showers in a day. It's not such a problem for us because we bring 40 cu metres of water from 30 miles away and all the waste water drains into two septic tanks. This is reused to water the plants. We have planted 400 drought-tolerant plants in all, including 70 date and Washington palms. I'm against cutting trees so we get our firewood from a farm 50km away where trees are grown and replanted.

Is environmental sensitivity taken seriously locally? The municipality collects aluminium cans for recycling twice a week and paper and boxes are burned. It hurts to see people who don't care about the environment – I hate seeing things dumped in the desert. We should bring in laws to enforce children to respect their environment – I think it's too late for my generation!

How does your camp contribute to the local community? I help local communities where I can: I provide extra income by using their 4WDs and camels and I market their blankets and carpets. The people of the desert are friendly and live by their tribal system, but they're proud and don't want to take part in tourism. For them it is difficult to carry a tray and be subservient, so we employ them as drivers and guards instead. I'm from Amman but I am a true Jordanian and we have lived all our lives with the Bedouin. I respect them and they respect us. Their lives have improved. They use computers and the internet at school. Times are changing and no-one wants to stop that.

In addition, vandalism and unwitting damage to sites such as Jerash and Petra (see the boxed text, p229), the effects of flash photography on fragile rock art, and rubbish left at hot springs and baths have made some wonder whether tourism is worth the trouble.

The RSCN has been at the forefront of attempts to promote a more sustainable form of tourism through its various ecotourism projects (see the boxed text, p74). Such projects provide a major means of funding environmental programs.

For more information on environmental issues in Jordan contact **Friends of the Earth** (☎ 06-5866602; info@ecowave.org; Amman) or www.foeme.org. In addition, Jordan's **Ministry of Environment** (www.environment.gov.jo) offers environmental overviews, a list of environmental organisations and regional reports.

Food & Drink

Our host stood by the circle, encouraging the appetite with pious ejaculations. At top speed we twisted, tore, cut and stuffed: never speaking, since conversation would insult a meal's quality, though it was proper to smile thanks when an intimate guest passed a select fragment.

TE Lawrence, Seven Pillars of Wisdom

Eating in Jordan is primarily a social experience, whether conducted over a chat in Amman's cafés or sitting in cross-legged silence in a Bedouin tent. Many travellers leave Jordan thinking that apart from the multicultural options in Amman and Aqaba, Jordanian food is a tedious affair of felafel sandwiches. Anyone venturing beyond the bus station kebab stands, however, will quickly find that not only is the food deliciously varied, but so is the company that they will inevitably share.

Recipes and Remembrances from an Eastern Mediterranean Kitchen: A Culinary Journey through Syria, Lebanon & Jordan by Sonia Uvezian is a high-quality introduction to the food of the Levant.

FOOD
On the crossroads of Arab caravans, bringing spices from India and rice from Egypt, Jordan's hybrid cuisine has absorbed many traditions from its neighbours. Travellers who have been in Lebanon and Turkey will quickly recognise the influence of these culinary goliaths on restaurant menus, while those with a taste for the organic will enjoy Jordan's home-grown fresh fruit and vegetables (see the boxed text, p78, for seasonal delights). There are two distinct cuisines in Jordan, which for argument's sake let's call Pan-Arab and Bedouin.

Pan-Arab
The day starts for most Jordanians with a breakfast of eggs and locally produced olives, cheese, sour cream and *foul madames* (fava-bean dish with olive oil) and of course bread. Arabic unleavened bread, *khobz*, is so ubiquitous at mealtimes it is sometimes called *a'aish* (life). A favourite breakfast staple is bread liberally sprinkled with *zaatar* (thyme blend) or sesame-encrusted rings of bread, which are often sold with a boiled egg.

Lunch is usually the main meal of the day, which could explain the habit of nap-taking in the afternoons. Invariably, lunch involves rice or potatoes and includes some form of seasonal vegetable, prepared as a slow-cooking stew with a meat bone or chicken. In a restaurant, or for a special occasion, *maqlubbeh* may be on the menu: a pyramid of steaming rice garnished with cardamom and sultanas, and topped with slivers of onion, meat, cauliflower and fresh herbs like thyme or parsley.

The evening meal is a ragged affair of competing interests – children snacking over schoolwork, mothers preparing dishes for surprise visitors and fathers sneaking out for a kebab with friends. At the weekend, Jordanians go out as a family. In cities that could mean a Thai curry, while in small towns it will be the chef's special. In an Arab-style restaurant, the evening is whiled away over mezze – a variety of exquisite little delicacies like peppery rucala leaves, aromatic chopped livers, spicy aubergine dips or a dish of freshly peeled almonds.

Meat dishes usually comprise mutton, goat, chicken or lamb, but never pork – which is *haram* (forbidden) for Muslims, though Jordan's Christian community is free to buy it – if they can find it.

The word 'mezze' is derived from the Arabic *t'mazza*, meaning 'to savour in little bites'.

Bedouin
Bedouin food consists of whatever is available at a particular time. Camel's milk and goat's cheese are staple parts of the diet, as are dried dates

and water. Water takes on a particularly precious quality when it is rationed, and the Bedouin are renowned for consuming very little, particularly during the day when only small sips are taken, mostly to rinse the mouth.

Bedouin specialities like *mensaf* – consisting of lamb, rice and pine nuts, combined with yogurt and the liquid fat from the cooked meat – was once reserved for special occasions. Now visitors can try such dishes in Wadi Rum and Wadi Musa.

Jordan is locally famous for its dairy products, especially salty white cheese. A popular soft white cheese is *kashkawan* (or *kishkeh*) while *haloumi* and Lebanese-style *shinklish* have a firmer texture.

Desserts

Jordanians have an incorrigibly sweet tooth, and there are pastry shops in every town dedicated to the sublime art of baklava. The giant circular trays of filo pastry, tickled with honey, syrup and/or rose water and cut into lozenges, are almost works of art.

The sweetest highlight of travel in Jordan is *kunafa*, a highly addictive dessert of shredded dough and cream cheese, smothered in syrup. Customers generally order desserts by weight: 250g is generally the smallest portion so have some friends (or a toothbrush) at the ready.

DRINKS
Nonalcoholic Drinks

All over Jordan, juice stalls sell freshly squeezed fruit juices *(aseer)*; these stalls are instantly recognisable by the string bags of fruit dangling from the awning. Popular juices include lemon, orange, banana, pomegranate and rockmelon: try a combination of them all and you won't want supper. Water is available in all restaurants and in earthenware ewers by the side of rural roads. You may prefer to stick to bottled water to avoid mild stomach upsets.

SEASONAL SPECIALITIES

Jordan is a great place for fresh produce. Forgetting time, transport and visas, the following could be some treats in store.

Start your taste tour at Bethany in winter, a good time to try the 'Baptism Fish', raised on local fish farms. Continue down the Dead Sea Highway: it may look like carnage on the roads, but it's actually tomatoes. Every January, crates of them line the roads around Safi, awaiting distribution. Glide on in to Aqaba for today's catch from the Red Sea, served with tomatoes and rice in a local dish called *sayadieh*.

Wait for spring before turning inland to Wadi Rum: lamb cooked in a *zerb* (ground oven) will ever after spoil your palate for mutton. Fresh, frothy camel's milk is also abundant in spring. Time your departure from Rum for May and pick up a giant watermelon from roadside fields near the Desert Highway.

Head into the hills around Dana for the summer fruit harvest. Pomegranates, pistachios, peaches, limes and oranges taste extra zestful when picked fresh from the trees. Give a ride to a farmer further up the King's Highway and he'll pay you in spring onions and coriander leaves from his small-holding.

Around Madaba, in late summer, pluck plump, dangling figs or pick grapes from the vine. During Ramadan, fast with the locals between dawn and dusk and see how hunger enhances the flavours of the traditional evening sweetmeats.

Spend the autumn in the north, sampling fresh corn drizzled with newly pressed olive oil from local groves. Escape the oncoming chill by descending to the fertile Jordan Valley, where bananas and mangoes ripen in the subtropical warmth.

Finish your culinary year over the border, in Jerusalem, where copper-coloured persimmons ripen in time for Christmas.

Alcoholic Drinks

There's an air of collusion about 'having a drink' in Jordan as it's *haram* for most of the (Islamic) population. The local wine, made for centuries by the Christian community in the Mt Nebo-Madaba area, won't win many prizes but it's an excellent way of easing down a heavy lunch and it is a feature of many a family's special occasion.

Arak mixed with water is the local aniseed firewater and is an instant ice-breaker with elderly locals. It's not for the faint-hearted, nor faint-headed. For something less potent, Amstel beer is brewed in Jordan or try the local Jordanian brews, Philadelphia or Petra (8% alcohol content).

There are bars in Amman (usually in hotels or doubling as coffee-shops), Christian towns like Madaba and all tourist destinations. Imbibing alcohol is a discreet pleasure in Jordan that is best kept that way to avoid giving offence to Muslims. Not all restaurants are licensed to sell alcohol, as you'll notice in the abstemious city of Aqaba.

Tea & Coffee

Tea and coffee are the major social lubricants in Jordan.

Tea *(shai)* is probably the more popular drink, taken without milk and in various degrees of sweetness: with sugar *(sukkar ziyada)*, a little sugar *(sukkar qaleel)* or no sugar *(bidoon sukkar)*. In most cafés you can ask for refreshing mint tea *(shai ma n'aana)*. Za'atar (thyme) and *marrameeya* (sage) herbal teas are especially delicious in Dana.

Coffee *(qahwa)* is served strong, sweet and flavoured with cardamom, and usually contains a thick sediment. You can specify a small espresso-sized cup *(finjan)* or large cup *(kassa kabira)*. In traditional Bedouin areas coffee is served in small porcelain bowls. Beans are traditionally roasted and then ground in a decorated pestle and mortar called a *mihbash*.

Sahlab is a delicious traditional winter drink, served hot with milk, nuts and cinnamon. Look for it at hot-drink vendors (recognisable by their silver samovars), who also offer takeaway shots of coffee or Lipton tea in white plastic cups.

> A Bedouin host will always refill his guest's coffee cup. A good guest will accept a minimum of three cups before gently tilting the cup from side to side (in Arabic 'dancing' the cup to indicate they've had their fill).

CELEBRATIONS

During the month of Ramadan (see p296 for a list of upcoming dates) Muslims fast during daylight hours. The daily evening meal during Ramadan, called *iftar* (breaking the fast), is always something of a celebration and it's a fun meal to share with hungry patrons in a busy restaurant. Most Jordanians stock up on an especially large pre-dawn breakfast called *suhur* and look forward to the hearty dish-of-the-day served at night.

The Ramadan fast is broken by the three-day festival of Eid al-Fitr, when everyone dresses in new clothes, visits friends and family, and enjoys a large family dinner.

> Out of respect for those fasting during Ramadan, visitors should refrain from eating, drinking and smoking in public. Restaurants catering to tourists serve customers during the day, but in rural areas they usually only open after sunset.

WHERE TO EAT & DRINK
Restaurants

There is a wide variety of restaurants in Amman, as you would expect of a fashionable, burgeoning capital. There's less choice in smaller towns, and in many rural areas self-catering may be your only option. With lots of wonderful fresh produce in the shops and markets, however, and some spectacular places to perch for a picnic, this is no hardship.

Coffeehouses

For men, Jordan's coffeehouses are great places to watch the world go by, write a letter, meet the locals and play a hand of cards, accompanied by

JORDAN'S BEST DINING EXPERIENCES *Jenny Walker*

The queue said it all: it was round the block and halfway back again when we came across the Hashem Restaurant in Amman. If a queue could be that good for a place that looked that bad, then the food must be worth waiting for. And indeed it was. From that moment, the quest was on to find other best eats similarly worth the wait, or indeed worth the effort to get there. This is our personal top 10 – in alphabetical order.

Ayola Coffeeshop & Bar (Madaba, p190) This is the quintessential Jordanian experience: a toasted *haloumi* sandwich in this lovable coffeeshop brings with it the affable tea and talk, the grumbling and gossiping, that makes Jordan Jordan.

Azraq Lodge (Azraq, p155) If anyone had told us we'd be raving about hospital food, then we'd have expected to be admitted – or committed. As it was, the Chechen dishes in this RSCN lodge (a former British military hospital) were simply the best we've ever eaten in Jordan.

Bait Ali (Wadi Rum, p272) Wrapped up in blanket coats, reclined on sheepskin, peering through the roaring fire at cloaked Arab men (a Saudi TV crew apparently) – this is the way to eat roasted meats, in the company of great storytellers.

Feinan Lodge (Dana Nature Reserve, p210) No beer and no meat didn't sound like our idea of a slap-up dinner after a six-hour hike. In the event, the vegetarian mezze in this candlelit lodge were well worth walking for.

Garden Triclinium (Petra, p232) If you like the sound of uninvited guests, unfurl a picnic cloth on the steps of this Nabataean funereal dining chamber. The chances are that only the local cats will come to the party, but then again…

Hashem Restaurant (Amman, p108) You haven't tried falafel until you've eaten here. To fit in with the locals, pop in a handful of mint leaves first, park a wedge of raw onion between your teeth and don't touch the scalding copper vats of beans (harder than you'd imagine given the space available).

Kir Heres (Karak, p203) 'Don't be scared of the tablecloths,' said the Karak-born chef. We weren't and even if the local dishes had cost double, it would've been worth it. Oh, for a pot of that basil!

Lebanese House (Jerash, p133) Nicknamed 'Umm Khalil', this restaurant, which has served over 500,000 customers since 1977, is a national treasure. If it's good enough for King Hussein, Kofi Annan and Richard Gere, it's certainly good enough for us! Try the fresh almonds.

Petra Kitchen (Wadi Musa, p238) There's nothing quite like cooking in the company of strangers. The Jordanian chef is on hand to make sure you don't make a camel's ear of the authentic Jordanian dishes.

Umm Qais Resthouse (Umm Qais, p143) This is one chow-with-wow! The open-air restaurant, set in Roman ruins and overlooking Lake Tiberias, is surrounded by flowers in spring that look good enough to sprinkle on the salad.

Afterthought You can't talk about dinner without dessert in sweet-loving Jordan. Any baklava shop with honey-dipped, pistachio-filled shredded wheat gets our vote for 'pudding'.

the incessant clacking of slammed domino and backgammon pieces and the gurgling of fruity *nargileh* (water pipes). Foreign women, with a bit of courage and modest attire, are usually welcome (see p305). Traditional coffeehouses don't generally serve food.

Western-style cafés are popping up in towns and cities. They serve meals and in Amman sometimes host live music or exhibitions.

Quick Eats

The two most popular local versions of 'fast food' are the shwarma and felafel. They are available in every town, usually from stands.

Shwarma comprises slices of lamb or chicken from a huge revolving spit, mixed with onions and tomato in bread. The vendor will slice off the meat (usually with a great flourish and much knife sharpening and waving), dip a piece of flat bread in the fat that has dripped off the meat, hold it against the gas flame so it flares, then fill it with meat and fillings.

Felafel are deep-fried balls of chickpea paste with spices, served in a piece of rolled-up *khobz* (bread) with varying combinations of pickled vegetables, tomato, salad and yogurt.

Chicken *(farooj)* is another popular quick eat, roasted on spits in large grills in front of the restaurant. The usual serving is half a chicken *(nuss farooj)*, which comes with bread, a side dish of raw onion, chillies and sometimes olives.

Kebabs are another favourite. These are spicy minced-lamb pieces pressed onto skewers and grilled over charcoal. *Shish tawooq* is loosely the chicken version of the same thing.

VEGETARIANS & VEGANS

Virtually no restaurants in Jordan specialise in vegetarian food (with the exception of Feinan Lodge – see Vegidex, p82), and there are few specific 'vegetarian' dishes. That said, meat is still a luxury for many people, so vegetable mezze, salads and soups are common. Hummus and *fuul* (fava-bean paste) are useful staples and there's a rich heritage of locally produced dairy products.

It is hard for a vegan to enjoy a varied diet in Jordan as dairy appears in many nonmeat dishes.

The Bedouin *zerb* oven consists of a hole in the sand and enough firewood to make glowing coals. The oven is sealed and the meat cooked for an hour or more. Most Bedouin camps in Wadi Rum cook food this way.

EATING WITH KIDS

You shouldn't have problems finding something the kids are willing to eat and the relative absence of fast-food chains outside the cities may be a good opportunity to wean them off bad habits! If they insist, however, you can always resort to chicken and chips. Grocery stores stock a wide range of imported Western foods.

HABITS & CUSTOMS

The most common way for a group to eat in a restaurant is to order mezze – a variety of small starters – followed by several mains to be shared by all present. In smaller towns, the dish of the day (usually a stew) is usually the best choice.

WHAT DOES A GIRL HAVE TO DO TO GET A BEER AROUND HERE? *Jenny Walker*

Diary Entries of 1995, near Jerash

Thankfully times have changed since my first trip to Jordan, and women on their own don't present quite such an unusual spectacle. Or is it that I've grown older and no-one's interested any more? Either way, girls be warned: eating on your own may bring more (or less) to your table than you expect. On the upside, travelling solo also means you are likely to be invited in for many wonderful home-cooked meals by locals who take pity on you.

20 April 1995 Despite the neatly laid tables there were no guests to warrant the preparation of food – except me. I braved a seat just before sunset and sat shivering over the tablecloth in the corner while the local police read the papers at a neighbouring table. Eventually a waiter greeted me brightly and brought me coffee. Shocked when I drank all the hot milk, he didn't return again and there was a limit to the length of time I could sit staring at the fairy lights intermittently beaming over the concrete grotto. The policeman went and another waiter came: 'Like to buy Roman coin,' he said (I was thinking rather more of a kebab – with chips). 'What about guide for tomorrow?' And finally, grabbing his crotch with gusto, 'Need a man?' I said, 'No thank you, but I wouldn't mind a beer'. That was the last I saw of him, too – or of anybody for that matter.

21 April 1995 Went down to breakfast with renewed hope of food and was glad to find it arrived without further negotiation from me. I could have done without the services of the hotel manager who felt it necessary to put most of the breakfast things on the table in such a way that he had to brush my left breast to rearrange them. After the third 'accident', I gave him the evil eye I learnt in Saudi and he went out grumbling. It's a silly detail but they do take liberties with lone women. Gobbled a few olives, tried mixing the strawberry jam with the soured goats' milk and popped a butter pat in whole thinking it was the local cheese. Another meal to remember in Jordan!

COOKING COURSES

You can learn how to cook a range of Jordanian mezze, main courses and desserts at a nightly cookery course held by local chefs at **Petra Kitchen** (☎ 2155700; www.petramoon.com/cuisinetours.htm, info@petramoon.com) in Wadi Musa. See p238 for details.

The New Book of Middle Eastern Food by Claudia Roden is a classic text that contains 800 mouth-watering recipes.

EAT YOUR WORDS
Useful Phrases

I'm a vegetarian.	*ana nabaatee* (m)/*ana nabateeyya* (f)
What is this?	*ma hadha?/shu hadha?*
breakfast	*al-futur*
restaurant	*al-matam*
daily special	*wajbet al-yum*

Menu Decoder

Note that, because of the imprecise nature of transliterating Arabic into English, spellings will vary. For example, what we give as *kibbeh* may appear variously as *kubbeh, kibba, kibby* or even *gibeh*.

MEZZE

baba ghanouj	(literally 'father's favourite') dip of mashed eggplant and tahini
balilah	snack of boiled salty legumes
basterma	pastrami, popular from Armenia to Lebanon
buraik	meat or cheese pie
fatayer	triangles of pastry filled with white cheese or spinach; also known as *buraik*

VEGIDEX

Jordan, like many countries in the region, has a strongly carnivorous bias in the national diet – at least, that is, in restaurants. At home, people enjoy their vegetables and dairy products (such as homemade cheese, yoghurt and *labneh*) and often consider meat as something to be afforded on high days and holidays. Delicious vegetable and dairy dishes can be found in many restaurants in Jordan, especially mezze, but the concept of 'vegetarian' is still an alien one. As such, there may well be meat stock within a soup or animal fats used to prepare pastries. The following restaurants are therefore recommended for the variety of their vegetarian options, but not for their nonmeat pedigree. Most of Jordan's top-end hotels offer excellent vegetarian options, so these are not listed here, although they are awarded a vegetarian icon in the eating reviews. As you would expect of an eco-enterprise, most of the nature-reserve restaurants have excellent vegetarian choices on the menu. Feinan Lodge gets the star prize as the outstanding vegetarian choice. Check out the following:

Ajloun Ajloun Nature Reserve restaurant (p136)
Amman Wild Jordan Café (p109); Hashem Restaurant (p108)
Aqaba Ali Baba Restaurant (p256); Blue Bay (p256); Formosa Restaurant (p256); Royal Yacht Club Restaurant (p256)
Azraq Azraq Lodge (p155)
Dana Nature Reserve Feinan Lodge (p210); Dana Guest House (p209); Rummana Campground (p210)
Jerash Lebanese House (p133)
Karak Kir Heres (p203)
Madaba Ayola Coffeeshop & Bar (p190); Haret Jdoudna (p191); Mystic Pizza (p190)
Mt Nebo Mount Moses Restaurant Siyagha (p194)
Petra Basin Restaurant (p234)
Umm Qais Umm Qais Resthouse (p143)
Wadi Musa Petra Kitchen (p238)
Wadi Rum Bait Ali (p272); Rum Gate Restaurant (p273)

EATING ETIQUETTE

Travel in Jordan for any length of time and inevitably you'll be invited home for a meal, especially if you are travelling alone, and most especially if you are a woman. Customs vary depending on who you are having supper with: the Bedouin, for example, share their meals from great aluminium dishes on the floor, whereas Christian communities in the hills may sit round a table. Whatever their own customs, however, Jordanians are very accommodating of other people's habits, though you will certainly impress your hosts if you manage a few of the following courtesies.

Eating in Someone's House

- Bring a small gift of baklava or, better still, a memento from home.
- It's polite to be seen to wash your hands before a meal.
- Use only the right hand for eating or accepting food. The left is reserved for ablutions.
- Don't put food back on the plate: discard in a napkin.
- Your host will often pass the tastiest morsels to you; it's polite to accept them.
- The best part – such as the meat – is usually saved until last, so don't take it until offered.
- If you're sitting on the ground, don't stretch your legs out until after the meal.

Eating in a Restaurant

- Picking your teeth after a meal is quite acceptable and toothpicks are often provided.
- It's traditional to lavish food upon a guest. If you're full, try one more mouthful!
- Leave a little food on your plate. Traditionally, a clean plate is thought to invite famine.
- It's polite to accept a cup of coffee after a meal and impolite to leave before it's served.

fatteh	garlicky yogurt and hummus, sometimes with chicken
fattoosh	salad with sumach (a red spice mix), tomatoes and shreds of crouton-like deep-fried bread
fuul medames	squashed fava beans with chillies, onions and olive oil with olive oil
gallai	sautéed tomato, garlic, onion and peppers topped with cheese and pine nuts on Arabic bread
hummus	cooked chickpeas ground into a paste and mixed with tahini (a sesame-seed paste), garlic and lemon
kibbeh	Lebanese-style kofta made with minced lamb, bulgur/cracked wheat and onion; served raw or deep fried
labneh	cream-cheese dip
makdous	pickled eggplant, walnut and olive-oil dip
manaqeesh	Arabic bread with herbs
manoucha/manaqish	baked breads or pies with thyme (*zaatar*) and cheese
mosabaha	hummus with whole chickpeas in it
mouhamara	walnut, olive oil and cumin dip
muttabal	eggplant dip similar to baba ghanouj but creamier
sambousek	meat and pine-nut pastry
shinklish	tangy and salty dried white cheese, sometimes grilled, sometimes in a salad
tabbouleh	salad of cracked (bulgur) wheat, parsley and tomato
treedah	egg, yogurt and meat
yalenjeh	stuffed vine leaves

Follow up a cookery course at Petra Kitchen with a copy of *Jordanian Cooking Step by Step* by Lina Chebaro Baydoun and Nada Mosbah Halawani.

MAIN DISHES

fareekeh	similar to maqlubbeh but with cracked wheat
fasoolyeh	bean stew

CHOPPING IT WITH THE BEST AT PETRA KITCHEN *Jenny Walker*

It was an inauspicious start one cold day in winter: the knives were seriously large, the onions eye-smartingly malevolent and the aubergines too big for their own good. But just as I was thinking this wasn't the activity for me, I caught sight of my fellow apprentice. With a smile of collusion across the basins of parsley, I took heart and placed myself in the hands of Mr Tariq, professional Petra chef and our teacher for the evening. Within moments, he had us shaving garlic with prodigious speed and chopping industrial quantities of tomatoes without them collapsing into ketchup.

On the menu this evening was green-wheat soup, Arabic salad, *mutabal* (smoky aubergine dip), *galaya bandura* (a tomato and pine-nut salsa), *foul madamas* (fava beans in oil) and pan-roasted chicken. The menu seemed to stretch into tomorrow's breakfast and it was impossible to see how it was all to be served before our husbands slid into oblivion over the Mt Nebo wine at the table. We may just about have managed the Arabic salad of tomatoes, peppers, parsley and mint on our own, but each of the other five dishes took constant supervision. There were pans of simmering beans on the stove, stock bubbling with heart-attack doses of salt on another ring and simultaneous mashing of eggplants and crushing of spices. Despite the dashing from one pan, vat, pot and plate to another, it is to the eternal credit of the chef that we not only managed to escape serious injury, serve up the six dishes on time and enjoy a glass of wine, but we also managed to have a good chat.

The whole experience of cooking a different kind of food in the company of strangers makes you realise that cooking isn't about the ingredients or recipe: it's about the inherited understanding of food and its preparation handed down from farmer to grocer, and from mother to daughter (or son). It's also about the good company of those one shares a kitchen with: as Sharon Stark, my fellow apprentice from New Zealand, said: 'If we'd tasted that meal at a restaurant, without all the fun of creating it, the four of us meeting/talking to each other and our hosts, it would still have been delicious but not as nice as it tasted that night.'

gallayah	traditional Bedouin meal of chicken with tomatoes, other vegetables, garlic and Arabic spices
kofta	meatballs, often in a stew
maqlubbeh	steamed rice topped with grilled slices of eggplant or meat, grilled tomato, cauliflower and pine nuts
mulukiyyeh	spinach stew with chicken or meat pieces
musakhan	baked chicken served on bread with onions, olive oil and pine nuts
sawani	meat or vegetables cooked on trays in a wood-burning oven
shish tawouq	grilled boneless chicken served with bread and onions
shwarma	chicken or lamb sliced off a spit and stuffed in a pocket of pita-type bread with chopped tomatoes and garnish

For the best *kunafa*, join the queues of sugar addicts at the takeaway branch of Habibah, hidden down an alley in downtown Amman (p108).

DESSERT

ftir jibneh	large pastries
haliwat al-jibneh	a soft doughy pastry filled with cream cheese
halva	soft sesame paste, like nougat
kunafa	shredded dough on top of cream cheese smothered in syrup
ma'amoul	biscuits stuffed with dates and pistachio nuts and dipped in rose water
m'shekel	a form of baklava
muhalabiyya	rice pudding, made with rose water
wharbat	triangular pastries with custard inside

Food Glossary
STAPLES

beid	egg
ejja	omelette

jibna	cheese
khobz	bread
labneh	yogurt
makarone	all varieties of pasta
ruz	rice
shurba	soup
sukkar	sugar

MEAT & FISH

farooj	chicken
hamour	a grouper-like fish from the Red Sea
kibda	liver
samak	fish

VEGETABLES

adas	lentils
banadura	tomato
batata	potato
khadrawat	vegetables
khiyar	cucumber

FRUIT

battikh	watermelon
burtuqal	orange
inab	grape
mish-mish	apricot
moz	banana
rumman	pomegranate
tamr	date
tin	fig
tufah	apple

OTHER DISHES & CONDIMENTS

fil fil	chillies
sumach	red-spice mix
tahini	sesame-seed paste
torshi	pink pickled vegetables
tum	garlic
zaatar	thyme blend
zayt	olive oil
zaytun	olives

DRINKS

asir	juice
maya at-ta'abiyya	mineral water
qahwa	coffee
sefeeha	lemon and mint drink
shai	tea

Amman

عمان

While neighbouring medieval cities Damascus and Cairo are steeped in rich antiquity, Amman is largely a modern construction devoid of grand Islamic architecture. Despite its Roman origins as the ancient city of Philadelphia, Amman was little more than a sleepy village prior to the arrival of the Hejaz Railway between Syria and Arabia in the early 20th century.

Following the formation of the state of Israel in 1948, Amman absorbed a massive flood of Palestinian refugees and its population doubled in two weeks. Indeed, the face of Amman has been shaped over the past 60 years by the arrival of hundreds of thousands of Palestinian refugees. Conservative and Islamic in its sympathies, Eastern Amman and the downtown areas are home to the vast majority of the urbanised poor.

However, residents talk openly of two Ammans. In contrast to the east, Western Amman is a world apart, with leafy residential districts, cafés, bars and art galleries. Fostered by a new generation of educated, tolerant and outward-looking youth, Western Amman pushes the boundaries of a cultural life that had been kept under close rein by Islamic conservatives.

Perspective is everything in Amman, and it's impossible to gain a full understanding of the city, or even Jordan, without visiting both Eastern and Western Amman. From the kinetic chaos of the earthy downtown to the stately calm of the urbane western suburbs, Amman is a multicultural city, home to Jordanians of varying backgrounds. While it's certainly not in the same league as emerging international centres like Dubai, Amman is a thoroughly modern Arab city with a diverse vision for the future.

HIGHLIGHTS

- Stand on top of **Jebel al-Qala'a** (p97), where you can visit the ruins of the Citadel while taking in views of the modern city

- Admire the engineering precision of the **Roman Theatre** (p98), Amman's most spectacular ancient monument

- Take in an art exhibition at **Darat al-Funun** (p101), and then sip a cappuccino in its café set amid Byzantine ruins

- Join the beautiful people for a glass of wine or a puff of the hubbly bubbly in the **bars and cafés** (p111) of Shmeisani and Abdoun

- Be one of the first visitors to the **National Museum** (p100), set to open in 2009

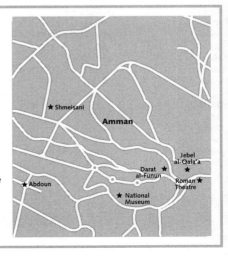

HISTORY

Excavations in and around the capital have turned up finds from as early as 8500 BC, when Neolithic farmers and herders lived near the Ain Ghazal spring in Eastern Amman. At the time, the settlement is reported to have been larger than nearby Jericho, and was home to a sophisticated culture that produced carvings from limestone and plaster. Today, you can see evidence of Amman's earliest inhabitants at the archaeology museum (p97).

The earliest inhabitants in Amman proper settled on Jebel al-Qala'a, the present site of the Citadel, around 1800 BC. There is archaeological evidence to suggest that this site was continuously inhabited through to at least the Bronze Age, and objects dated to this time show that the town was involved in trade with ancient Greece, Syria, Cyprus and Mesopotamia.

Biblical references indicate that by 1200 BC, Rabbath Ammon (the Great City of the

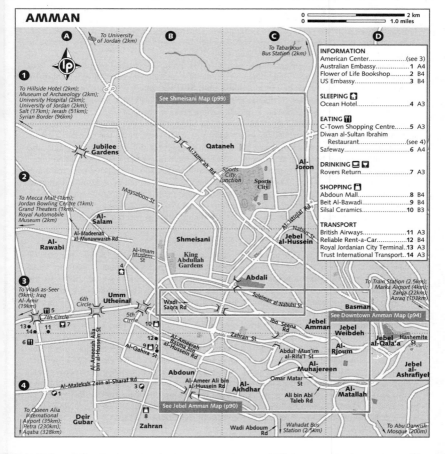

AMMAN

0 ___ 2 km
0 ___ 1.0 miles

To University of Jordan (2km)
To Tabarbour Bus Station (2km)

To Hillside Hotel (2km);
Museum of Archaeology (2km);
University Hospital (2km);
University of Jordan (2km);
Salt (17km); Jerash (51km);
Syrian Border (96km)

See Shmeisani Map (p99)

Jubilee Gardens

Qataneh

Al-Joron

To Mecca Mall (1km);
Jordan Bowling Centre (1km);
Grand Theaters (1km);
Royal Automobile Museum (2km)

Al-Salam

Al-Rawabi

Shmeisani

Jebel al-Hussein

King Abdullah Gardens

Abdali

To Wadi as-Seer (9km); Iraq Al-Amir (19km)

Umm Utheina

Wadi Saqra Rd

Basman

See Downtown Amman Map (p94)

To Train Station (2.5km);
Marka Airport (4km);
Zarqa (22km);
Azraq (103km)

Jebel Amman

Jebel Weibdeh

Jebel al-Qala'a

Jebel al-Ashrafiyeh

Al-Rjoum

Abdoun

Al-Akhdhar

Al-Muhajereen

Al-Matallah

To Queen Alia International Airport (35km);
Petra (230km);
Aqaba (328km)

Deir Gubar

Zahran

Wadi Abdoum Rd

Wahadat Bus Station (2.5km)

To Abu Darwish Mosque (200m)

INFORMATION
American Center........................(see 3)
Australian Embassy........................**1** A4
Flower of Life Bookshop..........**2** B4
US Embassy........................**3** B4

SLEEPING
Ocean Hotel........................**4** A3

EATING
C-Town Shopping Centre........**5** A3
Diwan al-Sultan Ibrahim
  Restaurant........................(see 4)
Safeway........................**6** A4

DRINKING
Rovers Return........................**7** A3

SHOPPING
Abdoun Mall........................**8** B4
Beit Al-Bawadi........................**9** B4
Silsal Ceramics........................**10** B3

TRANSPORT
British Airways........................**11** A3
Reliable Rent-a-Car........................**12** B4
Royal Jordanian City Terminal..**13** A3
Trust International Transport..**14** A3

Ammonites mentioned in the Old Testament) was the capital of the Ammonites. King David sent the Israelite armies to besiege Rabbath, after being insulted by the Ammonite king Nahash. After taking the town, David burnt many inhabitants alive in a brick kiln. Rabbath continued to flourish and supplied David with weapons for his ongoing wars. His successor Solomon erected a shrine in Jerusalem to the Ammonite god Molech. From here on, the only biblical references to Rabbath are

EXPLORING AMMAN

Keeping Perspective

Amman is all about perspective. In the *Pillars of Hercules,* the famed travelogue by the celebrated (and often criticised) Paul Theroux, Amman is described as being 'repulsively spick-and-span', a reference to the staid and orderly western suburbs. On the other hand, a number of our readers have criticised our descriptions of Amman as being a 'modern' and 'multicultural' city, especially in comparison to Gulf cities such as Dubai, Doha and Kuwait City. Clearly, the quality of your time in Amman is subject to a variety of factors.

For starters, your perception will be influenced by any past experiences you've had in the Arab world. If you're arriving in Amman from neighbouring Egypt or Syria, Amman is considerably more subdued and hassle-free. Since much of the city's infrastructure is less than 60 years old, Amman is also largely devoid of grand Islamic monuments, and more modern in appearance. With that said, Amman is a low-rise city scattered amid hills and valleys, and simply cannot be compared to the soaring skylines of the Gulf cities.

In regards to ethnicity, Jordanians are largely of Bedouin, Circassian, Palestinian and Iraqi descent, a heterogeneous mix that transcends national identity. Compared to other countries in the Middle East, Jordan embraces its multifaceted heritage, which is particularly evident in cosmopolitan Western Amman. Of course, the overwhelming majority of Jordanians are Muslim, which is a marked contrast to heavily internationalised cities in the Gulf.

It's also important to mention that Amman is really two different cities, which means that you should try to make an effort to equally explore both east and west. While the bustling markets and crowded cafés of the downtown area evoke classic images of Middle Eastern streetscapes, the grand boulevards and boutique restaurants of Western Amman are more European in nature.

Fortunately Amman is very conducive to exploration by taxi, and it shouldn't cost you more than a few dinars to cross from east to west. While the urban sprawl can be a bit intimidating to new arrivals, give yourself a day or two to get your bearings, which will help you scrape beneath the surface of this often-underrated Middle Eastern capital. And of course you should feel free to explore the city at your own pace; the following itinerary will help you get started.

Suggested Itinerary

On your first day in the city, take a taxi to the **Citadel** (p97), with its ruined Roman temple and Umayyad Palace, and check out the Archaeological Museum and views over downtown. Head east on foot and descend the series of steps to the aptly named downtown to check out the **Roman Theatre** (p98) and its worthwhile museums. Follow our **walking tour** (p103) in reverse and shop the *souqs* (markets) around the Hussein Mosque. Enjoy a cheap local lunch of hummus and mint tea at **Hashem Restaurant** (p108) or spend a bit more on an organic salad while visiting the **Wild Jordan Centre** (p95). In the afternoon, check out the **craft shops** (p114) around 2nd Circle, before dining in the swanky districts of **Shmeisani** (p109).

On the second day, take a taxi or drive to **Wadi as-Seer** (p118) to check out the ruined Hellenistic palace and handicrafts complex of Iraq al-Amir. Continue on to **Fuheis** (p122) for a lunch or dinner of *fatteh* (fried bread with yoghurt, hummus and chicken). Alternatively, you could make a great day trip out to the ruins at **Jerash** (p128), which was once a mighty Roman city in famed Decapolis. After a day's sightseeing, sweat it out in the opulent **Al-Pasha Turkish Bath** (p103), a quintessential Middle Eastern experience. After detoxing, put some poisons back into your blood with a chilled cocktail in any of Amman's chic Western-style **nightclubs** (p113).

prophecies of its destruction at the hands of the Babylonians.

The history of Amman between then (c 585 BC) and the time of the Ptolemies of Egypt is unclear. Ptolemy Philadelphus (283–246 BC) rebuilt the city during his reign, and it was named Philadelphia after him. The Ptolemy dynasty was succeeded by the Seleucids and, briefly, by the Nabataeans, before Amman was taken by Herod around 30 BC, and fell under the sway of Rome. The city, which even before Herod's arrival had felt Rome's influence as a member of the Decapolis (see p125), was totally replanned in typically grand Roman style, with a theatre, forum and Temple to Hercules. It soon became an important centre along the trade routes between the Red Sea and Syria.

Philadelphia was the seat of Christian bishops in the early Byzantine period, but the city declined and fell to the Sassanians (from Persia) in about AD 614. At the time of the Muslim invasion in about AD 636, the town, by then named Amman, was again thriving as a staging post on the caravan trade route. From about the 10th century, however, the city declined, and was soon reduced to a place of exile.

Amman was little more than a village of less than 2000 residents when a colony of Circassians resettled there in 1878. It boomed temporarily in the early 20th century when it became a stopover on the new Hejaz Railway between Damascus and Medina (Saudi Arabia). In 1921 it became the centre of Trans-Jordan when Emir Abdullah made it his headquarters. In 1948 many Palestinians settled in and around Amman and, two years later, it was officially declared the capital of the Hashemite kingdom.

During the 1950s and '60s, Amman sprawled well beyond its original borders as Palestinian refugees set about the business of making new lives outside of their homeland. Following Jordan's defeat in the Six Day War of 1967, the country lost Jerusalem and the West Bank, yet once again absorbed thousands of Palestinian refugees, the vast majority of which joined their displaced families in Amman. In 1970, the repercussions of the Israeli-Palestinian conflict were again felt during 'Black September' when major clashes between the Palestinian Liberation Organisation (PLO) and the Jordanian army erupted in the streets of Amman.

A third wave of Palestinian refugees arrived in 1991, this time from Kuwait as a consequence of the first Gulf War. Following the invasion and occupation of Iraq in 2003, more than 100,000 Iraqi refugees headed west to Jordan. This most recent wave was largely comprised of upper-class and educated refugees, who have set about internationalising Amman.

Largely in response to the constant influx of refugees, Amman is in the midst of a massive building and urban restoration campaign, particularly in the more well-to-do western suburbs. However, the city is facing severe water shortages, which are being compounded by the swelling population and generally poor urban planning. Fortunately, the US aid tap is flowing, the economy is liberalising and Amman is rapidly rising in prominence in both the Middle East and the world.

ORIENTATION

Like Rome, Amman was born on seven major *jebels* (hills), but today it spreads across over more than 20. It's not really a city to explore on foot, apart from the downtown area – known by locals as *il-balad*. A straight, flat road is almost unheard of in Amman. Indeed, the only way to make any sense of Amman in a short time is to pick out the major landmarks on the *jebels*.

The main hill is Jebel Amman, home to several embassies, a few hotels and trendy restaurants. The traffic roundabouts in this central area (some now replaced with tunnels and major intersections) are numbered west of downtown from 1st Circle to 8th Circle. If you're travelling in a taxi, street names will mean little so ask for the nearest 'circle' and walk from there, or give the driver a nearby landmark (like an embassy or hotel). For more information, see the boxed text, p92.

Jebel al-Hussein, northwest of downtown, has the Housing Bank Centre; its mossy, terraced facade sticks out a mile. This also marks the start of the upmarket Shmeisani area, which stretches out to the north as far as the leafy Sports City. It has plenty of restaurants, shops, top-end hotels and a few nightclubs. Another trendy and affluent area is Abdoun, a few hills south of Shmeisani and home to supercool cafés and several embassies.

JEBEL AMMAN

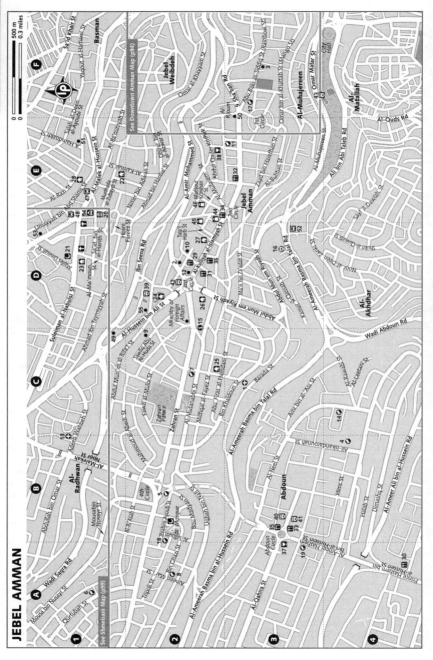

Closer to downtown is the grittier Abdali area, home to the Abdali bus station and topped by the distinctive blue dome of the King Abdullah Mosque.

In the far west is swanky Sweifieh, a booming shopping area. Further out, the city's outlying towns, suburbs and refugee camps have now pretty much merged into one sprawling urban area.

Maps

The maps in this guidebook should be sufficient for most casual visitors. If you plan to stay for some time, or intend to visit places out of the centre, the *Maps of Jordan, Amman and Aqaba* published by Luma Khalaf is worth picking up. It shows just about every street in the city, and pinpoints embassies and other landmarks, though it doesn't cover the southern or eastern suburbs. It's available from most bookshops.

INFORMATION
Bookshops

Amman has a good range of bookshops with titles in English.

Al-Aulama Bookshop (Map p94; ☎ 4636192; 44 Al-Amir Mohammed St, downtown; ⏱ 8am-8pm Sat-Thu) Good for hard-to-find locally produced (and Lonely Planet) guidebooks, maps and postcards.

Amman Bookshop (Map p90; ☎ 4644013; Al-Amir Mohammed St, Jebel Amman; ⏱ 9am-2pm & 3.30-6.30pm Sat-Thu) Just down from 3rd Circle, it has the best range of books and novels in Amman.

Books@café (Map p94; ☎ 4650457; Omar bin al-Khattab, downtown; ⏱ 10am-midnight) Has a large, eclectic selection, with a café and internet access.

Bustami's Library (Map p94; ☎ 4622649; Al-Amir Mohammed St, downtown; ⏱ 5am-6pm Sat-Thu) Right in the heart of downtown, this tiny bookstand is the place to go for up-to-date Western magazines and newspapers.

Flower of Life Bookshop (Map p87; ☎ 5921838; Abdoun Fawzi al-Qawoaji St, Abdoun; 10am-2pm & 4-7pm Sat-Thu) Strong on archaeology, spirituality and kids' books.

Cultural Centres

All of the following foreign cultural centres regularly organise film nights and lectures (generally in their own language), plus exhibitions and concerts (in their own language or Arabic). Tourists are normally welcome at these events, but it's always a good idea to ring the centre first. You will also find details of functions at the various cultural centres listed in the two main local English-language newspapers, the *Jordan Times* and the *Star*.

American Center (Map p87; ☎ 5859102; US Embassy, 20 Al-Umawiyeen St, Abdoun; ⏱ 1-4.30pm Sat-Wed,

9am-4pm Thu) Has a library with American newspapers and magazines.

British Council (Map p90; ☎ 4636147; www.british council.org.jo; Abu Bakr as-Siddiq St, Jebel Amman; ✆ 9am-6.30pm Sun-Wed, to 3.30pm Thu) Southeast of 1st Circle. Has a library with current English newspapers and a pleasant outdoor café. Library hours are noon to 6.30pm Sunday to Wednesday and 11am to 3.30pm Thursday.

Centre Culturel Français (Map p94; ☎ 4612658; www.cccljor-jo.org; Kulliyat al-Sharee'ah St, Jebel Weibdeh; ✆ 8.30am-2pm & 4-6pm Sat-Thu) By the roundabout at the top of Jebel Weibdeh. The library is open 4pm to 6pm Saturday, Sunday and Monday, 11am-1pm and 4pm to 6pm Tuesday and Wednesday, and 4pm to 8pm Thursday.

Goethe Institut (Map p90; ☎ 4641993; giammvw@ go.com.jo; 5 Abdul Mun'im al-Rifa'I St, Al-Radhwan; ✆ 9am-1pm Sun-Thu, 4.30-6.30pm Sun-Wed) Northwest of 3rd Circle.

Instituto Cervantes (Map p90; ☎ 4610858; http:// amman.cervantes.es; Mohammed Hafiz Ma'ath St, Jebel Amman; ✆ 9am-1pm & 4-7.30pm Sun-Thu) Behind Amman Surgical Hospital near 3rd Circle.

Emergency

The tourist police have an office at the Ministry of Tourism & Antiquities and there is a small tourist-police booth (Map p94) on Hashemi St near the Roman Theatre.

Ambulance (☎ 193)

Fire department (☎ 199, 4617101)

Ministry of Tourism & Antiquities (Map p90; ☎ 4642311, 4603360, ext 254; ground fl, Al-Mutanabbi St, Jebel Amman; ✆ 8am-9pm)

Police (☎ 192, 191)

Tourist police (☎ 0800 22228) You can contact the tourist police through the Halla Line, free if calling from a landline or public telephone.

Traffic police/accidents (☎ 190, 4896390)

Internet Access

Amman has plenty of internet cafés, particularly in downtown and by the university.

Books@café (Map p94; ☎ 4650457; Omar bin al-Khattab, downtown; per hr JD2; ✆ 10am-midnight) A professional set-up with fast connections.

WHEN CIRCLES ARE SQUARES

With its endless one-way streets, stairways, narrow lanes and *jebels*, Amman is confusing enough to get around anyway, but the ambiguous names for the streets and circles would challenge the navigational skills of even the most experienced explorer. We have used the more common names on maps and in the text, but if street signs, directions given by locals and queries from taxi drivers are still confusing you, refer to the list here.

Don't forget that Al-Malek means King, so King Faisal St is sometimes labelled Al-Malek Faisal St. Similarly, Al-Malekah is Queen and Al-Amir (Al-Emir) is Prince. And don't be too surprised that some 'circles' are now called 'squares' *(maidan)*...

Circles

- 1st Circle – Maidan al-Malek Abdullah
- 2nd Circle – Maidan Wasfi al-Tal
- 3rd Circle – Maidan al-Malek Talal
- 4th Circle – Maidan al-Emir Gazi bin Mohammed
- 5th Circle – Maidan al-Emir Faisal bin Hussein
- 6th Circle – Maidan al-Emir Rashid bin al-Hassan
- 7th Circle – Maidan al-Emir Talal bin Mohammed
- Ministry of the Interior Circle – Maidan Jamal Abdul Nasser
- Sports City Circle – Maidan al-Medina al-Riyadiyah

Streets

- Abu Bakr as-Siddiq St – Rainbow St
- Al-Kulliyah al-Islamiyah St – Zahran St
- Omar bin al-Khattab St – Mango St
- Quraysh St – Saqf Sayl St
- Suleiman al-Nabulsi St – Police St

Internet Yard (Map p94; ☎ 5509569; dweib@joinnet
.com.jo; Al-Amir Mohammed St, downtown; per hr JD1;
⏲ 9.30am-midnight)
Meeranet (Map p99; ☎ 5695956; Ilya Abu Madhi St,
Shmeisani; per hr JD2; ⏲ 24hr)
Welcome Internet (Map p94; ☎ 4620206; Al-Amir
Mohammed St, downtown; per hr JD1; ⏲ 10.30am-1am)

Laundry

Several tiny laundries and dry-cleaning
services are located in the various streets
and alleys of the downtown area. Some hotels, including the Palace Hotel (p106), offer
a laundry service.

Libraries

The gallery at Darat al-Funun (p101) has
terrific art books, while the main library at
the University of Jordan (p95) is your best
option for serious research. There are also
small libraries at the British Council and in
the American, French, Spanish and German cultural centres (p91).
Amman Central Library (Map p94; ☎ 4627718;
Hashemi St, downtown; ⏲ 9am-5pm Sat-Thu) Near the
Roman Theatre. The top floor holds an eclectic range of
English titles.

Media

Jordan Today (www.jordantoday.com.jo)
is a free monthly booklet that includes a
Yellow Pages listing of embassies, airlines,
travel agencies and car-rental companies in
both Amman and Aqaba, as well as restaurant listings and news of upcoming events.

The monthly *Where to Go* (www.w2go
.com) includes a useful collection of Amman
restaurant menus. To track down a copy of
either, ask at one of the tourist offices or at
top-end hotels and restaurants.

The English-language *Jordan Times* and
Star newspapers both print entertainment
listings and useful phone numbers.

Medical Services

Amman has more than 20 hospitals and
some of the best medical facilities available
in the Middle East. The English-language
Jordan Times and *Star* list hospitals and doctors on night duty throughout the capital.
They also publish a list of pharmacies open
after-hours.
Al-Khalidi Medical Centre (Map p90; ☎ 4644281;
www.kmc.jo; Bin Khaldoun St, Jebel Amman) Southwest
of 3rd Circle.

Islamic Hospital (Map p99; ☎ 5680127; just off Al-
Malek al-Hussein St, Jebel al-Hussein)
Italian Hospital (Map p94; ☎ 4777101; Italian St,
downtown)
Jacob's Pharmacy (Map p90; ☎ 4644945; 3rd
Circle, Jebel Amman; ⏲ 9am-3am) One of the more
conveniently located pharmacies.
Jordan Hospital & Medical Centre (Map p90;
☎ 5607550, 5620777; Al-Malekah Noor St, Jebel Amman)
Palestine Hospital (Map p99; ☎ 5607071;
Al-Malekah Alia St, Shmeisani)
University Hospital (off Map p87; ☎ 5353444; Univer-
sity of Jordan complex, northern Amman)

Money

Changing money in Amman is quick and
easy, especially since the downtown area
is awash with banks and moneychangers.
The Arab Bank, Jordan Gulf Bank and the
Housing Bank for Trade & Finance are
among those with widespread ATMs for
Visa and MasterCard, while Jordan National Bank and HSBC ATMs allow you to
extract dinars from your MasterCard and
are Cirrus compatible. The Housing Bank
has an ATM in the arrivals hall at Queen
Alia International Airport; you get there
after passing through customs so make sure
you have some cash to buy your Jordanian
visa if necessary.

Many moneychangers are located along
Al-Malek Faisal St in downtown.
Sahloul Exchange Co (Map p94; ground fl, Aicco Bldg,
Al-Malek Faisal St, downtown; ⏲ 9am-7pm Sat-Thu)
Good for travellers cheques.

Post

There are lots of small post offices around
town (ask your hotel for the nearest), including at the Jordan InterContinental
Hotel between 2nd and 3rd Circles in Jebel
Amman, and in the Housing Bank Centre
in Shmeisani.

To send a large parcel anywhere, first go
to the Parcel Post Office, in an alleyway behind the central post office in downtown (it
looks more like a shop, so look out for the
weighing machine on the counter), where
it's weighed. Then take it unwrapped to the
nearby Customs Office, diagonally opposite
(look for the sign with the word 'Customs'
in English on the crest), where a customs
declaration must be completed. Then take
the parcel back to the Parcel Post Office for
packing and paying.

DOWNTOWN AMMAN

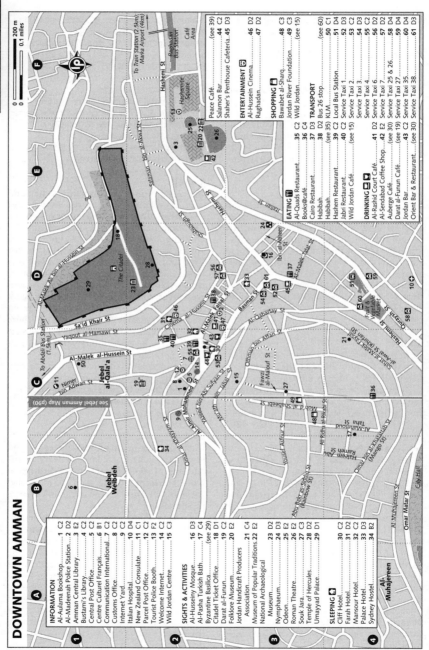

INFORMATION
Al-Aulama Bookshop...................	1	C2
Al-Madeenah Police Station........	2	D2
Amman Central Library...............	3	E2
Bustami's Library.........................	4	C2
Central Post Office.......................	5	C2
Centre Culturel Français..............	6	B1
Communication International........	7	C2
Customs Office.............................	8	C2
Internet Yard................................	9	C2
Italian Hospital............................	10	D4
New Zealand Consulate................	11	C1
Parcel Post Office.........................	12	C2
Tourist Police Booth....................	13	F2
Welcome Internet.........................	14	C2
Wild Jordan Centre......................	15	C3

SIGHTS & ACTIVITIES
Al-Husseiny Mosque....................	16	D3
Al-Pasha Turkish Bath................	17	C4
Byzantine Basilica......................	(see 29)	
Citadel Ticket Office..................	18	D1
Darat al-Funun...........................	19	C2
Folklore Museum.........................	20	E2
Jordan Handicraft Producers		
Association.................................	21	C4
Museum of Popular Traditions.22		E2
National Archaeological		
Museum..	23	D2
Nymphaeum.................................	24	D3
Odeon..	25	E2
Roman Theatre...........................	26	E2
Souk Jara....................................	27	C3
Temple of Hercules....................	28	D2
Umayyad Palace..........................	29	D1

SLEEPING 🏠
Cliff Hotel....................................	30	C2
Farah Hotel.................................	31	D2
Mansour Hotel............................	32	D3
Palace Hotel................................	33	D3
Sydney Hostel.............................	34	B2

EATING 🍴
Al-Quads Restaurant...................	35	C2
Books@café................................	36	C4
Cairo Restaurant........................	37	D3
Habibah.......................................	38	D2
Habibah.......................................	(see 35)	
Hashem Restaurant.....................	39	C2
Jabri Restaurant..........................	40	C2
Wild Jordan Café........................	(see 15)	

DRINKING 🍸🍴
Al-Rashid Court Café..................	41	D2
Al-Sendabad Coffee Shop..........	42	E2
Auberge Café..............................	(see 30)	
Darat al-Funun Café...................	(see 19)	
Jordan Bar...................................	43	C2
Orient Bar & Restaurant............	(see 30)	

Peace Café..................................	(see 39)	
Salamon Bar...............................	44	C2
Shaher's Penthouse Cafeteria.45		D3

ENTERTAINMENT 🎭
Al-Hussein Cinema.....................	46	D2
Raghadan....................................	47	D2

SHOPPING 🛍
Bawabet al-Sharq.......................	48	C3
Jordan River Foundation............	49	C3
Wild Jordan................................	(see 15)	

TRANSPORT
Bus 26 stop..................................	(see 60)	
KLM..	50	C1
Local Bus Station.......................	51	D4
Service Taxi 1..............................	52	D3
Service Taxi 2..............................	53	C2
Service Taxi 3..............................	54	D3
Service Taxi 4..............................	55	C2
Service Taxi 6..............................	56	D2
Service Taxi 7..............................	57	D2
Service Taxi 25 & 26...................	(see 30)	
Service Taxi 27............................	58	D4
Service Taxi 35............................	59	D4
Service Taxi 38............................	60	D4
	61	D3

Central Post Office (Map p94; ☎ 4624120; Al-Amir Mohammed St, downtown; ⏱ 7.30am-5pm Sat-Thu, 8am-1.30pm Fri)
Customs Office (Map p94; ⏱ 8am-2pm Thu-Sat) Diagonally opposite the Parcel Post Office.
Parcel Post Office (Map p94; Omar al-Khayyam St, downtown; ⏱ 8am-3pm Mon-Thu & Sun, to 2pm Sat)

Telephone

There is no central telephone office in Amman. To make a local call, use a telephone in your hotel (ask the price and minimum call length before dialling), or one of the numerous payphones (see p301 for more information). Telephone cards are available at shops close to telephone booths and grocery stores around town.

The private telephone agencies around downtown are the cheapest places for international and domestic calls.

Communication International (Map p94; Nimer Bin Adwan St, downtown) Charges 200 fils per minute to North America and Europe through a mobile phone.

Tourist Information

Ministry of Tourism & Antiquities (Map p90; ☎ 4642311, 4603360, ext 254; fax 4646264; ground fl, Al-Mutanabbi St, Jebel Amman; ⏱ 8am-9pm) The most useful place for information is this office, southwest of the 3rd Circle, which is also the centre for the tourist police. The staff is friendly, and speaks good English. You can also ask questions or lodge a tourism-related complaint at this office through the Halla (Welcome) Line ☎ 0800 22228; free if calling from a landline or public telephone.
Wild Jordan Centre (Map p94; ☎ 4616523; www .rscn.org.jo; Othman Bin Affan St, downtown) The place for information and bookings for activities and accommodation in any of Jordan's nature reserves, including Dana and Wadi Mujib. The centre is run by the Royal Society for the Conservation of Nature (RSCN; see p74). There's also a small crafts shop (p114) and organic café (p105) here.

Universities

The **University of Jordan** (Map p87; www.ju.edu.jo), one of the biggest universities in Jordan, is located about 10km northwest of downtown. It boasts a Museum of Archaeology (p102) and a massive library. It also offers language courses (see p293), and is a great place to meet young locals. Numerous internet cafés and Western fast-food outlets are dotted at various points along the main road, just opposite the university. Take any minibus or service taxi to Salt from either Raghadan or Abdali stations; the university is easy to spot from the main road.

Visa Extensions

If you're staying in Jordan for longer than 30 days, you must obtain a visa extension (see p304).

The process is simple but involves a little running around. First you will need to get staff at your hotel to write a short letter confirming where you are staying. They will also need to fill out two copies of a small card (or photocopy) that states all the hotel details. On the back of the card is the application form for an extension, which you must fill out. It's in Arabic but staff at your hotel should be able to help you fill it out and answers can be in English. That done, take the form, letter, photocopies of the front pages of your passport and the Jordanian visa page, and your passport to the relevant police station.

Which police station you visit depends on which area of Amman you're staying; ask at your hotel for directions to the relevant office. If you're staying downtown, go to the first floor of the **Al-Madeenah Police Station** (Map p94; ☎ 4657788; 1st fl, Al-Malek Faisal St, downtown), opposite the Arab Bank.

After getting the relevant stamp, take your passport off to the **Muhajireen Police Station** (Markaz Amn Muhajireen; Map p90; Al-Ameerah Basma bin Talal Rd, downtown), west of the downtown area. A taxi there from downtown should cost around 600 fils or take service taxi 35 along Quraysh St. A further stamp in your passport should see you with permission to remain in Jordan for an additional three months. Police stations are usually open for extensions from 10am to 3pm Saturday to Thursday, although it's best to go in the morning. Extensions are granted on the spot and you're unlikely to spend more than 10 minutes in each office.

DANGERS & ANNOYANCES

While neighbouring countries Iraq, Syria, Saudi Arabia, Egypt and Israel and the Palestinian Territories are regular headline grabbers the world over, Jordan is a comparatively peaceful country, even for foreign tourists. Since 2004, the Jordanian government has been involved in a massive promotion campaign aimed at doubling the tourism industry by 2010, and creating

AMMAN

CROSSING THE STREET IN AMMAN

When you first arrive in Amman, one of your greatest challenges is likely to be making it safely to the other side of the street. This is especially true of the downtown area, although the faster-moving thoroughfares elsewhere also pose a serious hazard to your health. Contrary to what you may think, Amman's drivers have no desire to run you over; they just want to get to their destination as quickly as possible.

The installation of more traffic lights has made the situation a little easier, but you'll still have a better chance of survival if you follow a few simple 'rules'. In slow-moving traffic, the name of the game is brinkmanship – whoever yields last will win. A car missing you by inches may scare the hell out of you but is actually a normal and precisely calculated course of events.

Cross wide roads a lane at a time – if you wait for a big gap you'll be there all day. Some unscrupulous travellers have even been known to hail a taxi so that it will block traffic and give them a lane's head start. Make your decision and then don't hesitate – Amman's drivers will make their decisions based on a reasonable assumption of what you'll do next.

Above all, have patience; an extra minute's wait is infinitely preferable to a nasty accident. And if all else fails, put your pride behind you and ask some old lady to lead you by the hand – or at least follow in their slipstream.

---

over US$2 billion in revenue and more than 50,000 additional jobs. However, suicide bombings in 2005 and a tourist shooting in 2007 have caused harm to Jordan's reputation as one of the safest travel destinations in the Middle East.

The bombings, a series of coordinated attacks on three hotels in Amman, were a worrying new development related to the turmoil in neighbouring Iraq – the export of terrorism. On 9 November 2005, suicide bombers killed 60 people and injured 115 others in near simultaneous attacks at the Grand Hyatt Hotel, the Radisson SAS Hotel, and the Days Inn. The worst attack was the suicide bomb at the Radisson, which exploded in the Philadelphia Ballroom during a wedding that was attended by hundreds of guests. The following day, an internet statement was released by the Iraqi wing of Al-Qaeda, claiming responsibility for the attack.

On 4 September 2007 lone gunman Nabil Ahmad Jaoura, who had no apparent ties to any terrorist organisation, randomly opened fire on a group of tourists at the Roman Theatre, killing one Briton and injuring six others. Jaoura, a Jordanian of Palestinian decent, claimed that he had carried out his crime in protest against Western interests in the region. According to police and government officials however, Jaoura originally hailed from Zarqa, the hometown of the notorious Al-Qaeda strongman Abu Musab Al-Zarqawi, who

was killed in Iraq a few months prior to the shooting. In December 2007, Jaoura was found guilty by a court of law and sentenced to death by hanging.

Tourist-targeted attacks can quickly destroy a country's reputation, which is why the Jordanian government has been quick to respond to these incidents. Since 2005, security presence has increased significantly at the vast majority of tourist hotels in Amman and throughout Jordan. Individuals entering hotels must now pass through a metal detector, and can be subjected to search if there is due cause. You can also expect to see a significant number of tourist police at major sites throughout the country, which sends a strong message that Jordan is committed to protecting foreigners within its borders.

The take-home message in all of this is that Jordan remains an extremely safe country in which to travel. In a world where terrorist attacks can occur any time and anywhere, Jordan is no more dangerous than any country in Western Europe or North America. In fact, crime of any sort in Amman is extremely rare, and Jordanians take great pride in reminding foreigners that their country remains an oasis of peace in a region torn apart by war and strife. If you still have any doubts about the present security situation in Jordan, you can always check the latest travel warnings online through your country's state department or ministry.

SIGHTS

A largely modern construction, Amman is home to few vistas that evoke images of grand empires. However, scattered amid the concrete-laden streetscapes are a couple of remainders of Philadelphia, particularly the ruins on top of Jebel al-Qala'a, and the Roman Theatre. Of course, if you're having problems imagining the ancient city, you can always stop by the National Archaeological Museum near the Citadel. Amman boasts several good museums, including the highly anticipated National Museum, set to open during the life of this book (for more information, see p100).

For sights around Amman, which make for pleasant day trips from the capital, see p118.

Citadel (Jebel al-Qala'a)

The area known as the **Citadel** (Map p94; ☎ 4638795; admission JD2; ☺ 8am-4pm Sat-Thu Oct-Mar, to 7pm Sat-Thu Apr-Sep; 10am-4pm Fri year-round) sits on the highest hill in Amman, Jebel al-Qala'a (about 850m above sea level), and is the site of ancient Rabbath-Ammon. Artefacts dating from the Bronze Age show that the hill was a fortress and/or agora (open space for commerce and politics) for thousands of years. The complex is surrounded by 1700m-long walls, which were rebuilt many times during the Bronze and Iron Ages, as well as the Roman, Byzantine and Umayyad periods. The Citadel ticket office is on the road leading up to the Citadel's entrance.

The Citadel's most impressive series of historic buildings is the **Umayyad Palace**, which stretches out behind the National Archaeological Museum. Believed to be the work of Umayyad Arabs and dating from about AD 720, the palace was an extensive complex of royal and residential buildings and was once home to the governor of Amman. Its life span was short – it was destroyed by an earthquake in AD 749 and was never fully rebuilt.

Coming from the south, the first major building belonging to the palace complex is the domed **audience hall**, designed to impress visitors to the royal palace. It is the most intact of the buildings on the site and is shaped like a cross because it was built over a Byzantine church. After much debate as to whether the central space had originally been covered or left open to the elements, consensus came down on the side of the ceiling dome, which was reconstructed by Spanish archaeologists.

A **courtyard** immediately north of the hall leads to the 10m-wide **colonnaded street**, lined with numerous arches and columns, and flanked by residential and administrative buildings. Further to the north is the former **governor's residence**, which includes the **throne room**.

East of the audience hall is the **Umayyad Cistern**, an enormous circular hole with steps leading down to the bottom, which once supplied water to the palace and surrounding areas. The small disc on the floor in the centre once supported a pillar that was used for measuring water levels.

Back towards the museum to the south is the small **Byzantine Basilica**, most of which has been destroyed by earthquakes. It dates from the 6th or 7th century AD, and contains a few dusty mosaics.

About 100m south of the basilica are the remaining pillars of the Roman **Temple of Hercules** (Map p94). Once connected to the Forum, the temple was built during the reign of Marcus Aurelius (AD 161–80). The only obvious remains are parts of the podium and the columns, which are visible from around town. Nearby is a **lookout** with sweeping views of the urban sprawl.

There are information boards in English and Spanish at a few places around the Umayyad Palace, though they can be a little confusing to follow. Guides (up to JD5, depending on the length of time and number of people) may approach you when you arrive (or you can ask at the museum), and can really enhance your visit.

The **National Archaeological Museum**, just northwest of the Temple of Hercules, has a good collection of items spanning all eras of Jordanian and regional history, ranging from 6000-year-old skulls from Jericho to Umayyad-period artwork. It also boasts some examples of the Dead Sea Scrolls found at Qumran in 1952, a copy of the Mesha Stele (see p199) and assorted artefacts from Petra and Jerash. Most exhibits are well labelled in English. The crown jewels of the collection are three of the Ain Ghazal statues, dating back to 6500 BC, and some of the world's earliest sculpture. Finds from the Citadel itself include the

AMMAN

TUNNEL UNDER AMMAN

In ancient Roman Philadelphia, royalty considered it beneath them to mingle with the general public unless they had to. To ease their path between the major sites, an underground tunnel was built to connect the Citadel high on the hill with the Nymphaeum and the Theatre. While modern visitors to Amman might welcome having such access without having to negotiate the streets of downtown, the tunnel's precise location and state of repair is a closely guarded secret. According to the rumour mill, locals living near Jebel al-Qala'a know about it, though few seem to know where it is, and most doubt that it even exists. Needless to say, those who might actually know don't seem to be too keen on telling anyone.

head from a statue of the Greek goddess Tyche and some Egyptian-style carvings. Note that there are rumours that this collection might one day be shifted to the new **National Museum** (see the boxed text, p100), though at the time of writing, there was little evidence of this happening soon.

The only access roads to the Citadel are from Al-Malek Ali bin al-Hussein St. It's better to hire a taxi for the trip up (less than JD1 from downtown), though it's a nice walk if you're headed downhill. Steps lead down from east of the Citadel complex, past a viewing platform to Hashemi St, opposite the Roman Theatre.

Roman Theatre & Museums

The restored **Roman Theatre** (Map p94; admission incl Folklore Museum & Museum of Popular Traditions JD1; ☾ 8am-4pm Sat-Thu & 10am-4pm Fri Oct-Mar, 8.30am-7pm Apr-Sep) is the most obvious and impressive remnant of Roman Philadelphia, and is the highlight of Amman for most foreign visitors. The theatre itself is cut into the northern side of a hill that once served as a necropolis, and has a seating capacity of 6000. It was built on three tiers: the rulers, of course, sat closest to the action, the military had the middle section, and the general public sat perched, squinting, way up the top.

The theatre was probably built in the 2nd century AD during the reign of Antoninus

Pius (AD 138–61). Theatres often had religious significance, and the small shrine above the top row of seats once housed a statue of the goddess Athena (now in the National Archaeological Museum), who was prominent in the religious life of the city.

Full restoration of the theatre began in 1957. Unfortunately, non-original materials were used, which means that the present reconstruction is partly inaccurate. However, the final product is certainly impressive, especially considering that the theatre has again become a place of entertainment in recent years. Productions are sometimes put on here in July and August – check with the tourist office or ask at your hotel.

The best time for photographs is the morning, when the light is soft – although the views from the top tiers just before sunset are also superb. During the night the theatre is floodlit, providing a spectacular backdrop to the modern downtown.

Immediately to the right as you enter the Roman Theatre is the **Folklore Museum** (Map p94; ☎ 4651742; Roman Theatre complex; ☾ 9am-7pm Sat-Thu & 10am-4pm Fri May-Sep, 9am-5pm Sat-Thu & 10am-4pm Fri Oct-Apr), which houses a modest collection of items illustrating traditional Jordanian life. They include a Bedouin goat-hair tent complete with tools; musical instruments such as the *rababa* (a one-stringed Bedouin instrument); looms; *mihbash* (coffee grinders); some weapons; and various costumes, including traditional Circassian dress. Don't miss the B&W photos of old Amman by the entrance. Captions are in English.

Immediately to the left as you enter the Roman Theatre is the **Museum of Popular Traditions** (Map p94; ☎ 4651670; Roman Theatre complex; ☾ 9am-7pm Sat-Thu & 10am-4pm Fri May-Sep, 9am-5pm Sat-Thu & 10am-4pm Fri Oct-Apr), which has well-presented displays of traditional costumes, jewellery, face masks and mosaics from Jerash.

The row of columns immediately in front (north) of the Roman Theatre is all that's left of the **Forum**, once one of the largest public squares (about 100m by 50m) in Imperial Rome. Built in AD 190, the square was flanked on three sides by columns, and on the fourth side by the Seil Amman stream, though almost everything lies underneath the modern streets.

On the eastern side of what was the Forum stands the 500-seat **Odeon** (Map p94;

SHMEISANI

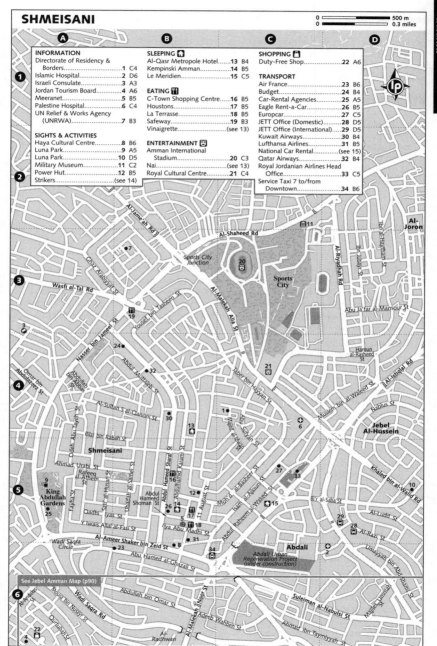

0 ____ 500 m
0 ____ 0.3 miles

INFORMATION
Directorate of Residency &
  Borders..1 C4
Islamic Hospital..............................2 D6
Israeli Consulate............................3 A3
Jordan Tourism Board...................4 A6
Meeranet...5 B5
Palestine Hospital..........................6 C4
UN Relief & Works Agency
  (UNRWA)..7 B3

SIGHTS & ACTIVITIES
Haya Cultural Centre...................8 B6
Luna Park...9 A5
Luna Park......................................10 D5
Military Museum...........................11 C2
Power Hut......................................12 B5
Strikers.......................................(see 14)

SLEEPING
Al-Qasr Metropole Hotel.......13 B4
Kempinski Amman.................14 B5
Le Meridien............................15 C5

EATING
C-Town Shopping Centre......16 B5
Houstons..................................17 B5
La Terrasse.............................18 B5
Safeway...................................19 B3
Vinaigrette..........................(see 13)

ENTERTAINMENT
Amman International
  Stadium.................................20 C3
Nai..(see 13)
Royal Cultural Centre............21 C4

SHOPPING
Duty-Free Shop..........................22 A6

TRANSPORT
Air France.....................................23 B6
Budget..24 B4
Car-Rental Agencies..................25 A5
Eagle Rent-a-Car.......................26 B5
Europcar.......................................27 C5
JETT Office (Domestic)...........28 D5
JETT Office (International).....29 D5
Kuwait Airways..........................30 B4
Lufthansa Airlines....................31 B5
National Car Rental............(see 15)
Qatar Airways.............................32 B4
Royal Jordanian Airlines Head
  Office.......................................33 C5
Service Taxi 7 to/from
  Downtown...............................34 B6

admission free). Built in the 2nd century AD, it served mainly as a venue for musical performances. The small amphitheatre was probably enclosed with a wooden or temporary tent roof to shield the performers and audience from the elements.

Nymphaeum

Built in AD 191, the **Nymphaeum** (Map p94; Quraysh St; admission free; ☺ daylight Sat-Thu) was once a large, two-storey complex with fountains, mosaics, stone carvings and possibly a 600 sq metre swimming pool – all dedicated to the nymphs (mythical young girls who lived in and around the rivers). Up until 1947, the ancient stream and Roman

bridge still stood where the road now runs. Excavations started in earnest in 1993, and restoration will continue for many years. Except for a few columns, an elegant archway and a few alcoves, there is little to see, though the workers toiling away may yet reveal hidden treasures in the years to come.

Al-Husseiny Mosque

Built by King Abdullah I in 1924, and restored in 1987, the **Al-Husseiny Mosque** (Map p94; Hashemi St, downtown; admission free) is in the heart of downtown on the site of a mosque built in AD 640 by 'Umar, the second caliph of Islam. The mosque is more interesting as a hive of activity than for any architectural

---

GIVING AMMAN A FACELIFT

With investment rates and rents skyrocketing, Amman is definitely a city on the rise. Here are some of the major construction projects that will be capturing headlines in the years to come:

- **National Museum** Amman's congested downtown is midway through a major makeover, though it will eventually be home to public gardens, panoramic vantage points and pedestrian trails linking the Citadel and the Roman Theatre. The highlight of this project will be the new international-standard National Museum, which will be located next to the City Hall. While construction delays have pushed back the opening of the museum, it is expected to welcome its first visitors sometime in 2009 (*in sha' Allah!*).

- **Raghadan Bus Station** As part of a massive Japanese-funded re-development campaign, the Raghadan bus station has been completely rebuilt with elegant corner towers, a tourist police booth, restaurants and shops. Many of the once grimy buildings in the area have been given a thorough cleaning, and the hope is that Raghadan will emerge as a major commercial hub in the near future. However, note that at the time of writing the bus station was not yet operating at full capacity – for more information see the boxed text, p115.

- **Abdali Urban Regeneration Project** In the western suburbs of Amman, the old and decaying Abdali bus station is being completely dismantled in a bid to regenerate the neighbourhood. The centrepiece of the project will be the new American University of Jordan, which will be surrounded by high-end shopping complexes, office parks, a public library and a performing-arts centre. Once again, note that at the time of writing the bus station was still partially operating – for more information, see the boxed text, p115.

- **Jordan Gate Towers** This high-profile US$1 billion business and retail complex at 6th Circle will feature twin 35-storey high-rise towers, a five-star Hilton Hotel and a boutique shopping mall. The Jordan Gate Towers will be the first skyscrapers the city has seen to date, and will surpass the Le Royale Hotel as the tallest building in the city. Largely financed by Kuwait and Bahrain, the towers are part of a larger Royal Metropolis project, which also includes an upmarket residential development on the outskirts of Amman as well as a new luxury spa and resort on the shores of the Dead Sea.

- **Queen Alia International Airport** In late 2007, the Jordanian government, in partnership with Royal Jordanian Airways, announced plans to construct a new US$600 million terminal. The aim of the project is to establish Amman as a major regional hub, and to construct larger runways capable of handling the new Airbus A380, the landmark plane of the Dubai-based airline Emirates. Once the new terminal is completed, Queen Alia will be able to handle around nine million passengers a year, nearly three times its current traffic.

splendour as the precinct is a popular local meeting place. Note that non-Muslims, while generally welcome any time except during prayers, may feel intrusive.

Abu Darwish Mosque

On top of Jebel al-Ashrafiyeh' is the striking **Abu Darwish Mosque** (off Map p87), built in 1961 with alternating layers of black and white stone. Non-Muslims are generally not permitted inside, but the views on the way up to the mosque are good. Take service taxi 25 or 26 from Italian St in downtown to the mosque, or charter a taxi. It's a very long and steep climb southeast of downtown if you decide to walk.

Darat al-Funun

On the hillside to the north of the downtown area, **Darat al-Funun** (House of Arts; Map p94; ☎ 4643251; www.daratalfunun.org; Nimer bin Adwan St, downtown; admission free; ⏰ 10am-7pm Sat-Wed, to 8pm Thu) is a superb complex dedicated to placing contemporary art at the heart of Jordan's cultural life. The main building features a small **art gallery** with works by Jordanian and other Arab artists, an art library, and workshops for Jordanian and visiting sculptors and painters. A schedule of upcoming exhibitions, lectures, films and public discussion forums is available on the website and in the *Jordan Times* newspaper.

Almost as significant as the centre's artistic endeavours are the architectural features of the site. At the base of the complex, near the entrance, are the excavated ruins of a 6th-century **Byzantine church**. Buildings further up the hill are mostly restored residences from the 1920s – it was in one of these that TE Lawrence wrote part of *Seven Pillars of Wisdom*. There is also a peaceful café (see p113) and gardens with superb views over Amman.

Access is easiest on foot. From near the southern end of Al-Malek al-Hussein St, head up the stairs under the 'Riviera Hotel' sign. At the top of the stairs, turn immediately right onto Nimer bin Adwan St and walk uphill for 50m where you need to take the left fork. The entrance gate (no English sign) is on the right after a few metres.

King Abdullah Mosque

Completed in 1989 as a memorial by the late King Hussein to his grandfather, the unmistakable blue-domed **mosque** (Map p90; Suleiman al-Nabulsi St, Jebel Weibdeh; admission JD2; ⏰ 8-11am & 12.30-2pm Sat-Thu, 8-10am Fri) can house up to 7000 worshippers inside, and another 3000 in the courtyard area. This is the only mosque in Amman that openly welcomes non-Muslim visitors.

The cavernous, octagonal prayer hall doesn't have any pillars, yet it's capped by a massive dome, 35m in diameter. The inscriptions quote verses from the Quran. The blue colour of the underside of the dome is said to represent the sky, while the golden lines running down to the base of the dome depict rays of light illuminating the 99 names of Allah. The huge three-ringed chandelier contains more Quranic inscriptions. There is also a small women's section for 500 worshippers, and a much smaller royal enclosure.

Inside the mosque is a small **Islamic Museum** (☎ 5672155), which has some pottery pieces, as well as photographs and personal effects of King Abdullah I. There are also a number of pieces of Muslim art, coins and stone engravings. The admission fee to the mosque includes access to the museum.

Women are required to cover their hair – headscarves are available at the entrance to the mosque. Additionally, everyone must remove their shoes before entering the prayer hall.

> **CRAFTY AMMAN**
>
> **JARA** (Jebel Amman Residents Association, www.jara-jordan.com) is a village initiative within a city. It spearheaded the now-famous **Souk Jara street market** (Fawiz al-Malouf Street; ⏰ 10am-10pm Fri May-Aug), among other projects.
>
> **Jordan Handicraft Producers Association** (☎ 4626295; 34 Khirfan Street, Jebel Amman; ⏰ 8am-4pm Sat-Thu) has 500 members working from home and small workshops. In 2008, it opened a showroom in a renovated, 120-year-old stone building.

Jordan National Gallery of Fine Arts

This small but visually impressive **gallery** (Map p90; ☎ 4630128; www.nationalgallery.org; Hosni Fareez St, Jebel Weibdeh; admission JD1; ⏰ 9am-5pm Sun-Thu) is a wonderful place to gain an appreciation of contemporary Jordanian painting, sculpture and pottery. Renovated in 2005, the attractive new space also highlights contemporary art from around the Middle East and the greater Muslim world. Temporary exhibitions here are of high quality, and serve as a valuable introduction (or refresher) to the world of Islamic art. An hour or so is probably enough time to take in most of the gallery, though you can slow down and appreciate your surroundings by relaxing at the on-site Art Café, or browsing the excellent gift shop.

The gallery is signposted from Suleiman al-Nabulsi St, opposite the King Abdullah Mosque.

Museum of Archaeology

While not as extensive as the National Archaeology Museum at the top of the Citadel, this younger sibling is still worth your time, especially if you happen to be visiting the area around the University of Jordan. Highlights of this small **museum** (Map p87; ☎ 5355000, ext 3412; 8am-5pm Sun-Thu) include models of the Temple of Artemis and Nymphaeum at Jerash, a copy of the Mesha Stele (see p199), and finds from Bronze Age Jericho and the 6th-century BC Ammonite fort at Tell al-Mazar. Don't miss the unmarked artefacts lying around outside the building, including several dolmens (ancient graves).

To get to the museum, take any minibus or service taxi heading towards Salt from Abdali or Raghadan stations, then get off at the main (west) entrance to the university and head for the clocktower; the museum is just behind it.

Military Museum

The simple and solemn Martyr's Memorial houses this small but interesting **museum** (Map p99; ☎ 5664240; admission free; 9am-4pm Sat-Thu), which chronicles Jordan's recent military history, from the Arab Revolt in 1916 (in which 10,000 Arab fighters were killed) through to the Arab-Israeli Wars. It does, however, airbrush over many of the controversial aspects of these conflicts – the 1948 and 1967 wars are hardly mentioned and the 1973 war only in passing.

The memorial is on the road to Zarqa, 1km east of the Sports City junction, in the grounds of the Sports City. Take any minibus or service taxi towards Zarqa, but check whether it goes past the Sports City (al-Medina al-Riyadiyah). A private taxi from downtown should cost a couple of dinar.

Other Sights

The **Museum of the Political History of HM Late King Abdullah bin al-Hussein** (Map p90; ☎ 4621151; Al-Kulliyah al-Islamiyah St, Jebel Amman; admission free; 9am-2pm Sun-Thu) is worth checking out for its coverage of Jordan's political life in the early 20th century. It's next to the Iraqi Embassy, west of 1st Circle.

Car enthusiasts will like the display of over 70 classic cars and motorbikes from the personal collection of King Hussein at the **Royal Automobile Museum** (off Map p87; ☎ 5411392; www.royalautomuseum.jo; King Hussein Park; admission JD1; 10am-7pm Wed-Mon). It's in the northwestern suburbs, north of 8th Circle.

Along King Fasyal street is **Duke's Diwan** (Map p94; admission free; dawn-dusk), a historic townhouse built in 1924 that has served as a post office, the Ministry of Finance and a hotel. Today, it has been restored with period furnishings by a prominent Jordanian businessman, who is also the duke of the village of Mukhaybeh.

ACTIVITIES

The top-end hotels allow non-guests to use their **swimming pools** for a small fee (JD10 to JD20 on average), which is a great way to kill an afternoon while beating the heat – for listings, see p107.

Sports City (Map p99; ☎ 5667181) in northern Amman has an Olympic-size pool. Non-members are charged JD5 to JD10, depending on how early you arrive in the day (it gets cheaper as the day goes on), and your fee also nets you a private locker. Note that women may feel uncomfortable swimming here. The Sports City complex also has tennis courts, which you can rent for JD2 per hour.

The **Bisharat Golf Course** (Map p119; ☎ 5520334) comprises of a nine-hole course, putting greens and even a golf pro. Nine holes with equipment rental will set you back around JD45, though the day becomes a bit more expensive if you factor in transportation costs. The club is located 14km south of downtown, and signposted from the Desert Highway on the way to Queen Alia airport – a taxi should cost around JD10 to JD15 each way.

The **Royal Racing Club** (Map p119; ☎ 5850630) holds horse and camel races in spring and summer, and offers horse-riding classes. Details are available from the club, located

GETTING A SCRUB DOWN AT THE TURKISH BATHS

A visit to a *hammam* (Turkish bath) is a quintessential Middle Eastern experience. An Ottoman creation based on prior Roman and Islamic designs, Turkish baths have existed as places of social gathering and ritual cleansing for centuries. While Amman lacks the storied bathhouses found in other Middle Eastern capitals, the city is home to the modern yet architecturally faithful **Al-Pasha Turkish Bath** (Map p94; ☎ 4633002; www.pashaturkishbath.com; Al-Mahmoud Taha St, Jebel Amman; ⏰ 9am-2am, last booking midnight). In the grand tradition of the healing *hammam*, Al-Pasha is the perfect pampering antidote to the hustle and bustle of Amman.

Your full-service treatment starts with a brief spell in the steam room, where you can sweat it out while sipping ice-cold *karkade* (sweetened hibiscus tea). A word of warning: steam does condense, so watch out for the occasional boiling-hot drops of water from the ceiling! The next step in the beautification process is to soak away in the Jacuzzi, which softens up your skin in preparation for the scrubbing to come. The bathhouse attendant will soon start calling bathers over one by one to the alcoves lining the wall.

This is where the fun begins. Using what can only be described as a glorified Brillo pad, the attendant will quite literally scour the visible surface area of your body until dead skin peels off. For a few extra dinars, they will even set to work on your callused feet with a precision file! After five to 10 minutes of thorough scrubbing, your skin will feel like a newborn baby's bottom. Of course, the fun continues as you're soon led over to the marble slabs for an olive-oil massage. Depending on how many bathers are in the queue, the massage lasts 10 to 15 minutes. For a few extra dinars, you can also request a facial or a full-body mud pack.

At the time of writing, the full service treatment cost JD22.50, though be advised that prices are on the rise in Amman. Generally speaking, women are welcome during the day, while evenings are men only. However, it's a good idea to book ahead as slots do fill up. Also, be sure to bring a modest swimming costume. Al-Pasha is easiest to find if you're coming along Abu Bakr as-Siddiq St (Rainbow St) from the 1st Circle; it's the fifth street on the right. Taxis know it as near Ahliya School for Girls.

off the Desert Highway and on the way to Queen Alia airport.

For tenpin bowling try **Strikers** (Map p99; ☎ 5200200; Kempinski Amman, Abdul Hamid Shouman St, Shmeisani) or the **Jordan Bowling Centre** (off Map p87; ☎ 5512987; Makkah al-Mukarramah Rd) at Mecca Mall in the northwestern suburbs. A game costs JD3.

Power Hut (Map p99; ☎ 5686349; powerhut@nets .com.jo; 11 August St, Shmeisani; ⏰ 5.30am-11pm Sun-Thu & Sat, 10am-6.30pm Fri) is one of the best gyms in town. A day/week pass costs JD10/25 and gives access to a wide range of machines, free weights, spin and taebo classes, and a sauna and steam room. The gym is women only from 9.30am to noon.

Club Olympus (Map p90; Grand Hyatt Amman, Al-Hussein bin Ali St, 3rd Circle, Jebel Amman; ⏰ 6am-10pm Sat-Thu, 7am-10pm Fri) charges JD20 for a day's use of its gym, indoor and outdoor pools, Jacuzzi and sauna.

WALKING TOUR

This walk takes you through the busiest part and most interesting sections of downtown's bustling *souqs*. It can be done in an hour (2km) but it's worth stopping, detouring and making a shopping trip out of it.

Start off by sitting down with a fortifying hummus and some mint tea at **Hashem Restaurant** (1; p108), before heading down Al-Malek (King) Faisal St. Just past the ornate Arab Bank, on the left, you'll see an alleyway perennially overflowing with men lining up like impatient addicts waiting for a plate of *kanafa* (shredded wheat and syrup dessert) from the takeaway branch of **Habibah** (2; p108); a few hundred fils or so will buy your very own sugar rush.

After another 80m, turn left into the dazzling **gold souq (3)**. After a quick window

WALK FACTS

Start Al Amir Mohammed St
Finish Citadel
Distance 2km
Duration One hour

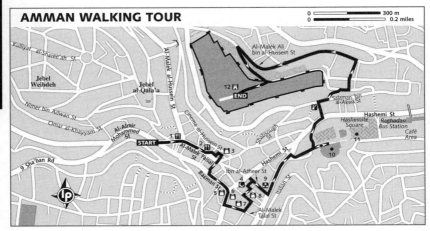

shop, cross the road and head up the alley directly opposite, by the Palace Hotel (the alley entrance is marked by a perfume stall). The eye-opening side alley is lined with risqué Islamic lingerie shops – sure to blow away any preconceived myths you have about prudish Arab women! Head up the flight of steps at the end of the alley and turn left onto Basman St, past several dress shops that stock some nice examples of Palestinian-style embroidery, to views of **Al-Husseiny Mosque (4**; p100). The area is particularly busy Friday lunchtime, when hundreds of men stream out of the mosque after the weekly sermon.

Right on the junction is the **Al-Afghani souvenir store (5)**, a tiny Aladdin's cave overflowing with tourist kitsch. The *souq* behind conceals a maze of other souvenir stores. Across the street, four shops from the souq, is a tiny but excellent **keffiyah shop (6)** – actually a converted stairwell!

Take your life into your hands, cross the street while dodging passing motorists, and head down Betra St. On the left is a traditional **Arabic medicine stall (7)**, recognisable by its dried alligators, starfish and drawers of herbs. At the junction take in the lovely aroma of the coffee roasters and spice grinders. Take a left past these and then another left, past a small bakery on the right, where the staff is continually pulling huge pitta breads out of the ovens. Take a right into the **vegetable market (8)**, past piles of Saudi dates, Iranian pistachios and Syrian olives.

A left and quick right takes you through the fruit *souq*. As you hit the main road, a left turn takes you to a couple of shops selling olives and cheeses; a right leads to the **Nymphaeum (9**; p100).

From the Nymphaeum, follow Quraysh St, then take a right along the busy road to the plaza in front of the **Roman Theatre (10**; p98). Beyond the theatre is **Hashemite Square (11)**, a place for locals to stroll, sip tea, smoke the *nargileh* (water pipe) and watch the world go by. If you're feeling fit, you can climb the steps across the road from the Roman Theatre up to a viewpoint, and then head up to the **Citadel (12**; p97).

AMMAN FOR CHILDREN

While Amman is not exactly the most exciting city for kids, Jordanians by nature love children, and will certainly make your little ones feel welcome. Of course, you do need to take care – traffic can be dangerous, and the sun's rays quickly dehydrate – but otherwise the capital is thoroughly family-friendly.

Amman Waves (Map p119; ☎ 64121704; www .ammanwaves.com; Airport Rd; adult/child JD14/8; ☉ 10am-7pm) Your children will love you for taking them to this Western-style waterpark, about 15km south of town on the highway to the airport. Note that adults should respect local sensibilities and wear appropriate swimwear (no Speedos or bikinis).

Haya Cultural Centre (Map p99; ☎ 5665195; Ilya Abu Madhi St, Shmeisani; admission free; ☉ 9am-6pm

Sat-Thu) Designed especially for children with a library, playground, an interactive eco-museum and an inflatable castle. It also organises regular activities and performances for kids.

Luna Park (Map p99; Khaled bin al-Walid Rd, Shmeisani; admission JD1; 🕙 10am-10pm) Has rides and amusements for the kids. Another branch is located at King Abdullah Gardens (Map p99).

Wild Jordan Café (p105) Offers a kid-friendly Friday brunch (9am to 11am) with entertainment and environmental education aimed at ages 8 to 11.

TOURS

The main backpacker hotels – the Cliff, Farah, Mansour and Palace – all offer a variety of day trips from Amman. The most popular are to the desert castles, Jerash, Ajlun and/or Umm Qais. Prices vary depending on the size of the party and the number of stops on the tour, though you can expect to pay somewhere around JD15 to JD20 per person. If you can find enough other interested people, you can also arrange trips to Madaba, Mt Nebo and the Dead Sea. Generally speaking, don't expect anything more than transport on these tours.

As an alternative to relying on public transport, all four hotels can also arrange tours to more far-flung destinations such as Petra, Wadi Mujib Gorge, Karak, Shobak and the Dana Nature Reserve. Some readers have recommended these tours as a quick and easy way to access Jordan's major sites, while others have complained of being rushed along from spot to spot. Make sure you understand the nature of the tour you're signing on to before you fork over your dinars.

The Palace Hotel also runs a day trip from Amman to Damascus for JD20 to 25 per person. Note that for most nationalities, Syria does not issue visas at the border, so be sure to make arrangements in advance if you're planning a trip to Damascus.

FESTIVALS & EVENTS

Concerts, plays and performances are occasionally held at the Odeon (p98) and the Roman Theatre (p98) in July and August. The Ministry of Tourism office, near 3rd Circle, is the best source of information, but also check out the English-language newspapers. See p129 for information about the Jerash Festival, Jordan's best-known cultural event (generally visited as a day trip from Amman).

SLEEPING

Choosing where to stay in Amman is an important decision, as it will strongly influence your perceptions of the city. Amman is roughly divided into east and west – the vast majority of the city's budget accommodation is located in the poorer downtown area, while upmarket options are located in the more fashionable districts of Jebel Amman, Shmeisani and the western suburbs.

Travellers often complain about the high prices of accommodation in Amman. While there are budget hotels catering to shoestringers, you don't get much for your money. Still, if you're happy with fan-cooled rooms, shared bathrooms and the occasional presence of hot water, you'll survive a night or two here. Room prices here include shared bathroom unless otherwise noted.

If you're looking for a few more creature comforts, midrange options offer en-suite facilities with hot water, air-conditioning and satellite TV. Another advantage of upgrading is that most midrange options are located in Western Amman between 1st and 5th Circles. Midrange accommodation is certainly not cheap, and high prices don't always mean value for money.

One thing Amman does have is a plethora of world-class four- and five-star hotels. Unlike neighbouring Damascus or Cairo, you can't expect to score a luxury suite here without parting with some serious cash. However, Amman is one place in Jordan where it's worth splurging if you have the capital, especially if you want to base yourself in trendy Shmeisani.

While our accommodation list is by no means comprehensive, we have strived to list places that meet our high standards for recommendation.

Budget

The following accommodation options are all located downtown.

Cliff Hotel (Map p94; ☎ 4624273; Al-Amir Mohammed St; mattress on roof/3-bed dm/s/d JD2/3/5/6) A long-standing shoestring favourite with a friendly and accommodating staff, Cliff remains one of the cheapest accommodation options in all of Amman. Of course, you shouldn't come here expecting much for your money – the cramped rooms are of questionable cleanliness, and it's a bit cheeky to charge a dinar to use the communal showers. But if your bank account is pushing red, or you're sticking to a tight budget, there is no better place to lay your head for the night.

Mansour Hotel (Map p94; ☎ 4621575; Al-Malek Faisal St; 4-bed dm JD5, s/d JD7/10, s/d with private bathroom JD9/14; 🖳 😂) A welcome change from the shabby hotels typically found at this price range, the Mansour is an old Arabic school that has been converted into an attractive budget accommodation. The new management receives glowing remarks from travellers, and its sheltered location away from the main road means that it's quieter than most downtown hotels. Rooms are extremely basic, though they're clean and comfortable, and will more than suffice if you're not too fussy.

Farah Hotel (Map p94; ☎ 4651443; farahhotel@ hotmail.com; Cinema al-Hussein St; 4- to 6-bed dm JD5, s/d JD9/15, s/d with private bathroom JD15/22; 🖳) This backpacker-savvy place, which has been spruced up over the past few years, gets consistently good reports from travellers. Private and shared rooms with varying amenities still appear as if they were furnished a generation ago, though the Farah more than makes up for this with its knowledgeable staff, warm communal feel and popular movie nights. The hotel is also a great place to organise day trips from Amman with like-minded travellers.

Sydney Hostel (Map p94; ☎ 4641122; sydney _hostel@yahoo.com; 9 Sha'ban St; dm JD7, s/d/tr JD17/24/30; 🖳) A relative newcomer to the Amman budget-hotel scene, the Sydney Hostel still needs a bit of time to work out the kinks, though it's certainly got potential to turn into a proper backpacker haunt. On one hand, the free internet is a nice perk, as is the small on-site restaurant where guests meet up to swap stories. However, travellers complain that the basic rooms are not kept as clean as they should be, and that the quality of the staff is hit and miss.

ourpick Palace Hotel (Map p94; ☎ 4624326; www .palacehotel.com.jo; Al-Malek Faisal St; s/d/tr JD10/15/18, s/d/tr with private bathroom JD17/24/30; 🖳 😂) The Palace is definitely the best budget option in the city, particularly because it's clued in to the needs of backpackers. The hotel offers reliable hot water, an on-site internet

café and the best value tours around the country. The fluorescent-lit rooms themselves aren't much to write home about, though they're kept fairly clean, and are well equipped with air-con and satellite TV. The price includes a simple but filling breakfast, which is served in an attractive lounge where travellers congregate in front of the tube.

Midrange

Unless otherwise stated, all of the following accommodation is located in the Jebel Amman area.

Caravan Hotel (Map p90; ☎ 5661195; caravan@ go.com.jo; Al-Ma'moun St; s/d JD24/30; 🅿 😂 🖳) Almost opposite the King Abdullah Mosque on the edges of Abdali bus station, the Caravan Hotel's location is something of compromise between the hectic downtown and the quieter Western districts. It's a good place to crash if you arrive at the station late, or if you don't want to shell out the cash for more upmarket midrange options. The Caravan is a good-value and reliable place with a family feel and pleasant rooms. Ask to see a few rooms as some are bigger than others.

Canary Hotel (Map p90; ☎ 4638353; canary_h@ hotmail.com; 17 Al-Karmali St; s/d JD24/31, ste JD40; 🅿 😂 🖳) In the leafy Jebel Weibdeh area, the cosy B&B-style Canary is pleasantly aloof from the chaos of the Abdali bus station, yet within easy walking distance of it. The rooms are more comfortable than luxurious, although everything is kept spick-and-span, including the bathrooms. Doubles are generally better value than the singles, though the best deal is the four-bed family suite.

Hisham Hotel (Map p90; ☎ 4644028; www.hisham hotel.com.jo; Mithqal al-Fayez St; s/d from 30/40, ste JD45; 😂 🖳) You can't go wrong in this excellent choice, in a leafy embassy district a couple of blocks south of the French Embassy. The rooms are comfortable and relaxed, and brought to life with small, personal touches. The hotel also has a dedicated following of frequent travellers, attracted to its central location and affordable price. Note that prices vary depending on the season, and are sometimes negotiable.

Toledo Hotel (Map p90; ☎ 4657777; www.toledo hotel.jo; Umayyah bin Abd Shams St; s/d from JD55/65; 😂 🖳 🦮) A major step-up in quality over cheaper options, the Moorish-style Toledo offers upmarket options at a midrange price. Modern rooms with soft and subdued lighting boast business-friendly amenities such as satellite TV and wireless internet, and the spacious bathrooms positively sparkle. If you are concerned about either a late arrival or early departure by bus (though there are taxis available at any time), the hotel is conveniently located right by the Abdali bus station.

Hillside Hotel (off Map p87; ☎ 5359481; www.hillsidehotel.com; University St; s/d J49/68; ❄ 🖳 🕸) While not as formal and sophisticated as the Toledo, the Hillside is an excellent option if you have any business to attend to on the campus of the University of Jordan. Located in the western suburbs across from the university hospital, this modest hotel with clean rooms is notable for its excellent amenities and attentive service. The ground floor is home to a huge swimming pool, while the restaurant serves up some serious buffets.

Ocean Hotel (Map p87; ☎ 5517280; www.oceanhotel.com.jo; Shatt al-Arab St, Umm Utheima; s/d from JD65/77; ❄ 🖳 🕸) Also located in the western suburbs, far from the hustle and bustle of the downtown, this upmarket midrange option is a good choice if you want peace and quiet. Rooms are warm and inviting as opposed to chic and luxurious, and are equipped with a full-range of amenities required by discerning travellers. The hotel is also home to the Diwan al-Sultan Ibrahim Restaurant, p111), regarded as one of the best Lebanese eating spots in the capital.

ourpick AlQasr Metropole Hotel (Map p99; ☎ 5689671; www.alqasr-hojo.com; 3 Arroub St, Shmeisani; s/d JD90/100; ❄ 🖳 🕸) Straddling the boundary between midrange and top end, the AlQasr Metropole Hotel is the closest thing to a boutique hotel in Amman. Located in the always fashionable Shmeisani, the AlQasr is home to only 70 rooms, a far cry from the larger and more impersonal luxury hotels. The rooms are artistically designed, incorporating pleasing design elements such as wood floors, crown moulding and soft lighting. The hotel also has an excellent range of restaurants and bars including Vinaigrette (p108) and Nai (p113).

Top End

All of the following accommodations are located in the Jebel Amman and Shmeisani

areas. Note that cheaper prices are sometimes available if you book in advance online.

Le Meridien (Map p99; ☎ 5696511; www.lemeridien.com; Al-Malekah Noor St, Shmeisani; r from JD120; 🖳 🖳 🕸) For those vital first impressions, the Le Meridien is grand and stylish, as are its elite surrounds in the Shmeisani district. While it's not as intimate as other top-end hotels, and primarily targets business travellers, the hotel is considerably more affordable than the competition, yet still manages to woo guests over with its flawless rooms and world-class service. Like other hotels in this category, the Meridien has a private gym, swimming pools and health spa.

ourpick Jordan InterContinental Hotel (Map p90; ☎ 4641361, 0800 22666; www.intercontinental.com; Al-Kulliyah al-Islamiyah St, Jebel Amman; r from JD140; ❄ 🖳 🕸) The grand-daddy of luxury hotels in Amman, the much revered and storied InterCon has been hosting foreign dignitaries since the early days of Jordan's founding. Today, it still attracts an interesting mix of distinguished guests, including top American brass on R&R from Iraq and visiting royalty from the Gulf. While it's certainly not the newest hotel, nor the most expensive on the block, there is an aged grace here not found at other top-end properties. A full refurbish in 2004 left the rooms as elegant as ever. Even if you're not staying here, you can always stop by and read the morning paper over a cappuccino in the grand lobby – there are usually some interesting people hanging out here.

Hotel Le Royal (Map p90; ☎ 4603000; www.leroyalhotel-amman.com; Zahran St, 3rd Circle, Jebel Amman; r from JD160; ❄ 🖳 🕸) Amman doesn't get more ostentatious than this huge ziggurat-shaped palace, currently the tallest building in Amman (the Jordan Gate towers, p100, will eventually top this). A favourite of visiting sheikhs and oil ministers, this is not the place for intimacy, but rather over-the-top indulgence. Opulent rooms incorporate traditional Middle Eastern design elements, though the highlight of the property is its award-winning health-and-beauty spa, which is the biggest in Amman.

Grand Hyatt Amman (Map p90; ☎ 4651234; www.hyatt.com; Al-Hussein bin Ali St, 3rd Circle, Jebel Amman; r from JD180; ❄ 🖳 🕸) An enormous complex with hundreds of rooms, suites and apartments as well as restaurants, bars, clubs, swimming pools and even a shopping mall, the Grand Hyatt is truly a class act. The majority of the hotel is constructed from polished Jerusalem sandstone, an elegant touch that tones down the sheer extravagance of it all. Of course, rooms are about as plush as they come, and certainly justify the high price tag.

Kempinski Amman (Map p99; ☎ 5200200; www.kempinski.com; Abdul Hamid Shouman St, Shmeisani; r from JD210; 🕱 🖳 🛎) Since its gala-opening in late 2005, the Kempinski Amman has earned the title of Amman's most chic and sophisticated accommodation option. This European-styled hotel is rightfully home in Shmeisani, and offers immaculate rooms with designer furnishings and positively regal bathrooms. The Kempinski also offers a wide range of upmarket bars and restaurants, as well as an impressive list of entertainment options including a bowling alley, a cinema and games centre for the kids.

EATING

Amman has a wide range of eating options, with budget places concentrated in downtown, while the more upmarket restaurants serving Arab and international cuisine are concentrated in Shmeisani and the western suburbs. If money's an issue, your mainstay in Amman will be felafel, shwarma and roast chicken – all of these fill the belly without hitting the wallet too hard. However, if you're partial to a good meal regardless of the expense, Amman serves up a good measure of high-quality Middle Eastern and international fare, ranging from Jordanian staples like boiled lamb and Lebanese-inspired mezzes to authentic Italian pastas and Japanese sushi spreads.

Note that many of the pub and bars in Amman also serve food – for listings, check out p111.

Budget

Habibah (Map p94; Al-Malek al-Hussein St, downtown; pastries from 300 fils) This legendary shop is your best bet for Middle Eastern sweets and pastries. Sweet tooths of all ages line up for honey-infused, pistachio-topped and filo-crusted variations on the region's most famous desserts. There is another branch on Al-Malek Faisel St.

Reem Cafeteria (Map p90; ☎ 4645725; 2nd Circle, Jebel Amman; shwarma JD1) There are hundreds of shoebox-sized shwarma dives in Amman but few that have the punters queuing down the street at 3am. Even the royal family are rumoured to have dropped in here for a late-night kebab. And if it's good enough for them…

ourpick Hashem Restaurant (Map p94; Al-Amir Mohammed St, downtown; mains JD1-3; 🕑 24hr) A legendary place that overflows into the alley, Hashem is incredibly popular with locals for felafel, hummus and *fuul* (fava-bean paste). A filling meal with bread and mint tea costs around JD1. As one reader extolled: 'nothing but bread, hummus, *fuul* and felafel, but everything is fresh and dirt cheap. We love this place!'

A NIGHT OUT AT KAN ZEMAN

The historic 19th-century inn of **Kan Zeman** (Map p119; ☎ 4128391; lunch/dinner from JD10/15; 🕑 noon-4pm & 7pm-midnight), is one of Amman's longest-standing restaurants. Resident expats give the food mixed reviews, and it's definitely aimed at tour groups, but the vaulted ceilings lend Kan Zeman a historic ambience that is difficult to find in modern Amman. The restaurant is brought to life each night when traditional live music fills the ancient halls.

While most diners opt for the hearty lunch and dinner buffets that highlight the best in Jordanian and Middle Eastern cuisine, you can also choose smaller snacks and drinks, such as *manaqeesh* (baked thyme pastry) washed down with a glass of *sefeeha* (a lemon and mint drink). Kan Zeman also produces its own signature red and white wine, which serves as a perfect complement to the food and song.

Kan Zeman is a bit of a hike from Amman, around 15km south of 8th Circle in the village of Al-Yadoudeh – 3km east of the Desert Highway – so you'll have to factor in a significant taxi fare (JD5 to J10 each way). If driving, take the signed turn-off to Al-Yadoudeh village and follow the signs for 3km to the hilltop site. It's sometimes known as the Sahtain Restaurant. The restaurant is part of a tourist complex with a few handicraft stores (most open after 6pm). While you can just turn up, it's advised that you phone ahead and make a reservation.

Jabri Restaurant (Map p94; ☎ 4624108; Al-Malek al-Hussein St, downtown; pastries from 500 fils, mains JD2-4; ☒ 8am-8pm Sat-Thu) Jabri is famed as a pastry place, and you certainly shouldn't miss the chance to stock up on a kilo or so of baklava and/or other local delicacies. However, the restaurant is also pretty good value for money, with attentive service and decent food that will only set you back a few dinars.

Al-Quds Restaurant (Map p94; ☎ 4630168; Al-Malek al-Hussein St, downtown; pastries from 500 fils, mains from JD2; ☒ 7am-10pm) The Jerusalem Restaurant is another famed place specialising in sweets and pastries, but with a large restaurant at the back. The menu is in Arabic, and most waiters can only be bothered to translate a couple of items before getting huffy. The speciality of the house is *mensaf*, a Bedouin dish of lamb on a bed of rice.

Cairo Restaurant (Map p94; ☎ 4624527; Al-Malek Talal St, downtown; meals JD2-5; ☒ 6am-10pm) This is one place we kept coming back to night after night for the best budget food in downtown. Most of the locals opt for the mutton stew and boiled goat's head, but take it from us – you're better off with the excellent *shish tawooq*, which is enough grilled chicken for two.

Midrange

Abu Ahmad Orient Restaurant (Map p90; ☎ 464 1879; 3rd Circle, Jebel Amman; mains JD4-6; ☒ noon-midnight) This excellent midrange Lebanese place has a nice outdoor terrace that bustles with life during the summer months. The standard grilled meats are all present here, but the real highlights are the hot and cold mezze – try a *buraik* (meat or cheese pie) or the *yalenjeh* (stuffed vine leaves).

Books@café (Map p94; ☎ 4650457; Omar bin al-Khattab, downtown; mains JD4-6; ☒ 10am-midnight) For a slice of coffeehouse chic and good Western food, this restaurant, bar and café is hard to beat. Genuine Italian pizzas and pasta are joined by good salads, and hot drinks are enjoyed by plenty of hip young Jordanians lounging on sofas in corners.

Ristorante Casereccio (Map p90; ☎ 5934722; Abdoun Circle, Jebel Amman; mains JD4-6; ☒ 1-4pm & 7pm-midnight) An unpretentious and casual pizza and pasta place just off the trendy Abdoun Circle attracts a mixed crowd, though everyone is here for the same reason, namely savoury pizza. Of course, if you've got a bit

of a sweet tooth, be sure to save space for the Nutella-stuffed pizza with strawberries – it's as delectable as its sounds!

our pick **Blue Fig Café** (Map p90; ☎ 5928800; Prince Hashem bin al-Hussein St, Jebel Amman; mains JD4-8; ☒ 8.30am-1am) Travellers always seem to appreciate the global coffeehouse vibe in this supercool place near Abdoun Circle, which offers an extensive and imaginative mix of world fusion dishes. Throw in some seductive world music and the occasional poetry reading, and you've got a winner. And, honestly, where else could you get a 'Kyoto green tea and mint flavoured crème brulée'?

Noodasia (Map p90; ☎ 5936999; Abdoun Circle, Jebel Amman; mains JD5-9) The shiny chrome and dark woods of this stylish pan-Asian diner feel like they have been lifted straight from the cooler quarters of Shanghai. However, the menu stretches across the Asian continent, and includes Chinese, Thai and Japanese snacks and main dishes such as green curries, sushi combos and the obligatory Chinese noodle dish.

Wild Jordan Café (Map p94; ☎ 4633542; Othman Bin Affan St, downtown; ☒ 11am-midnight; mains JD5-10; Ⓥ) After checking out the Wild Jordan Nature shop (p95), grab a bite at this stylish and modern café where the emphasis is on light and healthy, with smoothies, wraps and organic salads, plus strong veggie options like the spinach-and-mushroom salad. The glass walls and open-air terrace offer terrific views over Amman, particularly at night.

Vinaigrette (Map p99; ☎ 5695481; AlQasr Plaza Hotel, 3 Arroub St, Shmeisani; mains JD6-12) This stylish but affordable restaurant is located on the top floor of the AlQasr, and in keeping with the hotel's boutique theme, offers gourmet sushi and salads – build your own salad and sushi combo, or let the house choose for you. Mellow jazz complements the superb views over the city, making it a great place for a light dinner before hitting the dance floor downstairs at Nai (p113).

Top End

Houstons (Map p99; ☎ 5620610; off Abdul Hameed Shoman St, Shmeisani; mains JD9-15; ☒ noon-midnight) A popular American-style family restaurant that gets good reviews from homesick ex-pats. True to its Texan moniker, Houstons specialises in Tex-Mex dishes and margaritas, but it also does steaks, burgers and has

AMMAN

GEMS OF WISDOM FROM AMMAN'S TAXI DRIVERS *Matthew D Firestone*

On any given day, Jordan's capital is home to an estimated 16,000 yellow taxis and counting. One will never be far away, and they often find you before you find them – hopeful honking at tourists in case they missed the obvious is a favourite pastime. Most taxi drivers work hard for their money. A good day can yield JD35 (before overheads) in winter, and double that in summer. A bad day will bring as little as JD15 – not much for up to 15 hours' work. Most drivers are fast and friendly, often more interested in finding out where you're from than keeping an eye on the road ahead. Making the effort to talk with them is illuminating, from shedding light on the latest gossip or scandal to their take on the problems of the Middle East (many are Palestinians with stories to tell).

While updating the Amman chapter for this guidebook, I spent a good deal of time travelling in cabs, drinking from their fountain of collective knowledge, so to speak. To give you a taste as well, I've assembled this concise collection of notable quotables:

On the influence and greatness of America

- 'America needs to stop being Big Brother and leave us alone. It has no business in the Middle East and Iraq. The sooner it leaves, the happier everyone will be.'
- 'America and Jordan are great friends. But so are America and Israel. America needs to stop shaking everyone's hand and putting money in their pockets.'
- 'Most Americans can't find Iraq on a map. Jordan may not be a great country, but we know where Iraq is – it's right over there! Do you want to go there now?'
- 'USA is number one. They have great pizza and hamburgers. But our felafel is better. And we have some great shopping malls. Do you want to go there now?'

On the importance of choosing the right destination

- 'That hotel is too far away. Can't we go somewhere closer?'
- 'That hotel is too close. Can't we go somewhere farther?'
- 'That hotel burnt down. Can't we go somewhere else?'
- 'That hotel is a brothel. But we can go there if you want!'

On the subtle art of driving a taxi

- *(After breaking down)* 'I don't know much about cars, but that doesn't sound good. Do you know anything about cars? Do you mind taking a look at my engine?'
- *(After running out of petrol)* 'Good taxi drivers always remember to fill up their cars after every fare. Now, get out and help me push this car!'
- *(Driver is sipping a coffee and text messaging)* 'If you always keep your hands on the wheel, you will survive the roads here in Amman.'
- *(Driver is cut off)* 'Did you see that? I can't believe he did that!' *(Driver yells chain of expletives involving the other driver's mother and a camel)*

On the importance of carrying exact change

- *(Driver is given a JD20 note)* 'Don't you have anything smaller?'
- *(Driver is given a JD10 note)* 'Don't you have anything smaller?'
- *(Driver is given a DJ5 note)* 'Don't you have anything smaller?'
- *(Driver is given a JD1 coin)* 'Don't you have anything smaller?'

The take-home message in all of this is that you shouldn't be afraid to strike up a conversation with your local neighbourhood cabbie. While you should take their advice with a grain of salt, they should help you crack a smile.

a good salad bar – if you're from the States, you know the deal!

Bonita Inn (Map p90; ☎ 4615061; off Al-Kulliyah al-Islamiyah St, Jebel Amman; mains JD10-20; ☻ noon-midnight) This romantic spot with a rustic farmhouse feel is an excellent choice for European (primarily Spanish) cuisine. The steaks have a citywide reputation, while the paella Valenciana and gazpacho soup are as authentic as you'll get in the Middle East. Another highlight is the tapas menu, with plenty of calamari, octopus and salads.

La Terrasse (Map p99; ☎ 5662831; 11 August St, Shmeisani; mains JD20-25; ☻ 1pm-1am) This Shmeisani standard offers high-end European cuisine in pleasant surroundings emphasising low-key luxury. The wine list is extensive, with labels representing Jordan and much of the Mediterranean rim (JD20 to JD25 a bottle). Most nights after 10pm the tiny stage is given over to live Arab singers and musicians, making it a popular venue for well-to-do local families.

Diwan al-Sultan Ibrahim Restaurant (Map p87; ☎ 5517383; Ocean Hotel, Shatt al-Arab St, Umm Utheina; mains JD10-15; ☻ noon-midnight) The Diwan comes highly recommended by wealthy locals and expats for its high-quality Lebanese food. Among the meals are frogs legs with garlic and coriander, and deep-fried brains (the latter being something of an acquired taste). The fresh-fish selection is good, the *batrkh* (roe) is popular, and there are good salads and some Western dishes.

ourpick Romero Restaurant (Map p90; ☎ 4644227; www.romero-jordan.com; Mohammed Hussein Haikal St, Jebel Amman; pasta JD4, mains JD6-10) Without doubt the best Italian restaurant in town: upmarket, formal and a stone's throw from the InterContinental Hotel. The salads are imaginative (chicken, mushroom, orange and pine nuts in a honey balsamic dressing), as are the steaks, seafood (red snapper and mussels) and a wide range of pasta and risotto. Desserts are predictably wonderful – crêpes with crème de banana, Grand Marnier and Cointreau, or home-made hazelnut and vanilla ice cream. Reservations are recommended.

Self-Catering

Although there are small grocery stores throughout the capital, the larger supermarkets are located in the more affluent and remote suburbs.

There is a **Safeway outlet** (Map p99; ☎ 5685311; Nasser bin Jameel St, Shmeisani; ☻ 24hr) around 500m southwest of the Sports City junction.

C-Town Shopping Centre (Map p87; ☎ 5815558; Zahran St, Sweifieh; ☻ 7am-midnight) has a branch close to 7th Circle, and in Shmeisani (Map p99; Abdul Hameed Sharaf St; ☻ 7am-midnight).

More central is **Haboob Grand Stores** (Map p90; ☎ 4622221; Al-Kulliyah al-Islamiyah St, Jebel Amman; ☻ 7am-midnight), between 1st and 2nd circles; it sometimes closes on Friday.

DRINKING

There is plenty of nightlife in Amman, though little that's salubrious in the downtown area. On the other hand, the areas of Jebel Amman, Shmeisani and the western suburbs have numerous trendy cafés and bars, as well as few nightclubs and live houses that stay open late.

Bars

Several bars in downtown, patronised almost exclusively by men, are tucked away in the alleys near Al-Husseiny Mosque. If you're willing to move beyond downtown, there are a range of enjoyable options where women will feel much more comfortable.

MOSTLY MEN

Orient Bar & Restaurant (Map p94; ☎ 4636069; off Al-Amir Mohammed St, downtown; beer from JD2; ☻ 11am-late) Also known as Al-Sharq, this spit-and-sawdust bar serves a range of beers, spirits and the local arak (if you dare) – if you've had a bit to drink, mind your head on the stairs on the way down. Cheap meals are also available with the slowest service in central Amman thrown in at no extra cost.

Other local dives include the **Salamon Bar** (Map p94; ☎ 5902940; off Al-Amir Mohammed St, downtown; ☻ noon-midnight) and **Jordan Bar** (Map p94; ☎ 5796352; off Al-Amir Mohammed St, downtown; ☻ 10am-midnight). All of these places are fairly tiny and full of smoke, but they do exude a certain amount of charm.

WOMEN WELCOME

Rovers Return (Map p87; ☎ 5814844; Ali Nasouh al-Taher St, Sweifieh; drinks JD2-4, meals JD3-6; ☻ 1pm-late) A godsend for homesick *Coronation St* junkies, this is a popular and cosy English pub with wood panelling and a lively atmosphere. The comfort food includes authentic fish and chips, and roast beef with gravy.

The entrance is round the back of the building and can be hard to find – look for the red 'Comfort Suites' sign.

Big Fellow Irish Pub (Map p90; ☎ 5934766; Abdoun Circle, Jebel Amman; drinks JD2-4, meals JD3-6; ☺ noon-2am) It looks like an Irish pub, it even smells like an Irish pub, but with Arabic music sliding out of the stereo, it doesn't really sound like an Irish pub. If in doubt, tucking into a Guinness pie and a bread-and-butter pudding should put you in the right frame of mind.

Grappa (Map p90; ☎ 4651458; Abdul Qader Koshak St, Jebel Amman; beer JD2-4, mains JD3-8; ☺ 6pm-1.30am) Stylish wooden benches and B&W photos on the wall give this rustic bar a hip feel but it's the huge windows with views and the summer terrace seating that really draw the crowds. There are decent pizzas, salads and *manaqeesh* (Arabic bread with herbs) but the drinking takes priority.

our pick **Living Room** (Map p90; ☎ 4655988; Mohammed Hussein Haikal St, Jebel Amman; drinks JD3-5, mains JD6-10; ☺ 1pm-1am) Part lounge, part sushi bar and part study (think high-backed chairs, a fireplace and the daily newspaper), the Living Room is so understated that it's easily missed. It offers quality bar meals, from North American steaks to salmon with cream cheese, and the fine music seals it as a great place to hang out over a delicious iced tea with lemon grass and mint. Non-teetotallers can enjoy the full complement of expertly crafted cocktails on offer, which are served up strong with a healthy dose of style and refinement.

Blue Fig Café (see p109) is another great place to spend an evening, with a chic crowd, pleasant atmosphere and live music several times a week.

Cafés

Some of the cafés in downtown are great places to watch the world go by, write in your journal, smoke a scented nargileh, meet locals and play cards or backgammon. The first group of cafés listed here are generally men only with scarcely a local woman to be seen, although foreign women with some gumption and very modest attire, especially if accompanied by a male, will be welcome.

MOSTLY MEN

Auberge Café (Map p94; Al-Amir Mohammed St, downtown; ☺ 10am-midnight) One floor below the Cliff Hotel is this authentic Jordanian spot, popular with local men. You'll have to make your way through the tobacco haze to reach the balcony, which overlooks the main street, and is a particularly good place to smoke a nargileh (JD2). There are no pretensions to luxury, but it wears a certain downmarket authenticity as a result.

Peace Café (Map p94; ☎ 079 5297912; Al-Amir Mohammed St, downtown; ☺ 9am-midnight) This place is reached via a filthy staircase and is fairly basic, but if you can get one of the two balcony tables overlooking the street, you'll have one of the prime vantage points in downtown. Just like the Auberge Café, this is great place to take puffs from the nargileh (JD2) and just watch the world go by.

WOMEN WELCOME

Around Hashemite Sq and along Hashemi St, the dozen or more cafés are decent places for people-watching, especially in summer. The place in Amman to be seen at night is anywhere around Abdoun Circle where there are plenty of very cool cafés. Take your pick – fashions change frequently in this part of Amman.

Al-Rashid Court Café (Map p94; ☎ 4652994; Al-Malek Faisal St, downtown; tea or coffee 400 fils; ☺ 10am-midnight Sat-Thu, 1-11pm Fri) Also known as the Eco-Tourism Café, the 1st floor balcony here is the place to pass an afternoon and survey the chaos of the downtown area below, though competition for seats is fierce. This is one of the best places for the uninitiated to try a nargileh (JD2). Although you won't see any local women here, it's well accustomed to foreign tourists. To find it look for the flags of the world on the main facade; the entrance is down the side alley.

Al-Sendabad Coffee Shop (Map p94; downtown; ☎ 4632035; ☺ 10am-midnight) About 150m west of the Roman Theatre, this place has great views over the city (though not of the theatre itself), and is kept clean and comfortable by the friendly staff. It's a great place to smoke the nargileh (JD2), especially on the roof in summer, where you can soak up the sunshine while losing your head to syrupy sweet puffs of smoke.

Shaher's Penthouse Cafeteria (Map p94; Sahat al-Malek Faysal al-Awal St, downtown; coffee 500 fils; ☺ 9.30am-11pm) This cutesy café has a traditionally decorated indoor dining area as well as an outdoor terrace overlooking the street far below. Hussein, the resident musician, will happily play the oud (lute) or violin to provide a cultured counterpoint to the street noise below.

Darat al-Funun Café (Map p94; Nimer bin Adwan St, downtown; tea & coffee 500 fils, snacks JD1; ☻ 9.30am-11pm) Definitely the most peaceful place to escape from downtown, this scenic café is surrounded by the ruins of a Byzantine church that evokes the ghosts of the past. Drinks are cheap, which means you have little excuse not to take a break from your sightseeing to enjoy a hot drink.

Tche Tche Café (Map p90; ☎ 5932020; Abdoun Circle, Jebel Amman; snacks JD1-3; ☻ 10am-11pm) You'll have to arrive early to get a seat in this bright and buzzy café – far from a traditional teahouse, it's full of Jordanian women smoking the nargileh, sipping on fruit smoothies and nodding their heads to Arabic pop. The ice cream and pecan waffles are a great (if unconventional) accompaniment to apple tobacco.

ENTERTAINMENT
Cinemas

There are several modern cinema complexes that offer recent releases. Ticket prices vary, but are much less than their Western counterparts. Programs for cinemas are advertised in the English-language newspapers (see p93).

Century Cinemas (Map p90; ☎ 4613200; 3rd Circle, Jebel Amman) In the Zara Centre behind the Grand Hyatt, with several fast-food outlets.

Cine Le Royal (Map p90; ☎ 4603022; 3rd Circle, Jebel Amman) Part of the Le Royal Hotel.

Galleria (Map p90; ☎ 5934793; Abdoun Circle, Jebel Amman)

Grand Theaters (off Map p87; ☎ 5518411; Mecca Mall) Far from the downtown, though it's a nice break from the city.

A few other cinemas show kung fu flicks and other B-grade movies but these are often dubbed into Arabic and, apart from the violence, are heavily censored. In downtown, the better ones are **Al-Hussein Cinema** (Map p94; Cinema al-Hussein St) and the **Raghadan** (Map p94; Basman St).

Also in downtown, **Books@café** (p108) has film nights on Monday. The various cultural centres (p91) also show foreign films regularly.

Exhibitions & Music

Various foreign cultural centres organise lectures, exhibitions and musical recitals. The large, modern **Royal Cultural Centre** (Map p99; ☎ 5661026; Al-Malekah Alia St, Shmeisani) occasionally hosts concerts and plays, usually in Arabic, as does the **King Hussein Cultural Centre** (Map p90; ☎ 4739953; Omar Matar St, Al-Muhajareen). Events are sometimes advertised in the local English-language newspapers.

Darat al-Funun (p101) often features recitals of classical and traditional music; check with the gallery for a schedule of upcoming events. The Jordan National Gallery of Fine Arts (p101) sometimes has visiting exhibitions of contemporary art.

Nightclubs

The city's swankiest clubs and lounges tend to be found inside upmarket hotels, where the international atmosphere is more forgiving of Jordanians who want to let their hair down (both figuratively and literally). While Amman does remain a fairly conservative city in regards to homosexuality, attitudes relax a bit behind closed doors and under cover of night.

Note that cover charges vary depending on the night and the performing act, though you can generally expect to pay around JD5 to JD10. Amman becomes a fashionable city once the sun sets, so you'll get better treatment at the door if you dress to impress.

Although this list is by no means comprehensive, these are a few of the more established night spots.

JJ's (Map p90; Grand Hyatt Amman, Al-Hussein bin Ali St, Jebel Amman; ☻ 8.30pm-late Mon-Sat) The Grand Hyatt's disco is where you'll pay for the privilege of rubbing shoulders with Amman's rich and glamorous. The music varies greatly depending on the whims of the DJ, though it's always fresh, innovative and almost as beautiful as the clientele.

Harir Lounge (Map p90; ☎ 5925205; Abdoun Circle, Jebel Amman; ☻ 1pm-1am, to 3am Sat & Sun) You'll find less style and more glitz at this ostentatious upper-floor lounge and restaurant, which is a popular spot for Amman's upper crust. This is one spot where you're going to want to wear your best threads, especially if you want to mingle with the scenesters.

our pick Nai (Map p99; ☎ 5689671; AlQasr Plaza Hotel, 3 Arroub St, Shmeisani; ☻ 6pm-2am) A Howard Johnson hotel is not the first place you'd look for a superhip Ottoman-style lounge-club-mezze bar but Nai is definitely one of the hottest places in town. Renowned DJs get people off the sofas with the best in Middle Eastern and international beats. The daily drink specials (6pm to 9pm) will get you properly liquored up, while food specials including all-you-can-eat sushi spreads will make sure you're not too hungover the next day.

Kanabayé (Map p90; ☎ 4642830; 3rd Circle, Jebel Amman) A quieter, cool place for a drink, the couches (*kanabayé* in Arabic) and seductive lighting lend this lounge bar a sleek and sexy feel. In a bid to attract a savvy and international following, Kanabayé mixes it up nightly with everything from Arabic pop to salsa ballads.

Sport

Football (soccer) is followed religiously by most locals. The capital's two main teams are Wahadat (generally supported by Palestinians) and Faisaly (supported by other Jordanians). The games are mostly played on Friday at the **Amman International Stadium** (Map p99; tickets JD2), located near Sports City (see p102) in Shmeisani.

SHOPPING

Amman is the best place in Jordan to shop for souvenirs. There are several high-quality handicraft boutiques, concentrated on Rainbow St and near the InterContinental Hotel, which are run to benefit women, threatened communities and the environment. The main hotels also have branches of the top-end Souq Zara boutiques.

Mall mania is sweeping through areas of Amman. The biggest is **Mecca Mall** (off Map p87; ☎ 5527945; Makkah al-Mukarramah Rd) in the northwestern suburbs, with a cinema, bowling alley, video arcade and dozens of restaurants. **Abdoun Mall** (Map p87; ☎ 5920246; Al Umawiyeen St, Zahran) is a smaller version of the same thing. More are bound to follow.

Souvenirs

Al-Alaydi Jordan Craft Centre (Map p90; ☎/fax 4644555; off Al-Kulliyah al-Islamiyah St, Jebel Amman; ☾ 9am-6pm Sat-Thu) With an overwhelming selection spread over several floors, it's difficult to leave here without spending money. Items include jewellery, Hebron glassware, Palestinian embroidery, kilims,

wood carvings, old kitchen implements and Bedouin tent accessories. Prices are marked in both dinars and US dollars.

Al-Burgan (Map p90; ☎ 4652585; www.alburgan .com; 12 Tala't Harb St, Jebel Amman; ☾ 9.30am-6.30pm Sat-Thu) Has a smaller selection of items but the staff is knowledgeable and prices are reasonable. It's behind Jordan InterContinental Hotel.

Artisana (Map p90; ☎/fax 4647858; Mansour Kraishan St, Jebel Amman; ☾ 9.30am-6pm Sat-Thu) This excellent small showroom has a wide range that includes scarves, bottles of holy water from the Jordan River and reproductions of the famous 6000-year-old statues from Ain Ghazal.

Bawabet al-Sharq (Map p94; ☎ 4637424; Abu Bakr as-Siddiq St, downtown; ☾ 9am-7pm) The 'Gate of the Orient' has locally made (some on site) home décor items tending towards the kitsch. Sales benefit several Jordanian women's groups.

Beit al-Bawadi (Map p87; ☎ 5930070; Fawzi al-Qawoaji St, Jebel Amman; ☾ 9am-6pm Sat-Thu) The place for quality ceramics, created to support local artisans, who you can see working in the basement. Designs are both traditional and modern (lampshades and dinner sets), some decorated with Arabic calligraphy, and pieces cost around JD30 to JD60. The top floor has discounted items. Credit cards are accepted.

Jordan River Foundation (Map p94; ☎ 4613081; Bani Hamida House, Fawzi al-Malouf St, downtown; ☾ 8.30am-7pm Sat-Thu, 10am-6pm Fri) There's an emphasis on home design here, with cushions, camel bags, candles, embroidery, baskets (from Wadi Rayan in the Jordan Valley) and Dead Sea products, all at high prices to match the high quality.

Oriental Souvenirs Store (Map p90; ☎ 4642820; 3rd Circle, Jebel Amman; ☾ 8am-7pm Sat-Thu) This friendly, family-run store is more rustic than the others listed here, but it's something of an Aladdin's Cave.

Silsal Ceramics (Map p87; ☎ 5931128; Innabeh St, North Abdoun; ☾ 9am-6pm Sat-Thu) Has a small showroom of superb modern pottery with price tags that are surprisingly reasonable. If you're coming along Zahran St from 5th Circle, it's the third small street on the right.

Wild Jordan (Map p94; ☎ 4633587; Othman bin Affan St, downtown; ☾ 9am-7pm) The nature store at the Wild Jordan Centre sells eco-tourism products made in Jordan's nature reserves, including silver, organic herbs and jams from Dana, and candles made and decorated by Bedouin women as part of an income-generating project in Feinan. All profits go back to the craftspeople and to the nature-reserve projects.

GETTING THERE & AWAY

For information about international services to/from Amman, see p307.

Air

Amman is the main arrival and departure point for international flights, although some touch down in Aqaba as well.

The head office for **Royal Jordanian Airlines** (Map p99; ☎ 5607300; www.rja.com.jo; Al-Malekah Noor St, Shmeisani) is inconveniently located in the Housing Bank Centre (9th floor). There are more convenient offices in the **Jordan InterContinental** (Map p90; ☎ 4644267) and along **Al-Malek al-Hussein St** (Map p90; ☎ 5663525), up from the Abdali bus station.

The Royal Jordanian subsidiary, **Royal Wings** (www.royalwings.com.jo; ☎ 4875201), has an office at Marka Airport, but it's easier to book and confirm tickets at any Royal Jordanian office in town.

See p307 for contact details of airlines that fly to Amman.

Bus

For an explanation of the present and future transportation situation in Amman, see the boxed text, below.

BUS, MINIBUS & SERVICE TAXIS

At the time of research, the two main bus stations in Amman were Abdali bus station for transport to the north, and Wahadat bus station for the south. However, the Abdali bus station has been slated for closure for some years now, with services due to move to Tabarbour bus station in the northern outskirts, or possibly to the newly rebuilt Raghadan bus station in downtown. Ask at your hotel for the latest information.

Note that there is also limited service to the Dead Sea from the smaller Muhajireen bus station, as well as private coaches from the JETT and Trust offices.

Service taxis are generally faster, but they don't always follow fixed schedules. They depart from the same stations as the minibuses and departures are more frequent in the morning.

Abdali Bus Station

This **station** (Map p90; Al-Malek al-Hussein St, Jebel Amman) is a 20-minute walk (2km uphill) from downtown; service taxi 6 or 7 from Cinema al-Hussein St goes right by. Regular service taxis costing about 200 fils depart Abdali for Wahadat bus station throughout the day.

Minibuses take up the top end of the station, then (going downhill) there are the service taxis and private bus company offices.

From Abdali, fairly regular minibuses and service taxis leave for the following destinations, with all routes costing less

---

WARNING – THINGS CHANGE

The information presented here regarding bus schedules, departure points and prices is extremely vulnerable to change. At the time of writing, the entire transportation grid in Amman (and thus Jordan as a whole) was in the midst of a massive overhaul due to the renovation of Raghadan bus station and the gradual closing of Abdali bus station. To make matters even more complicated, Tabarbour bus station in the northern suburbs is handling the overflow during the transition, though it is difficult to speculate what its future role will be.

At the time of research, fuel prices in Jordan (and the rest of the world) were soaring due to factors such as the Iraq War, greater Middle Eastern instability and rampant inflation. As a result, it is almost certain that our published prices for bus routes will increase significantly during the shelf life of this book. Generally speaking however, all bus prices were researched during the same time frame, which means they are accurate in comparison to one another.

The message in all of this is that you should get local opinions, quotes and advice before parting with your cash – a good place to inquire is at your hotel. Tickets for private buses should always be booked at least one day in advance given the uncertainty of the transportation grid. Finally, the transport details given here should be regarded as pointers, and are not a substitute for your own careful, up-to-date research.

than JD1: Ajloun (two hours), Deir Alla (for Pella, one hour), Fuheis (45 minutes), Irbid (two hours), Jerash (1¼ hours), Madaba (45 minutes), Ramtha (two hours), Salt (45 minutes) and Zarqa (30 minutes).

From Abdali station, there are also transport links to various international destinations (see p309).

There are far fewer departures on Friday, when the lower half of the bus station is transformed into a giant flea market.

Muhajireen Bus Station

If you want to go to the Dead Sea, minibuses leave from this small station (Map p90) opposite the Muhajireen police station. You may find a local bus direct to Suweimah (JD1, one hour) or even Amman Beach – if not you'll have to go to Shuneh al-Janubiyyeh (South Shuna, JD1, 45 minutes) and change for Suweimah, from where you'll have to hire a taxi or hitch for the last stretch. Minibuses also leave frequently for Wadi as-Seer (less than JD1, 30 minutes).

Raghadan Bus Station

This newly renovated station (Map p94) in downtown Amman is a few minutes' walk east of the Roman Theatre. It had not fully reopened at time of research, but expect it to operate service taxis (for surrounding suburbs), local city buses and, most probably, minibuses to destination in the north of the country.

Tabarbour Bus Station

Located in the northern suburbs, this station (off Map p87) is temporarily handling the overflow of buses while the city gradually transitions its transport grid from Abdali to Raghadan. At the time of writing, it was impossible to speculate on the future role of this station. However, it is possible that during the shelf life of this book, Tabarbour will become an important part of the city's bus network. A private taxi here will cost around JD1 to JD2 from downtown.

Wahadat Bus Station

Almost all buses and service taxis headed south leave from this station (off Map p87), way out in the southern suburbs by Middle East Circle (Duwaar Sharq al-Awsat). To reach the station, take a service taxi or bus 23 from Abdali station, or service taxi

27 from Italian St (Map p94). A private taxi here will cost around JD1 to JD2 from downtown.

For Petra (actually Wadi Musa) minibuses and service taxis (JD4, four hours) depart when full from the far corner of the lot between around 7am and 4pm. Buses to Aqaba (JD5, five hours) leave every hour or so until midnight. There are regular buses to Karak (JD1, two hours), Shobak (JD2, 2½ hours) and Ma'an (JD3, three hours). Most services dry up around 4pm.

For Dana there is one bus a day at around 11am for Qadsiyya (JD3, three hours); otherwise take a bus to Tafila (JD2, 2½ hours) and change.

There are semiregular service taxis to Karak (JD2, two hours), Ma'an (JD3, three hours) and also infrequently to Aqaba (JD5, five hours).

PRIVATE COACHES

The domestic **JETT office** (Map p99; ☎ 5664146; Al-Malek al-Hussein St, Shmeisani) is about 500m northwest of the Abdali bus station. There are five buses daily to Aqaba (JD7, five hours) between 7am and 5pm, and one bus to King Hussein Bridge (JD8, one hour, 6.30am), for crossings into Israel and the Palestinian Territories.

A daily JETT bus connects Amman with Petra, largely designed for those wanting to visit on a day trip. The service leaves at 6.30am from Abdali Bus Station (single/return JD6/11) and drops passengers off at Petra Visitor Centre in Wadi Musa at 9.30am. The return bus leaves at 4.30pm.

Trust International Transport (Map p87; ☎ 581 3427) has seven daily buses to Aqaba (JD7, four hours) between 7.30am and 7pm. All buses leave from the office inconveniently located at 7th Circle, near the Safeway shopping centre – it's best to charter a taxi to/from downtown for a couple of dinars. Trust also has a **booking office** (Map p90; ☎ 4644627) at the Abdali bus station.

Car

Before getting behind the wheel, be sure to read our car-rental section, p319.

Charges, conditions and insurance costs (and waiver fees in case of accident) can vary considerably. Generally speaking, compact cars can be rented for as low as JD20 per day, though larger cars and 4WDs necessitate larger prices depending on the make and model.

Listed here are some of the more reliable car-rental agencies – all of them accept major credit cards, and offer cars less than three years old. Most companies have an office at King Abdullah Gardens (Map p99), where there is a collection of around 50 car-rental companies, allowing you to shop around and compare prices.

Avis (Map p99; ☎ 5699420, 24hr line 777-397405; www .avis.com.jo; King Abdullah Gardens, Shmeisani) Branches at the airport, Hotel Le Royal and Hotel InterContinental.

Budget (Map p99; ☎ 5698131; budget@go.com.jo; 125 Abdul Hameed Sharaf St, Shmeisani)

Eagle Rent-a-Car (Map p99; ☎ 5693399, 24hr line 079 5546021; eaglerentacar@wanadoo.jo; Abdul Hameed Sharaf St, Shmeisani)

Europcar (Map p99; ☎ 5655581; www.europcar.jo; Isam Al-Ajlouni St, Shmeisani) Branches at Radisson SAS and King Abdullah Gardens.

Firas Car Rental (Map p90; ☎ 4612927, 5846454; alamo@nets.com.jo; 1st Circle, Jebel Amman) The agent for Alamo Car Rental.

Hertz (Map p99; ☎ 5624191, 24hr line at airport 4711771; www.hertz.com; King Abdullah Gardens, Shmeisani). Offices at the airport, Grand Hyatt and Sheraton.

National Car Rental (Map p99; ☎ /fax 5601350, 24hr line 5591731; www.1stjordan.net/national) Offices at Amman Marriott, Le Meridien and Sheraton hotels.

Reliable Rent-a-Car (Map p87; ☎ 5929676, 5521358; www.reliable.com.jo; 19 Fawzi al-Qawoaji St, Abdoun) Cars JD20 to JD25, CDW JD5 extra.

Train

A train service leaves Amman for Damascus along the **Hejaz Railway** (www.jhr.gov.jo; one-way JD3; ☺ 8am Mon & Thu), but few travellers go this way as the dawdling service takes all day, with a change of trains at the border. The quaint old station is on King Abdullah I St, about 2.5km east of Raghadan bus station in Amman. The **ticket office** (☎ 06-4895413) is only open from 7am on the morning of departure, although you may find someone around at other times. To reach the station, take a service taxi from Raghadan bus station, or a private taxi (around JD1).

GETTING AROUND
To/From the Airports

Queen Alia International Airport is 35km south of the city. The **Airport Express bus** (Map p90; ☎ 0880 022006; 4451531) runs between the airport and the upper end of Abdali station,

passing through the 4th, 5th, 6th and 7th Circles en route. Buses (JD2, 45 minutes) run every 30 minutes or so between 7am and midnight. From the airport, buses depart from outside the arrivals hall of Terminal 2. Buy your ticket from the booth at the door. The last buses to the airport leave at 10pm and midnight; the first bus leaves at 6am.

With the impending scaling down of the Abdali bus station, the service could eventually shift to either the new station at Tabarbour or the Raghadan bus station.

Anyone travelling on Royal Jordanian can check in their bags and catch a shuttle bus (JD2, half-hourly between 8am and 9pm) to Queen Alia International Airport from the **Royal Jordanian city terminal** (Map p87; ☎ 5856855; fax 5857224), but it's inconveniently located on 7th Circle. Make sure to check in at least three hours before departure.

There are branches of **Avis** (☎ 4459040) and **Hertz** (☎ 4711771) at the airport and most other car-rental companies will meet you at the airport or otherwise let you pick up a car there.

The other option is a private taxi (JD15 to JD20), which is the quickest and easiest way to get to the airport, especially if you don't want to have to carry your luggage around the city.

To get to Marka Airport, take a service taxi for 200 fils from Raghadan station.

Public Transport
BUS

The local bus system is confusing, with nothing labelled in English. Buses 26, 27, 28, 41 and 43 can be useful for getting to downtown. If bus travel is your thing, ask around the bus section of Raghadan station to see what's headed your way, but you'll need patience and decent Arabic. Tickets cost around 50 fils.

For 7th circle, take bus 41 or anything headed to Wadi as-Seer.

Amman City Tour

The **Amman City Tour** (ticket JD10; ☺ 10am-8pm, to 6pm winter) is a circular bus route with 45 stops that encompasses a variety of locations from the Roman Theatre and the downtown to the shopping malls in the outer suburbs. The big red buses can be boarded using smart cards that are sold in hotels, and are valid for 24 hours after activation.

TAXI
Private Taxi

Most drivers of private taxis use the meter as a matter of course, but gently remind them when they don't. You need to be especially careful when you're laden with bags and searching for your hotel or heading out in the evening to an expensive restaurant.

The flagfall is 150 fils and fares are cheap; from downtown to Abdali cost less than JD1, while fares to Shmeisani shouldn't cost much more than JD2.

Service Taxi

Most fares cost 200 fils per seat, and you usually pay the full amount regardless of where you get off. After 8pm, the price for all service taxis goes up by 25%.

There can be long queues at rush hour (8am to 9am and 5pm to 6pm). The cars queue up and usually start at the bottom of a hill – you get into the last car and the whole line rolls back a car space and so on. Always double check that your taxi is going to your destination before climbing in.

SERVICE TAXI ROUTES

All departure points are listed on Map p94.

Service taxi 1 From Basman St for 4th Circle.

Service taxi 2 From Basman St for 1st and 2nd Circles.

Service taxi 3 From Basman St for 3rd and 4th Circles.

Service taxi 4 From the side street near the central post office for Jebel Weibdeh.

Service taxi 6 From Cinema al-Hussein St for the Ministry of the Interior Circle, past Abdali station and JETT international and domestic offices.

Service taxi 7 From Cinema al-Hussein St, up Al-Malek al-Hussein St, past Abdali station and King Abdullah Mosque, and along Suleiman al-Nabulsi St for Shmeisani.

Service taxis 25 & 26 From Italian St, downtown, to the top of Jebel al-Ashrafiyeh' and near Abu Darwish Mosque.

Service taxi 27 From Italian St to Middle East Circle for Wahadat station.

Service taxi 35 From opposite the Amman Palace Hotel, passing close to the Muhajireen Police Station.

Service taxi 38 From downtown to Makkah al-Mukarramah Rd.

AROUND AMMAN

Uncovering remnants of the ancients is no easy task in Amman, especially since the capital is largely a 20th-century creation. However, you don't have to look far beyond the city limits for historical reminders that you're in the Middle East. Indeed, the outskirts of the capital are home to Roman ruins, biblical landmarks, Byzantine churches and Ottoman structures, all of which are set against beautiful landscapes that are a world apart from the streets of Amman. All of the destinations listed in this section can be reached on a quick and easy day trip from Amman, and it is possible to visit a few different sights if you get an early enough start.

WADI AS-SEER & IRAQ AL-AMIR
وادي السير & عراق الأمير

West of the capital lies the fertile Wadi as-Seer, standing in marked contrast to the treeless plateau surrounding Amman. The stream-fed valley is lined with cypress trees, and dotted with fragrant orchards and olive groves. In the springtime, particularly April and May, as-Seer plays host to spectacular wildflower blooms that include the Jordanian national flower, the black iris.

The village itself, which is largely Circassian in origin, is now virtually part of sprawling western Amman. However, there still remains a fair measure of authenticity, especially in the Ottoman stone buildings and mosque that lie at the centre of the village. Wadi as-Seer is primarily a jumping-off point for the area's real highlights, which lie a bit further down the road.

About 4km past Wadi as-Seer, on the road to the village of Iraq al-Amir, is part of an ancient **Roman aqueduct** (Map p119). Shortly past the aqueduct, look up to the hillside on the left to a facade cut into the rock, known as **Ad-Deir** (monastery; Map p119), though it most likely served as a medieval dovecote (a place to house pigeons).

If you want to pause here and soak up the surroundings, you can grab a cup of hot *chai* and an apple nargileh (JD2) at the nearby **Al-Yanabeea** (meals JD1-4, ☺ dawn-dusk). This small but humble café and restaurant also serves up basic meals such as roasted chicken and hummus spreads.

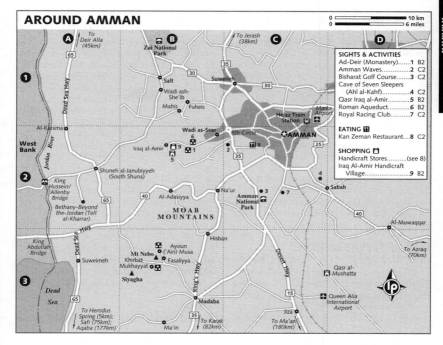

AROUND AMMAN

0 — 10 km
0 — 6 miles

SIGHTS & ACTIVITIES
Ad-Deir (Monastery)..........1 B2
Amman Waves................2 C2
Bisharat Golf Course.......3 C2
Cave of Seven Sleepers
(Ahl al-Kahf)..............4 C2
Qasr Iraq al-Amir..........5 B2
Roman Aqueduct............6 B2
Royal Racing Club.........7 C2

EATING
Kan Zeman Restaurant......8 C2

SHOPPING
Handicraft Stores..........(see 8)
Iraq Al-Amir Handicraft
Village..................9 B2

A further 6km down on the right side of the road are the **Iraq al-Amir** (Caves of the Prince). The caves are arranged in two tiers – the upper tier forms a long gallery (partially damaged during a mild earthquake in 1999) along the cliff face. The 11 caves were once used as cavalry stables, though locals have taken to using them to house their goats and store chaff. Steps lead up to the caves from the paved road – keep an eye out for the ancient Hebrew inscription near the entrance.

Opposite the caves is the village of Iraq al-Amir, home to the **Iraq al-Amir Handicraft Village** (Map p119; 8am-4pm, closed Fri), selling handmade pottery, fabrics, foodstuffs, carpets and paper products. The project was founded by the Noor al-Hussein Foundation, and employs dozens of women from the surrounding area.

About 700m further down the road, just visible from the caves, is the small but impressive **Qasr al-Abad** (Palace of the Slave; admission free; daylight hr), which is one of the very few examples of pre-Roman construction in Jordan.

Mystery surrounds the palace, and even its precise age isn't known, though most scholars believe that Hyrcanus of the powerful Jewish Tobiad family built it sometime between 187 and 175 BC as a villa or fortified palace. Although never completed, much of the palace has been reconstructed, and remains an impressive site.

The palace was built from some of the biggest blocks of any ancient structure in the Middle East – the largest is 7m by 3m. The blocks were, however, only 20cm or so thick, making the whole edifice quite flimsy, and susceptible to the earthquake that flattened it in AD 362. Today, the setting and the animal carvings on the exterior walls are the highlights. Look for the carved panther fountain on the ground floor, the eroded eagles on the corners and the lioness with cubs on the upper storey of the back side.

The gatekeeper will open the interior, as well as a small museum (which includes drawings of what the complex once looked like) for a tip of JD1. If he's not around, ask for the *miftah* (key) at the small shop near the gate.

Getting There & Away

Minibuses leave regularly from the **Muhajireen bus station** (Map p90; Al-Ameerah Basma bin Talal St, Amman) for Wadi as-Seer village (less than JD1, 30 minutes) and less frequently from the Raghadan bus station (Map p94) in downtown. From Wadi as-Seer, take another minibus – or walk about 10km, mostly downhill – to the caves. Look for the signpost to the Iraq al-Amir Handicraft Village, which is virtually opposite the stairs to the caves. Alternatively take bus 26 from Shabsough St in downtown to its terminus and then change to a bus for Wadi as-Seer or take a taxi. From the caves, it's an easy stroll down to the *qasr* (but a little steep back up).

If you're driving, head west from 8th Circle and follow the main road, which twists through Wadi as-Seer village.

CAVE OF SEVEN SLEEPERS (AHL AL-KAHF)   أهل الكهف

The legend of the 'seven sleepers' has several parallels throughout literature. It involves seven Christian boys who were persecuted by the Roman Emperor Trajan, then escaped to a cave and slept there for 309 years. This is one of several locations (the most famous being Ephesus in Turkey) that claim to be that cave. Inside the **main cave** (Map p119; admission free; 8am-6pm) – also known as *Ahl al-Kahf* (Cave of the People) – are eight smaller tombs that are sealed, though one has a hole in it through which you can see a creepy collection of human bones. Above and below the cave are the remains of two mosques. About 500m west of the cave is a large **Byzantine cemetery**, whose tombs are sadly full of rubbish.

The cave is to the right of a large new mosque complex in the village of Rajib, off the road from Amman to Sabah. Buses from Amman to Sabah pass 500m from the mosque; catch them at Wahadat bus station (less than JD1, 15 minutes). Alternatively, take a minibus from Quraysh St in downtown, ask for 'al-Kahf' and the driver will show you where to get off to change for a Sabah bus. The easiest way there is by chartered taxi (around JD5 each way).

SALT   السلط
☎ 05 / pop 70,000

Set in a steep-sided, narrow valley about 30km northwest of downtown Amman is the friendly and unpretentious town of Salt. During Ottoman rule, Salt was the region's administrative centre, but was passed over as the new capital of Trans-Jordan in favour of Amman. Consequently, Salt never experienced the intense wave of modernisation that swept across the capital, and as a result has retained much of its historic charm. Today, much of Salt's downtown remains a living museum of Ottoman-period architecture.

Salt is visited by few foreign tourists, and remains one of the undiscovered highlights of the Amman area. However, the face of Salt is about to change, thanks to a multmillion-dollar aid package that was awarded to the city in 2004 by Japan. The aid is being used to preserve many of the city's old buildings, and to create better tourist facilities. While tourist infrastructure is still somewhat lacking, the gears of development are starting to turn, and it is admirable that the residents of Salt have embraced their city's architectural heritage.

History

While you'd be forgiven for thinking that the town was named after the table condiment, Salt was named from either the Greek word *saltus* meaning 'forests' (although these are long gone), or from *sultana* for the grapes that were once abundant in the region.

Construction began on Salt's characteristic limestone buildings in the late-19th century when merchants from Nablus arrived on the scene. Over several decades, Salt began to thrive as trade networks sprang up between the city and neighbouring Palestine.

Following the establishment of Trans-Jordan, the new emir chose Amman as his capital due to its proximity to the railway. Almost overnight, Salt went into decline, though it managed to hold onto life for a few more decades. However, war with Israel separated Salt from the port of Haifa in 1948, and later from its trading partner of Nablus in 1967, ending Salt's significance as anything more than a village on the outskirts of Amman.

The friendly **tourist office** (☎ 3555652; Dayr St; 8am-3pm Sun-Thu) is upstairs in the impressive old residence of Beit Mismar, but is still a work in progress.

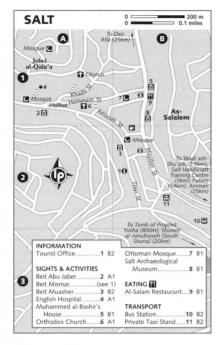

SALT

To Deir Alla (25km)

Mosque

Jebel al-Qala'a

Church

Khadir St

Mosque

Market Hammam St

Amaneh St

As-Salaem

Mosque

Maydan St

Dayr St

To Wadi ash-Shu'aib (2.5km);
Salt Handicraft
Training Centre
(3km); Fuheis
(14km); Amman
(25km)

To Tomb of Prophet
Yusha (800m); Shuneh
al-Janublyyeh (South
Shuna) (20km)

INFORMATION		
Tourist Office	1	B2
SIGHTS & ACTIVITIES		
Beit Abu Jaber	2	A1
Beit Mismar	(see 1)	
Beit Muasher	3	B2
English Hospital	4	A1
Muhammed al-Bashir's		
House	5	B1
Orthodox Church	6	A1

Ottoman Mosque	7	B1
Salt Archaeological		
Museum	8	B1
EATING		
Al-Salam Restaurant	9	B1
TRANSPORT		
Bus Station	10	B2
Private Taxi Stand	11	B2

Sights & Activities

There are some fine examples of **Ottoman architecture** (see the walking tour, right) in town dating from the late-19th and early-20th century. Few of these gracious limestone buildings are open to the public, but some of the facades are quite elegant. The town has recently renovated several facades and rebuilt a series of stairways leading up to fabulous views from atop Jebel al-Qala'a.

Salt Archaeological Museum (3555651; admission free; 8am-7pm May-Oct, to 4pm Nov-Apr) is well laid out in an Ottoman-era building. Downstairs focuses on glass and pottery (some dating back 5000 years), spanning the Roman, Byzantine and Islamic eras, mostly from around Salt but also from Deir Alla and Tell Nimrin (from where Joshua is thought to have led the Israelites across the River Jordan into the Promised Land). Upstairs are some examples of local traditional dress, displays on traditional farming activities and mosaics fragments from churches around Salt. Fifteen minutes should do it.

Visitors can watch weaving, pottery, mosaics and other handicrafts being made at the **Salt Handicraft Training Centre** (3550279; Nageb al-Daboor district; 8am-3pm Sun-Thu), 3km out of town. The centre specialises in both training and production and has a showroom for displaying the finished products. A taxi here costs JD1 to JD2 from the centre; ask for the Balkhar Islamic School (*Bejanib Maddaris al-Balkhar al-Islamiy*). The turn-off is at a set of traffic lights by a bridge, 2km from Salt along the road to Amman.

If you have a car it's worth exploring **Wadi ash-Shu'aib**, a refreshing valley named after the prophet Jethro (*Shu'aib* in Arabic), which offers some hiking opportunities and interesting caves. It's 2.5km southeast of Salt.

The **tomb** of Prophet Yusha (Joshua) is a 10-minute walk south of town, but is of little specific interest.

Walking Tour of Salt

The following route takes you on a circular tour of Salt's backstreets, taking in its bazaars and old Ottoman architecture. Budget around an hour, including a short visit to the museum.

From Salt bus station walk up Dayr St, past the impressive doorway of **Beit Mismar** and the lovely balcony columns of **Beit Muasher**, both grand old Ottoman residences. Continue along Dayr St as it passes the curved walls of Salt's Orthodox church to the recently restored **Beit Abu Jaber**, which houses a small local history museum. Head across the plaza and take the stairs up to the right of the mosque, curving round to the entry of the former **English Hospital** (look for the letters 'EH' on the green gate). From here you could wind your way uphill for fine views over the town.

Alternatively, return to the plaza and head down **Hammam St**, Salt's most atmospheric backstreet, past the ornate **Ottoman mosque** to the junction with Maydan St. Across the street is the colonnaded entry of **Muhammed al-Bashir's House** (built between 1890 and 1910), now a traditional coffeehouse (with a tree in front). Next door is Beit al-Sulibi (built between 1920 and 1930).

Break for lunch at the **Al-Salam Restaurant** (p122) and then visit the **archaeological museum** (left) before heading back to the bus station or taking a taxi to the **Salt Handicraft Training Centre** (above).

AMMAN

Sleeping & Eating

At the time of writing, there was nowhere to stay in Salt, though this is likely to change in the years to come.

The northern end of Maydan St is lined with traditional cafés, full of men drinking tea and smoking nargileh. Basic restaurants along the same street and by the bus station serve kebabs, though the best place in town for cheap Arabic food is the **Al-Salam Restaurant** (☎ 3552115; Maydan St; meals JD2-4; ⏱ 7am-10.30pm Sat-Thu), which serves up a good shish kebabs set.

Getting There & Away

The bus station is on the main road south of the town centre. There are minibuses to Salt (less than JD1, 45 minutes) from Amman's Abdali and Raghadan bus stations, via the University of Jordan, and occasional service taxis (450 fils) from Abdali. From Salt, minibuses head down the Jordan Valley to Shuneh al-Janubiyyeh (South Shuna; less than JD1, 45 minutes), and to Wadi as-Seer (less than JD1, 30 minutes) and Fuheis (less than JD1, 30 minutes), with which Salt can be combined as a day trip from Amman. Taxis can be chartered to Amman for around JD5 to JD10.

FUHEIS فحيص
☎ 06

Just 15km northwest of Amman, this pleasant village, located at a cool 1050m above sea level, is famous in Jordan for producing fruit and cement. For foreign visitors however, it is of more interest for its fine places to eat. First built in about 2000 BC, Fuheis is now an overwhelmingly Christian village, with several Orthodox and Catholic **churches**, three of which are just down from the minibus stop. However, the real reason you're here is to check out the town's two excellent restaurants, both easy to spot from the final minibus stop in the Al-Rawaq neighbourhood.

The food at the **Zuwwadeh Restaurant** (☎ 4721528; mains JD3-8; ⏱ 10am-midnight) is fabulous, especially the *fatteh* (fried bread) with hummus, meat or chicken and pine nuts, which is almost worth the trip from Amman on its own – the 'wedding *fatteh*' has tomato and cardamom added. You can choose between shady outdoor tables or a pleasant indoor dining area, and most nights there are live oud performances upstairs (after 7pm).

Similarly good and a little cheaper is the **Hakoura Restaurant** (☎ 4729152; mains JD2-6; ⏱ 10am-midnight), an artistic place with a commitment to traditional hospitality, soulful music and modern art – with some excellent food thrown in, of course.

Getting There & Away

Fuheis is easy to reach by minibus from Abdali bus station (Map p90) in Amman (less than JD1, 45 minutes). The town is also connected to Wadi as-Seer and Salt (less than JD1, 30 minutes), so you can visit all three places in a day. If you're eating at one of the restaurants until late, you may need to pre-arrange a chartered taxi back to Amman for around JD5 to JD10.

The minibus stop in the older Al-Rawaq neighbourhood (also known as *il-balad*) is at a roundabout, close to the two restaurants and marked by a statue of St George (known locally as Giorgis) slaying a dragon.

Jerash & the North
جرش & الشمال

Northern Jordan is the biblical land of Gilead, a mountainous region that is drained by the Yarmouk and Zerqa (Jabbok) Rivers, the two biggest tributaries of the River Jordan. Dotted by olive groves and pine forests, the hills of Gilead have been occupied since antiquity, and were once home to the Roman Decapolis. Largely established during the Hellenistic period, these 10 city-states flourished along the boundaries of the Greek and Semitic lands. However, the region didn't reach the height of its power until it fell under the influence of the Romans, who wanted their culture to prosper in the furthest reaches of the empire.

Today northern Jordan is the most densely populated area in the country, and is home to the major urban centre of Irbid as well as dozens of small towns and villages. However, scattered among the rolling hills are ancient tells and archaeological remains of the Decapolis, which include the ruined cities at Umm Qais (Gadara), Pella and Jerash. Often referred to as the 'Pompeii of Asia', Jerash is one of the most important and best–preserved Roman cities in the Near East, and is regarded as Jordan's most famous archaeological site after Petra.

Although there is a good public-transport network in the region, the north is best appreciated through the window of a rental car. The comfort and convenience of having your own wheels will enable you to explore some stunningly beautiful countryside, and to access some of Gilead's more far-flung ancient sites and monuments.

JERASH & THE NORTH

HIGHLIGHTS

- Wander the colonnaded streets of **Jerash** (p124), a wonderfully preserved Roman provincial city that is one of the finest in the Middle East

- Take in awesome views over the Sea of Galilee from the ruins of **Umm Qais** (p141), one of the historic cities of the Decapolis

- Hike along the shady trails of **Ajloun Nature Reserve** (p135) in search of the endangered roe deer

- Visit the fairy-tale castle of **Qala'at ar-Rabad** (p134), one of Jordan's most impressive Islamic structures

- Dig through layers of time at **Pella** (p146), an ancient site containing traces of all eras of Jordanian history

- Peruse the excellent exhibits at the **Museum of Archaeology & Anthropology** (p138), located on the vibrant campus of Yarmouk University in Irbid

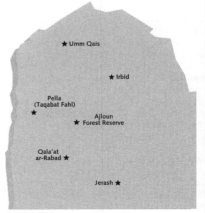

JERASH

The ruins at Jerash (known in Greco-Roman times as Gerasa) are one of Jordan's major attractions, and one of the Middle East's best examples of a Roman provincial city. Remarkably well preserved through the centuries by the dry desert air, Jerash is highlighted by stone monuments including a massive forum. Whether you're an aspiring archaeologist or simply an admirer of the ancients, the ruins at Jerash weave a powerful spell capable of evoking the ghosts of Rome. Although it's just a few hours north of Amman, Jerash is a world unto its own that beckons to be explored.

JERASH

جرش

☎ 02

At the height of its Roman heyday, Jerash (known as Gerasa) had a population of roughly 15,000 to 20,000 inhabitants. Although Jerash wasn't located on any major trade route, the city and its inhabitants thrived and prospered from the surrounding agricultural land. The famed hills of Gilead were (as they are today) extremely fertile, and the Mediterranean climate was conducive to farming. The resulting surplus of crops allowed Jerash to grow and diversify as a cosmopolitan city where Roman arts and culture could flourish at the furthest limit of the empire.

The walled city that survives today once served as the administrative, commercial, civic and religious centre of Jerash. In order to carry out these functions, it was equipped with public monuments including triumphal arches, temples and churches, colonnaded streets, amphitheatres, bathhouses, fountains and even a hippodrome. While there are certainly other surviving Roman cities that boast similar structures, Jerash is famous for its remarkable state of preservation, which has enabled both archaeologists and historians to piece together ancient life under the thumb of the Emperor.

The bulk of the Roman city's inhabitants once lived on the eastern side of Wadi Jerash outside the walled city. At the time, the two centres were linked by causeways and processional paths, which allowed commoners to access to the public monuments. Today the eastern retaining wall of

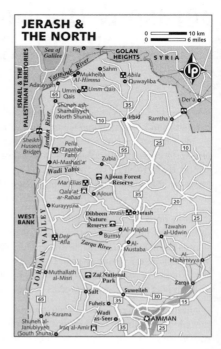

the ruins abuts the modern city of Jerash, which has also thrived and prospered from the surrounding agricultural land. As they've done through much of antiquity, the famed hills of Gilead support a lucrative olive industry, and if you squint your eyes just right (and use a bit of imagination!), there are parts of the region that are reminiscent of Tuscany.

History

Archaeological finds indicate that the site of Jerash was inhabited as early as Neolithic times, and may have been continuously inhabited throughout the Bronze and Iron Ages. However, the first major settlement is attributed to the Greeks, who founded Jerash during the time of Alexander the Great (333 BC). But in the truest sense Jerash is largely the creation of its Roman conquerors.

In the wake of the Roman general Pompey's conquest of the region in 64 BC, Gerasa became part of the Roman province of Syria, and then a city of the Decapolis. Over the next two centuries, trade with the

THE DECAPOLIS

The Roman commercial cities within modern Jordan, Syria and Israel and the Palestinian Territories became known collectively as the Decapolis in the 1st century AD. Despite the etymology of the word, it seems that the Decapolis consisted of more than 10 cities, and possibly as many as 18 (Decaoctodecapolis?!). No one knows for certain the reason behind such a grouping, though in all likelihood the league of cities served a double function: to unite Roman possessions and to enhance commerce in the region. In Jordan the main Decapolis cities were Philadelphia (Amman), Gadara (Umm Qais), Gerasa (Jerash), Pella (Taqabat Fil), and possibly Abila (Qweilbeh) and Capitolias (Beit Ras, near Irbid).

Convinced of Rome's everlasting greatness, the Emperor wanted Roman culture to flourish throughout the empire, which at the time included the Levant. As a result, Rome helped facilitate the growth of the Decapolis by granting the cities a surprising measure of political autonomy, albeit within the protective sphere of Rome. Each city operated more like a city-state, maintaining jurisdiction over the surrounding countryside and even minting its own coins. Indeed, coins from Decapolis cities often used words such as 'autonomous', 'free' and 'sovereign' to emphasise their self-governing status.

However, make no mistake about it – Rome became Rome through a campaign of cultural homogenisation, and it didn't take long for the Emperor to leave his mark on the Decapolis. True to Roman design, each city was rebuilt with gridded streets that were centred on well-funded public monuments.

The Roman engineers of the Decapolis also set about implementing the so-called 'imperial cult', which revolved around mandatory worship of the Roman emperor. This well-conceived practice unified cities in the Decapolis while simultaneously ensuring that its residents didn't forget the generosity of their Roman benefactors.

The cities of the Decapolis also enjoyed strong commercial ties, which were fostered by an extensive network of new Roman roads. Once again, this helped to establish fraternity within the Decapolis, which led to their common identification as a federation or league of city-states. However, due respect was given to Rome, which provided the necessary engineering skills to enable wagons and chariots to circulate rapidly.

Today, at the sites of Umm Qais and Jerash, the ruts carved by these vehicles can still be seen in the stones of the city streets.

At the height of its influence the Decapolis enjoyed a high living standard, which kept residents passive and obedient to Roman laws and values. As you wander the ruins of Jerash, try to imagine life 2000 years ago: the centre bustling with shops and merchants, and lined with cooling water fountains and dramatic painted facades. Picture today's empty niches filled with painted statues; buildings still clad in marble and decorated with carved peacocks and shell motifs; and churches topped with Tuscan-style, terracotta-tiled roofs. For a visual reconstruction of Jerash's finest buildings, check out the drawings at the visitor centre.

Eventually the term 'Decapolis' fell out of use when Emperor Trajan annexed Arabia in the 2nd century AD. Since the new province was east of the Levant, the cultural boundaries were pushed further from Rome, resulting in less attention being given to the Decapolis. However, the cities in the Levant continued to maintain connections with one another as well as with Rome, though major changes were ushered in following the adoption of Christianity across the empire.

In the New Testament gospels of Matthew, Mark and Luke, the Decapolis is mentioned by name as one of the ministries of Jesus. While much of the Levant was dominated at the time by the Jews, the gospels remark on the Roman-centric nature of the residents of the Decapolis. In Mark 5:1–20, Jesus is surprised to discover the gentile (non-Jewish) nature of the Decapolis when he comes across herds of pigs, animals that are expressly forbidden by kosher dietary laws.

Eventually the Decapolis fell into decline following the conquest of the Levant by the Umayyads in 641. At the time, the new Muslim Caliphate was based out of Damascus, which prompted the new rulers to shift money, goods and influence away from the Decapolis. The Caliphate was later moved to Baghdad as the entire Muslim world recentred itself, dealing the Decapolis a crippling final blow.

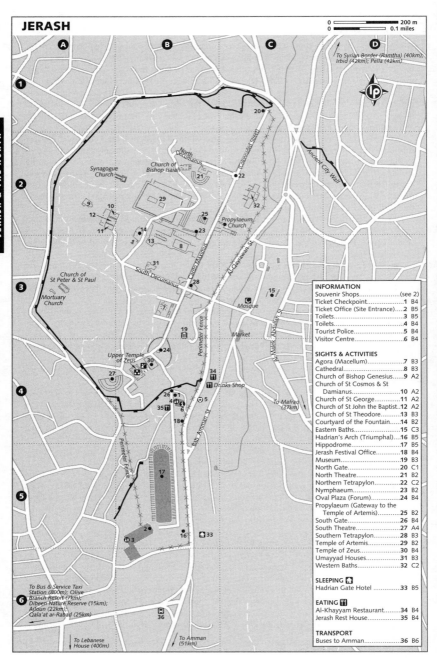

JERASH

0		200 m
0		0.1 miles

INFORMATION
Souvenir Shops	(see 2)	
Ticket Checkpoint	1	B4
Ticket Office (Site Entrance)	2	B5
Toilets	3	B5
Toilets	4	B4
Tourist Police	5	B4
Visitor Centre	6	B4

SIGHTS & ACTIVITIES
Agora (Macellum)	7	B3
Cathedral	8	B3
Church of Bishop Genesius	9	A2
Church of St Cosmos & St Damianus	10	A2
Church of St George	11	A2
Church of St John the Baptist	12	A2
Church of St Theodore	13	B3
Courtyard of the Fountain	14	B2
Eastern Baths	15	C3
Hadrian's Arch (Triumphal)	16	B5
Hippodrome	17	B5
Jerash Festival Office	18	B4
Museum	19	B3
North Gate	20	C1
North Theatre	21	B2
Northern Tetrapylon	22	C2
Nymphaeum	23	B2
Oval Plaza (Forum)	24	B4
Propylaeum (Gateway to the Temple of Artemis)	25	B2
South Gate	26	B4
South Theatre	27	A4
Southern Tetrapylon	28	B3
Temple of Artemis	29	B2
Temple of Zeus	30	B4
Umayyad Houses	31	B3
Western Baths	32	C2

SLEEPING
Hadrian Gate Hotel	33	B5

EATING
Al-Khayyam Restaurant	34	B4
Jerash Rest House	35	B4

TRANSPORT
Buses to Amman	36	B6

Nabataeans (the creators of Petra) flourished, and the city grew extremely wealthy. Local agriculture and iron-ore mining in the Ajloun area contributed to the city's well-being. In the 1st century AD a completely new city plan was drawn up, centred on the classical features of a colonnaded main north–south street intersected by two side streets running east–west.

When the emperor Trajan annexed the Nabataean kingdom around AD 106, more wealth found its way to Jerash. Many of the old buildings were torn down to be replaced by more imposing structures. Construction again flourished when Emperor Hadrian visited in AD 129. To mark a visit of such importance, the Triumphal Arch (Hadrian's Arch) at the southern end of the city was constructed.

Jerash reached its peak at the beginning of the 3rd century, when it was bestowed with the rank of Colony. However, its ascendancy was short lived due to disturbances such as the destruction of Palmyra (Syria) in 273, the demise of the overland caravans and the development of sea trade, all of which pushed the city into a slow decline. The only respite came during the reign of Diocletian (around 300), which saw a minor building boom.

From the middle of the 5th century, Christianity became the major religion of the Empire, and the construction of churches proceeded apace. Under the Byzantine emperor Justinian (527–65) seven churches were built, mostly out of stones pillaged from the earlier Roman temples and shrines. However, following the invasion of the Sassanians from Persia in 614, the Muslim conquest in 636 and the devastating earthquake in 747, Jerash's glory days passed into shadow, and its population shrank to about one-quarter of its former size.

Apart from a brief occupation by a Crusader garrison in the 12th century, the city was completely deserted until the arrival of the Circassians from Russia in 1878, after which the site's archaeological importance was realised and excavations began. Fortunately, the archaeological and historical value of Jerash was prioritised early on in modern history, which has significantly contributed to its stunning state of preservation.

Information
BOOKS & MAPS
Published by the Jordan Tourism Board, the free *Jerash* brochure includes a map, some photos and a recommended walking route. It can be found at the visitor centre in Jerash (below) or the Jordan Tourism Board in Amman (p95).

Anyone with a particular interest in the history of Jerash should pick up one of the three decent pocket-sized guides: *Jerash: The Roman City; Jerash: A Unique Example of a Roman City;* or the most comprehensive and readable *Jerash*. All three are available at bookshops in Amman. *Jerash* by Iain Browning is a more detailed and expensive historical book.

ENTRANCE
The entrance to the site is south of the ancient city, close to Hadrian's Arch. The **ticket office** (☎ 6351272; admission JD8; ⏰ 8am-4pm Oct-Apr, to 7pm May-Sep) is in the complex of souvenir shops, along with a post office and café. Tickets are checked later at the South Gate.

Next to the South Gate is the **visitor centre**, which has informative descriptions and reconstructions of many buildings in Jerash as well as a good relief map of the ancient city. There are toilets at the Jerash Rest House (p133), the visitor centre and the souvenir shops area at the site entrance.

Allow at least three hours to see everything in Jerash, and make sure you take plenty of water, especially in summer. It's best to visit Jerash before 10am or after 4pm, because it's cooler, glare is reduced in your photos and there'll be far fewer people at the site. Most of the buildings are at their best close to sunset. Remember, however, that public transport to Amman is limited after 5pm. It's possible to leave luggage at the Jerash Rest House, for no charge, while you visit the site.

GUIDES
Anyone with a special interest in the history of Jerash may wish to hire a guide, which costs approximately JD5 to JD10 depending on the length of the tour and the size of the group. Guides are available at the ticket checkpoint in front of the South Gate, and can do wonders in bringing the ruins to life.

Sights
HADRIAN'S ARCH & HIPPODROME

At the entrance to the site is the striking **Hadrian's Arch**, which is sometimes referred to as the Triumphal Arch. At 13m tall it's an imposing structure, though it was originally twice as high when first built in AD 129 to honour the visiting Emperor Hadrian.

The central arch was once supported by three enormous wooden doors, though only their stone frames remain. A distinguishing feature is the wreath of carved acanthus leaves above the base of each pillar, which is a traditional Roman design element. Interestingly enough, the arch was erected beyond the city walls as a new southern entrance to the city, though the area between the arch and the South Gate was never completed.

Behind the arch and also beyond the city walls is the **hippodrome**, built sometime between the 1st and 3rd centuries AD. This ancient sports field (244m by 50m) was once surrounded by seating for up to 15,000 spectators, and hosted mainly athletics competitions and chariot races. Recent excavations have unearthed remains of stables and pottery workshops, plus indications that it was used for polo by invading Sassanians from Persia during the early 7th century.

The hippodrome has undergone extensive renovation by the Jordanian Department of Antiquities, and is now one of the showpieces of the ruins at Jerash. For a taste of ancient Roman entertainment, be sure to pick up tickets for the daily chariot races, which re-create the sporting events of the Decapolis with surprising verisimilitude. For more information, see the boxed text, right.

SOUTH GATE & FORUM

About 250m beyond Hadrian's Arch is the **South Gate**, which was most likely constructed in AD 130, and originally served as one of four entrances along the city walls. Like Hadrian's Arch, it also bears acanthus-leaf decorations atop the pillar bases as tribute to Jerash's Roman roots, as well as three stone apertures that once contained massive wooden doors.

The **walls** themselves were also built around the same time as the South Gate, though they were extended several times as the city expanded. Most of what remains

---

THE RETURN OF BEN HUR

In the summer of 2005, chariot races returned to Jerash for the first time in around 1500 years, thanks to the vision of a joint Swedish-Jordanian venture. The **Roman Army & Chariot Experience** (www.jerash chariots.com; admission JD15; ☯ shows 11am & 2pm Wed, Thu & Sat-Mon, 10am Fri) runs chariot races in Jerash's hippodrome, re-created as authentically as possible, down to the use of Latin commands.

The show starts off with the entrance of around 40 Roman legionnaires (actually Jordanian special forces) who parade around the hippodrome and complete a range of military drills, from the tortoise manoeuvre to the use of a catapult, followed by four pairs of gladiators fighting it out with tridents, nets and *gladius* (sword). This is all a warm up for the main event: four chariots duking it out over seven laps around the hippodrome's central wooden *spina*.

There's currently space for about 500 spectators in the hippodrome, just 3% of the original capacity. You'll have to imagine the original crowd of 15,000 who packed in here; and while you're at it, just picture the spectacle of the Circus Maximus in Rome, which once roared with 157,000 spectators. That said, the Roman Army & Chariot Experience is an impressive effort to inject a bit of life into the old ruins at Jerash.

---

dates from the Byzantine era, though there is little evidence of the 24 towers that once stood guard along the walls. Today the remaining boundary walls are 3.5km long and 3m thick. Together, they encompass almost 1 sq km of the city.

The **Oval Plaza** or **Forum** is regarded as one of the icons of Jerash, especially since its oval shape and huge size (90m long and 80m at its widest point) is rather unusual. Some historians attribute this to the desire to gracefully link the *cardo maximus* (main north–south axis) with the Temple of Zeus, which would have enabled the Forum to serve as a place of sacrifice. Like all Roman cities, however, the Forum typically served as a marketplace: the heart of the city's social and political life.

Also constructed in the middle of the 1st century AD, the Forum is surrounded by 56 impressive Ionic columns, and paved with extremely high-quality limestone. It is centred on a large fountain, the plumbing of which is still visible below the podium, though this was added later on in the 7th century. Note the limestone paving slabs, which are wide in the outer areas of the Forum, but gradually get smaller and smaller as they approach the centre.

TEMPLE OF ZEUS & SOUTH THEATRE
On the south side of the Forum is the **Temple of Zeus**, which was built in AD 162 over the remains of an earlier Roman temple. The temple once had a magnificent monumental stairway leading up to it from a lower sacred enclosure, itself supported by a vaulted corridor built to compensate for the unhelpful local topography. The lower-level *temenos* (sacred courtyard) also had an altar, and served as a holy place of sacrifice. The temple itself is located on a colonnaded base measuring 40m by 30m that is clearly visible from anywhere within the city. Due to its prominent position at the summit of a hill, the temple was extremely prone to both erosion and earthquakes in previous centuries, and is currently a mere shell of its former grandeur. However, French excavations here have unearthed some extraordinary friezes of floral and figurative motifs, which may have been strongly influenced by the nearby Nabataeans.

The **south theatre**, located behind the Temple of Zeus, was built between AD 81 and 96, and opened up with a bang, housing 5000 spectators amid two storeys of seating. Although only the first level survived through the generations, the south theatre is still the largest and best preserved of the theatres at the Jerash. At present there are 32 rows of seats, many of which are still marked by Greek numbers, as well as an elaborately decorated bi-level stage. From the top of the theatre there are superb views of ancient and modern Jerash, particularly the Oval Plaza; just prior to sunset is the best time to visit.

The theatre is a testament to the wisdom of the ancients, boasting excellent acoustics as quickly becomes clear to anyone attending performances here during the **Jerash Festival of Culture & Arts** (see the boxed text, below). If you are lucky, you'll get to see the surreal Jordanian Scottish pipe band that sporadically belts out military tunes on the bagpipes to illustrate the excellent acoustics.

CARDO MAXIMUS
Heading northeast from the Forum, the **cardo maximus** (colonnaded street) is the city's main thoroughfare, and another of Jerash's highlights. Stretching for 800m from the Forum to the North Gate, it was originally built in the 1st century AD, and was redesigned and rebuilt several times after. The *cardo* is still paved with the original flagstones and the ruts worn by thousands of chariots are still clear, as are the manholes for the drains below.

JERASH FESTIVAL OF CULTURE & ARTS

Since 1981 the ancient city of Jerash has hosted the annual **Jerash Festival of Culture & Arts** (www.jerashfestival.com.jo), under the sponsorship of Queen Noor. Events are held in the South Theatre, North Theatre and Oval Plaza in Jerash, as well as the Royal Cultural Centre in Amman, and other places like Umm Qais and Mt Nebo. Special programs for children are also held at the Haya Cultural Centre in Amman.

The festival is held over 17 days from mid-July to mid-August, and features an eclectic array of performances including plays, poetry readings, opera and musical concerts from around the world. Events are listed in English in the official souvenir news sheet, the *Jerash Daily*, printed in English every day of the festival, and the English-language newspapers published in Amman.

Tickets cost about JD5 to JD10 for events in Jerash, and about JD20 to JD30 for more formal events in Amman and elsewhere. Since the events change from year to year, it is best to inquire online regarding the locations of ticketing venues. There is also a **festival office** next to the visitor centre near the South Gate, though it's not open at other times of the year. Also note that during the festival several bus companies, including JETT, offer special transport to Jerash, which is useful considering public transport usually finishes early in the evening.

Some of the 500 columns that once lined the street were deliberately built at an uneven height to complement the facades of the buildings that once stood behind them, though most of the columns you see today were reassembled in the 1960s. Just prior to the intersection with the **south decumanus** (main street, running from east to west), and where the columns are taller, is the entrance to the **agora** or **macellum**, where people gathered for public meetings around the central fountain.

Where the cardo maximus joins the south and north *decumanus,* ornamental *tetrapylons* (archway with four entrances) were built. The **southern tetrapylon** consisted of four bases, each supporting four pillars topped by a platform and a statue. They are in varying stages of reconstruction, though the southeastern one is the most complete. The more intact **northern tetrapylon**, dedicated to the Syrian wife of the emperor Septimus Severus, was probably built as a gateway to the north theatre. This *tetrapylon* differs in style from the southern one. If its condition looks too good to be true, that's because it is – it was rebuilt in 2000.

To the east of the intersection of the *cardo maximus* and south *decumanus* lay the former residential areas of Jerash, which are now buried beneath the modern town. To the west of the intersection are the ruins of some **Umayyad houses**, which date from the 7th and 8th centuries, well after the political and economic decline of Jerash.

CATHEDRAL & CHURCH OF ST THEODORE

The *cardo* gives way via an elaborate staircase to the city's only **cathedral**, which is actually little more than a modest Byzantine church, despite the elaborate name. Although the cathedral was constructed in the second half of the 4th century, the site was once home to the 2nd-century Temple of Dionysus, as well as an earlier temple to the Nabataean god Dushara. However, the temple was virtually dismantled for building materials following the adoption of Christianity by the Roman Empire, though parts of the original gate and steps remain.

Sadly, the cathedral has not weathered the storms of change that have swept across Jerash over the past millennium, though the standing walls do hint at the former grandeur of the structure. At the height of its glory, the cathedral consisted of a soaring basilica supported by three naves, and boasted a magnificent portal that was finely decorated with elaborate marble carvings.

Behind (west of) the cathedral is the **Church of St Theodore**, which was also built by the Byzantines in AD 496 during the Christianisation of the Roman Empire. Together with the much larger cathedral, the church was utilised as a sacred area for carrying out Christian rituals. Today little remains of St Theodore, aside from a skeletal frame adorned with limited mosaics, though here, too, once stood a large and soaring basilica.

Behind the church is the **Courtyard of the Fountain**, which is home to the modest remains of a square basin lying in the middle of a small atrium. During Byzantine times, the courtyard was used each year to commemorate the miracle of the marriage of Cana, where Jesus is reported by his disciples to have turned water into wine.

NYMPHAEUM, PROPYLAEUM & EASTERN BATHS

Also situated along the *cardo* is the elegant **nymphaeum**, the main ornamental fountain of the city that was dedicated to the water nymphs. Built in about AD 191, the two-storey construction was elaborately decorated, faced with marble slabs on the lower level, plastered on the upper level and topped with a half dome. Water would cascade over the facade into a large pool at the front, with the overflow pouring out through seven carved lions' heads into drains in the street below.

Although it's been quite some time since water poured forth from the nymphaeum, the well-preserved structure remains one of the highlights of Jerash. Several finely sculpted Corinthian columns still frame the fountain, and there is a lovely pink-granite basin at the base of the fountain, which was probably added by the Byzantines. At one point the entire structure was capped by a semi-dome in the shape of a shell, though you can still make out the elaborate capitals lining the base of the ceiling.

Further along to the west is the **propylaeum**, which was built in 150 AD as the monumental gateway to the Temple of Artemis (see opposite). In Roman times, a stairway, flanked by shops, originally ran from here to the eastern residential area. Today however, the portico lies in pieces in the street opposite the gateway, and a small Byzantine church occupies part of the original stairway.

From the stairway, you can still see the remains of the somewhat incongruous **eastern baths**, which lie in ruins beneath the shadow of a mosque in the modern town. In Roman times, public bathing fulfilled the role of a social club, and attracted a wide variety of people who gathered to exchange news and gossip, as well as to enjoy everything from music and lectures to sporting events and performances.

TEMPLE OF ARTEMIS & WESTERN BATHS

Behind the propylaeum on top of a small hill is the magnificent **Temple of Artemis**, which is dedicated to Artemis, the goddess of hunting and fertility, and the daughter of Zeus. Regarded as the most impressive temple in Jerash, it was built between AD 150 and 170, and was flanked by 12 (11 are still standing) elaborately carved Corinthian columns. The construction of the temple is particularly impressive given that large vaults had to be built to the north and south to make the courtyard level. At one point the whole of the building was covered in shining marble, and the vaults housed vast treasures in addition to prized statues of Artemis.

After the edict of Theodorius in AD 386 permitting the dismantling of pagan temples in an effort to promote Christianity in the newly dubbed Holy Roman Empire, many of the materials were taken away for construction elsewhere, especially the temple's highly prized marble floors. According to archaeologists, the Byzantines further disgraced this once-grand temple by converting it into a mere artisan workshop for kitchenware and crockery. In the 12th century the temple was brought back to life after being fortified by the Arabs, though it was subsequently destroyed by the invading Crusaders.

While visiting the Temple of Artemis, pay particular attention to the sacrificial altar located at the front of the building, which was common feature at temples in the Decapolis. Also note the holy water basins used for sacred ablutions, which are located in the temple courtyard. Below the central building there are also underground naves that can be accessed from the sides.

Just downhill (to the northeast) is the rubble of the huge **western baths**, measuring about 70m by 50m. Dating from the 2nd century AD, they represent one of the earliest examples of a dome atop a square room. Once an impressive complex of hot- (*calidarium*), warm- (*tepidarium*) and cold-water (*frigidarium*) baths, they were partially destroyed by various earthquakes.

NORTH THEATRE & NORTH GATE

Built in about AD 165 and enlarged in 235, the **north theatre** is smaller than the south theatre, though it differs considerably in shape and design. According to archaeologists and historians, the theatre was most likely used for government meetings rather than artistic performances. Originally it had 14 rows of seats with two vaulted passageways leading to the front of theatre, as well as five internal arched corridors leading to the upper rows.

Like many of the grand monuments at Jerash, the north theatre was destroyed by earthquakes and then partially dismantled for later Byzantine and Umayyad building projects. However, in recent years the north theatre has been magnificently restored and still maintains a capacity of about 2000 people. Take notice of the lower seats, which are inscribed with the names of the delegates who voted in the city council, as well as the exuberant carvings of musicians and dancers at the base of the stairs.

The *cardo maximus* ends at the comparatively unimpressive **North Gate**. Built in about AD 115, it has not been restored as well as its southern counterpart, though it remains an important monument. The gate was commissioned by Claudius Severus, who was responsible for building the road to Pella (see p146), also part of the Roman Decapolis.

CHURCHES

When Christianity became the official state religion under Emperor Constantine in AD 324, all Roman monuments that were tainted by so-called pagan practices were quickly abandoned. As history would have it, these structures were subsequently pilfered for building materials as Roman cities competed with one another to build glorious churches and cathedrals in the name of the Lord. As testament to the Byzantine presence in Jerash, a total of 15 churches have been uncovered among the ruins, though it's predicted that many more lie waiting to be discovered.

The **Church of St Cosmos & St Damianus** was consecrated in 533 in memory of twin brothers, both doctors, who devoted themselves to the care of the poor and the needy, and were martyred during the reign of Diocletian. The church is regarded as having the best-preserved mosaics at Jerash, which include zoomorphic figures, geometric designs and medical symbols. However, a good number of these are now housed in the Museum of Popular Tradition in Amman (p98).

The **Church of St John the Baptist** was built in about AD 531 under the jurisdiction of Bishop Paul, though it's now badly damaged. A simple building with a distinguishing horseshoe shape, its floor mosaics are difficult to make out, apart from a few depictions of flora and fauna, the changing seasons and several Egyptian cities.

The **Church of St George**, built in about AD 530, suffered the least amount of earthquake damage, and there is evidence that it was used as late as the 8th century. However, it was not spared from pilfering, which ravaged the church during the Umayyad dynasty. As a result the mosaics were damaged irreparably, while the debris on top of the other churches helped protect their mosaic floors.

Behind the three Byzantine churches is the humble **Church of Bishop Genesius**, which is believed to have been constructed in 611, based on the date inscribed in the mosaic floor. If this is true, it would imply that this was the last building constructed at Jerash prior to the arrival of the Persians.

MUSEUM

Before you finish exploring the ancient city, try to visit the small **museum** (☎ 6312267; admission free; ☺ 8.30am-6pm Oct-Apr, to 5pm May-Sep) just to the northeast of (and uphill from) the Oval Plaza. It houses a small but worthwhile selection of artefacts from the site, such as mosaics, glass, gold jewellery and coins found in a tomb near Hadrian's Arch. All items on display are well labelled in English, though no photography is allowed. Just as interesting as the exhibits are the inscriptions, tombs and pillars lying

higgledy-piggledy in the gardens outside the museum.

Sleeping

With an early start, you could cover Jerash in a day trip from Amman, though it's much more pleasurable to slow down, stay for the night and savour the full glory of the ruins. The modern town of Jerash, which comes to life after the sun sets and the air cools, is certainly worth exploring in the calm of the early evening.

our pick **Hadrian Gate Hotel** (☎ 77793907; walid friend.2007@yahoo.com; s/d/tr from JD18/35/45, breakfast JD2.75) Run by the always friendly and accommodating Walid, the first and only hotel in Jerash proper boasts a spectacular location directly across from the Hadrian's Gate. Private rooms with shared bathrooms are very simple and modest, so don't come here expecting lush quarters and luxurious amenities. However, this budget hotel gets our recommendation, simply because Walid will go out of his way to personally accommodate each and every one of his guests, and is more than happy to wake up early to prepare your breakfast. Although it's still something of a work in progress, this place has a lot of potential, especially if the rooftop garden overlooking the ruins is put to use.

Olive Branch Resort (☎ 6340555; www.olive branch.com.jo; s/d incl breakfast from JD20/40; 🏊 🐾) Around 7km from Jerash on the road to Ajloun, this secluded, low-key resort occupies a picturesque and tranquil location amid rolling Tuscan-like hills. Modern and comfortable rooms are surprisingly spacious, particularly the ones that come with en-suite bath tubs and private balconies. There is also an on-site restaurant that serves up country-inspired fare, especially if you want to sample the locally produced olive oil. If you don't have your own transport, a taxi from Jerash should only cost a few dinars. If you have your own wheels, drive 5km from Jerash towards Ajloun, turn right and continue for 1km, and then right again and continue for another 2km.

Eating

Modern Jerash is a bustling little city that's home to several outdoor markets, as well as the obligatory smattering of kebab and felafel shops. After the ruins have closed for the day and tourists retreat to their hotels, the town bursts to life and is a great place to walk around – just follow your nose and let your stomach do the thinking!

Al-Khayyam Restaurant (barbecued meats from JD2.50) Across the road from the city walls of Jerash, this popular spot specialises in charcoal-roasted chicken, lamb and mixed vegetables. Of course, those hot coals are also good for lighting up an apple *sheesha* (water pipe) – just the thing for lightening the head and settling the stomach.

our pick Lebanese House (☎ 6351301; starters JD1-3, mains JD3-5; ☽ noon-11pm) A five- to 10-minute walk from Jerash's centre, this is a much-loved favourite for local families, with outdoor seating and a kids' play area. The menu here (as its name implies) is decidedly Lebanese, and offers a broad range of mezzes including everything from frogs legs to *shinklish* (tangy white cheese). Culinary daredevils can try a pair of hot and buttery cow testicles, washed down by a glass of local Machereus white wine. Maybe just stick to the basics...

Jerash Rest House (☎ 6351437; buffet JD5; ☽ noon-5pm) Make no mistake about it – this restaurant located near Hadrian's Gate is an absolute tourist circus, though that doesn't mean you should steer clear. On the contrary, the all-you-can eat lunch buffet is a very good deal at JD5, and its convenient location will ensure that you have plenty of time to explore the adjacent ruins.

Getting There & Away

Jerash is located approximately 50km north of Amman, and the roads are well signed from the capital, especially from 8th Circle. If you're driving, be advised that this route can get extremely congested during the morning and afternoon rush hours, though it's certainly possible to tackle if you keep your wits about you and drive defensively.

From Abdali bus station in Amman, public buses and minibuses (less than JD1, 1¼ hours) leave regularly for Jerash, though they can take up to an hour just to fill up. Your best chance of minimising the waiting time is to show up in the morning hours when most people are getting ready to head up to Jerash for the day.

Jerash's relatively new bus and service-taxi station is a 15-minute walk southwest

of the site, at the second set of traffic lights, behind the big white building. You can pick up a minibus to the station from outside the visitor centre for a few coins. From here, there are also plenty of minibuses travelling regularly to Irbid (JD1, 45 minutes) and Ajloun (less than JD1, 30 minutes) until around 4pm. If you don't want to head to the bus station you can normally flag down the bus to Amman from the main junction in front of the site.

If you're still in Jerash after 5pm, transport drops off and you may have to hitch back to the capital. Service taxis sometimes leave as late as 8pm (usually later during Jerash Festival) from the bus station, but it's not guaranteed. The tourist police are usually happy to cajole a passing motorist into offering a free ride back to Amman, though you can always just grab a room at the Hadrian's Gate Hotel.

It is also possible to hire a private taxi between Amman and Jerash for around JD15 to JD20 each way, though you're going to have to bargain seriously hard. From Jerash, you can also grab a taxi to Irbid for around JD10 to JD15.

THE NORTH

Jordan's far-flung northern extents see few travellers aside from overlanders heading to Damascus in Syria. This is a shame as the region's rolling hills and verdant valleys are home to vast nature reserves, the ruins of Decapolis cities and the thriving university town of Irbid. The public-transport network is also extensive in this densely populated part of the country, though the freedom of having your own car will really bring the north to life. While you certainly shouldn't miss out of Jordan's top attractions, consider spending an extra few days exploring the heartland of biblical Gilead.

AJLOUN   عجلون
☎ 02

Roughly 30km west of Jerash, Ajloun (or Ajlun) is an ancient market town with more than a millennium of history that is centred on a 600-year old mosque. While this religious building is certainly impressive, it's overshadowed by nearby Qala'at ar-Rabad (Ajloun Castle), a spectacular example of

Islamic military architecture that's one of the highlights of the region. As if all of this wasn't enough to warrant a stopover in Ajloun, the town also serves as a jumping-off point for Mar Elias, which is regarded as the birthplace of the prophet Elijah.

The surrounding countryside of pine forest and olive groves is good for hiking, and is popular with picnicking locals in summer, especially since the hills are a few degrees cooler than Ajloun itself. However, if you really want to get a sense of the wonderful nature surrounding the town, consider pressing on to the nearby Ajloun Nature Reserve (see opposite) as well as the Dibeen Nature Reserve (see p137), southwest of Jerash.

Information

Just south of the main roundabout in Ajloun, the Housing Bank changes money and has an ATM. The **tourist office** (☎ /fax 6420115; 🕑 7am-1pm Sun-Thu) is in the restaurant complex at the foot of the castle.

Sights

QALA'AT AR-RABAD (AJLOUN CASTLE)

This historic **castle** (admission JD1; 🕑 8am-4pm Oct-Apr, to 7pm May-Sep) was built atop Mt 'Auf (1250m) between 1184 and 1188 by one of Saladin's generals (and also nephew), 'Izz ad-Din Usama bin Munqidh. It was enlarged in 1214 with the addition of a new gate in the southeastern corner, and once boasted seven towers as well as a surrounding 15m-deep dry moat.

The castle commands views of the Jordan Valley and three wadis leading into it – the Kufranjah, Rajeb and Al-Yabes – making it an important strategic link in the defensive chain against the Crusaders, and a counterpoint to the Crusader Belvoir Fort on the Sea of Galilee (Lake Tiberias) in present-day Israel and the Palestinian Territories. With its hilltop position, Qala'at ar-Rabad was one in a chain of beacons and pigeon posts that enabled messages to be transmitted from Damascus to Cairo in a single day.

After the Crusader threat subsided, the castle was largely destroyed by Mongol invaders in 1260, only to be almost immediately rebuilt by the Mamluks. In the 17th century an Ottoman garrison was stationed here, after which it was used by local villagers. The castle was 'rediscovered' by the

well-travelled JL Burckhardt, who also just happened to stumble across Petra. Earthquakes in 1837 and 1927 badly damaged the castle, though slow and steady restoration is continuing.

Note that there is a useful explanation in English just inside the main gate, although nothing else is signposted. However, not much explanation is needed to bring the castle to life, especially given that the views from these lofty heights are nothing short of spectacular.

The castle is a tough uphill walk (3km) from the town centre, but minibuses very occasionally go to the top (about 100 fils). Alternatively, take a taxi from Ajloun (JD1 to JD2 each way). A return trip by taxi from Ajloun (JD5), with about 30 minutes to look around, is money well spent.

MAR ELIAS

This little-visited **archaeological site** (admission free; 🕑 8am-7pm Apr-Oct, to 4pm Nov-Mar), the reported birthplace of the Prophet Elijah, gives you just the excuse you need to explore the countryside around Ajloun. To be honest, it's not a spectacular site by any stretch of the imagination, though it is certainly worth checking out solely for its religious and historical significance.

The prophet Elias is mentioned in both the Quran and the Old Testament, and is thought to have been born around 910 BC in the village of Lesteb, next to Mar Elias. The prophet died not far away in Wadi al-Kharrar (see p171), before supposedly ascending to heaven on a flaming chariot. During Byzantine times, a pilgrimage site grew up around the place under the guidance of the nearby Bishopric of Pella. In 1999 excavations unearthed a church complex dating back to the early 7th century.

From the car park, stairs lead up above the ruins of the earliest church, the apse of which has a tree growing directly above it. The foundations of the main cross-shaped church are easy to make out and are decorated with wonderfully fresh floor mosaics partially covered by plastic. Look for the tomb chambers to the back right of the church, and an earlier chapel with plain white tiles to the south. Water cisterns and bits of masonry dot the rest of the site.

There's no public transport to the site and it's only really worth a visit if you have a car and can combine a trip to Qala'at ar-Rabad (opposite) and the nearby Ajloun Nature Reserve (right). From Ajloun take a right by the Qalet al-Jabal Hotel, climb the hill for 1km and take a left at the junction, heading downhill after this for 2.7km. At the junction/army post take a right for another 1.8km until you see a signpost pointing left (the right branch leads to Ishfateena and the Ajloun Nature Reserve). After 1km take the left track for 400m up to the site (a total of 8.3km from Ajloun).

If you're headed on to Ajloun Nature Reserve take a left when you get back to the junction, 1.4km from the site, and head towards Ishfateena. After 1.6km you hit the main road; take a right here and after 5km you'll see the reserve signposted to the left, 300m before the main Irbid–Ajloun highway.

Mar Elias can also be reached by foot along the spectacular Prophet's Trail, which connects the site to the nearby Ajloun Nature Reserve (see right for more information).

Sleeping & Eating

There are two hotels on the road up to the castle, either of which are a good option if you want to enjoy the sunset.

Ajloun Hotel (☎ 6420524; s/d incl breakfast from JD18/30) The cheaper of the hotels is located 500m down the road from the castle. If you're sticking closely to your budget this isn't a bad option – assuming you don't mind the somewhat claustrophobic rooms and the unpredictable nature of the hot water. However, you can get a bit more value for your money by choosing one of the rooms on the top floor, which boast spectacular views of the countryside.

Qalet al-Jabal Hotel (☎ 6420202; s/d/tr from JD35/45/50) About 1km before the castle, this is a better option, though you're going to have to part with a bit more cash to stay here. If you can forgive the outdated decor, the rooms themselves are nicely equipped with private balconies and terraces, some of which overlook the castle lurking in the distance. The real highlight, however, is the outdoor terrace garden where slow-cooked meals are served – even if you're not staying here, you can certainly stop by for bite to eat.

Both **Abu-Alezz Restaurant** (meals JD2-3) and **Al-Raseed** (meals JD2-3) near the main roundabout

in Ajloun offer cheap and tasty standard Jordanian fare, including chicken, hummus and shwarma. There is also a small drink stand and snack shop next to the castle ticket office. A good alternative, however, is to scour the markets before heading into the surrounding hills for a picnic lunch.

Getting There & Away

Ajloun is approximately 75km northwest of Amman and 30km northwest of Jerash. The castle can be clearly seen from most places in the area. If you're driving or walking, take the signposted road (Al-Qala'a St) heading west at the main roundabout in the centre of Ajloun.

From the centre of Ajloun, minibuses travel regularly to Jerash (less than JD1, 30 minutes along a scenic road) and Irbid (less than JD1, 45 minutes). From Amman (JD1, two hours), minibuses leave a few times a day from the Abdali bus station.

AJLOUN NATURE RESERVE
محمية عجلون الطبيعية

Located in the Ajloun Highlands, this small (just 13 sq km) but vitally important **nature reserve** (☎ 02-6475673; ☺ year-round) was established by the Royal Society for the Conservation of Nature (RSCN) in 1988 to protect oak, carob, pistachio and strawberry forests. The reserve also acts a wildlife sanctuary for the endangered roe deer (which is being brought back from the brink of extinction through captive breeding programs) as well as wild boar, stone martens, polecats, jackals and even hyena and grey wolves.

The RSCN has been working hard to develop tourist infrastructure within the reserve, which is why Ajloun now boasts some swish new cabins – perfect for a romantic retreat. Of course, the real appeal of the reserve is its good hiking network, which offers a variety of trails suited to hikers of all skill levels. The scenery of rolling hills and lush forests is lovely, especially if you've been spending a few too many hours in Jordan's barren deserts or congested capital.

Orientation & Information

Getting here is a bit of an adventure in itself as no public transport goes directly to the reserve. If you have your own wheels, however, Ajloun is easily accessed from Amman, Jerash or Irbid in just a few hours, which means you can stop by either for the day or for a night or two.

You should book accommodation and meals in advance with the RSCN through its Wild Jordan Centre in Amman (see p95). If you're planning to take a guided hike, it's also a good idea to book. Note that a small fee applies to the guided hikes, which is determined by the size of your party.

At the entrance to the reserve is a modest **visitor centre** (dawn-dusk) where you'll find a small restaurant offering traditional Jordanian dishes and some local Ajloun specialities, as well as a nature shop selling locally produced handicrafts.

Activities
HIKING

If you're just stopping by for the day, the 2km-long **Scenic Viewpoint Trail** (year-round) takes about an hour and can be self-guided. It starts from the accommodation area, looping over a nearby hill – past a 1600-year-old stone wine press and lots of spring wildflowers (April) – and returning via a roe deer enclosure.

The **Rockrose Trail** is a longer trail of around 8km (four hours, open 1 April to 31 October) that involves some steep scrambling and requires a guide. This scenic route passes through heavily wooded valleys, rocky ridges and olive groves, all the while offering sweeping views of the Palestinian West Bank.

The **Village Orchards Tour** is a guided 12km trail (six hours, open from 1 April to 31 October) that takes in evergreen forests and fruit orchards, as well as offering a stopover in a local olive-oil soap workshop.

The **Soap Maker's Trail** is a self-guided 7km trail (four hours, open year-round) that combines several panoramic viewpoints along an evergreen-lined trail with visits to the soap workshop, where enterprising women make their eco-friendly products from natural resources and sell them at fair prices in the Ajloun Reserve shop.

The **Prophet's Trail** is the undisputed highlight of the reserve, especially since it terminates at the archaeological site of Mar Elias (see p134) where the prophet Elijah was reportedly born. An 8.5km guided route (four hours, open year-round), the Prophet's Trail begins at the visitor centre and slowly winds through fig and pear orchards.

However, once you reach Wadi Shiteau, the trail plunges into a dense forest of oak and strawberry trees. The sweeping valley itself is criss-crossed by stone dividing walls, though the going gets easier here as you can transfer all of your gear to donkeys. From here, you proceed to climb again to a distant ridge, which leads to the sacred birthplace.

After you've taken a breather and soaked up the spirituality of the site, a bus will pick you up and bring you back to the visitor centre. However, with prior arrangements (as well as the necessary discipline), it's also possible to continue hiking another 9.5km (four hours) through Wadi Al-Jubb to the distant Ajloun Castle (see p134). The terrain gets significantly steeper here, but it's worth the struggle for the privilege of arriving on foot at one of Jordan's most impressive monuments. A bus will pick you up from the castle and bring you back, so you'll have plenty of time to catch up on your sleep!

Sleeping & Eating

The reserve operates a set of **tented bungalows** (s/d/tr/q from JD20/30/40/50) that are perched on a tree house–style wooden platform. The bungalows are light and breezy, and are a short walk from an ablution block containing environmentally sound composting toilets and solar-heated showers. Note that the bungalows are only open from 1 April to 31 October. Also be sure to bring plenty of mosquito repellent during the summer months.

As part of the reserve's impressive overhaul, the RSCN has constructed a clutch of rustic **cabins** (s/d from JD55) that are equipped with private facilities and private terraces overlooking a patch of forest. These are certainly worth the extra money, especially if you're travelling with your better half.

Meals are available in the tented **rooftop restaurant** (meals JD4-7) if you give some notice, though you can always cook for yourself on the public barbecue grills. From the rooftop, check out the great views of snowcapped Jebel ash-Sheikh (Mt Hermon; 2814m) on the Syria–Lebanon border.

Getting There & Away

If you don't have a car, the best way to reach the reserve is to hire a taxi from Ajloun (9km) for a few dinars. You can ask the

THE JORDAN VALLEY

Forming a part of the Great Rift in Africa, the fertile valley of the Jordan River was of considerable significance in biblical times, and is now regarded as the food bowl of Jordan.

The hot dry summers and short mild winters make for ideal growing conditions, and (subject to water restrictions) two or three crops are grown every year. Thousands of tonnes of fruit and vegetables are produced annually, with the main crops being tomatoes, cucumbers, melons and citrus fruits. You'll see dozens of greenhouses and nurseries as you travel through the valley.

The Jordan River rises from several sources, mainly the Anti-Lebanon Range in Syria, and flows down into the Sea of Galilee (Lake Tiberias), 212m below sea level, before draining into the Dead Sea. The actual length of the river is 360km, but as the crow flies the distance between its source and the Dead Sea is only 200km.

It was in the Jordan Valley, some 10,000 years ago, that people first started to plant crops and abandon their nomadic lifestyle for permanent settlements. Villages were built and primitive irrigation schemes were undertaken; by 3000 BC produce from the valley was being exported to neighbouring regions, much as it is today.

The Jordan River is highly revered by Christians, mainly because Jesus was baptised in its waters by John the Baptist at the site of Bethany-Beyond-the-Jordan (see p169). Centuries earlier, Joshua also led the Israelite armies across the Jordan near Tell Nimrin (Beth Nimrah in the Bible) after the death of Moses, marking the symbolic transition from the wilderness to the land of milk and honey:

> And while all Israel were passing over on dry ground, the priests who bore the ark of the covenant of the Lord stood on dry ground in the midst of the Jordan, until all the nation finished passing over the Jordan.
>
> *Joshua 3: 17*

Since 1948 the Jordan River has marked the boundary between Jordan and Israel and the Palestinian Territories, from the Sea of Galilee to the Yarbis River. From there to the Dead Sea marked the 1967 ceasefire line between the two countries – it now marks the continuation of the official frontier with the Palestinian Territories.

During the 1967 war with Israel, Jordan lost the West Bank and the population on the Jordanian east bank of the valley dwindled from 60,000 before the war to 5000 by 1971. During the 1970s, new roads and fully serviced villages were built and the population has now soared to over 100,000.

reserve visitor centre to book one for your departure. If you're driving, take the road from Ajloun towards Irbid and take a left turn by a petrol station 4.8km from Ajloun towards the village of Ishfateena. About 300m from the junction take a right and follow the signs 3.8km to the reserve, which is next to the village of Umm al-Yanabi.

DIBEEN NATURE RESERVE متنزة دبين الوطني

Established in 2004, this small area (no more than 8 sq km) of Aleppo pine and oak forest is Jordan's newest **nature reserve** (☎ 02-6370017; year-round). Managed by the Royal Society for the Conservation of Nature (RSCN), Dibeen is representative of the wild forests that once covered much of the country's northern frontiers. Despite its small size, however, the reserve is recognised as a national biodiversity hot spot, and protects 17 endangered animals (including the Persian squirrel) and several rare orchids.

As Dibeen is still very much a work in progress, facilities are currently limited compared with other RSCN reserves. It's best to check in advance with the RSCN through the Wild Jordan Centre in Amman (p95) before heading out here, as new regulations or facilities might be in place.

There are some short marked (but unmapped) **hiking** trails through the park. In March and April carpets of red crown anemones fill the meadows beneath the pine-forested and sometimes snowcapped hills. Most trails are either small vehicle tracks or stony paths, some of which continue beyond the park's boundaries. The area is very popular with local picnickers on Fridays, and litter can be a problem.

In the middle of the park is **Dibeen Rest House** (☎ 6339710; d/tr from JD25/35), a comprehensive tourist complex with a children's playground and restaurant. The comfortable chalets (which sleep three) have simple but functional kitchens, large bathrooms with hot water, satellite TV and ceiling fans. It's worth negotiating as prices vary depending on the season. Visitors can pitch their own tent in the grounds for JD3 per person, and have access to toilets and hot showers.

Public transport here is limited. From Jerash, minibuses heading to the villages of Burma or Al-Majdal go through the park and can drop you off within 1km of the tourist-complex entrance – a detour to the complex can be arranged with the driver for a few extra dinars. Chartering a taxi from Jerash is the best idea, and will cost about JD5 to JD10 one way. If you're driving from Jerash, Ajloun or Amman, follow the initial signs close to Jerash and then ask directions to the Rest House – there are few signs.

IRBID   إربد
☎ 02 / pop 600,000

Irbid, Jordan's second-largest city, is in actuality something of a glorified university town. Home to Yarmouk University, which is regarded as one of the most elite centres of learning in the Middle East, Irbid is in many ways more lively and progressive than stodgy Amman. The campus, which is located just south of the city centre, is home to shady pedestrian streets lined with outdoor restaurants and cafes.

The area around Irbid has yielded artefacts and graves suggesting that the area has been inhabited since the Bronze Age, and both historians and archaeologists have identified the city as the Decapolis city of Arbela. Aside from the tell lying at the centre of town, however, there is little evidence in the town of such antiquity. Nevertheless, Irbid is a good base from which to explore Umm Qais, Al-Himma and Pella, and you can certainly have a fun time down at Yarmouk if you meet the right people.

Information

Irbid has plenty of banks for changing money and most have ATMs. The police station is above the market area, and offers great views of the city. There are literally dozens of internet cafés along the southern end of University St (Shafeeq Rshaidat St) near Yarmouk University; most are open year-round.

Post office (King Hussein St; ☾ 7.30am-5pm Sat-Thu, to 1.30pm Fri)

Royal Jordanian Airlines (☎ 7243202; cnr King Hussein & Al-Jaish Sts)

Sights

There are two museums in the grounds of the vast **Yarmouk University** (www.yu.edu.jo), which opened in 1977 and now boasts over 22,000 students from across the Middle East. Visitors, both domestic and foreign, are welcome to wander around the university, and it's a good place to meet young Jordanians.

The **Museum of Archaeology & Anthropology** (☎ 7271100, ext 4260; admission free; ☾ 10am-1.45pm & 3-4.30pm Sun-Thu) is highly recommended, and features exhibits from all eras of Jordanian history arranged in chronological order. The collection starts with 9000-year-old Neolithic statuettes found near present-day Amman, continues through to the Bronze and Iron Ages and the Mamluk and Ottoman occupations, and ends with more modern displays on rural Bedouin life. One of the highlights of the museum is a remarkable reconstruction of a traditional Arab pharmacy and smithy. Also, don't forget to head out back to the Numismatic Hall, which has some fascinating displays on the history of money over the last 2600 years. All displays are labelled in English.

Jordan Natural History Museum (☎ 7271100; admission free; ☾ 8am-5pm Sun-Thu) contains a range of stuffed animals, birds and insects, as well as rocks from the region, but very little is explained in English. It's good for birders, with some beautiful bee-eaters and rollers on display. The museum is in the huge green hangar No 23.

Beit Arar (off Al-Hashemi St; admission free; ☾ 9am-5pm Sun-Thu) was set up to host cultural events and is located in a superb old Damascene-style house. The rooms are set around a courtyard paved with volcanic black stones and there are manuscripts and photo displays of Arar, one of Jordan's finest poets.

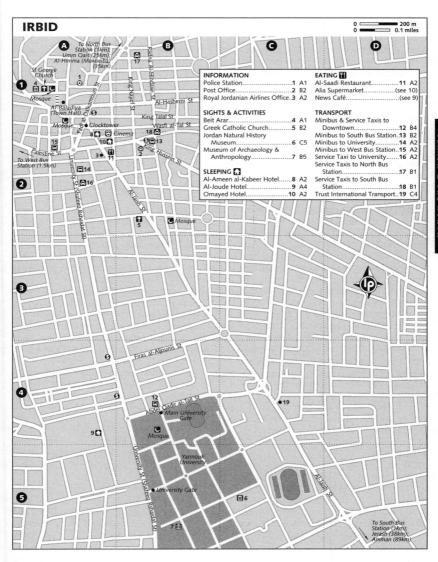

IRBID

INFORMATION			EATING 🍴		
Police Station	1	A1	Al-Saadi Restaurant	11	A2
Post Office	2	B2	Alia Supermarket	(see 10)	
Royal Jordanian Airlines Office	3	A2	News Café	(see 9)	

SIGHTS & ACTIVITIES			TRANSPORT		
Beit Arar	4	A1	Minibus & Service Taxis to		
Greek Catholic Church	5	B2	Downtown	12	B4
Jordan Natural History			Minibus to South Bus Station	13	B2
Museum	6	C5	Minibus to University	14	A2
Museum of Archaeology &			Minibus to West Bus Station	15	A2
Anthropology	7	B5	Service Taxi to University	16	A2
			Service Taxis to North Bus		
SLEEPING 🛏			Station	17	B1
Al-Ameen al-Kabeer Hotel	8	A2	Service Taxis to South Bus		
Al-Joude Hotel	9	A4	Station	18	B1
Omayed Hotel	10	A2	Trust International Transport	19	C4

JERASH & THE NORTH

Sleeping

The cheapest hotels are in the city centre in the blocks immediately north of King Hussein (Baghdad) St, while more comfortable (and expensive) lodgings are located on the fringes of the campus.

Al-Ameen al-Kabeer Hotel (☎ 7242384; Al-Jaish St; dm/s/d from D3/7/10) This is by far the best

of the downtown cheapies, mainly because the friendly management prides itself on giving personal and attentive service. Of course, this is very much a budget hotel with basic concrete rooms and shared bathrooms, though the property is well tended and there's a reliable supply of hot water. Be advised that the rooms overlooking the

JERASH & THE NORTH

street can be noisy before 9pm; also women may feel more comfortable at either of the more upmarket properties listed below.

Omayed Hotel (☎ 7245955; King Hussein St; s/d incl breakfast from JD20/25) This is a significant cut above the cheapies in terms of quality, especially since rooms at the Omayed boast satellite TV, as well as large picture windows overlooking the city. Rooms are still very basic, and they've definitely seen better decades, though the friendly staff goes out of its way to brighten up the place. Rooms towards the back of the property are a bit quieter – a good choice for light sleepers who don't want to be woken up by the sounds of the city.

our pick **Al-Joude Hotel** (☎ 7275515; off University St; s/d/tr from JD30/40/50, ste incl buffet breakfast JD75; 🗷 🖳) Located near the campus of Yarmouk University, Irbid's finest hotel proudly upholds its four-star status by offering a classy and sophisticated ambience. Primarily catering to the discerning families of visiting students, spacious rooms at al-Joude are kept spotless, and offer all of the modern amenities you'd expect at this price range. If you have the cash to burn, a suite here is a nice way to indulge in a bit of low-key luxury that might otherwise be out of your price range in more expensive destinations like Amman or Aqaba. The grounds are also home to a couple of good restaurants including the much-loved News Café (right), one of the best places in the city to sip an espresso while enjoying a bit of people-watching.

Eating

There are dozens of restaurants to suit most budgets along the southern end of University St. It's a great place in the evening when the street is crowded with young students. When we asked local university students which was their favourite place, most said, 'It will change tomorrow!' So rather than recommend a raft of particular places, we suggest that you do what the students do, and stroll along the university street until you find a place that looks sufficiently hip and trendy.

Al-Saadi Restaurant (King Hussein St; meals JD3-5; 🕑 8.30am-9.30pm) If you're staying in the downtown area, this is one of the better places for Jordanian staples including roasted lamb and chicken, felafel, humus and *fuul*.

BORDER CROSSINGS

Irbid serves as a convenient jumping-off point for travellers heading to either Syria or Israel and the Palestinian Territories. The office of **Trust International Transport** (☎ 7251878; Al-Jaish St) is your best source of up-to-date information – keep in mind that the situation changes daily (sometimes hourly) due to rising petrol prices and the ever-changing security situation along Jordan's borders. For more information, see the Getting There & Away section in the Transport chapter on p307.

Although it's a cheapie, the dining area is pleasant enough and the service is decent – perfect for a quick and informal meal.

our pick **News Café** (off University St; pizza JD2.500) Downstairs from the Al-Joude Hotel, this is one of the most popular gathering places for Irbid's cool set. Styled along the lines of a Western-style coffee shop, the News Café is warm and inviting, offering coffee, milkshakes, pizza and other snacks. True to its Middle Eastern roots, however, you can also indulge in the obligatory hookah here, which is a great way to lose an afternoon or evening to smoke-induced bliss.

Self-caterers and would-be picnickers should head to the **Alia Supermarket** (King Hussein St) near the Omayed Hotel, which has a good selection of local produce, including the region's justifiably famous olives.

Getting There & Away

Irbid, located approximately 85km north of Amman, is home to three main minibus/taxi stations.

From the North bus station, there are minibuses to Umm Qais (45 minutes), Mukheiba (for Al-Himma; one hour) and Quwayliba (for the ruins of Abila; 25 minutes), all of which shouldn't set you back more than a dinar.

From the large South bus station (New Amman bus station), air-conditioned Hijazi buses (JD2, 90 minutes) leave regularly for Amman's Abdali bus station until about 7pm. To Amman (Abdali) there are also less comfortable buses and minibuses (less than JD1, about two hours) and plenty of service taxis (JD1). Minibuses also leave the South station for Ajloun (45 minutes), Jerash

(45 minutes) and the Syrian border, all for less than one dinar.

From the West bus station (*Mujamma al-Gharb al-Jadid*), about 1.5km west of the centre, minibuses go to Al-Mashari'a (45 minutes) for the ruins at Pella, Sheikh Hussein Bridge (for Israel and the Palestinian Territories; 45 minutes) and Shuneh ash-Shamaliyyeh (North Shuna; one hour) for less than a dinar.

Getting Around

Getting between Irbid's various bus stations is easy, with service taxis (200 fils) and minibuses (100 fils) shuttling between them and the centre. Service taxis and minibuses to the South bus station can be picked up on Radna al-Hindawi St, while for the North station head to Prince Nayef St. For the West station take a bus from Palestine St, just west of the roundabout.

The standard taxi fare from the centre (*al-Bilad*) to the university (*al-Jammiya*) is 500 fils; few taxis use metres in Irbid. A minibus from University St to the university gate costs 150 fils. Otherwise it's a 25-minute walk.

If you have a car, be aware that the one-way roads and lack of parking can make driving a stressful experience.

ABILA (QUWAYLIBA)   (قويلبا) أبيلا

Lying just 10km north of Irbid, between the twin hills of Tell Abila and Tell Umm-al-Amad, are the ancient remains of the Decapolis city of **Abila** (admission free; ☉ daylight hr). At first glance you'd be forgiven for thinking that this site could only be enjoyed by the committed ruin hunter or the aspiring archaeologist. Indeed, little remains of this once-great city, especially since the earthquake of AD 747 did a pretty thorough job of turning Abila into a rock-strewn field.

To date, much of the Abila remains largely unexcavated and the site certainly isn't set up for visitors. Of course, you don't need a guide to find the Roman-Byzantine **theatre** or the scattered remains of **columns** from the markets, temples and baths lying around the site.

However, if you're looking to have a real Indiana Jones experience, definitely check out the eerie **tomb caves** that are carved into the hillsides surrounding the site. Independent exploration is possible if you bring along a good torch and your sense of adventure, though picking up a local guide in the nearby village of Quwayliba will certainly enhance the experience.

At one point the caves were full of corpses, but tomb raiders stripped them clean over the millennia. However, the spectacular **frescoes** adorning the walls and ceilings are marvellously intact, and made all the more dramatic by the fact there isn't a tourist in sight.

The Abila site is close to the village of Quwayliba, about 15km north of Irbid. Buses leave from the North bus station in Irbid (less than JD1, 25 minutes) for Quwayliba; ask the driver to drop you off at the ruins.

UMM QAIS (GADARA)   أم قيس
☎ 02

And when he came to the other side, to the country of the Gadarenes, two demon-possessed met him, coming out of the tombs, so fierce that no one could pass that way. And behold, they cried out, 'What have you to do with us, O Son of God? Have you come here to torment us before the time?' Now a herd of many swine was feeding at some distance from them. And the demons begged him, 'If you cast us out, send us away into the herd of swine'. And he said to them, 'Go.' So they came out and went into the swine; and behold, the whole herd rushed down the steep bank into the sea, and perished in the waters.
Matthew 8:28–32

In the northwest corner of Jordan are the ruins of yet another Decapolis city, namely Gadara (now called Umm Qais). Although the ruins are less visually impressive than those at Jerash, they are particularly striking due to the juxtaposition of the ruined Roman city and a relatively intact yet abandoned Ottoman-era village. Furthermore, there is a good chance that you can indulge in the luxury of having the site virtually to yourself as few foreign tourists visit this remote corner of the country.

Umm Qais is also famous for its sweeping views over the Israeli-occupied Golan Heights (*Murtafa-at al-Jawlan*) as well as the Sea of Galilee (Lake Tiberias) in Israel proper. Since approximately two-thirds of Jordanians can claim Palestinian descent, Umm Qais has recently emerged as a pilgrimage site for Jordanians yearning for a glimpse of their former homeland. From the Resthouse, a popular restaurant located amid the ruins, families congregate to swap stories of the holy land. For more information on the Palestinian situation, see the boxed text, p144.

History

The ancient town of Gadara was captured from the Ptolemies by the Seleucids in 198 BC, then the Jews under Hyrcanus captured it in 100 BC. Under the Romans, the fortunes of Gadara, taken from the Jews in 63 BC, increased rapidly and building was undertaken on a typically grand scale.

Herod the Great was given Gadara following a naval victory and he ruled over it until his death in 4 BC – much to the disgruntlement of locals who tried everything to put him out of favour with Rome. On his death the city reverted to semi-autonomy as part of the Roman province of Syria.

According to the Bible, it was at Gadara that Jesus performed one of his greatest miracles: casting demons from two men into a herd of pigs. Since the first millennium, Gadara has resultantly been a Christian place of pilgrimage, though an alternative Israeli site on the eastern shore of Lake Galilee also claims this miracle.

With the downfall of the Nabataean kingdom in AD 106, Gadara continued to flourish and was the seat of a bishopric until the 7th century. By the time of the Muslim conquest, however, it was little more than a small backwater village. Throughout the Ottoman period the village was substantially rebuilt, and today much of this impressive architecture remains preserved.

In 1806 Gadara was 'discovered' by Western explorers, and the local inhabitants claim to have formed the first government in Jordan, as well as signing the first agreement with the British in 1920. However, excavation did not commence until the early 1980s, and Umm Qais has never received even a fraction of the attention (and funding) as nearby Jerash.

Today the ruins have been marvellously restored through the aid of German funding, though the future of the Ottoman village remains undecided. When excavation began, the Jordanian government paid for local residents to temporarily relocate, and later flirted with the idea of creating a tourist village centred on a luxury resort hotel.

Following strong local protests, as well as a recent downturn in Middle East tourism, much of the government's ambitious plans have been tabled. As the time of research, the Ottoman village (aside from the Resthouse) was somewhat reminiscent of a ghost town, though there are quiet rumblings that change is on the horizon.

Information

The easiest way to enter ancient **Gadara** (admission JD1) is from the western end of the car park. The site is open 24 hours and there are no ticket checks.

There are few signs in English. However the brochure about Umm Qais published by the Jordan Tourism Board is useful for guiding yourself around the site. *Umm Qais: Gadara of the Decapolis,* published by Al-Kutba (JD3), is ideal for anyone who wants further information. Guides (JD5 per 10 people) are also available at the ticket office in the car park.

There are toilets at the Umm Qais Resthouse. The tourist police are along the laneway between the museum and the resthouse.

The souvenir shop, just east of the parking area, is run by the former site curator who is a great source of informal information on the area's archaeology.

Sights

The first thing you come to from the south is the well-restored and brooding **west theatre**, which once seated about 3000 people. Like the north theatre, it was made from black basalt.

Just to the north is the **basilica terrace** complex, about 95m by 35m, with a **colonnaded courtyard** of lovely limestone, marble and basalt colours. The western section housed a row of **shops** (the shells of which remain), but the most interesting remains are of the 6th-century **church**, with an unusual octagonal interior sanctum, marked today by the remaining basalt columns. The church was destroyed by earthquakes in the 8th century.

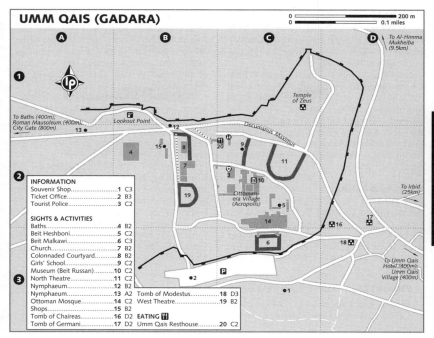

You'll soon hit the **decumanus maximus**, the main road that once linked Gadara with other nearby ancient cities such as Abila and Pella, and eventually reached the Mediterranean coast.

West along the *decumanus maximus* are the overgrown **baths**. Built in the 4th century, this was an impressive complex of fountains, statues and baths, but little remains after the various earthquakes. Almost opposite is the decrepit **nymphaeum** (the eastern of the two nymphaeums).

The *decumanus maximus* continues west for another 1km or so, leading to some ruins of limited interest, including **baths**, **mausoleums** and **gates**. Japanese and Iraqi archaeologists are currently excavating here. Most interesting is the basilica built above a **Roman mausoleum**. You can peer down into the subterranean tomb through a hole in the basilica floor. The sarcophagus of Helladis that once lay here can be seen in the Museum of Anthropology & Archaeology in Irbid.

When you find yourself flagging, head back and grab a reviving drink at the **Umm Qais Resthouse** with its stunning views over Galilee, the Golan and the snowcapped peaks of Lebanon beyond. From the resthouse, you can see the minarets of al-Himmah below and the lakeshore city of Tiberias in the distance.

From the resthouse continue on to Beit Russan, a former residence of an Ottoman governor, and now a **museum** (☎ 7500072; admission free; ⊗ 8am-5pm Oct-Apr, to 6pm May-Sep). It is set around an elegant and tranquil courtyard. The main mosaic on display (dating from the 4th century and found in one of the tombs) contains the names of early Christian notables. Another highlight is the headless white marble statue of the Hellenic goddess Tyche, which was found sitting in the front row of the west theatre. Also look out for the wonderful carved basalt door. Exhibits are labelled in English and Arabic.

Surrounding the museum are the ruins of the **Ottoman village** dating from the 18th and 19th centuries, and also known as the Acropolis. If you have the time and interest you can check out two intact houses,

Beit Malkawi (now used as an office for archaeological groups) and the nearby **Beit Heshboni**. In the southeast corner is the **Ottoman mosque**, and in the far north are the remains of the **girls' school**.

Northeast of the museum is the **north theatre**, now overgrown and without its original black basalt rocks, which were cannibalised by villagers in other constructions.

Finally, around the eastern entrance from the main road are several tombs, including the **Tomb of Germani** and the **Tomb of Modestus**. About 50m further west, the **Tomb of Chaireas** dates from AD 154.

Sleeping & Eating

Umm Qais Hotel (☎ 7500080; s/d from JD10/15) Few people choose to spend the night in Umm Qais, especially since the ruins can easily be accessed on a day trip from either Amman or Irbid. However, if you want to slow down and enjoy a bit of peace and quiet, this modest option on the main street of the modern village is a decent choice. Bright and airy rooms (some with en suites) are complemented by a friendly management, and guests can also take advantage of the small ground-floor restaurant and rooftop café.

our pick **Umm Qais Resthouse** (☎ 7500555; meals JD5-10; ☺ 10am-7pm, to 10pm Jun-Sep) A much loved Umm Qais institution, the Resthouse is located inside a converted Ottoman house that lies alongside the ruins of Gadara. Famed for its stunning views of Israel and the Palestinian Territories, this is a popular place for Palestinian families to swap news, stories and gossip while indulging in nostalgic views of the homeland. Part of the Romero group, a famed consortium of top-notch restaurants across Jordan, the Resthouse offers an impressive seasonal menu highlighting fresh produce and locally raised meats.

EMPOWERING PALESTINIAN REFUGEES   *Hassan Ansah*

Roughly two-thirds of Jordanians can claim either Palestinian descent or ancestry, a striking statistic that reflects the intimate and complex relationship between Jordan and Israel and the Palestinian Territories. Since the formation of the state of Israel in 1948, Jordan has hosted successive waves of Palestinian refugees, though viable and sustainable economic integration has proved to be a difficult task. Hassan Ansah reports here on how microfinance programs are empowering Palestinian refugees in the region.

A Grassroots Approach

The **Ibdaa Cultural Center** (www.ibdaa194.org) is a Palestinian non-governmental organisation (NGO) based out of the Dheisheh Refugee Camp in the West Bank, near the city of Bethlehem. In Arabic *ibdaa* means 'to create something out of nothing', a fitting name given that the NGO strives to empower Palestinian women and children with the necessary self-confidence and life skills to face their difficult future, while simultaneously informing the international community about the plight of Palestinian refugees.

Ibdaa began in 1994 as a cultural exchange project that sent 30 children from the Dheisheh refugee camp to Paris, where they performed folk dance and theatrical choreography in order to artistically communicate the plight of Palestinian refugees. Today Ibdaa serves over 2000 women and children per year by providing microfinance loans aimed at stimulating income-generating projects.

Ibdaa is also determined to provide an open environment in which men and women can work together to promote gender equality, human rights and social justice. Since its inception, the organisation has challenged conservative social values and norms in the camp, which has subsequently begun to transform the mindset of the larger Dheisheh community.

An Entrepreneurial Spirit

I interviewed one of Ibdaa's newest members, Ms Halima El Manar. Halima is an innovative and resourceful entrepreneur originally from the Sheikh Radwan area of Gaza City. In 1998 Halima took her first steps as businessperson when she decided to start selling secondhand clothes to women in her neighbourhood from a small room in her home. Later, as the sewing industry developed in Gaza, she began selling locally manufactured children's and women's clothing.

Getting There & Away

Umm Qais village, and the ruins 200m to the west, are about 25km northwest of Irbid, and about 110km north of Amman. Minibuses leave Irbid's North bus station (less than JD1, 45 minutes) on a regular basis. There's no direct transport from Amman.

With a car you can drive direct from Umm Qais to Pella along the Jordan Valley road, via the village of Adasiyyeh. The occasional minibus runs down this road to Shuneh ash-Shamaliyyeh but if you are relying on public transport to get to Pella you'll most likely have to backtrack to Irbid and take another minibus from there.

AL-HIMMA (MUKHEIBA)   الحمى (مخيبا)

☎ 02

In Roman and Byzantine times, the ancient hot-spring town of al-Himma was the site of Gadara's bath complex, which was famous throughout the empire for its lavish design and architecture. However, as history would have it, most of the ruins today lie across the border in the Israeli-occupied Golan Heights. While the Jordanian side may not bear testament to its former grandeur, a soak here in the hot springs remains the perfect antidote for travel-worn bones. The springs have been famous for millennia for their health-giving properties.

Today the al-Himma hot springs are located in the pleasant village of Mukheiba, which is literally a stone's throw from the Golan Heights. In contrast to the bare, steeply rising plateau of the Golan to the north, the area is subtropical, lush and surprisingly dotted with banana trees. While soaking in the springs can be a bit unpleasant during the muggy summer months, a therapeutic trip to Mukheiba is certainly worth the effort, especially if you're a borderholic looking to get up close to the Golan.

Halima is a veteran at accessing diverse microfinance programs in the region, some from small locally developed grassroots organisations, and others from larger, better known NGOs such as the UN Relief and Works Agency (UNRWA). Halima, like many other Palestinian small traders, used to travel abroad to buy popular goods that she could resell in Gaza. Because of the relative freedom and the higher standard of living of Palestinian refugees in Jordan, the country was one of her favourite places to visit.

In Jordan, Halima used to purchase desirable household items that are difficult to come by in Gaza, such as Western clothing, copper cookers, embroidered dresses and bedspreads. For 12 years her business expanded, and she was able to regularly pay back her loan in fixed instalments, earning a monthly profit of around US$400. She quickly became a role model within her community, and would always speak about the importance of paying back her loans on time to other aspiring entrepreneurs.

Closed Borders

When Hamas won the Palestinian government elections in January 2006, Israel essentially sealed off Gaza from the outside world, ceased contact with the Palestinian Authority and halted all internal tax revenue transfers. In April of the same year, international donor funding, including that from Jordan, was suspended indefinitely.

With the Gaza borders closed, Halima could no longer travel abroad to Jordan, or even to neighbouring Egypt. After selling her entire inventory of foreign goods, she resorted to selling locally manufactured goods, which brought in considerably less profit. For the first time in 12 years, Halima was unable to repay her monthly loan instalments on time, due to circumstances completely beyond her control.

However, thanks to the extraordinary generosity of Ibdaa, Halima has not only been granted access to Jordanian goods but has also found a new source of microfinance loans. 'I've been working as a trader for 30 years,' says Halima. 'Because of Ibdaa, I can continue to pursue the only livelihood that I know.'

Hassan Ansah is a freelance writer and journalist who has taught at the Western International University in Phoenix, Arizona and at the American University of Cairo (AUC).

Activities

The village's public **baths** (☎ 7500505; admission JD1; ☉ 8am-8pm) consist of three indoor hot pools and one natural outdoor hot pool. There are separate bathing times for men and women, which alternate every two hours. At the time of research, men ruled the roost from 10am to noon, 2pm to 4pm and 6pm to 8pm, with women welcome at other times. The baths are on the right as you enter the village – don't forget to bring modest and appropriate bathing costumes (best to leave the Speedos and bikinis at home!). Note that the place is overrun with local tourists (mostly young men) on Friday, and you may find accommodation full on Thursday and Friday nights.

For the past few years, there have been rumours flying around that a foreign company was interested in upgrading the facilities, and offering a complete Dead Sea–style spa experience. While there is little evidence that these lofty plans are anywhere near close to materialising, there is a chance that al-Himma could get a drastic makeover in the years to come.

Sleeping & Eating

Sah al-Noum Hotel (☎ 7500510; d/tr from JD5/10) The Sah al-Noum is probably your best bet if you want to spend the night in town and maximise your soaking time. Barebones rooms have squat toilets and fans, though they're well ventilated, and you certainly don't have to worry about blowing your budget. The grounds are also home to a shady restaurant and a private bathing area out the back. The hotel is signposted at the fork in the road near the public baths.

Chalets (☎ 7500505; d/tr from JD10/15, family apt JD25-35; ☷) Part of the hot-springs complex, these basic chalets overlook the public baths, though they are rundown and not very inspiring. However, if you're travelling in a large group, the family apartments are a significant step up in quality. Each apartment is equipped with en suite, satellite TV and air-con, and there are cosy private porches where you can unwind and take in the surrounding views.

Al-Hameh Restaurant (☎ 7500512; meals JD1-5; ☉ 9am-8pm) The town's only real formal restaurant, al-Hameh is centred on a bright and airy terrace overlooking the baths, and

serves your standard offering of Jordanian staples. However, the nicest part of the restaurant is the cold beer in the fridge, which goes down really smoothly after a soak in the hot springs.

Getting There & Away

Mukheiba is 10km north of Umm Qais, down the hill towards the Golan via a very scenic road. There are reasonably regular minibuses (less than JD1, 15 minutes) between Mukheiba and Umm Qais on most days, with plenty on Friday. Direct minibuses from Irbid's North station (less than JD1, one hour) also pass along the main street of Umm Qais.

Make sure you bring your passport as there's a military checkpoint just past the turn-off to the Umm Qais ruins. This is also a good place to hitch a ride.

PELLA (TAQABAT FAHL)   بيلا
☎ 02

In the midst of the Jordan Valley are the ruins of the ancient city of Pella (Taqabat Fahl), one of the 10 cities of the fabled Roman Decapolis. Although not as spectacular as Jerash, Pella is far more important to archaeologists as it has revealed evidence of over 6000 years of continuous settlement. In fact, it's regarded as the most historically significant site in the whole of Jordan. Centred on a large tell (hill), and surrounded by fertile valleys that together comprise a rich watershed, Pella has fostered human civilisation from the Stone Age through to the medieval Islamic period.

Many of the ruins are spread out and in need of excavation, so some walking and imagination are required to get the most from the site. Unlike Jerash, which overwhelms visitors with its monumental glory and exacting precision, Pella requires a bit of imagination to visualise the city at the height of its greatness. With that said, the natural setting is superb and there are some fine views over the Jordan Valley.

The **site** (admission free) is officially open from 8am to 6pm, but if the main entrance is closed you can enter via the Pella Rest House on the hill.

Anyone with a specific interest should buy *Pella* (JD3), which is published by Al-Kutba and available in major bookshops around Jordan.

History

Pella was inhabited as early as a million years ago by groups of early human hunters and gathers, who followed herds of game animals through the Stone Age forests and savannahs. By 5000 BC, however, there is evidence of permanent Neolithic farming villages around the tell. In fact, the significance of Pella was known to the Egyptians, who referred to the site in written texts in the 2nd millennium BC.

Prior to the rise of the Greeks, Pella throve due to its strategic position on the trade routes running between Arabia, Syria, Egypt and the Mediterranean. According to artefacts uncovered by archaeologists, Pella was a prosperous settlement throughout the Bronze and Iron Ages. Luxury items including ivory sculpture and gold jewellery have all been excavated from the site.

However, the city wasn't truly a city until the Greek period, which is the first time that the name Pella is attributed to the site. In 218 BC, King Antiochus captured Pella as part of his expansionist campaign through the Levant. After being annexed to the Seleucid Empire, Pella was completely Hellenised and named after the birthplace of Alexander the Great.

At the behest of the Hasmonean leader Alexander Jannaeus, the Jews largely destroyed Pella in 83 BC because the inhabitants were not inclined to adopt the customs of their conquerors. Twenty years later, the legions of Roman Emperor Pompey swept into the Levant and rebuilt Pella, along with neighbouring cities in the Decapolis.

Life under the Romans was embraced in Pella and the city enjoyed an era of political and economic stability, and a rich cultural life. As evidenced by archaeological finds, Pella also enjoyed a remarkable degree of autonomy, and even had the power to mint its own coins.

It was to Pella that Christians fled persecution from the Roman army in Jerusalem in AD 66. Although they later returned to Jerusalem, they left a strong mark on Pella, which helped to ease the city's adoption of Christianity a few centuries later.

Pella reached its peak during the Byzantine era, and by the year 451 the city was influential enough to warrant its own bishop. The population at this time may have been as high as 25,000, and there is evidence that Pella was part of a massive trade route that encompassed most of Asia Minor as well as North Africa.

The defeat of the Byzantines in the Levant by the invading Islamic army in 635 was quickly followed by the knockout blow at the Battle of Yarmouk (near modern Mukheiba) the following year. As a result, the city quickly fell into decline.

Pella survived under the Umayyads, though the city was virtually destroyed by the massive earthquake that shook the whole region in 747. However, Pella has always endured, and archaeological finds show that even after the earthquake, the city remained inhabited on a modest scale by subsistence farmers.

The last occupiers of Pella were the Mamluks, who set up shop during the 13th and 14th centuries. While Pella enjoyed a brief renaissance, the defeat of the Mamluks by the Ottomans caused the residents of Pella to flee, ending more than 600 years of continuous settlement. Today the ruins of Pella lie a few kilometres away from the modern Arab village of Taqabat Fahl.

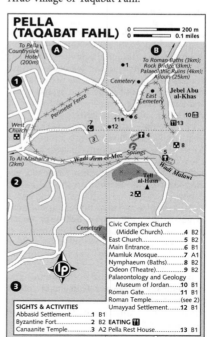

PELLA (TAQABAT FAHL)

0 — 200 m
0 — 0.1 miles

SIGHTS & ACTIVITIES
Abbasid Settlement..............1 B1
Byzantine Fort.....................2 B2
Canaanite Temple.............3 A2
Civic Complex Church (Middle Church)...........4 B2
East Church.....................5 B2
Main Entrance..................6 B1
Mamluk Mosque...........7 A1
Nymphaeum (Baths)........8 B2
Odeon (Theatre)............9 B2
Palaeontology and Geology Museum of Jordan....10 B1
Roman Gate....................11 B1
Roman Temple............(see 2)
Umayyad Settlement.......12 B1

EATING
Pella Rest House..............13 B1

Sights

THE RUINS

At the base of the main mound (on your right as you pass through the main entrance) are the limited remains of a **Roman gate** to the city. Atop the hill are the ruins of an **Umayyad settlement**, which consisted of shops, residences and storehouses. The small, square **Mamluk mosque** to the west dates from the 14th century. Carved into the south side of the hill is the recently excavated **Canaanite temple**, which was constructed in around 1270 BC, and dedicated to the Canaanite god Baal.

The main structure, and indeed one of the better preserved of the ruins at Pella, is the Byzantine **civic complex church** (or **middle church**), which was built atop an earlier Roman civic complex in the 5th century AD, and modified several times in the subsequent two centuries. Adjacent is the **odeon** (a small theatre used for musical performances). It once held 400 spectators, but you will need considerable imagination to picture this now. East of the civic complex church are the low-lying remains of a Roman **nymphaeum**.

Up the hill to the southeast is the 5th-century **east church**, which has a lovely setting perched high above the lower city. From there a trail leads down into Wadi Malawi and then climbs **Tell al-Husn** (note the remains of tombs cut into the hillside), atop which are the stones of a **Byzantine fort** and **Roman temple**. There are good views of the Jordan Valley from here.

Outside the main site, there are the ruins of a small **Abbasid settlement** about 200m north of the main entrance. There are also a few limited **Palaeolithic ruins** (4km), **Roman baths** and a **rock bridge** (3km) reached via the road past the turn-off to the Pella Rest House.

Also inquire at the rest house about how to get to the rubble of a **Hellenistic temple** high on Jebel Sartaba to the southeast. From there, Jerusalem is visible on a clear day – figure on a couple of hours for the return hike.

Behind the rest house is the brand new **Palaeontology & Geology Museum of Jordan** (☎ 65695134; www.pellamuseum.org; 9am-5pm), which is the brainchild of famous Jordanian architect Ammar Khammash. While archaeology has certainly brought Jordan's ancient past to life, the concept behind the museum was to focus instead on the natural history of Jordan. Displays depict Jordan's unique palaeontological and geological record, which provide fascinating insight into this truly prehistoric land.

Sleeping & Eating

our pick **Pella Countryside Hotel** (☎ 079-5574145; s/d from JD25/30) The manager of the famous Pella Rest House also runs this charmer of a B&B from the back of his house, which has a lovely family feel and splendid views out towards the ruins. The seven comfortable rooms are well kept, with private en suites, hot showers and plenty of country-style flourishes. It's a good place to kick back for a few days; the family can arrange picnics in the surrounding hills. From February to May, black irises, the national flower of Jordan, bloom in the owner's garden. The hotel is well signposted on the road to the site.

Pella Rest House (☎ 079-5574145; meals JD4-8; noon-7pm) This famous restaurant is renowned for its exceptional views over Pella and the Jordan Valley – Israel and the Palestinian Territories is visible to the right of the communications towers, the West Bank is to the left, and the Jenin Heights and Nablus are in the middle. Of course, you shouldn't let the views distract you too much from the enticing menu, which highlights regional cuisine – fresh St Peter's fish from the Jordan River is about as local as it gets.

Getting There & Away

From Irbid's West bus station, minibuses go to Al-Mashari'a (less than JD1, 45 minutes), though be sure to get off before Al-Mashari'a at the junction. Pella is a steep 2km walk up from the signposted turn-off, but you should be able to find a seat in a minibus up to town or the rest house for a few hundred fils. With that said, check the price first as many of these unlicensed drivers are sharks. Note that there is no direct transport from Amman.

With your own car, the ruins are an easy day trip from Amman, or from nearby Irbid of Jerash. You can also take the scenic back roads to Ajloun (25km), but it's best to get good directions from the rest house before setting off – this route gets tricky to follow in parts.

The Desert Castles
القصور الصحراوية

A string of ruined pavilions, caravanserais (merchants' inns), hunting lodges and forts – known collectively (if a little erroneously) as the desert castles – peppers the deserts of eastern Jordan, and is one of the country's most surreal attractions. Dating back to the Damascus-based Umayyads (AD 661–750) in the earliest years of Islam, the desert castles were once richly decorated with mosaics, frescoes, marble, plaster and painted stucco, providing oases of pleasure in the harsh and inhospitable desert. Here, the elite could pursue their pastimes of hawking, hunting and horse racing during the day, while evenings were spent in wild festivities with plenty of wine, women, poetry and song.

The early Arab rulers were still Bedouin at heart, and their love of the desert may have led them to build these pleasure palaces, which once teemed with orchards and wild game. Historians have also suggested that the rulers may have come to avoid epidemics in the big cities, or to maintain links with, and power over, the Bedouin – the bedrock of their support in the conquered lands. The desert castles also served as staging posts for pilgrimages to Mecca, and along trade routes to Syria, Arabia and Iraq – never underestimate the luxury of a hot bath in the desert!

Today, the desert castles represent the furthest fringes of tourism of Jordan, especially since public transport in this unforgiving wilderness is virtually non-existent. However, if you're keen to rent a sturdy vehicle, and you have some confidence in your navigation skills, Jordan's eastern deserts are ripe for independent exploration.

THE DESERT CASTLES

HIGHLIGHTS

- Clamber through the brooding basalt ruins of **Umm al-Jimal** (p151), an ancient town of shimmering black stone
- Admire the risqué frescoes in the bathhouse of **Qusayr Amra** (p161), a Unesco World Heritage site
- Explore the desert castle of **Qasr al-Azraq** (p159), the former headquarters of the enigmatic Lawrence of Arabia
- Wander the maze-like corridors of **Qasr Kharana** (p163), a mighty fortress in the lonely desert
- Spot the endangered Arabian oryx at the **Shaumari Wildlife Reserve** (p156), a vital ecotourism venture

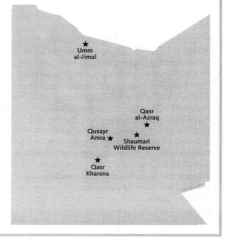

★ Umm al-Jimal

Qasr al-Azraq ★

Qusayr Amra ★

★ Shaumari Wildlife Reserve

★ Qasr Kharana

THE EASTERN DESERT

شرقي الأردن

To the east of Amman, the suburbs gradually peter out, replaced by the *Badia* – a stony, black basalt desert that stretches to Iraq and Saudi Arabia. The desolate region has long been criss-crossed by pilgrimage and trade routes to Mecca and Baghdad, though today it's the Trans-Arabia Pipeline and the increasingly strategic Hwy 10 to Iraq that cut across the region. If not for the pipeline and the highway, eastern Jordan would probably be left to the Bedouin and their goats.

Out here in the middle of nowhere, you are very quickly reminded that Jordan's harsh deserts make up 80% of the country's land, yet support only 5% of its population.

ZARQA

الزرقاء

☎ 09 / pop 750,000

The third-largest city in Jordan after Amman and Irbid, Zarqa is now virtually part of the continuous urban sprawl of northern Amman. There's not much to this gritty working-class city that merits anything more than a passing glance, but you may need to change buses here if you're heading east on public transport.

Zarqa is currently most (in)famous for being the home town of Jordanian terrorist Abu Musab al-Zarqawi, thought to be behind many of the kidnappings and bombings in neighbouring Iraq. Zarqawi spent six years in jail in Jordan during the 1990s before being released in an amnesty.

In Zarqa, there are two terminals for buses, minibuses and service taxis. Transport to/from both Raghadan and Abdali bus stations in Amman (around JD1, 30 minutes) use the New (Amman) station.

THE DESERT CASTLES

EXPLORING THE DESERT CASTLES

The desert castles are scattered among the gravel plains of the Eastern Desert, a region with an immense size and scope that occasionally deter independent travellers. However, it's far easier to plan a trip here than you'd imagine, especially if you stick to some of the more accessible castles. The desert castles that most visitors see are **Qasr al-Hallabat** (p158), **Qasr al-Azraq** (p159), **Qusayr Amra** (p161) and **Qasr Kharana** (p163) – starting and ending in Amman, you will need a day to visit all four. If you start early in the morning, it may also be possible to visit the **Shaumari Wildlife Reserve** (p156) and/or **Umm al-Jimal** (opposite).

It is also feasible to visit the four main castles in a single day using a combination of minibuses and hitching, though only the castles at Hallabat and Azraq are directly accessible by public transport. You could also base yourself in the town of **Azraq** (p153) and use public transport, hitch or charter a vehicle from there. However, travelling around in a rental car or on an organised tour is a much better option.

If you have a rental car, consider keeping it for an extra day or two for a jaunt around the castles and reserves. From Amman, head east of Raghadan bus station towards **Zarqa** (above), and follow the signs to the individual castles. A 2WD is sufficient for visiting the four main castles. However, you will need a 4WD if you plan to leave the highway and visit some of the more remote castles.

Jumping on an organised tour of the desert castles from Amman also makes a lot of sense, and is one of the few times when an independent traveller on a tight budget will find it worthwhile to bite the bullet and pay for a tour. Tours can be arranged at the Palace, Farah, Mansour and Cliff hotels in Amman (see p105), which charge about JD15 to JD20 per person for a full-day trip. You're unlikely to get a better deal by negotiating directly with the driver of a service taxi or private taxi in Amman, and regular taxi drivers may not speak English or know the way.

If you want to slow down and develop a greater appreciation for the beauty and isolation of the region, there are a handful of attractive accommodation options in Azraq. The other advantage of staying in town is that you could spend more time at the nearby Azraq Wetland Reserve and the Shaumari Wildlife Reserve, which both offer rare chances to spot some impressive desert wildlife including the oryx and wild ass, both reintroduced from the brink of extinction.

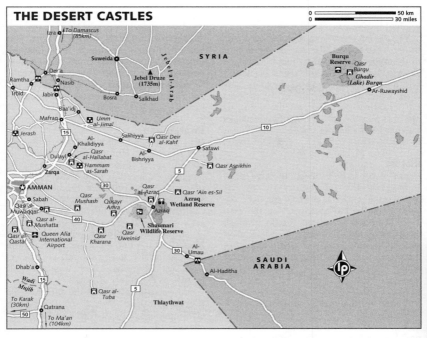

THE DESERT CASTLES

From the Old station in Zarqa, there is public transport to smaller villages in the region, such as Hallabat (for Qasr al-Hallabat and Hammam as-Sarah), Mafraq and Azraq. Minibuses shuttle between the two terminals in Zarqa every few minutes.

MAFRAQ   المفرق

☎ 04 / pop 35,000

Mafraq is much smaller than Zarqa, which means that there is even less to see in this dusty and congested frontier town. However, like Zarqa, you may have to change buses here if you're heading east on public transport.

Mafraq has two terminals for buses, minibuses and service taxis. The larger Bedouin station has minibuses and service taxis to Abdali and Raghadan bus stations in Amman (around JD1, one hour) as well as to Zarqa, Umm al-Jimal, Deir al-Kahf (for Qasr Deir al-Kahf) and Ar-Ruwayshid (for Qasr Burqu). From the Fellahin station, buses, minibuses and service taxis go to places in northern Jordan, such as Jerash, Irbid and the Syrian border.

UMM AL-JIMAL   أم الجمال

Comparatively little is known about the ruined city of **Umm al-Jimal** (Mother of Camels; admission free; ☯ daylight hr), which has been referred to by archaeologists as the 'Black Gem of the Desert'. An extensive rural settlement in the lava lands east of Mafraq, Umm al-Jimal is located on the edge of a series of volcanic basalt flows that slope down from the Jebel Druze. Despite its remote location, this chosen site was ideal as it provided ancient labourers with high-quality building materials and a steady supply of clean drinking water.

Umm al-Jimal lacks the elaborate temples, colonnaded streets and grand amphitheatres found at Jerash, and much of what remains is unpretentious urban architecture. However, over 150 buildings standing one to three stories above ground remain, including 128 houses and 15 churches. Together, these buildings provide a fascinating insight into rural life during the Roman, Byzantine and early Islamic periods. Compared to other archaeological sites in the region, Umm al-Jimal was rarely looted or vandalised, which has left much of the original layout intact.

The famed American archaeologist HC Butler once wrote: 'Far out in the desert, in the midst of the rolling plain, there is a deserted city all of basalt, rising black and forbidding from the grey of the plain.' Indeed, Umm al-Jimal is one of the region's most captivating sites, and the opportunity to scramble across huge basalt blocks warmed by the heat of the desert sun is not to be missed.

History

Umm al-Jimal is believed to have been founded in the 1st century BC by the Nabataeans, and was notable for the 'corbelling' method of constructing inverted V-shaped roofs from large bricks of black basalt. Soon after its founding, it was taken over by the Romans, who used it as part of their defensive cordon against the desert tribes. Queen Zenobia of Palmyra's rebellion against Rome highlighted the need to have a fortified frontier, which contributed to Umm al-Jimal's early growth as a garrisoned town.

As the centuries passed, the town prospered as an important trading station for Bedouin and passing caravans. From Umm al-Jimal, roads led north to Bosra (in present-day Syria) and southwest to Philadelphia (modern Amman), which firmly established the town on most of the region's major trade routes.

The city grew even further during the Byzantine period when churches were constructed and Roman buildings were demilitarised. At the peak of growth, this thriving agricultural city boasted some 3000 inhabitants. According to archaeologists, the key to Umm al-Jimal's prosperity lay in its sophisticated method of storing water, which was a necessity for surviving the long periods between rainfall, and for irrigating staple crops. Even today, many of the ancient town's reservoirs are still virtually intact.

As history would have it, Umm al-Jimal declined soon after the invasion by the Sassanians from Persia in the early 7th century AD, which also happened to coincide with a deadly outbreak of the bubonic plague. The city's death knell was later sounded by an earthquake in 747, which forced the surviving inhabitants to flee the city and take up residence elsewhere.

Prior to the 1920s, Umm al-Jimal was virtually abandoned, though the ruins were quickly occupied by Druze refugees fleeing persecution in Syria. In the subsequent years, a small modern town sprung up around the ruins, which was occasionally used as a military outpost by French soldiers.

Information

It's a good idea to allow at least an hour or two to explore Umm al-Jimal, though its enormous size (800m by 500m) does invite lengthier exploration. One of the highlights of a visit to the ruins is scrambling across the shimmering black rocks, which radiate a surprising amount of warmth. With that said, it's best to visit early in the morning, or late in the afternoon, when the black basalt isn't too hot. Note that there is little shade at the site, so you should take precautions against sunburn and sunstroke, and be sure to drink lots of water.

For more details about the site, look for the hard-to-find booklet *Umm el-Jimal* (JD3), published by Al-Kutba and available sporadically at bookshops in Amman.

Sights

The large structure just past the southern entrance is the **barracks**, built by the Romans. The towers were added later and, like the castle at Azraq, it has a swinging basalt door that still functions. The **barracks chapel** was added to the east of the barracks during the Byzantine period (around the 5th century), and is inscribed with the names of the archangels Gabriel, Raphael, Michael and Uriel.

About 150m to the left (west) of the barracks is what some archaeologists believe is a **Nabataean temple** because of the altar in the middle. About 100m north of the barracks is the **Numerianos church**, one of several ruined Byzantine churches. Another 100m to the northeast is the **double church**, recognisable by its two semicircular naves, a wonderful structure that was renovated and extended several times over the centuries. About 80m to the right (east) is **house XVII**, whose double-door entrance, interior courtyard, fine corbelled ceilings, decorated doorways and carved pillars indicate that it was built by a wealthy family.

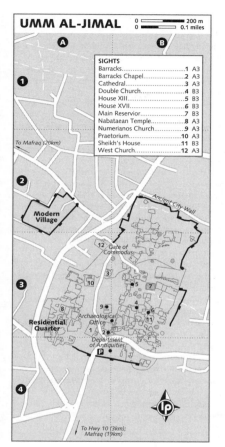

UMM AL-JIMAL

0 —————— 200 m
0 —————— 0.1 miles

SIGHTS

Barracks	1	A3
Barracks Chapel	2	A3
Cathedral	3	A3
Double Church	4	B3
House XIII	5	B3
House XVII	6	B3
Main Reservoir	7	B3
Nabataean Temple	8	A3
Numerianos Church	9	A3
Praetorium	10	A3
Sheikh's House	11	B3
West Church	12	A3

To Mafraq (20km)

Modern Village

Ancient City Wall

Gate of Commodus

Residential Quarter

Archaeological Office

Department of Antiquities

To Hwy 10 (3km); Mafraq (19km)

ventilation screen, which was used to separate the manger from the living space.

To the west (about 100m) is the **cathedral**, built in about AD 556, but now mostly in ruins – look for the lintel stone detailing the Roman emperors that ruled over the region. The **praetorium** (military headquarters) is less than 100m to the southwest. Built in the late 2nd century AD by the Romans, it was extended by the Byzantines, and features a triple doorway. About 200m to the north, through one of the old city gates, is the **west church**, easily identifiable with its four arches and ornate Byzantine crosses.

Getting There & Away

Umm al-Jimal is only 10km from the Syrian border, and about 20km east of Mafraq. With an early start, it is possible to do a day trip from Amman by public transport. From the Abdali or Raghadan bus stations in Amman, catch a bus or minibus to Bedouin station in Mafraq (possibly with a connection in Zarqa), and from Mafraq catch another minibus to Umm al-Jimal.

If you're driving, head east of Mafraq along Hwy 10 for 16km towards Safawi, then take the signed turn-off north for 3km to Umm al-Jimal. If you have chartered a taxi from Amman for a day trip around the desert castles, it is possible to include Umm al-Jimal on the itinerary for a little extra (about JD5 to JD10) – but start early to fit it all in.

AZRAQ   الأزرق
☎ 05 / pop 8000

Meaning 'blue' in Arabic, the former oasis of Azraq was once an important crossroads of trade routes from Baghdad to Jerusalem, as well as a strategic stop on the pilgrimage route to Mecca. Prior to its environmental collapse in the 1990s (see the boxed text, p154), Azraq was the region's most important permanent source of water, and had been fiercely guarded from the Palaeolithic period through to the Middle Ages. In WWI, TE Lawrence launched his attack against the Turks in Damascus from Azraq, while Druze, Chechens, Palestinians and Syrians settled here in more recent years.

Today, Azraq very much remains a crossroads, though the belching camels have been all but replaced by belching trucks. Approximately 100km east of Amman, Azraq forms a junction of roads heading northeast

A few metres to the south is the **sheikh's house**, notable for its expansive courtyard, stables and stairways. Look for the gravity-defying stairs to the north and the precarious corner tower. You can just make out a double stairway to the east of the courtyard. After exiting the building you get a good view of the lovely arched window and vaulted semicircular basement in the exterior eastern wall.

About 150m north of the double church, steps lead down to the **main reservoir**, one of several around the city. Less than 100m to the left (southwest) is **house XIII**, originally a stable for domestic goats and sheep, and later renovated and used as a residence by Druze settlers. Here, take notice of the stone

THE DESERT CASTLES

WHAT HAPPENED TO THE OASIS?

The **Azraq Oasis** and surrounding wetlands originally fanned out over 12,710 sq km (an area larger than Lebanon), and was once regarded as the most important source of water in the region. Excavations indicate that it was home to communities as early as 200,000 years ago, and once supported roaming herds of animals including elephants, cheetahs, lions and hippos. Sadly, the Azraq Oasis is regarded today as a total ecological disaster.

Extraction of water from the wetlands to the developing cities of Amman and Irbid started in 1963, though in the early years there was little evidence that the water levels were dropping. However, all of this changed in 1967 when hundreds of thousands of Palestinian refugees fled to Jordan after the conclusion of the Six Day War. The country was not able to provide clean water for its swollen population, and the oasis was tapped in desperation. By 1975, Azraq was supplying as much as one quarter of Amman's water.

The major unforeseen problem was that much of the water at Azraq was 'fossil water' – around 10,000 years old – which meant that it was being replaced less than half as quickly as it was being pumped out. Experts estimated that 3000 cu metres of water filled the wetlands every year about 40 years ago; this figure plummeted to a catastrophic 10 cu metres per year in 1980. Even worse was the fact that three years prior, the Jordanian government signed an international wetlands-protection treaty that led to the establishment of the **Azraq Wetland Reserve** (p156). At the same time, Azraq's reputation as a thriving agricultural centre was spreading, which led to many Jordanians settling in the area, and sinking private (and illegal) wells.

A generation ago, Azraq was home to a vast oasis; by 1991 the water table had dropped to over 10m below the ground, and the wetlands had dried up completely. Salt was added to the wound, quite literally, when over-pumping destroyed the natural balance between the freshwater aquifer and the underground brine. As a direct result, salt water seeped into the wetlands, making the now brackish water unpalatable for wildlife, and hopeless for drinking and irrigation.

The effect on wildlife has been devastating. The oasis was once a staging post for migratory birds en route from Europe to sub-Saharan Africa, but a simple statistic tells the tale: on 2 February 1967 there were 347,000 birds present in the wetlands; on 2 February 2000, there were 1200 birds. The wetlands were also home to a species of killifish (*Aphanius sirhani*), a small fish of only 4cm to 5cm in length and found nowhere in the world outside Azraq. Believed extinct in the late 1990s, a few somehow survived and the **Royal Society for the Conservation of Nature** (RSCN; www.rscn.org.jo) is trying to ensure the killifish population is again able to grow.

Fortunately, there is hope that this once great oasis can be restored to its former glory. Since 1994, serious funding and a commitment from the UN Development Program (UNDP), Jordanian government and RSCN have successfully halted the pumping of water from the wetlands to urban centres. A new pipeline between Diseh (near Wadi Rum) and Amman, which was constructed through a generous Libyan aid package, has also helped ease Amman's insatiable thirst for clean drinking water.

Around 1.5 million cu metres of fresh water is now being pumped back into the wetlands every year by the Jordanian Ministry of Water, an ongoing process aimed at restoring about 10% of the wetlands to their former state. If estimates by scientists are correct, this restoration of wetland habitat will also help decrease ground salinity, which would facilitate the return of wildlife again to the region. However, a major hurdle are the estimated 500 illegal deep wells that still operate in the area.

to Iraq and southeast to Saudi Arabia. The town itself is fairly unattractive, but it is home to Qasr al-Azraq (p159), an iconic desert castle, as well as the region's best (and only) accommodation options. Azraq also serves as a jumping-off point for the nearby Shaumari Wildlife Reserve (p156) and Azraq Wetland Reserve (p156).

The town is divided into two settlements located north and south of the T-intersection of Hwy 5 from Safawi and Hwy 30 from Amman. South Azraq is basically a glorified truck stop, with a strip of restaurants and mechanics. North Azraq isn't much different, though it has a bit more dignity due to the presence of Qsar al-Azraq.

History

Since the start of the new millennium, archaeological excavations in the Azraq area have revealed assemblages of both Palaeolithic and Neolithic sites containing stone tools and simple cooking pits. However, early populations on the shores on the oasis were anything but primitive, with evidence that Azraq was an ancient processing centre for malachite.

The next major occupation of Azraq was by the Romans, who built a large fort on the present-day site of Qasr al-Azraq. This site was later occupied by the Byzantines and then the Umayyads, though its present form was largely the result of the Damascus-based Ayyubids, who fortified the site in 1237 as a defence against the Crusaders. Azraq was later occupied by Mamluks and then the Ottomans, though the height of its glory came during the winter of 1917–18 when it served as a staging area for Lawrence of Arabia and his Arab army.

Azraq ash-Shomali (North Azraq) began to take shape after WWI when Druze refugees fleeing French-controlled Syria began to settle the area. During its early years, the Druze community garnered huge profits by distributing locally produced salt throughout Jordan and Iraq, though this industry collapsed following the establishment of the much larger Safi salt works near the Dead Sea.

Azraq al-Janubi (South Azraq) was founded shortly after the arrival of the Druze, though this community was spearheaded by Chechens fleeing Russian persecution. Since the Chechens had made their living in Russia as farmers and fishermen, the majority chose to eke out a living by doing the same on the shores of the oasis.

Starting in the 1950s, the racial lines separating these two communities were slowly eliminated by successive waves of Palestinian and Syrian immigrants, while the eventual death of the oasis caused much of the local population to seek subsistence elsewhere. Today, Azraq clings to life as a mere transport hub, though there is hope that increased tourism in the region may inject a measure of life back into the town.

Sleeping

The majority of tourists striking out to visit the desert castles do so on a day trip from Amman. However, spending a night in Azraq, the region's only real accommodation centre, allows you the luxury of slowing down and savouring the beauty of the Eastern Desert. Having a base in Azraq also makes it feasible to strike out on a 4WD expedition to some of the more far-flung desert castles.

Zoubi Hotel (☎ 3835012; r from JD10) Apart from several less-than-inviting truck stops, this is the only real budget accommodation in town. However, the rooms on offer at this modest, family-run hotel are comfortable, with clean bathrooms and charming old-fashioned furniture. The Zoubi is located behind the Refa'i Restaurant in South Azraq, about 800m south of the T-intersection.

Al-Azraq Resthouse (☎ 3834006; s/d/tr with breakfast from JD30/35/50; 🔀 🏊) This semi-luxurious resort, which is a definite step up in quality from the Zoubi, is comprised of spacious chalets equipped with satellite TV and aircon. The highlight of the property is the pleasantly landscaped swimming pool – a godsend in the midst of the desert, assuming you don't ask where the water comes from! The turn-off is located about 2km north of the T-intersection, from where it's a further 1.5km to the Resthouse.

our pick Azraq Lodge (☎ 3835017; s/d with breakfast from JD48/60; 🔀) This former British military hospital in south Azraq has recently been renovated by the Royal Society for the Conservation of Nature (RSCN) as a base from which to explore the Eastern Desert. It's a nostalgic lodge with a 1940s colonial feel – the RSCN has done an exemplary job of preserving the historic building while incorporating modern amenities and furnishings. The lodge is run by a delightful family of Chechen descent, who serve up their traditional cuisine in the on-site restaurant (meals JD5 to JD10). Although tourism in the Eastern Desert is still in its infancy, the RSCN is hoping that the Azraq Lodge will emerge as the preferred base for travellers visiting the desert castles as well as nearby Shaumari Wildlife Reserve and Azraq Wetland Reserve. The lodge is also home to a small **handicraft workshop** (☎ 3835017; ⏱ 9am-5pm) where women from the local community sell silk screens, ostrich-egg carvings and traditional textiles.

Eating

A bunch of local restaurants serving modest fare lines the 1km stretch of road south of the T-intersection, rich with the aroma of grilled mutton and diesel. High-quality meals aimed at visiting tourists are also available at the Al-Azraq Resthouse and the Azraq Lodge.

Azraq Palace Restaurant (☎ 079 5030356; buffet JD8, plates JD2-5; ☺ noon-4pm & 6-11pm) This is the best place to eat in town, which is why you're likely to share the restaurant with busloads of tourists taking a break from their desert-castle excursion. The lunch buffet will fill your stomach to the brim, and the cold beer on offer will make your parched throat a distant memory.

Getting There & Away

Minibuses run up and down the road along northern and southern Azraq in search of passengers before hitting the highway to Zarqa (less than JD1, 1½ hours). If you're driving, Azraq is a long and straight shot along Route 30 from Zarqa. Although the temptation is to put the pedal to the metal out here, be advised that if you're not careful, shifting sands beneath your tyres can end your travels quicker than you'd like.

AZRAQ WETLAND RESERVE   محمية واحة الأزرق

For several millennia, the Qa'al Azraq (Azraq Basin) comprised a huge area of mudflats, pools and marshlands, which lead to the establishment of Azraq as one of the most important oasis towns in the Levant. Although the basin was declared an 'internationally important wetland' by the Jordanian government in 1977, this largely token gesture couldn't stop the horrific environmental destruction that was being wrought on the area. In an effort to provide fresh drinking water to the burgeoning cities of Amman and Irbid, the wetlands suffered appalling ecological damage in a remarkably short time, and were virtually bone dry by 1991. For more information on the history of this ecological disaster, see p154.

In recent years, the RSCN has seized control of the wetlands, and established a small **nature reserve** (☎ 3835017; admission JD2; ☺ 9am-sunset) to help facilitate the recovery of the wetlands. Sadly, until more water is pumped in to attract larger and more stable bird populations, the wetlands are a meagre reflection of their past glory. However, an environmental recovery project of this magnitude is certainly worth your support, and the on-site visitor centre has well-documented (if somewhat tragic) exhibits detailing the history of the basin's demise.

Information

An attractive visitor centre run by the RSCN marks the entrance to the reserve. It contains an informative interpretation room and an education room (to raise awareness of the wetlands plight and for the training of guides) as well as a gift shop selling local crafts and artwork.

Sights & Activities

The RSCN estimates that about 300 species of resident and migratory birds still use the wetlands during their winter migration from Europe to Africa. They include raptors, larks, warblers, finches, harriers, eagles, plovers and ducks. A few buffaloes also wallow in the marshy environs, and jackals and gerbils are occasionally spotted in the late evening. The best time to see birdlife is in winter (December to February) and early spring (March and April), though large flocks of raptors steadily arrive in May. Ultimately, however, bird populations are dependent on the water levels in the reserve.

The **Marsh Trail**, a 1.5km pathway through the reserve, is ideal for bird-watching. Serious birding enthusiasts can stop at the bird hide and various places along the pathway. Also of interest is the viewing platform overlooking the Shishan springs, which once watered the entire marshlands, as well as the ancient Roman control wall that runs alongside the path.

Getting There & Away

The Azraq Wetland Reserve is located 500m east of Azraq. For information on getting to Azraq, see left.

SHAUMARI WILDLIFE RESERVE   محمية الشومري

Established in 1975 by the RSCN, the 22 sq km **Shaumari Wildlife Reserve** (Mahmiyyat ash-Shaumari; www.rscn.org.jo; ☺ 8am-4pm) aims to reintroduce wildlife that has disappeared

THE DESERT CASTLES

SAVING THE ARABIAN ORYX

The Arabian oryx is a majestic animal that stands about 1m high at the shoulder, and weighs around 70kg. Oryxes are distinguished by their luminous white coats, which serve as a vital form of camouflage against the pale backdrop of the scorching desert. The undersides and legs of oryxes are pale brown, and there are black stripes along the neck, the forehead and face, though the most distinguishing feature of the animal is its enormous horns, which project over half a metre into the air. Interestingly enough, biblical scholars have postulated that the legend of the unicorn may have stemmed from oryxes, which appear to only have a single horn when seen in profile.

The oryx is an herbivore that relies primarily on a diet of grass, though it occasionally seeks out young leaves, fruit, tubers and roots from the parched desert. The animal is supremely adapted to the harshest of environments, and can survive for several weeks without the slightest drop of liquid water. In times of drought, oryxes have been known to survive almost two years without water, obtaining moisture solely from plants and leaves. Remarkably, the animals have an uncanny ability to sense rain on the wind – one herd is recorded as having travelled up to 155km, led by a dominant female, to a recent rainfall!

Oryxes are classic herd animals, preferring groups of 10 or less, but occasionally numbering as many as 100. They also adhere to a strict hierarchical structure – every two to three years younger males challenge the leader of the herd for dominance, locking horns in a battle in which the loser often dies. These battles are often grim and the stakes are extremely high, especially since the winner is guaranteed access to breeding females as well as the best grazing lands. Most oryx calves, which can weigh up to 5kg, are born in winter with an 8½-month gestation period. Mothers leave the herd just prior to birth to make a small nest, returning to the herd two or three months after the birth.

In the wild the only natural predator of the oryx is the wolf, which means that the animal once enjoyed a long and healthy lifespan, sometimes living for 20 years. However, their shimmering white coats and long horns were not ignored by hunters in Arabia, thus precipitating the demise of the oryx. The last time the Arabian oryx was seen in the wild in Jordan was in 1920, when hunting drove the animal to local extinction. In 1972, the last wild Arabian oryx was killed by hunters in Oman, which led officials to declare the oryx extinct in the wild. However, in a remarkable conservation effort, the nine oryxes left in captivity were pooled together, and taken to the Arizona Zoo for a captive breeding program.

Today the Arizona Zoo is largely credited with saving the Arabian oryx from extinction. The original nine oryx taken to the USA became known as the 'World Oryx Herd,' and eventually grew to over 200 strong. In 1978, four male and four female oryxes from this herd were transported to Jordan in an effort to help re-establish the country's wild population. Under the auspices of the RSCN (www.rscn.org.jo), the first calf, Dusha, was born at Shaumari Wildlife Reserve the following year, which initiated the precarious road to recovery. Five years later, there were no less than 31 oryxes at Shaumari. Since then they have been treated as wild animals to facilitate their eventual release into the wild.

In a significant landmark for environmentalists the world over, a breeding group of oryxes was reintroduced into the wild in the Wadi Rum Protected Area in 2002. The next step is to introduce the oryx in other protected areas throughout the country, which has prompted the RSCN to significantly overhaul its facilities at Shaumari in the hopes of attracting greater interest and funding in its vital conservation project.

THE DESERT CASTLES

from the region, most notably the highly endangered Arabian oryx (see above). Despite intense funding hurdles, natural predators and the continuous threat of poaching, oryx, Persian onagers (wild ass), goitered gazelle and ostrich have flourished here – a testament to RSCN efforts.

Shaumari's small size means that it is not the place to go to see wildlife roaming the plains unhindered, but it is certainly worth a visit, even if only to catch a rare glimpse of some of the region's most endangered wildlife. The environmentally significant work being conducted here by the RSCN also deserves your financial and moral support, especially considering that the conservation movement in Jordan is still in its infancy, and at times is an intense uphill struggle.

At the entrance to the reserve is a shop selling RSCN products. To the right as you pass through the gate is the nature centre, detailing the fight to save the oryx. Further in is a small picnic area and children's playground, which leads to the observation tower and telescope, from where most of the animal species can be seen, including the ornery ostriches.

At the time of research, Shaumari Wildlife Reserve was temporarily closed to visitors, and undergoing extensive renovation and restoration. According to RSCN staff, the new face of Shaumari will be significantly more attractive to tourists, and will figure prominently in the organisation's prominent drive to develop tourism in the Eastern Desert. Since the reserve should be fully operational by the time this book hits the shelves, be sure to stop by Shaumari, and let us know what's happening on the ground.

Sights & Activities

Shaumari was established as a private reserve to protect the Arabian oryx, though since then it has become the home of bluenecked and red-necked ostriches, Sabgutu Rosa and Dorcas gazelles, and Persian onagers (wild ass). Due to its proximity to the Azraq Wetland Reserve, dozens of bird species have been identified on the grounds including raptors, golden eagles and Egyptian vultures.

When Shaumari reopens to the public, the main attraction will once again be its towering **observation platform**, a lofty spot for scoping animals and birdlife. The highlight of any visit however is the **Oryx Safari**, which is a magical experience, either day or night.

Sleeping & Eating

Prior to closing, Shaumari was home to a modest campground, which will continue to operate after the relaunch. However, staff at the Wild Jordan Centre in Amman confirms that the new Shaumari will feature more upscale lodging and an on-site restaurant.

Getting There & Away

Shaumari is well signposted on the road from Azraq south to the Saudi border. From the T-junction in Azraq, the turn-off is 7km to the south, while the small road to the reserve runs for a further 6km – the last kilometre is gravel, but is easily manageable in a 2WD. The reserve is best accessed by private vehicle, though it is not a problem to charter a taxi to the reserve from Azraq for a few dinars.

DESERT CASTLES
القصور الصحراوية

Some of Jordan's most enigmatic sights, the famed desert castles are scattered amid the country's expansive Eastern Desert, and stand as a testament to the early flourishing of Islamic civilisation. The desert castles were largely constructed by the Umayyads (AD 661–750), and are among the earliest standing monuments of Islamic art. At the height of this dynasty, the caravan stations, bathhouses and hunting lodges that comprise the desert castles were spectacularly landscaped, and furnished with great treasures from across the empire. Here, elite rulers hoping to rekindle their Bedouin roots could indulge in nostalgia by returning to the humble desert. They may also have used visits to the desert castles as a means of avoiding epidemics in the cities.

Getting There & Away

For information on tours and transport to the castles, see the boxed text, p150.

QASR AL-HALLABAT   قصر الحلابات

Lying 55km northwest of Azraq, Qasr-al Hallabat (along with nearby Hammam as-Sarah) is the first stop for many visitors from Amman. At the height of its glory Hallabat boasted elaborate baths, intricate frescoes and mosaics, a towering mosque and several reservoirs, and served as the centrepiece for a thriving farming community.

Today the ruins are sadly little more than a jumble of crumbling walls and fallen stones, though Hallabat remains a good first stop on the desert-castle circuit. Restoration of the site under Spanish direction also promises to restore some of the faded grandeur to this once mighty castle.

During the reign of the Roman Emperor Caracalla (AD 198–217), the *qasr* (fort) was originally built as a defence against raiding desert tribes. However, there is evidence to suggest that Emperor Trajan before him established a post on the site of a Nabataean emplacement. In the 6th century, Hallabat was converted by the Byzantines into a monastery, but was abandoned a century later during the Sassanian invasion from Persia.

Following the rise of the Umayyads, the hedonistic caliph Walid II converted Hallabat into a veritable pleasure palace that contained four large towers, and soared three storeys high. In an impressive building program, the Umayyads also constructed a large mosque with cusped arches, an agricultural enclosure fed by an elaborate irrigation system, and the adjacent bath complex of Hammam as-Sarah.

Today the sight is distinguished by the white limestone of the **Umayyad castle** (built on top of the existing black basalt of the earlier **Byzantine monastery**), as well as the mosaics above the large central cistern and the ruins of the original **Roman fort**. Also look out for the rectangular **mosque** hailing from the 8th century – three walls are still standing, and the foundations of the original mihrab remain. Scattered around the fort, you can still spot the **ruins** of several cisterns, a huge reservoir and a village that was home to an entire community of palace servants.

Getting There & Away

Qasr al-Hallabat is located in the village of Hallabat, and is one of the few castles that can be visited by public transport. From Amman (either Abdali or Raghadan bus station), take a minibus to the New (Amman) station in Zarqa, another minibus to the Old station in Zarqa, and another to Hallabat village. If you're driving, the castle is located off Route 30.

HAMMAM AS-SARAH   حمام الصرح

Hammam as-Sarah is an ancient *hammam* (bathhouse) and hunting lodge that was built by the Umayyads, and linked to the complex at Qasr al-Hallabat. Constructed originally from high-quality limestone, the building was pilfered for its stones in

the 1950s. Fortunately, it has since been well restored, and today you can still see the underfloor piping system that was used to heat the hot, cold and tepid bathing rooms. Outside the main building is a **well**, nearly 20m deep, an elevated tank and the remains of a nearby **mosque**.

The building is located along the main road to Hallabat village, about 3km east of Qasr al-Hallabat and 5km from the main road. The minibus to Hallabat village drives past Hammam as-Sarah, and can drop you off (ask the driver) at the turn-off.

QASR AL-AZRAQ   قصر الأزرق

It was to be Ali's first view of Azraq, and we hurried up the stony ridge in high excitement, talking of the wars and songs and passions of the early shepherd kings, with names like music, who had loved this place; and of the Roman legionaries who languished here as garrison in yet earlier times.

> *TE Lawrence,*
> *Seven Pillars of Wisdom*

This imposing **fort** (admission JD1, ticket also valid for Qusayr Amra & Qasr Kharana; ☼ daylight hr) is where TE Lawrence and Sharif Hussein bin Ali based themselves in the winter of 1917–18 during the Arab Revolt against the Turks. Lawrence set up his quarters in the room above the southern entrance, while his loyal followers braved the elements in other areas of the fort. They were holed up here for several months in crowded conditions with little shelter from the intense cold – gaping holes in the roof were patched up with nothing but palm branches and clay.

Despite the hardships endured during his stay at Azraq, TE Lawrence writes fondly about the time spent with his men at arms. In the evenings everyone would assemble before a great fire in the open courtyard and break bread while swapping stories of war, peace and love. At the time, the castle also commanded sweeping views of the nearby palm-fringed oasis at Azraq.

Unfortunately, the ancient fort was almost destroyed in 1927 following a violent earthquake, and the Azraq oasis all but dried up in 1991 following decades of pumping. Today the remains of the fort are plonked next to the highway on the edge of a rather drab and dusty little town, though

A BRIEF HISTORY OF THE UMAYYADS

At the height of their power, the Umayyads (AD 661–750) ruled over a vast empire stretching from Portugal and Morocco in the east to Arabia and Persia in the west. Centred on its glorious capital of Damascus, the empire was home to nearly 30% of the world's population, and to date remains the third-largest contiguous empire ever to exist. The impact of Umayyads is still felt throughout the Middle East and the world today, as the dynasty was largely responsible for the Sunni-Shiite split in Islam.

Following the assassination of Uthman in 656, the cousin and son-in-law of Muhammad, namely Ali, was appointed as the fourth ruler of the Muslim caliphate. However, his ascension to caliph was met by extreme resistance, which prompted him to move the capital from Medina to Kufa.

Conflict ensued, and the resulting civil war became known as the First Fitna or 'Time of Trial,' which marked the end of unity in the Islamic nation. While Ali was praying at a mosque in Kufa on the 19th day of Ramadan in 661, he was struck down with a poison-coated sword, and died two days later.

Ali believed that the descendants of Muhammad were entitled to rule the caliphate, which prompted Kufi Muslims to pledge allegiance to Ali's eldest son Hasan. At the same time, Muawiyah of the powerful Umayyad family also declared himself caliph. As the commander of the largest army in the empire, Muawiyah controlled the Levant and Egypt, and proceeded to march into Iraq intent on overthrowing Hasan.

In the end, Hasan was forced to concede to the power and influence of Muawiyah and the Umayyads. However, this schism regarding ascension to the caliphate is the very foundation for the Sunni-Shiite split that has remained divisive 1350 years later. At the time, the majority of Muslims (Sunnis) accepted Muawiyah and the Umayyads as the rightful heirs to the caliphate, while a small minority (Shiite) maintained that Hasan and the descendents of Ali should have retained control.

The primary thrust of the Umayyads was territorial expansion, which led the majority of their subjects to believe that they were primarily a dynastic rather than a religious caliphate. However, the Umayyads are credited with establishing Arabic as the administrative language of the Middle East, as well as implementing a campaign of mass conversions that brought a large influx of Muslims to the caliphate.

The Umayyads also launched an impressive building campaign across the empire, which resulted in the building of the Dome of the Rock in Jerusalem, and the Umayyad Mosque in Damascus.

However, resistance to the dynasty grew increasingly bitter on both sides of the Sunni-Shiite split. For the majority Sunni, public opinion was that the Umayyad rulers after Muawiyah were dim-witted sinners who were largely concerned with mere earthly delights. For the minority Shiite, the lack of discord in the Muslim nation and the denial of Ali's heirs were grave injustices that simply could not be forgiven. In 747, a huge rebellion was incited by outlying peoples of the caliphate, who gambled that Damascus could not continue to exert influence over such a vast empire.

In 750, the army of Caliph Marwan II fought against a combined force of Persians, Shiites and Abbasid soldiers at the River Zab. The Abbasids, who advanced the claim that they were directly descended from Muhammad, rode this wave of morale to victory over the thinly stretched Umayyad army. Caliph Marwan escaped the battle alive, though he was eventually hunted down and killed – forever ending Umayyad rule in the Middle East. This subsequently ushered in the Baghdad-based Abbasids as the second great Muslim caliphate.

In the modern era, Arab nationalists regard the Umayyads as part of a greater Arab Golden Age that many are keen to see restored. In fact, the colour white, which appears on the flags of most Arab countries, is considered to represent the Umayyads' dynasty. However, the most prominent legacy of the Umayyads is the material remains of their vast empire, which include the impressive desert castles that are scattered across the Eastern Desert of Jordan.

there is a fair measure of magic still in the air, particularly in the late afternoon when the castle interior is lit up by the setting sun. And of course, it's humbling to explore the hallowed grounds of the former dwelling of the famous Lawrence of Arabia.

History

Despite being one of the most famous and accessible of the desert castles, comparatively little is known about the history of Qsar al-Azraq, and there's been little excavation and renovation. What is known is that Greek and Latin inscriptions date earlier constructions on the site to around AD 300, which coincides with the reign of the Romans.

The structure was renovated later during the Byzantine period, and yet again by the Umayyad caliph Walid II, who used it for hunting and as a military base. Its present form dates to 1237 when it was heavily reconstructed by the Damascus-based Ayyubids, though its fortifications didn't hold up against the Ottoman Turks, who stationed a garrison here in the 16th century. In 1918, it was from this building that the Arab Revolt launched their attack on Damascus against the very same Ottoman Turks.

Sights

This large building was constructed out of black basalt stone, and was originally three storeys high. Some **paving stones** in the main entrance have small indentations, carved by former gatekeepers who played a board game using pebbles to pass the time. By the courtyard entrance, look for the carvings of animals and various inscriptions.

Above the entrance is **Lawrence's Room**, strategically overlooking the entry and offset with arrow slits for defence. Opposite the entrance, and just to the left, are the remains of a small **altar**, built in the 3rd century AD by the Romans. In the middle of the expansive **courtyard** is a small **mosque**, angled to face Mecca – it dates to the Ayyubid period (early 13th century), but was built on the ruins of a Byzantine church. In the northeast corner of the courtyard, a hole with stairs leads down to a **well**, full of water until about 20 years ago. In the northwest corner are the ruins of the **prison**.

The northern sections are residential areas with barely discernible ruins of a **kitchen** and **dining room**, and nearby **store-**rooms and **stables**. The **tower** in the western wall is the most spectacular, and features a huge **door** made of a single massive slab of basalt. Lawrence describes in his book *Seven Pillars of Wisdom* how it 'went shut with a clang and crash that made tremble the west wall of the castle'.

Getting There & Away

The fort is situated in Azraq ash-Shomali (North Azraq), about 5km north of the T-junction at the end of the highway from Amman. For information on getting to and from Azraq, as well as listings for accommodation and restaurants in the area, see p153.

QUSAYR AMRA   قصر عمرا

One of the best-preserved desert buildings of the Umayyads, the Unesco World Heritage Site of Qusayr Amra is the highlight of any trip out into the Eastern Desert. Part of a much greater complex that served as a caravanserai, bathhouse and hunting lodge, the *qusayr* (little castle) is famous for its hedonistic (and somewhat risqué!) 8th-century frescoes of wine, women and wild good times. According to some historians, only out here in the isolated wilds of the desert did the caliphs feel comfortable about flouting Islam's edicts.

Qusayr Amra seems to rise incongruously from the parched, dry desert plains, though in ancient times the site was adjacent to a lush wadi famed for its wild pistachio trees. At the time the water table was much higher, which allowed the builders to tap the ground, enabling the steady supply of water needed to supply the bathhouse. Even today, you can still see the 25m deep masonry-lined well, which stands as a testament to the impressive engineering skills of the Umayyads.

Of course, what would otherwise be a fairly modest site is seriously spiced up by its floor-to-ceiling frescoes, which have captivated visitors for over a millennium. The original painters were highly skilled, and took an immense amount of time to capture even the most subtle of details. As the result of an impressive restoration effort, the frescoes have been returned to their former state, and continue to depict elaborate scenes ranging from hunting motifs to depictions of women in their full glory.

For more information on the frescoes of Qusayr Amra, see the boxed text, opposite.

History

There exists a small measure of archaeological evidence suggesting that the site of Qusayr Amra was occupied prior to the arrival of the Umayyads. The general consensus amongst historians however is that the present-day structure was constructed around AD 711 during the reign of Walid I (AD 705–15). Walid was a fierce proponent of the Muslim caliphate, and launched an impressive building campaign across the empire that resulted in the Umayyad Mosque at his capital of Damascus, and the Dome of the Rock in Jerusalem. Of course, even overworked caliphs need some down time every once in awhile!

In a sharp contrast to the orthodox murals of the Umayyad Mosque, which depict vast motifs of devoted Muslims ascending to the Kingdom of Heaven, the frescoes at Amra highlight the pleasures of the earth. Coincidentally, it was Walid's successor that ordained the destruction of such imagery in Islam, though the far-reaching hand of Damascus fortunately spared this remote outpost in the furthest reaches of the Jordanian desert.

Excavation at the site began in the mid-1970s, and was spearheaded by a team of Spanish archaeologists. Since then, the frescoes have been restored with the assistance of governments and private institutions from Austria, France and Spain. In 1985, the frescoes were recognised as being a 'masterpiece of human creative genius', which prompted Unesco to designate Qusayr Amra as a World Heritage Site.

Orientation & Information

Heading back towards Amman from Azraq along Hwy 30, a turn-off south leads to Hwy 40 and **Qusayr Amra** (admission JD1, ticket also valid for Qsar al-Azraq & Qasr Kharana; ☻ 8am-6pm May-Sep, to 4pm Oct-Apr). However, the complex is only signposted coming from Amman, so keep an eye out as you are likely to speed past it if coming from Azraq.

Entrance to the complex is through the excellent **visitor centre**, which has a relief map of the site, some detailed descriptions of the site's history and the frescoes, plus some public toilets.

Photography of the interior of Qusayr Amra doesn't seem to be regulated, but bear in mind that flash photography will harm the frescoes.

Sights

The entrance of the main building opens immediately to the frescoed **audience hall**, where meetings, parties, exhibitions and meals were held.

As your eyes grow accustomed to the light you are greeted by two topless women painted on the arches, holding bowls of food (or money) against a blue background – look for the rich details in the cloth. On the right side of the right wall is a scene of wrestlers warming up. To the left is the image of a woman bathing in what looks like an 8th-century thong.

To the left of this painting are the defaced images of the Umayyad caliph surrounded by **six great rulers**, four of whom have been identified – Caesar, a Byzantine emperor; the Visigoth king, Roderick; the Persian emperor, Chosroes; and the Negus of Abyssinia. The fresco either implies that the Umayyad ruler was their equal or better, or it is simply a pictorial list of Islam's enemies.

Above is a hunting scene. The left corner depicts a reclining woman with two attendants holding fans. Above her are twin peacocks and the Greek word for victory.

The main chamber alcove here features women's faces on a barrel vault topped off by a king seated on a throne surrounded by floral motifs.

The entire left wall is a huge hunting scene with dogs driving wild onagers into a trap of nets. The ceiling has a clear depiction of the construction of the baths, from the quarrying, moving the stones by camel, to carpentry and plastering of the walls.

A small doorway leads to the left through the three small rooms that made up the baths. The **apodyterium** (changing room) has three blackened faces on the ceiling, said to depict the three stages of man's life. Local Christians believe the central figure to be a depiction of Christ. The left wall has a crazy hallucinogenic painting of an exuberant bear playing the banjo, egged on by an applauding monkey. The right wall depicts a musician and female dancer.

The **tepidarium** (where warm water was offered and warm air circulated beneath the floor) has scenes of naked women bathing a child.

The final room is the hot-water **calidarium**, which is closest to the furnace outside. The highlight here is the Dome of Heaven, upon which is depicted a map of the northern-hemisphere sky accompanied by the signs of the zodiac – one of the earliest known attempts to represent the universe on anything other than a flat surface. You can make out the centaur-like Sagittarius, the Great Bear and several other zodiac signs (see the map in the visitor centre for details).

Outside, a few metres north of the main building, is a partially restored 36m-deep stone **well** and a restored *saqiyah* – a pump turned by a donkey, which raised the water to a cistern that supplied water for the baths and for passing caravans.

Getting There & Away

Qusayr Amra is right on the main road – it's on the north side of the road, 26km from Azraq, southwest of the junctions of Hwys 30 and 40. If you don't have a private car or are not part of a private tour, bear in mind that there are no buses stopping here so you'll have to hitch along Hwy 40. From Azraq, take a minibus towards Zarqa as far as the junction, then hitch. You could also charter a taxi from Azraq, and combine it with a visit to Qasr Kharana.

QASR KHARANA   قصر خرانه

Located in the middle of a vast, treeless plain, this mighty fortress was most likely the inspiration for the somewhat incorrect 'desert castles' moniker. The intimidating two-storey structure is marked by round, defensive towers and narrow windows that appear to be arrow slits. If you take a closer look, however, you'll soon realise that the towers are completely solid, which means that they couldn't be manned by armed soldiers. Furthermore, it would be impossible to fire bows from the bizarrely shaped 'arrow slits,' meaning that they most likely served as air and light ducts.

Although it clearly isn't a castle, Kharana was nevertheless a vital building for the Umayyads as evidenced by its dramatic size and shape. Historians have had a difficult time postulating as to why the early Islamic rulers chose to fortify such a remote location. Despite the fact that it has the ap-

---

THE FRESCOES OF QUSAYR AMRA

The information boards in the visitor centre at Qusayr Amra assure the visitor that: 'None of the paintings of Qusayr Amra portray scenes of unbridled loose-living or carryings-on'. Given the context of early Islam's prohibition of any illustrations of living beings, it's difficult to agree.

Just how far these boundaries were pushed is evident on the western wall of the audience hall, where there is a depiction of a nude woman bathing. Some historians speculate that she may have been modelled on the favourite concubine of the ruler of Amra. The more your eyes roam the walls, past images of musicians, naked dancers, cherubs, baskets of fruit (and even a bear playing a banjo!) the more the heresy of the frescoes becomes apparent.

And the purpose of all these paintings? Some Islamic scholars blame the Ghassanids, a pagan Arab tribe that ruled the region at the time of Rome, others mumble about rogue rulers who were not true to Islam. But most admit privately that it seems as though the rulers were simply enjoying themselves on a boys' night out, away from the confines of the court.

---

pearance of a *khan* (caravanserai), Kharana wasn't located on any major trade route, and there appears to be a total absence of structures for water storage. However, a recent supposition is that the building served as a meeting space for Damascus elite and local Bedouin.

Regardless of its origins, Kharana has been impeccably restored, and is arguably the most photogenic of all the desert castles. Named after the *harra* (surrounding gravel plains), Kharana lords imposingly over a harsh and barren moonscape that appears ill-equipped for human habitation. However, a brief stroll through its graceful interior courtyard can be a calming experience, especially if the tour groups are elsewhere, allowing you to soak up the centuries of history clinging to the stones.

History

Compared with nearby Umayyad monuments, very little is known about the origins of Qsar Kharana, which contributes to the mystery surrounding the site. However, a painted inscription above one of the doors on the upper floor mentions the date AD 710, making it one of the earliest forts of the Islamic era. The presence of stones with Greek inscriptions in the main entrance also suggests it was built on the site of a Roman or Byzantine building, possibly as a private residence.

Orientation & Information
Heading back towards Amman along Hwy 30, a turn-off south leads to Hwy 40 and **Qusayr Kharana** (admission JD1, ticket also valid for Qusayr Amra & Qasr al-Azraq; 8am-6pm May-Sep, to 4pm Oct-Apr). The complex is only signposted coming from Amman, so keep an eye out as you are likely to miss it if coming from Azraq.

Entrance to the complex is through the **visitor centre**, which has some displays on local history in addition to a few public toilets.

Sights
About 60 **rooms** (known as *beit*) surround the **courtyard** inside the castle, and most likely served as meeting spaces for visiting delegations. The long rooms either side of the arched **entrance** were used as **stables**, and in the centre of the courtyard was a **basin** for collecting rainwater. Remarkably, the interior is much smaller than you'd imagine as the walls are deceptively thick, though again, the building was probably not used for defensive purposes.

Make sure you climb to the top levels along one of the elegant **stairways**, passing en route some rooms with vaulted ceilings. Most of the rooms in the upper levels are decorated with well-restored **carved plaster medallions**, set around the top of the walls, which are said to indicate Mesopotamian influence.

Also in one of the rooms on the second floor is a few lines of Arabic **graffiti**, which were crucial in helping to establish the age of the fortress. Above the door in simple black script is the inscription 'Abd al-Malik the son of Ubayd wrote it on Monday three days from Muharram of the year 92'.

Stairs in the southeast and southwest corners lead to the 2nd floor and the roof, from which there are great **views** of the surrounding desert. Unfortunately, the nearby highway and power station spoil the ambience somewhat.

Getting There & Away
The castle is 16km further west along Hwy 40 from Qusayr Amra. Like Qusayr Amra, there's no public transport along the highway. If you don't have a private vehicle or are not part of a tour, either hitch from Amman or Azraq, or charter a vehicle from Azraq and combine it with a visit to Qusayr Amra.

QASR AL-MUSHATTA قصر المشتى
Of the five major desert castles, the 'winter palace' of **Qasr al-Mushatta** (admission free; daylight hr) is the most difficult and time consuming to reach, and thus usually not part of most organised tours. But this is not to say that Mushatta is located in the middle of nowhere – on the contrary, it's actually the closest of the desert castles to Amman. In fact, if you're travelling around Jordan in a rental car, the ruins may be the last thing you see in the country as they're located right next to Queen Alia International Airport!

The construction of Qasr al-Mushatta is believed to have started in about AD 743, under Caliph Walid II, who intended to establish a large city in the area. Although the fort was planned as the biggest and most lavish of all the desert castles, it was never finished. In 744, Walid II was assassinated by angry labourers, many of whose colleagues had died during construction due to a lack of water in the area. If you ignore the occasional sound of jumbo jets soaring over head, the extensive ruins hint at the vast potential of the caliph's grand vision.

Many pieces have disappeared over the years, ending up in museums around the world. The elaborate carving on the facade was shipped off to Berlin (it's now in the Pergamon Museum) after the palace was 'given' to Kaiser Wilhelm in 1903 by Sultan Abd al-Hamid of Turkey. Mushatta was also partially destroyed by earthquakes, and most of the columns and watchtowers have long since collapsed. However, the huge exterior wall and carved facades still hint at the original grandeur and beauty of the site.

Right of the entrance are the ruins of a mosque, with its obviously rebuilt mihrab (niche in mosque, indicating direction of Mecca). The northern sections have the remains of a vaulted **audience hall** and **residences**. Segmented pillars lie scattered around like broken vertebrae. One unusual feature of the site is that the vaults were made from burnt bricks (an uncommon material in buildings of this style) rather than black basalt. And of course, be sure not to miss the ancient **toilets** (complete with drains!), which are located at the back of the hall.

Getting There & Away

Qasr al-Mushatta is impossible to reach by public transport or hitching. As the castle is located near sensitive areas – primarily the airport – make sure you have your passport ready to show the guards at the military checkpoints along the route.

If you're driving from Amman, head towards the Queen Alia International Airport, turn left off the Desert Highway to the airport, then turn right at the roundabout just past the Alia Hotel. Leave your passport at the first security check and then follow the road for 12km around the perimeter of the airport, turning right by the second and third check posts.

An alternative is to charter a taxi from the airport – a great idea if you have a long wait for a flight – or combine a taxi to the airport with a visit to the ruins. A visit can be made from the airport in an hour.

OTHER CASTLES

While the more popular desert castles attract the bulk of the tourists in the Eastern Desert, there are numerous other off-the-beaten-path castles in this off-the-beaten-path region. For the most part, the 'other castles' lie in virtual ruin, are inaccessible by public transport, and attract few people beyond aspiring archaeologists and adventure seekers. However, that is precisely why you should put this book down and spend some time exploring the furthest reaches of Jordan's Eastern Desert.

Qasr 'Ain es-Sil   قصر عين السيل

This is not really a castle or a fort, but rather a humble farmhouse built by the Umayyads, possibly over the existing fortifications of a Roman building. Rather small (17 sq metres) and built from simple basalt brick, there are ruins here of a courtyard (flanked by seven rooms), equipment for making bread and olive oil, and some baths. It is located just off the main road through Azraq ash-Shomali (North Azraq), and about 2km from Qasr al-Azraq.

Qasr Aseikhin   قصر الشيخين

This small Roman fort, built from basalt in the 3rd century over the ruins of a 1st-century Nabataean building, is worth visiting if you're a fan of 4WD adventure. The small structure is about 22km northeast of North Azraq, but you will need a high-clearance vehicle and some local advice before setting out. Go along the road north of Qasr al-Azraq for about 15km, and follow the signs to the fort. It's a tough ride out here, but after arriving at the fort you'll be rewarded by sweeping views of the surrounding nothingness.

THE DESERT CASTLES

WINSTON'S HICCUP

When Winston Churchill was serving as British Colonial Secretary in the early 1920s, he once boasted that he had 'created Trans-Jordan with the stroke of a pen on a Sunday afternoon in Cairo'. As Churchill had something of a reputation for enjoying 'liquid lunches', a rumour started to fly that he had hiccuped while attempting to draw the border, and stubbornly refused to allow it to be redefined. The resulting zigzag in Jordan's eastern border subsequently became known as **Winston's Hiccup**.

Of course, Churchill was anything but drunk and foolish. The zigzag was precisely plotted to excise Wadi Sirhan, an age-old Incense Route and vital communication highway between French-controlled Syria and Arabia, from Jordan. The masterful pen stroke also created a panhandle between Azraq and Iraq, which meant that the British now controlled an unbroken corridor between the Mediterranean Sea and Persian Gulf.

Today Jordan's erratic boundaries with Syria, Iraq and Saudi Arabia are of little political consequence, at least in comparison to the heightened emotions surrounding the border line with Israel. However, Winston's Hiccup does stand as testament to a time when little to no lip service was given to the colonial division of occupied foreign lands.

Qasr Deir al-Kahf   قصر دير الكهف

Built in the 4th century, the 'Monastery of Caves' is another purpose-built Roman fort that primarily served as a sentry post. Like its famous neighbour Umm al-Jimal, Deir al-Kahf is also constructed of black basalt, though the ruins here are not nearly as extensive. However, the scattered remains of the fort are atmospheric, and serve as a nice diversion. There is an access road north of Hwy 10, or look for the signs along the back roads east of Umm al-Jimal.

Qasr Mushash   قصر موشاش

Although this rather large (2 sq km) Umayyad settlement was once a grand city in the desert, today Mushash sadly lies in virtual ruin. However, it's still possible to get a sense of the original layout, and there are a number of impressive buildings left standing including the remains of a palace, a large courtyard surrounded by a dozen rooms, baths, cisterns and walls built to protect against possible flooding. Only accessible by 4WD, Mushash can be reached via an access road along Hwy 40.

Qasr al-Muwaqqar   قصر الموقر

Not much is known about this former Umayyad caravanserai as its remains are fairly decrepit, and look like they've seen much better centuries. If you squint your eyes, you can still make out the shapes of some ancient reservoirs and a column or two, though there is little else to see. However, a 10m stone tower with Kufic inscriptions, which now stands in the National Archaeological Museum (p97) in Amman, was found by archaeologists at the site. The ruins are located about 2km north of Hwy 40.

Qasr al-Qastal   قصر القسطل

This ruined Umayyad settlement is unique, as it was ornately renovated by the Mamluks in the 13th century AD. Sadly, time has not been kind to the beautiful palace that once stood, though you can still get a sense of its former majesty. The site, located just to the west of the Desert Highway before the turnoff to the airport, is also home to the ruins of an Islamic cemetery and bathhouse.

Qasr al-Tuba   قصر التوبة

Easily the most impressive of the lesser-known castles, Tuba is located approximately 75km southeast of Amman in the absolute middle of nowhere. This is precisely why it's worth making an expedition out here – with little to no surrounding development, Tuba captures the original essence of 'luxury in the desert' that drove the Umayyads to launch their massive building campaign.

Tuba was erected by Caliph Walid II in about AD 743, though like Qasr al-Mushatta, it was left to waste following his sudden assassination. Despite its seemingly remote location, however, the castle was probably going to be a caravanserai, which would have served as a vital staging post on the Incense Route between Syria and Arabia. The structure is unique for its sun-baked mud bricks, a sturdy building material that is surprisingly absent from other desert castles. You can see an impressive doorway from the site at Amman's National Archaeological Museum (p97).

An excellent detour from Tuba – assuming you have proper GPS equipment and a local guide – is Thalathwat, a remote desert area that is the sole nesting place in Jordan of the rare **Houbara bustard**. Even if you're not a die-hard birder, these bizarre flightless birds are a strange sight, especially if you catch them in the midst of a mad-dash flapping frenzy. Note however that bustards are highly endangered, which means that you will need a measure of luck to actually see one.

Tuba is only accessible by 4WD along a poorly signed dirt track (35km) west of the Desert Highway, or an unsigned dirt track south (50km) of Hwy 40. Because the roads are so difficult to find and follow, a knowledgeable guide is recommended, though most local villagers can point out the castle to you. Travelling with a local also increases your chances of spotting the Houbara bustard.

Qasr 'Uweinid   قصر عويند

This Roman military fort was built in the 3rd century AD to protect the source of Wadi as-Sirhan (now in Saudi Arabia), but was abandoned less than 100 years later. However, it remains as one of the oldest standing desert castles, and is a powerful reminder of the past Roman occupation of the area. Uweinid is only accessible by 4WD, and is located about 15km southwest of Azraq al-Janubi (South Azraq) – look for the turn-off along the road towards Shaumari Wildlife Reserve.

Qasr Burqu   قصر بورقو

You have to be pretty dedicated to visit this brooding black basalt fort, which stands guard over the silent shores of Ghadir (Lake) Burqu. Of course, the apparent incongruity of the lake in the harsh desert is what makes this place so special. With a tent, some basic survival gear and a reliable 4WD, you could have a serious adventure out here. It is precisely for this reason that the RSCN has been fighting to establish Burqu as a protected reserve, which would fit nicely into its plans to develop tourism in the Eastern Desert. At the time of writing, however, it was not possible to organise trips to Qasr Burqu from the RSCN base in Azraq, though this may change in the years to come.

The reason for the lake's existence is an ancient dam that was constructed by the Romans in the 3rd century as a means of securing water for caravans heading between Syria and Arabia. In order to secure this vital water source, the Romans also built a small fort here, though it became a monastery during the Byzantine period, and was later restored by the Umayyads in about AD 700. Remarkably, an inscription on one of the walls of the fort suggests that it may have been occupied as late as 1409.

The lake itself is home to a number of bird species (including finches, storks, sandpipers, larks, cranes, buzzards, pelicans, eagles and vultures) that come to roost because the water level rarely changes, even in summer. The harshness of the surrounding landscape, as well as the lack of properly graded roads, has acted as a strong deterrent against poaching. The area also has all the makings of a successful wildlife preserve, as it's already home to gazelles, desert hares, foxes, hyenas and even caracals.

The good news for the flora and fauna – and the bad news for would-be visitors – is that Burqu is only accessible by 4WD. The lake and castle are about 15km northwest of Ar-Ruwayshid, which is on the road from Mafraq to the Iraqi border. Although public transport is available between Mafraq and Ar-Ruwayshid, there is no chance of even hitching north of the highway to Burqu, and the access road to Burqu is very rough. If you're heading this way, you need to be completely self-sufficient, ideally be travelling with a knowledgeable local, and be prepared for any situation that might arise out here on the fringes of civilisation.

For the latest information on the state of Qasr Burqu, it is best to contact the RSCN at the Wild Jordan Centre in Amman (see p95). If anything does change during the shelf life of this book, contact us with an update on the situation.

Dead Sea Highway

الطريق البحر الميت

Fleeing across the mosaic map of Madaba is a gazelle who turns towards a lion (identifiable only by its tail) in hot pursuit. They're running through the Jordan Valley towards the Dead Sea, just above the place where Apostle John baptised Jesus, and are symbolic, perhaps, of the human flight that has marked this poignant patch of land for centuries.

There are no lions today and you are unlikely to see a gazelle, but standing on the high ground above the polished, glass-smooth sea, it's easy to sense the antiquity of a region that has supported human endeavour for thousands of years. All along the highway, fresh water springs bring a hopeful abundance of life (as at Wadi Mujib) in vivid contrast to the surrounding barren escarpment. In season, the parched soil is threaded with blood red crates of tomatoes and glossy-coated aubergines.

Belying its name, even the Dead Sea has contributed to the pattern of human civilisation. Known to the ancients as the Sea of Asphalt, it produced bitumen harvested by the Nabataeans and sold to neighbours for embalming processes in a nascent oil industry. Travel along the Dead Sea Highway today, with its proximity to the Israel and Palestinian Territories, and you quickly feel how oil, albeit of a different kind, defines the territory still. Police checks, border posts, cautious eyes across the Rift Valley – this is disputed soil, a land cleaved in two, geologically, historically and politically.

Float in peace in a Dead Sea spa and you can't help but be aware that the calm has been bought at a high price.

DEAD SEA HIGHWAY

HIGHLIGHTS

- Scoop a handful of history from the water at **Bethany-Beyond-the-Jordan** (opposite), where Jesus was baptised

- Descend to the depths for a bob in the **Dead Sea** (p172), at the lowest point on earth, before scaling the heights with a cocktail at a lavish spa resort

- Place the Dead Sea in a historical and geographical context at the informative **Dead Sea Panorama** (p177)

- Splash through the canyon pools of **Wadi Mujib Nature Reserve** (p179), keeping an eye open for ibex

- Taste a freshly plucked tomato before exploring the rainbow hills of **Wadi Araba** (p181)

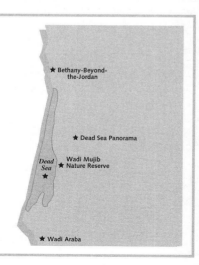

★ Bethany-Beyond-
the-Jordan

★ Dead Sea Panorama

Dead
Sea
★ Wadi Mujib
Nature Reserve
★

★ Wadi Araba

Getting Around

The best way to explore the Dead Sea Highway (Hwy 65) is with a car, as there's no public transport along the route. The Dead Sea Highway runs along the edge of the Dead Sea, between the honey-coloured Moab Mountains and the distant cliffs of Judaea on the West Bank, and offers an interesting alternative to the Desert Highway between Amman and Aqaba.

If you're not in a hurry, there are some spectacular roads that link the Dead Sea Highway with the King's Highway. With the intimate insight these roads afford into Bedouin communities and striking desert landscape, they are almost destinations in their own right.

Due to the proximity of the Israel and Palestinian Territories border, there are numerous police checkpoints in the area. Keep your passport, driver's licence, rental contract and *ruksa* (car registration card) handy on any of the roads near or along the Dead Sea Highway.

There are few petrol stations in the vicinity, and little accommodation (except at the Dead Sea Resorts and within the National Parks of Wadi Mujib and Wadi Dana). Amman, Madaba, Karak and Wadi Mousa make suitable bases for exploring the region.

BETHANY-BEYOND-THE-JORDAN (AL-MAGHTAS) المغطس

Then Jesus came from the Galilee to the Jordan to be baptised by John.
(Matthew 3:13)

This took place in Bethany beyond the Jordan, where John was baptising.
(John 1:28)

Whatever one's religious persuasions, it's hard not to be moved by this minimal pile of ruins with its preposterously long name. This is the site, archaeologists assure us, where John the Baptist preached, where Jesus was baptised, where the first five apostles met and where, thereby, the foundations of the early Christian faith were laid. They chose an auspicious spot as many also believe that this was the place from where prophet Elijah (who was born in Mar Elias in north Jordan) ascended to heaven in a whirlwind:

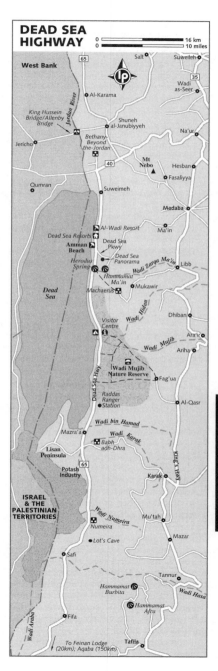

DEAD SEA HIGHWAY

DRIVING BELOW ZERO

The switchback roads that link the high ground with the low ground (often below sea level) are a highlight of Jordan, especially if you are driving and can stop to admire the panoramic views. The roads twist through terraced fields of onions, hug contours of sheep-cropped hills, edge past nomadic communities of Bedouin with their black tents and attendant goats, before spiralling into a painted desert, vermilion with iron ore, olive green with copper oxides and laced with hanging gardens. Here is a summary of the best of these drives. You won't find the roads indicated on all maps but they are all well paved, suitable for a 2WD car (beware sharp bends) and usually marked 'Dead Sea' or 'Wadi Araba' on signs. Remember to carry your passport with you as there are numerous checkpoints along the roads that access the Jordan Valley and Dead Sea Highway.

Salt to Bethany

90 minutes, 23km descent and 45km along the Jordan Valley

A varied drive along a busy road of Aleppo pines, red-barked strawberry trees and gardens of early-summer hollyhocks, giving way to tamarisks and acacias. Let your brakes cool at the sea-level marker and enjoy the view of the fertile Jordan Valley, lit up with flowering flame trees in May.

Follow signs for Zay National Park and Dayr 'Alla on Hwy 30 from Salt. Watch out for truck drivers on their mobiles on the hairpin bends! Add a 14km detour (well signposted) to Mountain Breeze Country Club for a tea break.

Mt Nebo to Dead Sea Resorts

30 minutes, 21 km

An easy drive, passing wildflowers and clumps of prickly pear, and driving through Bedouin grazing grounds before descending to a colourful, semi-arid desert with spectacular Dead Sea views.

The start of the descent is to the left of the Mt Nebo entrance gate. After 14.5km, turn left for the Dead Sea Resorts or right for Bethany.

Madaba to Dead Sea Panorama

50 minutes (half-day with stops), 30km plus 5km return trip to Hammamat Ma'in

The best of the Dead Sea drives, through avenues of windswept junipers and firs, vines and olive groves, and alongside a wadi decorated with flowering oleander. Don't miss the steep descent of the sulphurous hillside to Hammamat Mai'in (p177). Recover at the aptly named Panorama Restaurant (p177).

And as they still went on and talked, behold, a chariot of fire and horses of fire separated the two of them. And Eli'jah went up by a whirlwind into heaven.
(2 Kings 2:11)

Although John was later beheaded by Herod at Machaerus (see p195) and Jesus was crucified in Jerusalem, the meeting between the two men at this spot in the fertile Jordan Valley was one of hope and new beginnings. It is little surprise, then, that it became a focus for early pilgrimage, and remains so to this day.

The name Bethany comes from the Aramaic *Beit Anniya* (House of the Crossing). As you stand by the almost-stagnant river at this point, Israel and the Palestinian Territories is almost within arms' reach. Pilgrim churches, guesthouses and a 6th-century pilgrim road developed around the crossing as pilgrims broke their journey between Jerusalem and Mt Nebo. Today, there's little visible evidence of the early passage of pilgrims but the sense of crossing is still disturbingly apparent: as one traveller, Nathalie Ollier, remarked, 'It's hard for Christian visitors on either side of the water to pray when watched over by Jewish and Muslim armed guards intent on making sure you don't cross the border'.

The site has only relatively recently been identified. Some ancient ruins were discov-

Follow signs for Hammamat Mai'in from King's Hwy, 1km south of Madaba. The new road is incorrectly shown on most maps. Use low gear if you're making a detour to Hammamat Ma'in. Continue to Dead Sea Resorts (7km), Bethany (25km) or Amman (60km).

Karak to Safi
30 minutes, 40km
This is an easy drive along steep-sided wadi, with expansive views of potash production. Take a side trip to Lot's Cave (p181).

Time this drive for midafternoon, when the sunset turns the sandstone to molten gold. Follow signs from the King's Highway in Karak to 'Al Mazraa' or 'Dead Sea' along Hwy 50. Turn left at the Dead Sea Highway for Safi.

Tafila to Fife
40 minutes, 26km
Descend from cypress woodland, through weather-beaten rock formations and palm oases to tomato fields at Fifa.

Give extra time to this trip – it's a veritable geography lesson in habitats at different altitudes. Take Hwy 60 from the centre of Tafila, following signs for Wadi Araba; take care on the sharp bends.

Little Petra to Wadi Araba
One hour 15 minutes (half-day with stops), 45km plus 2km return to Little Petra and 20km return to Feinan Lodge
This fantastic drive begins with Nabataean sites such as the Elephant Rock and a side trip to the Siq at Little Petra (p244). Look out for rock-cut wine presses and dams through Siq Umm Al-Alda, decorated with ancient carob trees. Pass through the psychedelically green landscape surrounding a reclaimed-water project and visit a pre-pottery Neolithic tell (look for a wire fence on the left of the road) at Shkarat Msaiad. The mountain road thereafter twists through magnificent rainbow rocks before gliding into Wadi Araba, dotted with Bedouin camps, acacia trees and sand dunes.

Head through Umm Sayhoun to Little Petra. Turn right to Hesha and Bayder and immediately left to Wadi Araba. The road, which doesn't appear on most maps, is damaged but not impassable at the bottom. At the junction in Wadi Araba, turn right to Qurayqira to stay at Feinan Lodge (p210) or left to reach the Dead Sea Highway. From the highway junction, it is 130km to Aqaba.

ered in 1899 but it wasn't until the clearing of landmines (following the 1994 peace treaty with Israel and the Palestinian Territories) that the remains of churches, caves, extensive wells and several baptism pools were unearthed. After much debate, scholars identified the site of John the Baptist's mission and Jesus' baptism from descriptions in the Bible and from 3rd- to 10th-century pilgrim accounts. Pope John Paul II sanctified the claim with an open-air mass at the site in the spring of 2000.

Information
Entry to the **site** (adult/child under 12 JD7/free; ⏰ 8am-4pm Nov-Mar & Ramadan, to 6pm Apr-Oct) includes a one-hour guided tour and shuttle bus service to the main complex, close to the sensitive border with Israel and the Palestinian Territories. Collect a brochure and map at the main gate, where there are toilets, souvenir shops and a restaurant. The flies here are of plague proportions in spring.

The Site
The shuttle bus makes a brief stop at Tell Elias (see p172), where Elijah is said to have ascended to heaven, and then continues to a modern baptism pool with filtered water from the Jordan River (the river is badly polluted). The tour continues on foot (hot

in summer so take a hat and water) to the **Spring of John the Baptist**, one of several places where John is believed to have carried out baptisms. Most baptisms were conducted in the spring-fed waters of Wadi al-Kharrar, rather than in the Jordan River. The path leads through thickets of tamarisk and *argul* (wild cherry) and the yellow rose of Jericho in spring.

The main archaeological site comprises the remains of three churches, one on top of the other. Steps lead down to the original water level and a building nearby marks the likely **site of Jesus' baptism**. Byzantine churches were built to mark the site during the 5th and 6th centuries, and rebuilt on the same site after they were destroyed by flooding. All that remains today are traces of original mosaic.

The walking trail passes a golden-roofed Greek Orthodox church and leads, under the watchful eye of border guards, to the **Jordan River** – little more than a stagnant ditch. It's not very inviting but you can be baptised in the Jordan if accompanied by a priest. Across the river (and the border) is a rival Israeli baptism complex. This is the only place where civilians can currently touch the Jordan River as the remainder runs through a military no-man's-land.

Tours often return via the **House of Mary the Egyptian**, a 'reformed sinner' who lived and died in the two-room house in the 4th century. The trail continues left, up some wooden stairs to a two-room **hermit cave** burrowed into the soft rock.

On the way back, ask to be dropped at **Tell Elias** (Elijah's Hill). The rebuilt arch marks the 5th- to 6th-century pilgrim chapel, where the late Pope John Paul II authenticated the site in March 2000. The nearby 3rd-century rectangular prayer hall is one of the earliest Christian places of worship ever discovered, dating from a period when Christianity was still illegal.

The hill behind holds the presumed cave of John the Baptist, a 5th-century monastery (built around the site) and the **Rhotorios Monastery**, which has a mosaic floor with Greek inscriptions. In the 3rd to 4th century, the plaster-lined pools were used by pilgrims for bathing. In the early years of Christianity, John was a more celebrated figure than Jesus and this was the more important of the two pilgrimage sites.

Eating

John's Retreat (mains JD3-5; 8am-4pm) Within the Bethany complex, John's is good for a sandwich. Cool and clean, it lives up to its name if the flies are giving you grief.

Bethany Touristic Restaurant (079 6076060; fish JD10; 10am-midnight). Attached to a thriving fish farm, this place specialises in excellent tilapia (*talloubi* in Arabic), locally known as Baptism fish. The fish is fried, or baked with sweet peppers and fresh coriander. It's a popular spot at weekends, particularly at dusk when the sun sets over distant Jerusalem. Look for signs along the road halfway between the baptism site and the main Amman–Dead Sea road.

Getting There & Away

Follow signs to the 'Baptism Site' along the road from Amman to the Dead Sea. A taxi from Amman or Madaba to the site, taking in the Dead Sea and Mt Nebo en route, costs around JD30. Getting there by public transport is more difficult. Take any minibus to Suweimah and ask to be dropped at the Al-Maghtas junction. The Dead Sea is to the left of the junction, the baptism site to the right. There's no public transport for the 5km trip to the visitor centre. Take plenty of water if you intend to walk or hitch.

SHUNEH AL-JANUBIYYEH (SOUTH SHUNA)   الشونة الجنوبية
05 / pop 6000

Serving as a junction for public transport to the Dead Sea, Jordan Valley and King Hussein Bridge, this town is well connected by minibus with Amman's Muhajireen bus station (500 fils, 45 minutes), as well as Madaba (350 fils, 45 minutes) and Salt (250 fils, 45 minutes). There are also frequent minibuses to Suweimeh, 3km from the Dead Sea resorts.

There are a few simple restaurants and groceries in town. Consider chartering a taxi (if you can find one) for a few hours from Shuneh al-Janubiyyeh to places like Bethany-Beyond-the-Jordan (JD10) and Amman Beach (JD10).

DEAD SEA   البحر الميت
05

It would be a travesty to come to Jordan and miss the Dead Sea. This extraordinary body of intense blue water, polished smooth like

THE DEAD SEA IS DYING *Dr Alon Tal*

The Dead Sea is the lowest place on earth, and probably one of the hottest. The resulting evaporation produces an astonishing salinity of 31%, about nine times higher than the oceans, making a dip in the Dead Sea a very salty experience. The high mineral concentrations mean incredible buoyancy and great photo opportunities – get a snapshot of your travel companions happily sitting upright on the water reading newspapers. The waters' oily minerals also contain salubrious properties. German health insurance covers periodic visits to the Dead Sea for psoriasis patients to visit and luxuriate in the healing waters.

Sadly, no natural resource in the Middle East shows more signs of relentless population growth and economic development than the Dead Sea. Technically, the sea is a 'terminal lake' into which the Jordan River, along with other more arid watersheds, deposit their flow. Despite the folk song's characterisation of the River Jordan as 'deep and wide', in fact it has never been much of a gusher. When Israeli and Jordanian farmers began to divert its water to produce a new agricultural economy in the 1950s, the flow was reduced to a putrid trickle and the Dead Sea began to dry up.

In 1900, the river discharged 1.2 trillion litres a year into the Dead Sea, but water levels in the river today are hardly 10% of the natural flow. The Jordanian and Israeli potash industries in the southern, largely industrial Dead Sea region exacerbate the water loss by accelerating evaporation in their production processes. The impact is manifested in sink holes, created when underground salt gets washed away by the infiltrating subsurface freshwater flow. Particularly ubiquitous on the western (Israeli side) of the sea, the ground literally opens up – with people, farming equipment and even trucks falling in. Perhaps the most acute environmental consequence though is the 27m drop in the sea's water level, and the long and discouraging walks now required to reach the edge of the retreating beach.

Several solutions have been considered to bring water back to the Dead Sea. A 'Med–Dead' canal utilising the height drop from the Mediterranean Sea was discarded because of the prohibitively expensive price tag. But a similar pipeline from the Red Sea is seriously being considered. Dubbed the 'Peace Conduit', the project would pipe water from the Gulf of Aqaba to the Dead Sea's southern shore, producing hydroelectricity as well as a desalination plant that would provide water to Amman. Environmentalists question the anticipated unnatural water chemistry reaction and the seismic instability of the area. The World Bank, however, recently decided that the US$5 billion project was sufficiently serious to justify a $15 million feasibility study.

Dr Alon Tal is a professor in the Desert Ecology Department at Israel's Ben-Gurion University. For more biographical information, see p341.

oiled skin on a windless day in winter or ruffled into salty whitecaps during the summer winds, is a sea like no other. The extreme salinity of the water (31%, or nine times that of the ocean) makes for an almost intolerable environment for all but the most microscopic of life forms. Indeed, the only things you're likely to see in the Dead Sea are a few over-buoyant tourists.

The concentration of salt has nothing to do with the Dead Sea being below sea level; rather it comes about because of the high evaporation rate. Dead Sea salts and minerals have long been exploited for their skin-friendly properties – although they don't always feel that friendly. While swimming in the sea, you'll discover cuts you never

knew you had (don't shave before visiting), and if any water gets in your eyes, be prepared for a few minutes of agony.

Swimming is probably a misnomer – bobbing is nearer the mark. The buoyancy experienced in the Dead Sea makes it difficult to move through the water and any attempt at breaststroke results in being flipped over like a kipper.

The best way to visit the Dead Sea is to stay at one of the luxury resorts at the northeastern end of the sea. Here you can enjoy a spa treatment, watch the sunset across the water, and toast the rising night lights of Jerusalem, perched 1200m above the West Bank.

Alternatively, the Dead Sea can be reached as an easy day trip from Amman or Madaba. The public facilities of the newly refurbished Amman Beach, about 5km south of Suweimah, mean that you no longer have to put up with an embarrassed dip by the roadside. See p32 for the history of the Dead Sea area.

Information

The best time to visit the Dead Sea is October and November, and March to early May. During these times the weather is idyllic. In the winter months, the area is noticeably warmer than the rest of Jordan and the sea and sky are a brilliant blue. The summer is too hot for comfort for most people (nearing 50°C) and the area is generally deserted. On Friday and public holidays the hotels and public areas are crowded. Carry lots of water at any time of the year as there's little shade.

Activities

SWIMMING

After a dip in the Dead Sea, you'll find yourself coated in uncomfortable encrustations of salt that are best washed off as soon as possible. For this reason, although you

---

FAST FACTS

- The Dead Sea is part of the Great Rift Valley; it is the lowest spot on earth at 408m below sea level and more than 390m deep
- It is not actually a sea but a lake filled with incoming water with no outlet
- It is the second-saltiest body of water on earth (after Lake Aral in Djibouti) with a salt content of 31%
- Egyptians used Dead Sea mud (bitumen) in their mummification process; the last lump of floating bitumen surfaced in 1936
- The majority of Dead Sea minerals (including calcium and magnesium) occur naturally in our bodies and have health-giving properties
- The Dead Sea is 3 million years old but it has shrunk by 30% in recent years (half a metre per year) due to evaporation and the demands of the potash industry, one of Jordan's most valuable commodities

---

can take a dip anywhere along the Dead Sea coast, it's better to reserve your swim for the comfort of the Dead Sea resorts or at Amman Beach where freshwater showers are available and where access to the sea is generally cleared of sharp and lethally slippery rocks.

Most of the resorts offer day rates. The Mövenpick charges JD35 for access to the excellent spa, pools and beach (JD30 excluding the spa). The Marriott charges JD40 (JD20 entrance only; JD20 for use of spa). The Dead Sea Spa Hotel charges JD15 (JD7.500 for children); with a snack and a drink thrown in it costs JD20 (JD12 for children). All the hotels have mud pots on the beach where you can self-administer a full-body mud-pack. Leave it in place to bake under the sun for five to 10 minutes and then wash it off in the sea. It tightens the skin and leaves it feeling smooth, tingling and refreshed.

SPA TREATMENTS

Many people go to the Dead Sea area for the therapeutic treatments on offer in the Dead Sea spas. The low levels of UV rays and high oxygen levels are good for the health, and the Dead Sea mud contains high concentrations of minerals. These include calcium and magnesium, helpful remedies against allergies and bronchial infections; pungent bromine that promotes relaxation; iodine which alleviates certain glandular ailments; and bitumen that has skin rejuvenating properties. Many of these Dead Sea properties are made into easy-to-use preparations such as soaps, shampoos and lotions, and sold at the Dead Sea spas and in tourist shops throughout Jordan.

Of course, you don't need to be under-the-weather to enjoy the benefits of a spa treatment. If you feel like a scrub or a massage, or just a bit of pampering, it's easy to book in for an hour or two.

The most luxurious spa is the **Zara Spa** (☎ 3491310; www.zaraspa.com; Mövenpick Resort & Spa; ✆ 8.30am-8.30pm). It offers a range of facilities and treatments in a beautiful environment (see opposite) and costs JD25 for guests and JD35 for nonguests. These rates include access to a gym, private beach, pool, sauna, steam room, foot-massage pool, infinity pool and aqua-pressure pool. Extra services include a mud wrap (one hour, JD60), dry

---

IT'S A TOUGH JOB – BUT SOMEONE HAS TO DO IT   *Jenny Walker*

I have to say that as a die-hard, old-school traveller who felt that succumbing to a bed with a soft mattress was a sign of weakness, I was deeply suspicious of the whole spa circus. But if they were good enough for Herod the Great and Cleopatra, they ought to be good enough for a Lonely Planet author, so in the spirit of in-depth research, I forced myself out of the hiking boots and into the fluffy bathrobes of the Zara Spa (see opposite).

Stepping gingerly into the clinically white, marble entrance hall, I half expected to be routed by the security guard – but not a bit of it. Without a hint of irony, I was served courteously with a mint tea, given my own spa bag to stow boots and notebook, and shown to the changing rooms. Within moments of entering the marble corridors of this opulent modern bathhouse I realised that this wasn't going to be a swim in the municipal pool back home.

I started my spa experience in the cradling waters of the Dead Sea saltwater pool (27% salt), followed up with a foot spa and a float in the Damascene-tiled Jacuzzi. I then stepped outside for a bust up with a variety of bullying jet sprays that exercised parts they probably shouldn't have. Best of all were the little pots that bubble when you sit in them and really ought to be X-rated.

Luxury of this kind is an extreme sport and by the time I reached the spa's private infinity pool, I was so seduced by the ambience I hadn't the energy to try the saunas, steam rooms and tropical sprays, let alone the private gym. I lay under the oleander by the pool, sipping a chilled carrot juice and wondered where the next tough assignment would take me.

---

flotation, hot-stone therapy, shiatsu and other massages (from JD60 for 50 minutes). A day package costs JD190 for 3½ hours of treatments; a three-day package is JD365.

Spa (☎ 3560400; Dead Sea Marriot; ☼ 8.30am-10pm, treatments 10.30am-10pm) is free for guests and JD25 for nonguests (it costs an extra JD20 for access to the beach, pools and gym). The spa includes a heated pool, Dead Sea saltwater pool, Jacuzzi, steam room and sauna. Treatments include massage (JD70, 55 minutes), body wraps, salt scrubs, phytomer facials, mud facials, dry flotation and hydro baths. Day packages range from JD150 to JD225; a week package costs around JD750.

Dead Sea Spa (☎ 3561000; Dead Sea Spa Hotel; ☼ 9am-6pm) focuses primarily on medical treatments, with an in-house dermatologist and physiotherapist. Entry to the beach, pools and spa costs JD40 and includes a fitness room, solarium and Dead Sea saltwater pool. A full-body Swedish massage (JD25) and mud application (JD30) are also available.

Keep an eye open for the second-largest spa in the Middle East, about to open at the Kempinski.

AMMAN BEACH   شاطئ عمان
This newly upgraded public facility goes under the full title of **Amman Beach Tourism Resort, Restaurant & Pools** (☎ 3560800; adult/child

JD10/6; ☼ 8am-midnight). The beach, 2km south of the main resort strip, is run by Amman municipality to give affordable access to the Dead Sea. The grounds are attractively landscaped and the beach is clean, with sun umbrellas, freshwater showers and a vibrant local flavour, making it a great place to strike up conversation with a Jordanian family.

There are also a number of swimming pools, a restaurant (JD10 buffet), some drinks stalls, basketball courts and an amusement park next door. It gets very busy at weekends (especially Thursday night and Friday).

Locals will generally swim fully clothed, though foreigners shouldn't feel uncomfortable in a modest swimming costume. Women on their own may attract less unwanted attention in shorts and a T-shirt.

Amman Beach is the finishing line for the annual Dead Sea Marathon. See p291 for more details.

AL-WADI RESORT
Newly opened, this **public resort** (adult/child JD25/18; ☼ 9am-6pm Sat-Thur, to 7pm Fri) has a variety of water games, including a wave machine and slides, in pleasantly landscaped surroundings. There are two restaurants (open 9am to midnight), one selling snacks and the other offering an Arabic menu. Children are measured on entry: those

under 95cm are admitted free! The resort is about 500m north of the Convention Centre at the head of the Resort strip.

HERODUS (ZARA) SPRING   نبع هيرودوس

These hot springs, 10km south of Amman Beach, have been famous for centuries, and are even marked on the Madaba mosaic map. Indeed, nearby is the site of ancient **Callirhöe**, a favourite spa of the ancients. Herod came here in 4 BC to find treatment for, according to Josephus, 'an unbearable itching all over his body' – quite possibly psoriasis. Little remains to be seen at the archaeological site (discovered in 1807) other than remnants of Roman bathhouses and the ancient harbour from which Herod's boats sailed. But with a bit of imagination, it's easy enough to conjure poor Herod's itching form being led to the therapeutic hillside.

Despite the popularity of the spot with locals, especially on Friday, it's hard to recommend swimming here either in the hotspring pools (which are unclean), or at the beach, which affords no privacy from the road. There is no public transport.

Sleeping & Eating

About 5km south of Suweimah along the Dead Sea Highway are a number of first-class resorts. They don't look much from the highway, but once inside, they tumble into landscaped gardens, terraced sun spots, cascading pools and pristine Dead Sea beaches. They all have excellent restaurants and offer vantage points for watching the sun set over the hills of Judaea. Reservations are necessary at weekends (Thursday, Friday and Saturday). At other times, discounts are often offered for walk-in customers.

Dead Sea Spa Hotel (☎ 3561000; www.jordandeadsea.com; s/d JD71/85, ste from JD156; ✖ 🖭) Not as refined as its neighbours, this hotel is pleasant nonetheless. There's a medical/ dermatological spa, private beach access, a big pool and separate kids' pool with slides. Choose from rooms in the main block or bungalows. There's a Lebanese restaurant and a buffet (JD13).

Dead Sea Marriott (☎ 3560400; www.mariotthotels.com; s/d from JD175/190; ✖ 🖳 🖭 Ⓥ) Polished marble floors, brass fixtures and fittings, and spacious rooms contribute to the general opulence of this much-loved resort. Eating spots include sea-view cafés

and a brasserie–style French restaurant. Two cinemas, high-speed internet access, a jungle playground, mini waterfall and family pool ensure the kids are kept happy while parents luxuriate in the spa.

OUR PICK Mövenpick Resort & Spa (☎ 3561111; www.moevenpick-deadsea.com; r from JD215; ✖ 🖳 🖭 Ⓥ) This wonderful haven of dates and hibiscus boasts a river that ambles through the village-style complex of rustic two-storey apartments. Wooden screens and balconies allow guests to enjoy the view (of sea or gardens) in private while secluded seating areas around a superb infinity pool add to the ambience of discreet, gentle pleasure. The Zara Spa (p174) is justifiably renowned as one of the best in the Middle East. Culinary high points include Al-Saraya buffet (JD25), a Thursday night barbecue and prodigious Friday brunch (JD28). If five-star luxury is your thing, you won't want to stay anywhere else.

Kempinski Hotel Ishtar (☎ 3568888; www.kempinski.com; s/d from JD200/220; ✖ 🖳 🖭 Ⓥ) Dominating the shore, this grand resort is not shy in its bid to be the best. Floor-to-ceiling windows stretch the length of the Dead Sea vista, a Sumerian-style lobby overlooks a spectacular, circular infinity

---

A HIGH PRICE TO PAY FOR LUXURY

There's no doubt that the luxury Dead Sea resorts are helping visitors to enjoy access to the Dead Sea, bringing development to the area and much needed revenue to national coffers. It is also a fact that the spas offer a valuable therapeutic service for many 'health tourists' in search of relief from skin ailments and chronic joint problems. Unfortunately, however, the rapid development along the resort strip is beginning to add to the environmental woes of the area (see p173). All of the freshwater requirements of these resorts – showers, pools, baths, laundry and gardens – is being met by water piped from Wadi Mujib. The Royal Society for the Conservation of Nature (RSCN), which protested against the use of this resource, now notes that water levels in Wadi Mujib are decreasing. As one ranger at Wadi Mujib put it, the natural environment appears to being picking up the tab for our very human taste for luxury.

pool, and a series of water features tumbles down to the Dead Sea, making this a palace among hotels. Each of the modern rooms has a semi-shaded balcony and semi-sunken bath. Champagne is served with breakfast and the cuisine, from the Thai restaurant to the Mediterranean restaurant at sea level, is excellent. Visit at night time when a walk through the floodlit grounds is like participating in a piece of conceptual art.

Getting There & Away
BUS & MINIBUS
Buses (1½ hours) from Amman direct to Amman Beach leave on a demand-only basis from Muhajireen bus station between 7am and 9am. The last bus returns to Amman around 5pm (4pm in winter). JETT buses from Amman leave twice a week at 8am, returning at 6pm; in July, there is a daily service. Check with the JETT office in Amman (p116) for the latest timetable.

Minibuses only run as far as Suweimah. For details of getting to/from the Dead Sea from Amman, see p116. See p192 for details on reaching the Dead Sea from Madaba.

CAR
From Amman, it takes about an hour to reach the Dead Sea Resorts, along Hwy 40 and Hwy 65. Alternatively, you can drive from Madaba via Mt Nebo (see p170). If you choose this route, your first view of the Dead Sea will be a spectacular blue lozenge beyond the iron-coloured hills.

HITCHING
If you miss the last bus back to Amman from Amman Beach, you can try hitching. Friday and Sunday are the best days, but don't rely on this in summer or winter.

TAXI
A return taxi from Amman costs about JD30 for the day or JD15 for a one-way journey. From Shuneh al-Janubiyyeh, taxis cost from JD30 for the day, including side trips to Bethany-Beyond-the-Jordan and the Dead Sea Panorama.

TOURS
Some budget hotels in Amman and Madaba organise day trips (see p105 and p192) via Mt Nebo, the Dead Sea Panorama and Hammamat Mai'in.

DEAD SEA PANORAMA
البحر الميت بانوراما

Walk among the cacti to this **lookout** (admission per person JD2; ◷ 8am-midnight), high above the Dead Sea, watch the raptors wheel in the wadis below and you will have to pinch yourself to think that you are standing at sea level. This wonderful museum and restaurant complex offers some breathtaking views, especially on a crisp day in winter when the Judaea Mountains across the water seem as if they are an arm's stretch away.

For an excellent introduction to the geology, history and environment of the Dead Sea, spare an hour for the **Dead Sea Museum** (◷ 8am-4.30pm) and lay hands on a set of touchable stones. Drive the roads in the area (see p170) and you'll notice the rich pattern, texture and hue of the exposed rocks alongside the road. This is particularly the case on the Dead Sea Parkway, which extends above the Dead Sea Panorama to Hammamat Ma'in and Madaba or below to the Dead Sea Highway. Along the cut of the steepest section of road, rich layers of sedimentary rock create natural murals that add to the beauty of the journey. In the museum, you can identify and touch specimens of this geological treasure.

If reading about the threat to the Dead Sea gets too depressing, the **Panorama Restaurant** (☎ 3245500; mains JD6-12; ◷ noon-11pm; **V**), with its splendid view, will lift your spirits. The excellent cuisine makes it a popular venue for weekend lunch and dinner. Try the mashed-walnut dip (JD2.500) or *shanklish* (local blue cheese mixed with tomatoes, onion and parsley, JD2), and follow it up with marinated, locally reared lamb chops (JD10).

The complex is clearly signposted off the Dead Sea Highway, about 10km south of the Dead Sea Resorts. The Dead Sea Panorama makes a worthwhile stop on a day circuit from Madaba, Mt Nebo, Bethany, the Dead Sea and Hammamat Ma'in, either by hired car or taxi (JD50 through Charl at the Mariam Hotel – see p190). There is no public transport.

HAMMAMAT MA'IN
حمامات ماعين (زرقاء ماعين)

☎ 05

Drive anywhere in the hills above the Dead Sea and you'll notice occasional livid green belts of vegetation, a trickle of water as it

DEAD SEA HIGHWAY

catches the sunlight, or a curtain of ferns across a disintegrating landscape of sulphurous rock. On closer inspection, you may catch a puff of steam and the hiss of underground water. These hills are alive with the sound of thermal springs – there are about 60 of them suppurating below the surface, breaking ground with various degrees of violence.

The most famous spring is **Hammamat Ma'in** (admission per person JD10; ☑ 8am-11pm), a resort in Wadi Zarqa Ma'in. The water, ranging from 45°C to a blistering 60°C, tumbles off the hillside in a series of waterfalls and less assuming trickles, and is collected in a variety of pools for public bathing. It contains potassium, magnesium and calcium.

The entrance fee permits use of the Roman baths at the base of the waterfall closest to the entrance. There's a separate charge for use of the swimming pool (JD13). The entry fee also includes a sandwich and a cold drink from the complex shop. Visitors are requested not to bring their own picnic, but this is rarely enforced. The valley is hugely popular on Friday during spring and autumn.

Activities

Two main baths are open to the public. The **Roman baths** have clean, indoor, hot baths (separate for men and women). There is also a small **family pool** beside a waterfall (turn left after the entrance), restricted to women, families and couples.

The large, clean, cold-water **swimming pool** closes around 4pm. A steaming waterfall

downstream makes a striking backdrop for tea on the terrace of the hotel.

It's possible to **hike** the 8km from the springs through Wadi Zarqa Ma'in to Herodus Spring on the Dead Sea Highway. The seven-hour trail involves negotiating deep pools, reed beds and slippery surfaces and is closed during winter (November to March). The trail (closed at the time of research due to refurbishment of the resort), requires a guide, but you can explore the upper 3km of the wadi on your own.

Sleeping & Eating

The ugly, concrete **Janna Spa & Resort** (☎ 3245500; www.jannaspa.com) rather blights the wadi, but the glamorous interior compensates. Windows onto the waterfalls bring the hot springs to your table. Many of the rooms – with sumptuous bathrooms – share a view of the piping, sulphurous hillsides. The hotel, chalets and spa were closed at the time of writing for refurbishment.

Minimal snacks and soft drinks are for sale in the shop near the entrance of Hammamat Ma'in.

Getting There & Away

The resort is 18.5km from the Dead Sea Resorts and 27km from Madaba, and well signposted in either direction. If you're driving, the 2.5km descent into Hammamat Ma'in is scenic (with bands of green, yellow and red streaking the hillside) but very steep, so use low gear.

AN UNCERTAIN FUTURE AT WADI MUJIB NATURE RESERVE

One of the most spectacular parts of the King's Highway is the point at which the road crosses the great Wadi Mujib (see p198). Midway through the crossing, the road scales the side of a brand-new dam. Picturesque though this startling band of blue might be in the barren landscape, it is the source of grave concern for the Wadi Mujib Nature Reserve, the vast 215 sq km of protected land between the dam and the wadi's outlet on the Dead Sea Highway. It's too early to gauge the impact of the dam, but already water in the permanently flowing wadis of the reserve has significantly reduced as water is siphoned off for use in Amman and the Dead Sea Resorts. If the water dries up completely, this would spell disaster for the rich flora and fauna that currently characterise the reserve.

With other challenges to the reserve's ecosystems, such as illegal hunting by local Bedouin tribes, overgrazing of livestock and the demands of mining companies for licenses to start mineral extraction, the future of the park is looking precarious. The RSCN is doing a first-class job in managing the park and it can only be hoped that increased tourism to the reserve – with its crystal-clear pools of water, hanging gardens and desert escarpments – will increase the pressure on the government to safeguard its long-term protection.

A WALK ON THE WET SIDE *Jenny Walker*

It's 100°F in the shade and the tarmac is rippling off the road ahead. The silence is alarming, as if all living things have retreated to the safety of higher ground, leaving only mad dogs – and English folk writing guidebooks – under the desiccating sun. This clearly wasn't the best time to be hiking in Wadi Mujib, we thought. In fact we were wrong. Late spring and summer is the perfect time for hiking, at least for the reserve's so-called 'wet trails'. And by wet, they really mean wet.

Leave your valuables behind (you can leave a locked backpack behind at reception), wrap your camera in a watertight bag, wear hiking sandals rather than leather hiking boots and give the 2km **Siq Trail**, the shortest hike in the reserve, a go.

The Bad Bits:

- Even on a summer morning it gets surprisingly cold wading between the canyon walls
- Ignore the macho types telling you it's just a 'gentle splash': depending on water levels, it's more like an assault course
- There are three or four points where you need a steadying hand to help cross fast-moving water (ask for a guide if you're on your own)
- Several giant, slippery boulders or obstructions at best require inelegant scrambling, shunting and stretching, and at worst invite a dislocated hip or shoulder
- Watching the clearly insane abseil down the waterfall you felt so pleased to reach the bottom of

The Good Bits:

- 'Petra with water' is how the reserve ranger described the Siq Trail, and the comparison is a fair one
- Beautiful pockets of lime-green reeds harbouring toads and the occasional snake
- Outrageously banded rock, scooped out and smoothed by the water
- Adrenalin rush as the water thunders past a precarious foothold
- Exhilarating descents, being pushed by the water from one rock pool to the next
- Relief on surfacing easily from the bubbling cauldrons of water
- Happy the pictures came out even though the camera didn't make it

So was it worthwhile? Without doubt! We're fit but not great water-goers so we were surprised by how benignly exciting it was to be alone in a raging torrent, bounced down small waterfalls and flipped into gorgeous pools of sunlight in what must be one of the region's most accessible little adventures.

From Madaba a taxi costs JD10 one way, or JD20 for a return journey including around an hour's waiting time. There is no public transport.

WADI MUJIB NATURE RESERVE
محمية الموجب

This wonderful reserve, which ranges from an altitude of 900m above sea level to 400m below, was originally established by the RSCN for the captive breeding of the Nubian ibex, but it also supports a surprising variety of over 400 species of plants (including rare orchids), 186 species of birds and 250 animal species, including the Syrian wolf, striped hyena, caracal and Blandford's fox. It's also an important staging post for migratory birds travelling between Africa and Europe.

The reserve faces several challenges (see p74) but it's encouraging to see parties of schoolchildren here, as the future of Jordan's ecological heritage is in their hands.

Information

The **visitor centre** (☎ 07-77422125) is along the Dead Sea Highway, about 20km south of the Dead Sea resorts, beside a suspension bridge across Wadi Mujib. Guides are compulsory for all but the Siq Trail and should be booked in advance through the RSCN (see p95). Only 25 people per day are allowed on each trail and there's a minimum group size of three on some trails. Apart from the Ibex Trail, children under 16 are not allowed. Life jackets are provided.

There are three wet trails (open between 1 April and 31 October) and two dry (1 November to 31 March). The best time to visit is April and May, although February and March, and October and November are the high seasons. The region is extremely hot and dry for most of the year, so guided treks usually begin early in the morning. For the wet trails, you may be wading up to your chest in water (or swimming) so bring a swimming costume, towel, walking shoes that can get wet, and a waterproof bag for your valuables and camera. A spare set of clothes is also recommended.

Hiking
The easiest hike on offer is the wet **Siq Trail** (per person JD12), an exciting 2km wade and scramble into the gorge, ending at a dramatic waterfall (see p179).

The wet **Malaqi Trail** (per person JD53) is the reserve's most popular hike. It's a half-day trip involving a hot and unremitting climb into the wadi, a visit to the natural swimming pools of Wadi Hidan and descent (often swimming) through the *siq*. The finale involves rappelling down the 18m waterfall (not suitable for non-swimmers or those with a fear of heights). If you have limited time, tackle the wet **Canyon Trail** (per

person JD35) instead. The trails start 3km south of the visitor centre.

Other options include the winter dry **Ibex Trail** (per person JD9.500), a half-day guided hike that leads up to a Nubian ibex enclosure at the Raddas ranger station, along a ridge with views of the Dead Sea, and optional excursion to the ruined Qasr Riyash.

The dry **Mujib Trail** (from JD35) starts from the ranger station at Fag'ua near the King's Highway and descends through a number of wadis to the Raddas ranger station or Wadi Mujib gorge.

Sleeping
The reserve operates 15 brand-new **chalets** (☎ 07-97203888; s/d with breakfast JD84/95; ⊠) on the windy shores of the Dead Sea. You need to book in advance, either by calling the chalet manager direct, or when booking your hike through the RSCN. The chalets have twin beds, a fridge and a shaded patio overlooking the Dead Sea in a plot that is still under development. The communal shower block has hot and cold water, and there are freshwater showers by the beach. The small restaurant serves early breakfast (open 7am to 8.30am) for hikers. For JD25.500, guests can also order a lunch or dinner of chicken, salad and mezze.

Getting There & Away
There's no public transport to the reserve: hire a car or take a taxi from Amman (125km), the Dead Sea Resorts, Madaba or Karak.

LISAN PENINSULA
ليسان شبه جزيرة

From Wadi Mujib, the Dead Sea Highway continues along the remaining length of the sea until it veers inland at the Lisan Peninsula. This area, together with the shallow waters of the Southern Ghor (Depression), is now dominated by the potash plant. Huge quantities of potassium chloride (Jordan's most valuable commodity), calcium and bromide are reclaimed from the Dead Sea through solar evaporation, leaving piles of discarded rock salt along the shoreline. The area was once settled during the early-Byzantine period and a number of minor ruins are scattered across the landscape.

The fields to the south of the Lisan Peninsula are highly fertile and produce tomatoes in biblical quantities, as well as aubergines,

---

OASES OF THE DEAD SEA HIGHWAY

There are limited eating and sleeping stops along the southern part of the Dead Sea Highway.

Feinan Lodge (run by Dana Nature Reserve, see p210) is the only sleeping option south of Wadi Mujib. Set in magnificent multihued desert, it's 22km off the Dead Sea Highway.

For a pit stop an hour's drive north of Aqaba, **Beir Mathkour** (☎ 03-2063650) has a restaurant, craft shop and service station within a garden of palms.

IN SEARCH OF SODOM

Say the words 'Sodom and Gomorrah' and dens of iniquity spring to mind. The Book of Genesis (Gen 19:24–25), responsible for the wicked reputation of these two terrible towns, describes the last straw – namely, when local Sodomites demanded to have sex with the angels sent by God to visit Lot. In response 'the Lord rained upon Sodom and upon Gomorrah brimstone and fire…and he overthrew those cities, and all the plain, and all the inhabitants of the cities, and that which grew upon the ground…'

Fanciful legends of a fevered biblical imagination? Not necessarily. The whole area is located on a major fault line, and it's possible that the towns were swallowed up by collapsing soil. Another possibility is that an earthquake released large amounts of underground flammable gas and bitumen (the infamous 'slime pits' referred to in the Old Testament), which were ignited by fire or a lightning strike.

Whatever the cause of their demise, archaeologists have long speculated as to the location of the world's most sinful cities. Many archaeologists favour the southern shore of the Dead Sea. But there's also the Bronze Age site of Babh adh-Dhra, on the edge of Wadi Karak. This town (population roughly 1000) was destroyed in 2300 BC, but intriguingly it holds the remains of 20,000 tombs, containing an estimated half a million bodies – as such it's odds-on favourite for Sodom. Both Babh adh-Dhra and the nearby site of Numeira, believed to be Gomorrah, are covered in a foot-deep layer of ash, suggesting the cities ended in a great blaze.

Natural disaster or the wrath of God? Some believe it amounts to the same thing.

---

cucumbers and potatoes, groves of bananas and date palms. It's a colourful region to visit during the winter harvest (January) when trucks, laden with produce, lumber up the mountain roads, leaving a trail of off-loaded vegetables strewn behind them.

LOT'S CAVE   كهف لوط

Now Lot went up out of Zo'ar, and dwelt in the hills with his two daughters, for he was afraid to dwell in Zo'ar; so he dwelt in a cave with his two daughters.
(Genesis 19:30)

Lot, the nephew of Abraham, features repeatedly in the colourful annals of the Dead Sea's southern shores. **Lot's Cave** (admission free; ☼ daylight hr), just past the Lisan Peninsula, is where he and his daughters apparently lived after fleeing the destruction of Sodom and Gomorrah (see the boxed text, above). Lot's wife famously turned into a pillar of salt after looking back at the smouldering city.

In an eyebrow-raising incident of incest that's remarkable even for the Bible, Lot's two daughters spiked their father's drink, had sex with him and then nine months later gave birth to his grandsons/sons Moab and Ben-Ammi, the forefathers of the Moabite and Ammonite peoples.

The cave, a 10-minute climb up a steep flight of steps, is surrounded by the ruins of a small Byzantine church (5th to 8th centuries), a reservoir and some mosaics, which were excavated by the British Museum. Remains from the cave date to the early Bronze Age (3300–2000 BC) and an inscription in the cave mentions Lot by name.

The **Lowest Point on Earth Museum**, at the base of the hill, was closed at the time of research.

The cave is 2km northeast of Safi and well signposted from the Dead Sea Highway. Look for the circular museum building on the hillside. Regular minibuses run between Karak and Safi (550 fils, one hour). If you're relying on public transport, be prepared for a 2km walk from the highway.

WADI ARABA   وادى عربة

Beyond the town of Safi, the Dead Sea Highway enters the arid landscape of Wadi Araba, and the desert quickly reasserts its dominance. The odd sand dune encroaches upon the road, the escarpment recedes to the distance and the sky assumes the epic quality of uninterrupted space. As such, there is not much to see along the final run into Aqaba – although the sensation of driving uphill to the Red Sea is an odd one. You can make the journey more interesting by diverting to the King's Highway, along the remarkable roads to Karak, Tafila or Little Petra (see p170 for details of these routes).

King's Highway
الطريق الملوكي

There is a point on the King's Highway, just before you reach the lip of the great Wadi Mujib, where the landscape could best be described as quintessentially Jordanian. Neat olive groves wrap around the contours of the gently undulating hills; sheep, driven in liquid streams of good-natured bleating, pour through the rural network of paths; a village, with washing flapping outside the flat-roofed, ochre-coloured houses, sleeps through the hottest part of the day. Only the lizards disturb the peace as they rustle through the fallen masonry of antiquity, watched by pied wagtails that bob over a mosaic of parched earth.

There is another point on the King's Highway, just after the great yawning gap of Wadi Mujib, where the avenues of poplars, the prickly pear–fences and the sleepy market towns resume. It's as if they form part of a seamless continuum along the surface of the upper plateau, uninterrupted by the great hiatus that divides the northern highway from the south.

There is surely no better metaphor for the continuity and tenacity of human life along this ancient highway. The highway has for the past 3000 years been traversed by the Israelites en route to the Promised Land; by Nabataeans to and from their sacred city at Petra; by Christian faithful on pilgrimage to Moses' memorial at Mt Nebo; by Crusaders to their castle fortifications; and by Muslim pilgrims heading to and from Mecca. Travel the road today, with all its difficulties, and you follow in the path of human beliefs, hopes and dreams.

HIGHLIGHTS

- Piece together early Christian history in the mosaics of **Madaba** (p184) and visit a modern workshop to see how they were made

- Survey the Promised Land from Moses' memorial at **Mt Nebo** (p193): the promised land that took almost 2000 years to deliver and cost the region dearly

- Dance with Salome's ghost at **Mukawir** (p195), before unveiling the spot where a reluctant Herod beheaded John the Baptist

- Listen to the thunder of ghostly hooves at **Karak castle** (p201) and **Shobak castle** (p211), Jordan's most impressive Crusader castles

- Find peace (and ibex if you're lucky) at **Dana Nature Reserve** (p205), on a hike from the temperate high-ground to the desert landscape of Wadi Araba

Getting Around

Of Jordan's three highways running north to south, the King's Highway is by far the most interesting, with a host of historical attractions lying on the road or nearby (see p44 for the history of this ancient thoroughfare). The highway connects the mosaic town of Madaba to the pink city of Petra via Crusader castles, Roman forts, biblical sites, a windswept Nabataean temple and some epic landscapes – including the majestic Wadi Mujib.

Unfortunately, Wadi Mujib is to blame for the lack of public transport along this road: minibuses serve the communities on either side of the wadi, while through traffic uses the Desert Highway. Chartering a taxi for the day is more feasible (see p192). The Palace Hotel (and other budget hotels in Amman, see p105) run minibus tours that stop in Wadi Mujib and Karak (and sometimes Dana and Shobak) en route to Petra.

The most convenient way to explore the King's Highway is to hire a car. This allows for longer, circular trips that combine the King's Highway with the Dead Sea Highway along spectacular hairpin roads (see p170).

If all else fails, hitching is possible but be prepared for long waits on deserted stretches – not advisable in the extreme temperatures of summer or winter. To explore all of the sites covered in this chapter on public transport could easily take a week.

MADABA   مأدبا

☎ 05 / Pop 70,000

The amiable market town of Madaba is best known for a collection of superb, Byzantine-era mosaics. The most famous of these is the mosaic map on the floor of St George's Church, but there are many other mosaics carpeting different parts of the town, many of which are even more complete and vibrant in colour.

One third of Madaba's population is Christian (the other two thirds are Muslim), making it one of the largest Christian communities in Jordan. The town's long tradition of religious tolerance is joyfully – and loudly – expressed on Friday. This is one day when you shouldn't expect a lie-in. The imam summons the faithful before a sliver of dawn leavens the sky. Then the carillon bells bid the Orthodox Christians

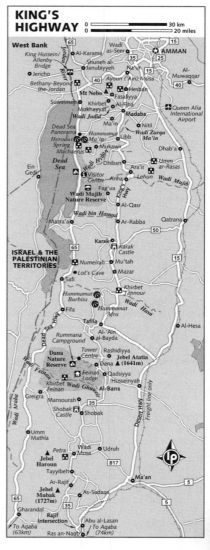

to rise, and finally Mammon gets a look in with the honks and groans of traffic. The rest of the day is punctured with yelps to buy apricots, and friendly greetings from children.

Madaba is easily explored on foot. With its lively shops dangling with strings of shoes; skinned goats tended by men in white Wellington boots; sewing machines rattling off repairs by the roadside; piles of fat cabbages; and giant aluminium pots and pans, Madaba is a typical King's Highway town. Unlike most other towns along the highway, however, it has a good choice of hotels and restaurants and many people find they stay longer than planned.

Madaba is less than an hour by public transport from Amman and makes an alternative base for exploring local sights including Mt Nebo, Mukawir and Umm ar-Rasas as well as Dead Sea highlights. You can even come by taxi from Queen Alia International Airport, bypassing Amman altogether.

History

The region around Madaba has been inhabited for around 4500 years. The biblical Moabite town of Medeba was one of the towns divided among the 12 tribes of Israel at the time of the Exodus, mentioned on the famous Meshe Stele of 850 BC (see p199) commemorating Meshe's victory over the Israelites.

The region passed from Ammonites to Israelites, Nabataeans and eventually, by AD 106, to Romans, under whom Madaba became a prosperous provincial town with the usual colonnaded streets and impressive public buildings. The prosperity continued during the Christian Byzantine period, with the construction of churches – and the lavish mosaics that decorated them.

The town was abandoned for about 1100 years after a devastating earthquake in AD 747. In the late 19th century, 2000 Christians from Karak migrated to Madaba after a bloody dispute with Karak's Muslims. The new arrivals found the town's signature mosaics when they started digging foundations for houses. News that a mosaic map of the Holy Land had been found in St George's Church in Madaba reached Europe in 1897, leading to a flurry of excavation that continues to this day. Various NGOs have assisted in restoration and rejuvenation projects in Madaba; at the time of writing, US Aid was taking an active initiative in this field. To find out more, see www.jordan.usaid.gov.

Information

Collect a brochure called *Madaba and Mount Nebo*, summarising Madaba's attrac-

tions, from the visitor centre. Other good Jordan Tourist Board brochures include *Madaba Mosaic Map* and *Mount Nebo*.

The American Center of Oriental Research publishes the definitive *Madaba: Cultural Heritage* (around JD20). More portable is the *Mosaic Map of Madaba* by Herbert Donner (JD7 to JD10), with a fold-out reproduction of the map and detailed text. Also recommended is the pocket-sized *Madaba, Mt Nebo* published by Al-Kutba (JD3).

The bookshop opposite the Burnt Palace sells a range of international newspapers.

Arab Bank (Palestine St) Accepts Visa and MasterCard, and has an ATM.

Bank of Jordan (cnr Palestine & King Abdullah Sts) Changes cash and travellers cheques.

Housing Bank (Palestine St) Accepts Visa; has an ATM.

Jordan National Bank (cnr King Abdullah & Talal Sts) Changes cash and travellers cheques.

Ministry of Tourism & Antiquities (☎ /fax 3252687; www.tourism.jo) Has an office above the Burnt Palace for specialised information about Madaba's preservation efforts.

Post office (Palestine St; ☾ 8am-5pm) Long-distance telephone calls can be made from here.

Tour.Dot Internet (Talal St; per hr 500 fils; ☾ 9am-2am)

Tourist Police Office (☎ 191; Talal St; ☾ 24hr) Just north of St George's Church.

Visitor Centre (☎ 3253563; Abu Bakr as-Seddiq St; ☾ 8am-5pm Oct-Apr, to 7pm May-Sep) This helpful information office has a range of brochures and some informative displays. Ask to see the 10-minute film that sets Madaba in the context of the surrounding highlights. There are toilets and a handy car park.

Sights

Most tourists file dutifully in and out of St George's Church and pay scant attention to the rest of Madaba. This is good news for the discerning visitor who can pore over the town's other stunning mosaics, untroubled by the crowds. A combined ticket to the Archaeological Park, Madaba Museum and Church of the Apostles costs JD2 (for one or all the sites). Children under 12 are free. There's no student discount.

ST GEORGE'S CHURCH & MOSAIC MAP

It's easy to understand why this rather modest 19th-century **Greek Orthodox church** (Talal St; admission JD1; ☾ 8am-5pm Sat-Thu Nov-Mar, 7.30am-6pm Sat-Thu Apr-Oct, 9.30am-5pm Fri year-round) has such a magnetic attraction. Imagine the excitement in 1884 when Christian builders came across the remnants of an old

MADABA

0 — 200 m
0 — 0.1 miles

INFORMATION	
Arab Bank	1 A2
Bank of Jordan	2 A2
Bookshop	3 A3
Housing Bank	(see 1)
Jordan National Bank	4 A2
Ministry of Tourism &	
Antiquities	(see 10)
Post Office	5 A2
Tour.Net Internet	6 A2
Tourist Police Office	7 A2
Visitor Centre	8 B3

SIGHTS & ACTIVITIES	
Archaeological Park	9 B3
Burnt Palace & Martyrs	
Church	10 A3
Church of the Apostles	11 B4
Madaba Institute for	
Mosaic Art &	
Restoration (MIMAR)	12 B3

Madaba Museum	13 A3
Madaba Turkish Bath	14 A3
New Orthodox School	(see 15)
St George's Church &	
Mosaic Map	15 A3
Tell Madaba	16 A3

SLEEPING	
Black Iris Hotel	17 A2
Madaba Hotel	18 A3
Madaba Inn Hotel	19 A2
Mariam Hotel	20 B1
Moab Land Hotel	21 A2
Mosaic City Hotel	22 A2
Queen Ayola Hotel	23 A3
Salome Hotel	24 B1
St George's Church Pilgrim	
House	(see 15)

EATING	
Al-Baraka Sweets	25 A2
Ayola Coffeeshop & Bar	26 A3
Bowabit Restaurant	(see 26)
El Cardo Restaurant	27 B3
Haret Jdoudna	28 A3
Mystic Pizza	29 A3
Petra Restaurant	(see 6)
Stop & Go	30 A3

SHOPPING	
Al-Baraka Dates	31 B3
Hanania Silver Shop	32 B3
Haret Jdoudna	(see 28)
Holy Treasures Centre	(see 21)
Madaba Studio & Lab	33 B3
Rug Shops	34 B3

TRANSPORT	
Local Bus Station	35 B3
Minibus & service taxi to	
Fasaliyya	36 A2
Minibus Stop to Fasaliyya	(see 2)

Byzantine church on the site of their new construction. Among the rubble, having survived wilful destruction, fire and neglect, the mosaic they discovered wasn't just another mosaic, it was one with extraordinary significance: to this day, it represents the oldest map of Palestine in existence and provides many historical insights into the region.

Crafted in AD 560, the map has 157 captions (in Greek) depicting all the major biblical sites of the Middle East from Egypt to Palestine. It was originally around 15m to 25m long and 6m wide, and once contained more than two million pieces. Although much of the mosaic has been lost, enough remains to sense the majesty of the whole.

Before viewing the map, take a look at the full-size replica in the ticket office and spot the details that you want to home in on in the church.

On Friday and Sunday morning the church opens at 7am for Mass (visitors welcome); viewing the map at these times is not permitted. A small shop by the exit sells copies of the map and reproduction Orthodox icons.

ARCHAEOLOGICAL PARK
Some careful restoration and excavation in the early 1990s led to the creation of the **Archaeological Park** (☎ 3246681; Hussein bin Ali St; combined ticket JD2; ☽ 8am-4pm Oct-Apr, to 5pm May-Sep), a collection of ruins and mosaics from the Madaba area.

KING'S HIGHWAY

NAVIGATING THE MADABA MAP

Step inside St George's Church and instinct dictates that you will look at the mosaic map spread across the church floor expecting north to be in front of you, towards the altar. In fact, the map, and indeed the church itself, is oriented towards the east. Imagine, therefore, as you approach the map, that you are in the hills above Jerusalem, looking over the crenulated tops of the great city residences towards the Dead Sea and the River Jordan (north, or far left). Today's Jordan lies beyond, at the 'top' of the mosaic (east, or nearest the altar), with the walled town of Karak in the uppermost portion of the map. Look for the fish in the mosaic rivers to the far right (south). They are swimming in the Nile Delta. Follow the perimeter of the fragments west (back towards the front the church) and you will come across a snippet of the Mediterranean, completing your tour of the Holy Land.

The most exquisitely detailed part of the map is that depicting Jerusalem, complete with city walls, gates, the central road (cardo) and the Church of the Holy Sepulchre in the northeast of the city. South of Jerusalem is Bethlehem (marked in red letters) and Judah. Above Jerusalem are Nablus, Hebron and the oasis of Jericho, surrounded by palm trees.

Above Jericho is one of the most touching and humorous parts of the mosaic. Look for the fish in the River Jordan, scampering back upstream from the lethal waters of the Dead Sea. They swim under the cable-drawn ferries of the river crossing – marked today by King Hussein Bridge. Spare time for the bodiless lion forever pursuing a pensive gazelle above the site of Jesus' baptism (marked as 'Sapsafas' on the map). Becalmed on the waters of the Dead Sea, their oars at the ready, lie two boats going nowhere. Perhaps they were trying to ferry Herod to the spa at Callirhöe (Zara), marked by three springs and two palm trees. Lot's Cave, where the old man was seduced by his two daughters, lies just above the settlement of Safi (Balak or Zoara). One of the 'Five Cities of the Plain', Balak is also distinguished by palm trees, just as Safi is today.

And so to Mt Sinai, recognisable by the multi-coloured mountains from which Moses descended with the Ten Commandments. Almost fragmented from the rest of the Holy Land by damage, but resolutely connected to Egypt and the Mediterranean Sea, is Gaza. This accident of history gives the map a kind of presentiment that matches its historical vision.

As you enter, you'll see a 1st-century BC mosaic from Machaerus, which is said to be the oldest mosaic found in Jordan. Follow the walkway to the right, above the Roman street. This street once ran east to west between the Roman city gates and was lined with columns. Continue past the faded but elegant mosaics of the **Church of the Prophet Elias** (built AD 607), pausing to enjoy the details (such as the fine green bird) and then descend to the crypt (AD 595).

The large, roofed structure in front of you contains the most impressive mosaics on the site, including those of **Hippolytus Hall**, an early-6th-century Byzantine villa. Spot the four seasons in each corner and notice the beautiful depictions of flowers and birds. The middle section shows characters from the classic Greek oedipal tragedy of Phaedra and Hippolytus. The upper image shows Adonis and a topless Aphrodite spanking naughty, winged Eros, while the Three Graces (daughters of Zeus, representing joy, charm and beauty) float nearby.

The **Church of the Virgin Mary** was built in the 6th century and was unearthed beneath the floor of someone's house in 1887. The central mosaic, thought to date from AD 767, is a masterpiece of geometric design.

CHURCH OF THE APOSTLES

Near the King's Highway, this **church** (Al-Nuzha St; combined ticket JD2; ☻ 9am-4pm Oct-Apr, 8am-5pm May-Sep) contains a remarkable mosaic dedicated to the 12 apostles. The embroidery-like mosaic was created in AD 568 and is one of the few instances where the name of the craftsman (Salomios) is included. The central portion shows Thalassa, a female personification of the sea, surrounded by fish and slippery marine creatures. Native animals, birds, flowers and fruits, and cherubic faces decorate the corners.

MADABA MUSEUM

The **Madaba Museum** (☎ 3244189; Al-Baiqa' St; combined ticket JD2; ☻ 9am-5pm) is housed in several old Madaba residences.

Some highlights of the museum include a 6th-century mosaic depicting a naked satyr, a saucy (and partially damaged) mosaic of Ariadne, dancing with cymbals on her hands and feet, and a mosaic in the courtyard depicting two rams tied to a tree – a popular image recalling Abraham's sacrifice.

Spare a few minutes in the **Folklore Museum**, housed at the Madaba Museum and included in the admission price. It features jewellery, traditional costumes and a copy of the Mesha Stele (see p199).

There have long been plans to move the museum to the Saray, but nothing has come of this yet. It may explain, however, why the museum is rather under par.

BURNT PALACE & MARTYRS CHURCH

The **Burnt Palace** (Hussein bin Ali St; admission free; 8am-5pm Sun-Thu Oct-Apr, to 7pm Sun-Thu May-Sep) was a late-6th-century luxury private mansion destroyed by fire and earthquake around AD 749. Walkways lead around the ruins for viewing the assorted mosaics, the best of which are the hunting sequences in the east wing, and the lion attacking a bull in the west wing.

On the site is the continuation of the ancient **Roman road** that runs through what is now the Archaeological Park, as well as the 6th-century **Martyrs Church**, which was destroyed in the 8th century. The site requires more imagination than most; five minutes should do it.

MAKING MOSAICS *Jenny Walker*

Push the door open on a mosaic workshop and it's like entering the Hall of the Mountain King. Clouds of dust plume up from the masonry saws and the workspace echoes with the screech of metal against rock and the persistent snapping of the workers' pincers as they cut stone rods into tiny, coloured squares. During our visit, all the workers engaged in this dedicated craft, from the stone-cutters to the assembly teams, were women. They looked up with beaming smiles and giggled into the chilly air. One of the ladies dusted her hands against her overcoat and, parking her mobile phone in among the tweezers, the paste brush and the glue pot, gave us an ad hoc tour of the workshop.

Mosaics, Mayzoon explained, are traditionally made from tiny squares of naturally coloured rock called tesserae. The first part of the process is preparing the stone, which is hewn in blocks from the rock face and then cut into thin cuboid rods in the workshop. These are then snipped by pincers into the tesserae. The smallest tesserae make the most intricate designs but they are much harder to work with and the mosaics take longer to assemble. It's rather like the knots on a carpet – the more tesserae there are per centimetre, the finer and more valuable the mosaic is.

Artists sketch a design freehand or trace the image from books, in the same way as their ancient predecessors would have copied scenes from pattern books. Designs usually feature scenes from everyday life, with surprisingly poetic depictions of plants and animals (look for the chicken – almost every mosaic seems to feature one). Hunting and viniculture, personification of the seasons, and various religious or mythological scenes are all fair game for the mosaic designer. But it's the detail that is so captivating – the bell on a gazelle's neck, the palm trees at an oasis, the wry smile on a human face.

Once the design is in place, the tesserae are then painstakingly arranged – traditionally on a thick coating of wet lime and ash to form a permanent and enduring flooring. Today they are more likely to be attached to wet plaster and affixed to wooden boards that can be used as table tops or wall decorations.

The tour concluded, Mayzoon returned to her friends round the assembly table. 'You took our photograph, no?' one of the ladies said. I was about to apologise when she added 'Please, you take it again. This time we want one of all of us!' A shaft of brilliant sunshine cut through the dusty air, lighting up the eight faces gathered in intense concentration around the half-built mosaic. The team of women worked rhythmically together, tapping and snapping, inching and coaxing the stones into a tree of life. With a little definition in olive green malachite and an ochre-coloured sandstone for their headdresses, they could for all the world have found their own immortalisation in stone.

MADABA INSTITUTE FOR MOSAIC ART & RESTORATION (MIMAR)

Originally set up as a school in 1992 by the Jordanian Government, **MIMAR** (☎ 3240723, Abu Bakr as-Seddiq St; admission free; ⏱ 8am-3pm Sun-Thu) has recently been upgraded to an institute. Its primary aims are to train Jordanian artists in the production and restoration of mosaics, spread awareness of mosaics in Jordan and actively preserve mosaics throughout the country. The restoration work of the school's artisans is evident in the Archaeological Park, the Church of the Apostles and at Khirbet Mukhayyat.

The institute consists of a workshop, which includes a partial reproduction of the mosaic map in St George's Church; it is displayed on the wall, making it easier to photograph. This is an active school so all visitors should first visit the administration office staff who are usually happy to show visitors around, although the classrooms are off limits.

TELL MADABA

This important archaeological site in the heart of Madaba was under excavation at the time of research, and there's not much to see. Like many sites around Madaba, it was discovered by accident when a local started digging the foundations for his house. It contains remains of a **Byzantine villa** and parts of an **Iron Age wall** or fortification, the largest of its kind in Jordan and visible from above the arch on the top level.

To get the most from this site you'll need a trained eye. For more on the excavations see www.utoronto.ca/tmap. Tread carefully as much remains to be excavated.

Activities

TURKISH BATHS

If you've had just about enough mosaics for one day, you could always enjoy closely knit tiles of a modern kind at **Madaba Turkish Bath** (☎ 3250999; Hashmi St; ⏱ 11am-11pm; without/with massage JD15/20). These small and cosy baths are clean and intimate but opening times, like elsewhere in Madaba, are flexible. Call ahead to reserve the baths for an hour or so. Women can choose a female or male attendant and couples can share the facilities if they wish. You begin with a shower, sweat it out for a few minutes in the steam room, relax on a heated marble slab, lounge in the

Jacuzzi and finally lie down at the mercy of the masseur. If you behave nicely, you'll be rewarded with mint tea in the comfortable *majlis* (lounge) area.

VOLUNTEER WORK

For those who like Madaba well enough to stay, there's an opportunity to teach English at the **New Orthodox School** (☎ 3250636; Talal St) that would make for an excellent gap-year experience. Run by Father Innocent (Innokentios) and attached to St George's Church, the school promotes 'mutual respect and peaceful coexistence' among youngsters of different religious communities. The school is a non-profit organisation, supporting needy students. Volunteers receive free accommodation, pocket money and private Arabic lessons. Email Father Innocent for details (diodoros@wanadoo.jo).

Walking Tour

All the main attractions in Madaba can easily be visited on foot. Allow two to three hours for the walk, longer if you want to spend more time admiring the mosaics.

The obvious place to start is **St George's Church** (1; p184), with its mosaic map. From there, head south along Talal St and visit the complex of restaurants and craft shops in **Haret Jdoudna** (2; p191), a wonderfully restored example of traditional Madaba architecture. Return north along Talal St, and then turn right (southeast) along Hussein bin Ali St. This takes you to the **Burnt**

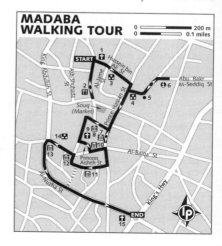

MADABA WALKING TOUR

Palace & Martyrs Church (**3**; p187). Further down the hill, at the end of Hussein bin Ali St, turn right (southwest) into Prince Hassan St, then immediately left to reach the **Archaeological Park** (**4**; p185). Next door is the **Madaba Institute for Mosaic Art & Restoration** (**5**; opposite), adjacent to the **Madaba Visitor Centre** (**6**; p184). Return to Prince Hassan St and head up the hill, past the new mosque, to the decaying but elegant 1898–1904 **Beit al-Farah** (**7**) at the corner to the right (west).

For a detour, backtrack up the hill to the solid **Saray** (**8**), built in 1896 and now the police station, and curve round the building, turning left, past **John the Baptist Catholic Church** (**9**), with its Roman column fragments built into the walls. Turn left onto Princess Aisheh St and Al-Baiqa' St, with the 1916–20 **Beit Shweikat** (**10**) on the corner. Turn right back onto Prince Hassan St and right again, passing the 1913–22 **Beit Alamat** (**11**) to the left (south) and the lonely ruins known as the 'cathedral' on the right. The road curves round to rejoin Al-Baiqa' St.

Down an alley running left (south) off Al-Baiqa' St is the entrance to **Madaba Museum** (**12**; p186). Continue further west along Al-Baiqa' St to the junction with An-Nuzha St passing more old houses, including **Beit Sawaihah** (**13**). Around 50m northeast of the junction, above an open patch of ground, are the ruins of **Tell Madaba** (**14**; opposite). Al-Nuzha St leads south and then southwest, to the junction with the King's Highway, where the **Church of the Apostles** (**15**; p186) stands.

Sleeping

Madaba has a good range of hotels, mostly run by Christian families, and all within easy walking distance of Madaba's main sights. Prices include breakfast and private bathroom unless otherwise noted

Madaba Hotel (☎ /fax 3240643; Al-Jame St; s/d JD10/18, s/d/tr with shared bathroom from JD8/16/21) This eight-room, family-run guesthouse (the first hotel in Madaba) was set up for Peace Corps visitors and not much has changed since. That said, the spartan rooms are clean with dorm-style beds and a heater. The shared bathrooms have hot water in the morning and evening. There's a ground-floor lounge and kitchen that guests can use. Breakfast (JD1) is better enjoyed elsewhere.

Queen Ayola Hotel (☎ 3244087; www.queenayola hotel.com; Talal St; s/d JD12/20, with shared bathroom

JD10/18) The Astroturf stairs say much about this run-down hotel. One or two rooms have balconies onto the busy street – the best that can be said for this charmless place. Keep it in mind only if everywhere else is full.

St George's Church Pilgrim House (☎ /fax 3245956; Talal St; s/d JD15/24) For a characterful place to stay, consider this pilgrim house, attached to St George's Church. Although it receives mainly Christian pilgrims, travellers can expect a warm welcome too. Rooms are ascetically simple with crisp linen and freshly laundered towels, and small bathrooms with hot water. Some rooms have a church view, others extend from a sliver of courtyard, bright with geraniums. If you encounter the patron of the house, the urbane and charming Father Innocent (self-confessedly 'Innocent by name, Guilty by every other means'), then your stay will find an extra blessing! Profits made by the guesthouse are invested in the neighbouring church school (see opposite for information about an interesting gap-year opportunity).

Black Iris Hotel (☎ 3241959; www.blackirishotel .com; Al-Mouhafada Circle; s/d/tr JD18/25/35) For a 'home away from home' feeling, it's hard to beat this family-run hotel. The carpeted rooms, with thick blankets and fresh towels, are cosy and there's a spacious sitting area where guests can drink coffee and read up on the town without being harassed. With its 'very special breakfast', made by the landlady, home-cooked Jordanian dishes (by request) in the evening, and warm assistance in organising onward travel, this hotel deserves its popularity with readers. Arrive in spring, and you may spot the national flowers of Jordan – the namesake of this hotel. Women travelling alone will feel comfortable here. The hotel is easy to spot from Al-Mouhafada Circle.

Moab Land Hotel (☎ /fax 3251318; moabland hotel@wanadoo.jo; Talal St; s/d/t JD20/25/30) With grand views of St George's Church and beyond, this family-run hotel couldn't be more central if it tried. The bright, recently refurbished rooms, painted pale yellow, have proper sprung mattresses and pine furniture and there's a cosy communal area with TV. The prize draw of this establishment, apart from the welcome, is the glorious rooftop terrace where breakfast is served in summer. The reception is on the upper floor.

KING'S HIGHWAY

Salome Hotel (☎ 3248606; www.salomehotel.com; Aisha Umm al-Mumeneen St; s/d JD18/25; ✹ ▢) With the family-run appeal of a small residential hotel, the Salome is a good choice for a quiet stay. It may lack the buzz of fellow travellers plotting their onward routes, but it nonetheless has a welcoming reception-cum-lounge and a licensed restaurant. The small rooms all have TV and spotless bathrooms. Notice the fossils in the garden: geology is a family passion. The hotel is located in a quiet residential district, an easy five-minute walk from the town centre.

our pick Mariam Hotel (☎ 3251529; www.mariam hotel.com; Aisha Umm al-Mumeneen St; s/d/tr JD25/30/36; ✹ ▢ ✹) The Mariam has grown a prodigious reputation over the years and has expanded to meet the demands of a constant stream of visitors. Inevitably, a bigger business leaves less time for the personal touch but the super-friendly reputation of the owners is largely undiminished. The hotel offers excellent facilities, including a bar, restaurant by the pool and internet access in a cheerful communal lobby area. The modern, no-nonsense rooms have comfortable beds, TV and sparkling bathrooms. Reservations are recommended. The hotel can organise a taxi to/from the airport (around JD12) and transport to Petra (see p192). Ask Charl, the owner, about a trip to see the local dolmens (p195) – a subject he is knowledgeable and passionate about.

Mosaic City Hotel (☎ 3251313; www.mosaiccity hotel.com; Yarmouk St; s/d JD25/35, extra bed JD10; ✹) This attractive, family-run, 21-room hotel is a welcome new addition to Madaba's midrange accommodation. Some of the bright and spacious rooms (with matching curtains and bedspreads) have balconies overlooking lively Yarmouk St. There's a small restaurant for breakfast and dinner, homemade on request). The 1st-floor reception is above the shops; access is from the neighbouring street.

Madaba Inn Hotel (☎ 3259003; www.madaba inn.com; Talal St; s/d/t JD45/60/75; ✹ ▢) This efficiently managed, 33-room hotel has brought a new dimension to tourism in Madaba, allowing for tour groups to stay overnight and thereby encouraging much-needed investment in town. Outside high season, this affable hotel is quiet and reservations are not necessary. The comfortable rooms (all with TV and minibar) have ex-

cellent views across the Madaba plain. The restaurant offers a generous breakfast of homemade staples including local cheese, olives and yoghurt.

Eating & Drinking

Madaba is a good place to sample traditional Jordanian food. Many restaurants organise a good-value lunch buffet (largely catering to tour groups) which offers a chance to sample various local dishes. Most of Madaba's restaurants serve beer, some interesting local wines and arak.

Stop & Go (☎ 776530034; Prince Hassan St; snacks 500 fils) The doughnuts may not always be today's, but the frank and thoroughly likeable owner is the first to tell you as much – while he fills you in on the gossip of Madaba. A cup of coffee in the upper gallery of this tiny café is like the pause for tea in a carpet shop: an essential experience of being in town.

Petra Restaurant (Talal St; ✹ 8am-midnight; snacks JD1) Cheap and cheerful, this restaurant serves reliable fare. The kebab sandwiches (JD1) fill the gap and you can pick up dessert from the Arabic sweet shops round the corner. Note that the sign here reads King Shwarma.

our pick Ayola Coffee Shop & Bar (☎ 3251843; ayola@hotmail.com; Talal St; snacks around JD2; ✹ 8am-11pm; Ⓥ) If you want a toasted sandwich (JD2), Turkish coffee (JD1), glass of arak with locals, or simply a cosy perch on which to while away some time with fellow travellers, then this is the place to come. With festoons of hand-loomed kilims draped from the ceiling, creeping vines and the aroma of *sheesha* (water pipe) it captures the very essence of Jordan. There's free internet access if you have a laptop.

Bowabit Restaurant (☎ 32403335; Talal St; mains JD7; ✹ 9am-midnight) With two tables overhanging the road opposite St George's Church, photographs of old Madaba on the wall and excellent Italian-style coffee (cappuccino JD2.500), this is a number-one place to relax after strolling round town. Alternatively, make a night of it over a dish of Madaba chicken (JD7) and a beer (JD3).

Mystic Pizza (☎ 3243249; Prince Hassan St; small/medium/large pizza around JD3/6/8; ✹ 9am-midnight; Ⓥ) This tiny, trendy new venue with its heavy wood chairs and flat-screen TV prepares delicious pizzas (including a fire-roasted vegetarian pizza), onion rings (JD3), lentil soup (JD2) and garlic bread

(JD1). Follow it up with the best frappacino in town (JD2.500).

El Cardo Restaurant (☎ 3251006; Hussein bin Ali St; buffet/mains JD8/5; ☯ 8am-midnight) Come to the upper gallery of this typical old-house restaurant at lunchtime in season, and you can expect a good buffet of baked chicken or lamb, fresh hummus and local salads. The measure of the chef to our mind, however, was the ability to rustle up something expert on a dark night in winter and the willingness of the aging patrons to give us an out-of-hours welcome. The restaurant is opposite the Archaeological Park.

Haret Jdoudna Complex (☎ 3248650; Talal St; mains JD5-10, plus 26% tax; ☯ 9am-midnight; **V**) This attractive complex of craft shops (right), also runs a bar and a restaurant set in one of Madaba's restored old houses. The interesting menu includes *mutaffi bethanjan* (fried eggplant with sesame), *fatteh* (fried bread with garlic-laced yoghurt and hummus, sometimes with chicken) and *sawani* (meat or vegetables cooked on trays in a wood-burning oven). Sit indoors by a roaring fire in winter (if the staff allows you) or in the shaded courtyard in summer. Though popular with locals and discerning diners from Amman, the persistently surly attitude of restaurant staff can ruin the experience.

There are a number of snack shops along Yamouk St and the King's Highway, selling felafel, shwarma and roasted chicken. For freshly baked Arabic bread, head for the ovens opposite the Church of the Apostles. There are several grocery stores in town. The most convenient for visitors is the so-called 'Tourist Supermarket' next to the Coffee Shop Ayola. Fresh fruit and veg for a picnic can be bought along King Abdullah St.

Don't miss out on the Arabic sweet shops, like **Al-Baraka Sweets** (cnr Palestine & King Abdullah Sts) where you'll find round trays of honey-drizzled pastries, some filled with local cheese, other with nuts and sugar.

There's little going on in Madaba after dark, except drinks in the bar at Coffee Shop Ayola or poolside at the Mariam Hotel.

Shopping
You can visit private mosaic workshops (with no obligation to buy), such as **Lawrence Arts & Crafts** (☎ 79 5504121; fax 4903753; King's Highway) and purchase your own copy of the Madaba map or a more modest Tree of Life (from JD8, depending on size). Another large handicraft centre specialising in mosaics is the **Al-Mukhayat Handicraft Centre** (☎ 3250247) located 1km before Mt Nebo on the road from Madaba.

Madaba is also famous for its colourful hand-loomed kilims (see p66), which flap and dance outside shops throughout town (especially between the Burnt Palace and St George's Church). Buying one of these rugs is more than just a purchase, it's a great way to get under the skin of the town: chats and tea with the rug-sellers are *de rigueur*.

The **Haret Jdoudna Complex** (☎ /fax 3248650; Talal St; ☯ 9am-9pm) sells an extensive range of crafts including mosaics, ceramics, textiles and clothing. Look out particularly for some exquisite embroidery; many of these items are sponsored by the Arab Cultural Society, which supports Jordanian war widows. Indeed, most items come from local non-profit organisations, including the Noor Al-Hussein Foundation (see p259).

There are a number of quality shops in town including a locally renowned master silversmith at **Hanania Silver Shop** (Prince Hassan St), opposite Al-Baraka Dates. There is little on display in the window but every piece is hand-crafted to the highest standards. **Holy Treasures Centre** (☎ 3248481; Talal St), opposite St George Church, has an extensive range of Dead Sea products. It also sells consecrated holy water from the River Jordan.

Madaba Studio & Lab (☎ 3245932; Talal St; ☯ 8am-8.30pm) has memory cards (1GB for JD20) and batteries for digital cameras. It's near the Moab Land Hotel.

For an unusual present, take back a selection of spices or freshly ground coffee beans from **Spice** (Palestine St), opposite the Housing Bank. Another good buy are the attractively packaged dried dates (JD3 for a box of eight) from **Al-Baraka Dates** (Prince Hassan St). Spare some time to amble along Al-Yarmuk St: here you will find water pipes, women's headscarves and shops selling Jordanian sweets. The street comes alive at night and it's a good place to mingle with local shoppers to gain a flavour of the town.

There are a couple of warehouse-like emporiums selling handicrafts but they are mainly intended for tour groups and lack the personal touch of shops in town. If you are into one-stop shopping, however, then you can find these outlets along the road to Mt Nebo.

Getting There & Away

The local bus station is about 15 minutes' walk east of the of the town centre, on the King's Highway. A taxi from town to the station costs around JD1. A taxi to the new bus station, 3km from the town centre, is JD1.500. This bus station services longer-distance routes.

Most attractions around Madaba (with the exception of Mt Nebo and Mukawir) are time-consuming to reach by infrequent public transport. It's easy, however, to charter a taxi in Madaba. Ask at your hotel for help.

TO/FROM THE AIRPORT

If you want to bypass the bustle of Amman, it's possible to reach Madaba from Queen Alia International Airport by private taxi (day JD15, night JD20). Most hotels in Madaba can arrange a taxi from the airport if you contact them in advance.

TO/FROM AMMAN

From Raghadan, Wahadat and, less often, Abdali bus stations in Amman, there are regular buses and minibuses (400 fils, one hour) throughout the day for Madaba. Minibuses return to Amman from the new bus station until around 9pm (earlier on Friday). Taxis cost JD12 during the day, JD15 at night.

TO/FROM THE DEAD SEA

Minibuses leave from the new bus station to Shuneh al-Janubiyyeh (South Shuna; 500 fils, 45 minutes), from where you can catch another minibus to Suweimah (300 fils, 30 minutes). Returning to Madaba is more problematic: take a minibus (before 5pm) for Amman and ask the driver to let you out just before Na'ur. Here you'll have to wait for a minibus to take you to Madaba (total of JD2, 1½ hours). To visit the Dead Sea by taxi, including two hours' waiting time, costs JD25.

One popular trip to the Dead Sea is via Mt Nebo and Bethany, returning via the Dead Sea Panorama and Hammamat Ma'in (JD50). The Black Iris Hotel and the Mariam Hotel can organise these taxi tours with a one hour stop at each site.

With your own transport, you can drive to the Dead Sea via Mt Nebo and return along the Dead Sea Panorama road. Alternatively, you can make a longer but equally stunning drive via Karak (see p170).

SOUTH ALONG THE KING'S HIGHWAY

There is no public transport linking Madaba with Karak along the King's Highway. If you wish to go this way, you must take a minibus to Dhiban (450 fils, 45 minutes) and then charter a taxi to cross Wadi Mujib to Ariha and wait for an onward minibus to Karak. From Karak, minibuses run to Tafila, where you can find transport for Qadsiyya (access to Dana). Public transport south of Qadsiyya is infrequent, so you may need to take a minibus to Ma'an and then another to Wadi Musa (Petra).

One option is to take the service organised by the Mariam Hotel (you don't have to be a guest). Leaving at 10am, it goes to Petra (arriving around 6pm), with stops at Wadi Mujib for photos, and an hour in Karak. You can get off at Dana, but you'll have to pay the full fare. The service requires a minimum of three people (the hotel rings around Madaba to find other passengers) and costs JD15 per person. Alternatively, the Black Iris Hotel can organise a taxi for JD60. If you can find two passengers to join you, the price is JD20 per person. A normal taxi fare for this service is JD90 per car.

TO/FROM ELSEWHERE

It is possible to travel to Karak on a twice-weekly minibus (Sunday and Thursday, JD2, two hours) from the new bus station, although it travels via the less interesting Desert Highway. The bus, which usually leaves sometime around 6am, is the university bus for Mu'tah, but it stops at (or close to) the minibus station in Karak. Note that it often doesn't run during university holidays.

From the local bus station in Madaba, minibuses go to Mukawir (for Machaerus castle, 600 fils, one hour) several times a day, the last at around 5pm. A taxi costs JD20 with one hour of waiting time.

See p194 for details of getting to and from Mt Nebo.

Getting Around

If you're laden with bags, private taxis are plentiful; from the new bus station to the centre of town costs around JD1. If you are driving, note that it is not possible to park outside some of the cheaper hotels as they are on busy, narrow streets.

MT NEBO   جبل نيبو

> Go up unto…Mount Nebo in Moab, across from Jericho, and view Canaan, the land I am giving the Israelites as their own possession. There on the mountain that you have climbed you will die.
>
> *(Deuteronomy 32:49–50).*

Mt Nebo (admission JD1; 🕙 8am-4.30pm Oct-Apr, to 7pm May-Sep) is where Moses is said to have seen the Promised Land, a land he was himself forbidden to enter. He died (allegedly aged 120) and was later buried in the area, although the exact location of the burial site is the subject of conjecture. The site flickered briefly into the international spotlight with the visit of Pope John Paul II in 2000.

The Mt Nebo region features several peaks, including Siyagha (the local name of the site, meaning 'monastery'). This is where you will find the Moses Memorial Church. It's a pleasant side trip from Madaba, just 9km away, and the mosaics are magnificent. Aside from its religious significance, Mt Nebo commands sweeping views of the ancient lands of Gilead, Judah, Jericho and the Negev – the Promised Land.

History
A Roman nun, Etheria, stumbled across the original three-apsed church on this site during a pilgrimage in AD 393. A nave was added in the 5th century, the first baptistery chapel (with the mosaic) in 530, and the main basilica in 597, together with a large monastery.

By this time Nebo had grown into an important pilgrimage site, even earning a signpost off the main Roman road through the region (a Roman mile marker lies in the church courtyard). Pilgrims would travel to Jerusalem, Jericho, Bethany, Ayoun Musa and Mt Nebo, before descending to Hammamat Ma'in for post-pilgrimage bathing.

The church was abandoned by the 16th century and only relocated in the 20th century, using 4th- and 5th-century pilgrim travelogues. The Franciscans bought the site in 1932 and have excavated most of the ruins of the church and the monastery, as well as reconstructing much of the basilica.

Information
The entrance to the complex is signposted from the Madaba–Dead Sea road, next to a visitor centre (not yet opened at the time of research). Smoking and mobile phones are not allowed in the complex. Toilets can be found next to the entrance.

The authoritative *Town of Nebo* by Fr Sylvestre J Salter and Fr Bellarmiro Bagatti details this and other Christian sites in Jordan. More portable is *Mount Nebo* by Michelle Piccirillo. Both are usually available for sale inside the church. The Jordan Tourism Board publishes an excellent pamphlet entitled *Mount Nebo,* which summarises the site's significance. The encyclopaedic *Mosaics of Madaba* is on display inside the church.

Sights
Before you enter **Moses Memorial Church,** visit the **museum** which has a good collection of mosaics from around Nebo and a 3-D map of the area.

The nave and the presbytery mark the oldest section of the **basilica,** built around 4th-century foundations in AD 597. Pilgrims light candles near the altar in continuance of a tradition that dates back some 1500 years. Note the beautiful braided-cross mosaic next to the altar.

Enter the old baptistery to see the exceptionally well preserved main **mosaic** (AD 530). Measuring about 9m by 3m, it depicts hunting and herding scenes interspersed with an assortment of African fauna, including a zebu (humped ox), lions, tigers, bears, boars, zebras, an ostrich on a leash and a camel-shaped giraffe. The inscription below names the artist. Even to the untrained eye, it's clear that this is a masterpiece.

The newer **baptistery** to the southeast has smaller mosaics, with a fine image of a gazelle and pomegranate trees.

From the **lookout** in the **courtyard**, the views across the undulating hills to the Dead Sea, Jericho, the Jordan River and Jerusalem (just 46km away), are superb, especially in winter when the air is clear from heat haze. A helpful direction finder indicates which way to look. Nearby, an Italian-designed **bronze memorial** symbolises the suffering and death of Jesus on the cross and the serpent that 'Moses lifted up' in the desert.

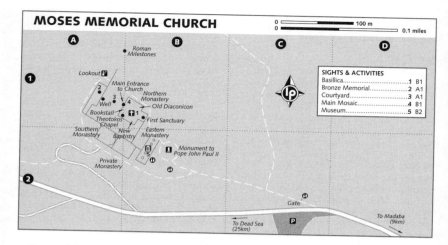

Some of the complex is part of a functioning monastery and is therefore off limits to visitors.

To enjoy the views away from the crowds, pack a picnic and hike along the road downhill from the site (towards the Dead Sea) for 100m and take the track to the left to the nearby hilltop.

Eating
If you happen to be around Mt Nebo at lunchtime, call into the recommended **Mount Moses Restaurant Siyagha** (☎ 3250226; buffet JD9; ☷ 8am-5pm; **V**). Every day it produces an excellent buffet, which includes Jordan's famous *maqlubbeh* (upside-down dish) and a variety of vegetarian options, served piping hot under copper lids in this trestle-tabled restaurant. The stone pillars and reed ceiling add to the 'been here forever' ambience and you can take a glass of after-lunch wine and stretch out on the *majlis* cushions.

The restaurant is attached to a craft shop (selling largely imported goods from across the Middle East) and a mosaic workshop, 1km back along the road towards Madaba.

Getting There & Away
From Madaba shared taxis run to the mosque at Fasaliyya, for 250 fils a seat. For an extra JD1 or so the service will drop you at Mt Nebo, 3km further.

A return trip in a private taxi from Madaba, with about 30 minutes waiting time, shouldn't cost more than JD5 per vehicle.

From Mt Nebo the road continues for 17km into the Jordan Valley to meet the main Amman–Dead Sea Highway, offering excellent views of the Dead Sea. The drive takes you from the tree line of olives and root vegetables, past a rocky landscape of prickly pears to the ochre-coloured hills of the Dead Sea depression. The yellow turns to red as the road twists past iron-rich escarpments and finally descends to the highly cultivated Jordan Valley, dotted with greenhouse plastic. There is no reliable public transport along this route.

AROUND MT NEBO
Khirbet Mukhayyat   خربة مخيط
The village of Khirbet Mukhayyat marks the original site of ancient Nebo village, as mentioned on the 9th-century BC Mesha Stele (see p199) and in the Bible. Also here is the **Church of SS Lot & Procopius**, which was originally built in AD 557. Inside this unremarkable building is a remarkable **mosaic**, with scenes of daily life such as agriculture, fishing and wine-making (the cutting and carrying of grapes).

The turn-off to Khirbet Mukhayyat is signposted 'Al-Makhyt', about 6km from Madaba and 3km before reaching the church complex at Mt Nebo. A good road leads 2.5km along the edge of the village to a car park surrounded by juniper trees. There is no public transport.

Sadly, the mosaics have been damaged by rainwater in recent years and the church was closed for restoration at the time of writing.

Ayoun ('Ain) Musa   عين موسى

Ayoun Musa (Spring of Moses) is one of two places where the great man is believed to have obtained water by striking a rock (see also p237). Six giant eucalyptus trees mark the spot and there's an occasional waterfall over the lip of the rocks. The littered site is disfigured by discarded concrete buildings and there's little to see except the low-lying **ruins** of a couple of churches nearby.

To reach the site, turn right about 1km before the church at Mt Nebo, opposite the Siyagha Restaurant. A 2.4km switchback road to Ayoun Musa is steep (but tarmacked) and it offers a close-up view of Bedouin encampments, hunkered down against the elements. Arums grow in abundance among the rocky patches of tilled ground, and small, fertile wadis bristle with citrus and olive trees.

There is no public transport to the site. Walking down from the main road is easy; coming back is a killer.

Hesban   حسبان

Amateur archaeologists will like **Tell Hesban** (admission free; ☼ daylight hr), 9km north of Madaba. Over the centuries this strategic hill has been a Bronze Age settlement, an Amorite capital (900–500 BC), a Hellenistic fortress (198–63 BC), a Roman settlement called Esbus (63 BC–AD 350), a Byzantine ecclesiastical centre (AD 350–650), an Umayyad market town (650–750), a regional capital of the Abbasids (750–1260) and Mamluks (1260–1500) and, finally, an Ottoman village. All these layers of history are on view, albeit faintly.

The site is well signed, indicating the remains of a Byzantine church (the mosaics are displayed in Madaba), Roman temple and Hellenistic fort. There are lots of caves and cisterns both here and in neighbouring Wadi Majar. The largest Bronze Age cave can be explored with a torch (flashlight). Read up on the site beforehand at www.hesban.org.

Minibuses run frequently from Madaba (200 fils, 20 minutes) to Hesban or otherwise take a taxi for JD5. Coming from Madaba, the tell is on the left side of the road; if you are driving, turn left at the first set of traffic lights after the pedestrian bridge in the modern town of Hesban and follow your nose up the hill.

WADI JADID   وادي جديد

More terraced fields than wadi, Wadi Jadid is locally renowned for its remarkable collection of early Bronze Age burial chambers and stone memorials. Known as **dolmens**, these stone structures date back to around 5000 to 3000 BC and consist of two upright stones capped by a bridging stone. The term 'dolmen' means stone table and it remains a mystery as to how the huge bridging stones were winched into position: little wonder that social anthropologists regard them as proof of early social cohesion. There are about 40 dolmens scattered across the unmarked site, with at least 12 in good condition. There are thousands more scattered across Jordan, especially around ar-Rawdah.

From the road, it takes about 30 minutes to walk to the nearest dolmen, and an hour to reach more distant groups. The site is near the village of Al-Fiha, 10km southwest of Madaba, but you need to be 'in the know' to find it. The best way to visit is by taking a taxi (JD20 per car) organised by Mariam Hotel (p190). Chat with the hotel owner, Charl, before making the trip: as a geologist, he is passionate about dolmens and it was he who rediscovered this remarkable site for tourists.

If you have a car, follow the guide from Mariam Hotel and after visiting the dolmens, continue downhill to the Dead Sea (30 minutes). The road is narrow and potholed towards the end but it threads through beautiful and varied terrain, with Bedouin camps, green valleys of grapevines, olive groves and citrus orchards. As it descends to the desert floor, the road passes a spring with a small waterfall – almost miraculous in the arid landscape.

MUKAWIR (MACHAERUS)   مكاور (مكاريوس)

☎ 05 / pop 5000

Just beyond the village of Mukawir (pronounced mu-kar-wir) is the spectacular 700m-high hilltop perch of Machaerus, the castle of Herod the Great, and the place where Salome danced for the head of John the Baptist.

The pudding basin of a hill was first fortified in about 100 BC, and expanded by Herod the Great in 30 BC. The ruins themselves are of minor interest, but the setting, with the wind blowing through the columns like one of Salome's seven veils, is both haunting and breathtakingly beautiful. Most days you'll be alone with the ghosts.

Machaerus is known locally as Qala'at al-Meshneq (Castle of the Gallows), a fitting name given that it is renowned as the place where John the Baptist was beheaded by Herod Antipas, the successor of Herod the Great. John the Baptist had denounced Herod Antipas' marriage to his brother's wife, Herodias, as Jewish law forbade a man marrying his brother's wife while he lived. Bewitched by his stepdaughter Salome's skill as a dancer, the king promised to grant her anything she wished. To take revenge on the Baptist, Herodias told her daughter to ask for his head on a platter:

> And she went out, and said to her mother, "What shall I ask?" And she said, "The head of John the Baptiser."
> *(Mark 6:24)*

So, at the request of Salome, John was killed at Herod's castle, Machaerus. Provocative Salome has inspired painters and writers ever since.

There is nowhere to stay in Mukawir and only a few basic grocery stores, so bring your own provisions.

Sights & Activities
From the car park, a stone staircase leads down to the main path, which climbs the hill in a clockwise direction. Near the base of the climb, a small track leads around the main hill to the right, past a number of **caves**. Legend has it that it was in one of these that the gruesome execution took place. Flocks of choughs wheel through the air in suitably ominous fashion.

The main path climbs eventually to the **castle**. At the top, the modest ruins are unlabelled. The reconstructed columns southwest of the deep cistern mark the site of Herod Antipas' **palace triclinium**; this is the site where Salome danced. You can also make out the low-lying remains of the eastern **baths** and defensive **walls**.

The Romans built a **siege ramp** on the western side of the hill when taking the fort from Jewish rebels in AD 72 and the remains are still visible.

The castle is about 2km past Mukawir village and easy to spot. If you don't feel in the mood for a climb, it's worth coming this way just to see the hilltop fortress framed by sea and sky beyond.

This is a great area for **hiking**, with plenty of shepherds' trails snaking around hilly contours. One particularly worthwhile track leads steeply down the west side of the castle hill from the top and along a ridge line towards the Dead Sea. The views are magnificent, particularly at sunset.

It's also possible to follow the shepherds' trails (or the 4WD road) to the hot springs at Hammamat Ma'in. You must exercise extreme caution if taking any of these trails as the terrain falls steeply away and many paths are only for the sure-footed. Women are advised not to hike alone.

You can arrange with a private tour operator to hike from Mukawir to Zara/Herodus Hot Springs, a hard three- to four-hour trek. See p290 for a list of recommended hiking agencies.

Shopping
In Mukawir village, by the side of the road leading to the castle, is a weaving centre and gallery. This women's cooperative is run by the Bani Hamida Centre (see opposite) and the gorgeous, colourful kilims and cushions are on sale in the attached **gallery** (☎ 3210155; www.jordanriver.jo; ☼ 8am-3pm Sun-Thu). The women who run the centre speak little English, but welcome you to the workshop. There's also a display video explaining the work of the cooperative. For an excellent anthropological perspective on the Bani Hamida story, it's worth picking up a copy of *A Bedouin Perspective* (JD5) by Sue Jones who worked with the Jebel Bani Hamida women in the early 1990s. This booklet is on sale in the showroom.

Getting There & Away
Frequent minibuses (600 fils, one hour) leave from outside the local bus station in Madaba for the village of Mukawir, via Libb (the last is around 5pm). From there, it's a pleasant downhill stroll to the foot of the castle, or ask the minibus driver to take you

WEAVING A FUTURE: THE WOMEN OF BANI HAMIDA

When the Bani Hamida initiative was first established in 1985 with help from Save the Children, it was a pioneering venture aimed at bringing paid work to the newly settled Bedouin women of Mukawir district. The project began with only 12 women, elders in their community and experienced hand-loom weavers. Ten years later, the cooperative involved 1500 women from the surrounding hillsides involved in the process of washing, carding, spinning and dying the sheeps wool, weaving and finishing the rugs, and making tassels for the complex designs. All these activities took place around the usual business of looking after husband, family and home. The project now employs 24 full-time staff, responsible for the coordination of the project, marketing in an international arena and promoting the vision of the enterprise.

Despite this impressive growth, the project, which was initially set up with the help of international agencies and is now run by the Jordan River Valley Foundation, has not been without difficulties. The cooperative has had to contend with competition from subsequent initiatives, keen to cash in on Bani Hamida's success. It has faced declining tourism in recent years due to the instability of the region. Cheaper carpets are on sale in every shop in Madaba, so the weavers have had to find ways of measuring up to a more sophisticated market with modern tastes in order to stay distinctive and viable. They now import a certain amount of wool from New Zealand and dyes from Europe to produce the lively modern designs that appeal to a wider range of buyers.

These challenges notwithstanding, the project continues to be a success story, empowering women in proportion to their involvement in the project. Earning even a little extra money has given many women more independence and social manoeuvrability, allowing them to make changes to their lives. When asked what the project meant for her family, one weaver at the showroom in Mukawir explained that her house now had a kitchen and she could afford to buy new pans from Madaba.

Most significantly, the project has helped women think about the choices they can make for their children, from providing the basics at school to making a university education possible. It has also enabled them to seek specialist health care instead of relying on local remedies. In short, the project has helped an entire community avail themselves of the benefits of a settled life in the 21st century. This has been achieved by harnessing, rather than rejecting, the traditional skills that have been handed from mother to daughter since the days of Abraham, and which have helped define the Bedouin identity. As such, buying a Bani Hamida rug is more than just making a purchase; it is affirming of an ancient but evolving way of life.

the extra distance for a few fils more. There is no return traffic between the castle car park and the village, although one delighted traveller reported that the bus driver kindly waited for her while she spent 30 minutes looking round the ruins.

UMM AR-RASAS   أم الرصاص

Umm ar-Rasas is one of those delightful surprises that crops up along the King's Highway. Despite being designated a Unesco World Heritage site in 2004, it's not as well promoted as other sites along the highway. This is about to change, however, as a grand new visitor centre is set to open at end of 2008, allowing for much-needed interpretation of the archaeology of the site.

The ruined **Church of St Stephen** (admission free; ☾ 8am-5pm), protected by an ugly hangar, is one of four churches in the original village. Inside, the magnificent **mosaics** date back to about AD 785. If you have mosaic fatigue after Madaba and Mt Nebo, try to muster up one last flurry of enthusiasm for this well-preserved masterpiece. There are depictions of hunting, fishing and agriculture; scenes of daily life (such as boys enjoying a boat ride, a man astride an ostrich); and the names of those who helped pay for the mosaic. A panel consisting of 10 cities in the region includes Umm ar-Rasas, Philadelphia (Amman), Madaba, Esbounta (Hesban), Belemounta (Ma'in), Areopolis (Ar-Rabba) and Charac Moaba (Karak). A northern panel depicts Jerusalem, Nablus, Casearea, Gaza and others.

Beyond are the expansive ruins of **Kastron Mefaa** (mentioned in the Bible as the

KING'S HIGHWAY

Roman military outpost of Mephaath), with another four churches and impressive city walls. Arches rise up randomly from the rubble like sea monsters and you can spot cisterns and door lintels everywhere, although a lack of signposts makes it hard to grasp the structure of the town.

About 1.5km north of the ruins is an enigmatic 15m-tall **stone tower**, the purpose of which baffles archaeologists as there are no stairs inside but several windows at the top. It was most likely a retreat for stylites, early Christian hermits who lived in seclusion on the top of pillars. Crosses decorate the side of the tower and several ruined monastery buildings lie nearby.

As part of the development of facilities at Umm ar-Rasas, a new museum is planned for the archaeological site of **Lehun**. Lehun was a garrison town built in AD 300 to house the 4th Roman Legion, forming part of a line of Roman forts called the Limes Arabicus which defended the most remote borders of Rome. The site is 7km east of Dhiban and is worth a visit not so much for the random excavations as for the panoramic view across Wadi Mujib.

Getting There & Away

The easiest way to get to get to either Umm Ar-Rasas or Lehun is to drive or charter a private taxi from Madaba, 32km to the north. The turning is clearly signposted off either the King's Highway or the Desert Highway (Umm Ar-Rasas lies halfway between the two).

A few minibuses go directly to Umm ar-Rasas via Nitil from the local bus station in Madaba. Alternatively, catch anything going to Dhiban, and try arranging a taxi (if you can find one) from there. It costs around JD7/10 one way/return, including waiting time. Failing that you could try hitching, although the road to Ar-Rasas is not a busy one.

WADI MUJIB   وادي الموجيب

Stretching across Jordan from the Desert Highway to the Dead Sea (covering a distance of over 70km) is the vast Wadi Mujib, proudly known as the 'Grand Canyon of Jordan'. Aside from being spectacular, it is also significant as the historic boundary between the ancient Amorites (to the north) and the Moabites (to the south). Moses is

also believed to have walked through Wadi Mujib, when it was known as the Arnon Valley. The King's Highway crosses the upper reaches of the wadi while the lower reaches fall within the Wadi Mujib Nature Reserve (see p179) – normally accessed from the Dead Sea Highway.

The canyon measures 1km deep and 4km wide, but it takes the King's Highway 18km of road to switchback down one wall of the wadi, across the dam at the bottom and up the other side. From the picturesque olive groves of the upper plateau, either side of the wadi, there is no hint of the sublime upheaval that renders the land in two.

Travelling south, **Dhiban** is the last town you'll pass through before the descent into Wadi Mujib. Once the powerful capital of an empire carved out by King Mesha in the 9th century BC, Dhiban is where the Mesha Stele was discovered (see opposite). There is nothing now left of the ancient city and it's hard to imagine this unexceptional little town had such an illustrious past.

Even if you are not intending to make the crossing, it's worth travelling to the canyon rim. Just after Dhiban, the road descends after 3km to an awesome **lookout** over Wadi Mujib. Some enterprising traders have set up a tea stall here and an assortment of fossils and minerals from the canyon walls are for sale. This is the easiest point on the road to stop to absorb the view, take a photograph and turn round if you're heading back to Madaba.

Climbing out of the gorge on the southern side, you will come to the strategically placed **Trajan Rest House & Restaurant** (☎ 03 2310295, 079 5903302; trajan_resthouse@yahoo.com; bed in shared room JD5, with breakfast JD10). Perched like an eyrie on the canyon rim, the rest house is mainly visited for its restaurant, a cavernous grotto of Bedouin artefacts, with hand-loomed rugs and cushions, and benches at the long trestle tables. Every day the hospitable owner, Mr Awad, and his family prepare open buffets (mostly intended for tour groups) including local dishes of spicy meatballs and herb chicken. The accommodation here is basic, with curtains for doors, but the views from the canyon rim on an early morning walk easily compensate. For those hitching along the highway, you may find a ride across the valley from here.

A STELE AT TWICE THE PRICE

The original Mesha Stele was found by a missionary at Dhiban in 1868. It was a major discovery because it not only provided historical detail of the battles between the Moabites and the kings of Israel, but was also the earliest example of Hebrew script to be unearthed. After surviving intact from about 850 BC (when it was commissioned by King Mesha of Moab to advertise his successes against Israel) to AD 1868, it quickly came to a rather unfortunate end.

After finding the stele, the missionary reported it to Charles Clermont-Ganneau at the French consulate in Jerusalem, who made a mould of the chest-high, black basalt tablet of stone and returned to Jerusalem to raise the money to buy it. While he was away, local families, arguing over who was to benefit by the sale, lit a fire under the stone and poured water over it, causing it to shatter. Although most pieces were recovered, inevitably some were lost. The remnants were collected and shipped off to France, and the reconstructed stone is now on display in the Louvre in Paris. Copies can be seen in the museums at Amman, Madaba and Karak.

Ariha is the nearest village to the canyon rim on the southern side of Wadi Mujib, although the village is about 2.5km off the main King's Highway.

Getting There & Away

Dhiban is where almost all transport south of Madaba stops. The only way to cross the mighty Wadi Mujib from Dhiban to Ariha is to charter a taxi for JD8 (bargain hard) each way. Finding a taxi in Ariha is even harder. Hitching is possible, but expect long waits.

AR-RABBA   عرابه

The holy and historic city of Ar-Rabba came under the rule of King Mesha (9th century BC), then Alexander the Great (mid-4th century BC) and later the Nabataeans (from the 2nd century BC to the 2nd century AD). The Greeks named it Areopolis after Ares, the god of war, and the Romans based their Arab governorate here.

At the northern end of town are the minimal **ruins** of a Roman temple from the end of the 3rd century AD (two niches contained statues of the Roman emperors Diocletian and Maximilian), and other Roman and Byzantine buildings. None of the ruins are signposted.

The site is permanently open, free to enter and located by the side of the main road. Ar-Rabba is accessible by minibus from Karak, 16km to the south, but is best visited on a 15-minute stop en route between Madaba and Karak.

KARAK   الكرك
☎ 03 / pop 23,000

The ancient Crusader stronghold of Karak (or Kerak) lies within the walls of the old city and is one of the highlights of Jordan. The fortified castle that dominates the town was a place of legend in the battles between the Crusaders (Franks) and the Islamic armies of Saladin (Salah ad-Din). Now among one of the most famous Crusader castles, the castle at Karak was just one in a long line built by the Crusaders, stretching from Aqaba in the south to Turkey in the north.

Often ignored by travellers speeding south towards Petra, Karak deserves a detour.

History

Karak lies on the ancient caravan routes between Egypt and Syria, and was used by the Greeks and Romans. The city is mentioned several times in the Bible as Kir, Kir Moab and Kir Heres, capital of the Moabites, and later emerges as a Roman provincial town, Charac Moaba. The city also features in the famous mosaic map in St George's Church in Madaba.

The arrival of the Crusaders gave the city renewed prominence, especially after Crusader king Baldwin I of Jerusalem built the castle in AD 1142. Standing midway between Shobak and Jerusalem, Karak's commanding position and strategic value are obvious: it soon became the capital of the Crusader district of Oultrejourdain and, with the taxes levied on passing caravans and food grown in the district, helped Jerusalem to prosper.

The castle was inherited by the de Milly family and through marriage fell into the sadistic hands of Renauld de Chatillon. Hated by Saladin for his treachery, de Chatillon arrived from France in 1148 to take

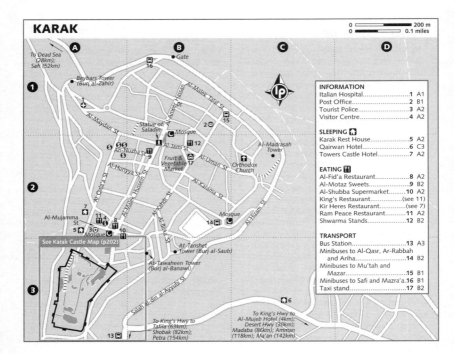

KARAK

0 | 200 m
0 | 0.1 miles

INFORMATION
Italian Hospital..........................1 A1
Post Office...............................2 B1
Tourist Police...........................3 A2
Visitor Centre...........................4 A2

SLEEPING
Karak Rest House......................5 A2
Qairwan Hotel..........................6 C3
Towers Castle Hotel..................7 A2

EATING
Al-Fid'a Restaurant...................8 A2
Al-Motaz Sweets.......................9 B2
Al-Shubba Supermarket............10 A2
King's Restaurant................(see 11)
Kir Heres Restaurant...........(see 7)
Ram Peace Restaurant.............11 A2
Shwarma Stands.....................12 B2

TRANSPORT
Bus Station.............................13 A3
Minibuses to Al-Qasr, Ar-Rabbah
and Ariha............................14 B2
Minibuses to Mu'tah and
Mazar..................................15 B1
Minibuses to Safi and Mazra'a.16 B1
Taxi stand.............................17 B2

part in the Crusades and from Karak he was able to control the trade routes to Egypt and Mecca, thereby severely disrupting the supply lines of the Islamic armies. De Chatillon delighted in torturing prisoners and throwing them off the walls into the valley 450m below; he even went to the trouble of having a wooden box fastened over their heads so they wouldn't lose consciousness before hitting the ground.

De Chatillon was later executed at the hands of Saladin (the only Crusader leader to suffer such a fate). Saladin's Muslim armies took the castle in 1183 after an epic siege. The Mamluk sultan Beybars took the fort in 1263 and strengthened the fortress, deepening the moat and adding the lower courtyard, but three towers collapsed in an earthquake in AD 1293.

Little more is known of the castle until Jean Louis Burckhardt (the Swiss explorer who rediscovered Petra) passed through Karak in 1812, describing the castle as 'shattered but imposing'.

In the 1880s, religious fighting compelled the Christians of Karak to flee north to re-settle in Madaba and Ma'in; peace was only restored after thousands of Turkish troops were stationed in Karak.

Orientation & Information

The old city of Karak is easy to get around on foot but has a maddening one-way system if you are driving. The friendly, busy and chaotic town centre radiates around the statue of Saladin. The plaza near the entrance to the castle has been redeveloped, and it's in the surrounding streets that you'll find most of the tourist hotels and restaurants. Qala'a St is also known by the English name, Castle Street.

Look for signs in the suburbs to two panorama points just southeast and north-west of town, providing grand views of the castle.

There are at least four banks that change money on An-Nuzha St, one block south of the Saladin roundabout, and most have an ATM for Visa and MasterCard.

Italian Hospital (Al-Maydan St)

Post office (Al-Khadr St) In the lower (northern) part of town.

Tourist police (☎ 191; Al Qala'a St)
Visitor centre (☎ 2354263; Al Qala'a St; ☻ 8am-4pm
Sat-Thu)

Sights

The entrance to the **Karak Castle** (☎ 2351216;
admission JD1; ☻ 8am-4pm Oct-Mar, to 7pm Apr-Sep) is
at the southern end of Al Qala'a St.

Throughout the castle, informative display boards give detailed descriptions of
the history and function of each structure.
Bring a torch (flashlight) to explore the
darker regions, and watch your head on low
doorways. Reconstruction and excavation
work within the castle is ongoing.

The main entrance, **Ottoman's Gate**, is
reached via a bridge over the dry moat. The
Crusader's Gate (old entrance) is not open to
the public.

From Ottoman's Gate, pass the ticket office and take the path to the left. Resist the
temptation to head into the vaulted corridor straight ahead and instead turn left and
enter the **Crusader Gallery** (stables).

Near the far end of the gallery, steps lead
down to the Crusader's Gate. Those entering the castle did so via a narrow winding passage (separated from the Crusader
Gallery by a wall). This restrictive access
is typical of Crusader castles, ensuring the
entrance could be easily defended. On the
north wall is a (now headless) **carved figure**
that local legend claims to be Saladin, but
which actually dates from the 2nd century
AD and is believed by scholars to be a Nabataean funerary carving.

A small staircase leads up to the site of
the ruined **northeast tower** while a long passageway leads southwest to the **soldiers barracks**. Note the small holes for light, walls of
limestone and straw, and a few Byzantine
rock inscriptions on the walls. Across the corridor is the **kitchen**, which contains large,
round stones used for grinding olives, and
huge storage areas for oil and wheat. In a
dark tunnel (only visible with a torch) are
some **Greek inscriptions** of unknown meaning. A door from the kitchen leads to a
giant **oven**.

Continuing southwest along the main
passage, leave the cool, covered area and
emerge into the light. Peer over the parapet
at the **glacis**, the dizzyingly steep rocky slope
that prevented invaders from climbing up
to the castle and prisoners from climbing

down. This is where Renauld de Chatillon
delighted in expelling undesirables.

Turn right into the overgrown **upper court**,
which has a large **cistern** and the largely unexcavated domestic **residences** of the castle.
At the northern end of the castle is the
terrace, directly above the Crusader Gallery, with fine views. Above the far (southern) end of the castle rises **Umm al-Thallaja**
(Mother of Snows), the hill which posed
the greatest threat to the castle's defences
during times of siege. To the west is the
village of **Al-Shabiya**, which was once called
Al-Ifranj because many Crusaders (Franks)
settled here after the fall of the castle.

Returning to where you emerged from
the long corridor, head southwest. On the
left is a **tower** and what is believed to have
been a **Mamluk mosque**. On the right is the
castle's main **Crusader church** with a **sacristy**
down the stairs to the right (north). Note
how in this lowered room there are arrow
slits in the walls, suggesting that this originally formed part of the castle's outer wall.

Continue to the southern end of the castle towards the impressive, reconstructed
Mamluk keep. Because it faces Umm al-
Thallaja, it was here that the defences were
strongest, with 6.5m-thick walls, arrow slits
on all four levels and a crenellated section
at the top. The keep was built from 1260 by
the Mamluk sultan Beybars.

From the keep, find the stairs leading
down to the **Mamluk palace**, built for Sultan
al-Nasir Muhammad in 1311. The open-
air **reception hall** is a variation of the classic
Islamic design of four *iwans* (chambers)
off the main hall; on two sides are barrel-
vaulted rooms. The **mosque** here, with a
clearly visible mihrab (niche) facing Mecca,
was probably reserved for palace notables.

Pause near the top of the stairs for good
views of Wadi Karak and the alleged site
of the condemned cities of Sodom and
Gomorrah (see p181). Return to the main
Crusader church and you will find two corridors. The left (east) corridor leads past
seven **prison cells** and the **prison administration
office**. The right (west) corridor leads from
the foot of the stairs through the **Rosettes
Gallery**, named after the carved rosette at the
bottom of the staircase.

If you're game, take the third passage to
the left of the steps, which leads northwest
through the bowels of the castle, roughly

KARAK CASTLE

0 ——— 50 m

SIGHTS & ACTIVITIES

Carved Figure.........................1	C2
Cistern..................................2	B2
Crusader Church....................3	B3
Crusader Gallery (Stables)......4	B2
Crusader's Gate.....................5	C1
Dry Moat..............................6	B1
Glacis...................................7	B3
Greek Inscriptions.................8	C2
Islamic Museum.....................9	A2
Kitchen...............................10	B2
Mamluk Keep.......................11	B4
Mamluk Mosque.............(see 25)	
Mamluk Palace.....................12	A3
Marketplace.........................13	B3
Mosque...............................14	B3
Northeast Tower...................15	C2
Ottoman's Gate (Main	
Entrance).........................16	B1
Oven...................................17	C2
Prison Administration Office..18	B3
Prison Cells..........................19	B3
Reception Hall...............(see 12)	
Residences...........................20	B2
Rosettes Gallery....................21	B3
Sacristy...............................22	B2
Soldiers' Barracks.................23	C2
Terrace (1st Floor)............(see 4)	
Ticket Office........................24	B1
Tower.................................25	B3

EATING

King's Castle Restaurant........26 C1

underneath the church. The corridor turns right (north) and emerges into the better-lit areas of the delightful underground **market-place** with various **shops** and **cellars**.

At the northern end of the market, the path leads back to the entrance (also the exit) or you can detour down the hill to the **Mamluk ruins** and the excellent **Islamic Museum** (☽ 8am until 1 hr before castle closing time).

Sleeping

Towers Castle Hotel (☎ /fax 2354293; Al-Qala'a St; s/d/tr JD12/20/27; ☒) Near to the castle, this friendly, budget hotel is good meeting place for younger travellers. Don't be put off by the dingy reception area: the rooms, with their floral motifs, are spick and span and many open onto balconies with views

across Wadi Karak. You can find help with onward travel from here.

Qairwan Hotel (☎ /fax2396022; King's Highway; s/d/tr JD18/24/30; 5-bed Jacuzzi suite with kitchen JD35; ☒) Also spelt 'Cairwan', this eccentric, family-run hotel, with its tiled pitched roof, exotic, gilt-edged furniture, and homely etceteras, is Karak's answer to a boutique hotel. Each of the nine rooms is unique, with matching curtains, carpets and quilts, painted walls and tiled bathrooms. All come with satellite TV and fridge. Quite unexpectedly, stairs lead down to an enormous, cavernous basement with disco and function rooms. Check whether a wedding is expected before banking on a quiet night's sleep. The hotel is 500m from the bus station, outside the main town of Karak: the walk into town is an uphill struggle in summer. Breakfast is not included.

Al-Mujeb Hotel (☎ 2386090, fax 2386091; King's Highway; s/d/tr JD22/35/37; **P** 🏠) Although this sprawling, three-storey hotel has seen better days, the charming Egyptian management and an assortment of interesting guests give the place character, especially when the guests are huddled round the gas heater in the foyer on a cold winter's evening. The large rooms have enormous beds, satellite TV, towels, a fridge and full-length windows overlooking the road. The hotel is around 5km from Karak, by the junction on the road to Ar-Rabba. If you are driving, consider parking here and taking a taxi (JD3 to JD4 one way) into town.

`our pick` **Karak Rest House** (☎ 2351148; karak castle@gmail.com; Al-Qala'a St; s/d JD28/47; 🏠) You won't find a more convenient bed for the night than in this extravagantly decorated hotel, right next door to the castle. With fantastic sweeping views of Wadi Karak from many of the rooms, elaborate Middle Eastern–style fixtures and fittings, and an elegant lobby area, this hotel prefigures Karak's rejuvenation as the next tourist hot spot in Jordan. Enjoy a cup of Egyptian tea under the pergola outside the hotel and watch the goings-on of the busy street.

Eating

Most restaurants are near the castle on Al-Mujamma St or near the statue of Saladin. Shwarma stands are clustered around Al-Jami St.

King's Restaurant (☎ 2354293; Al-Mujamma St; mezze JD1, mains JD4; 🕓 8am-10pm) Opposite an open area called Castle Plaza, this boulevard restaurant with tables on the pavement attracts travellers at all times of the day and night. It offers grills, pizzas and sandwiches, and local, home-cooked Jordanian dishes like *maqlubbeh*. The freshly squeezed orange juice is welcome after hot climbs up and down Al-Qala'a Street.

`our pick` **Kir Heres Restaurant** (☎ 2355595; Al-Qala'a St; mains JD5-7; 🕓 9am-10pm; **V**) A cut above the rest, this award-winning restaurant is a surprise find in Karak. The chef (and owner), Saddam, is from Karak and he has a passion for food, reflected in the inventive menu. There are ostrich steaks (JD7) and chicken dishes prepared with local herbs (JD5.550). Vegetarians can

choose from dishes including fried *haloumi* (salty cheese; JD2.250), and mushrooms with garlic and thyme (JD2.250). The owner laments that people take fright at the smart tablecloths, serviettes and tasteful interior of draped kilims and imagine the prices will be prohibitive. The secret is out, however, among the discerning palates of Karak, and a reservation is necessary at weekends. This is also the only restaurant in town selling alcohol. Try the locally-produced sweet white wine (JD3 per glass) in the upper gallery at lunchtime and you can forget about visiting the castle afterwards!

King's Castle Restaurant (Map p202; ☎ 2396070; lunch buffet JD10; 🕓 noon-4pm) The daily buffet here is popular with tour groups. With pleasant outdoor seating, castle views and over 20 salads to choose from, it's easy to understand why. The eastern building is worth a visit for its impressive relief display of the castle.

Ram Peace Restaurant (☎ 353789; Al-Mujamma St; mezze JD1, mains JD3; 🕓 8am-10pm) and **Al-Fid'a Restaurant** (☎ 079 5037622; Al-Mujamma St; mains JD3; 🕓 8am-10pm) are other popular places selling standard local fare of chicken, dips and salads. Arabic pastry shop **Al-Motaz Sweets** (☎ 2353388; An-Nuzha St; 🕓 8am-10pm) is a must for those with a sweet tooth.

Al-Shubba supermarket (Al-Mujamma St) is ideal for stocking up on supplies for the next leg of the King's Highway.

Shopping

While there is a small selection of souvenirs around the castle area, for an idea of how the people of Karak like to spend their money, try a walk down Al-Malak Hussein St – the road that leads from Castle Plaza to the Saladin statue. Here you will find tailors stitching fake fur to collars; leather jackets and red woollen sweaters dangling in the wind; vendors with rakishly tied headscarves and broken-backed shoes (the local answer to slip-ons); bushy green bundles of coriander hanging from butchers' shops; fennel, turnips and shaggy-mopped carrots begging to be bought for a picnic; and locally gathered herbs in textile bags flagging the outside of spice and coffee bean shops. There is even a small gold *souq* – selling mostly silver.

Getting There & Away

Karak is difficult but not impossible to reach by public transport. The main bus station is outside the town, at the bottom of the hill, by the junction of the King's Highway. If you are driving, there is a highly scenic road (Route 50) that leads from Karak down to the Dead Sea (see p170).

BUS & MINIBUS

From the main bus station, a daily bus goes direct to Amman's Wahadat station (JD1, around two hours) via the Desert Highway, leaving around 1.30pm. Minibuses also run about every hour along the King's Highway from Karak to Tafila (750 fils, one hour), the best place for connections to Qadsiyya (for Dana Nature Reserve) and Shobak. To Wadi Musa (for Petra), take a minibus to Ma'an (JD2, two hours) which leaves around 1pm daily, and change there. Alternatively, leapfrog on minibuses to Tafila, Shobak and Wadi Musa.

Buses to Aqaba (JD2.500, three hours) travel in the mornings via the Dead Sea Highway about four times a day. In the afternoon it's better to take the Amman bus to Qatrana on the Desert Highway and change to a southbound bus to Aqaba.

There are smaller minibus stands (Map p200) around town for services to Safi (600 fils) and Mazra'a (400 fils) on the Dead Sea Highway, south along the King's Highway to Mu'tah (200 fils) and Mazar (200 fils), and north to Al-Qasr, Ar-Rabba and Ariha.

TAXI

From Amman it's possible (with considerable bargaining) to charter a taxi to Karak via the Desert Highway for about JD30 one way. From Amman via the King's Highway, with a stop at Madaba and Wadi Mujib, it costs at least JD55.

From Karak, taxi fares cost around JD35 to Amman or Madaba, JD30 to Dana and JD50 to Petra.

Getting Around

The old city of Karak has a tricky system of narrow one-way streets. To avoid serious frustration if you're driving, park outside town and take a taxi.

MU'TAH مؤته

☎ 03 / pop 20,000

Mu'tah is a nondescript town that boasts one of Jordan's best universities, **Mu'tah University** (www.mutah.edu.jo) home to 12,000 students. Mu'tah is also famous as the location of a battle in AD 632 (although some historians say AD 629), when Christianity first clashed with the armies of Islam (the Byzantine forces defeated the Arab Muslims but the tables were turned four years later). At the main junction in the south of Mu'tah, you'll find a **monument** commemorating the battle and its *shaheed* (martyrs).

On the outskirts of Mu'tah (3km south of the town centre), the main road passes through the impressive mosque complex of **Mazar** (meaning 'tomb'), containing the **tombs** of some of the Prophet Mohammed's companions killed in battle.

Minibuses regularly run between Karak and Mu'tah. From Madaba, try the university minibus (JD2, two hours) on Sunday and Thursday, from the main bus station, which travels via the Desert Highway. Beware, however, that it often doesn't operate during university holidays.

KHIRBET TANNOUR خربة التنور

Travelling south from Karak, the King's Highway gradually descends from a brooding piece of black volcanic hillside into the impressive but arid Wadi Hasa (the biblical Zered Valley). Attempts at tomato growing are in evidence but it's hard to encourage the rocky topsoil into production, and the discarded and wind-strewn strips of plastic are a sorry blight on an otherwise wild landscape.

The highway skirts a reservoir, above which looms a small, conical-shaped hill. A track leads off to the right of the highway from where a steep 15-minute hike leads to the top of the hill. At the top are the neglected ruins of the 2000-year-old Nabataean temple of **Khirbet Tannour** (admission free; 🕒 daylight hr). A famous statue of Nike was found here, a copy of which is housed in Amman's National Archaeological Museum; the original is in Cincinnati. A statue of the goddess Atargatis (currently in Amman's National Archaeological Museum) was also unearthed from this auspicious little hilltop.

In truth there's not much to see here except for column bases and the outlines of a temple courtyard with adjoining rooms. Despite this, most people will relish the windswept site and epic location. In fact the term 'most people' is misleading: there is the strong suggestion among the scampering lizards and the desert larks, that no one ever comes up here – except a conscientious guidebook writer or two. Even the dogs herding sheep along the fertile wadi to the south keep their distance, running in contours around the lower hills.

Access is only viable with private transport. The turn-off is 36km south of Karak town, at the crest of the hill. It is marked as 'AT TA NOURAN I QUI ES SI', which isn't a Latin inscription, but a weather-beaten version of 'At-Tannour Antiquities Site'. The 1.5km access road is potholed but you can park off the track quite easily. Walk up to the communication tower and the path up the hill becomes obvious.

HAMMAMAT BURBITA & HAMMAMAT AFRA

حمامات بربيتا & حمامات عفرا

Hammamat Burbita (or Burbayta) and Hammamat Afra are two thermal hot springs near Wadi Hasa. Recently improved facilities at Wadi Afra (JD5 per person) include private pools for men and women, changing rooms and picnic areas. It's very popular with locals at weekends and there's little chance of escaping the party as wardens prohibit you exploring the wadi upstream. Women on their own are likely to feel conspicuous.

The two springs are signposted about 23km north of Tafila; from the turn-off it's about 13km to Burbita; a green oasis at the base of a wadi with a small, uninviting rock pool marks the spot. The road continues for 5km to an entry gate where you pay the entrance fee and show your passport before continuing the extra 1km to the more picturesque Hammamat Afra. You can't see the springs from the road.

There is no public transport to either spot but it is adequately signposted if you are driving. A chartered taxi from Tafila to Afra costs around JD20 return, including waiting time.

TAFILA

الطفيله

☎ 03 / pop 25,000

Wrapped around a steep-sided wadi, Tafila (also spelled Tafileh) is a busy market centre and transport junction. There is nothing to see, except the decrepit exterior of a ruined **Crusader castle** (closed to visitors). It was in Tafila that one of the Prophet Mohammed's emissaries was beheaded, leading to the military conquest by the Islamic armies from AD 632.

The drab **Afra Hotel** (s/d with shared bath JD8/11) is the only place to stay and is not recommended. Plenty of stalls sell felafel and shwarma around town. The **Aboud Palace Restaurant** and the **Adom Rest House**, at the southern end of Tafila on the highway to Dana, can muster a coffee and a *sheesha* but you are best saving your appetite for your next destination.

Minibuses from Karak (750 fils, one hour) to Tafila cross the inspiring desert scenery of Wadi Hasa. There are also direct minibuses to/from Wahadat station in Amman (JD2, 2½ hours) via the Desert Highway; Aqaba (JD1.500, 2½ hours) via the Dead Sea Highway; Ma'an (JD1.100, one hour) via the Desert Highway; and Shobak (JD1, one hour) and Qadsiyya (for Dana Nature Reserve, JD1, 30 minutes) along the King's Highway.

DANA NATURE RESERVE

محمية دانا الطبيعية

☎ 03

The **Dana Nature Reserve** (adult/student JD5.800/ 3.200; free for guests staying in RSCN accommodation) is one of Jordan's hidden gems. The focal point of the reserve is the charming 15th-century stone village of **Dana**, which dangles beneath the King's Highway on a precipice, commanding exceptional views of the valley below.

The reserve is the largest in Jordan and includes a variety of terrain, from sandstone cliffs over 1500m high near Dana to a low point of 50m below sea level in Wadi Araba. Sheltered within the red rock escarpments are protected valleys that are home to a surprisingly diverse ecosystem. About 600 species of plants (ranging from citrus trees and juniper, to desert acacias and date palms) thrive in the reserve, together with 180 species of birds. Over 45 species of mammals (25 of which are endangered) also inhabit the reserve, including ibex, mountain gazelle, sand cat, red fox and wolf.

In addition to the natural wonders of Dana, there are almost 100 archaeological sites in the reserve, most still being excavated by British teams. The ruins of **Khirbet Feinan**, at the mouth of Wadi Feinan and

A WARDEN'S TALE

Malik Al-Nanah was born and brought up in the village of Qadisya, and is the centre manager at Dana Nature Reserve. He loves the reserve like a second home and was keen to tell us more about it.

Why did you choose to work at Dana? I graduated in biology from Ma'an University and Dana is a good place to continue scientific study. When you work here, you work with like-minded people who understand how to be around nature – no high voices or loud music, no littering.

What was your first day like? The driver who brought me here congratulated me for getting the job, scolded me for throwing out an empty carton of juice and swerved to avoid a rockmartin chick on the road. I knew then that I had a lot to learn.

What has been your most exciting wildlife encounter at Dana? I've had many: I've seen wolf, wild cat and horned viper – all rare animals. But the best was probably seeing, at 5am one morning, a family of ibex. I was surprised because the animals were not afraid.

What's your favourite time of year here? All year is a favourite time! In summer, there is the bird migration, the skies are cloudy and the sunsets are fantastic. You may see up to 40 griffin vultures and even short-eared owls.

Who visits the reserve? All sorts, but there's been a change in the kind of tourists who come: more and more nature lovers visit to take pictures or to research special species.

Tell us about the cement factory. It's owned by a French company and there are many rules in place to minimise its effect. Water springs include heavy elements released from the factory, but good filters have helped reduce the dust clouds.

What role does the community cooperative play in the preservation of this reserve? We hold workshops and plan how to include the local community by increasing employment – in transportation, for example, or by using local shops for supplies. The whole philosophy of the RSCN is to protect nature by supporting local people. We also have initiatives with local schools to get children interested in nature.

We understand that there has been royal involvement in this project. Yes, they are very supportive. The royal family have stayed here – in Room 9 – and the king sends guests here too.

What does the future hold for the reserve? Dana is unique because it has four ecosystems – Arabian, Iranian/Asian, Semi-Desert and Desert – ranging from altitudes of 1700m to -50m, all of which occur within a very compact distance. As such, we hope Dana will soon achieve official 'biodiversity reserve' status and within five years become the first national park in the Middle East.

In summary, why should people visit Dana? Dana offers a different experience: clean air, waking up early, seeing animals and hearing bird song, watching the local people at work – in short, you can learn the meaning of nature here.

What if they can't make it to Dana? They should go and visit the RSCN's Wild Jordan centre in Amman – we've taken nature to the city there and it's really inspiring!

At the end of the interview, Mr Malik took us to see a rockmartin nest, with three wide-mouthed chicks, attached to the roof of the lodge – a fitting metaphor perhaps for the intimate relationship being nurtured between people and nature at Dana.

Wadi Ghuweir, are particularly interesting: the copper mines here date back 6000 years, when they were the largest metal-smelting operations in the Near East (they are mentioned in the Bible). The Romans later worked the mines using Christian slaves. You can explore the ruins of three churches, a Roman tower and slag heaps where the copper was mined. The main mines of Umm al-Amad are visited on a 13km return hike in the hills surrounding Feinan Lodge (p210). The hills still contain copper, but despite lobbying from mining companies, the Jordanian government has agreed not to allow mining in the reserve. A growing cement factory which quarries along the rim of the reserve is the nearest incursion permitted in this wildlife haven.

Dana village itself dates from the Ottoman period but was largely abandoned less than a generation ago as locals moved to nearby Qadsiyya in search of jobs. The village, home to only a handful of remaining residents, is in need of some care and attention. The neighbouring terraces, however, grow abundant produce, including pistachio, almond, walnut, pomegranate, lemon and apple crops.

About 50 Bedouin families remain inside the lower reaches of the reserve. They are only permitted to herd their livestock in the Dana Valley at certain times of the year to allow the vegetation to recover.

The RSCN assumed control of the reserve in 1993 in an attempt to promote ecotourism, protect wildlife and improve the lives of local villagers in an integrated project. The reserve directly or indirectly employs over 40 locals, and income from tourism is helping to rebuild Dana village and provide environmental education in local schools. Villagers also make quality local crafts (organic herbs, fruit rolls, jams, olive-oil soaps, candles and silver jewellery) that are sold by the RSCN throughout Jordan. The leather goods and candles produced by local Bedouin women at Feinan Lodge, in particular, give local women a degree of economic independence and an incentive to move away from goat rearing, which is detrimental to the fragile environment.

In short, the reserve is a wonderful place to spend a few days hiking or simply reading and relaxing en route from Madaba or the Dead Sea to Petra, Wadi Rum and Aqaba.

Information

The **visitor centre** (☎ 2270497; dhana@rscn.org.jo; www.rscn.org.jo; ◷ 8am-3pm) in the guesthouse complex in Dana village includes an **RSCN shop**, nature exhibits, craft workshops (closed by 3.30pm) and a food-drying centre for making organic food. This is also the place to obtain further information about the reserve and its hiking trails, and to arrange a guide. The staff at the centre is knowledgeable, enthusiastic and friendly, and you sense a genuine commitment to the cause.

Spare 10 minutes for the wonderful little **museum** that illustrates the various wildlife at 1500m on the King's Highway, at 1100m at Dana Village and 50m below sea level in Wadi Araba. It also explains the peculiar challenges to the ecosystem in a reserve that experiences 350mm of rain per year in winter on the mountaintops, and soaring desert temperatures and 10mm of rain per year at sea level.

The best time to visit Dana is in the spring, when the hillsides bloom with flowers, or during the autumn, when the auburn foliage thins out, making it easier to spot wildlife. The winter can be bitterly cold and some of the trails are closed, while the summer is simply too hot for comfort in the lower part of the reserve.

Guides are available (and compulsory on some hiking and cycling trails) to give visitors a deeper understanding of the reserve. They cost JD15 for up to two hours, JD25 for three to four hours, JD35 for five to six hours. It costs JD85 for a guide for a full day.

If you are sufficiently seduced by the atmosphere of Dana to want to stay longer, you could consider a three-month posting as a volunteer. **Voluntary work** includes training as a guide, working on the reception desk and helping out in the visitor centre. For more details, contact the centre manager, **Mr Malik Al-Nanah** (☎ 2270497; dhana@rscn .org.jo); the post includes board and lodging.

Activities

HIKING

The reserve begs to be explored on foot. It's only by getting out in the thick of it that you feel the special beauty of the terrain and invite the chance encounter with Dana's diverse wildlife.

The visitor centre can give information on a range of **hikes**, most of which are guided. The trails from Al-Barra require a short drive to get to the trailhead (RSCN charges JD11.600 for a shuttle). The major trails include the following.

Easy Trails

Rummana Campground Trail (1-2hr, self-guided; 1 Mar-31 Oct) This spectacular walk traces the fluted edge of Wadi Dana's canyons, circling through the trees and rock formations around the campground, and giving plenty of opportunities for a quiet sit among untroubled wildlife. Look out for griffon vultures wheeling above the stone turrets of Wadi Dana, brilliant turquoise agamas (like a lizard) basking on rocks, jewel beetles and, if you get really lucky, an early-morning ibex in the creases and folds of neighbouring canyons.

Wadi Dana Trail (14km, 6hr, self-guided year-round) Although this is the most popular trail, you are still likely to have this long hike through majestic Wadi Dana to yourself (see below). The trail is easy to follow, partially along a disused road, and latterly via Bedouin grazing paths. Although no scrambling is involved, beware that the trail involves a relentless one-hour's descent at the beginning of the hike that gives toes, calves and knees a good bruising. It's not feasible to complete the walk in both directions in a day unless you are super fit or plainly masochistic. Either stay the night at Feinan Lodge, at the bottom of the walk, or arrange with the RSCN office for a car (JD46) to bring you back to Dana either via Tafila (2½ hours) or Shobak (2¾ hours).

A WALK IN THE PARK   *Jenny Walker*

One of the most popular trails at Dana is the 14km, 'easy hike' Wadi Dana Trail, from Dana to Feinan Lodge. As it's downhill all the way, it ought to be a mere walk in the park, but don't be deceived – it's not as easy as it looks! Start the walk after lunch: that way, you'll reach the hotter part of the walk in the cooler part of the day. Take more water than you think you'll need and wear a hat. Don't forget, in your planning, that it takes three hours, partly by 4WD, to return to Dana by road.

The Bad Bits:

- Interminable initial descent on a potholed vehicle track, wishing you'd worn thicker socks
- Blazing heat with little shade (there's only one tree in the first hour)
- Not having time to stop to chat with the Bedouin (some one-dinar notes for tea would've been handy)
- The end of the wadi is nowhere near where you think it is
- Being overtaken by an encouraging old couple on a donkey saying '*Funduq* (hotel) – only five minutes', when you're an hour's walk from Feinan
- The prospect of no beer and no meat at the inn

The Good Bits:

- A lizard sunning itself in the ash of an old fireplace
- A crest of goats martialled into camera by an entrepreneurial herdsman
- Carnival pink oleander flowers, waving like bunting along the entire lower wadi
- Secret gardens of reeds and oleander and huge, spreading trees
- A barefoot race by two local lads conducted for the sheer fun of running
- A Sinai agama (lizard), whose brilliant turquoise livery demanded a second look
- The same encouraging couple returning on the donkey saying '*Funduq* – only five minutes'
- The sampling of delicious cool water and superb vegetarian food at Feinan Lodge

So was it worthwhile? Without doubt! We walked in peak season but had the reserve to ourselves. Anyone who has hiked main trails in other popularly visited destinations will know what a treat that is.

Moderate Trails

Rummana Mountain Trail (2.5km, 1-2hr, self-guided; 🕐 1 Mar-31 Oct) From Rummana Campground to the nearby Rummana (Pomegranate) Peak, this trail gives great views over Wadi Araba. One Rummmana receptionist, Mahmoun, described the trail as a good metaphor for life: lots of ups and downs but greatly rewarding when you reach your goal.

Feinan Eco-Lodge Copper Mine Tour (1-2hr, guide required; 🕐 closed Jul & Aug) This trail visits ancient copper mines, Iron Age sites and a Roman tower around Feinan Lodge. Appealing to budding archaeologists, the tour is very hot for much of the year.

Waterfalls Trail (2.5km, 2½hr, guide required; 🕐 year-round) This great short walk, from Al-Barra to the luscious springs and Nabataean ruins of Nawatef, involves a steep uphill walk back to Dana.

Steppe Trail (8km, 3hr, guide required; 🕐 1 Mar-31 Oct) Taking you past dramatic wadi escarpments surrounding Rummana Campground, through the beautiful terraced gardens of Dana village, this trail leads through waist-high vegetation to Dana Guesthouse.

Hard trails

Mysterious Nabataean Tomb Tour (2.5km, 2hr, guide required; 🕐 year-round) This short but strenuous hike leads from Al-Barra to Shaq al-Reesh and is not for the faint-hearted.

Palm Trees Wadi Tour (16km, 6-8hr, guide required; 🕐 year-round) A spectacular but highly taxing trail leading from Al-Barra through the oases, palm groves and pools of Wadi Ghuweir to Feinan Lodge.

In addition to the above, there's an ambitious two-day hike to Feinan Lodge, via Wadi Ghuweir, overnighting at the lodge and returning via Wadi Dana. Hotels in Dana can help organise longer treks to Shobak (two days) via Wadi Feinan, Wadi Ghuweir and the village of Mansourah, and even on to Petra (four days).

CYCLING

A new **mountain-bike trail** (guide required) offers cyclists three opportunities to explore the park on saddleback: a short ride (7km, two hours), medium ride (15km, three to four hours) and a long ride (30km, four to six hours). The trail starts at Feinan Lodge and uses gravel tracks past the archaeological site of Khirbet Feinan, ending at the villages of Rashaydeh and Greigra. There are opportunities to stop en route to hike or have tea with the Bedouin. The lodge has 10 bikes available (JD11.600 per day

plus guide fees). The trail is closed in July and August.

Sleeping & Eating

The RSCN operates three excellent places to stay, each of which should be booked in advance through the Wild Jordan Centre in Amman (see p95). In addition, there are two privately run budget hotels in Dana village. Camping in the reserve, except at the Rummana Campground, is not allowed.

Dana Tower Hotel (☎ 2270226, 079 5688853; dana_tower2@hotmail.com; s/d/tr with shared bathroom JD5/10/12, summer rooftop camping JD1) This quirky assembly of rooms, sitting areas and tiny, leafy courtyards has its own appeal, with a *majlis* (meeting room) draped in memorabilia, including plastic roses, *sheesha* bottles and backgammon sets. There's even a stuffed Syrian eagle keeping watch in reception. With names like 'Flying Carpet' and 'Sunset Royal', the small, unheated rooms, some of which are decorated with travellers' graffiti, are a winner with younger backpackers. There's free tea, a washing machine, shared hot showers and rooftop seating. Lunch and dinner of chicken, salad and dips (JD3) can be provided on request.

Dana Hotel (☎ 2270537, 079 6730547; www.dana village.piczo.com; s/d JD12/20) This 17-room, no-frills hotel is run by the Sons of Dana, a village cooperative that provides medical and social programmes to around 150 local residents. It's the oldest hotel in Dana and is in need of some refurbishment. It takes a leap of faith, for example, to commit to the corroding metal staircase leading to the 1st floor. The spotless rooms are stark and plain with metal bedposts and there's no heating in winter. That said, this is a friendly establishment and it feels good to be giving patronage to a worthy self-help project. Meals, in a commodious dining room with en-suite *majlis* on the 1st floor, cost JD5 for the usual fare of chicken, salad and mezze.

ourpick Dana Guest House (☎ 2270497; dhana@ rscn.org.jo; s/d/tr with shared bathroom JD35/45/55, d with private bathroom JD60) With panoramic views across the reserve and a great roaring fire in winter, a welcome from enthusiastic park rangers and a collection of like-minded fellow travellers, this is one ecolodge that lives up to its hearty reputation. Run by the RSCN, the lodge is set into the hillside with the balcony and dining-room on the ground floor and minimalist, stone-walled rooms on the floor below. All but the two single rooms have a balcony on which you can shiver in the dawn before sneaking back to bed before breakfast. The heating and hot water is provided by solar panels. A selection of fresh salads, local cheese, *labneh* and *halva* can be expected for breakfast (included in the room rates). Dinner (JD9) is shared around long trestle tables.

Rummana Campground (s/d/tr tent incl breakfast & park entry fee JD20/35/50; 🌙 1 Mar-31 Oct; Ⓥ) Location, location, location is what this wonderful RSCN campsite is all about. The price may seem steep given the minimal facilities but when you wake up to the sound of Dana's copious wildlife singing in your ear, it's easy to see why you have to book in advance during high season. With some fantastic hiking trails just beyond the tent pegs, you can step out of your dreams and into the cloudscape as the mist rises from the valley floor. Tents come with mattresses, copious bedding and kerosene lamps, and there's a cold-water shower block with locally made olive-oil soap. Dinner (JD9) and breakfast (included in the camp fee) are whisked up by a jolly cook intent on beefing you up for another day's exertions; meals are surprisingly lavish affairs of freshly prepared Jordanian specialities. You can drive here (see right) or hike in three hours from Dana village (p209). You can use the barbecue grills if you bring your own food and fuel. There's a 45% discount for students.

our pick Feinan Lodge (☎ 2270497; Wadi Feinan; s/d/tr incl breakfast & park entry fee JD40/50/65; 🌙 1 Sep-30 Jun; 🍽 Ⓥ) This remarkable one-of-a-kind ecolodge, run by the RSCN, is only accessible on foot from Dana or by 4WD from the Dead Sea Highway via the Bedouin village of Greigra. The 26 adobe rooms are quirky in design, with patchwork mirrors and 'balconies' that are integral to the room rather than appended to the outside. At night the lodge is lit solely by locally made candles (they go through more than 4000 a month!), adding to the reverential atmosphere somewhere between medieval monastery and desert fortress. It gets very hot here in summer (air-conditioning is available in extreme temperatures only) and you should bring a torch and mosquito repellent. The hot water (available

between 11am and 7pm) is solar-heated. Dinner comprises a delicious vegetarian feast of potato, rice, aubergine, tomato and bean dishes, garnished with local herbs, and served with wafer-thin Arabic bread. Staff is recruited from local Bedouin tribes; food and supplies are purchased locally and all profits from tourism are invested in the care of Dana Reserve.

If all the accommodation at Dana village is full, consider staying at **Al-Nawatef Camp** (☎ 2270413, 77-7240378; nawatefcamp@hotmail.com; half board JD15). Perched on the edge of a neighbouring wadi to Dana, this small camp has a fabulous location and is run by an enterprising local man who knows the area 'because', he says, 'it runs in my blood'. The camp comprises a few goat-hair chalets with comfortable beds (and balconies overlooking the exceptional view), and a shared shower block. In spring, the camp is surrounded by black iris. Tea and coffee is available all day, delicious dinners are rustled up from the ground oven and a free transport service is offered to Dana village. You can set your own tent up in the grounds for JD5 and order dinner (JD5) or breakfast (JD1.500) to suit. The camp also organises several excellent guided hikes in Wadi Ghuweir and Wadi Hamra. Ask about Rasmi's Walk, an ambitious three-day hike to Petra (JD180 to JD200 per person for a minimum group of six), including guide, camping facilities, all meals and transportation of luggage. The camp is signposted 2km off the King's Highway, 1km south of Qadsiyya. The owner can collect you from the main road. He also organises onward travel via local buses and will drop you at the relevant junction.

Getting There & Away

The easiest way to get to Dana by public transport is from Tafila. Minibuses run every hour or so between Tafila and Qadsiyya (JD1, 30 minutes). The turn-off to Dana village (the faded sign simply says 'Dana Hotel') is 1km north of Qadsiyya; from here it's a 2.8km steep, downhill walk to Dana village (there's no bus). Alternatively, you can take a private car with one of the locals in Qadsiyya for JD4. Heading out of Dana, ask around at the hotels for a ride as you won't want to walk back up that hill. A daily bus to Amman (JD3, three hours) leaves Qadsiyya between 6am and 7am.

A taxi to Dana from Karak costs around JD30 one way. The Dana Tower Hotel will pick up travellers for free from Qadsiyya if you ring in advance and stay at its hotel. It can arrange a taxi to Petra (JD30).

If you're driving from Tafila or Karak, the first signpost you'll see off to the right goes to the Rummana Campground. A few kilometres beyond this turning, pull over by the side of the highway at a gap in the pines. If you don't have time to visit Dana, you can at least enjoy the spectacular view from the viewpoint here. It's especially inspiring at sunset. The turn-off to Dana Nature Reserve is signposted, just before the village of Qadsiyya. Beware, it is a steep descent: use low gear instead of relying on your brakes.

To get to Rummana Campground from Dana village, head 4.5km north of Qadsiyya along the King's Highway and turn left at the signpost. The campground is 6km along a road partially shared by cement factory traffic. RSCN can arrange transport from Dana village for JD10.500 (for one to four people).

SHOBAK CASTLE شوبك

☎ 03

Perched in a wild, remote landscape, **Shobak Castle** (admission free; ☾ daylight hr) wins over even the most castle-weary, despite being less complete than its sister fortification at Karak (p201). Formerly called Mons Realis (Mont Real, or Montreal – the Royal Mountain), it was built by the Crusader king Baldwin I in AD 1115. It withstood numerous attacks from the armies of Saladin before succumbing in 1189 (a year after Karak), after an 18-month siege. It was later occupied in the 14th century by the Mamluks, who built over many of the Crusader buildings.

Built on a small knoll at the edge of a plateau, the castle is especially imposing when seen from a distance. Restoration work is ongoing and hopefully this will include some explanatory signs. In the meantime, the caretaker shows visitors around for about JD10. Bring a torch for exploring the castle's many dark corners.

As you climb up from the entrance, there are some **wells** on the left. Soon after passing these, you'll see the reconstructed **church**, one of two in the castle, down to the left. It has an elegant apse supported by two smaller alcoves. The room leading off to the west was the **baptistery**; on the north wall there are traces of water channels leading from above.

Returning to the main path, turn left. After passing under the arches, a door leads into the extensive **market**. Turn left and descend 375 steps into an amazing **secret passageway** that leads to a subterranean spring, finally surfacing via a ladder outside the castle, beside the road to Shobak town. Tread carefully, use a torch and don't even think about coming down here if you're claustrophobic. Alternatively, continue past the tunnel for 50m and you'll pass a large two-storey building with archways, built by the Crusaders but adapted by the Mamluks as a **school**.

At the northern end of the castle is the semicircular **keep** with four arrow slits. Outside, dark steps lead down to the **prison**. Head to the northeast corner of the castle to see **Quranic inscriptions**, possibly dating from the time of Saladin, carved in Kufic script around the outside of the keep. Following south along the eastern perimeter, you'll pass the entrance to the **court of Baldwin I**, which has been partly reconstructed. The court was later used as a **Mamluk school**.

Continuing south, you'll pass some **baths** on the right. Off to the left is a reconstructed **Mamluk watchtower**. Just past the tower is the second **church**. On a room to the left as you enter, you can see above a door in the east wall a weathered carving of a **Crusader cross**. In the church proper, the arches have been reconstructed.

Beneath the church are **catacombs**, which contain Islamic tablets, Christian carvings, large spherical rocks used in catapults, and what is said to be Saladin's very simple throne. From the catacombs, the path leads back to the gate.

A new **visitor centre** (☾ 9am-5pm Nov-Mar, to 7pm Apr-Oct) has just opened with limited facilities (and no telephone). The caretaker can rustle up a Turkish coffee in the attractive courtyard with great views of the castle. At the time of research, it looked as though a small café with snacks was opening soon.

Sleeping & Eating

There is limited accommodation in Shobak (properly known as Musallath) village but that is soon to change when the **Montréal Hotel**, on the approach road to the Jaya Tourist Camp, is finally completed (rumoured to open in mid-2009). In the meantime, **Jaya Tourist Camp** (☎ 2164082/79 5958958; jaya_camp@ yahoo.com; JD15) has 15 tents in a tranquil spot on high ground opposite Shobak Castle, and has a clean shower block and Bedouin goat-hair tent for relaxing. The camp also runs a number of hikes, including from Shobak to Feinan Lodge or to Little Petra (JD30 per day for a guide) and can organise transport of luggage (JD70 per day). If you want to gain a better insight into the nomadic way of life, consider visiting a local Bedouin family (JD5 including meal; JD30 to stay overnight).

To reach the camp, follow the signs for the Shobak Castle Campground (not apparently functioning at the time of research), signposted from the King's Highway, and after 300m turn left and immediate right. The road passes the new hotel and ends after 1km at the camp.

There are a few grocery stores and cheap restaurants in Shobak village.

Getting There & Away

Occasional minibuses link Shobak village with Amman's Wahadat station (JD2, 2½ hours), Aqaba and Karak. Some minibuses travelling between Wadi Musa and Ma'an also pass through Shobak. There are less reliable minibuses between Shobak and Tafila (JD1, one hour). For the 3km from Shobak village to the castle, you can charter a taxi (around JD5 return including waiting time) or walk.

If driving, there are two well-signposted roads from the King's Highway to the castle and there are signs from Shobak village.

Petra بترا

It is early morning. The path winds down towards the Siq, the dramatic rift in the land that leads towards the hidden city of Petra. The only sounds are the ringing of hooves on cobblestones as horse carts pass into the narrow gorge. The corridor of narrowing stone squeezes out the sky and the sun casts long shadows across the sacred way. At length, the path slithers into the sunlight and there, bathed in all the glory of first light, stands the Treasury, a beacon of hope to the ancients and a promise of 'wonderful things' for the modern visitor.

The sublime experience of emerging from the Siq is a hard act to follow, although Petra has other spectacles waiting in the wings, not least the Theatre and the Royal Tombs. Magnificent as they are, however, these dramatic gestures of immortality may prove to be less memorable than the asides that Petra whispers to the discerning visitor: the quiet amble through forgotten tombs, the chance illumination of a candy swirl of rock, the aroma from a chain of cloves or the sense of sheer satisfaction, perched on top of a High Place, of energy well spent. From this lofty vantage point, you can watch the everyday dramas of camel handlers arguing with their mounts, young children moving goats from one patch of sparse vegetation to the next and Bedouin stallholders regaling the unsuspecting traveller. They each move beyond the languishing tombs of ordinary folk, far too mindful of the needs of the living to worry much about the forgotten hopes of the ancient dead.

HIGHLIGHTS

- Tread the path of history by winding through the **Siq** (p223), the sheer-sided chasm leading to an ancient world
- Catch the early-morning sun slanting off the pillars of the **Treasury** (p223), the sublime spectacle at the end of the Siq
- Climb the processional way to the **High Place of Sacrifice** (p225), pause for tea with the Bedouin and return to the valley floor through a garden of wildflowers
- Search the **Royal Tombs** (p226) for spirits, lurking in the rainbow-coloured hollows
- Make the pilgrimage to the **Monastery** (p230) and watch the weather-burnished stones catch alight at sunset
- Let your soul glide through the Siq's shadows, guided by music and candle-light on tour with **Petra by Night** (p238)

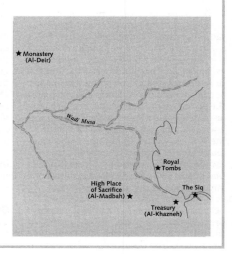

History

Mention Petra and the Nabataeans immediately spring to mind, but they were not the first people to settle in the area. In fact, Neolithic villages dating from around 7000 BC can be traced to the surrounding wadis and hillsides of Petra. Remains of the most famous of these, excavated in the 1950s, can be seen at Al-Beidha, just north of Petra (see p245). Built at the same time as Jericho on the West Bank, Al-Beidha is one of the earliest known farming communities in the Middle East.

In the Iron Age the area was home to the Edomites. The Edomite capital Sela (mentioned in the Bible) was once thought to have been on top of Umm al-Biyara (p233), although research now suggests a location 10km south of Tafila.

The Edomites were pushed west into Judea by the Nabataeans, a nomadic tribe from western Arabia who settled in the area around the 6th century BC. The Nabataeans organised traders (see p37) and over the next 500 years they used their accumulated wealth to build the city of Petra. In its heyday, under King Aretas IV (8 BC–AD 40), the city was home to around 30,000 people, including scribes (the Nabataeans created their own cursive script; the forerunner of Arabic) and expert hydraulic engineers who built dams, cisterns and water channels to protect the site and its magnificent buildings.

The Nabataeans faced many challenges in retaining their coveted trade routes, the most lucrative in the region. At first, under King Aretas III, they were able to buy off the Romans, led by General Pompey, in exchange for independence. The Romans in return exerted a deep cultural influence, as evidenced in the buildings and coinage of the period. In the next scuffle, the Nabataeans sided against Rome in the Parthian war and were obliged to pay heavy tribute to the Roman victors. When the Nabataeans fell behind in paying the tribute, they were invaded twice by Herod the Great. The second attack, in 31 BC, led to his control of a large portion of Nabataean territory.

By the time of the Nabataean King Rabbel II, the Nabataeans had lost much of their commercial power. Palmyra assumed the role of entrepôt of the Silk Road trade from Asia, and knowledge of monsoon winds opened sea trade routes via the Red Sea to Rome, bypassing Petra altogether. Inevitably, in AD 106, the Romans took Petra, creating the province of Arabia Petraea, with a capital at Bosra (Syria). Far from abandoning the city of Petra, however, the invaders invested in recasting the ancient city with familiar Roman features, including a colonnaded street and baths. The city was honoured by a visit from Emperor Hadrian in AD 131, and in the 3rd century Petra once again became a capital city – this time of the newly created province of Palaestrina Tertia.

During the Byzantine period, a bishopric was created in Petra and some Nabataean buildings were turned into churches. Earthquakes in 363 and 551 ruined much of the city and, by the time of the Muslim invasion in the 7th century, Petra was a backwater. The only mention of Petra in the next 500 years was in the 12th century when the Crusaders built two forts.

From 1189 (when Saladin conquered the Crusader castles) until the early 19th century, Petra was a forgotten outpost, a 'lost city' known only to local Bedouin. These descendants of the Nabataeans were reluctant to reveal its existence because they feared (perhaps not without reason) that the influx of foreigners might interfere with their livelihood. In 1812, however, a young Swiss explorer, JL Burckhardt, ended Petra's splendid isolation, riding into the city disguised as a Muslim holy man.

Throughout the 19th century, Petra became the focus of the Western European obsession with the Arabic Orient and the site was pored over by numerous archaeologists, travellers, poets and artists (including the famed British painter David Roberts in 1839). The first English archaeological team arrived in 1929 and excavations have continued unabated to the present day. In 1992 the mosaics of the Petra Church were unveiled and in 2003 a tomb complex was found underneath the Treasury. Part of the continuing allure of the 'rose red city' is that despite nearly a century and a half of scrutiny, Petra still has many secrets not unearthed.

Orientation

The town of Wadi Musa (p234) is the transport and accommodation hub for Petra, as well as for other attractions in the vicinity

'IBRAHIM' BURCKHARDT – EXPLORER EXTRAORDINAIRE

There can't be many explorers in history who can match the remarkable exploits of Jean Louis Burckhardt. Born in Lausanne, Switzerland in 1784, and educated at university in Leipzig and Göttingen, he soon became part of a European obsession with the Arabic Orient. 'No one can now pretend,' wrote one contemporary writer, 'to have seen the world who has not…taken a ride on camel-back across the Syrian desert.' This may have been enough for most travellers, but it wasn't to satisfy Burckhardt who wanted to get under the skin of Arabian culture.

Burckhardt went to England in 1806, where he joined the so-called African Association to help find the source of the River Niger. Understanding he wasn't going to get far as a European and an infidel, Burckhardt prepared for this expedition by studying Arabic and attending lectures on science and medicine at Cambridge University. In 1809 he moved to Aleppo, converted to Islam and took the name Sheikh Ibrahim bin Abdullah. Over the next two years he became a master of disguise, adopting local customs and putting his alias to the test among local Bedouin.

In 1812 Burckhardt set out from Damascus for Cairo, visiting Jerash, Salt, Amman and Shobak en route. At Karak he was detained for 20 days by the local sheikh and forced to sleep in different houses each night to appease the locals' numerous offers of hospitality. In his posthumously published journal, *Travels in Syria and the Holy Land,* he regretted being relieved of his watch and compass – and 'as to cash, I have not a single farthing in my pocket'. He even had to sell his saddle for payment.

On the way south, he heard locals tell of fantastic ruins hidden in the mountains of Wadi Musa. Determined to see for himself, he had to think of a ploy to allay the suspicions of his guide and porters:

> I, therefore, pretended to have made a vow to have slaughtered a goat in honour of Haroun (Aaron), whose tomb I knew was situated at the extremity of the valley, and by this stratagem I thought that I should have the means of seeing the valley on the way to the tomb.

The plan worked and soon he was riding down the Siq, trying hard to hide his astonishment. His guide wasn't fooled for long, and imagined that the pale Syrian had come hunting for treasure, declaring: 'I see now clearly that you are an infidel, who have [sic] some particular business amongst the ruins.' To avoid occasioning more suspicion, Burckhardt had to confine his curiosity to the briefest examination of Petra's monuments. What he saw, however, was enough for him to conclude (based no doubt on his knowledge of classical literature):

> This place is very interesting for its antiquities and the remains of an ancient city, which I conjecture to be Petra, the capital of Arbia Peetraea, a place which, as far as I know, no European traveller has ever visited.

This letter to his employees, written on 22 August 1812, when he was aged just 27, betrays nothing of the excitement of his monumental discovery. Despite being a man not given to literary flourishes, his journals are a little more revealing:

> The situation and beauty of [the Treasury] are calculated to make an extraordinary impression upon the traveller, after having traversed…such a gloomy and almost subterranean passage [the Siq]…it is one of the most elegant remains of antiquity existing.

For many an explorer, this expedition would have been a lifetime's achievement – but not for Burckhardt. He continued his aim to find the source of the Niger and later stumbled on the magnificent Ramses II temple at Abu Simbel in Egypt. He also explored, still under disguise, Mecca and Medina, sending home the most accurate contemporary accounts of Islam's holy cities. In 1815 he contracted dysentery in Cairo, while completing his journals and assembling a collection of 800 Oriental manuscripts (bequeathed to Cambridge University). The dysentery returned with fatal consequences in 1817 and he was buried as a Muslim in the Islamic Cemetery in Cairo. He was only 33 years old.

FINDING YOUR OWN PACE IN PETRA

Instead of trying to tick off all the top spots (the quickest way to 'monument-fatigue'), make Petra your own by sparing time to amble among unnamed tombs, have a picnic in the shade of a flowering oleander or sip tea at a stall on the valley floor and watch everyone else toiling to 'see it all'.

The following suggestions combine some of the obvious highlights with some off-the-beaten-track exploration. See the boxed text, p222 for tips about distances and best times to visit.

Half Day (five hours) Amble through the Siq, absorbing its special atmosphere and savouring the moment of revelation at the Treasury. Resist the temptation to head for the Theatre; instead, climb the steps to the High Place of Sacrifice. Pause for tea by the Obelisk and take the path into Wadi Farasa, enjoying wildflowers and the Garden Tomb en route. The path reaches the Colonnaded Street via a paintbox of rock formations. If there's time remaining, visit the Royal Tombs then return to the valley floor for a chat with Bedouin stallholders and a hunt for the perfect sand bottle.

One Day (eight hours) Spend the morning completing the half-day itinerary, but pack a picnic. After visiting the Royal Tombs, walk along to Qasr al-Bint and hike along the broad wadi that leads to Jebel Haroun as far as Snake Monument – an ideal perch for a snack and a snooze. Return to Qasr al-Bint and slip into the nearby Nabataean Museum to find out more about the snake you shared lunch with. Save some energy for the climb to the Monastery, a fitting finale for any visit to Petra.

Two Days Spend a second day scrambling through exciting Wadi Muthlim and restore your energies over a barbecue in the Basin Restaurant. Walk off lunch exploring the hidden beauty of Wadi Siyagh with its pools of water before strolling back along the Street of Façades. Sit in the Theatre to watch the sun go down on the Royal Tombs opposite – the best spectacle in Petra.

(like Little Petra, p244). The town is split roughly into three parts. The upper part comprises a few top-end hotels lining the main road, each of which has spectacular views of the weathered sandstone landscape. The town centre is where most of the cheaper hotels, the bus station and shops are located. The lower part of town, a 10-minute walk from the town centre, is where you'll find most of the top-end and midrange hotels, together with souvenir shops, tourist restaurants and the famed Cave Bar.

Beyond this is the Petra Visitor Centre and entrance to Petra. The Ancient City is reached via the Siq, or gorge, which begins after a 15-minute walk (or horse ride) from the entrance (see the boxed text, p222, for details of walking times).

In the 1980s many of the Bdoul Bedouin, who had lived in Petra for generations, were resettled in villages such as neighbouring Umm Sayhoun. At the end of this village, there is a **new access road** into the old city of Petra. It would be a pity to enter Petra this way on your first day (as the Siq is Petra's most spectacular highlight), but if you want a shortcut to the Monastery thereafter, take a taxi to the gate at the top of this road and walk down. Note that you can't buy tickets here and you can't enter without one.

Dangers & Annoyances

Some travellers have complained of over-charging and hard-sell techniques (not to mention persistent local children!). This rarely tends to be aggressive and waxes and wanes with the fortunes of local traders. When we visited in winter, people were too busy keeping warm to worry about sales. In the competitive high season, however, traders and animal handlers were making up for lost time. Invariably, after establishing contact with a smile, greeting or snippet of conversation, you'll find almost all will reciprocate in kind.

Locals have a mischievous sense of humour, offering camels as 'air-conditioned taxis' and donkeys as 'Mercedes Benz'. Handicrafts are often prefaced with the words 'buy one for the wife and one for the girlfriend'. 'Happy hour prices' are also charged for souvenirs that can cost double when leaving Petra Valley in the evening.

When hiking from November to March and in September and October, pay careful attention to the weather as the narrow wadis are susceptible to flash flooding.

Getting There & Away

Petra is a three-hour drive from Amman, two hours from Aqaba and 1½ hours from Wadi Rum. See p242 for transport details. If driving to or from the Dead Sea, consider travelling along the spectacular and seldom-used road that links Little Petra with Wadi Araba (see the boxed text, p169, for details).

Getting Around

If you book through Petra Visitor Centre, a horse ride for the 800m stretch between the main entrance and the start of the Siq costs JD7 return (arrange a return time with the handler). If you walk down, you can usually find a ride back to the entrance for around JD3. Horses and carriages with drivers travel between the main entrance and the Treasury (2km) for JD20, and to the museum for JD50 per carriage (which seats two people). It costs JD30 for a two- to three-hour horse ride around the surrounding hills.

Unofficial donkey rides (with handlers) are available all around Petra for negotiable prices. Donkeys can reach the High Place of Sacrifice (from JD5 one way) and the top of the Monastery (between JD5 and JD10 one way). They can also be rented for longer trips to the Snake Monument and Jebel Haroun (from JD30). Leading donkeys is a genuine occupation for local Bedouin, who prize their animals as an important part of their livelihood; there is an animal clinic near Petra Visitor Centre called the Brooke Hospital for Animals.

Magnificently bedecked camels are available for rides between Qasr al-Bint and the Treasury (about JD10) and they will pause for a photograph near the Theatre. You may be able to hitch a ride on something four-legged back along the Siq for a few dinars at the end of the day.

THE ANCIENT CITY

The ancient city of Petra is strewn over a vast area of mountains and wadis, but there's just the one main access point. As such, be careful not to underestimate the amount of time it takes to walk between sights, nor the uphill return journey when you're tired (see the boxed text, p222 for details of walking times).

In general the best time to visit Petra is from mid-October to the end of November, and late January to the end of May. This avoids the coldest and wettest (when floods are possible) and hottest times of the year. Petra is open every day unless it rains heavily – rare but disappointing occasions if you only allow one day for your visit in winter.

Sturdy footwear, sunscreen and water are essential at any time of year and a warm coat is needed in winter. Take spare batteries and memory cards with you as supplies are limited beyond the Siq.

ONE OF THE WORLD'S SEVEN WONDERS

Petra is officially one of the new Seven Wonders of the World. At least, that's according to a popularity poll organised by the privately run New 7 Wonders Foundation in Switzerland. The winners – Chichen Itza in Mexico, Christ the Redeemer in Brazil, the Colosseum in Italy, the Great Wall of China, Machu Picchu in Peru and the Taj Mahal in India – were selected in 2007 through a staggering 100 million votes cast by internet or telephone, the largest such poll on record.

To qualify for nomination, each wonder had to be manmade, completed before 2000 and in an 'acceptable state of preservation'. Jordan's nomination of Petra, backed by Queen Rania, was a consistent favourite throughout the campaign, although how 14 million votes were cast from within a country of only 7 million in population is a mystery. Indeed, detractors (including Unesco) immediately questioned the validity of a poll that permitted the casting of multiple votes by citizens, tourist agencies and even government bodies while disenfranchising people without access to modern communications.

The criticisms haven't dented the organisers' enthusiasm, however. Already a list of seven *natural* wonders is being compiled, and authorities in Wadi Rum are eagerly eyeing the prize. The boost the 7 Wonders project has brought to local tourism is undeniable: 'I changed my name to Seven Wonders,' said one café owner in Petra, 'in celebration of our success' – and he's not the only one cashing in. Prices have risen, hotels are full and that's at least partly thanks to Petra's newly endorsed status as one of the world's best-loved treasures.

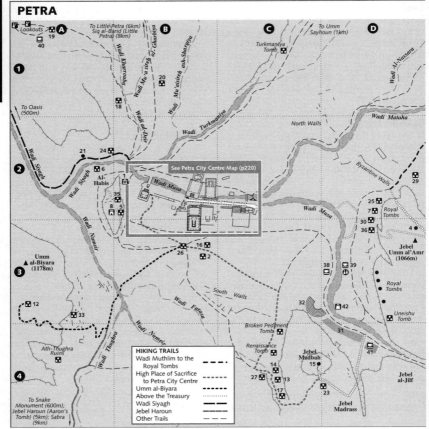

Start your visit to Petra at the visitor centre plaza in Wadi Musa, across from the Mövenpick Hotel. This is where you can buy tickets, get leaflets and a map, and use the toilets (there are very few inside the ancient city).

Information

The **ticket office** (Map p236; ☎ /fax 2156029; ⏰ 6am-5pm) is in the visitor centre at Wadi Musa. Although tickets are not sold after 5pm, you can remain in Petra until sunset.

Entry fees are JD21/26/31 for one-/two-/three-day passes (payable only in Jordanian currency). Multiday tickets are non-transferable. Children under 15 are admitted free. If you're contemplating trying to enter Petra without paying, please

don't. The ongoing preservation of Petra depends on the income from tourists and this is where responsible tourism begins.

You can hire an **official guide** (per 2/4hr JD20/50), from the visitor centre; these guides have a lot of knowledge and experience, and can bring a different dimension to your visit. Guided tours are available in English, Spanish, French and Arabic.

BOOKS

There is some interesting literature about Petra, together with beautiful souvenir books, available at shops and stalls around Wadi Musa and Petra.

One of the best guidebooks, *Petra: A Traveller's Guide* by Rosalyn Maqsood,

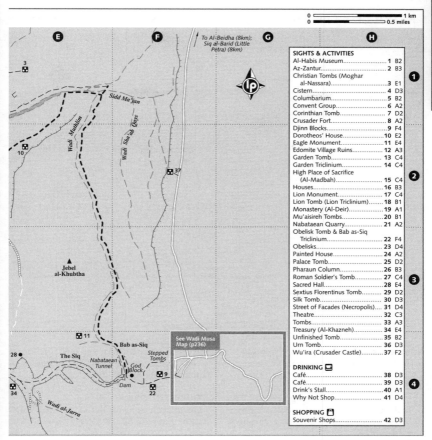

covers the history and culture of the site and describes several hikes. The pocket-sized *Petra: The Rose-Red City,* by Christian Auge and Jean-Marie Dentzer, is excellent on Petra's historical context. Jane Taylor's *Petra* (JD12) is another good paperback introduction to the site. Taylor also writes the authoritative *Petra & the Lost Kingdoms of the Nabataeans.* There's a chapter on hiking in Petra in Tony Howard and Di Taylor's *Jordan – Walks, Treks, Climbs & Canyons.*

For an engaging account of the Bdoul Bedouin who once lived in the caves surrounding the Petra valley and who now live on the rim of the ancient city, *Married to a Bedouin* is a recommended read. The author, Marguerite van Geldermalsen, raised three children among the Bdoul and ran the local clinic. Since the book's publication in 2006, Marguerite has become a local celebrity in Jordan (see the boxed text, p221) and runs tours for those wanting to see the places she wrote about (see Tours, p237).

INTERNET RESOURCES
American Museum of Natural History (www.amnh .org/exhibitions/petra) See its online Petra exhibition.
Brown University (www.brown.edu/Departments /Anthropology/Petra) Take an online tour of the excavations of the Great Temple.
Complete Petra (www.isidore-of-seville.com/petra) A great collection of current and archived links on Petra.
Go 2 Petra (www.go2petra.com) For background and general travel info on Petra.

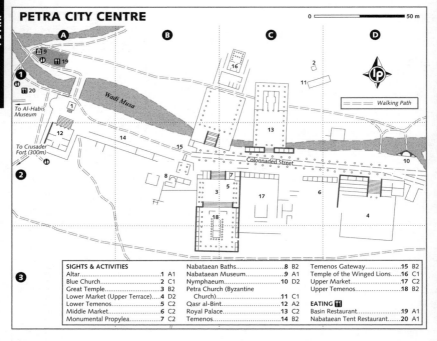

PETRA CITY CENTRE

SIGHTS & ACTIVITIES							
Altar	1	A1	Nabataean Baths	8	B2	Temenos Gateway	15	B2
Blue Church	2	C1	Nabataean Museum	9	A1	Temple of the Winged Lions	16	C1
Great Temple	3	B2	Nymphaeum	10	D2	Upper Market	17	C2
Lower Market (Upper Terrace)	4	D2	Petra Church (Byzantine			Upper Temenos	18	B2
Lower Temenos	5	C2	Church)	11	C1			
Middle Market	6	C2	Qasr al-Bint	12	A2	EATING		
Monumental Propylea	7	C2	Royal Palace	13	C2	Basin Restaurant	19	A1
			Temenos	14	B2	Nabataean Tent Restaurant	20	A1

Nabataea Net (http://nabataea.net) Everything you wanted to know about the Nabataean Empire.

MAPS

Very little in Petra is signposted or captioned, so a map and guidebook are essential. For most visitors the maps in this book should suffice.

If you plan to hike long distances in Petra without a guide, the best map is the Royal Jordanian Geographic Centre's contoured 1:5000 *Map of Petra* (2005; JD3). It's usually available at bookshops in Wadi Musa and at the stand outside the Nabataean Museum.

The *Petra* brochure, published by the Ministry of Tourism & Antiquities, has an easy-to-read map with useful photos that help identify certain monuments. Pick one up before coming to Petra as the visitor centre often runs out.

TOILETS

There are toilets at the visitor centre (Map p236); opposite the Theatre, in a gorgeous rock-hewn cave (Map pp218–19); at the back of Qasr al-Bint (Map p220); and at the two nearby cafés (Map pp218–19). Please avoid going to the toilet elsewhere as it spoils the site for others.

TOURIST INFORMATION

Information is available at the **Petra Visitor Centre** (Map p236; ☎ 2156020; fax 2156060; ☺ 6am-9pm), just before the entrance. It houses the ticket office, a helpful information counter, a couple of shops and toilets.

Sights

There are over 800 registered sites in Petra, including some 500 tombs, but the best things to see are easy to find and easy to reach. From the gate, a path winds 800m downhill through an area called **Bab as-Siq** (Gateway to the siq; Map pp218–19), punctuated with the first signs of the old city.

See the boxed text, p339, for a handy explanation of archaeological terminology used in this chapter.

DJINN BLOCKS

Just past the entrance, look out for three enormous, squat monuments, known as

Djinn Blocks (Map pp218–19). Standing guard beside the path, they take their name from the Arabic word for spirit, the source of the English word 'genie'. Other than the fact they were built by the Nabataeans in the 1st century AD, little is known about their why or wherefore – they could have been tombs, or funerary dedications, or even related to the worship of water and fertility. Whatever their intended function, they are the lodestar for the modern visitor – a tantalising taste of the monuments to come, and announcing journey's end on your weary way back.

OBELISK TOMB & BAB AS-SIQ TRICLINIUM

Further along the path to the left is a tomb (Map pp218–19) with four pyramidal obelisks, built as funerary symbols by the Nabataeans in the 1st century BC. The four obelisks, together with the eroded human figure in the centre, most probably represent the five people buried in the tomb. The monument comes into its own at sunset when the obelisks are thrown into relief.

The obelisk tomb at first appears to be multistorey. In fact it was built on top of a much earlier structure, with a Doric

---

MARRIED TO A BEDOUIN *Jenny Walker*

It's a classic travellers' fantasy – meeting your soul mate and being whisked off to live an exotic life far from the mundane realities of home. But few of us are lucky enough, or plucky enough, to make the dream a reality. Not so Marguerite van Geldermalsen, a backpacker from New Zealand who in 1978 met and subsequently married Mohammed, a witty and charming Bdoul Bedouin from Petra who had the temerity to ask her to stay the night in his cave. I caught up with Marguerite, author of the best-selling *Married to a Bedouin*, 30 years later in her home in Umm Sayhoun. I asked her what it was like living an 'other life' as Umm Raami (mother of her eldest son, Raami) and how she felt towards the community that adopted her as their own.

I notice you're wearing Western clothes today, unlike the pictures in the book. It's the fashion, just as youngsters in Umm Sayhoun wear jeans now! In fact, I've worn jeans for years, ever since I got a washing machine to deal with them. It's important, I think, not to be sentimental about the 'good old days' – people want education, warmth, comfortable housing. I can tell you, it wasn't easy in the cave at night, with a crying baby, trying to change a nappy without light.

Have the Bdoul accepted the changes to their lives since settling in Umm Sayhoun? Actually, that's the subject of my new book! Life has undoubtedly changed, and the experience I had with the Bedouin – the nomadic life in and around the caves of Petra – has slowly melted back into the landscape. I think that's why so many Jordanians thanked me for telling their story, because it's a record of a social history – their history.

You said in your book that after the death of your husband, your reason for being in Petra had gone. But you're back! Yes, that was six years ago. At that time I needed to leave, and being away gave me an unexpected chance to reminisce about our 'cave years' and the life we led. I couldn't have completed a memoir here, with all the constant interruptions – children everywhere, the extended family and village life that you become part of. I miss being able to watch a program from start to finish as I can do in New Zealand, but I love my life here: climbing to the Monastery through the clouds, being part of a tight social network. This is my home and my son has married a Bedouin girl from the village.

You've met members of the Jordanian royal family and even the Queen of England. What do you make of your fame? I've always been something of a local celebrity, because of the life I lead; in the old days, people would just turn up at the cave and say, 'We heard of you in Turkey', or they'd come to look at me from across the road. There are always places you can disappear to though – it's easy to get off the beaten track in Petra. I'm surprised these days how many people have read my book. Life's not so different really, whether you're celebrating a party in tents or in the room of your house – we're all just people trying to get on with life and have some fun.

PETRA

BUILD YOUR OWN ITINERARY IN PETRA

To make the most of Petra you need to walk. The good news is that you don't have to be a serious hiker with a week to spare to have a 'Burckhardt moment' in the ancient city – you just need to know where to go and when. Times in the following table indicate one-way walks (unless stated otherwise) at a leisurely pace. Add 15 minutes to stroll from Petra Visitor Centre to the dam (Siq entrance). If in a hurry, you can walk at a fast without stopping from Petra Visitor Centre to the Treasury in 20 minutes, and the museum in 40 minutes. See Map pp218–19.

	Highlights	Beat the Crowd	Be Surprised
Short Distance	**Siq & Treasury** Emerging from the narrow Siq (opposite) into daylight opposite the Treasury (opposite) is Petra's most exceptional experience. (20 minutes Siq entrance to Treasury)	**Petra by Day** The Treasury is sunlit in the morning; you may have seen photos but the real thing is indescribably magical. Tip: go before the 8am tours arrive. **Petra by Night** (p238) Catch the spirit of Petra by candlelight. Tip: warm coat needed in winter.	**Amble** Meander along the Siq in early afternoon and you may have the processional path to yourself (20 minutes/easy). **Hike** Clamber above the Treasury and look down on everyone else looking up (1 hour/strenuous). **Horse ride** Stand on four-legged tiptoe (p237) above the Treasury for a unique of vertiginous glimpse of the Siq (3 hours/strenuous).
	Royal Tombs These rock-hewn tombs (p226) rank among the most impressive monuments in Petra. (40 minutes Treasury to Royal Tombs)	**Photogenic Petra** Mid-afternoon and most of Petra's weary guests have returned to base. Those who linger catch the finale when the Royal Tombs become the rose red tombs of sunset. Tip: the sun sets around 6pm in summer and 5pm in winter.	**Amble** Climb the steps between the Royal Tombs and Sextius Florentinus tomb for a regal-eyed view of Petra. Continue to the cistern and descend to the Urn Tomb (1 to 1½ hours/strenuous). **Hike** As an alternative to the Siq, squeeze through sinuous Wadi Muthlim (p231) to reach the Royal Tombs (1½ hours/moderate).
Medium Distance	**High Place of Sacrifice** This lofty plateau (p225) offers stunning views of Petra. (45 minutes Treasury to Obelisk)	**Petra on High** The Siq, Street of Facades and museum all lie brooding in the wadi bottom. Climb a few steps, hike to a high place, sit on a camel and you'll find a whole new dimension to Petra. Tip: the Theatre seats give grandstand views.	**Amble** Walk beyond the High Place altar onto the solitary edge of the escarpment for a wide-angle view of Petra (15 minutes from Obelisk/easy). **Hike** Ramble to Petra City Centre via enchanting Wadi Farasa, passing rainbow-coloured rocks, Lion Monument and Garden Tomb (1 hour from Obelisk/easy).
	Monastery This fabled rock-hewn tomb (p230) is at its best in late afternoon. (30 minutes Treasury to museum/40 minutes museum to Monastery)	**Hidden Petra** Petra doesn't give up its secrets easily and most visitors leave without discovering the myriad excavations around the corner, or, in the case of the Monastery, at the top of 800 hand-hewn steps. Tip: for a surprise view over Wadi Araba, stroll the extra 15 minutes to the lookouts.	**Amble** Get a head-start to the Monastery via Umm Sayhoun access road, passing at Turkmaniya Tomb, famous for its long Nabataean inscription (20 minutes/easy). **Hike** For a rare glimpse of how tombs like the Monastery were cut, walk round Al-Habis to see the Unfinished Tomb (40 minutes return to museum/easy to moderate).
Longer Distance	**Siq al-Barid** Surrounded by oases of fig and carob and sporting its own siq, Little Petra (p244) is a haven for wildlife. (5 hours museum to Little Petra)	**Green Petra** Explore a parallel world where crickets wheeze through the daytime and toads croak through the night. Lizards, snakes and scorpions are common but shy residents of Petra. Tip: the magnificent pink oleander flowers in late spring and summer.	**Amble** Push past oleanders to discover permanent pools of water in fertile Wadi Siyagh (p233) (2 to 3 hours return from museum/easy to moderate) **Hike** Reach Little Petra the ancient way either via the Monastery (3 hours) or the hidden tombs of Wadi Muaisireh al-Gharbiya (5 hours from museum/ strenuous/guide necessary).
	Jebel Haroun Hike across Bedouin territory to reach this mountaintop shrine (p233). (30 minutes museum to Snake Monument/2½ hours Snake Monument to Shrine)	**Living Petra** Petra may be a pile of ruins to some, but for others, it's home. Take Marguerite's Tour (p237) to see how the Bdoul Bedouin interact with their famous monuments. Tip: say yes to tea with the Bedouin and participate in Petra's most ancient ritual.	**Amble** For a taste of Jebel Haroun without going the whole distance, climb Umm al-Biyara (p233) (3 hours return from museum/strenuous). **Hike** Discover where trade caravans once unloaded their precious cargo in the Nabataean suburbs of Sabra (p234) (5 hours return from museum/ strenuous/guide necessary).

columned facade. This building is known as a triclinium, or dining room, and is one of several in Petra. This is where annual feasts were held to commemorate the dead, although it's hard to imagine the conviviality of a banquet in the silent hollow that remains.

Further down the track, a signposted detour to the right leads to several stepped tombs carved into the tops of domed hills. It's a secret little place, missed by almost everyone in their rush to get to the Siq.

THE SIQ

The 1.2km *siq* (Map pp218–19) starts at an obvious bridge, beside a modern dam. The dam was built in 1963, on top of a Nabataean dam dated AD 50, to stop floodwater from Wadi Musa flowing through the Siq. To the right, Wadi Muthlim heads invitingly through a Nabataean tunnel – the start (or finish) of an exciting hike (see p231).

The entrance to the Siq was once marked by a Nabataean monumental arch. It survived until the end of the 19th century, and some remains can be seen at twin niches on either side of the entrance.

Technically, the Siq, with its 200m high walls, is not a canyon (a gorge carved out by water), but a single block that has been rent apart by tectonic forces. At various points you can see where the grain of the rock on one side matches the other – it's easiest to spot when the Siq narrows to 2m wide.

The original channels cut into the walls to bring water into Petra are visible, and in some places the 2000-year-old terracotta pipes are still in place. A section of Roman paving was revealed after excavations in 1997 removed 2m of floor accumulation.

At one point the Siq opens out to reveal a square tomb next to a lone fig tree. A little further on, look for a weathered carving of a camel and caravan man on the left wall. The water channel passes behind the carving. Hereafter, the walls almost appear to meet overhead, shutting out the sound and light and helping to build the anticipation of a first glimpse of the Treasury. It's a sublime introduction to the ancient city.

TREASURY (AL-KHAZNEH)

Tucked into a confined space, the Treasury (known locally as Al-Khazneh; Map pp218–19) is protected from the ravages of the ele-

---

NABATAEAN RELIGIOUS PROCESSIONS

Some historians speculate that the primary function of the Siq was akin to the ancient Graeco-Roman Sacred Way. Some of the most important rituals of Petra's spiritual life began as a procession through the narrow canyon, and it also represented the end point for Nabataean pilgrims. Many of the wall niches that are still visible today along the Siq's walls were designed to hold figures or representations (called *baetyls*) of the main Nabataean god, Dushara. These small sacred sites served as touchstones of the sacred for pilgrims and priests, offering them a link to the more ornate temples, tombs and sanctuaries in the city's heart, reminding them that they were leaving the outside world, and on the threshold of what was for many a holy city.

---

ments, and it is here that most visitors fall in love with Petra. The Hellenistic facade is an astonishing piece of craftsmanship of a scale and grandeur guaranteed to take your breath away.

As you pause to take in the view, the individual details become more apparent. Atop the six columns at ground level are floral capitals, while the triangular pediment depicts a gorgon's head. The carved figures at ground level are thought to be the sons of Zeus, while the figures on the top tier, in the sunken niches, depict two winged Victories and four figures of unknown origin. The central figure above the entrance pediment is the source of much speculation; most scholars believe it to be an assimilation of the Egyptian goddess Isis and the Nabataean goddess Al-'Uzza, while others suggest Tyche, the Roman goddess of fortune. Two eroded eagles stand sentry at the very top. Regularly spaced niches on either side of the facade are suggestive of scaffolding.

Although carved out of iron-laden sandstone to serve as a tomb for the Nabataean King Aretas III (c 100 BC to AD 200), the Treasury derives its name from the story that an Egyptian pharaoh hid his treasure here (in the urn in the middle of the second level) while pursuing the Israelites. Some locals clearly believed the tale because the 3.5m-high urn is pockmarked by rifle shots, the results of vain attempts to break open the secret.

As with all the rock-hewn monuments in Petra, it's the facade that captivates; the interior is just an unadorned square hall with a smaller room at the back. The Treasury, which is 43m high and about 30m wide, is at its most photogenic in full sunlight between about 9am and 11am.

From the Treasury, the Siq veers to the right; diagonally opposite is a **Sacred Hall**, which may have had ritual connections with the Treasury.

One of the great experiences of Petra is watching the beaming smiles on the faces of those emerging from the Siq. This can be easily enjoyed from the steps of the Treasury (though the smiles quickly change to grimaces if you're sitting in someone's picture) or better still from up high. You can either hike to an aerial viewpoint (see p232) or take a daring ride on horseback (see the boxed text, p237).

STREET OF FAÇADES

From the Treasury, the passage broadens into what is commonly referred to as the Outer Siq. Riddling the walls of the Outer Siq are over 40 tombs and houses built by the Nabataeans in a 'crow step' style reminiscent of Assyrian architecture. Colloquially known as the Street of Façades (Map pp218–19), they are pleasingly accessible. That said, most people ignore them, lured on by the majestic Theatre a few paces further on.

For those who prefer to savour the moment, there are a couple of tombs worth exploring. The first tomb (number 67) is unusual in that it has a funeral chamber in the upper story. The low entryway highlights how the valley floor has risen over the centuries thanks to the debris washed down during flash floods. Nearby, tomb 70 is unusual in that it is freestanding, with a ziggurat-style top that makes it look like a miniature fort.

VERTIGO ON HORSEBACK   *Jenny Walker*

Diary Entry – January 2008

She didn't look capable of much when I slipped into the saddle, but I should have known better than to underestimate a glossy chestnut Arab with a star on her nose. 'You can ride, no?' asked Mahmoud as we edged the horses uphill, in the opposite direction to the Siq. An odd time to be asking the question, I thought, as we broke into a trot on the makeshift bridlepath out of town.

I hadn't intended to go riding, but when offered a different way to reach the Treasury I'd hopped into the saddle without a second thought. 'You first person ever to say yes' said Mahmoud pointing his horse in the direction of a distant plateau. 'You must be crazy woman!' It was breathtakingly beautiful, high above the stone turrets of Petra, the crisp winter sun drawing the colours from the rocky outcrops like a magnet.

Suddenly we reached the edge of the plateau and the horses lurched immediately from a canter into a gallop, snorting breath into the cut-glass air. I just about remembered to lift out of the saddle, leaning forward as one whole magnificent horsepower urged at full speed across the slight rise. Caught somewhere between fear and exhilaration, I noticed the plateau was large…but not that large, and that it was surrounded on three sides by the end of the world. It was towards this aerial vacancy that we were now charging at full speed.

The path narrowed, the vague outline of Petra's tortured rock formations passed below on either side of us and the edge loomed terrifyingly into view. 'Stop. Stop! Sto…!' The last 'p' disappeared over the rim of the plateau, together with heart, lungs and stomach. The rest of me came to a perfectly poised four-legged tiptoe on the vertical edge. We dismounted. 'Come,' said Mahmoud, 'let me show you *my* Petra.' Flattened out against the rock and gingerly looking down, I spotted two climbers below us on the opposite ledge. They, too, were looking down. Somewhere in the dark end-of-day gloom, a trail of tiny figures marched in single file up through the gap in the rock. 'I said I'd bring you to the Treasury,' said Mahmoud, triumphantly dangling over the ledge, high above the monument. 'Coming down?' In the circumstances, I decided I'd got about as close to the Treasury as I wanted for one day.

If you can stay your curiosity even longer, take the steps up to the High Place of Sacrifice from here (while you have the energy) and leave the Theatre either for the way down or the way back from Petra city centre.

HIGH PLACE OF SACRIFICE (AL-MADBAH)

The most accessible of the many mountain-top sites at Petra is the High Place of Sacrifice (Map pp218–19), referred to locally as Al-Madbah (the Altar). The Nabataeans levelled the top of Jebel Madbah to make a platform, digging large depressions with drains to channel the blood of sacrificial animals. At first there doesn't seem much to see except some weathered steps, but this is in fact one of the best-preserved sacred sacrificial sites from ancient times.

Look first for two **obelisks** that mark the entrance to the site. Over 6m high, these are remarkable structures because they are carved out of the rock face, not built upon it: looking at the negative space surrounding them, you can understand the truly epic scale of excavation involved. Dedicated to the Nabataean gods Dushara and Al-'Uzza, their iron-rich stone glows in the sun and they act like totems of this once-hallowed ground.

The altar area includes a large rectangular triclinium, where celebrants at the sacrifice shared a communal supper. In the middle of the High Place, there's a large stone block preceded by three steps. This is a *motab,* or repository, where the god statues involved in the procession would have been kept. Next to it is the circular altar, reached by another three steps; stone water-basins nearby were used for cleansing and purifying.

The faint bleat of sheep or the clunk of a goat bell evokes the ancient scene – except that no ordinary person would have been permitted to enter this holy of holies at that time. Cast an eye across the superb panorama in front of you – far above the mortal goings-on of both ancient and modern city – and it's easy to see how this site must have seemed closer to the sky than the earth.

To reach the High Place of Sacrifice, look for a flight of steps between the Why Not shop and the Theatre. The steps are well maintained, if unremitting, and it takes about 45 minutes up through the crevices and folds of the mountain to reach the obelisks. From here, you fork right to reach the altar area. The route is steep but not exposed, so is manageable even without a head for heights. You can ascend by donkey (about JD10 return), but you'll sacrifice both the sense of achievement on reaching the summit and the good humour of your poor old transport. From the altar area, descend the shelves of rock to a broad rim: about 50m down are regal views of the Royal Tombs.

Return to the obelisks and continue to the city centre via a group of interesting tombs in beautiful Wadi Farasa. See p232 for details of this highly recommended hike.

THEATRE

Originally built by the Nabataeans (not the Romans) over 2000 years ago, the weathered Theatre (Map pp218–19) was cut out of rock, slicing through many caves and tombs in the process. The seating area had an original capacity of about 3000 in 45 rows of seats, with three horizontal sections separated by two corridors. The orchestra section was carved from the rock, but the backdrop to the *frons scaenae* (stage, which is no longer intact) was constructed (as opposed to carved) in three storeys with frescoed niches and columns overlaid by marble. The performers entered through one of three entrances, the outlines of which are still partially visible.

The Theatre was renovated and enlarged (to hold about 8500, around 30% of the population of Petra) by the Romans soon after they arrived in AD 106. To make room for the upper seating tiers, they sliced through more tombs. Under the stage floor were storerooms and a slot through which a curtain could be lowered at the start of a performance. From near the slot, an almost-complete statue of Hercules was recovered.

The Theatre was badly damaged by an earthquake in AD 363, and parts of it were then removed to help build other structures in Petra. With a backdrop worthy of a David Roberts canvas (see the boxed text, p226), the Theatre offers a vantage point from which to watch a modern tragicomedy of the ill-costumed, cursing their high-heeled footwear; the ill-cast, yawning at tedious tour guides; and the ill-tempered – mainly in the form of irritable camels and their peevish owners.

PETRA

DAVID ROBERTS (1796–1864) *Jenny Walker*

Stand in certain parts of Petra and it's almost impossible not to imagine striped-robed Arabs from the 19th century lounging languidly in the foreground. Sit in the cafés and hotel lobbies of Wadi Musa and you'll see the same characters and landscapes writ large across otherwise-vacant walls. And who do we have to thank for this 'picturesque' peopling of ancient Petra? The culprit is one David Roberts, artist, Scot and much-beloved topographer of the late Romantic era.

Given the continuing popularity of his images with tourists, it's safe to say that Roberts had the common touch. This may have had something to do with his seven-year apprenticeship as a housepainter, or perhaps his stint as a scenery painter at the Theatre Royal in Edinburgh. Whatever the reason, his compositions are full of human interest – an unloaded caravan, friends waving across a wadi, a quarrel between traders cast against a backdrop of exaggerated landscape.

Roberts, partly inspired by the paintings of European landscape painters such as Linant de Bellefonds and Laborde, visited Petra in 1839 as part of a longer visit to the Arabic Orient. He dressed as an Arab, in the tradition of Burckhardt just two decades earlier, and travelled with a caravan of 20 camels and local bodyguards. Petra was the high point of his journey, but the visit was cut short due to trouble with local tribes. On his return to Britain, his watercolours, magnificently interpreted in lithograph by the Belgian engraver Louis Haghe, were exhibited in 1840 and won instant critical acclaim.

Postscript. On my way back from Jebel Haroun in 1988, I passed an English artist near Snake Monument wearing the headdress and flowing robes not of a modern Bedouin woman but of a Roberts painting. She seemed living proof of how Roberts' images have passed into the visual vocabulary of one of the world's most treasured sites. For a shoemaker's son with no formal art training who began life painting houses, that's a formidable legacy.

ROYAL TOMBS

Downhill from the Theatre, the wadi widens out to create a larger thoroughfare. To the right, the great massif of Jebel al-Khubtha looms over the valley. Within its west-facing cliffs are burrowed some of the most impressive burial places in Petra, known collectively as the 'Royal Tombs' (Map pp218–19).

The most distinctive of these tombs is the **Urn Tomb**, recognisable by the enormous urn on top of the pediment. It was probably built in about AD 70 for King Malichos II (AD 40–70) or Aretas IV (8 BC–AD 40). Part of what makes it such a grand structure is the flanking Doric portico cut into rock face on the left of the tomb, and the huge open terrace in front of it – a feature that encouraged its use, according to a Greek inscription inside the tomb, as a cathedral in AD 447. The double layer of vaults was added at a later date by the Byzantines. Look towards the top of the building and you'll see three inaccessible openings carved between the pillars. These are tombs, the central one of which still has the closing stone intact, depicting the king dressed in a toga. The naturally patterned interior of the Urn Tomb measures a vast 18m by 20m.

Spare some time to admire the neighbouring **Silk Tomb** – noteworthy for the stunning swirls of pink, white and yellow veined rock in its facade – and the badly damaged **Corinthian Tomb**. The latter is something of a hybrid, with elements of both Hellenistic and Nabataean influences. The portico on the lower level of the tomb is distinctively local in origin, while the upper decorative features are more Hellenistic in style. The tomb gets its name from the Corinthian capitals adorned with floral motifs.

Nearby is the delightful three-storey imitation of a Roman or Hellenistic palace, known as the **Palace Tomb**. Its rock-hewn facade, the largest in Petra, is thought to owe more to ornamental exuberance than to any religious significance. The two central doorways are topped by triangular pediments, while the two on either side have arched pediments. The doors lead into typically simple funerary chambers. The 18 columns on the upper level are the most distinctive and visually arresting elements of the tomb. Notice the top-left corner: pragmatically, it is built – rather than cut out – of stone because the rock face didn't extend far enough to complete the facade.

Continue a few hundred metres around the hill to reach the seldom-visited **Sextius Florentinus Tomb**, built from AD 126 to 130 for a Roman governor of Arabia, whose exploits are glorified in an inscription above the entrance. Have a cup of tea with the Bedouin grandmother who has set up shop here and admire the dazzling veining of the tomb in peace. The gorgon's head in the centre of the facade above the columns is eroded, but it's still possible to distinguish the vine tendrils emanating from the head. The horned capitals are a uniquely Nabataean creation. Unlike many other tombs, the interior is worth a look for the clearly discernible *loculi* (graves); there are five carved into the back wall and three on the right as you enter.

The Royal Tombs are reached via a set of steps that ascends from the valley floor, near the Theatre. A fantastic hike from the Royal Tombs leads up to the numerous places of worship on the flattened High Place of Jebel Khubtha, together with a spectacular view of the Treasury. The steps are clearly marked between the Palace and Sextius Florentinus tombs – see p232. The Royal Tombs also can be reached via the adventurous hike through Wadi Muthlim – see p231.

COLONNADED STREET

Continuing downhill from the Theatre, the Colonnaded Street (Map p220) marks Petra's city centre. The street was built in about AD 106 (contemporaneous with the Colonnaded Street in Jerash), over an existing Nabataean thoroughfare. It follows the standard Roman pattern of an east–west *decumanus,* but without the normal *cardo maximus* (north–south axis). Columns of marble-clad sandstone originally lined the 6m-wide carriageway, and covered porticoes gave access to shops.

At the start of the Colonnaded Street is the **Nymphaeum**, a public fountain built in the 2nd century AD and fed by water channelled from the Siq. Little can be seen today, although it's recognisable by the huge 450-year-old **pistachio tree**, giving welcome shade in summer.

Also along the colonnaded street are the limited remains of the market area and the unrecognisable ruins of the **Royal Palace.**

THE TOMBS OF PETRA

There are more tombs dotted around Petra than any other type of structure and for years visitors assumed that the city was a vast necropolis. One plausible reason why so few dwellings have been discovered is that many of the Nabataeans lived in tents, much like some Bedouin do today.

Petra's earliest rock tombs date from the 3rd century BC. The size and design of the tombs depended on the social status and financial resources of the deceased, ranging from simple cave-like tombs to the ornate facades of the Royal Tombs, the high point of Nabataean funerary architecture.

More sculptors than architects, the Nabataeans quickly realised that it was easier to carve tombs out of the soft sandstone rock than to build free-standing structures that were vulnerable to earthquakes. The larger tombs were carved out of the rock from the top down, using scaffolding support, and the facades were then plastered and painted (almost none of this decoration remains).

The dead were buried in *loculi* (small, separate cavities) carved from the plain walls inside the tomb, while the exterior decoration was made to represent the soul (and sometimes likeness) of the deceased. All but the most simple tombs contained banqueting halls where funerals and annual commemorative feasts were held. Some rooms were frescoed and you can still see traces of coloured decoration in Wadi Siyagh's Painted House (see p233) and in the Siq el-Barid in Little Petra (p244).

The Nabataeans were a nomadic desert people without an architectural heritage of their own, but as traders they were a cosmopolitan people who readily borrowed elements of art and architecture from neighbours. Thus you'll see Egyptian, Assyrian, Mesopotamian, Hellenistic and Roman styles throughout Petra, as well as unique local architectural inventions such as the Nabataean horned column. If you combine this eclecticism with the organic nature of Petra's cave-like tombs, the stunning natural colour of the rock and natural grandeur of the landscape, it's easy to see how Petra has captured the imagination of generations of travellers.

PETRA

The street ends at the **Temenos Gateway**. Built in the 2nd century AD, the gateway originally had huge wooden doors and side towers. It marked the entrance to the *temenos* (sacred courtyard) of the Qasr al-Bint, separating the commercial area of the city from the sacred area of the temple. Look closely for the few remaining floral friezes and a figure with an arrow, which suggest that this was once a very grand structure. Opposite are the minimal ruins of the **Nabataean baths**.

GREAT TEMPLE

Excavations of the Great Temple (Map p220) have been under way since 1993 and have yielded impressive results. It was built as a major Nabataean temple in the 1st century BC and, despite being badly damaged by an earthquake not long after, was in use (albeit in different forms) until the late Byzantine period. The first set of stairs was fronted by a monumental *propylaeum* (gateway) while the courtyard at the top of the first stairs marked the lower *temenos*, flanked by a triple colonnade. The upper level housed the temple's sacred enclosure, with four huge columns (made from stone discs and clad in marble) at the entrance. A *theatron* (miniature theatre) stands in the centre. The temple was once 18m high, and the enclosure was 40m by 28m. The interior was originally covered with striking red-and-white stuccowork.

QASR AL-BINT

One of the few free-standing structures in Petra, Qasr al-Bint (Map p220) was built in around 30 BC by the Nabataeans, adapted to the cult of Roman emperors and destroyed in about the 3rd century AD. Despite the name given to it by the local Bedouin – Qasr al-Bint al-Pharaun (Castle of the Pharaoh's Daughter) – it was built as a dedication to Nabataean gods and was one of the most important temples in the ancient city. In its original form, it stood 23m high and had marble staircases, imposing columns topped with floral capitals, a raised platform for worship, and ornate plaster and stone reliefs and friezes – small traces of which are still evident. The central 'holy of holies', known as an *adyton,* would have housed an image of the deities. The sacrificial altar in front, once overlaid with

marble, indicates that it was probably the main place of worship in the Nabataean city and its location at street level suggests that the whole precinct (and not just the temple interior) was considered sacred.

TEMPLE OF THE WINGED LIONS

The recently excavated Temple of the Winged Lions (Map p220), built in about AD 27, is named after the carved lions that once topped the capitals of each of the columns. The temple was probably dedicated to the fertility goddess, Atargatis, the partner of the male god Dushara.

This was a very important temple, centred around a raised altar, and with a colonnaded entry of arches and porticoes that extended across the wadi. Fragments of decorative stone and painted plaster found on the site, and now on display in the Nabataean Museum, suggest that both the temple and entry were handsomely decorated.

PETRA CHURCH

An awning covers the remains of Petra Church (also known as the Byzantine Church; Map p220). The structure was originally built by the Nabataeans, and then redesigned and expanded by the Byzantines around AD 530. It eventually burned down, and was then destroyed by repeated earthquakes. It has recently been restored by the American Center of Oriental Research in Amman.

Inside the church are some exquisite Byzantine floor **mosaics**, some of the best in the region. The mosaics originally continued up the walls. A helpful map and explanations in English are located inside the church.

AL-HABIS

Beyond Qasr al-Bint is the small hill of Al-Habis (the Prison; Map pp218–19). From the Nabataean Tent Restaurant (p234), steps lead up the hill to the small **Al-Habis Museum** (8am-4pm), the smaller of Petra's two museums. The classical statues, tiny figurines and painted stuccowork on display lend a human dimension to the huge scale of the site.

If you continue up the steps, beyond the museum, a little-used path leads around the back of Al-Habis, with striking views of fertile Wadi Siyagh and the junction with Wadi Numeir. The path soon skirts the teashop and comfortable **cave home** of Bdoul

Mofleh, one of the last residents of Petra. Asked why he didn't leave when the rest of his family were relocated to Umm Sayhoun, he replied, 'Why would I? This is my home; I've always lived here.' With a view to die for, and a garden of flowering jasmine, it's easy to see why this hardy resident chose to stay. Notice the red-capped aloe, standing to attention in early summer, billeted across the cliffs opposite.

The path continues round the hill, past the **Convent Group** of tombs to a flight of steps. These lead in turn (via a wooden plank bridge) to the top of Al-Habis, another of Petra's many High Places. At the summit (allow 10 to 15 minutes to reach the top) are the limited ruins of a small **Crusader fort**, built in AD 1116 by Baldwin I.

The ruins are not impressive, but the views across the city certainly are.

From here you can either hike, via **Pharaun Column** (a good landmark), to Snake Monument in Wadi Thughra or along Wadi Farasa to the High Place of Sacrifice (see p232 and the boxed text, p231).

Alternatively, complete the circuit of Al-Habis by descending the hill behind Qasr al-Bint. On your way down, look out for the **Unfinished Tomb**. It offers a rare glimpse at the way the Nabataeans constructed their rock tombs, starting at the top on a platform of scaffolding and working their way down. Nearby is the enigmatic **Columbarium**, whose multiple niches remain a mystery; some suppose they housed votive images or urns, others say this was a dovecote for pigeons.

LOVING PETRA TO DEATH

It seems ironic that after nearly 1000 years of obscurity, if not neglect, Petra owes its current fragility to a renaissance of interest in the site. In a 'good' year half a million people visit, putting a huge strain on the management of one of the world's best-loved antiquities. The combination of thousands of footprints a day, increased humidity levels from the breath of tourists in the most popular tombs and the effects of adventurous travellers clambering over tombs and steep hillsides continues to accelerate severe erosion at the site.

Aware of these threats to the long-term future of Petra, a number of bodies cooperate in protecting and enhancing the site. About 25% of Petra's ticket revenue filters back to the Petra Regional Authority, which is responsible for developing tourism in a 853 sq km area – 264 sq km of which have been designated as an 'Archaeological Park'. The private Petra National Trust is involved in training guides, studying the impact on Petra from tourism, managing the number of souvenir stalls (due to be redeveloped shortly into permanent kiosks, much to the disgruntlement of locals) and creating dedicated walking trails. Various foreign governments and NGOs are also contributing to Petra's preservation; the Swiss in particular share a sense of responsibility towards a site rediscovered by one of their nationals (see p215), and the German-Jordanian Conservation and Restoration Centre in Petra (CARCIP) offers specialist advice on technical reconstruction.

Anyone who has visited the site over the past 20 years or so can take heart that, despite the internal wrangling of interested parties, many visible improvements are in place. One obvious difference is that the site for the most part is now spotlessly clean, thanks to constant maintenance, more toilet facilities on site and a shift in attitude from visitors, who largely carry their rubbish back out with them. Other improvements include the use of an invisible mortar to conserve fragile masonry and replace unsightly cement used in previous restoration attempts; major shoring up of the Siq; and ongoing conservation of tomb façades. Rampant development in Wadi Musa has also been checked, an infrastructure of drainage and sewerage systems installed and a moratorium enforced on the building of unsightly hotels that impinge on the sense of seclusion in Petra. Rumours of better signage and trail markers are yet to put in an appearance.

Few of the conservation measures, however, are likely to save Petra for future generations without the cooperation of visitors. Each tourist can play their part by sticking to trails, avoiding clambering over the monuments, resisting the temptation to touch crumbling masonry, removing their litter and using designated toilet facilities. These things sound obvious, but judging by a piece of graffiti that reads 'Daniel 2008' on top of one of the High Places, responsible tourism may still be a long time coming.

PETRA

NABATAEAN MUSEUM

This **museum** (Map p220; 9am-5pm, to 4pm Oct-Mar) has an interesting display of artefacts from the region, including mosaics. Explanations are in English. The museum, together with a shop selling detailed maps and fixed-price, handmade jewellery sponsored by the Queen Noor Foundation, shares the same building as the Basin Restaurant (see p234).

MONASTERY (AL-DEIR)

Beyond the museum, hidden high up in the hills, is one of the legendary monuments of Petra. The spectacular Monastery (known locally as Al-Deir; Map pp218–19) is similar in design to the Treasury but far bigger (50m wide and 45m high). Built in the 3rd century BC as a Nabataean tomb, perhaps for King Obodas I (r 96–86 BC), the Monastery derives its name from the crosses carved on the inside walls, suggesting that the building was used as a church in Byzantine times. The courtyard in front of the Monastery was once surrounded by columns and was probably used for sacred ceremonies.

Opposite the Monastery there's a strategically placed drinks stall in a cave with a row of seats outside where you can sit and contemplate the majestic Hellenistic facade. It's particularly spectacular from mid- to late afternoon when the setting sun draws out the colour of the sandstone. Behind the drinks stand, tomb 468 is worth exploring for another fine facade, some defaced carvings and excellent views.

Beyond the drinks stand a trail leads up to two lookouts, with stunning views west over Wadi Araba towards Israel and the Palestinian Territories and south to the peak of Jebel Haroun, topped by a small white shrine.

The easy-to-follow **trail** to the Monastery starts from the Nabataean Museum and takes about 40 minutes (if in doubt, look for weary hikers coming down). Alternatively, donkeys (with a guide) can be hired for about JD3/5 one way/return. The trip is best started in mid-afternoon when there is welcome shade and the Monastery is at its most photogenic. The remarkable ancient rock-cut path of more than 800 steps follows the old processional route and is a spectacle of weird and wonderfully tortured stone. There are several side paths to explore, including a detour to the **Lion Tomb** (Lion Triclinium), set in a gully. The two weather-beaten lions that lend the tomb its name face each other at the base of the monument.

An exciting 6km **hike** leads from the Monastery to Little Petra (it takes about 2½ hours and involves some easy scrambling). Ask at Petra Visitor Centre or at local travel agencies for a guide as the route is difficult to find.

Hiking

Anyone wanting to see some stunning landscapes, explore unexcavated tombs and meet the Bedouin should pack an extra bottle of water and go hiking.

FIVE TIPS FROM FELLOW TRAVELLERS

Imagine Ancient Caravans Hidden in the sandstone wilderness of Jordan is the ancient trading city of Petra, whose buildings and beautiful facades are carved out of the rock. Do yourself a favour and spend a few days exploring it while imagining the bustle of caravans full of exotic merchandise (*Wornoutboots79*).

Pretend to be Indiana Jones Visiting the ancient ruins of Petra was a dream come true. No, really – since watching Indiana Jones it was a lifetime goal! The immense structures carved straight out of the mountainside are stunning and, yup, I saw where they filmed (*evilthecat*).

Give Yourself Time Give yourself at least three days and explore the further-off bits. Tip: hire a donkey if you're too tired to climb up all the steps [to the Monastery]. In decent shape? Then ask a local for the 'secret' path [above Royal Tombs] to overlook the Treasury (*santamonica811*).

Be There at Sunset The rose red city turns into a palette of deep colours as the day ends. The sun's rays reach into areas of the carved facades unseen in the harsh desert light, and as the sun sets a band of golden light gradually snakes to the top of the valley (*mscott*).

Visit the Best Sunset Spot A beautiful and surprisingly peaceful view is from the main road south of Wadi Musa. The sun turns the rocks from red into a spectacular glowing red as it slowly sinks behind mountains into Wadi Araba (*louby_lou35*).

None of the following hikes is all that strenuous and none involves camping overnight (which is not permitted within Petra). Only the hikes to Sabra or Little Petra require a guide. Hikers should pick up the contoured *Map of Petra* mentioned on p220. Note that the approximate hiking times are just that, and do not include time for pottering.

Experienced multilingual guides can be hired from Petra Visitor Centre (p220) for JD20/50 for two/four hours, or from local travel agencies (see p237). Unofficial Bedouin 'guides' may charge considerably less than the official rates: occasionally they are very good but there's no guarantee. Women on their own should be cautious of hiking with unregistered guides, particularly as most of the hikes involve spending time in isolated parts of Petra.

Please stick to trails and remove your litter to avoid degradation of the site.

WADI MUTHLIM TO THE ROYAL TOMBS

This adventurous 1½-hour canyon hike (Map pp218–19) is an exciting alternative route into Petra if you've already taken the main Siq path, or a rewarding way out of the site if you still have energy. The hike is not difficult or strenuous, but there are several boulder blockages and in winter you may need to wade through pools of water.

The trail starts from the dam, just before entering the Siq. Before entering the ancient, 88m-long **Nabataean tunnel**, it's possible to make a short detour (veer right and double-back over the top of the tunnel) to the **Eagle Monument**, with its eponymous carvings.

Back on the hike, walk through the tunnel and you'll emerge into the sunlight of Wadi Muthlim with its thick ribbon of oleander. The wadi gradually narrows into a metre-wide *siq* and in three places you'll have to lower yourself down 2m-high boulder blockages. The first is easy enough to negotiate; the other two take a bit more strategy – not impossible if you have someone to lean on, but tricky on your own. If you're not comfortable on the second boulder, turn back or you could get stuck between boulder blockage two and three for quite some time before help arrives!

After 25 minutes from the start of the hike, look for the remains of a Nabataean

dam above the trail. Five minutes later, you'll meet a T-intersection where the trail joins Wadi Mataha. Follow the painted arrow to the left. This is the most exciting part of the hike as the *siq* narrows to little more than a crack in the rock. You can see here how treacherous this hike would be in a flash flood as there is little space between you and the parallel walls. At certain times of the year you may have to splash through residual pools of water here until at length you pass into the perfect picnic point. Surrounded by Nabataean niches, and shaded on two sides almost all day, this little square of ancient Petra has a presence far bigger than its dimensions.

From here, follow the cliff face to the left, past a series of little-visited tombs, including **Dorotheos' House** and the **Tomb of Sextius Florentinus**, until you reach the Royal Tombs. Alternatively, you can turn northeast on a small track that begins from the wadi almost opposite the Tomb of Sextius Florentinus, and explore the interesting so-called 'Christian Tombs' of Moghar al-Nassara where excavations are ongoing.

Note that if you are doing this hike in the opposite direction, you can find the entry to

---

HEAR IT FROM A PROFESSIONAL

Striding up the road in Wadi Musa, with a big grin and a half-finished bottle of water in hand, a sturdy-looking man from Northern England exclaimed: 'That was one of the best hikes I've ever done – in fact, it has to be one of my all-time top six.' Normally such a comment would raise little more than a warm smile of shared enjoyment. But the comment came from one Gordon Miller, Secretary of the International Rangers Federation. Over the course of his 30+ years of hiking, he has clocked up thousands of miles in multiple countries. So when he says this was one of his all-time top-six hikes, it's more than just a casual accolade!

So where did he walk? Start at Al-Habis (p228), walking round the hill in an anticlockwise direction. Hike from there to the Pharaun Column, then take the Wadi Farasa path up to the High Place of Sacrifice (p232). The good news is that none of this requires more than average fitness and each part of the route is detailed in this chapter.

the *siq* after Dorotheos' House by following the curved wall around to the right – niches mark the entry to the *siq*.

Some parts of the *siq* may be impassable if it's been raining. Flash floods occur along Wadi Muthlim because the dam at the start of Petra's main *siq* deliberately diverts water along this wadi. As such, it's imperative that you don't start this trek if it's been raining, is raining or is likely to rain soon. If in doubt, check with the Visitor Centre before setting off.

HIGH PLACE OF SACRIFICE TO PETRA CITY CENTRE

This one-hour hike (Map pp218–19) starts from the High Place of Sacrifice and is a must. Refer to p225 for information about getting to the High Place via the steps near the Theatre. It's also possible to do this hike in reverse, making for a grand afternoon exit from the site.

From the top of the path, near the obelisks, a trail with steps heads down towards Wadi Farasa (Butterfly Valley). The start of the trail is not obvious, so look for the helpful piles of stones indicating the trail, or ask for directions at the drinks stand.

The hike is immediately rewarding with magnificent veined rock formations and wild gardens of flowers. After about 10 minutes of descent, you'll come to the 5m-long **Lion Monument**, where water was channelled to pour out of the lion's mouth from the rock face above – an example of Nabataean engineering at its most sophisticated. A stone altar diagonally opposite suggests the fountain had some religious function. The steps wind further down the side of the cliff to the **Garden Tomb** (more likely to have been a temple) and the remains of a giant water cistern.

A little further down, on the left, is the elegant **Roman Soldier's Tomb**, named after the statue over the door. Almost opposite is the **Garden Triclinium**, a hall used for annual feasts to honour the dead placed in the Soldier's Tomb. The hall is unique in Petra because it has carved decoration on the interior walls. The tomb and triclinium were once linked by a colonnaded courtyard.

Hereafter, the trail branches to the right, above the dry wadi floor. A teashop here sells handmade strings of cloves, a good sniff of which is surprisingly reviving. The path

forks at the ridge ahead. The right fork leads past some outrageously colourful but dilapidated tombs and descends eventually to the Colonnaded Street. The left fork passes **Az-Zantur**, a 1st century AD palace that's still under excavation. Nearby is a collection of ruined Nabataean and Roman houses, one of the few traces of habitations so far discovered in Petra. The trail continues west along the ridge to the **Pharaun Column**, the lone surviving column of another Nabataean temple. From here you can turn left to Snake Monument for a longer hike or go straight on for Qasr al-Bint (see p228) and Al-Habis (p228). If you're disoriented, look for Petra Church, north of the Colonnaded Street: its pale green awning makes a good landmark.

ABOVE THE TREASURY

There are two vantage points (Map pp218–19) from which to admire the Treasury. The first is a steep 20-minute hike and scramble. To reach the trail, turn left at the bottom of the Siq, passing the Treasury on your right, and look for a steep flight of steps in rock face ahead of you. At the top of the steps, scramble over the wall that blocks Wadi al-Jarra and head for a small, flattened plateau. The handkerchief-sized lookout above the vertical cliff won't be a favourite for those with vertigo, but the sense of being transported above the crowds quickly quells the fear of falling.

For an even more dramatic and unusual view of the Treasury, make this 1½-hour return hike from the Palace Tomb, with the option of returning via the Urn Tomb. Start this hike in the early morning to catch the Treasury in sunlight.

A recently renovated set of processional steps leads steeply uphill from about 150m northeast of the Palace Tomb (they are signposted). The stiff climb takes about 20 minutes and flattens out at a hilltop Nabataean cistern. Along the way there are wonderful views of the Roman Theatre.

Continue south from the cistern (currently occupied by a helpful Bedouin teashop owner) along a less obvious dirt path. Descend through the dry wadi for about 15 minutes and then pass into a small ravine; suddenly you will reach a dramatic lookout about 200m above the Treasury, with fantastic views of the mighty edifice. Watch your step and look out for landmarks on the way down as it's disorienting finding the path back to the top of the steps.

Back at the cistern, a tiny cleft in the rock reveals worn steps leading down a gully and along the rock face to a point next to the **Urn Tomb**. The trail isn't all that clear (and is rather dirty at the outset), but it is navigable with a bit of common sense. The author, lacking in this quality, ended up on a Nabataean drain dangling over a vertical drop. Of course, you can always return the way you came.

UMM AL-BIYARA

He the Judaean king, Amaziah was the one who defeated ten thousand Edomites in the Valley of the Salt and captured Sela in battle…

2 Kings 14:7

Umm al-Biyara (Map pp218–19) is the flat-topped mountain (1178m) in the southwest of Petra. Legend maintains that it was once the Edomite capital of Sela, from where the Judaean king Amaziah (r 796–81 BC) threw 10,000 prisoners to their deaths over the precipice. There are ruins of a 7th-century BC **Edomite village** at the top as well as several cisterns. There are also many unexcavated **tombs** along the base of the eastern cliffs.

The return trip from Qasr al-Bint to Umm al-Biyara (the Mother of Cisterns) takes about three hours and offers stunning mountaintop views over Petra (you can even spot the Monastery). It's a fairly strenuous hike up hundreds of steps, but the trail is easy to follow. Start the hike in the mid-afternoon when most of the path is in shade but don't leave it too late as you don't want to be coming down in poor light.

From behind Qasr al-Bint, head to the Pharaun Column and descend to the road that leads along Wadi Thughra towards Snake Monument. The path up the rock face starts from the left of the largest of the rock-cut tombs on the southeast face of the mountain.

WADI SIYAGH

For a leg-stretcher that doesn't require a vertical take-off, try the trail (Map pp218–19) that follows the dry riverbed of Wadi Siyagh beneath Al-Habis hill. Once a residential suburb of Petra, the wadi and the nearby slopes have unexcavated tombs and

residences to explore and offer some peaceful picnic spots once you pass the noisy restaurant generator.

Enter Wadi Siyagh opposite the Basin Restaurant (Map p220). You'll soon see steps on the right leading to the **Painted House**, one of the very few tombs in Petra that still has traces of Nabataean frescoes. Further down, at a bend in the valley, is a **Nabataean quarry**.

The main attraction further along the valley is the dense oasis of green bushes, water pools and even waterfalls (in winter). In spring, the flowers are beautiful and in May and June it's worth making the hike just to enjoy the oleander and seams of aloe.

The trail along Wadi Siyagh is easy to follow, but becomes a bit rough in parts as it ascends the wadi walls. Don't attempt the hike if rain is imminent because flash floods are possible.

JEBEL HAROUN

Aaron will be gathered to his people: he will die there. Moses did as the Lord commanded: they went up to Mount Hor in the sight of the whole community.

Numbers 20:26–27

Jebel Haroun (1350m) is thought to be biblical Mt Hor, where Moses' brother Aaron (Haroun to Muslims) is believed to be buried. The small white shrine on top of Jebel Haroun (off Map pp218–19) was built in the 14th century, apparently over Aaron's tomb, and some people consider this a place of pilgrimage. For most, however, the big drawcard of Jebel Haroun is the superb panoramic view from the top.

The trip from Qasr al-Bint takes around six hours return. Some people hire a guide with a donkey or even a camel for the trip, but if you're reasonably fit and not fazed by working out your own route from the network of goat tracks that head in the general direction, then this really isn't necessary.

The trail to Jebel Haroun starts at Pharaun Column, and follows the dirt road past Bedouin settlements to **Snake Monument**, a curled stone on a rock pedestal that resembles a snake. Continue to the southwest towards the obvious white shrine (which looks deceptively close); the trail is not as steep as it looks. At the bottom of the mountain, find the caretaker if you want to enter the shrine.

SABRA

The trip from Qasr al-Bint to the remote Nabataean suburbs of Sabra (off Map pp218–19) takes a minimum of five hours return. This was where trade caravans once unloaded their precious cargoes at the fringes of the main city and the remains here include some ruined walls, temples, bridges and a small Roman theatre. A guide is needed even to find the trail from Snake Monument. A return trip on donkey costs from around JD50, depending on your powers of negotiation.

An exciting option offered by some travel agencies is the adventurous two-day hike from Tayyibeh, through the *siq*-like Wadi Tibn, to Sabra, camping overnight and continuing on to Petra the next day.

WADI MUSA وادي موسى

☎ 03 / pop 15,600

The village that has sprung up around Petra is called Wadi Musa (Valley of Moses). It's an easy-going assemblage of hotels, restaurants and shops stretching about 5km from

'Ain Musa to the main entrance of Petra at the bottom of the wadi.

Wadi Musa's fortunes depend almost entirely on tourism. Dozens of new hotels were hastily erected in the late 1990s (after the peace treaty with Israel), often with no aesthetic or social sensitivity. Many locals bought into the new opportunities that mass tourism offered only to be stung in the tourism slump after 9/11. Tourism is currently on the rise again, however, and a mood of cautious optimism prevails in town. A moratorium on hotel building is in place until 2012 in an effort to curb rampant expansion and to shift the focus to improving services rather than simply 'packing them in'.

Prices in Wadi Musa are inevitably higher than in other tourist destinations in Jordan, reflecting its status as guardian to one of the new Seven Wonders of the World (see the boxed text, p217).

Orientation

The commercial centre of Wadi Musa is Shaheed roundabout, around 3km from the entrance to Petra. There is a second collec-

---

PICNIC AT PETRA

There are lots of ways to enjoy alfresco dining in Petra, from a simple take-your-own picnic to fine dining (well nearly) at the two Petra Valley restaurants.

For breakfast, spread your cloth in the little opening at the end of Wadi Muthlim; overlooked by god niches (see p231), you may host unexpected guests. Entertain the wind for lunch on top of Umm Al-Biyara (see p233) and have high tea (or at least tea-on-high) with the Bedouin stallholder above the Royal Tombs. For dinner with a difference, choose a Nabataean dining room (the Garden Triclinium is a good bet – p232) or share a candlelight supper. For the latter, join the Petra by Night tour (p238) and spread your tablecloth in the middle of the Siq while the crowds race to the Treasury.

If a picnic takes too much forethought, try the **Basin Restaurant** (Map p220; lunch buffet JD12.800, fresh orange juice JD2.500; ⏰ 11am-4pm; Ⓥ), run by the Crown Plaza Resort. It serves a healthy selection of salads, fresh felafel and barbecued spicy sausage, followed by fruit and *umm ali* (bread pudding-like dessert). Groups sit by the ravine under canvas; independent travellers are given tables under the trees. Flies can be a problem.

The **Nabataean Tent Restaurant** (Map p220; lunch buffet JD10, drinks JD2; ⏰ 11am-4pm) is similar, with a slightly less appetising spread but a lovely spot under blue-flowering jacaranda trees (they flower in May).

In the neighbouring village of Umm Sayhoun, north of the city centre, you can try the original flavours of Petra in a Bedouin family home, prepared by the mother of the house (see p237). Not content just to watch? Then cook the food yourself at Petra Kitchen (p238) in Wadi Musa.

Throughout Petra, including at the High Place of Sacrifice and the Monastery, stalls sell bottled water (around JD1.500), soft drinks and snacks. Best of all they sell sweet black tea laced with herbs; sharing a quite conversation with the aged or infant vendor is a guaranteed highlight of the ancient city.

tion of midrange and top-end hotels, restaurants and souvenir shops 2km downhill, close to the Petra entrance. There are also a number of four- and five-star hotels on the 'rim' of Wadi Musa, on the road towards Wadi Rum.

Information

BOOKSHOPS

Books on Petra can be found in the shops behind the visitor centre and along the main road through Wadi Musa. See p218 for information about maps and books.

EMERGENCY

Main police station (☎ 2156551, emergency 191) In Wadi Musa, adjacent to the Police roundabout.
Tourist police station (☎ 2156441, emergency 196; 8am-midnight) Opposite Petra Visitor Centre. A few tourist police can be found lounging around in the shade inside Petra.

INTERNET ACCESS

There are lots of internet cafés around the town centre including **Rum Internet** (per hr JD1; 10am-midnight), located downhill from Shaheed roundabout. **Seven Wonders Restaurant** (per hr JD3.500; 9am-11pm), near the entrance to Petra, a few doors up from the Mövenpick Hotel, also serves a luxury hot chocolate (JD2.500).

LAUNDRY

Most hotels will do laundry for around JD1.500 per piece, through the drycleaners at Amra Palace Hotel.

MEDICAL FACILITIES

Queen Rania Hospital High-standard healthcare; open for emergencies without referral. Located 5km from the Police roundabout on the road to Tayyibeh.
Wadi Musa Pharmacy Has a wide range of medications and toiletries. Located near the Shaheed roundabout.

MONEY

Many hotels will change money, albeit at a poor rate. It's generally better to change travellers cheques before arriving in Petra.

The Housing Bank and Jordan Islamic Bank up from the Shaheed roundabout are good for money exchange; both have ATMs. The Arab Bank is downhill from the roundabout. Closer to the Petra entrance, the Cairo-Amman Bank in the Mövenpick Hotel and the Arab Jordan Investment Bank both change cash and (usually) travellers cheques with a minimum of fuss. The banks are open from about 8am to 2pm Sunday to Thursday and (sometimes) 9am to 11am on Friday. A couple of moneychangers near the Silk Road Hotel keep longer hours.

POST

Main post office (8am-5pm Sat-Thu) Located inside a mini-plaza on the Shaheed roundabout.
Post office (8am-5pm Sat-Thu) Small office by the Mussa Spring Hotel in 'Ain Musa.
Visitors centre post office (7.30am-5pm) The attraction of using the small post office behind Petra Visitor Centre is that mail is postmarked 'Petra Touristic Post Office', rather than Wadi Musa.

TELEPHONE

International telephone calls can be made from private agencies along the main streets of Wadi Musa. The cheapest and easiest way to make a call is to buy a prepaid phonecard called Ma'alak for JD3.

TOURIST INFORMATION

The best source of information is the main Petra Visitor Centre near the entrance to Petra (p220). The easiest way to find information about minibuses and other transport is to ask at your hotel or one of the restaurants around the Shaheed roundabout. You can also log on to **Jordan Jubilee** (www.jordanjubilee.com); the author of the site, Ruth, is a long-term resident of Wadi Musa and local oracle.

Activities

HAMMAMS

A Turkish bath (see the boxed text, p292, for an idea of what to expect) is the perfect way to ease aching muscles after a hard day's walking in Petra. The service includes steam bath, massage, hot stones, scrubbing and 'body conditioning' for a standard JD20 for one hour. The baths are popular with tourists and locals alike, so book in advance; women can request a female attendant.

In the passage under the Silk Road Hotel, near the entrance of Petra, **Petra Turkish Bath** (☎ 2157085; 3-10pm) has a completely separate bath area for women, with female attendants.

Salome Turkish Bath (☎ 2157342; 4pm-10pm), entered via a grotto displaying old farming implements, has an atmospheric sitting area

PETRA

WADI MUSA

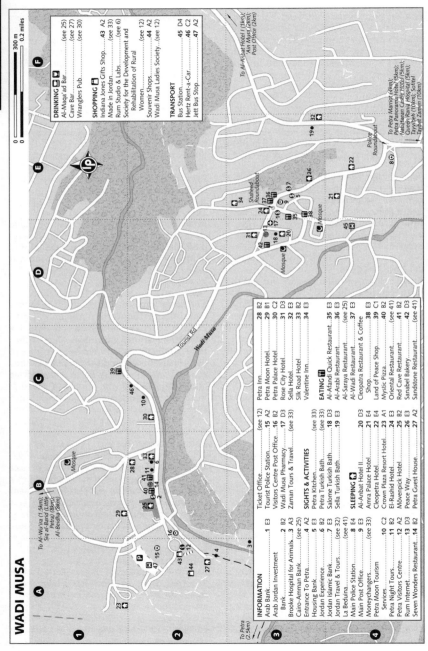

0   300 m
0   0.2 miles

To Al-Wu'ira (1.5km);
Sig al-Barid (Little
Sig) al-Petra (8km);
Al-Beidha (8km)

To Petra
(2.5km)

Mosque

Mosque

Tourist Rd

Wadi Musa

Mosque

Shaheed
Roundabout

Police
Roundabout

Mosque

To Al-Anbat Hotel (1km);
Ain Musa (2km);
Post Office (2km)

To Petra Marriot (4km);
Petra Panorama Hotel (5km);
Nabataean Castle Hotel (5km);
Guest House Hospital (5km);
Taybeh (10km); Sofitel
Taybet Zaman (10km)

for relaxing with a herb tea after bathing. It's located near Al-Anbat Hotel II.

The **Sella Turkish Bath** (☎ 2157170; www.sella hotel.com; ☽ 3-10pm) has the newest facility in town with a comprehensive list of services including sauna and separate baths for men and women. There's discount for groups of three or more (JD16 per person). Dead Sea products are on sale here.

The Amra Palace Hotel (p240) has an excellent *hammam*, with separate sections for men and women.

Tours

The most professional agency in Wadi Musa for arranging trips inside Petra and around Jordan (including Wadi Rum and Aqaba) is **Petra Moon Tourism Services** (☎ 2156665; www .petramoon.com). The office is on the main road to Petra. It can arrange horses to Jebel Haroun, fully supported treks to Dana (four to five days), hikes from Tayyibeh to Petra and camel treks to Wadi Rum.

Other reliable agencies:

Jordan Experience (☎ 2155005; www.jordan experience.com.jo) On the main road to Petra.

Jordan Travel & Tours (www.jordantravelandtours .com) In addition to local tours, it organises tours to six countries (including visas) and daily trips to Israel and the Palestinian Territories and Syria. Near the Sella Hotel.

La Beduina (☎ 2157099; www.labeduinatours.com) Near the Red Cave Restaurant.

Petra Night Tours (☎ 2154010; www.pntours.com) On the main road to Petra.

Raami Tours (☎ 796 203790; raami_manajah@ hotmail.com) Can organise traditional meals for visitors who want real homecooking and don't mind a few children around.

Zaman Tours & Travel (☎ 2157723; www.zaman tours.com) In the same building as the Silk Road Hotel.

A couple of the budget (and a few midrange and top-end) hotels can also arrange simple day trips around Petra and further afield.

For a fascinating insight into the life of the local Bedouin from the perspective of an expatriate who married into the Bdoul, consider taking a tour with **Marguerite van Geldermalsen** (tours@marriedtoabedouin.com). Marguerite adapts a six-hour tour to your fitness and interests, and takes in many of the sites mentioned in her book, *Married to a Bedouin* (see the boxed text, p221). Reservations need to be made by email in advance.

> **THE SPRING OF MOSES**
>
> Then Moses raised his arm and struck the rock twice with his staff. Water gushed out, and the community and their livestock drank.
>
> *Numbers 20:11*
>
> 'Ain Musa (Spring of Moses) is one of two possible locations in Jordan for the site where Moses supposedly struck the rock with his staff and water gushed forth to the thirsty Israelites (the other possible site is near Mt Nebo). The simple site is marked by a modern three-domed building occasionally visited by local pilgrims, but there's not a great deal to see. The site is located near the Golden Tulip Hotel, alongside the King's Highway at the main junction into Wadi Musa from the north.

There are many excellent local guides working independently in the Petra area. These include **Mahmoud Twaissi** (☎ 077-254658; mat65petra@yahoo.com), who has a well-earned reputation not just as a guide but also as a fixer for large-scale projects throughout the country (he is currently National Field Coordinator for the Abraham's Path project, see p52). Equally well regarded is **Mohammed Al-Hasanat** (☎ 2156567; explorer one69@yahoo.com), who has been a licensed national guide since 1979. He has a passion for hiking and has had plenty of practice: 'I took my first steps aged six,' he says, 'and I've been walking ever since.' Both these guides are reliable, knowledgeable both of the historical and cultural contexts of the areas they cover, and experienced in catering to the needs of individual or groups with special interests. They can organise camping tours over several days including camel and horse safaris.

Experienced horse-riders looking for an adventure should contact **Mahmoud al-Hamadeen** (☎ 077-79247417). Mahmoud offers two-hour sunset rides (JD25), three-hour rides to the High Place of Sacrifice (JD35), half- day trips to Little Petra (JD75) and day trips to Jebel Haroun (JD120). If you're looking for an adrenalin rush, be careful what you wish for! (See the boxed text, p224.)

If you were wondering what Petra would be like under the stars, then you are not

PETRA

PETRA BY NIGHT *Jenny Walker*

Like a grumbling camel caravan of snorting, coughing, laughing and farting miscreants, 200 people and one jubilantly crying baby make their way down the Siq 'in silence'. Asked to walk in single file behind the leader, breakaway contingents surge ahead to make sure they enjoy the experience 'on their own'. And eventually, sitting in 'reverential awe' outside the Treasury, the collected company show its appreciation of Arabic classical music by lighting cigarettes from the paper bag lanterns, chatting energetically, flashing their cameras and audibly farting some more.

Welcome to public entertainment in the Middle East! If you really want the Siq to yourself, come in the winter, go at 2pm or take a virtual tour on the internet.

But despite the promotional literature to the contrary, silence and solitude is not what Petra by Night is all about. What this exceptional and highly memorable tour does give you is the fantastic opportunity of experiencing one of the most sublime spectacles on earth in the fever of other people's excitement. Huddles of whispering devotees stare up at the candlelit god blocks, elderly participants are helped over polished lozenges of paving stones, the sound of a flute wafts along the neck-hairs of fellow celebrants – this is surely much nearer to the original experience of the ancient city of Petra than walking through the icy stone corridor alone.

---

alone. The extremely popular tour **Petra by Night** (adult/child under 12 JD12/free) was introduced in response to numerous requests from visitors wanting to see Petra by moonlight. The magical tour of the old city starts from Petra Visitor Centre at 8.30pm on Monday, Wednesday and Thursday nights (it doesn't run when it's raining), and lasts two hours. It takes you along the Siq (lined with 1500 candles) in as much silence as is possible given the crowds, as far as the Treasury. Here traditional Bedouin music is played and mint tea served. The performance of Bedouin storytelling depends on the mood of the raconteur. Tickets are available from travel agencies in town, or from Petra Visitor Centre before 5pm. Also see the boxed text, above.

Courses

If you've always wanted to know how to whip up wonderful hummus or bake the perfect baklava, **Petra Kitchen** (☎ 2155700; www.petrakitchen.com; cookery course per person JD30; JD10 for partners of participants; Ⓥ) is for you. Located 100m up the main road from the Mövenpick Hotel, Petra Kitchen offers nightly cookery courses to those wanting to learn from locals how to cook Jordanian mezze, soup and main courses in a relaxed family-style atmosphere. Dishes (including delicious vegetarian fare) change daily. It starts at 6.30pm (7.30pm in summer) and the price includes food and soft drinks. Better still, buy a bottle of Mt Nebo to share

with your fellow apprentice chefs. Reservations are recommended. See the boxed text, p84, for a first-hand account of the experience.

Sleeping

In 1908 Macmillan's guide, *Palestine and Syria,* had the following advice:

> At Petra, there is no sleeping accommodation to be found, and travellers therefore have to bring with them camp equipment, unless they prefer to put up with the inconvenience of sleeping in the Bedwin huts at Elji, half an hour distant from Petra, or spend the night in some of the numerous temples. Such a course cannot be recommended to European travellers, especially if ladies are in the party.

Even as recently as 1991, there were only four official hotels in Wadi Musa. Visitors now have a choice of over 70 hotels and camping is no longer permitted inside Petra.

The high season is generally from April to mid-May and October to November. Outside these times, prices can drop quickly from the official rates, especially if you're staying more than a couple of nights. That said, with the steady increase in tourism, the 'low season' is shrinking. Most hotels have a variety of rooms in a variety of sizes; some with a balcony, some with no natural light, so ask to see some options.

The prices quoted in this chapter are for high-season accommodation in an average room (neither the hotel's best nor worst) with breakfast.

In winter (November to March), make sure there's heating that works. Few places have fans and only the more expensive hotels have air-conditioning. Note that the views advertised by some hotels are of Wadi Musa valley, not of Petra itself.

Hotels beyond walking distance of the entrance to Petra often offer free transport to and from the gate (usually once a day in either direction). Although many hotels offer 'half board' (which includes breakfast and dinner), you can always obtain a room-only rate if you prefer.

One last point: if you get off the minibus at the Shaheed roundabout in Wadi Musa with a backpack, then you will be besieged by persuasive touts. Decide on your choice of hotel in advance if you want to be left alone.

BUDGET

The budget hotels listed here are clean and generally well run. Women travelling alone need to be more on their guard in budget hotels here than in other towns (make sure doors lock properly). Most offer free shuttles to/from Petra and video viewings of *Indiana Jones and the Last Crusade*. Prices include shared bathroom and breakfast unless otherwise noted.

Valentine Inn (☎ 2156423; valentineinn@hotmail .com; s/d/tr incl breakfast JD10/15/18; dm JD3/4; P) Still struggling to slough off its image as a mainly-for-men hostel, the Valentine is the quintessential backpackers hotel with a raft of add-on services, including tours along the King's Highway. Rooftop sleeping costs JD2 and home-cooked dinner is JD4. There's a pleasant sitting area outside.

Cleopetra Hotel (☎ 2157090; www.cleopetra.jeeran .com; s/d/tr JD12/16/21) This has to be one of the friendliest budget hotels in town. The rooms here, all with private bathroom (with hot water), are on the small side but there's a cosy communal sitting area that feels like your aunt's front room. You can sleep on the roof for JD4 or JD5 with breakfast. They organise overnight 4WD trips to Wadi Rum (JD40 per person for a minimum of three) that travellers have recommended.

Peace Way (☎ 2156963; www.peacewayhotel.com; s/d JD15/20) The interior of this quirky hotel

(with stuffed eagle in the lobby and trip-over kilims on the stairs) doesn't live up to the fresh, modern exterior. A favourite with Japanese and Chinese travellers, it has some bright rooms at the front and a pleasant outside sitting area.

Al-Anbat Hotel II (☎ 2157200; www.alanbat.com; s/d/tr JD15/20/30, breakfast JD1) The bright, white-marble lobby promises better accommodation than the small rooms with turquoise doors deliver – particularly as the plumbing needs some attention and the staff is conspicuous by its absence. That said, the double rooms at the front aren't bad and there's an excellent Turkish bath opposite.

Rose City Hotel (☎ 2156440; fax 2014133; s/d/tr JD18/20/25) The delightful staff makes this a good-value hotel. Rooms vary considerably, but all have private bathrooms. The pink corridors may just disappear with the renovations currently under way.

Al-Anbat Hotel I (☎ 2156265; www.alanbat.com; s/d/tr JD18/30/36, buffet dinner JD6; P ✕ ☐ ☑) Located some way out of town, on the road between 'Ain Musa and Wadi Musa, this three-storey resort offers midrange quality for budget prices. The large rooms (mostly with views) have satellite TV and come with a balcony. Other facilities include a Turkish bath (JD18 for guests) and small pool. Free transport to/from Petra is available. Campers (JD5 per person) can use a designated area with showers and a kitchen, and you can park a campervan.

MIDRANGE

There are some excellent-value hotels in this price range. All include private bathrooms and breakfast.

El-Rashid Hotel (☎ 2156800; wailln@hotmail.com; s/d/tr from JD20/35/45) This well-run, friendly hotel has an attractive, marble-floored lobby and elegant furniture. The rooms are not quite so appealing, but the satellite TV will take your mind off the lime-green walls. It's popular with French tour groups.

Petra Moon Hotel (☎ 2156220; www.petramoon hotel.com; s/d/tr JD25/35/45) Behind the Mövenpick Hotel, this friendly establishment is convenient for the entrance to Petra and is perennially popular with travellers (reservations are advisable). The comfortable rooms have fridge, TV and two windows that are good for enjoying the sunset. Best of all, the pillared foyer is a great meeting point for travellers. Discounts are possible for longer stays.

Petra Inn (☎ 2156401; www.petrainn.com; s/d/tr JD30/45/60; ❄) The brass jardinières decorating the foyer set the tone for this good-value hotel, just uphill from the entrance to Petra. With all new furniture, the rooms are comfortable if rather dark with small windows. Ask about the brighter end rooms, which offer 120-degree views. The roof terrace is a great place to catch the sunset in summer.

Sella Hotel (☎ 2157170; www.sellahotel.com; s/d/tr JD40/55/67; P ❄ 🖳) This new hotel is out of the town centre, but compensates with great views across Wadi Musa. The spacious rooms (some with connecting doors) are decorated in maroon and share the same furnishings as the Crowne Plaza – for some obscure reason! Free tea and coffee is available. The hotel runs the spotless Turkish baths opposite.

Amra Palace Hotel (☎ 2157070; www.amrapalace.com; s/d JD42/65, d with extra bed JD90; P ❄ 🖳 🛋) This lovely hotel lives up to its name with magnificent lobby, marble pillars, giant brass coffeepots and Damascene-style furniture. The brothers who have run this establishment for 12 years take a personal interest in the details and they have a fine sense of interior design. Each room has spotless linen that's changed every day (there's a laundry on site), wooden headboards, upholstered furniture and satellite TV. Most rooms have views across the valley. Services include heated pool, Jacuzzi, summer terrace and excellent Turkish bath (JD20 per person). There's also a fun cave-style internet café. With pretty gardens of roses and jasmine, this is undoubtedly one of the best hotels in Wadi Musa.

Petra Palace Hotel (☎ 2156723; www.petrapalace.com.jo; s/d/tr JD42/63/85; P ❄ 🖳 🛋) Located on the main street, 500m from the entrance to Petra, this attractive hotel – with its palm-tree entrance, big bright foyer and helpful management – is an excellent choice. The corridors are tired, but the newly renovated rooms have a rag-rolled finish and lots of useful furniture. Ask about the 'garden rooms' that open onto a terrace with two swimming pools. The bar and restaurant are another drawcard.

Silk Road Hotel (☎ 2157222; www.petrasilkroad.com; s/d/tr JD60/70/90; P ❄) Hand-painted

panels of Bedouin camps stretch across the foyer and restaurant walls of this old favourite, 300m from the entrance to Petra. The common areas are showing signs of age but the rooms all sport new furniture and big bathtubs. Some rooms are very dark so ask for one with a view. Buffet in the restaurant (JD10) is popular with tour groups.

TOP END

There are some surprising bargains to be found when business is quiet in the hotels below, with discounted rates of up to 20% on prices quoted here.

Petra Guest House (☎ 2156266; www.crowneplaza.com; s/d/tr JD120/150/180; P ❄ 🖳 🛋) You can't get closer to the entrance to Petra without sleeping in a cave. Although not the same quality as its sister, the Crown Plaza, the guesthouse does offer use of the latter's facilities. Choose from motel-like chalets or rooms in the recently renovated main building.

Crowne Plaza Resort Hotel (☎ 2156266; www.crowneplaza.com; s/d/tr JD140/170/210; P ❄ 🖳 🛋 Ⓥ) A great location (close to the entrance to Petra and overlooking sandstone bluffs) makes this a popular top-end choice, although the rooms are not as luxurious as one might expect for the price. The heated swimming pool is useful outside of high summer and a lovely terrace offers summer barbecues. The hotel also has a Jacuzzi, sauna, tennis courts, coffee makers in rooms and self-service laundry facilities. Breakfast (JD10) isn't included in the room rate.

Mövenpick Hotel (☎ 2157111; www.moevenpick-petra.com; s/d JD155/170; P ❄ 🖳 🛋 Ⓥ) This beautifully crafted Arabian-style hotel, 100m from the entrance to Petra, is worth a visit simply to admire the inlaid furniture, marble fountains, wooden screens, and brass salvers. Petals are floated daily in the jardinière, a roaring fire welcomes residents to the Burckhardt Library (a lounge on the upper floor) and pleasant views are afforded from the roof garden. As the hotel is in the bottom of the valley, there are no views but the large and super-luxurious rooms all have huge windows regardless. There's a children's playground and small arcade of quality gift shops. The buffet breakfast and dinner are exceptional.

The following four luxury hotels are on the scenic road between Tayyibeh and Wadi

Musa, a five- to 10-minute drive from the entrance to Petra. Perched at around 1400m above sea level, they offer fine views over the Rift Valley (the terraces are fantastic places for a sunset drink). Transport can be inconvenient if you don't have your own car. Some close in the winter. Unfortunately, lovely though the hotels are, they have somewhat blighted the once-secluded view from inside Petra.

Nabataean Castle Hotel (☎ 2157201; www .movenpick-hotels.com; s/d incl half board JD120/135; P ⓟ ⏛ ⏛ V) Mövenpick runs this often fully booked hotel. With the region's only heated indoor pool, it is an opulent choice although it plays second fiddle to its sister hotel near the entrance to Petra. Most rooms have views over the valley, but the windows are surprisingly small. There's a daily shuttle bus to and from Petra.

Petra Panorama Hotel (☎ 2157393; www.petra panorama.com; r incl breakfast/half board JD120/140; P ⏛ ⏛ ⏛ V) Popular with European tour groups, this hotel was designed for the package tourist with cavernous corridors, little finesse and a *Marie Celeste* atmosphere during the day. That said, the rooms, which cascade in tiers down the mountain, are bright and spacious and they all come with unmatchable views. Most open onto terraces where you can enjoy your own private sunset.

Petra Marriott (☎ 2156407; www.marriott.com; s/d JD125/140; P ⏛ ⏛ ⏛ V) One of the most elegant hotels in the area, services include an outdoor pool, several restaurants, a Turkish bath and even a cinema for free use by guests.

ourpick **Sofitel Taybet Zaman** (☎ 2150111; reservation@taybetzaman.com; s/d US$180/200, extra bed US$53; P ⏛ ⏛ ⏛ V) One of the unique hotels in Jordan, the Taybet Zaman is a stylish and evocative reconstruction of a traditional Ottoman stone village, with luxurious rooms, handicraft shops, swimming pool and Turkish bath. Set in tranquil gardens of fruiting figs and flowering plumbago with views across the Rift Valley, it is something of a rural idyll. The hotel is located in Tayyibeh village; a taxi from Petra (10km) costs about JD10 one way. Ask to pause at the spectacular viewpoint, just below the junction for the hospital. The delightful terrace restaurant called Sahtain, with cavernous, vaulted interior, special-

ises in traditional Arabic and international home-cooked specialities. Simpler fare for lunch includes the chef's salad (JD2.700) and there's a dinner buffet (JD19).

Eating
The main road through Wadi Musa is dotted with grocery stores where you can buy the necessaries for a picnic in Petra; there's also a supermarket next to Al-Anbat Hotel I, slightly out of town on the road to 'Ain Musa. Some hotels can arrange snackboxes with a boiled egg, bread and tomato. A felafel sandwich travels well and makes a filling lunch. Buy your dessert course at **Sanabel Bakery** (☉ 5am-midnight), which sells a delicious range of Arab sweets round the corner from Rum Internet.

After a hot day's hiking in Petra, it's hard to resist a Swiss ice cream (JD2) from the window outside the Mövenpick Hotel.

If you're climbing the hill between Petra Visitor Centre and Shaheed Roundabout, you might like to stop at the **Land of Peace Shop** (☎ 079-5738934; ☉ 8am-midnight), a halfway house with a small craft shop, café with seating on the pavement, and four clean loos!

BUDGET
The cheapest places to eat are around Shaheed roundabout and Sanabel bakery.

Al-Wadi Restaurant (☎ 2157151; salads JD1, mains JD4-5; ☉ 7am-late) Right on Shaheed roundabout, this lively spot offers pasta and pizza, as well as a range of vegetarian dishes and local Bedouin specialities such as *gallayah* and *mensaf*, most of which come with salad and rice.

Al-Arabi Restaurant (☎ 2157661; mains from JD1; ☉ 6am-midnight) Similar to next-door neighbour Al-Wadi Restaurant, it offers discounts to repeat customers.

Al-Afandi Quick Restaurant (meals from JD2) This simple and friendly place located off the Shaheed roundabout offers hummus, felafel and shwarma.

Cleopatra Restaurant & Coffee Shop (☎ 079-5318775; buffet JD5; ☉ 6am-11pm) This canteen offers a reasonable open buffet, with a range of Bedouin specialties.

MIDRANGE
All of the places listed here are close together and similar in menu and price. They are near the entrance to Petra.

PETRA

Red Cave Restaurant (☎ 2157799; starters JD1, mains JD4-5; ☻ 9am-10pm) Cavernous, cool and friendly, this restaurant specialises in local Bedouin specialities including *mensaf* and *maqlubbeh* (steamed rice with meat) and is a popular travellers' meeting place.

Mystic Pizza (☎ 2155757; ☻ 8.30am-11pm; **V**) A welcoming new establishment serving fresh, tasty pizza from around JD3 for a small, JD6 for a medium and JD8 for a large. It also has vegetarian options, including lentil soup (JD2).

The **Oriental Restaurant** (☎ 2157087; mains JD4-5, pizzas from JD2.500; ☻ 11am-9.30pm), together with neighbouring **Sandstone Restaurant** (☎ 079-5542277; entrees/mains JD1/6; ☻ 8am-midnight), offers simple fare of tasty mixed grills, salad and mezze with pleasant outdoor seating. These are good places for a beer and a good-natured chuckle at the menu.

TOP END

Al-Saraya Restaurant (☎ 2157111; ☻ lunch/dinner JD12.500/16.250; **V**) Serves a top-notch international buffet or you can opt for salad, soup and bread for JD6. Leave time for a nightcap in the magnificent bar afterwards.

Two other high-quality dining options include **Sahtain** (☎ 2150111; buffet JD19; **V**) at the Sofitel Taybet Zaman (see p241 for details) and Petra Kitchen (p238), where you can cook your own Jordanian specialities.

Drinking

There's not a lot to do in the evening, other than plan your next day in Petra. Some hotels organise DVDs or other entertainment, but only when there are enough takers.

our pick **Cave Bar** (☎ 2156266; beer/cocktails JD4.5007; ☻ 8am-midnight; **☒**) You can't come to Petra and miss the oldest bar in the world. Occupying a 2000-year-old Nabataean rock tomb, this blue-lit Petra hot spot has been known to stay open until 4am on busy summer nights. Sit among the spirits, alcoholic or otherwise, and you'll soon be getting a flavour of Petra you hadn't bargained on (including the 26% tax and service charge!). There's live Bedouin music from 9pm (except Saturday). They also serve food, including a special menu of 'Nabataean food' served in clay bowls – reserve this a half day in advance. The bar is next to the entrance

to Petra Guest House, behind Petra Visitor Centre.

Wranglers Pub (☎ 2156723; beer JD3-5; ☻ 2pm-midnight) The Petra Palace Hotel runs this sociable bar, decorated with assorted local memorabilia.

Al-Maqa'ad Bar (☎ 2157111; beer from JD2.500) The Mövenpick hotel bar has a superb Moroccan-style interior with carved wooden grills and a chandelier: it's worth having a cocktail just to enjoy the ambience. The ice-cream specials are unforgettable. It also has a 26% tax and service charge.

Shopping

There are many souvenir shops near the entrance to Petra and ad hoc stalls run by local Bedouin inside Petra. Throughout Wadi Musa you'll see craftsmen patiently pouring coloured sand into glass bottles; they will write your name if you give them time. Top-end hotels sell good-quality handicrafts. Ask for Umm Raami's concession inside Petra where you can buy contemporary silver jewellery inspired by ancient Nabataean designs and crafted by local women originally trained through a Noor al-Hussein Foundation project.

Made in Jordan (☎ 2155700; www.madeinjordan .com) This excellent shop sells quality crafts from various local enterprises. Products include olive oil, soap, paper, ceramics, table runners, nature products from Wild Jordan in Amman, jewellery from Wadi Musa, embroidery from Safi, camel hair shawls, and bags from Aqaba. The fixed prices reflect the quality and uniqueness of each piece; credit cards are accepted.

The **Wadi Musa Ladies Society** (☻ 6am-9pm) and the **Society for the Development & Rehabilitation of Rural Women** (☻ 6am-9pm) both have shops at the visitor centre selling a range of souvenirs, books and crafts.

At the **Indiana Jones Gifts Shop** (☎ 2155069; ☻ 8am-10pm), you can buy a video of the main sites in Petra.

Rum Studio & Labs (☎ 2157467; ☻ 8.30am-10pm) A range of digital accessories is available here; the shop is located in front of the Silk Road Hotel on the main road.

Getting There & Away

Public transport to and from Wadi Musa is less frequent than you'd expect, given that it's the number-one tourist attrac-

PETRA: PUBLIC TRANSPORT AT A GLANCE

To/From	Duration	Frequency	Notes
Amman (210km) (via Desert Hwy)	3 hours	1 buses daily/ 11 minibuses daily	**JETT Bus**: Leaves 6.30am from Abdali Bus Station. Returns 4.30pm from Petra Visitor Centre. **Minibus**: Leaves between 6am and 1pm to/from Wahadat Station in Amman and Wadi Musa bus station. Leaves only when full.
Wadi Rum (90km)	2 hours	1 daily	**Minibus**: Leaves 6.30am from Wadi Musa bus station. Leaves 8.30am from Wadi Rum Petra Visitor Centre. May only leave if full: ask hotel/camp owner to contact bus driver in advance.
To/From Aqaba (120km)	2½ hours	4 daily	**Minibus**: Leaves between 6.30am & 8.30am, with one midafternoon to/from Wadi Musa bus station and Aqaba minibus station. Leaves only when full.

tion in Jordan. For a guide to transport between Petra and Jerusalem, see the boxed text, p316.

BUS & MINIBUS

A daily JETT bus connects Amman with Petra, largely designed for those wanting to visit on a day trip. The service leaves at 6.30am from Abdali Bus Station (single/ return JD6/11) and drops passengers off at Petra Visitor Centre in Wadi Musa at 9.30am. The return bus leaves at 4.30pm.

Minibuses leave from the bus station in central Wadi Musa. Most minibuses won't leave unless they're at least half full, so be prepared for a wait. If there are insufficient passengers, they may not leave at all, or you may be approached to pay for the empty seats. This is not a scam: it's just an attempt by the driver to cover the cost of the journey. You should establish the fare you are being charged before you depart. There are far fewer services on Fridays.

About 11 minibuses travel every day between Amman (Wahadat station) and Wadi Musa (JD5, four hours) via the Desert Highway. These buses leave Amman and Wadi Musa when full every hour or so between 6am and 1pm.

Minibuses leave Wadi Musa for Ma'an (JD1, 45 minutes) fairly frequently throughout the day (more often in the morning), stopping briefly at the university, about 10km from Ma'an. From Ma'an there are connections to Amman, Aqaba and (indirectly) Wadi Rum. Minibuses also leave Wadi Musa for Aqaba (JD4, 2½ hours),

via Tayyibeh, at about 6.30am, 8.30am and 3pm – ask around the day before to confirm or check through your hotel.

For Wadi Rum (JD5, two hours), there is a daily minibus some time around 6.30am. It's a good idea to reserve a seat the day before – your hotel should be able to ring the driver. Be wary of anyone who tries to charge you extra for 'luggage', offers to buy you overpriced water or hooks you onto a substandard tour – these are common complaints made by many readers. If you miss this bus, or the service isn't operating, take the minibus to Aqaba, get off at the Ar-Rashidiyyah junction and catch another minibus or hitch the remainder of the journey to Rum. Cleopatra Hotel (p239), among other budget hotels, organises overnight tours to Wadi Rum.

To Karak, a minibus sometimes leaves at around 8am (JD3), but demand is low so it doesn't leave every day. Alternatively, travel via Ma'an.

CAR

Hertz Rent-a-Car (☎ 2156981; ☒ 8am-6pm) rents out cars from JD30 per day. A 4WD costs around JD160 per day.

Petra and Wadi Musa are well signposted along the main highways. The road from Petra to Little Petra extends to the Wadi Musa to Shobak road offering a scenic alternative route out of town. A spectacular new road winds into Wadi Araba for direct access to the Dead Sea Highway (see the boxed text, p170). The road to Tayyibeh is also particularly scenic.

TAXI

Private (yellow) taxis are easy to find in Wadi Musa. A few 4WD taxis are available for much the same cost, but they are not of much benefit now that all 4WD transport in Wadi Rum is regulated from Petra Visitor Centre. One-way taxi fares cost JD40 to Wadi Rum (one hour) or Aqaba (1½ hours); JD7 to Shobak (JD12 return including a one-hour wait); and JD50 to Karak (1½ hours). If you want to travel to Madaba or Amman via the King's Highway, with stops at Shobak, Dana and Karak, the fare is around JD90.

Getting Around

The standard, non-negotiable fare anywhere around central Wadi Musa is JD1; it costs a little more if you go as far as 'Ain Musa. There are usually plenty of private (yellow) unmetered taxis travelling up and down the main road, especially in the late afternoon.

AL-WU'IRA (CRUSADER CASTLE) وعره

Built by the Crusaders in AD 1116, **Al-Wu'ira** (Map pp218-19; admission free; daylight hr) was overrun by Muslim forces 73 years later. A fantastic bridge (previously a drawbridge) leads over the gorge to a gatehouse and the limited ruins.

Look for the unsigned turn-off, about 1.5km north of the Mövenpick Hotel, and on the left side of the road leading to Siq al-Barid (Little Petra).

SIQ AL-BARID (LITTLE PETRA)

سيق البيضاء (البتراء الصغيرة)

Siq al-Barid (Cold Canyon) is colloquially known as **Little Petra** (admission free; daylight hr) and is well worth a visit. It was thought to have served as an agricultural centre, trading suburb and resupply post for camel caravans visiting Petra. The surrounding area is picturesque and fun to explore.

From the car park, an obvious path leads to the 400m-long *siq*, which opens out into larger areas. The first open area has a **temple**, which archaeologists know little about. Four **triclinia** – one on the left and three on the right – are in the second open area, and were probably used as dining rooms to feed hungry merchants and travellers. About 50m further along the *siq* is the **Painted House**, another small dining room, which is reached by some exterior steps. The faded but still vivid frescoes of vines, flowers and birds on the underside of the interior arch are a rare example of Nabataean painting, though the walls have been blackened by Bedouin campfires. Cut into the rock opposite the room is a large **cistern**; there are also worn water channels at various points along the *siq*.

At the end of Siq al-Barid are some steps. If you climb to the top, there are some great views and plenty of picnicking opportunities. If you have extra time and interest you could explore the Nabataean quarries and cisterns of Umm Qusa, located just before the entrance to Siq al-Barid.

A DOZEN UNUSUAL WAYS TO ENJOY PETRA

- Enter Petra via the hairstreak Wadi Muthlim (p231) instead of the Siq.
- Gain an eagle-eye view of the Treasury from the path above the Royal Tombs (p232).
- Gallop across a plateau on horseback, high above the Treasury (p237).
- Descend from the High Place of Sacrifice via the garden valley of Wadi Farasa (p232).
- Take tea with one of the few remaining residents of Petra behind Al-Habis (p228).
- Unfurl a portable feast in a triclinium, a banqueting hall for honouring the dead.
- Hike with a guide to Little Petra (above) from the Monastery.
- Find your own secret garden beyond the *siq* at Little Petra (above).
- Saddle up a donkey for the two-day hike to Sabra via Wadi Tibn (p234).
- Leave Petra with the Bdoul via the road to Umm Sayhoun.
- Walk between Umm Sayhoun and Wadi Musa for a sublime view of Petra at sunset.
- Stop at the viewpoint on the scenic road to Tayyibeh for the ultimate Petra panorama.

If you come prepared, it's possible to **hike** from Siq al-Barid to Petra's Monastery (Al-Deir), or to Petra centre via Wadi Mu'aisireh al-Gharbiya. You'll need a guide (ask at the car park by the entry to Siq al-Barid) as route-finding is tricky. You must also have a valid ticket to Petra (you can't get one at Siq al-Barid).

A 10-minute walk from Little Petra is the **Ammarin Bedouin Camp** (☎ 079-5667771, 2131229; www.bedouincamp.net; half board per person in tent US$50) in the next-door Siq al-Amti. Accommodation is a mattress and blankets in a Bedouin tent, but there is a shower and toilet block. A small ethnographic museum on site spotlights the local Ammarin tribe. The camp offers guided hikes in the surrounding hills. Reservations are essential.

Hidden in the mountains on the road between Umm Sayhoun and Little Petra is **King Aretas IV Luxury Camp** (☎ 06-4631435; kingaretas camp@gmail.com; per person US$65, half board per person US$125, minimum 2 people). Formerly the Hilali Camp, its new management has brought a touch of class to this secluded complex. It offers camping in style with army tents that sport proper beds with mattresses and full-length wood-rimmed mirrors. The spotless shower blocks have hot water. Dinner is prepared in a cave and served with finesse in a variety of dining areas, including romantic caverns. Ring ahead if you want to try their speciality dinner of meat prepared in ground ovens (JD30).

Getting There & Away

Some hotels in Wadi Musa organise tours to Little Petra. If not, a private taxi costs about JD12 one way or JD16 return, including an hour's waiting time.

If you're driving, take the road north of the Mövenpick Hotel and follow the signs to 'Beda' or 'Al-Beidha'. Turn left at the junction from where it's just under 1km to the car park.

Alternatively, it's a pleasant 8km walk following the road. The route passes the village of Umm Sayhoun, the 'Elephant Rock' formation and then 'Ain Dibdibah, which once supplied Petra with much of its water. You can shortcut across fields to the left about 1km before the junction to Al-Beidha.

Hitching is possible, especially on Friday when local families head out for a picnic.

AL-BEIDHA   البيدا

The Neolithic ruins of **Al-Beidha** (admission free; ☉ daylight hr) date back some 9000 years and, along with Jericho, constitute one of the oldest archaeological sites in the Middle East. The remains of around 65 round (and later rectangular) structures are especially significant because they pinpoint the physical transition from hunter-gatherer to settled herder-agriculturalist. The settlement was abandoned around 6000 BC, which is why it's still intact (latter civilisations never built upon it). For the casual visitor, the ruins require imagination. Follow the marked trails as the site is fragile.

To reach the site, follow the trail starting to the left of the entrance to Little Petra for about 15 minutes.

Aqaba, Wadi Rum & the Desert Highway

العقبة وادي رم & الطريق الصحراء

There is a magnificent road (A35) that leads from Wadi Musa, with westerly glimpses across expansive Wadi Araba, to the escarpment of Jebel Batra. Here the road joins the Desert Highway and hand in hand they sweep onto the majestic floor of what is commonly called the Southern Desert. This is the home of the Bedouin, whose legendary courage and bravado were made famous by TE Lawrence in *Seven Pillars of Wisdom*; this is where a pan-Arab ideal was most convincingly expressed during the 20th-century Arabic Revolt; it's where the cry of 'to Aqaba' still rings between the towering walls of Wadi Rum, carried in the whistle of the freight train as it winds along the now-placid tracks of the Hejaz Railway.

But put history aside and still the Southern Desert casts a spell on those who visit. This is the quintessential desert of sand dunes, oases and weathered escarpments, beautiful at sunset and awe-inspiringly extreme in midsummer. A trip to Wadi Rum makes all but the most unromantic at heart long to leave the modern world behind and attempt the life of a nomad.

Make no mistake, however: the desert, much of which is characterised not by the picturesque features of Wadi Rum but by inhospitable plains, doesn't take prisoners. Life here is hard, even for the Bedouin and, in the words of Lawrence, 'a death in life' for strangers. Take the journey along the Desert Highway, along the edge of the mighty Badia, and you'll quickly learn a new respect for this extreme environment – and for the people and wildlife who have adapted to its privations.

HIGHLIGHTS

- Live a 'Lawrence moment' by riding through **Wadi Rum** (p260) on a camel, visiting the places made famous in *Seven Pillars of Wisdom*

- Enjoy the banter between Bedouin drivers on a **4WD excursion** (p267) through Wadi Rum

- Book a private tent and personally delivered dinner on your own sand dune in **Diseh** (p275) for the ultimate candlelit supper

- Taste fresh tuna steaks in one of the excellent fish restaurants of **Aqaba** (p256), and ruin your love for the tinned version

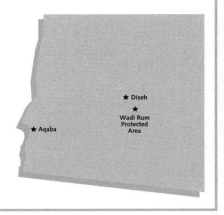

AQABA
العقبة

☎ 03 / pop 105,000

Aqaba is the most important city in southern Jordan and, with feverish development underway, is being groomed as the country's second city, if not in size at least in terms of status, revenue and tourism potential. Perched on the edge of the Gulf of Aqaba, ringed by high desert mountains and enjoying a pleasant climate for most of the year, Aqaba has what it takes to make a major resort – a fact not lost on hotel chains: a new InterContinental hotel is up and running and a neighbouring Kempinski hotel was nearly finished at the time of research. In addition, the $2.5 billion Saraya Project, which includes lagoons, marina, golf course and a British university, was taking shape in the heart of town when we visited and to the south, the Tala Bay hotel and residential development (unopened at the time of writing) will also help Aqaba in its bid to become Jordan's answer to Eilat.

Surprisingly, given this radical makeover, Aqaba retains the relaxed small-town atmosphere of a popular local holiday destination. For the visitor, although there's not much to 'do' as such, the town offers a sociable stopover en route to the diving and snorkelling clubs to the south, and the big destinations of Wadi Rum and Petra to the northeast. It's also an obvious place to break a journey to/from Israel and the Palestinian Territories or Egypt. There's plenty of good-value accommodation in the town centre and some excellent restaurants. The port mars the view a little and the beaches close to town are fairly unappealing (except at the top-end hotels), but overall you'll probably find you end up staying a day or two longer than you originally planned.

While Amman shivers in winter with temperatures around 5°C and the occasional snowfall, the daytime temperature in Aqaba rarely goes below 20°C and is often quite a few degrees warmer. In summer the weather is hot, with daytime temperatures over 35°C, but the sea breezes make it bearable. It also helps to follow the traditional siesta: everything shuts down around 2pm and reopens after the afternoon nap, from around 6pm.

History

And king Solomon made a navy of ships in Ezion-Geber, which is beside Eloth (Eilat), on the shore of the Red Sea, in the land of Edom

1 Kings 9:26

Excavations at Tell al-Khalifa, 4km west of central Aqaba and right on the border of Jordan and Israel and the Palestinian Territories, have revealed the ancient world's largest copper-smelting site, thought to be the biblical site of Ezion Geber. Smelting was carried out here from the 10th to 5th centuries BC, processing ore from mines in Wadi Araba. Ezion Geber was also the ancient port from which King Solomon's fleet departed for the gold mines of Ophir (an unidentified location, possibly Sudan, Ethiopia, Eritrea or Yemen).

As trade with southern Arabia and Sheba (present-day Yemen) developed, the area around Aqaba thrived thanks to its position on one of the Middle East's major trade routes, with spurs leading north to Petra, Damascus and Bosra; west to Egypt and Palestine; and south to Arabia. The discovery in Aqaba of ceramics from China and

AQABA, WADI RUM & THE DESERT HIGHWAY

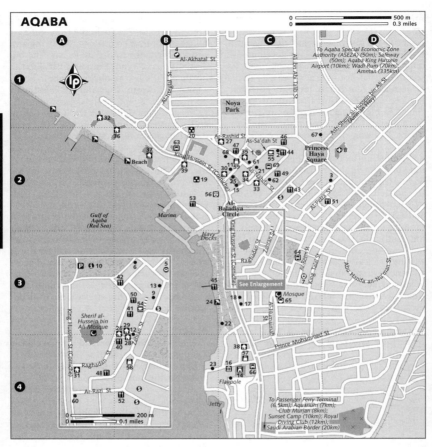

Aksumite coins from Ethiopia highlights the cosmopolitan nature of the port.

The town was occupied by the Ptolemies from Egypt during the 2nd and 3rd centuries BC, and then the Nabataeans from about the 3rd to 1st centuries BC. During Roman times, the town was renamed Aqabat Ayla (Pass of Alia) and it housed a garrison of legionaries.

Intriguingly, archaeologists working at Ayla unearthed a late-3rd-century church, thought to be the world's oldest purpose-built church (earlier churches have been found but these were built for other purposes and later converted). The sanctuary was used for less than a century before the church was destroyed by an earthquake.

In the 10th century, a Muslim traveller described Aqaba as 'a great city' and a meeting place of pilgrims en route to and from Mecca. In AD 1024 the town was sacked by local tribes and in 1068 a huge earthquake split the old city of Ayla in two, consigning the town to a minor historical role.

The Crusaders occupied the town in 1116 and fortified a small island nearby – then called Ile de Graye, but now known as Pharaoh's Island (p254). By 1170 both the port and island were in the hands of the Ayyubids, under Saladin (Salah ad-Din). In 1250 the Mamluks took over. By the beginning of the 16th century the town had been swallowed up by the Ottoman Empire, and lost much of its significance when the main trading area of the region was moved to Baghdad in the middle of the 16th century.

For about 500 years, until the Arab Revolt during WWI, Aqaba remained an insignificant fishing village. Ottoman forces occupying the town were forced to retreat after a raid by the Arabs and TE Lawrence in 1917. From then on, the British used Aqaba as a supply centre from Egypt for the push up through the Trans-Jordan and Palestine regions.

After WWI, the border between Trans-Jordan and Saudi Arabia had still not been defined, so Britain arbitrarily drew a line a few kilometres south of Aqaba. The Saudis disputed the claim but took no action. As the port of Aqaba grew, the limited coastline proved insufficient, so in 1965 King Hussein traded 6000 sq km of Jordanian desert for another 12km of coastline with Saudi Arabia.

Orientation

The centre of Aqaba is compact and easy to cover on foot. King Hussein St (also known as the Corniche) is the main axis of Aqaba.

It follows the languid Gulf from the border with Israel and the Palestinian Territories to the border with Saudi Arabia. In the centre of town, a walking path parallels King Hussein St, cutting inland around private hotel beaches, the marina and navy docks, and passing through incongruous allotments of spinach and alfalfa. With its intermittent access to public beaches, local-style cafés and kebab stalls, it offers a good introduction to the town. A huge Jordanian flag marks the southern end of the path, where you'll find a pleasant plaza, the remains of old Aqaba and the tourist office. The disappointingly obtrusive port is a few kilometres south of the centre. Most of the fashionable new eating and drinking venues are around As-Sadah St while the budget haunts are near to the *souq* in the older centre of town.

Information
BOOKSHOPS

Aqaba has two excellent bookshops that sell a range of international newspapers as well as books about Jordan and the region.

LAWRENCE OF ARABIA

Born in 1888 into a wealthy English family, Thomas Edward Lawrence ('TE' to his friends) nurtured an early passion for the Middle East. He studied archaeology at Oxford (where he later became a fellow of All Souls College) and journeyed in 1909 to Syria, Lebanon and Jordan to research his thesis on Crusader castles. Bewitched by the region, he returned to the Syria–Turkey border in 1910 as part of a British Museum excavations project on the Euphrates. With the outbreak of WWI, Lawrence became a natural choice for the intelligence service in Cairo, where he quickly earned a commission and became attached to the Hejaz Expeditionary Force.

Lawrence felt a natural sympathy towards the fomenting Arab Revolt, the objective of which (at least from an Arab perspective) was to create a Sunni Arab state. Learning to ride camels with the best of them, and wearing Arab clothing like so many other English adventurers before him, Lawrence accompanied the armies of the great Arab warrior (and later statesman) Emir Faisal (p45). Despite adopting the life of the Arab raiding parties whom he grew to love, however, Lawrence never forgot he was English and answerable to General Allenby, the veteran British commander-in-chief, responsible for securing British interests in the Middle East. From his headquarters in Cairo, Allenby recognised the value of Arab assistance in defeating the Turks and gave Lawrence his tacit, and sometimes reluctant, blessing to participate in the Arab conquest of Aqaba.

After Aqaba, Lawrence continued to be committed to the cause, joining various Arab contingents all the way to Damascus, where the Ottoman Turks were finally routed. Although the Arabs won the war, they were partially robbed of the peace. The settlement at the Paris Peace Conference of 1919 fell far short of the independent nation that the Arabs had been encouraged to fight for, not least by Lawrence. As he admits in the introduction to *Seven Pillars of Wisdom*, his famous account of the Desert Revolt:

'It was evident from the beginning that if we won the war these promises would be dead paper, and had I been an honest adviser of the Arabs I would have advised them to go home and not risk their lives fighting for such stuff…'

Seven Pillars of Wisdom

Seven Pillars of Wisdom was printed privately in 1926 and, largely thanks to the promotional endeavours of an American journalist looking for a story, the Lawrence legend was born. In this adventurous account of derring-do, the first draft of which was allegedly lost at Reading train station near London in the UK, Lawrence casts himself in the role of trusted adviser, brave soldier and ultimately a messiah figure of the Arab cause. However, that was not necessarily how he was regarded from an Arab perspective. Indeed for some he was 'Lawrence Who?' – one among 100,000 Arabs, 10% of whom died in their epic struggle to build a nation. Some say that Lawrence was embarrassed by the hero status conferred upon him by an adoring English public (in 1927 he changed his name to Shaw and chose to enrol as a private in the RAF); others say he did nothing to put his contribution into a more historically accurate perspective. When Lawrence writes: 'On the whole I prefer lies to truth particularly when they concern me', it's hard not to have some sympathy with his detractors.

In 1927 he left on a mission to India, but returned home after only a short secondment because of rumours that he had encouraged an uprising of Afghan tribes. Lawrence settled into a quiet life as an uncommissioned aircraftsman in Dorset, England, until leaving the RAF in February 1935. He died three months later in a motorcycle accident – a lone and isolated figure, by all accounts, who never fully found in peacetime the sense of purpose and passion he experienced with his Arab comrades in the desert. Lawrence's legacy is best judged not so much in terms of his disputed military accomplishments, eccentric and brave though they may be, but in the way he has immortalised (at least for Western readers) some of the great characters of modern Arab history. But it is not just the hallowed names of Auda and Faisal that ring out of the desert at Wadi Rum; to his credit, Lawrence also describes with great tenderness the ordinary foot soldier of the Arab cause who gave their lives for a brave new world.

Redwan Bookshop (☎ 2013704; redwanbook@
hotmail.com; Zahran St; ☼ 7.30am-12.30pm & 4-9pm)
One of the best in Jordan with an extensive selection of
newspapers, hard-to-find Jordanian titles, Lonely Planet
guidebooks, and English, German and French novels.
Yamani Library (☎ /fax 2012221; Zahran St; ☼ 9am-
2.30pm & 6-10pm) A few doors to the north; has a better
range of English novels.

EMERGENCY
Police station (☎ 2012411, 191; Ar-Reem St) Opposite
the bus station.
Princess Haya Hospital (☎ 2014111 ; Ash-Shrif
al-Hussein bin Ali St) Well equipped and modern. It's just
north of Princess Haya Square roundabout.

INTERNET ACCESS
Aqaba has a good sprinkling of internet
cafés, particularly along As-Sadah St, most of
which charge around JD1 to JD2 per hour.
10zll Internet Café (☎ 2022009; As-Sadah St; per hr
JD1, ☼ 24hr) Next to Days Inn, this large establishment
has coffee and soft drinks.

LAUNDRY
Most visitors stay long enough in Aqaba to
get some laundry done – especially useful
if you've gathered layers of dust and sand
from Wadi Rum.
Ayla Dryclean (☎ 2062200; As-Sadah St; ☼ 9am-
midnight Sat-Thu, 2pm-5pm Fri) Trousers cost JD2,
complete with pencil-sharp creases (not necessarily where
you want them). Shirts or T-shirts cost JD1.
Frindes Laundry (☎ 2015051; Al-Petra St; ☼ 8am-1pm
& 4pm-10pm Sat-Thu) Offers similar services to Ayla Dryclean.

MONEY
There are dozens of banks and ATMs around
the city. Many are located along the southern side of Al-Hammamat al-Tunisieh St.

Numerous moneychangers are congre-
gated around the corner of Zahran and Ar-
Razi Sts. They keep longer hours than the
banks, and most change travellers cheques
without commission, though check the
rate first.

POST
DHL (☎ 2012039, 2011385; Al-Petra St)
General post office (☼ 7.30am-7pm Sat-Thu, to
1.30pm Fri) Opposite Zahran St in the centre of town.

TELEPHONE
There are a number of telephone booths
outside the general post office, and several

stalls nearby sell telephone cards. Other private telephone agencies are located on the
main streets, and some moneychangers also
offer telephone services. Note that international calls from Aqaba are up to five times
cheaper than in Wadi Rum.

TOURIST INFORMATION
Tourist office (☎ /fax 2013363; Baladiya Circle;
☼ 8am-2.30pm Sun-Thu) Located in a kiosk in the middle
of a new park between carriageways, the brand new
tourist office just east of the roundabout has lots of leaflets
and precious little else despite friendly staff. There's
another branch inside Aqaba Museum.

VISA EXTENSIONS
Aqaba Special Economic Zone Authority (ASEZA;
☎ 2091000, 2091031; www.aqabazone.com; Ash-Sherif
al-Hussein bin Ali St—Amman Hwy) Opposite Safeway. You
need to register here if you were given a free visa on arrival
in Aqaba and plan to stay in Jordan for more than 14 days.
The website has some useful information about Aqaba.
Police station (☎ 2012411; Ar-Reem St; ☼ 7am-9pm
Sat-Thu) Opposite the bus station. This is the place to come
for an extension of your visa for up to three months. These
extensions are usually available on the spot and are free.
It's best to go earlier in the day (8am to 3pm). Aqaba is
the only reliable place to get your visa extended outside
Amman.

Dangers & Annoyances
Women travellers have reported varying
degrees of harassment from local lads on
the public beaches. Foreign women may
feel less conspicuous wearing loose shirts
and baggy shorts over a swimsuit or, better still, using the facilities of one of the
hotels.

Activities
BEACHES
Look at pictures of Aqaba in a brochure,
and you may imagine that the town has
already achieved resort status. While there
are some good facilities in the top-end
hotels, and plenty more in the pipeline, the
public beaches at present are more about
fully dressed bathing on board your own
inflatable lilo, rather than jet-skiing in designer swimwear across palm-fringed bays.

The main free **public beach** is the stretch
of sand lined with cafés between the navy
docks and Aqaba Castle. Forget the swimming and join the Jordanians at leisure
instead. There are macho youths trotting

ON A RAINY DAY IN AQABA ...

...you could picnic under the clouds with delighted locals, or if this doesn't do it for you, then how about spending a couple of hours rooting out some of Aqaba's history? To be fair, there isn't too much to see or do (most people come to Aqaba to go snorkelling or diving – see p277) but if you tack the following sites onto a promenade along the corniche, it's a pleasant enough way to spend a morning. If you don't feel like walking from one site to another, take a **horse and cart** (JD8 for 30 minutes) from outside Al-Cazar Hotel.

■ **Aqaba Fort** (just west of King Hussein St; admission JD1, includes Aqaba Museum; ☯ 8am-4pm Sat-Thu, 10am-4pm Fri) This squat fortification, at the other end of the Corniche to Ayla, measures around 50m by 50m, and is unusual in having sides of slightly uneven length. Construction of the original castle is generally attributed to the Mamluks during the reign of Sultan Qansur al-Ghuri (1510–17), as attested by the Arabic inscriptions inside the gateway of double wooden doors with metal reinforcements. In one of the eastern rooms off the main courtyard are further inscriptions suggesting that the castle was renovated and enlarged by the Ottomans in both 1587 and 1628. In subsequent centuries the castle was used as a *khan* (travellers inn) for travelling pilgrims, especially Egyptians, on their way between their homeland and Mecca. The Ottomans occupied the castle until WWI when, in 1917, the fortress was substantially destroyed by shelling from the British Royal Navy. The Hashemite coat of arms above the main entrance commemorates the Arab Revolt that swept through Aqaba, ousting the Turks. The aged eucalyptus tree in the castle courtyard could tell a tale or two.

■ **Aqaba Museum** (Museum of Aqaba Antiquities; just west of King Hussein St; admission JD1; ☯ 8am-4pm Sat-Thu, 10am-4pm Fri) The museum, part of the Aqaba Fort complex, was previously the home of Sherif Hussein bin Ali – the great-great-grandfather of the present king, Abdullah II – who lived here for a period of time after WWI. The collection of artefacts includes coins from Iraq and Egypt, ceramics from the excavations of Ayla, 8th-century Islamic stone tablets and some late Byzantine reliefs. Anyone who has travelled the King's Highway may be interested to see an inscribed milestone from the Trajan Road (the Roman incarnation of this famous thoroughfare). There's also small tourist-information centre housed at the museum.

■ **Ayla** (admission free; ☯ 24 hr) Located along the Corniche, and incongruously squeezed between the marina and the Mövenpick Resort, Ayla is the site of the early medieval port of Aqaba. The ruins are limited, but noticeboards in English clearly pinpoint items of interest. At the back of the parking space behind the JETT bus office is another small section of the old city, including the city wall and the ruins of an ancient church.

■ **Jordan Experience Show** (☎ 2022200; Aqaba Gateway; admission JD7; ☯ shows noon, 1pm, 3pm, 4pm & 5pm) If it really is raining, then consider taking the kids to watch this 35-minute film featuring the highlights of Jordan. The multimedia experience begins with a Disney-style walk through the Siq, followed by a simulated flying-carpet tour of Jordan, complete with movable seats. At least four people are needed for the shows to run.

rudely along the beach in pointed, shiny leather shoes; babies being carried carefully in sports bags and wicker holdalls; footballers of all ages, congregating under the giant flag at the end of the beach; men in corduroy coats, sitting cross-legged on the seawall; pink-jacketed children racing between poles of fairyfloss; young women seated demurely on a variety of four-legged transport; and listless vendors half bothering to wave snacks or Chinese trinkets at whoever passes by. Inevitably, given the garrulous and hospitable nature of Jordanian people, you won't be left by yourself for long.

If you are determined to bare some skin and take a dip in the Gulf, then you are better off at a private beach attached to one of the hotels. The **Aquamarina Beach Hotel** (☎ 2016254; www.aquamarina-group.com; King

Hussein St; ☼ 6am until sunset) offers use of its tiny scrap of sand, concrete pontoon, pool and restaurant for a day rate of JD5.

The **Mövenpick Resort Hotel** (☎ /fax 2034020; www.movenpick-aqaba.com; King Hussein St; ☼ 7am until sunset) charges JD19 for day use of a clean beach, three pools, health club, sauna and Jacuzzi and includes a JD5 drink voucher.

Keep your eyes opened for the opening of the Tala Bay complex, south of Aqaba; it features a huge sandy bay in attractively landscaped gardens. See p254 for beach options further south.

WATER SPORTS

The top-end hotels and the Aquamarina Beach Hotel are well equipped for various water sports (prices start from JD8 per hour). Water-skiing, jet-skiing, windsurfing and kayaking are some of the water sports on offer. All hotels can organise snorkelling and diving, although these activities are best carried out from the diving clubs south of the town (see p278).

CRUISES

A local company **Sindbad** (☎ 2050077; www .sinbadjo.com; marina) operates a number of popular cruises around the Gulf of Aqaba. Prices range from JD15 per person for a two-hour sunset cruise, to JD29 for a half-day trip with snorkelling (equipment included) and barbecue. The cruises operate on a daily basis and depart from the end of the pier. Most hotels can book you on these trips, or simply turn up 30 minutes before departure (1pm for barbecue trip; 6pm for a sunset cruise) and buy a ticket from the Sindbad staff.

GLASS-BOTTOM BOATS

If you can't spare time to go diving or snorkelling, the next best thing is a glass-bottom boat. The ride is fun, but the amount of fish and coral is usually disappointing unless you get away from central Aqaba. This entails hiring a boat for at least two to three hours.

Boats, which operate between 6.30am and 5pm, congregate along the central public beach or at a jetty in front of Aqaba Castle. The posted rate for a boat (holding about 10 people) is JD10 per 30 minutes, JD15 for 45 minutes and JD25 for an hour.

A three-hour trip costs JD75 and a half-day trip is JD100. During any of the trips, you can swim, snorkel or fish (bring or hire your own equipment) and it makes a great excursion if you can get a group together.

HAMMAM

Aqaba Turkish Baths (☎ 2031605; King Hussein St; ☼ 10am-10pm) offers the full works – massage, steam bath and scrubbing – for a very reasonable JD12. Women are theoretically welcome to attend, but as 'special arrangements' need to be made (single men are evacuated for the session and a female attendant found), entry isn't guaranteed. Book a couple of hours ahead on a quiet day and you could be in luck. Couples can make similar arrangements.

Tours

There are a number of good travel agents in town offering diving and snorkelling trips (see p278 for a list of dive centres), tours in Jordan (including to Wadi Rum, see p274), and longer trips to neighbouring Egypt, and Israel and the Palestinian Territories. Some agencies also organise day trips to Petra (JD35 per person for a minimum of three; JD75 for one); these trips are worth considering if you only have one day to spend at Petra and don't want to spend half of it waiting for public transport. Bear in mind that the price doesn't include entrance fees and you'll find the amount of time you get to spend at the site is disappointingly brief. Some of the more experienced agencies:

International Traders (☎ 2013757; aqaba.office@ traders.com.jo; Al-Hammamat al-Tunisieh St) The price reflects the reliable and quality service.

Nyazi Tours (☎ 2022801; www.nyazi.com.jo; King Hussein St) Recommended adventure tour company run by Nyazi Shaba'an, former Director of Antiquities & Tourism in Petra. Camping, hiking, jeep tours and camel trips along Wadi Umran.

Wadi Rum Desert Services (☎ 2063882; wadi rumsafari.com; ☼ 8.30am-11pm) Located round the corner from Al-Cazar Hotel, between King Hussein and An-Nahda Sts, this is another long-standing agency that offers a variety of reliable services, particularly, though not exclusively, to Wadi Rum. It's worth paying this agency a visit just to admire the Iranian furniture in the office! There's another branch near Al-Shami Restaurant, off Zahran St.

ON A SUNNY DAY AROUND AQABA... *Matthew D Firestone*

- **Aqaba Marine Park Visitors Centre** (Map p281; ☎ 03-2035801) The headquarters of the Aqaba Marine Park, around 12km south of Aqaba, has the largest section of free public beach, with sun shades and a jetty, museum, café, gift shop and park offices. There's another large, free, public beach just to the south, with several cafés. Both beaches can be very busy on Friday.

- **Aquarium** (Map p281; ☎ 2015145; admission JD2; ◷ 8am-5pm) Part of the Marine Science Station complex, the aquarium has definitely seen better decades, though it's still good for a quick visit, especially if you're looking for an introduction to the local fauna. The tanks provide a colourful glimpse of coral, moray eels, turtles and stonefish. The aquarium is located about 7.5km south of Aqaba, 500m south of the ferry passenger terminal.

- **Club Murjan** (Map p281; ☎ 03 2012794) About 1.3km south of the Marine Science Station, this beach and diving centre is run by Al-Cazar Hotel in Aqaba (opposite). Guests of the hotel, and divers using the hotel's diving centre, can enjoy the facilities at Club Murjan for no charge, while the public can use the good beach, swimming pool and showers during the day for JD4, including return transport from Al-Cazar Hotel. Hire of snorkelling gear costs JD7 per day. Water-sports gear such as canoes and paragliders is available for a small fee, and there is an on-site bar and restaurant.

- **Pharaoh's Island** (Map p281) This picturesque island (*Jazirat Fara'un* in Arabic) is 15km south of Aqaba, but only a few hundred metres from Taba, in Egypt. It's actually in Egyptian waters, but travelling to or from Egypt this way is not permitted. Excavations suggest that the island was inhabited as far back as the Bronze Age. The fantastic Crusader Salah ad-Din Fort is fun to explore; and there is good swimming and snorkelling in the lagoon, and diving further out that is only accessible by boat. Top-end and good midrange hotels can book day trips to the island for around JD30 per person, which includes the entrance fee to the island, Egyptian visa, lunch and transport. Note that two days' notice is often required to allow time for the visas to be processed.

- **Royal Diving Club** (Map p281; ☎ 2017035; www.rdc.jo) Located about 12km south of Aqaba, and close to the Saudi border, this club is an excellent place for swimming, diving and snorkelling. It has a lovely swimming pool, restaurant and a decent beach where women are able to feel relaxed. The entrance fee of JD7/3.5 for adults/children (aged five to 12) allows guests to use the facilities. Entrance and transport is free for anyone diving with the Royal Diving Club (see p279).

Sleeping

Aqaba is a popular place for Jordanian and Saudi tourists in winter (October to March), with the season (and hotel rates) peaking in April, May, October and November. Holiday-makers also flock to Aqaba from northern Jordan during long weekends and public holidays, especially around Eid al-Adha (immediately after the haj). At these times, prices may increase by as much as 30% and you must book in advance.

Campers, overlanders, beach bums and dive junkies should consider staying at one of the camps along the beach south of Aqaba (see p283). Enjoy the end of an era: this whole area is due for up-market redevelopment.

BUDGET

Unless otherwise stated, places listed here offer (non-satellite) TV, air-conditioning and private bathroom with hot water. Most hotels don't include breakfast but can usually rustle up something uninspiring for around JD2 to JD5; better still, go for beans and *labneh* in the nearest café.

Al-Amer Hotel (☎ /fax 2014821; Raghadan St; s/d/tr JD12/15/20; ✷) Don't get too excited at the powder blue reception with its chandelier: the French Rococo stops here! That said, the bright, clean rooms, especially at the front, make this a quality budget option. If you get peckish in the night, the Syrian Palace Restaurant is right next door.

Al-Kholil Hotel (☎ /fax 2030152; Zahran St; s/d/tr JD14/16/22; ✷) This very basic hotel is at least central. The low ceilings are a serious inconvenience to tall people and the white tiles in reception make it look more like a public loo than a hotel. If you ignore the damp patches on the wall and the smell of food pervading the rooms, however, then this is a clean option if you get stuck for somewhere cheap.

Moon Beach Hotel (☎ 2013316; ashraf.saad77@yahoo.com; King Hussein St; s/d/tr with sea view JD17/25/30; ☒) Nearly next to the castle, this is undoubtedly the best of the budget options. The foyer is a welcoming mixture of striped settees, matching drapes and some interesting photographs of old Aqaba. Most rooms have sea views, satellite TV, a fridge and soap, though the dark red furnishings, faded carpet, chocolate paint and odd plastic-panelled corridors won't be to everyone's liking. The delightful management easily makes up for the dodgy decor.

Aqaba Star (☎ 2016480; fax 2018147; King Hussein St; s/d/tr JD20/25/35; ☒) This modern, Arabian-style, two-storey hotel with its plaster pillars and blue linoleum tiles caters mainly for Arabic clientele. The staff isn't very friendly but the rooms are reasonable, if underdecorated. Ask for a room with sea views and a balcony.

Al-Shula Hotel (☎ 2015153; alshula@wanadoo.jo; Raghadan St; s/d/tr JD20/27/34; ☒) With its black-and-white marble reception desk and painted mirrors, the hotel promises well enough but the rest of the hotel is rather utilitarian, with stark, unfriendly corridors. The rooms have hideous bed canopies and plastic seats but they do at least come with TV, fridge and mostly with good views.

MIDRANGE
On the whole, midrange accommodation in Aqaba offers better value for money. Every place listed here has a fridge, air-con, TV (usually satellite), telephone and private bathroom with hot water. Prices include breakfast (usually buffet) unless otherwise stated.

Al-Cazar Hotel (☎ 2014131; www.alcazarhotel.com; An-Nahda St; s/d/tr from JD25/35/45; ☒ ☒) If you're looking to stay somewhere with a bit of character, this faded old grand dame of Aqaba – with two dozen overgrown Washington palms in the front garden, an enormous, empty lobby and a bar with outrageous filigree plaster – is the place to

come. The spacious rooms have bathrooms with multiple mirrors and marble surfaces that must have looked grand in their day. One big plus is that guests are entitled to free access to Club Murjan, a beachfront sports centre south of Aqaba, to which the hotel runs transport twice a day at 9.30am and 1.30pm.

Aquamarina Beach Hotel (☎ 2016254; www.aquamarina-group.com; King Hussein St; s/d JD37/64; ☒ ☒) There's very little to commend this ugly, substandard Euro-resort except that it is the only midrange option to have beach access – well, access to the sea via a concrete pontoon, to be more accurate. The facilities include a water-sports centre and a bar with questionable night-time 'entertainment'. Ask for a room with sea views. Women on their own may feel uncomfortable here.

Aquamarina IV (☎ 2051620; www.aqamarina-group.com; An-Nahda St; s/d JD40/60; ☒) Besides the smell of stale smoke, the rooms in this functional, new hotel are clean and comfortable. The lime green walls and yellow ceilings are designed to appeal to Ukrainian taste, apparently, which explains the Cyrillic script in the lifts.

Captain's Hotel (☎ 2060710; www.captains-jo.com; An-Nahda St; s/d JD60/70; ☒ ☒ ☒) Aqaba's version of a boutique hotel, the Captain's began life as a fish restaurant (still functioning on the ground floor and with an excellent reputation) and then evolved, one storey at a time, into this stylish new accommodation. With a bronze horse in the foyer and copper-tiled flooring; compact rooms (with flat-screen TV), Arabian-style furniture and wonderful bathrooms with massage showers, this is an up-market choice for a midrange price. Other facilities include an attractive pool, sauna and Jacuzzi.

Golden Tulip (☎ 2051234; www.goldentulip.com; As-Sadah St; s/d JD65/80, discounted to JD35/50; ☒ ☒) This thoroughly recommended hotel in the centre of town is comfortable and modern. It has a fashionable foyer (complete with vocal African Grey parrot) and tasteful karaoke bar where the teetotal bartender mixes a superb cocktail. The rooms are cosy and bright but beware knees and elbows in the surprisingly mean-sized bathrooms. The reception desk is manned by a uniformly charming staff.

Aqaba Gulf Hotel (☎ 2016636; www.aqabagulf.com; King Hussein St; r JD80; ☒ ☒ ☒) This excellent hotel is just across the road from the Aqaba Gateway complex. It was the first hotel to be built in Aqaba and it has quite an honour roll of guests. The stained-wood, split-level dining room looks thoroughly dated, like the rest of the common-use areas, but this is not a criticism. The large, extremely comfortable room (ask for a double-window corner room for great sunsets), copious breakfasts and an excellent staff make this more of a lower-top-end option.

TOP END

our pick InterContinental Hotel (☎ 2092222; www .intercontinental.com; King Hussein St; standard/deluxe US$162/175; ☒ ☐ ☎ ♥) An imposing full stop at the end of the bay, the InterCon boasts less of an infinity pool than an 'infinity sea': on a calm day, the Gulf of Aqaba stretches in one seamless ripple all the way to Egypt. With exceptional landscape gardening, pools, a lazy river and a terracotta army of fully grown palm trees, the InterCon has stolen the top spot in Aqaba's luxury accommodation, providing the kind of practical service that has made this chain a favourite throughout the Middle East. With six restaurants and a shopping arcade among its many amenities, you won't want to move on in a hurry.

Mövenpick Resort Hotel (☎ 2034020; www.moven pick-aqaba.com; King Hussein St; standard/seaview/ superior US$226/254/283; ☒ ☐ ☎ ♥) This stylish hotel, spreadeagled across the main road, has a palatial interior decorated with mosaics and Moroccan lamps. The huge pool and beach complex has three pools, a gym (open 6am to 10pm), lovely gardens and the Red Sea Grill. Other restaurants include the Palm Court, and Italian and Lebanese restaurants, both with outdoor terrace. Disabled-access rooms are available.

Watch out for the **Kempinski Hotel**, expected to rival its neighbours on completion some time in 2009.

Eating

Aqaba has a large range of places to eat to suit all budgets. The seafood is particularly delicious: try Aqaba's signature dish of *sayadieh* (fish layered onto rice with a tomato, onion and pepper sauce).

BUDGET

For shwarma, grills and snacks, the dusty array of stalls and restaurants along King Hussein St spill onto the pavement and are popular with locals. For a wider choice of budget meals, have a prowl along Raghadan St and pick the restaurant you fancy: the eateries range from little more than a collection of open-air tables, serving tea, hummus, *fuul* (fava-bean paste) and felafel, to the larger restaurants listed here.

Syrian Palace Restaurant (☎ /fax 2014788; mains JD2-6; ☽ 10am-midnight) As the name implies, this is a good option for Syrian and Jordanian food, including fish dishes. It's next to the Al-Amer Hotel.

Ali Baba Restaurant (☎ 2013901; mains JD3-7 ☽ 8am-midnight; ☒ ♥) With its wooden awning, leafy cannas and potted palm trees, this favourite still draws the crowds. It has a large outdoor seating area wrapped round the corner facade and offers a large menu of mezze, grilled meats and fish, including *sayadieh* (JD8). It's a sociable place to come for breakfast, a fresh juice or a cake between meals, but it really comes into its own in the evening.

Al-Mabrouk Beach Touristic Restaurant (☎ 20063304; mains JD8; ☽ 9am-11.30pm; ☒) This smart new restaurant is a friendly and popular place for a large fish supper, with glass-top tables decorated with shells outside or air-conditioned dining indoors. A local favourite is a pot of Al-Mabrouk fish, mussels, calamari and tomatoes (JD11).

If a takeaway is more your style, call into the **Al-Tarboosh Restaurant** (☎ 2018518; Raghadan St; pastries around 200 fils; ☽ 7.30am-midnight), one of two neighbouring pastry shops that offer a great range of meat, cheese and vegetable pastries that can be heated up for you in the huge oven.

MIDRANGE & TOP END

There are plenty of modern and sophisticated restaurants in the newer part of town, especially along either side of As-Sadah St, and in the Aqaba Gateway complex. The following all serve excellent seafood, together with international meat and vegetarian dishes. Note that many restaurants do not have a license to sell alcohol.

Formosa Restaurant (☎ 2060098; Aqaba Gateway complex; mains JD3-8; ☽ 8am-midnight; ☒ ♥) For a really excellent Chinese perspective on seafood (and with plenty of meat and vegetable options on the menu too), you couldn't better this cosy, intimate restaurant.

Captain's Restaurant (☎ 2016905; An-Nahda St; mains JD5-6; ⏲ 8am-midnight; ❄) Serving consistently good quality seafood, including *sayadieh* and seafood salad, this is a perennially popular choice for locals with something to celebrate. Breakfast is also served (from JD3).

Floka Restaurant (☎ 2030860; An-Nahda St; mains JD5-11; ⏲ 12.30pm-11.30pm; ❄) Choose from the catch of the day (which normally includes sea bream, silver snapper, grouper and goatfish) and select how you would like it cooked. Service can be a little slow but it's a friendly, unpretentious establishment. There's indoor and outdoor seating.

ourpick **Blue Bay** (☎ 2070755; As-Sadah St; mains JD6; ⏲ am-midnight; ❄ Ⓥ) The seafood menu here is a cut above the rest with large portions of beautifully prepared catch-of-the-day, presented with finesse. The sleek glass tables and open-plan upper seating area attract Jordan's in-crowd and groups of 'in-the-know' expats. Imaginative salads make this a good choice for vegetarians.

Royal Yacht Club Restaurant (☎ 2022404; www .romero-jordan.com; Royal Yacht Club; mains JD6-12; ⏲ noon-4.30pm & 6-11pm; ❄ Ⓥ) With views of the marina, this elegant, wood-panelled restaurant is the place to savour a romantic sunset and mingle with Aqaba's nouveau riche. The mostly-Italian menu includes Mediterranean favourites like crab, avocado, shrimp and artichoke salad, mussels Provençale, and homemade vegetarian pasta. Reservations are recommended.

SELF-CATERING

The best supermarket is **Humam Supermarket** (☎ 2015721; Al-Petra St; ⏲ 8.30am-2.30pm & 4-11pm). **Safeway** (⏲ 8am-midnight) is quite a hike away, 750m north of Princess Haya Hospital. A couple of modern American–style malls are putting in an appearance in and around town.

The **fruit and vegetable souq**, hidden at the southern end of Raghadan St, is the best place to buy healthy, locally grown items for a picnic. There are lots of **bakeries** around, including one on Al-Hammamat al-Tunisieh St.

For up-market nuts scooped from wooden drawers, call in at **Eibal Coffee** (☎ 2035555; As-Sadah St; 1kg nuts from JD6.500; ⏲ 10am-midnight). Try the smoked nuts: a kilo of pistachio, cashew and almonds costs JD8 but they are irresistibly moreish. Ask for them to be bagged in 250g bags to avoid them going soft in the humidity.

CAFÉS & ICE-CREAM PARLOURS

There are popular **beachfront cafés** between Aqaba Castle and the marina. The front-row seats are so close to the water that you can wet your toes while you whet your whistle. No alcohol is served at these public places.

The **juice stands** (750 fils-JD1.500) on Ar-Razi St are popular meeting places for travellers.

On a hot day, stop by **Hani Ali** (Raghadan St), a sugar addict's paradise of traditional sweets and delicious ice cream, or **Gelato Uno** (off An-Nahda St) behind the Hertz car-rental office. For something even more sublime, row the boat out at the **ice-cream parlour** and **cake shop** at the Mövenpick Resort Hotel (you don't have to enter the hotel – there's access from King Hussein St) and order a 'special'.

Drinking

Many of the midrange and all the top-end hotels have bars, and most offer some kind of happy hour from 6pm to 7.30pm. Around the As-Sadah St loop, there are a number of open-air coffee shops with armchairs on the pavement, selling *sheesha*, coffee and soft drinks.

Al-Fardos Coffee Shop (coffee 500 fils), just off Zahran St, is a traditional coffeehouse where local men sip *qahwa*, play backgammon and stare open-mouthed at Arabic music videos. It has a pleasant outdoor setting, and foreign women are welcome.

Friends (☎ 2013466; upper storey, Aqaba Gateway; beer JD2.500-3; ⏲ 3.30pm-3am) This relaxed and friendly place, with sensible prices, is on a lovely terrace that captures the sea breezes. Try the Dizzy Buddah (JD7); have two, and you may as well sleep over.

Rovers Return (☎ 2032030; Aqaba Gateway; pint of Amstel/Guinness JD3/5; ⏲ 3pm-midnight) An aerial version of the Amman expat favourite (it's located in a mock lighthouse), this pub attracts a young crowd. If you're British and feeling homesick, stay for fish and chips or bangers and mash (JD7) and watch three-screen football. The only downside is that the compact space can get oppressively smoky.

Royal Yacht Club bar (☎ 2022404; ⏲ opens around 5pm; beer JD2.500-3.500) Above the Romero

Restaurant in the marina, this is an elegant rendezvous, with a harbourside view of the sunset. It closes around 11pm.

If you want to get off the road for a bit of peace and quiet, try the cosy **Wisalak Café** (☎ 2022600; sheesha JD2; milkshakes from JD1.600; 🕑 3pm-midnight; 🕸), which has an upstairs seating area.

Entertainment

There's not too much in the way of entertainment in Aqaba, although **Aqaba Gateway** (☎ 2012200; Al-Baladiah Circle) has a popular collection of restaurants, fast-food outlets, shops, two bars and a cinema. If you want to see the kind of entertainment popular with Middle Eastern men, call in on the nightclub at the **Aquamarina Beach Hotel** (☎ 2016250; www.aquamarina-group.com; King Hussein St). You can gauge the idea from the posters in the foyer: the 'cabaret' performances are generally quite tame, usually involving poorly executed belly-dancing or multipurpose gyrating in time to electronic Arab-pop.

Shopping

Aqaba is a fun place to do some shopping, especially at night when Jordanian holidaymakers treat the shops as an excuse to cruise along in large groups, enjoying the company of strangers. Head for the *souq* in the older part of town, where shops are bulging at the seams with loofahs, colourful Arab headscarves, Dead Sea products, denim and cotton clothing, and of course nuts and spices.

Aqaba is also a good place to buy jewellery, with a few gold and silver shops in the *souq* and several shops selling beautiful beads (see below).

The shop owner in the arcade outside Al-Cazar Hotel will make a necklace of your design, or for something more refined, visit **Sam's Jewellers** (☎ 2012100; next to Wadi Rum Desert Services, between King Hussein St & An-Nahda St; 🕑 9.30am-11pm), round the corner from Al-Cazar Hotel. With designs 'inspired by my mother and my aunts', the jeweller takes a personal pride in his very unusual necklaces of silver, coral, amber and semiprecious

---

BUYING BEADS IN AQABA

Walk around Aqaba's *souq* in the middle of town, and your eye will soon be drawn to chaotic windows festooned with brightly coloured beads. There are strings of royal blue lapis lazuli with tiny flecks of gold; creamy caramels of tiger's eye; glittering goldstone that spangles in the sunlight; and smooth round beads of red or pink coral, draped next to their plastic imitations. There are also cloudy butter-coloured beads of amber, vying with more lucent resins of embalmed insects, and polished agate, turquoise, green malachite, jet, amethyst and even polka dots of jade. Most of these magnificent beads of natural stone are imported from neighbouring countries but they are usually crafted locally into necklaces, earrings and bracelets, often by the shop owners themselves. If a piece is not 'Made in Jordan', the vendor is usually quick to tell you so.

If you have the time, ask the bead-shop owner to make a piece from your own design. Think 'Bedouin', and add a few silver beads among the stones, or think 'ethnic' and rope the stones onto leather or camel-hair cord. The price of beads depends on the quality of the stones used and the intricacy of the work but a simple strand starts at around JD5, while a multiple strand necklace of good stones can cost JD100 or more. Men not fond of wearing jewellery needn't feel left out: *misbah* (prayer beads – usually in sets of 33, 66 or 99 in honour of the 99 names and attributes of Allah) make a handy introduction into Arab society across the Middle East. Or you could buy an ever-popular agate ring. Note that the stones are almost invariably clasped in silver as it is considered *haram* (forbidden) for Muslim men to wear gold.

Jewellery may seem like 'mere decoration' but beware that this may not be the way the locals look at it. Choose a necklace with a central medallion inscribed with Allah's name, for example, and you may be exhorted to remove the necklace before using the bathroom; if you admire someone else's jewellery, they may feel obliged to give it to you; ubiquitous eye-ball beads are accorded almost mystic powers in fending off the 'evil eye'. If the bead vendor is particularly pleased with the way a piece hangs about your neck, he or she may well say 'ma sha'Allah' to protect you from the envy of onlookers. In fact, enter a bead shop in Jordan and you quickly realise that jewellery is less about decorating the body than making a statement of the soul.

stones, which combine traditional motifs with modern settings.

For a fine selection of handicrafts, visit **Noor Al-Hussein Foundation shop** (☎ 2012601; ◷ 8am-6pm, to 7pm May-Sep), located in the Aqaba Fort complex, opposite the museum. Profits go to help supporting marginalised communities throughout Jordan. Items include silver jewellery from Wadi Musa, petroglyph designs from Wadi Rum, kilims, clothes, embroidery, basketware and ceramics. Credit cards are accepted.

If you want to go snorkelling but have forgotten your swimsuit, visit Ipanema Brazil, a classy cossie shop in the Aqaba Gateway complex. The Brazilian owner is married to a Jordanian and can advise women on what booty to shake and where.

Photo Hagop (☎ 2012025; Zahran St; ◷ 8.30am-11pm) has several branches around town and offers digital accessories.

Getting There & Away

AIR

Aqaba has Jordan's only commercial **airport** (☎ 2012111) outside Amman, although it only awakes from slumber when a flight is about to leave or arrive. There are daily flights to Amman and intermittent charter flights. The airport is 10km north of town.

Royal Jordanian (☎ 2014477; www.rja.com.jo; Ash-Sherif al-Hussein bin Ali St; ◷ 9am-5pm Sun-Thu) Operates flights to Amman's Queen Alia International Airport on Friday and Saturday. This is the place to buy, confirm or change Royal Jordanian or Royal Wings air tickets. Tickets to Amman cost JD55 one way.

Royal Wings (www.royalwings.com.jo) A subsidiary of Royal Jordanian, flies between Aqaba and Amman twice daily.

BOAT

There are two daily boat services to Nuweiba in Egypt. For information about these services, see p314.

Buy your ticket at the ferry terminal when departing, except during haj (see p296) when you may need to book in advance.

BUS

There are buses to Amman and Irbid from Aqaba. It's worth paying for the comfort, speed and air-conditioning of a JETT or Trust private bus. Book tickets for these at least a day in advance. Buses for both companies leave from outside their offices.

From the **JETT bus office** (☎ 2015223; King Hussein St), next to the Mövenpick Resort Hotel, buses run five times daily to Amman (JD7, four hours), between 7am and 5pm. The office is a 10-minute walk from the centre.

Trust International Transport (☎ 2032200; just off An-Nahda St) has four daily buses to Amman (JD7.500, four hours), at 7.30am, 11.30am, 2.30pm and 7pm. There are also buses to Irbid (JD11, 5½ hours) at 8.30am and 3.30pm.

Ordinary public buses travel between the main bus/minibus station in Aqaba and Amman's Wahadat station (JD5, five hours) about every hour between 7am and 3pm, sometimes later.

CAR

Aqaba has branches of all the major car-hire agencies. Most charge a 'drop fee' (JD25) if you wish to leave the car in Amman or at Queen Alia International Airport. Hiring in Aqaba makes some sense as public transport in the south of the country is less frequent and requires more connections than in the north. Aqaba is also far easier to drive around than Amman. The cost of car hire is between JD25 to JD35 per day plus Collision Damage Waiver (average JD7 per day). Enquire about seasonal discounts.

Al-Cazar Car Rental (☎ 2014131; An-Nahda St)
Avis (☎ 2022883; www.avis.com.jo; King Hussein St) Located inside the Housing Bank Centre.
Europcar (☎ 2019988; www.europcar.com.jo; An-Nahda St)
Hertz (☎ 2016206; www.hertz.com.jo; An-Nahda St)
Thrifty (☎ 2030313; An-Nahda St) Opposite the Al-Cazar Hotel.

MINIBUS

To Wadi Musa (for Petra), minibuses (JD4, two hours) leave when full between 7am and 2pm; the exact departure times depend on the number of passengers and you may have to wait an hour or two. Otherwise, get a connection in Ma'an (JD2, 80 minutes) for which there are hourly departures throughout the day.

Two minibuses go to Wadi Rum (JD1.500, one hour) at around 6.30am and, more reliably, 11am. You may find afternoon buses at 1pm and 3pm. On Friday there is usually only one minibus a day. At other times, catch a minibus towards Ma'an, get off at the turn-off to Wadi Rum at Ar-Rashidiyya and then hitch a ride to Rum village (30km) from there.

Minibuses to Amman (JD5, five hours) leave hourly throughout the day.

All of the above minibuses leave from the main Aqaba bus/minibus station on Ar-Reem St. Minibuses to Karak (JD2, three hours), via Safi and the Dead Sea Highway, are the exception, leaving from the small station next to the mosque on Al-Humaimah St.

TAXI & SERVICE TAXI

From the main bus/minibus station, service taxis head to Amman (JD7, five hours), but far less regularly than buses and minibuses. To Karak (JD5, three hours) they leave from the small station on Al-Humaimah St. Service taxis start lining up at either station at 6am and many have left by 8am, so get there early. Chartering a taxi costs around JD40 one way to Petra and JD25 to Wadi Rum return.

Chartering a taxi between Aqaba and the Israel and the Palestinian Territories border costs around JD5. For details on crossing the southern border to/from Israel and the Palestinian Territories, see p310.

Getting Around
TO/FROM THE AIRPORT

Aqaba's **King Hussein Airport** (☎ 2012111) is located 10km north of town, close to the border with Israel and the Palestinian Territories. There's a bus to the airport, so take service taxi 8 (15 minutes, around JD1.500) from the main bus/minibus station, or take a taxi for around JD5 to JD8.

TO/FROM THE FERRY TERMINAL & SOUTHERN COAST

Minibuses (JD1) leave from near the entrance to Aqaba Castle on King Hussein St for the Saudi border via the southern beaches, camps, dive sites and Royal Diving Centre, passing en route the ferry terminal for boats to Egypt. Minibuses returning to Aqaba can be full of construction workers heading off shift from 2pm to 3pm. A taxi from central Aqaba to the ferry terminal shouldn't cost more than JD5.

TAXI

Hundreds of private (blue and green) taxis cruise the streets beeping at any tourist (Jordanian or foreign) silly enough to walk around in the heat rather than take an air-conditioned taxi. Taxis are unmetered so prices are entirely negotiable, and the drivers in Aqaba enjoy the sport. Most rides cost between around JD1 to JD2.

WADI RUM   وادي رم
☎ 03

Western visitors have been fascinated by the magnificent desert and mountain landscape of Wadi Rum ever since TE Lawrence wrote so evocatively about its sculpted rocks, dunes and Bedouin encampments in *Seven Pillars of Wisdom* in the early 20th century:

> The crags were capped in nests of domes, less hotly red than the body of the hill; rather grey and shallow. They gave the finishing semblance of Byzantine architecture to this irresistible place: this processional way greater than imagination…Our little caravan grew self-conscious, and fell dead quiet, afraid and ashamed to flaunt its smallness in the presence of the stupendous hills.

The name Wadi Rum lends itself not just to the broad valley flanked on either side by the towering, domed pillars of Lawrence's description, but to a whole series of beautiful broad valleys, stretching north to south for over 100km. The central valley, 900m above sea level, fans into an arena dominated by Jebel Rum (1754m), once considered the highest peak in Jordan – an accolade that now goes to Jebel Umm Adaami (1832m), on the Saudi border.

Wadi Rum is everything you'd expect of a quintessential desert: it is extreme in summer heat and winter cold; it is violent and moody as the sun slices through chiselled *siqs* in the early morning or melts the division between rock and sand at sunset; it is exacting on the Bedouin who live in it and vengeful on those who ignore its dangers. For most visitors, on half- or full-day trips from Aqaba or Petra, Wadi Rum offers one of the easiest and safest glimpses of the desert afforded in the region. For the lucky few who can afford a day or two in their itinerary to sleep over at one of the desert camps, it can be an unforgettable way of stripping the soul back to basics.

WADI RUM

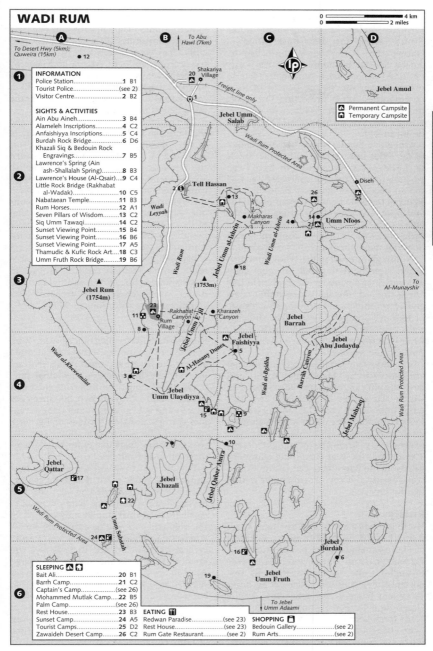

0 ——— 4 km
0 ——— 2 miles

INFORMATION
Police Station.........................1 B1
Tourist Police.....................(see 2)
Visitor Centre.......................2 B2

SIGHTS & ACTIVITIES
Ain Abu Aineh.......................3 B4
Alameleh Inscriptions...........4 C2
Anfaishiyya Inscriptions.........5 C4
Burdah Rock Bridge.............6 D6
Khazali Siq & Bedouin Rock
  Engravings..........................7 B5
Lawrence's Spring (Ain
  ash-Shallalah Spring)..........8 B3
Lawrence's House (Al-Qsair)...9 C4
Little Rock Bridge (Rakhabat
  al-Wadak)..........................10 C5
Nabataean Temple...............11 B3
Rum Horses...........................12 A1
Seven Pillars of Wisdom.......13 C2
Siq Umm Tawaqi..................14 C2
Sunset Viewing Point............15 B4
Sunset Viewing Point............16 B6
Sunset Viewing Point............17 A5
Thamudic & Kufic Rock Art...18 C3
Umm Fruth Rock Bridge........19 B6

To Desert Hwy (5km);
Quweira (15km) • 12

To Abu
Hawl (7km)

Shakariya
Village

Freight line only

Jebel Amud

Permanent Campsite
Temporary Campsite

Jebel Umm
Salab

Wadi Rum Protected Area

Diseh

Tell Hassan

26

25

Wadi
Leyyah

14
21
Umm Nfoos

Wadi Rum

Wadi Umm al-Ishrin

Makharas
Canyon

4

18

Wadi Umm al-Ishrin

To
Al-Munayshir

Jebel Rum
(1754m)

(1753m)

23
Rakhabat
Canyon
Rum
Village

11
8

Kharazeh
Canyon

Jebel
Barrah

Jebel
Abu Judayda

Jebel
Faishiyya
5

Al-Hasany Dunes

3

Jebel Umm Ejil

Wadi al-Bgdha

Barrah Canyon

Wadi al-Kharseinthar

Jebel
Umm Ulaydiyya

15 9

Wadi Rum Protected Area

Jebel Mahraq

7

10

Jebel
Qattar
17

Jebel
Khazali

Jebel Qabar Amra

22

Umm Sabtah

Wadi Rum Protected Area

24

16

Jebel
Burdah
6

Jebel
Umm Fruth

19

To Jebel
Umm Adaami

SLEEPING
Bait Ali...............................20 B1
Barrh Camp........................21 C2
Captain's Camp...............(see 26)
Mohammed Mutlak Camp...22 B5
Palm Camp.......................(see 26)
Rest House.........................23 B3
Sunset Camp......................24 A5
Tourist Camps....................25 D2
Zawaideh Desert Camp.......26 C2

EATING
Redwan Paradise..............(see 23)
Rest House........................(see 23)
Rum Gate Restaurant.........(see 2)

SHOPPING
Bedouin Gallery.................(see 2)
Rum Arts...........................(see 2)

AQABA, WADI RUM &
THE DESERT HIGHWAY

The area has been protected since 1988, formerly under the management of the Royal Society for the Conservation of Nature (RSCN) but now controlled by Aqaba Special Economic Zone Authority (ASEZA), which has a similar mandate to promote tourism for the benefit of local communities, while protecting the fragile desert environment. With over 100,000 visitors per year using 600 4WDs, this is no mean feat.

Of course the desert has had a caretaker of far older lineage than either the RSCN or ASEZA: the local Bedouin have been roaming in this area for centuries (see p55 for an account of modern Bedouin life). Many of the 5000 Bedouin remaining in the area have now opted for a settled life in the villages of Rum, Diseh and Shakriyyeh but, certainly as far as they are concerned, this does not make them any the less Bedouin.

Although not part of the Wadi Rum protected area, the desert spills in equal magnificence into neighbouring areas including Diseh. Indeed, the sandstone monuments and intervening sand dunes are a feature of Jordan's Southern Desert that stretches right up to the Saudi border to the south while running out into the plains of the Badia in the northeast.

The most comfortable months for a visit are early spring (March and April) and late autumn (October and November). In winter (December to February) it is bitterly, unbearably cold. In the hot season (May to September) daytime temperatures often soar above 40°C: this is when you really come to know the meaning of desert! Throughout the year (including summer), night-time temperatures can fall to 0°C, so come prepared if you're camping or watching the sunset.

History

With its many wells and springs, Wadi Rum (known in ancient times as Iram) has been inhabited since prehistoric times. Petroglyphs and burial mounds appear throughout the area, indicating its importance as a hunting and meeting point in ancient times. It was referred to by the Greeks and Romans, who noted its vineyards (now gone), and olive and pine trees (some of which remain on the mountaintops), and some Islamic scholars claim that this is the location of 'Ad', described in the Quran. About 30,000 inscriptions decorate the soft sandstone surface of Wadi Rum's cliffs. They were made firstly by Thamudic tribes from Southern Arabia and later by the Nabataeans who settled in Wadi Rum by about the 4th century BC. The two tribes lived peacefully side by side, honouring the same deities of Lat and Dushara.

The region owes its current fame to the indefatigable TE Lawrence, who stayed here in 1917 during the Arab Revolt – a campaign led by King Hussein bin Ali against the Ottoman Turks in a bid to establish an independent Arab nation. The king's camel- and horse-mounted troops passed through Wadi Rum on their way to conquer Aqaba and some units (including that of Lawrence) returned to use the area as a temporary base before moving north towards Damascus.

The serendipitous discovery of a Nabataean temple (behind the Rest House) in 1933 briefly returned the spotlight to the desert. A French team of archaeologists completed the excavations in 1997.

Wildlife

Despite its barren appearance, Wadi Rum is home to a complex ecosystem. Dotted among the desert are small plants that are used by the Bedouin for medicinal purposes, and during the infrequent rains parts of the desert bloom with over 200 species of flowers and wild grasses. Around the perennial springs, hanging gardens of fig, fern, mint and wild watermelon topple over the rocks, creating shaded lairs for small mammals, birds and reptiles.

For most of the year, the extreme heat and lack of water mean that animals only venture out at night. If you sit tight, you may well see a hedgehog, hare or hyrax (a small furry animal implausibly related to the elephant). If you're extremely lucky, you could catch a glimpse of a jackal, wolf, caracal or giant-horned ibex. Sadly, you are not likely to see the highly endangered Arabian oryx, a small group of which were released into Wadi Rum in 2002 (see p157) but which didn't like the new accommodation and set out for the rocky plains of neighbouring Saudi Arabia. A new program of reintroduction was underway at the time of research.

DESERT BUT NOT DESERTED

Gaze across the empty sands of Wadi Rum in the rippling heat of midday, and you may be forgiven for thinking that the desert is bereft of life. But take five minutes to climb out of the 4WD and crouch close to the sand and you'll soon see that it is criss-crossed with the tufted paw prints of hares and foxes, and ribbed with the S-bends of vipers. In among the highways and byways of Wadi Rum's desert floor, you may be lucky to spot the fast lane, left by the hooves of a newcomer.

In 2007 ASEZA – in collaboration with the RSCN – launched a new project to reintroduce the oryx, the majestic rapier-horned antelope of the desert, to Wadi Rum. The first attempt at reintroduction in 2004/05 was not overly successful as the animals roamed south in search of water and eventually died. Having learnt some lessons from this attempt, a new introduction program is in place (using stock imported from Abu Dhabi) involving the staggered release of animals from a large enclosure. As the herds acclimatise to their new environment, well out of sight of the main areas of tourist interest, they will be released little by little into the wild – a process that will be ongoing over the next two to three years.

The oryx are part of a scheme not just to make the desert more attractive to visitors, but also to bring about a greater awareness of the desert as habitat rather than as empty space. The oryx will be a magnificent *visual* reminder of that fact, but, as you race across the desert from one 'sight' to another, keep your other senses open too – for Wadi Rum's smaller inhabitants. Listen for the 'pew' of a raptor overhead, the smell of crushed lavender underfoot and the texture of lichen on stone, unravished by a thoughtless penknife.

This is big-bird country and there is usually a raptor or two (including sooty falcons, kestrels and eagle owls) circling on the thermals above the desert floor, on the lookout for the desert's plentiful geckos, agamas and lizards. If you see a scorpion, snake or camel spider, count yourself lucky as they are all shy residents of Rum.

Orientation

Wadi Rum is accessed from a tarmac road off the main Desert Highway, an hour's drive from Aqaba. The road is flanked at first by fields of watermelons, but shortly after crossing the Hejaz railway line the splendid scenery begins, becoming more and more spectacular as you reach the mouth of Wadi Rum. The road passes a police post and the junction for the small village of Diseh and continues towards the visitor centre. This is where all visitors to Wadi Rum must report before venturing farther into the valley. This is also from where you can book a one-, two-, three- or four-hour tour of the desert in a 4WD or by camel (no prior reservations necessary) and arrange a guide for hiking, scrambling or climbing (best to book in advance, especially if you want a particular guide).

Even if you don't have time to spend a whole day at Wadi Rum, it is worth coming as far as the visitor centre. From this attractive, sympathetic complex you can see Lawrence's Seven Pillars of Wisdom (a striking rock formation at the head of the valley), visit the museum, watch a short film about the desert, have lunch and get an idea of what Rum is all about. This is also where you pay the admission fee if you want to proceed further into the valley.

Beyond the visitor centre, the road is initially lined by a battered set of 4WDs, accompanied by their Bedouin drivers awaiting their next fare in strict rotation. The tarmac road continues for 7km to the village of Rum. The village, wedged between the towering dome-capped pillars of Wadi Rum, has a few concrete houses, a school, some shops and the *Beau Geste*–style fort, headquarters of the much-photographed Desert Patrol.

Again, if you haven't much time or can't afford one of the 4WD tours, consider at least reaching the village (you can drive in your own car, hitch or walk). In the village, there's a pleasant rest house with an outside terrace and camping facilities where you can watch the sun draw out the colours of the sandstone pillars of rock opposite, as the day comes to a close.

To penetrate the desert beyond the village of Rum, you must either have organised a

4WD trip from the visitor centre, booked a camel or be prepared for an exhausting hike through soft sand. Alternatively, if you entered in your own 4WD you can make your own way into the desert, presuming you know how to navigate and drive off-road in soft sand and have the necessary back-up equipment with you.

Beyond the village of Rum, the tarmac runs out and numerous tracks take over, slithering through the soft sand of Wadi Rum to an open area of converging valleys. From here, tracks lead to various points of interest such as windblown formations like rock bridges, desert mushrooms and yardangs. Most 4WD and camel tours make a circular route through the intersecting wadis of the area before returning to the visitor centre.

Outside this heavily visited area is a portion of desert known as the Wilderness Area. It is forbidden to take a 4WD into this protected zone but you can hike there with a guide.

If you have time to stay overnight, there are several Bedouin campsites with rudimentary facilities within the Wadi Rum area which can be booked from the visitor centre. Alternatively, you can make private arrangements to stay at one of the camps in the neighbouring Diseh area (see p275), on the rim of the reserve.

BOOKS & MAPS

If you are planning any short hikes and scrambles, bring a detailed guidebook and map; if you intend to do some serious hiking and rock climbing, it's vital to organise a guide in advance.

British climber Tony Howard has spent a lot of time exploring Wadi Rum, and has co-written with Di Taylor the excellent and detailed *Treks & Climbs in Wadi Rum, Jordan*. The condensed, pocket-sized version of this is called *Walks & Scrambles in Wadi Rum*. Treks and climbs around Wadi Rum are also mentioned in Howard and Taylor's *Walking in Jordan*. Buy these books before arriving in Wadi Rum.

The free Wadi Rum brochure has a map showing the major sites and is available from the visitor centre, or you can buy ASEZA's *Wadi Rum Destination Guide* (JD3). The 1997 *Map of Rum* is contoured and detailed for a small section of northern Wadi Rum (ie around Rum village). The most detailed and informative map is *Wadi Rum Tourist Plan*, published by Interna-

---

WADI RUM ITINERARY BUILDER

It is worth making the effort to visit Wadi Rum, even if you only have a few hours to spend. Below is a suggestion of what you can do in a given time under your own steam. For 4WD and camel excursions lasting from one hour to one day, see the boxed text on p269 & p270. Obviously, the longer you stay, the more your eyes (and heart) open to the desert.

With this time...	You can go this far...	And do this much...
En route to elsewhere	Visitor Centre (opposite)	Have a panoramic view of Wadi Rum (lit up magnificently at sunset).
One hour	Visitor Centre (opposite)	Enjoy a leisurely lunch overlooking Wadi Rum, then visit the museum.
Two hours	Rum Village (opposite)	Walk through Wadi Rum on the tarmac road (7km) as far as Rum Village, snack at the Guest House and hitch a lift back.
Three hours	Lawrence's Spring (p266)	Hitch a ride to Rum Village and hike through the sand to Nabataean Temple & Lawrence's Spring.
Half day	Red Sands (p266)	Time your hike from Rum Village to the sands to coincide with sunset.
Overnight	Desert Camp (p272)	Book your accommodation at a Wadi Rum camp through the visitor centre (4WD transport included) or pay extra to ride there by camel.
Two days	Wadi Rum & Diseh Area (p274)	Choose a Wadi Rum camp near Barrah Canyon, then hike through the canyon (5km) to a Diseh camp for the following night.

DESERT PATROL

The camel-mounted Desert Patrol was set up to keep dissident tribes in order and to patrol the border. Today they've exchanged their camels for blue armoured patrol vehicles and concentrate on smugglers along the Saudi border, though they occasionally rescue a lost tourist.

The men of the Desert Patrol can be quite a sight in their traditional full-length khaki robes, dagger at the waist, pistol and rifle slung over the shoulder – but mostly they now wear just ordinary khaki uniforms. They still revel in their photogenic nature and are happy to pose for those who spend some time with them over tea.

---

tional Traditional Services Corp, but it's not widely available in Jordan.

Information

Admission to **Wadi Rum Protected Area** (per person JD2; children under 12 free) is strictly controlled and all vehicles, camels and guides must be arranged either through or with the approval of the visitor centre (below). Essential items to bring along include a hat, preferably with a brim or a flap to keep the sun off your neck, sunscreen, sturdy footwear and plenty of water. If you are camping (including at the rest house), bring along a torch (flashlight), a book to read and a padlock (many tents are lockable).

The Bedouin are a conservative people, so dress appropriately. Loose shorts and tops for men and women are acceptable around the rest house, but baggy trousers/ skirts and modest shirts/blouses will, besides preventing serious sunburn, earn you more respect from the Bedouin, especially out in the desert. You often need a heavy coat, scarf, hat and gloves in the winter.

Police station (☎ 2017050) Located in the old police fort 400m south of the rest house. They will not receive complaints (go to the tourist police), but they will come looking for you if you get lost.

Tourist police (☎ 2018215) At the visitor centre.

Visitor Centre (☎ /fax 2090600; www.wadirum.jo; ◷ 7am-7pm) Situated at the entry to the protected area, about 30km east of the Desert Highway and 7km north of Rum village. This is where you buy your entry ticket to the reserve, book a 4WD or camel excursion, organise accommodation at a camp and book a guide. There is a

restaurant, craft shops, an excellent museum, clean toilets and parking area. You can also ask to see a 10-minute film on some of the highlights of Wadi Rum, shown in the purpose-built cinema.

Sights

For the distance between each of the following sights and the visitor centre, together with the time it takes to get there by 4WD or camel, see p269 and p270.

SEVEN PILLARS OF WISDOM

Named in honour of Lawrence's book, this large rock formation, with seven fluted turrets, is easy to see from the visitor centre. If you fancy a closer look, ask at the visitor centre for information on the rewarding three- to four-hour **hike** that circumnavigates the mountain. The trail cuts through **Makharas Canyon** (take the left branch of the wadi), curves around the northern tip of Jebel Umm al-Ishrin and meanders back to the visitor centre.

The Seven Pillars rock is connected to the deeply crevassed **Jebel Umm Ishrin** (Mother of Twenty), a 20-domed mountain forming the east flank of Wadi Rum. The mountain acquired its name, according to local legend, after a woman killed 19 suitors; she was outwitted by the 20th, so she married him. The whole range turns a magnificent white-capped auburn during sunset.

The western flank of Wadi Rum is formed by **Jebel Rum** (1754m) which towers over Wadi Rum village. It is a popular destination for scramblers and climbers who tackle parts of the ancient Thamudic Way to the summit (guide required – ask at the visitor centre). Similar pathways, once used for hunting ibex and collecting medicinal plants, link one massif to another throughout the area, giving limitless scope for hiking, scrambling and climbing (see p267).

Other landmark mountains deeper in the desert include Jebel Khazali, El Qattar (off-limits at the time of research) and Jebel Umm Adaami (1830m), the highest mountain in Jordan (see p271) on the Saudi border.

RUM VILLAGE & VILLAGE PLAZA

Rum village, in the middle of Wadi Rum, houses a small community of Bedouin who have chosen to settle, rather than continue a more traditional nomadic life. The village has a rest house, restaurants and a couple of grocery shops. It also has the last piece of tarmac before the desert proper.

Built in the former police station, a new complex in the middle of Rum village will eventually house a museum displaying artefacts from Rum's history, and a local handicrafts centre. It was closed at the time of writing.

NABATAEAN TEMPLE

On a small hill in Rum village, located about 400m behind the Rest House (follow the telephone poles) are the limited ruins of a 2000-year-old **Nabataean temple**, dedicated to the deity Lat. Before you set out for the site, read the information board (in English and French) inside the Rest House for a helpful description of the temple and its excavation. The ruins are important because they are evidence of a permanent Nabataean settlement, built on the earlier foundations of a temple built by the Arab tribe of Ad. The baths in a villa behind the temple are the earliest so far discovered in Jordan. Near the temple are some **inscriptions** by hunters and nomads dating back to the 2nd century BC.

LAWRENCE'S SPRING (AIN ASH-SHALLALAH)

A short walk from the Nabataean temple, you'll see a white water tank at the opening of Wadi Shallalah. After the tank, a path climbs the hill to **Lawrence's Spring**, so-named in honour of Lawrence's evocative description of it in the *Seven Pillars of Wisdom*:

In front of us a path, pale with use, zigzagged up the cliff-plinth ... From between [the] trees, in hidden crannies of the rock, issued strange cries; the echoes, turned into music, of the voices of the Arabs watering camels at the springs which there flowed out three hundred feet above ground.

Together with other springs in the area, this natural water spout that tumbles into a leafy 'paradise just five feet square' allowed Rum to become an important waterhole for caravans travelling between Syria and Arabia. Look out for a small shrine dedicated to Lat, an aqueduct used to channel the water from the spring, and inscriptions on

the rock face. Notice too the smell of mint in the air: it grows wild among the ferns and trees of this shady place. To walk to the spring and back (2.5km) from the Rest House takes about 1½ hours.

OTHER SPRINGS

There are many other springs in the area. Another famous one, often mistakenly called Lawrence's Spring, is **Ain Abu Aineh**. The water is piped down the mountain into a large tank for Bedouin sheep, goats and camels. Look out for a large boulder near the tank: it is covered with Thamudic inscriptions, proving the spring has been used for a similar purpose for millennia. To reach Ain Abu Aineh, head south from the Rest House and follow the eastern side of Jebel Rum for 3km (a 1½-hour walk in soft sand). The site in itself is not particularly special but the views across to Jebel Khazali are wonderful, especially at sunset when the whole amphitheatre of stone and sand is lit up like an epic drama.

LAWRENCE'S HOUSE (AL-QSAIR)

There is little left of this building, built on the Nabataean ruins of a water cistern. Nonetheless, legend has it that Lawrence stayed here during the Desert Revolt and that makes it a must on the regular 4WD circuits of the area. Near the building is a Nabataean inscription that mentions the area's ancient name of Iram. The remote location and supreme view of the **red sand dunes** are the main attraction.

SAND DUNES

While there are sand dunes in several places around Wadi Rum, the most striking are the red **Al-Hasany Dunes** that bank up against Jebel Umm Ulaydiyya. If you are in a 4WD, drivers will stop near a pristine slope for you to plod your way to the crest of the dune. They take about three hours to reach on foot, partly through soft sand.

ROCK INSCRIPTIONS

Thamudic and Nabataean inscriptions, depicting camel caravans, hunting warriors and various animals, are common throughout the Wadi Rum area. The **Alameleh inscriptions**, near to the Seven Pillars of Wisdom and on the edge of the Diseh district, are some of the most comprehensive and best preserved.

Another wonderful set, the **Anfaishiyya inscriptions**, is scratched into the smooth surface of a huge, vertical rock face.

ROCK BRIDGES

There are many remarkable rock formations in the area, where the wind has whittled away the softer parts of the sandstone, leaving the tortured forms of harder rock behind. The most striking of these formations are the rock bridges that arch from one rock mass to another. You can see several of these bridges around the area but there are three famous ones.

The largest of the three is the **Burdah Rock Bridge**, precariously perched about 80m above surrounding rock. The top can be reached (up the western side) without equipment by anyone in decent shape who has a head for heights.

The smaller **Umm Fruth Rock Bridge** is tucked away in a remote corner of the desert and can easily be climbed without gear or a guide. Although it can be a busy spot at lunchtime, the best time to see it is in the late afternoon when full sunlight hits the rear side of the arch.

Little Rock Bridge (Rakhabat al-Wadak) is easier to climb and more accessible than Burdah Rock Bridge, but is not as impressive. The views, however, across a broad expanse of desert valley, are superb.

SIQS & CANYONS

An easy *siq* to explore is the narrow fissure that cuts into **Jebel Khazali**. You can explore on foot for about 150m, far enough to appreciate the shade and the cool and to see inscriptions made by the ancients who used the *siq* for the same purpose. Look out for drawings of ostriches, pairs of feet and a woman giving birth. You need ropes and a guide to penetrate the *siq* farther and 4WD transport to reach the *siq*.

A popular destination by 4WD is **Siq Umm Tawaqi**, a beautiful area with mature trees sprouting apparently from the rock face. Locals have carved the humorous likeness of TE Lawrence (complete with Arab headdress), and two other prominent figures of the Arab Revolt, into a stone plinth in the middle of the *siq*.

Numerous other canyons riddle the area, including the 5km-long **Barrah Canyon**; they all offer opportunities for hiking, camel

trekking, climbing or simply napping in the shade and absorbing the special atmosphere of Wadi Rum's hidden heartland.

SUNSET & SUNRISE VANTAGE POINTS

Dusk and dawn are the most magical (and cooler) times to be in the desert. The best vantage points differ according to the time of year but you can't go far wrong if you park yourself at Umm Sabatah. Jeep drivers can take you there and either wait or pick you up later (they are reliable about such things); or arrange a sunset tour which can include a traditional Bedouin dinner for a negotiable price.

Activities

Although you could have a pleasant day out in the Wadi Rum area by calling in at the visitor centre and ambling along to the village of Rum, you will have a more interesting experience if you penetrate deeper into the desert. This requires going 'off-road' or, in other words, leaving the tarmac behind. You can do this most effectively by hiring a 4WD vehicle with driver; by hiring a camel or a horse with a mounted escort; or by hiking, scrambling or climbing with or without a guide. For a list of guides, see p274.

A word of warning: although there is nothing to stop you driving your own 4WD in the desert or striking off on your own two feet, you should not attempt this unless you are experienced in the terrain. Soft sand is difficult to drive in and exhausting to walk through. If you get stuck or run out of steam, it may be a long time before anyone finds you – a serious danger if you are short of water in midsummer. Furthermore, it can be highly disorienting trying to navigate through the labyrinthine passages. Make sure you have a compass and map before attempting even a simple route on your own.

4WD EXCURSIONS

The easiest way to see the largest number of sights in the least amount of time is to arrange a 4WD trip. This is easily done through the excursion office in the visitor centre on arrival. You can either hire the vehicle (with driver) for a whole day, choosing your own set of destinations, or you can select a destination from two prescribed routes (listed as 'Operator 1' and 'Operator 2'

HAND OVER HAND IN THE DESERT *Jenny Walker*

We threw our faces to the bitter winter wind of Wadi Rum and gripped the mangled rails of 'Vehicle Number 1', safe in the hands of our expert Bedouin driver. Having written our own off-road guide (to Oman), we were surprised at his angle of approach in heading for a sandy rise and we knew exactly what the driver would be thinking: is it the right speed for the incline, will the engine cope with the drag, could we reverse downhill if necessary? But today it wasn't our responsibility so when Vehicle Number 1 ground to a halt, spraying sand from all four wheels independently, we simply laughed.

Our driver did what all drivers do in that situation (unless their lives depend on it) – he tried to coax the vehicle out of the sand with the result that we were then really stuck. Time for Vehicle Number 2: with a derisory flick of the wrist at Driver Number 1, a kind stranger bundled us into his cosy cab and sailed competently over the dune, finding time with one hand to wrap me up in a goat-hair blanket while answering his mobile with the other. He was 'on business' at a nearby camp but detoured out of his way to unload us into Vehicle Number 3.

Vehicle Number 3 was a work of art, with a dashboard padded out with sheepskin; festoons of love hearts, Chinese bunting and various talismans against the evil eye dangling in the front windscreen; there was a boarded-up back windscreen; a door held on with masking tape and a total absence of hand brake. Unfortunately, there appeared to be an absence of petrol too and so we unwrapped our picnic, resigned to a long wait. One bite into a cows-cheese triangle and Vehicle Number 4 arrived, lurching towards us like a bucking bronco. In a remote spot, 30 minutes later, it backfired like a mule on chilli and relieved itself of the drive shaft.

The sun was beginning to sink behind the great auburn pillars of Wadi Rum's outer rim and it was already mind-numbingly cold so we were relieved when a whistle went up and some shadowy figures appeared on the horizon. Moments later Vehicle Number 5 turned up – with its 14-year-old driver. With superb skill, he delivered us to base and drove off before we had a chance to thank him.

Our memorable journey was a seamless display of care and concern. None of the drivers asked us for money; none of them waited for an explanation: they simply delivered us hand over hand into safety. That has been our experience of the Bedouin throughout 20 years of living in the Middle East. The Bedouin don't pay lip service to 'hospitality' – they live it.

---

routes). The driver will stop at any sights en route to your furthest point. Make sure you and the driver agree about where you are going before you set off. Note also that drivers may speak some English but they are not trained guides. If you would like a guide to accompany you, then enquire about costs from the excursion office.

It's unlikely that anything will go wrong with your trip as the drivers are highly experienced in the desert terrain. Some of the vehicles, however, have seen better days so if you are involved in a breakdown try to avoid heated confrontation: the Bedouin take their responsibility towards the visitor very seriously and they will quickly arrange for a replacement – if everyone remains amicable! You can always lodge a complaint later, if necessary, at the visitor centre.

Rates for 4WD excursions are fixed and listed on a board outside the excursion office in the visitor centre. The prices are per

vehicle, not per person, so it can help with costs if you put together a group in Wadi Musa or Aqaba (not easy to do on arrival at Wadi Rum). Most 4WDs seat six people; some have bench seats in the back offering better views than the closed-in cabs but they are fearfully cold or boiling hot in extreme seasons.

If you take the vehicle for a day, don't forget to pack food and water for you and your driver. You can buy the basics of a rudimentary picnic in Rum village on your way into the desert.

You may be approached by the odd freelance guide in Rum village. Prices may be cheaper but there are no guarantees regarding the safety or quality of the trip and more importantly, it cheats the lads waiting patiently in line at the visitor centre of a fare. In addition, 60% of the profit from excursions goes back to the cooperative of drivers: someone who jumps the queue robs the community at large of that revenue. Rangers tour the Wadi Rum area, checking people have tickets. Entering without one is not only unethical, it is also illegal.

You can easily add on an overnight stay at a Bedouin camp (ask at the visitor centre when booking your vehicle). Your driver will simply drop you off in the afternoon and pick you up the next morning. See p272 for details and costs.

CAMEL TREKKING

If you have the time, travelling around Wadi Rum by camel is highly recommended. Apart from being ecologically sound, it will enable you to experience Wadi Rum as the Bedouin have for centuries, and to appreciate the silent gravitas of the desert. That said, a ride of more than about four hours will leave you sore in places you never knew existed.

Rates for camel-trekking excursions are fixed and listed on a board outside the excursion office in the visitor centre. The prices are per person. You'll enjoy your ride much more if you ride yourself rather than being led. This will cost a bit more as you need to pay for your guide's camel but it's well worth the extra cost.

You can easily add on an overnight stay at a Bedouin camp (ask at the visitor centre when booking your camel). If you want to return by 4WD then you have to pay the price of returning the camel to where you collected it from. If you have a lot of gear, it's better to hire an additional camel (at the same rate) to bear the load.

It is also possible to arrange longer camel excursions from Wadi Rum to Aqaba (three to six nights depending on the route); or towards Wadi Musa (for Petra; about five nights). Sunset Camp (p272) has a two-day

---

4WD EXCURSIONS AROUND WADI RUM

The routes listed below are those suggested by the Wadi Rum visitor centre. You can choose any combination of sights but most people choose either an 'Operator 1' route around the central areas of Wadi Rum, or an 'Operator 2' route to more outlying (but just as beautiful) areas. Distances are measured from the visitor centre. Maximum times are given: you could rush round the main sights of Wadi Rum in a few hours but the trip will be much more rewarding if you get out of the vehicle and explore each of the sights on foot, or simply sit and enjoy the peace and quiet. The prices quoted below were correct at the time of research. Don't forget that drivers queue up for their fare outside the visitor centre in strict rotation. You may get a driver who speaks English and is knowledgeable about the desert or you may not. If you want a guide to accompany you, then you need to tell the visitor centre this or book one in advance (see p274).

Site	Km	Time	Price per vehicle
Operator 1 Routes			
Lawrence's Spring	14km	1 hour	JD25
Khazali Canyon	30km	2 hours	JD35
Sunset sites of Rum	35km	2½ hours	JD44
Little Rock Bridge	35km	3 hours	JD44
Red Dunes	40km	3½ hours	JD51
Lawrence's House	45km	3½ hours	JD59
Umm Fruth Rock Bridge	50km	4 hours	JD67
Burdah Rock Bridge	60km	5 hours	JD75
Burdah Canyon	65km	8 hours	JD80
Operator 2 Routes			
Alameleh inscriptions	15km	1 hour	JD25
Siq Umm Tawagi	18km	2 hours	JD35
Sunset sites of Diseh	20km	2½ hours	JD44
Barrah Canyon	49km	3 hours	JD51
Burdah Rock Bridge	50km	4 hours	JD67
Full-day tour	60km	8 hours	JD80

CAMEL TREKS AROUND WADI RUM

Camel routes are sorted into two circuits for 'operational' purposes. Camel excursions normally begin from Rum village and distances are measured from the rest house. Prices are on the rise due to transportation of fodder.

Site	Km	Time	Price (max)
Operator 1 Routes			
Nabataean Temple	1km	30 minutes	JD2
Lawrence's Spring	6km	2 hours	JD7
Khazali Canyon	14km	4 hours	JD16
Sunset sites	22km	overnight	JD40
Red Dunes	25km	5 hours	JD20
Burdah Rock Bridge	40km	overnight	JD40
Full-day tour	unlimited	8 hours	JD20
Luggage camel		8 hours	JD20
Operator 2 Routes			
Alameleh inscriptions	6km	1 hour	JD7
Sunset sites	8km	1½ hours	JD10
Sunrise sites	9km	1½ hours	JD10
Umm Salab	14km	4 hours	JD16
Burrah Canyon	25km	8 hours	JD20
Burdah Rock Bridge	40km	overnight	JD40

trip to Aqaba, completing the last part of the trip by taxi. Call ahead for a quote.

Camel races are held weekly in winter, generally on a Friday, at the camel track near Diseh. Ask at the visitor centre for details.

HORSE TREKKING

An alternative and memorable mode of four-legged transport through Wadi Rum and surrounding areas is by horse. A hack costs around JD20 per hour. These trips are for people who have some experience of riding, and novices should not underestimate the challenge of riding high-spirited Arab horses in open country. Among the agencies or guides who can organise such an expedition is **Rum Horses** (☎ 2033508, 077-7471960; www.desertguides.com), a professional French-run trekking, camel- and horse-trekking agency located on the approach road to Wadi Rum visitor centre, about 10km from the Desert Highway. Look for a signboard beside the road.

HIKING

For those who prefer 'Shank's pony' to the real thing, there are many wonderful places to explore on foot. You can walk unguided to several of the main sights in Wadi Rum

if you have time, or you can hire a 4WD and a guide from the visitor centre to get you off-the-beaten-track – a great way to learn about how the Bedouin interact with the desert environment.

There is only space in this chapter to highlight a couple of hikes but if you're serious about hiking (or scrambling and climbing), invest in one of the excellent books by Tony Howard and Di Taylor (p264).

Avoid the extreme heat of summer (May to September). Remember that it's very easy to get disoriented amid the dozens of craggy peaks; temperatures (cold as well as hot) can be extreme; natural water supplies are not common and sometimes undrinkable; passing traffic is rare; and maps are often inaccurate. Walking in sand is particularly exhausting.

Makharas Canyon Hike

One excellent do-it-yourself option is to hike southeast across the plain from the visitor centre towards the Seven Pillars of Wisdom and then head up Makharas Canyon (take the left-hand wadi when it branches). The wadi narrows after about an hour from the visitor centre and then pops out onto a patch of gorgeous red sand with fabulous views of Jebel Barrah and Umm Nfoos to the east. From here cut north over the sand dunes and plod your way around the northern tip of Jebel Umm Ishrin until you get back to the Seven Pillars of Wisdom. This hike takes about 2½ hours.

Jebel Rum Round Trip
Another possible DIY hike is the circumambulation of the southern half of Jebel Rum via Wadi Leyyah, starting from Rum village and passing Lawrence's Spring and Ain Abu Aineh. The route takes eight hours and offers some stunning 'big country' scenery.

Jebel Umm Adaami Ascent
One great 4WD-hiking trip is to hike up Jebel Umm Adaami (1832m), Jordan's highest peak, on the rarely visited southern border with Saudi Arabia. The hourlong uphill hike is marked by cairns and offers fabulous views of Wadi Rum to the north and Saudi Arabia to the south. Find a driver who knows the 45-minute 4WD route south to Wadi Saabet, where the hike starts. On the way back, stop off at the rock carvings of nearby Siq al-Barid, a lovely spot for a picnic.

SCRAMBLING
Scrambling lies somewhere between hiking and climbing. No technical skills are required but you may have to pull yourself up short rock faces on the following trips.

Burdah Rock Bridge
If you take a 4WD excursion to Burdah Rock Bridge, it's well worth making the hour-long scramble up to the bridge itself. There's nothing technical about the scramble but you'll need a guide to find the route up and will need a head for heights on one spot just before the bridge. There are fabulous views from the route up and from the top of the bridge. To continue beyond the bridge you'll need ropes and some climbing skills (one climber fell to his death here in 1999).

Rakhabat Canyon
With a local guide or a copy of Tony Howard's *Walking in Jordan* you can navigate the labyrinthine *siqs* of Rakhabat Canyon for an exciting half-day trip through the heart of Jebel Umm al-Ishrin. The western mouth of the canyon is just by Rum village, but don't confuse it with the more obvious Makhman Canyon to the north. At the far (eastern) end of the canyon you can hike across the valley to the Anfaishiyya inscriptions, 600m south of the Bedouin camp, and then return on foot to Rum via the southern point of Jebel Umm al-Ishrin, with a possible detour to Ain Abu Aineh en route. Alternatively, with a guide and some experience of abseiling you can head back west through the mountain ridge along the Kharazeh Canyon for a great loop route.

ROCK CLIMBING
Wadi Rum offers some challenging rock climbing with a vast array of climbs up to Grade 8. Although the Bedouin have been climbing in the area for centuries, climbing as a modern sport is still relatively undeveloped in the area. That said, there are now several accredited climbing guides, most of whom have been trained in the UK. To arrange a climbing trip, contact the visitor centre a few days in advance; they will put you in touch with a guide with whom you can negotiate the price and organise camping gear, equipment and transport. Costs start at around JD150 for one to two days' climbing.

Guides often suggest Jebel Rum for less experienced climbers: minimal gear is needed and it's close to the Rest House. Another popular climbing location is Jebel Barrah. For information on routes see Tony Howard and Di Taylor's books (p264); also check out www.wadi rum.net.

OTHER ACTIVITIES
For a magnificent eagle-eye view of Wadi Rum, take to the air by balloon (JD130 per person for a minimum of two people) or try a 20-minute 'flip' by microlight or ultralight. **Bait Ali** (☎ 2022626, 079-5548133; www .desertexplorer.net) acts as the local facilitator for the **Royal Aero Sports Club of Jordan** (☎ 2058050; www.royalaeroclub.com), providing the easiest way of making a booking for these sports. Bait Alia also rents out sand yachts, mountain bikes and quad bikes, along with maps of possible routes in the dry mud flats north of the camp.

The annual **Jebel Ishrin Marathon** (www.whmf .org in German) takes place each September and the **Wadi Rum Endurance Race** (www.fei.org), a 120km-in-a-day FEI event, may interest horse enthusiasts.

Sleeping

There is no hotel in Wadi Rum, nor in the neighbouring village of Diseh, so if you want to spend a couple of days in the area you have to be prepared to camp. Camping can range from a goat-hair blanket under the stars at an isolated Bedouin camp, a mattress under partitioned canvas in a 'party tent' at Diseh, to a comfortable cabin at Bait Ali, just outside Wadi Rum. You can even pitch your own tent in designated areas (enquire about locations at the visitor centre). Mattress, blankets and food are provided by the camps but bring your own linen. It's also a good idea to bring a torch and a padlock (many tents are lockable).

RUM VILLAGE

The frayed tents at the back of the **Rest House** (☎ 2018867; mattress & blankets in 2-person tent per person JD3) offer the most accessible accommodation, but they're only recommended if you arrive in Wadi Rum too late to head into the desert. Some of the mattresses are very thin. You can pitch your own tent for JD1, which includes use of toilets and shower block. The site has little security so keep your valuables with you.

IN THE DESERT

The best way to experience the desert is by sleeping in it. You can do this by staying at one of the camps run by the Bedouin, all of which have to conform to certain standards and are checked regularly. There are two types of camps – permanent (which usually have toilet-shower blocks and operate year-round) and temporary (used only occasionally by Bedouin groups or tourists). The camps are only permitted in certain areas and these fall either within Wadi Rum or within neighbouring Diseh. The Wadi Rum camps are best booked through the visitor centre, either in advance (especially if you want to stay at a particular camp), or on arrival. For camps in the Diseh area, see p275.

The price of accommodation at these camps, including food, tents and blankets, is generally around JD30 per person per night. Camps advertising half-board generally provide a simple barbecue supper with salads and Arabic bread, coffee or tea and a piece of fruit, and a breakfast of jam, cheese, bread and coffee. For groups staying in a temporary camp, there is an additional charge for the transportation of camping items to the campsite each day. If you have your own sleeping bag, tent and food, all you should have to pay is the cost of your four-wheeled or four-legged transport.

As there are many camps, all offering similar services in similarly beautiful parts of the desert, it is hard to recommend one over another.

Sunset Camp (☎ 077-7314688; www.mohammed wadirum.8m.com) Near Umm Sabatah, this well-run camp has been recommended. It offers a half-/full-day 4WD excursion, half-board accommodation and food at the camp, and a lift back to Rum village the next morning with prices dependent on the size of the group. It's best to contact the camp in advance for a quote.

Mohammed Mutlak Camp (☎ 077-7424837; www .wadirum.org) In a beautiful spot overlooking Jebel Qattar, this camp is run by brothers who speak English well. Half board costs JD30 per person and dinner may, if you're lucky, include delicious lamb cooked in a *zerb* (oven buried in the ground). Transport by 4WD to the camp is free if you don't visit anywhere en route. You can come by camel (JD20, two hours and 15 minutes). Hiking opportunities include a 45-minute hike to see the merging of red and white sand dunes. There is no electricity, but light is provided by gas lamp.

Tour operators run their own camps scattered around the desert – see p274.

AROUND WADI RUM

our pick **Bait Ali** (☎ 2022626, 079-5548133; www .baitali.com; half board in tent/chalet JD25/27; ☒ Ⓥ) If you want to stay in the area but are not wild about roughing it, then Bait Ali offers a wonderful compromise. Tucked behind a hill, with a sublime view of the wilderness, this up-market, eco-friendly camp is clearly signposted just off the road, 15km from the Desert Highway and 9km from the Wadi Rum visitor centre. The accommodation (either in army tents or twin-bed cabins) is basic but spotless (and includes linen) and a separate shower block with hot water for men and women. The facilities include an excellent restaurant with an extensive nightly barbecue, a circular meeting hall with a central fire, a bar and comfortable, cushion-filled Bedouin tents that add an exotic Arabian Nights atmosphere to the camp. There is even an attractively designed swimming pool. You can pitch your own tent (JD8) or park a camper van (JD8) and use the shower block. The owners are delightful and can advise on bike rides, hikes, ballooning and other activities in the local area. The hike around Lion Mountain (12km, three hours) is particularly recommended. For an interview with the owner on how the camp keeps a green profile, see p76.

Eating

Apart from the good Rum Gate Restaurant at the visitor centre, there are limited eating options in Wadi Rum.

Rest House (☎/fax 2018867; breakfast JD3, lunch JD8, dinner buffet JD10; ☾ 6am-midnight) Dining here is open-air and buffet-style. Sipping a large Amstel beer (JD2.500) while watching the sun's rays light up Jebel Umm al-Ishrin is the perfect way to finish the day.

Redwan Paradise (☾ 6am-1am) Along the main road of Rum village, this cheap and local place serves tea, hummus and felafel for around JD1, and is where the younger Bedouin guides go to unwind.

ourpick **Rum Gate Restaurant** (☎ 2015995; Wadi Rum visitor centre; buffet lunch JD10; ☾ 8am-5pm; ✷ Ⓥ) A fine selection of dishes is offered in the buffet between noon and 4pm (popular with tour groups); outside this time, the restaurant is a buzzing meeting place for guides, weary hikers and independent travellers who congregate over a non-alcoholic beer (JD2) and a chicken sandwich (JD4.500).

The small grocery stores along the main road through Rum village have mineral water and basic supplies, though you'll have a greater variety of imported goods if you stock up elsewhere en route to Wadi Rum. The area around Diseh has some of the cleanest aquifer water in Jordan so it's generally not a problem drinking spring water in Wadi Rum.

While out in the desert you may be lucky enough to try a *zerb* – a Bedouin barbecue, cooked in an oven buried in the sand.

Shopping

Rum Arts (☎ 2032918; ☾ 8am-5pm) at the visitor centre is a good place to look for quality silver items, embroidered bags and glass designs. Most items are made by local women to whom most of the profits are returned. It's possible to visit the workshop in Rum village if you are interested (closed Friday and Saturday) – ask for directions here or at the Rest House. Almost adjacent, the **Bedouin Gallery** sells a fine selection of textiles and Bedouin goat-hair rugs.

Getting There & Away

Public transport is limited because Rum village has a small population and many visitors come on tours organised by agencies or hotels from Wadi Musa or Aqaba. Public transport stops briefly at the visitor centre before continuing to Rum village.

There is talk of a passenger train between Rum and Aqaba operating along the existing goods line, but don't hold your breath!

CAR

The most convenient way to get to Wadi Rum as an independent traveller is by car. You can hire a car in Aqaba and, if you intend to continue to Petra, you are well advised to keep the car for the round-trip. This will save you considerable time and frustration trying to fathom the limited public transport.

If you are accustomed to desert navigation and off-road driving in sandy conditions, you could hire a 4WD in Aqaba and drive into the desert yourself, providing you state your intention at the visitor centre at Wadi Rum and pay the JD2 (per person) entrance fee. Do not attempt this if you have no prior knowledge of desert driving.

HITCHING

Because of the limited public transport to and from Rum village, many travellers (including locals) are obliged to hitch – a normal form of transport in this part of Jordan.

The well-signposted turn-off to Wadi Rum is along the Desert Highway at Ar-Rashidiyya, 5km south of Quweira. From Aqaba, take any minibus heading along the highway (except JETT buses, which won't stop here) and get out at the turn-off (JD1.500); from Wadi Musa or other towns to the north; anything headed towards Aqaba will pass the Rum turn-off. From the crossroads you should be able to find a minibus headed your way for around JD2 per person; otherwise hitch and negotiate a fare for the 30km ride.

You can normally hitch a lift in a pick-up between the visitor centre and Rum village for around JD1.500.

MINIBUS

At the time of research, there was at least one minibus a day to Aqaba (JD1.500, one hour) at around 7.30am. A second one may run at 8.30am. To Wadi Musa (JD5, 1½ hours) there is a fairly reliable daily minibus at 8.30am. Check current departure times at the visitor centre or Rest House when you arrive in Wadi Rum.

For Ma'an, Karak or Amman, the minibuses to either Aqaba or Wadi Musa can drop you off at the Ar-Rashidiyya crossroads with the Desert Highway (JD1.500, 20 minutes), where it is easy to hail onward transport.

TAXI

Occasionally taxis hang around the visitor centre (and very occasionally the Rest House) waiting for a fare back to wherever they came from – normally Aqaba, Wadi Musa or Ma'an. It costs about JD25 to Aqaba, and JD40 to Wadi Musa (Petra). A

taxi from Rum village to the Ar-Rashidiyya crossroads with the Desert Highway costs around JD5.

TOURS

If you have limited time, you may find it easier to arrange a tour to Wadi Rum from Aqaba. Prices start from JD45 per person per day (including transport, food and entrance fee) and can include an overnight stay in the desert (JD10 for facilities and breakfast). **Wadi Rum Desert Services** (☎ 2063882; http://wadirumsafari.com) has one of the better reputations for these tours.

Some tours overnight at Diseh and do not even enter the main protected area of Wadi Rum. Diseh has some good camps in beautiful scenery but the fact remains that it is not part of the reserve area. As such, you should be clear about what the tour entails to avoid disappointment.

DISEH   الديسي

Diseh is northwest of Rum village, about 12km as the vulture flies but 22km by road. The scenery is almost as spectacular as it is at Wadi Rum, and there are plenty of places to hike outside the official Wadi Rum protected area. There are seven camps in the desert near Diseh that offer basic facilities. If you stay at one of these, you can organise transport to Wadi Rum visitor centre and book your desert excursion from there.

AGENCIES & GUIDES

Jeep drivers and camel escorts do a good job of looking after visitors, but if you want more detailed or specialised information about Wadi Rum, or help in organising a particular activity, then you may prefer to hire the services of a guide. Staff at the visitor centre can help you locate a guide, or you can contact one of the guides listed here (recommended by our readers). Contact the guide at least 48 hours in advance and carry a copy of your email correspondence in case the staff at the visitor centre asks for it. For longer excursions, some planning is required on the part of the guide (eg buying provisions, arranging camels). April, September and October are the busiest seasons for guides.

Al-Hillawi Desert Services (☎ /fax 2018867, 079-5940117) Agency with several desert camps, run by the management of the Rest House.

Attayak Ali (☎ 079-5899723; www.bedouinroads.com) One of the best climbing and adventure guides.

Attayak Aouda (☎ 079-5834736; www.rumguides.com) Recommended as one of the best (if not the best) climbing guide in Rum.

Hassan Al-Zawaidh (☎ 077-9711374, 077 7390357; hrummagic@yahoo.com) A knowledgeable guide in the Wadi Rum area.

Hilal Zawaedh (☎ 079-5413563; hzawaydeh@yahoo.com) As president of the Diseh Villages Touristic Cooperative, this guide can help put you in touch with almost anybody in the Wadi Rum-Diseh area.

Sabagh Eid (☎ /fax 2016238) Official climbing guide.

The paved road to Diseh from the turn-off to Rum offers a few accessible *jebels* and landscapes, which are easy to explore. Locals will happily (for a negotiable price) drive you out into the desert area north of the railway line, which is dotted with Nabataean and Roman dams, artificial rock bridges, rock carvings and inscriptions. The landscape around **Jebel Amud** is the most interesting. A longer trip could take in the 2m-high rock carvings at **Abu Hawl** (Father of Terror), 7km north of the Bait Ali camp, and on to a rock bridge at Jebel Kharazeh. A three-hour 4WD trip costs around JD45.

Sleeping & Eating

A number of camps outside Diseh have been recommended by readers. The camps, numbered one to seven, are wrapped round a hill with only the first three accessible by 2WD. They all offer traditional sitting areas with cushions, beds either in cramped individual tents (or larger communal Bedouin tents), and clean shower-toilet blocks. The first three are next to each other a couple of kilometres southeast of Diseh village.

Zawaideh Desert Camp (☎ 079-5840664; zawaideh _camp@yahoo.com; half-board per person JD14) Simple but atmospheric camp in the undercliff of the escarpment, on the edge of a wide plain.

Captain's Camp (☎ 2016905, 079-5510432; captains @jo.com.jo; half-board per person JD30) A well-run midrange camp with hot showers, a clean bathroom block and good buffets. It's popular with large tour groups. The camp also offers a romantic tent for two (JD90 per person) in the middle of the desert, with a candlelit supper delivered to the tent flaps.

Palm Camp (☎ 077-7244605; www.jordandesertpalm camp.com; half-board per person JD15) A sociable place with a central campfire and lounging area, but with more cramped accommodation.

Camps four to seven are located progressively farther away from the road in more isolated parts of the desert. Number Seven is one of the most appealing of these; known as **Barrh Camp** (☎ 077-6031246; hzawaydeh@yahoo.com; half board per person JD25), it is tucked discreetly at the end of Siq Umm Tawaqi, beside a giant vertical slice of rock and is within walking distance of some fine rock inscriptions. The camp is run by Hilal Zawaedh, the president of the Diseh Village Touristic Cooperative, a group that ensures profits are returned to the local community.

Getting There & Away

You're unlikely to find a minibus or service taxi headed all the way to Diseh, so follow the instructions for getting to Wadi Rum as far as the turn-off to Diseh (the police checkpoint 16km after leaving the Desert Highway). From there you'll have to hitch 8km (be prepared for quite a wait), or the police might, if you ask nicely, ring ahead to one of the camps where someone is usually happy to come out and pick you up.

Minibuses often run from Diseh to the Desert Highway for JD1.500 per person. A single bus runs to Aqaba daily at around 7.30am. Check at your camp for the latest information.

MA'AN   معان
☎ 03 / pop 28,000

Ma'an has been a transport junction and trading centre for many centuries, and is now one of the larger towns and administrative centres in southern Jordan. There's little of specific interest here, but the centre of town is pleasant enough and some travellers may have to stay overnight while waiting for transport to Wadi Rum, Wadi Musa (for Petra) and Aqaba. The town is particularly busy during haj as it lies on the main pilgrimage route from Jordan and Syria to Mecca in Saudi Arabia.

Orientation & Information

The main north–south thoroughfare is King Hussein St, centred somewhere around the mosque and the communication tower. Here you'll find restaurants and several banks with ATMs. To get here from the bus station head two blocks west then one block north (a five-minute walk) to the southern end of King Hussein St, where it meets Palestine St. The Hotel Kreashan is a further five minutes' walk north of here.

Horizon Internet Centre (☎ 2131700; King Hussein St; per hr JD1; ◷ 9am-10pm), opposite the Housing Bank, has fast connections.

Sleeping & Eating

Hotel Kreashan (Krishan Hotel; ☎ 2132043; Al-Bayyarah St; r from JD12) There's really no need to look further than this good central choice, with a variety of simple and sunny rooms and clean, shared bathrooms. It's a small block east of the mosque off the northern end of King Hussein St.

Grill and chicken restaurants abound along King Hussein St, including **Alroz-Al Bokhary** (King Hussein St; mains JD2-3). There's a tempting sweets shop diagonally opposite the corner of King Hussein and Palestine Sts, and fruit shops nearby.

Getting There & Away

If you can't get a direct bus to where you want to go in Jordan, there's a good chance that you can find a connection in Ma'an.

The station for buses, minibuses and service taxis is a five-minute walk southeast of the centre. Departures from Ma'an start to peter out around 2pm and stop completely around 5pm.

There are regular minibuses (JD3, three hours) and less frequent service taxis (JD5, three hours) to/from Amman's Wahadat bus station. To Aqaba, minibuses (JD2, 80 minutes) and service taxis (JD1.500) are also frequent. For Wadi Rum, take an Aqaba-bound minibus to the junc-

tion at Ar-Rashidiyya (JD1.500) then take a minibus or hitch from here. For Petra, minibuses to Wadi Musa (JD1, 45 minutes) leave fairly frequently when full and stop briefly at the university en route. To Karak, there are occasional service taxis (JD2, two hours) and three minibuses a day, via Tafila (JD1.100).

A chartered taxi to Petra/Wadi Musa costs around JD10, and JD25 to Karak or Aqaba.

QATRANA   القطرانه

☎ 03 / pop 5000

One of the few towns along the Desert Highway is Qatrana, a couple of kilometres north of the turn-off to Karak, and a former stop on the pilgrim road between Damascus and Mecca. The only reason to stop here (if you have your own transport) is to have a quick look at **Qatrana Castle** (admission free), built in 1531 by the Ottomans. It has been nicely restored, but there are no explanation boards.

The **Ba'albaki Tourist Complex** (☎ 2394156; r with private bathroom & breakfast JD35), about 8km north of Qatrana on the highway, has souvenir shops and a restaurant (buffet JD10).

Diving & Snorkelling

With Jordan's living history stretching back several millennia, it's no wonder that a good number of tourists never give thought to exploring its underwater world. Of course, while landlubbers are busy sweating bullets in the desert, divers and snorkellers are plunging into the Red Sea's clear depths, and finding themselves surrounded by one of nature's most magnificent sights. The Red Sea has a legendary reputation among underwater enthusiasts, and deserves its status as one of the world's premier marine destinations. King Abdullah II himself is an avid diver, and was instrumental in the establishment of Jordan's premier artificial reef, the wreck of the *Cedar Pride*.

Unlike neighbouring Egypt, which is widely regarded in diving circles as one of the world's premier dive destinations, Jordan is comparatively off-the-beaten-path. Truth be told, Jordan can't compete with the sheer breadth and diversity of underwater sites that Egypt boasts, though this is not to say that Jordan isn't a spectacular diving and snorkelling destination. On the contrary, the relatively small number of visitors that Jordan receives each year ensures the pristine nature of its reef system is retained, and the Jordanian section of the Red Sea is home to the majority of flora and fauna that inhabit Egyptian waters.

Perhaps the biggest appeal of diving and snorkelling in Jordan is that it's nearly always a low-key experience. As a result, novice and first-time divers and snorkellers will feel calm and comfortable on the reefs, while intermediate and more advanced divers will appreciate the down-tempo pace and relaxed environment. So, even if you're a huge desert junkie or an aspiring Lawrence of Arabia, be sure to save at least a few days for getting wet!

DIVING & SNORKELLING

HIGHLIGHTS

- Explore the coral-encrusted remains of the **Cedar Pride** (p282), Jordan's most famous dive site
- Look for rare black corals in the sheer blue depths of **Big Bay** (p282)
- Scout for cruising hammerheads and sea turtles along the **Saudi Border Wall** (p283)
- Hover about the discarded shell of an old Russian tank at **Oliver's Canyon** (p282)
- Chill out with like-minded backpackers and divers at the **Bedouin Garden Village** (p283)

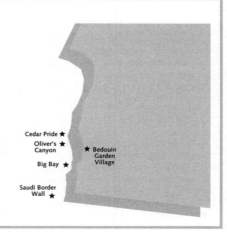

Cedar Pride ★
Oliver's ★
Canyon   ★ Bedouin
                Garden
Big Bay ★   Village

Saudi Border
Wall ★

ORIENTATION

There is only 27km of Jordanian coastline between Israel and the Palestinian Territories and Saudi Arabia. Sadly, however, much of the northern section of shoreline is paved over by the town and container ports of Aqaba, which has damaged the marine environment. However, there is plenty of unspoiled coastline to the south, between the port and the Saudi border. This stretch of coast is protected within the Red Sea Marine Peace Park, and is run in cooperation with Israel and the Palestinian Territories – reefs here are in excellent condition, and the soft corals, especially those found on the Cedar Pride, are fantastic.

INFORMATION

The northern end of the Gulf of Aqaba enjoys high salinity, and the winds from the north and minimal tides means the water stays clear. The water temperature is warm (an average 22.5°C in winter and 26°C in summer), attracting a vast array of fish, and helping to preserve the coral.

According to the **Jordan Royal Ecological Society** (☎ 06-5679142; www.jreds.org), the gulf has over 110 species of hard coral, 120 species of soft coral and about 1000 species of fish. These include colourful goatfish, leopard flounder, clownfish, triggerfish; various species of butterfly fish, parrotfish, angelfish; and the less endearing spiky sea urchin, poisonous stonefish, scorpionfish, sea snakes, jellyfish and moray eels. Green

turtles and hermit crabs can also be found and even (harmless) whale sharks pay a visit in summer.

One unwelcome natural visitor in the area is the crown of thorns starfish (known as COTS), which feeds on and kills local coral. Divers should notify their divemaster if they spot these starfish.

The **Aqaba Marine Park Visitors Centre** (☎ 03-2035801) has a jetty, museum, cafe, gift shop and park offices.

For information on other sights and activities along the coast, see p252 and p254.

Dive Centres

As development in the Aqaba area reaches breakneck speed, the number of independent diver operators is likely to mushroom. At present count, there are already a staggering number of dive centres in town, offering services of varying quality and professionalism. For the most part, however, the standard set by operators in Aqaba tends to be very high, though it's always a good idea to shop around a bit before settling on a particular dive centre.

Generally speaking, prices and services are fairly standardised in the Aqaba area, with a one-/two-tank shore dive costing around JD20/35, and an additional JD10 for full equipment rental. There are significantly cheaper packages available if you're planning on diving for several days, which is always a good way to maximise your underwater time while minimising the blow to your wallet.

MARE ROSTRUM – THE RED SEA

Surrounded by desert on three sides, the Red Sea was formed some 40 million years ago when the Arabian Peninsula split from Africa, allowing the waters of the Indian Ocean to rush in. Bordered at its southern end by the 25km Bab al-Mandab Strait, the Red Sea is the only tropical sea that is almost entirely closed. No river flows into it and the influx of water from the Indian Ocean is slight. These unique geographical features, combined with the arid desert climate and high temperatures, make the sea extremely salty. It is also windy – on average the sea is flat for only 50 days a year.

In 1989 a panel of scientists and conservationists selected the northern portion of this 1800km-long body of water as one of the Seven Underwater Wonders of the World. Here, in the depths of the Red Sea, divers and snorkellers alike will find coral mountains rising from the seabed, shallow reefs swarming with brightly coloured fish, sheer drop-offs disappearing into unplumbed depths and coral-encrusted shipwrecks, all bathed in an ethereal blue hue.

In regards to its name, there are two competing schools of thought regarding etymology. Some believe that the sea was named after the red-rock mountain ranges that surround it. Others insist it was named for the periodic algae blooms that tinge the water a reddish brown. Whatever the spark, it inspired ancient mariners to dub these waters *Mare Rostrum* – the Red Sea.

RED SEA AQABA MARINE PARK

Jordan's only stretch of coastline is the northern part of the Gulf of Aqaba, and it's home to over 300 types of coral, and numerous species of fish and marine life. Jordan's only port (and the region's major shipping lane) and resort cause real problems for the fragile marine environment.

In an attempt to halt the damage, the **Aqaba Marine Park** (Map p281; ☎ 03-2019405) was established in 1997. The park stretches for about 8.5km, from the Marine Science Station to the Royal Diving Club, and extends about 350m offshore and 50m inland. The park contains about 80% of Jordan's public beaches and most of the decent diving and snorkelling spots, so the park managers are trying to find the right balance between promoting tourism and preserving the marine environment.

Local and foreign environmentalists have managed to ban fishing and limit boating in the park, and have established jetties into the sea so that divers and snorkellers can jump into the water rather than wade out over coral from the beach. Park rangers ensure that visitors and locals obey the strict environmental-protection laws.

In the future, the park managers also hope to conduct a public-awareness campaign for locals (particularly children) and all divers and snorkellers, lobby the government to enforce local environmental laws, and conduct further research into the damage caused by tourism and pollution. The Marine Science Station, south of Aqaba, is also involved in the preservation of the marine environment.

If you are interested in taking a dive course, PADI Open Water courses are fairly priced at around JD200. Advanced Open Water courses cost around JD160, while Rescue Dive courses are around JD180. Several centres also offer divemaster training, which can be completed in about two weeks, and starts at around JD350.

Here are some tips to help you choose a respectable dive centre:

- Take your time when choosing a dive centre and dive sites, and don't let yourself be pressured into accepting something, or someone, you're not comfortable with.
- Don't choose a dive centre based solely on cost. Safety should be the paramount concern; if a dive outfit cuts corners to keep prices low, you could be in danger.
- If you haven't dived for more than three months, take a check-out dive. This is for your own safety (and is required by many operators), and the cost is usually applied towards later dives.
- If you're taking lessons, ensure that the instructor speaks your language well. If you can't understand them, request another.
- Check that all equipment is clean and stored away from the sun, and check all hoses, mouthpieces and valves for cuts and leakage.
- Confirm that wet suits are in good condition. Some divers have reported getting hypothermia because of dry, cracked suits.
- Check that there is oxygen on the dive boat in case of accidents.

Be aware that there are dozens of dive clubs in Aqaba and along the Red Sea Coast. It's only possible to list a few here, and we have chosen dive centres with a long-standing reputation for excellence, though there are certainly other dive clubs worth checking out.

Aqaba Adventure Divers (Map p248; ☎ 079-5843724; www.aqaba-divers.com) Operates dives in conjunction with Bedouin Garden Village.

Aqaba International Dive Centre (Map p248; ☎ 03-2031213; www.aqabadivingcenter.com) Popular, well-equipped and one of Aqaba's best.

Arab Divers (Map p248; ☎ 03-2031808; www.aqaba-arabdivers.com) Highly recommended year after year by Lonely Planet readers.

Dive Aqaba (Map p248; ☎ 079-6600701; www.diveaqaba.com) A highly professional training centre known for its high-quality teaching staff.

Red Sea Diving Centre (Map p248; ☎ 03-2022323; www.redseadivecentre.com) One of the most established dive centres in Aqaba.

Royal Diving Club (Map p281; ☎ 03-2017035; www.rdc.jo) Around 12km south of the city, this is one of Aqaba's most famous institutions.

Books

Lonely Planet's *Diving and Snorkelling Guide to the Red Sea* concentrates on sites along the Egyptian coast, but also has a

DIVING & SNORKELLING

detailed section about diving around the Gulf of Aqaba. The major bookshops in Aqaba (see p249) have a good range of books about diving, including *Introduction to the Marine Life of Aqaba*. Keep an eye out for the plastic *Red Sea Fishwatchers Field Guide*, which can be taken underwater to identify species of fish and coral. *The Red Sea: Underwater Paradise* by Angelo Mojetta is one of the better glossy coffee-table books, with beautiful photos of marine flora and fauna.

Internet Resources

H₂0 Magazine (www.h2o-mag.com) The website of the quarterly publication of the Red Sea Association for Diving and Watersports, with articles and updates on diving in the region.

Reef Check (www.reefcheck.org) A membership organisation working to save coral reefs in the Red Sea and elsewhere in the world.

Health & Safety

One of the biggest concerns among divers in Aqaba isn't getting bitten by a ferocious shark, but rather stepping on a nasty bugger of a creature known as a stonefish. This poison-packing fish has a nasty habit of lying half submerged in the sand, so wear something on your feet if you're walking into the sea (as opposed to jumping into the deep water from a jetty or boat). If stung by a stonefish, see a doctor immediately.

Other nasty creatures to avoid include lionfish, which have poisonous spikes like stonefish, and jellyfish, whose sting can be painful. If stung by either, douse the rash in vinegar to deactivate any stingers which have not 'fired'. Calamine lotion, antihistamines and analgesics (and urine) may reduce the reaction and relieve the pain. Coral cuts are notoriously slow to heal and, if they're not adequately cleaned, small pieces of coral can become embedded in the wound.

The excellent **Princess Haya Hospital** (Map p248; ☎ 03-2014111) in Aqaba is well equipped for diving mishaps, including cuts, bits and stings. It also has a **decompression chamber** (☎ 03-2014117), where staff is trained to deal with diving accidents. The reputable dive centres are equipped with emergency oxygen tanks, a first-aid kit and a mobile phone.

The most important thing to remember when diving in the Red Sea is to use common sense. More often that not, most diving fatalities are caused by divers simply forgetting (or disregarding) some of the basic rules. The following are a few tips for safe diving:

- Do not fly within 24 hours of diving.
- Don't drink and dive. Alcohol dehydrates, especially in a dry climate such as Jordan's, and increases your susceptibility to decompression sickness.
- Be sure you are healthy and feel comfortable diving. If you are taking prescription drugs, inform your medical examiner that you intend to be diving. Sometimes diving can affect your metabolism and your dosage might need to be changed.
- Dive within your scope of experience. The Red Sea's clear waters and high visibility often lull divers into going too deep. The depth limit for casual divers is 30m – stick to it.
- Make sure you can recognise your boat from in the water. Some dive sites get crowded and boats can look similar from underneath. It's not unknown for divers to get left behind because they didn't realise that their boat was leaving.
- Be aware that underwater conditions vary tremendously from site to site, and that both daily and seasonal weather and current changes can significantly alter any site and dive conditions. These differences influence not only which sites you can dive on any particular day, but the way you'll need to dress for a dive and the necessary dive techniques.
- Be insured. If something happens to you, treatment in the decompression chamber

> ### DRIVING & DIVING: A WORD OF CAUTION
>
> Altitude can kill, particularly if your body is full of residual nitrogen. If you've been diving recently, be advised that most roads out of Aqaba are high enough to induce decompression sickness. As a general rule, wait at least 12 hours before leaving town, and longer if you've been deep diving. Although this may complicate your travel plans, trust us – you'll be delayed a lot longer if you end up confined in a hyperbaric chamber, and decompression sickness is anything but fun.

can cost thousands. If you hadn't planned to dive before arriving in Jordan, many of the better clubs can provide insurance.

WATCHING MARINE LIFE

The Red Sea is teeming with more than 1000 species of marine life, and is an amazing spectacle of colour and form. Fish, sharks, turtles, stingrays, dolphins, corals, sponges, sea cucumbers and molluscs all thrive in these waters.

Coral is what makes a reef a reef – though thought for centuries to be some form of flowering plant, it is in fact an animal. Both hard and soft corals exist, their common denominator being that they are made up of polyps, which are tiny cylinders ringed by waving tentacles that sting their prey and draw it into their stomach. During the day, corals retract into their tube, only displaying their real colours at night.

Most of the bewildering variety of fish species in the Red Sea – including many that are not found elsewhere – are closely associated with the coral reef, and live and breed in the reefs or nearby seagrass beds. These include such commonly sighted species as the grouper, wrasse, parrotfish and snapper. Others, such as tuna and barracuda, live in open waters and usually only venture into the reefs to feed or breed.

When snorkelling or diving, the sharks you're most likely to encounter are the white- or black-tipped reef sharks. Tiger sharks, and the enormous, plankton-eating whale sharks, are generally found only in deeper waters. If you're skittish about these apex predators, you can take comfort in the fact that shark attacks in the Red Sea are extremely rare.

The most common type of turtle found in these waters is the green turtle, although the leatherback and hawksbill are occasionally sighted. Turtles are protected in Jordan, and although they're not deliberately hunted, they are sometimes caught in nets and end up on menus in restaurants in Aqaba.

As intriguing as they may seem, there are some creatures that should be avoided, especially moray eels, sea urchins, fire coral, blowfish, triggerfish, feathery lionfish, turkeyfish and stonefish. It's a good idea to familiarise yourself with pictures of these creatures before snorkelling or diving –

single-page colour guides to the Red Sea's common marine hazards can be bought in hotel bookshops around diving areas.

DIVE SITES

The coast between Aqaba and the Saudi Arabian border boasts about 30 diving and snorkelling sites, the majority of which can be enjoyed by snorkellers, and are easily accessible from either a jetty or the beach. Sites are not signposted, nor are they remotely obvious from the road. If you want to dive or snorkel independently you'll have to ask for directions, or take your chances and search for obvious offshore reefs.

The following are brief descriptions of some of Jordan's more popular diving destinations (see Map p281), listed from north to south – keep in mind that this list is by no means comprehensive. Although we've given a general indication of difficulty, you should always seek local advice when deciding where to go. Remember too that strong currents or winds can make an otherwise

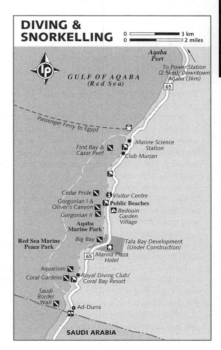

fairly tame site dangerous and, at times, undiveable.

THE POWER STATION
Location: Just south of Aqaba
Rating: Intermediate
Access: Shore

From a shallow fringing reef of fire coral, a sloping plateau of coral and sand patches leads down to a sheer wall, which drops from 12m to a narrow shelf at 40m. Keep an eye out for napoleonfish, turtles and huge schools of fusiliers, as well as a large outcrop at 22m – home to schools of glassfish and bright orange anthias.

FIRST BAY & CAZAR REEF
Location: Opposite the Club Murjan
Rating: Novice
Access: Shore or boat

First Bay is a shallow reef plateau with miniature lagoons and sandy channels leading to a fringing reef of fire coral. Just south of here is Cazar Reef, noted for its black coral trees, ghost pipefish and frogfish, as well as more common reef dwellers including lionfish, glassfish and coral groupers.

GORGONIANS I AND II & OLIVER'S CANYON
Location: 3km north of the Royal Diving Club
Rating: Novice
Access: Shore or boat

Gorgonian I takes its name from a large, solitary fan that sits at 18m – from here a sand channel leads to Gorgonian II, which is home to two large, solitary fans at 20m and 33m. A short swim south is Oliver's Canyon, which features a deep-sided canyon leading to a drop-off at 40m – in the shallows are several pinnacles and the shell of a Russian tank!

BIG BAY
Location: 1km north of the Royal Diving Club
Rating: Intermediate
Access: Shore or boat

There are four main sites in Big Bay: the first is **Blue Coral**, named for a resident species of lacy blue coral, while further south is **Kalli's Place**, comprising two small reefs and several coral outcrops. Further south is **Moon Valley**, a gently sloping reef marked by undulating sand valleys, and **Paradise**, which features beautiful strands of black corals.

CEDAR PRIDE
Location: 4km north of the Royal Diving Club
Rating: Intermediate
Access: Shore

Completely intact and festooned with soft corals, the *Cedar Pride* is one of the most colourful and impressive wrecks in the Red Sea.

Originally called the *San Bruno*, this Spanish-built ship was renamed after it was purchased by a Lebanese company in 1982. Just a few months later, however, a fire broke out in the engine room while the ship was hauling a cargo of phosphates and potassium. The resulting blaze raged for several days and claimed one life, though the ship refused to go down. With few options available, the owners simply abandoned the *Cedar Pride* along the shoreline, where it sat and rusted for four years.

Fortunately for divers, in 1986 the World Wildlife Fund (WWF) in Jordan launched an initiative to sink the *Cedar Pride*. After receiving the king's backing, the boat was towed back out to sea and sunk as an artificial reef. Today, the freighter lies on her port side at a depth of 25m, within easy reach from the shore.

On your descent, you'll first notice the stern bathed in sunlight. As you move forward along the deck, look for the remains of one of the lifeboats sitting alongside the ship, as well as the main mast and crow's nest, which are adorned in soft corals of every hue and texture.

Following a sand channel underneath the wreck, look for a lovely pink soft coral that drapes down from the hull like a massive Christmas decoration. Moving along the reef toward the bow, you'll find a magnificent garden of sea fans, basket stars and wire corals growing from the wreck's hull and the seafloor.

Fish life is generally excellent throughout the wreck – local residents include lionfish, angelfish, barracuda, napoleonfish, large snappers, schools of doublebar bream and geometric moray eels.

RESPONSIBLE DIVING & SNORKELLING

The Red Sea's natural wonders are just as magnificent as Jordan's historical and cultural splendours. However, care is needed if the delicate world of coral reefs and fish is not to be permanently damaged. Divers and snorkellers should heed the requests of instructors *not* to touch or tread on coral – if you kill the coral, you'll eventually kill or chase away the fish, too. Overall, the paramount guideline for preserving the ecology and beauty of reefs is to take nothing with you, leave nothing behind. Other considerations:

- Do not touch or feed fish, and minimise your disturbance of marine animals. In particular, do not ride on the backs of turtles as this causes them great anxiety. Feeding fish may disturb their normal eating habits, encourage aggressive behaviour or be detrimental to their health.

- Do not touch or remove any marine life or coral, dead or alive, from the sea or beach. Dragging equipment across the reef can also do serious damage. Polyps can be damaged by even the gentlest of contact. Never stand on coral – instead use a jetty (or boat) to reach the water, even if the coral looks solid and robust.

- Be conscious of your fins. Even without contact, the surge from heavy fin strokes near the reef can damage delicate organisms. When treading water in shallow reef areas, take care not to kick up clouds of sand. Settling sand can easily smother the delicate organisms of the reef.

- Do not throw any rubbish into the sea or leave it on the beach. Plastics in particular are a serious threat to marine life. Turtles can mistake plastic for jellyfish and eat it.

- Ensure that boat anchors are on buoys, and not attached to precious coral, and take care not to ground boats on coral.

- Practise and maintain proper buoyancy control. Major damage can be done by divers descending too fast and colliding with the reef.

- Resist the temptation to buy coral or shells. Aside from the ecological damage, taking marine souvenirs depletes the beauty of a site and spoils the enjoyment of others – and is illegal in Jordan.

THE AQUARIUM & CORAL GARDENS
Location: Offshore from the Royal Diving Club
Rating: Intermediate
Access: Shore or boat

The Aquarium is home to two main reefs separated by sand channels, and a spectacular fringing reef, distinguished by its giant wall of fire corals. Immediately south lies Coral Gardens, where a sloping bed of seagrass gives way to a scattering of bizarre coral heads adorned with purple and pink soft corals.

THE SAUDI BORDER WALL
Location: Just north of the Saudi Arabian border
Rating: Intermediate
Access: Shore or boat

Offering hard coral formations and dramatic scenery, the Saudi Border Wall is characterised by a sloping reef that drops quickly to a sheer wall. Turtles and napoleonfish often pass by, as do schools of jacks and the occasional white-tip reef or hammerhead shark.

SNORKELLING

Since the vast majority of dive sights in Jordan are accessible from the shore, snorkelling is an easy and rewarding way to explore the Red Sea. Note that all of the sites mentioned above are suitable for snorkelling.

Diving centres hire out flippers, mask and snorkel for around JD5 per day. Although you can simply enter the water at any spot along the coast, snorkellers tend to gravitate towards the private beaches at the Royal Diving Club and Club Murjan.

If you're interested in hiring a guide, ask at the dive centres about the cost of joining a scuba-diving trip. Diving staff are generally happy to take a few snorkellers along, and some spots are easier to access if you have a local point them out.

SLEEPING & EATING

One decision that divers and snorkellers will inevitably have to make is choosing to stay either in Aqaba (p254) or south along the coast.

DIVING & SNORKELLING

The main advantage of staying in Aqaba is that you can choose from a wide variety of accommodation and eating options. Along the coast, however, you are more limited, though all three places described here are picturesque and tranquil spots to spend a few nights, and all have on-site bars and restaurants.

The other thing to consider is transport. If you're staying along the coast, it is helpful to have a car if you want to head into town. However, you can always call a cab, and hotels will pick you up in Aqaba with advanced reservations. If you're staying in Aqaba and planning on going diving, note that most operators will arrange transport to the dive sites.

Bedouin Garden Village (☎ 079 5602521; camping per person JD3, dm JD12, d JD36; meals around JD5; 🏊 ✖) Sun worshippers and dive bums alike will love this funky little spot, which aims to bring a bit of Dahab-style Bedouin flair to Jordan. Drawing inspiration from the famous backpacker town in the Sinai, the Bedouin Garden Village offers a clutch of cosy rooms and camping pitches. However, the real appeal of the village is swapping stories with fellow travellers beneath the canopy of the Bedouin tent.

Marina Plaza Hotel (☎ 2017222; www.talabay .jo; s/d from JD85/115; 🏊 ✖ 💻) This boutique hotel is the first property to open at Tala Bay, an ambitious project that will eventu-ally include several hotels and residences, a marina, a golf course and a water-sports club. Fortunately, the developers are work-ing hard to minimise their impact upon the environment as demanded by the Red Sea Aqaba Marine Park management. Al-though Tala Bay is still very much a work in progress, the understated luxury on offer at the Marina Plaza is a promising sign of things to come.

Coral Bay Resort (☎ 2017035; s/d from JD55/65; 🏊 ✖ 💻) Part of the Royal Diving Club, this excellent midrange option is a quin-tessential divers' paradise. If you're plan-ning on taking a dive course, or arranging a lengthy dive package, you couldn't ask for a better base. Simple, elegant rooms are awash in bright motifs, though guests here seem determined to spend as much time as possible exploring the ocean depths.

GETTING AROUND

Minibuses (less than JD1) leave from near the entrance to Aqaba castle on King Hus-sein St for the Saudi border via the southern beaches, camps, dive sites and Royal Diving Club, passing en route the ferry terminal for boats to Egypt. Minibuses returning to Aqaba can be full of construction work-ers heading off shift from 2pm to 3pm. A private taxi from central Aqaba to the ferry terminal shouldn't cost more than a few dinars.

Directory

CONTENTS

> **BOOK YOUR STAY ONLINE**
>
> For more accommodation reviews and recommendations by Lonely Planet authors, check out lonelyplanet.com/hotels. You'll find the true, insider lowdown on the best places to stay. Reviews are thorough and independent. Best of all, you can book online.

ACCOMMODATION

Jordan has accommodation to suit most budgets, although away from the main tourist centres there's limited choice. Jordan is so compact, however, that most attractions can easily be visited in day trips from the main towns.

Prices are highest during the two peak seasons, which are from September to October and from March to mid-May. Holiday weekends are also peak times in Aqaba and at the Dead Sea resorts.

High inflation and increased tourism are contributing to escalating prices. Although prices were accurate at the time of writing, expect increased prices.

Camping

For many people, spending a night under the stars – or at least under canvas – is a highlight of a trip to Jordan. One popular option is to sleep in a traditional 'house of hair' at a Bedouin camp in Wadi Rum. Facilities in these goat-wool tents are basic but it's a great experience – see p272 for details.

Another beautiful area for camping is Dana Nature Reserve (open March to November). Intended for those who are happy to pay extra to wake up in the wilds, the tents fill up quickly. Book in advance through Wild Jordan (p95).

Camping with your own tent is permitted in a few places in southern Jordan, especially in the desert surrounding Wadi Rum. Camping 'off piste' in the north is more problematic, not least because you'll have competition for the best spots from the Bedouin and it's surprisingly hard to find a secluded place to pitch a tent.

Bringing a tent to save money on accommodation isn't cost effective as camping is rarely possible without your own transport. Besides, cheap rooms are plentiful in areas close to the major sites of interest.

Hotels

From opulent pleasure palaces on the Dead Sea to eco-friendly lodges in the nature reserves, Jordan offers some interesting hotel accommodation. Reservations are recommended during peak seasons, especially at the Dead Sea Resorts, and for midrange and top-end hotels in Aqaba, Wadi Musa and the nature reserves.

PRACTICALITIES

- **Electricity** Jordan's electricity supply is 220V, 50 AC. Sockets are mostly of a local two-pronged variety, although some places use European two-pronged and British three-pronged sockets.

- **Newspapers & Magazines** There are several English-language papers available, including the daily *Jordan Times* (250 fils). Imported newspapers include *The Times* (JD4), *Guardian Weekly* (JD2), *Le Monde* (JD2.700) and *Le Figaro* (JD2.250). The *International Herald Tribune* (JD1.250) has a regional section from Lebanon's *Daily Star*. Magazines include *Time* (JD2.700) and *Newsweek* (JD2.900).

- **Radio** Radio Jordan is on 96.3 FM and the BBC World Service is on 1323AM. Try 99.6 FM for popular hits.

- **TV** Channel 2 of Jordan TV broadcasts programs in French and English. Satellite stations such as the BBC, CNN, MTV and Al-Jazeera can be found in most midrange and top-end hotels.

- **Weights & Measures** Jordan uses the metric system. See the inside front cover for a conversion table.

Accommodation prices in this book (see inside front cover) include breakfast, unless otherwise stated. Breakfast varies from a humble round of bread with a triangle of processed cheese in budget hotels to a delicious assortment of locally made yoghurt, hummus, *fuul* and olives in midrange hotels. The buffet-style breakfasts at top-end hotels can set a hungry hiker up for a week.

Hotels indicated as offering 'air-con' have both cooling and heating appliances available in at least some of their rooms.

BUDGET

Budget rooms are available in most towns and vary from stark and basic to simple and homely. Most are spotlessly clean.

Private rooms start from JD8/16 for singles/doubles, with less stark rooms with a private bathroom costing around JD20/25. Prices are negotiable, especially during quieter seasons. Dorm rooms are not common, but most budget places have 'triples'

(rooms with three beds), which you can ask to share with other travellers, cutting the cost of accommodation considerably. In summer you can even sleep on the roof in some places for about JD3 per person. There are no youth hostels in Jordan.

Some things to consider: many budget places are located above shops and cafés that can be noisy at night; avoid windowless rooms that are stifling hot in summer; and winter in Jordan is bitterly cold so ensure the heater is working before checking in.

Payment usually needs to be made in cash in Jordanian dinars.

MIDRANGE

Midrange hotels offer the best value for money in Jordan. They are often privately owned by families who take pride in welcoming their guests. The owners are a fount of local knowledge and can provide assistance in catching transport or advising on sights of interest. Some even organise their own tours. Most family-run hotels offer some kind of home cooking for breakfast and guests may even be asked to join the family if they have ordered an evening meal.

There is at least one midrange hotel in towns you're likely to visit, with a good selection in Amman, Madaba, Wadi Musa (near Petra) and Aqaba. Rooms in midrange hotels usually have colour TV (sometimes featuring satellite stations such as CNN), fridge, heater (essential in winter), telephone, reliable hot water and a private bathroom.

Prices start at about JD30/45 for singles/doubles. Negotiation is usually possible, especially if you're staying for several days. Many midrange hotels are starting to accept credit cards, but it's best to ask before checking in.

TOP END

There are some excellent top-end hotels in Amman, Wadi Musa (near Petra) and Aqaba (for the Dead Sea, see opposite). With liveried staff, welcome drinks on arrival, marble foyers and luxurious rooms, they live up to their counterparts in other parts of the Middle East. Most have a travel agency within their shopping arcades from where you can hire a car and organise hotel bookings for the next part of your trip.

Most of the top-end hotels are owned by international chains, but they invariably reflect the local character of Jordan, with Arabian-style interior design, options for high-quality Middle Eastern dining, shops selling fine Jordanian handicrafts and bookshops with a selection of English language titles on Jordan.

Independent travellers can often negotiate a walk-in rate. Outside peak seasons and holidays (when booking is essential), you may find a world-class room for a midrange price.

A tax and service charge of 26% (see p298) is added to the bill in top-end hotels, although it's worth checking to see if this has already been included in a discounted rate. Major credit cards are accepted in all top-end hotels.

Rental Accommodation

In Amman, the best places to check for apartments and houses to rent are the accommodation listings in the English-language newspapers, cultural centre noticeboards (p91), and the noticeboard at Books@café (p109). There is also a useful noticeboard in the office of the University of Jordan Language Center (p293). For longer stays, wander around the suburbs of Shmeisani, or between the 1st and 5th circles: signs advertising places to rent are often displayed in residence or shop windows.

It costs about JD200 to JD400 per month for a furnished apartment in a reasonable area of Amman; a little less if it's unfurnished. A furnished apartment or small house in a less salubrious area is possible for as little as JD100 to JD200 per month, but for this price don't expect everything to work.

Short-term rentals are available in Aqaba, where prices for a furnished two-bedroom apartment with a kitchen start at JD15 per night in the low season and JD25 in the peak season. Most apartments in Aqaba can only be rented for a minimum of one week, however, and must be pre-booked in the peak season.

Resorts

If you have only one night's luxury during your visit to Jordan, plan to stay in one of the Dead Sea resorts (see p176). Not only are these state-of-the-art hotels worth a visit in their own right, but they also offer the best access to the Dead Sea – an area where there is next to no alternative accommodation. Residents of one resort can also use the facilities of the neighbouring hotels, which can take care of several nights'

TOP FIVE PLACES TO STAY

In Jordan, top beds don't necessarily cost top dollar. The following high five are drawn from all categories of accommodation and have been chosen because of the uniqueness of the experience they offer.

Bedouin camp, Wadi Rum (p272) The sky's the limit for those who stay in one of the Bedouin camps in Wadi Rum. Unfurl your mat under the stars and let singing youths, together with the snorts of grumbling camels and the whistle of mint tea over the fire, lull you to sleep.

Feinan Lodge, Dana (p210) Found at the end of a long, hard day's hike through the Dana Nature Reserve, this lodge is more grail than guesthouse. With its monastic appearance and vegetarian supper served by candlelight (electric lights are not used), this eco-lodge offers an experience that hovers on the sublime. If hiking is not your thing, you can always cheat and drive round the long way – at the risk of losing much of the magic.

Mövenpick Resort & Spa, Dead Sea (p176) While floating in one of the infinity pools, with a carrot cocktail in one hand and a jet of water massaging the other, it's easy to see why the spa at the heart of this resort is billed as the best in the Middle East. Begin in the primordial mud at the Dead Sea shore-side and work your way up to heaven in the hotel's spangled-ceiling bar.

Sofitel Taybet Zaman, Tayyibeh village (p241) With the rose-tinted sandstone typical of Petra's famous landscape spread beneath the lintels of this unusual hotel, you won't mind being a half-hour drive from the entrance to the site. Indeed, the sequestered nature of the accommodation, in renovated local village houses, is part of its unique appeal.

St George's Church Pilgrim House, Madaba (p189) For those who want their night's sleep to matter, there's no better place to head for than this ascetic guesthouse, located beside St George's Church, home of Madaba's famous mosaic map. If Father Innocent is in residence, he'll happily explain how the guesthouse profits are used to benefit local underprivileged boys.

worth of entertainment in an area with no local nightlife.

Apart from the Dead Sea, there are also resorts in and around Aqaba (p256) – including the flagship resorts of the Mövenpick and Intercontinental chains. With access to the calm waters of the Red Sea, multiple pools, gyms and a selection of top-notch restaurants, they are bringing a touch of class to Jordan's second city.

ACTIVITIES

Jordan offers some of the best outdoor activities in the Middle East, from hiking and climbing in stunning landscapes to painstakingly piecing together the past on an archaeological dig. Don't head home without trying at least a couple of these fantastic adventures. For information on scuba diving and snorkelling, see the Diving & Snorkelling chapter (p277).

Aero Sports

The **Royal Aero Sports Club of Jordan** (☎ 03-2058050; www.royalaeroclub.com) offers microlighting, skydiving, gliding, paragliding and even hot-air ballooning (by arrangement) over the dramatic scenery of Wadi Rum. Ballooning costs about JD130 per person for a minimum of two people and rides take from one to two hours depending on the weather.

Archaeological Digs

Real-life archaeological fieldwork is nothing like an Indiana Jones movie, though it can be an incredibly rewarding activity, especially if you uncover the material remains of the ancients. In Jordan, this is in fact a very real possibility as a significant number of sites across the country are in the process of being excavated. Even if you don't have an extensive background in archaeology, it's not too difficult to grab a spot on one of these digs.

If you're interested in conducting archaeological fieldwork, keep in mind two very important things: first, you will need to plan well ahead if you want to participate in an expedition; and second, you will most likely need to pay a fee for your volunteer placement. In order to gain access to sites, project leaders must obtain permits and complete security forms, which can take up to six months for all possible bureaucratic

niceties. Furthermore, while archaeologists are happy to support energetic and motivated amateurs, there are a limited number of volunteer positions available. However, if you are an aspiring archaeologist, or you simply want to gain exposure to this fascinating discipline, it's certainly worth the effort to join a dig.

For starters, do your homework and find out who is conducting which digs, and where and when they are taking place. To help facilitate your search, we've included a list below of various organisations involved in Jordanian archaeology. When you contact project leaders, be sure to sell yourself as there is strong competition for openings. If you have special skills (like photography or drafting), have travelled in the region or worked on other digs (or similar group projects), let them know – it'll certainly increase your chances of landing a spot.

American Center for Oriental Research (ACOR; www.bu.edu/acor) Prepares an extensive annual listing of field-work opportunities in Jordan and the Middle East.

American Schools of Oriental Research (www.asor .org) This organisation supports the study of the culture and history of the Near East.

JORDANIAN ARCHAEOLOGY ON THE WEB

- **East of the Jordan** (www.asor.org/pubs /macdonald.pdf) Has the full text of Burton MacDonald's book on the territories and sites of the Hebrew scriptures.

- **Franciscan Archaeological Institute** (http://198.62.75.5/opt/xampp/custodia/01fai .php) Presents exquisite detail on excavations in the Madaba and Mt Nebo regions.

- **Madaba Plains Project** (www.madaba plains.org/hesban) An overview of Andrews University's excavation at Tell Hesban on the Madaba Plains.

- **Petra: The Great Temple Excavation** (www.brown.edu/departments/anthropology /petra) The history of Brown University's excavation of the Great Temple of Petra.

- **Virtual Karak Resources Project** (www .vkrp.org) A comprehensive website dedicated to the archaeological and historical study of Karak Castle.

Archaeological Institute of America (AIA; www
.archaeological.org) The largest and oldest archaeology organisation in America is a valuable resource for information.
Biblical Archaeological Society (www.bib-arch.org)
Produces the magazine *Biblical Archaeological Review*, runs
archaeological tours and lists volunteer openings.
Council for British Research in the Levant (CBRL;
www.cbrl.org.uk) British Academy–sponsored institute
with research centres in Amman & Jerusalem.
University of Jordan (Map p87; ☎ 06-5355000; www
.ju.edu.jo) The archaeology department at this Amman-
based university is a good contact point.
University of Sydney (www.arts.usyd.edu.au/departs
/archaeology) This prestigious Australian university runs a
highly reputable field project at Pella.

Camel Treks

The camel is no longer a common form
of transport for Bedouin; most now prefer
the ubiquitous pick-up truck – in fact, it's
not unusual to see a Bedouin transporting
a prized camel in the back of a Toyota. For
visitors, however, one truly rewarding experience is a camel trek. This costs about JD30
for two hours: choose a mounted rather
than a walking guide for a more authentic
experience. Enterprising Bedouin are happy
to take visitors on three- to six-night camel
treks from Wadi Rum to Aqaba or Petra (see
p269), as well as shorter trips.

Cycling

There are some great places to cycle in
Jordan, but it's not what one could call a
developed sport here. Most cycling involves
bringing your own bicycle and spare parts,
and sorting out a route along roads with
few amenities that are too hot or too cold
for comfort for half the year. If none of
this fazes you, then contact the **Cycling Association** (www.cycling-jordan.com) for help with
route-planning and see p315 for more
information.

Dana Nature Reserve has a guided desert
cycling trail and there are 10 mountain bikes
for hire from Feinan Lodge (see Cycling,
p209).

Hiking

Hiking is an exhilarating activity in Jordan, not least because of the pristine and
varied quality of the landscape and the historical allusions that underlie almost every
path. Don't expect an organised network of
routes, with signposts and watering holes

en route: most hiking in Jordan is an unso-
phisticated, ad hoc affair passing through
small villages where the welcome is often
as warm as the weather.

Hikes in Jordan take longer, and take
more out of you, than you'd imagine –
walking in sand is not easy, nor is going uphill in the hot sun. Allow plenty of time to
linger and enjoy the view, chat with passers-
by or simply sit in the shade during the
heat of the day.

Although finding reliable maps is a
problem, there are some good books detailing the most popular routes (see Books,
below). It's best to buy both maps and books
abroad as their availability in Jordan is
sporadic.

Most wadis are unsafe during winter
(November to February) due to the danger
of flash floods. Paths are often washed away
and so routes change frequently. Bear in
mind that Global Positioning System (GPS)
units and mobile phones may not function
between steep canyon walls.

The best places for hiking in Jordan
are Ajloun Nature Reserve (p135), Dana
Nature Reserve (p207) and Wadi Mujib
Nature Reserve (p180) where most trails require a guide. For more DIY options, there
are some exciting hikes in Petra (p230) and
in Wadi Rum (p270). Bedouin guides also
offer accompanied hikes along the old caravan routes that link these two spectacular
places. Also see the boxed text, p12, for
Jordan's top five-day hikes.

Several longer routes are also possible
with a tent. In particular, Dana to Petra is
an excellent four-day trek that takes you
through Wadi Feinan, Wadi Ghuweir and
Little Petra. Also see the boxed text, p290.

BOOKS

British climbers Tony Howard and Di Taylor have spent much of their lives exploring and mapping the hiking, trekking and
rock-climbing possibilities in Jordan. Their
books include the detailed *Treks & Climbs
in Wadi Rum* and the more condensed
Walks & Scrambles in Wadi Rum, published
in Jordan by Al-Kutba. They have also
produced the highly usable *Jordan: Walks,
Treks, Caves, Climbs & Canyons,* published
by Cicerone (published by Interlink in the
USA as *Walking in Jordan*). These books
are only sporadically available in Jordan.

WADI WALKING

Jordan's most exciting hikes are via the lush gorges, waterfalls, pools and palm trees of its dramatic wadis (seasonally dry riverbeds). You'll need some help arranging a hike in a wadi (see Tours, p314 and Hiking Agencies, below), largely because you need transport to drop you off at the beginning and pick you up at the end of your hike (generally a different location and accessed from different roads). Moreover, route-finding is difficult (there are no defined trails) and trails change year to year due to seasonal flooding. Hikes are only safe from late March or early April to early October, and you should always check the weather forecast for rain and get local advice before heading off on a hike.

The following are Jordan's best wadi options and the routes are fully described in Di Taylor and Tony Howard's *Jordan: Walks, Treks, Caves, Climbs, Canyons*.

Wadi bin Hammad A 10km day-hike from a set of hot springs to the Dead Sea Highway, 6km north of Mazra'a. The hot springs and upper (eastern) stretches are popular with day trippers, especially on Fridays. The full hike ends at the Dead Sea, or alternatively you can just do the first 90 minutes through the dramatic narrow gorge. It's a one-hour drive from the King's Highway to the start of the trail, but it's hard to find without a guide; the turn-off is 11km north of Karak.

Wadi Ghuweir This full-day hike (12km, 7hrs) from Mansoura (near Shobak) to Wadi Feinan takes you past dramatic geological formations. The trail is accessed from near Shobak via a steep downhill drive, or you can start from Dana Nature Reserve (p205).

Wadi Hasa This moderate two-day, 24km trek runs through one of the most beautiful wadis in Jordan. It's all downhill, often in water, through a water playground of pools and waterfalls (including a hot waterfall) and changing scenery. There is currently a police check along the road to the start of the trail. The full trek ends near Safi.

Wadi Numeira This wadi starts 10km north of Lot's Cave (p181) and quickly leads to a dramatic *siq* with pools and waterfalls. The upper wadi is only accessed via a 1.5m rope ladder.

Wadi Yabis This day-hike (12km, 6-7hrs) is accessed from Hallaweh village, 15km from Ishfateena, north of Ajloun. The trail descends 700m past a spring and 2000-year-old olive trees, down a canyon to a 50m waterfall and on to Wadi Rayyan dam. Spring brings wonderful wildflowers and is the best time to visit.

Wadi Zarqa Ma'in This hike (4km, 4hrs) runs from the hot-spring resort of Hammamat Ma'in to the Dead Sea. Check trail regulations at the Hammamat Ma'in spa.

Although it can be difficult to find, *Trekking & Canyoning in the Jordanian Dead Sea Rift* by Itai Haviv contains numerous trekking and canyoning routes in the wadis of Central Jordan; its cultural and environmental insights alone make it worth the trouble to find.

HIKING AGENCIES

The **Royal Society for the Conservation of Nature** (RSCN; Map p94; ☎ 06-4616523; www.rscn.org.jo; PO Box 1215, Amman 11941) offers a wide range of guided hikes in Jordan's nature reserves and can also arrange long-distance treks if given prior notice. Rates vary from JD15 for a two-hour guided hike up to JD85 for a full-day trek.

For individual or group adventure hikes that include abseiling and canyoning, **Terhaal Encounters** (☎ 06-5866607; www.terhaal.com) is recommended. Their aim is to make Jordan's natural wonders accessible while minimising environmental impact and bringing benefits to local communities.

Desert Guides Company (☎ 06-5527230; www.desertguidescompany.com) also specialises in adventure hikes, treks and climbs throughout Jordan.

The best way to organise a trek in Petra or Wadi Rum is to arrange one through the respective visitor centre (see p220 and p251). If you engage a Bedouin guide independently, make sure you understand exactly what services are on offer to avoid disappointment on either side. Rates vary (and are negotiable) between JD30 to JD100, depending on the skills required for each hike or scramble.

Yamaan Safady (☎ 077-7222101; www.adventurejordan.com) is of the best hiking guides. From March to October he leads weekly hiking trips for expats and locals to places such as Wadi Yabis, Wadi Hasa and beyond, as part of the Adventure Jordan Hiking Club. Costs for day hikes generally start at JD25 per person including transport and guide.

For a list of general agencies overseas, see p314.

WHAT TO BRING

Lightweight trousers and long-sleeved shirts are culturally sensitive and best for the terrain. Other essentials include a hat, sunscreen, water bottle, torch (flashlight) and insect repellent. Lightweight walking boots are ideal, together with hiking sandals and a watertight bag for wet wadi walks.

WHEN TO GO

The best time for hiking is the middle of spring (mid-March to late April), when it's not too hot, the rains have finished, flowers are blooming and wells are full. Always check local conditions before setting out as flash floods can occur throughout the spring and may make wadis impassable.

Another good time is from late September to mid-October when it's dry but not excessively hot.

Rain occurs from November to March, making it dangerous to hike or camp in narrow wadis as flash floods can sweep unheralded out of the hills. It's also very cold for camping.

Horse Riding

It's possible to explore the deserts around Wadi Rum on Arabian stallions, though this recommended for experienced riders only. **Rum Horses** (☎ 03-2033508, 077-7471960; www.desertguides.com) is a professional camel- and horse-trekking agency located on the approach road to Wadi Rum.

There are also opportunities to ride in the hills above Petra. Several of the Bedouin horse owners at Petra will saddle you up with a spirited horse, but again, prior knowledge of horse riding is necessary and don't expect a helmet (see p237).

Hot Springs

Jordan boasts dozens of thermal hot-water springs, where the water is usually about 35°C to 45°C. The water contains potassium, magnesium and calcium, among other minerals with reputed health benefits. The most popular spring is Hammamat Ma'in, near the Dead Sea (see p177). Other popular spots around Jordan include Hammamat Burbita and Hammamat Afra, west of the King's Highway near Tafila (see p205), and Al-Himma springs, close to the northern border with Israel and the Palestinian Territories (see p145).

Women are likely to feel most comfortable at Hammamat Ma'in, which has an area for families and unaccompanied women, and the public baths at Al-Himma, which allocates special times solely for ladies.

Rock Climbing

Wadi Rum offers some challenging and unique rock climbing. The most accessible and popular climbs are detailed in the excellent books written by Tony Howard and Di Taylor (see Books, p289). Guides are necessary, and you'll need to bring your own climbing gear. See p271 for more details.

For more information go to www.rumguides.com and www.wadirum.net.

Running

Long-distance runners can combine a trip to Jordan with the annual Dead Sea Marathon. Starting at the 7th Circle in Amman, it involves a 50km run (individually or in a relay) to the Dead Sea at Amman Beach, as well as a half marathon, a 10km fun run and a kids run of 4km. In case you think that this is the preserve of a few mad locals, bear in mind that around 1000 runners take part annually. The race generally takes place on the second Friday in April so if you fancy running below zero, check the official website (www.deadseamarathon .com) for details.

The local branch of the **Hash House Harriers** (http://hashemitehhh.googlepages.com), dubbed 'drinkers with a running problem' on their website, organise local runs each Monday from Amman.

Turkish Baths

A great antidote for aching muscles, the *hammam* is otherwise known as a Turkish bath. The best baths are in Amman, Madaba, Wadi Musa and Aqaba and prices are around JD20, including a massage. At the better places you'll sweat it out in a dry- or wet-steam bath and then be scrubbed with woollen gloves, soaped with olive-oil soap, massaged and laid to rest on a hot marble platform.

Women are welcome, usually at separate times to men; call ahead so that a female attendant can be organised. See the boxed texts, p292 and p103, for personal accounts by the authors!

DIRECTORY

BATHING WITH BRUISERS IN JORDAN'S HAMMANS   *Jenny Walker*

If you thought you felt sore after a long day's hike, then just wait until you see what they do with you at the local *hammam* (Turkish bath). The large, muscular attendants (male or female, depending on your sex) could easily retrain as Sumo wrestlers and you can rely on them to find parts of the body you didn't know you had.

In fact, they'll remove parts of the body you didn't know you had, as the art of extreme exfoliation counts as one of their many talents.

Don't expect phrases like 'no' and 'please don't' – uttered in either Arabic or English – to help you: more often they invite an almost sadistic acceleration of pummelling, scrubbing and slap-ping, accompanied by snorts of laughter. In fact, a sense of humour seems to be a prerequisite on both sides of the fluffy white towels handed out so thoughtfully in the antechamber of the baths: in emergencies (as when a nose hair is plucked without warning or two ears are lifted independently of the scalp) these towels can be used as a flag of surrender by battered bathers to signal that enough is enough.

Don't try to strut off with attitude, though, nor look back in anger, as there is always enough soap on the polished marble tiles to make sure you aren't the one having the last laugh.

If, by now, the prospect of being bullied in the bath is putting you off the idea altogether, don't let it. The bizarre part about the experience is that the moment you step out of the steaming pools of indistinct water, the minute you expose your newly scraped and kneaded flesh to the outside air, you'll feel so rejuvenated that you'll be booking your next appointment before you leave.

BUSINESS HOURS

Opening times vary from town to town, and from office to office across the country, but the following table gives an idea of business hours in Jordan. Many sights, government departments and banks close earlier in winter.

During the month of Ramadan, working hours are greatly reduced.

OPENING TIMES

Place	Times	Days	Notes
Banks	8.30am-3pm	Sun-Thu	
Government departments	8am-3pm	Sat-Thu	Some close Sat
Money-changers	9pm-9pm	daily	
Post offices	8am-6pm	Sun-Thu	Some open Fri until 2pm
Shops & businesses	9am-8pm	Sat-Thu	Some close 2-4pm
Souqs (markets)	9am-8pm	daily	
Tourist offices	8am-3pm	Sat-Thu	
Visitor centres	8am-6pm	daily	See relevant destination

CHILDREN

In common with the rest of the Middle East, children are universally adored in Jordan.

Children are instant ice-breakers and they'll invite plenty of contact with local people – especially as so few visitors bring their youngsters here. People will go out of their way to help you or make your family feel welcome, especially on buses and in shops, hotels and restaurants.

A few precautions can help make travelling with children a success: avoid the extreme heat of summer, stick to bottled mineral water, avoid peeled fresh fruit and washed salads (the most likely source of stomach complaints), and check that fresh dairy products are made with pasteurised milk.

Powdered milk is available, but disposable nappies (diapers) are hard to find outside Amman and Aqaba.

Although there are very few designated attractions for children beyond playground swings, the novelty of floating in the Dead Sea, playing on the beach or hotel pools at Aqaba, snorkelling in the Red Sea, exploring castles at Karak, Shobak and Ajloun, riding a camel at Wadi Rum or donkey at Petra, and checking out the ostriches and oryx at Shaumari Wildlife Reserve should keep most kids amused.

See also Amman for Children, p104, for activities in the capital city.

For more comprehensive advice about travelling with children, pick up a copy of Lonely Planet's *Travel with Children* by Cathy Lanigan.

CLIMATE CHARTS

Spring (March to mid-May) is a wonderful time to visit Jordan as the climate in all parts of the country is clement, with the occasional shower, and the countryside is studded with wildflowers, including Jordan's famous black iris.

The other good time to visit is autumn (September to mid-November) when the temperature cools off after the heat of summer and the Dead Sea and Red Sea are pleasantly warm.

Climate in Jordan is conditioned partly by altitude, with the lowest areas such as the Jordan Valley and Gulf of Aqaba experiencing the most extreme summer heat and humidity (mid-May to August). The hilly central and northern areas, in contrast, can be very cold in winter (November to February) when snow often falls over the high ground.

Also see When to Go, p20, for more information on the best time to travel.

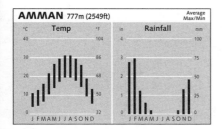

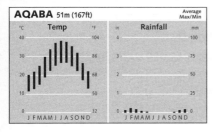

COURSES
Cooking

For details about the fun and worthwhile cooking course in Petra, see the boxed text, p84.

Language

For those enchanted enough by the Arab world to want to learn the language, there are some opportunities in Amman:

British Council (☎ 06-4636147; www.britishcouncil.org /jordan.htm) Can put individuals in touch with a private tutor.

University of Jordan Language Center (☎ 06-5355000, ext 2370; www.ju.edu.jo; University of Amman) Offers tailormade courses with private instruction for individuals and small groups, geared to students' special interests. Rates are US$50 per hour per group, for groups of one to six students.

CUSTOMS REGULATIONS

Drugs and weapons are prohibited, as are pornographic films, tapes (cassettes) and magazines.

Duty-free allowances for 'nonresidents' (tourists) are: 200 cigarettes or 25 cigars or 200g of tobacco (a charge of JD3.75 for each additional 200 cigarettes, up to a maximum of 2000); 1L of alcohol (a charge of JD2.91 for each additional litre, up to a maximum of 4L); a 'reasonable amount of perfume for personal use'; and gifts up to the value of JD50 or the equivalent of US$150.

DANGERS & ANNOYANCES

Jordan is very safe to visit and, despite local dissatisfaction with Iraqi immigration, you are unlikely to feel any hint of the turmoil of neighbouring countries.

Two incidents in Amman in recent times (the 2005 Al-Qaeda suicide bombing of three hotels, and the 2007 shooting of tourists by a lone gunman – see p95) momentarily cast doubt over Jordan's peaceful reputation. With so much at stake in terms of revenue, however, every effort is being made by Jordanian authorities to ensure the safety of travellers within the country.

The best general advice for travellers is to be vigilant in the cities without being paranoid (by cooperating, for example, with security checks in hotel foyers). Conversations of a stridently political nature should also be avoided with casual acquaintances.

DIRECTORY

GOVERNMENT TRAVEL ADVICE

The following government websites offer travel advisories and information on current hot spots.

Australian Department of Foreign Affairs & Trade (☎ 1300 139 281; www.smarttraveller.gov.au)

British Foreign & Commonwealth Office (☎ 0845-850-2829; www.fco.gov.uk/countryadvice)

Canadian Department of Foreign Affairs & International Trade (☎ 800-267 6788; www.dfait-maeci.gc.ca)

US State Department (☎ 888-407 4747; http://travel.state.gov)

Minefields

A minefield comprising 86,756 mines along the Jordan–Syria border is well off the tourist trail, but if you're in the area take heed of warnings not to enter. It's hoped that Jordan will be mine free by May 2009, the 10-year anniversary of Jordan's signature of the UN mine-ban convention.

Public Disorder

During rare political or economic crises, occasional protests and acts of civil disobedience occur. There are also frequent demonstrations in support of the Palestinians. These usually take place in Karak, Tafila and Ma'an, and in the university areas of Irbid, Mu'tah and northern Amman. Foreigners are unlikely to be targeted during these protests, but it is best not to get involved.

The best sources of current information are the English-language newspapers published in Amman or your embassy/consulate in Jordan.

Sexual Harassment

Women who have travelled in other Middle Eastern countries, especially Turkey and Israel, will find that Jordan is comparatively relaxed and hassle free. Women who have not visited the region before, however, may be annoyed at the leering and harassment from local men. See p301 and p304 later in this chapter for more advice for solo and women travellers.

Theft & Crime

As with Arab Muslims across the region, Jordanians prize honesty and are anxious to make visitors feel secure in their country. That said, given their relative poverty there is a great temptation for some people in tourist areas to make a quick buck either through scams or petty theft. One scam to be wary of is during taxi rides in Amman and other towns. The fare quoted on the meter is in fils, not in dinars, and visitors often misunderstand this when paying. Perhaps understandably, it is rare for a taxi driver to point out this mistake. Another minor scam is to claim something is genuinely locally crafted as part of a profit-share scheme, when in fact it is imported from abroad. Similarly, so-called 'ancient' oil lamps and coins are seldom what they seem.

Theft is less common, but it doesn't harm to take some simple precautions, like carrying wallets or purses in a front pocket, and avoiding carrying too much cash. A cotton money belt is a good idea and so is hiding some cash and a copy of your passport in a pair of socks in your luggage.

Leaving your bag under the watchful eye of a member of staff at a bus station or hotel is generally safe, but a shared hotel room is only as good as your fellow travellers: avoid jumping to conclusions about the hotel staff if something goes missing. Be careful late at night outside nightclubs in Amman: pickpockets and muggers are attracted by the patronage of intoxicated, vulnerable and comparatively wealthy foreigners.

The military keep a low profile and you're unlikely to experience anything but friendliness, honesty and hospitality from them, in common with their compatriots. It's generally safe for men to walk around day or night in well-lit areas of Amman and other towns, but women should be more cautious.

DISCOUNT CARDS

Student discounts are occasionally available at tourist sites on production of an International Student Identity Card (ISIC) – university ID cards are not accepted.

EMBASSIES & CONSULATES

The following embassies and consulates are in Amman. Egypt also has a consulate in Aqaba (see the boxed text, p303, for visas for neighbouring countries). In general, offices are open 9am to 11am Sunday to

Thursday for visa applications and 1pm to 3pm for collecting visas.

Australia (Map p87; ☎ 06-5807000; www.jordan .embassy.gov.au; 3 Youssef Abu Shahhout, Deir Ghbar)

Egypt Consulate (Map p248; ☎ 03-2016171; cnr Al-Isteglal & Al-Akhatal Sts, Aqaba; ☼ 8am-3pm Sun-Thu) Embassy (Map p90; ☎ 06-5605175; fax 5604082; 22 Qortubah St, Jebel Amman; ☼ 9am-noon Sun-Thu) Between 4th and 5th circles.

France (Map p90; ☎ 06-4604630; www.ambafrance -jo.org; Al-Mutanabbi St, Jebel Amman)

Germany (Map p90; ☎ 06-5930367; www.amman .diplo.de; 31 Bin Ghazi St, Jebel Amman) Between 4th and 5th circles.

Iraq (Map p90; ☎ 06-4623175; fax 4619172; Al-Kulliyah al-Islamiyah St, Jebel Amman) Near the 1st circle.

Israel Consulate (Map p99; ☎ 06-5503529; Maysaloon St, Shmeisani)

Lebanon (Map p90; ☎ 06-5929111; fax 5929113; Al-Neel St, Abdoun) Near the UK embassy.

Netherlands (Map p90; ☎ 06-5902200; www .netherlandsembassy.com.jo; 22 Ibrahim Ayoub St) Near the 4th circle.

New Zealand Consulate (Map p94; ☎ 06-4636720; fax 4634349; 99 Al-Malek al-Hussein St, Downtown) On the 4th floor of the Khalaf Building.

Saudi Arabia Consulate (Map p90; ☎ 06-5924154; fax 5921154; 1st Circle, Jebel Amman)

Syria (Map p90; ☎ 06-5920684; Abdoun Prince Hashem bin Al-Hussein St, Jebel Amman) Near the 4th circle.

UK (Map p90; ☎ 06-5909200; www.britain.org.jo; Dimashq St, Wadi Abdoun, Abdoun)

USA (Map p87; ☎ 06-5906000; http://usembassy -amman.org.jo; 20 Al-Umawiyeen St, Abdoun)

Yemen (Map p90; ☎ 06-5923771; Al-Ameer Hashem bin al-Hussein St, Abdoun Circle)

FESTIVALS & EVENTS

Jordan's best-known cultural event is the Jerash Festival of Culture and Arts (see the boxed text, p129). In summer (July and August), traditional concerts and plays are held at the Odeon and Roman Theatre in Amman, as well as in the towns of Salt and Fuheis.

Another summer festival is the **Global Village** (www.globalvillagejo.com) in the Marj al-Hamam area of Amman. Held in July and August it comprises an international carnival with funfair, shopping opportunities, theatre and local cultural entertainments.

A brand-new addition to the events circuit in Jordan is the **Jordan Rally** (www.jordan rally.com) held in April and organised by the

FIA World Rally Championship. See p67 for details.

A festival that may be of interest to music-loving travellers is **Distant Heat** (www .distantheat.com). Whether or not it lives up to its billing as one of the top 10 festivals in the Middle East, it's a fun event that 'highlights Jordan as a peaceful destination' and attracts a young crowd from around the region. The all-night party, featuring top international and local electronic-dance-music artists, is held at the end of July each year in Wadi Rum and often continues next day with beach pool parties in Aqaba.

FOOD

In this guide restaurants are ordered by price (not by author preference), starting with the cheapest. Venues have been chosen for the quality of the experience on offer in terms of the food, atmosphere and service, as well as their value for money.

A kebab sandwich or budget meal of roast chicken costs JD1 to JD3; a main dish in a midrange restaurant costs around JD4 to JD6; and a meal in a top-end restaurant costs from JD8 upwards. See p77 for more detailed information, and p296 for restrictions on eating and drinking during Ramadan.

GAY & LESBIAN TRAVELLERS

Homosexuality is illegal in most Islamic countries in the Middle East, but in Jordan (according to most sources) gay sex is legal and the age of consent is 16. Public displays of affection by heterosexuals are frowned upon and the same rules apply to gays and lesbians, although same-sex hand-holding is a common sign of friendship in Jordan.

There is a subdued underground gay scene in Amman – if you're keen to explore it, keep your enquiries discreet. Gay-friendly venues that attract young, gay and straight crowds include the multipurpose Books@café (p109) and the Blue Fig Café (p109). Other suggested meeting places are the top-end hotel bars in Amman.

Check www.gaymiddleeast.com and the gay and lesbian thread of Lonely Planet's Thorn Tree bulletin board (www.lonely planet.com) for more information.

HOLIDAYS

As the Islamic Hejira calendar is 11 days shorter than the Gregorian calendar, each

DIRECTORY

TABLE OF ISLAMIC HOLIDAYS					
Hejira Year	New Year	Prophet's Birthday	Ramadan Begins	Eid al-Fitr	Eid al-Adha
1430	29.12.08	09.03.09	22.08.09	20.09.09	27.11.09
1431	18.12.09	26.02.10	11.08.10	10.09.10	16.11.10
1432	07.12.10	15.02.11	01.08.11	31.08.11	05.11.11
1433	20.10.11	04.02.12	21.07.12	20.08.12	23.10.12

year Islamic holidays fall 11 days earlier than the previous year. The precise dates are only fixed a short time beforehand because they depend upon the sighting of the moon.

Public Holidays

During the public holidays listed below, government offices and banks close. Shops, moneychangers and restaurants generally remain open, and public transport functions normally. During Eid al-Fitr and Eid al-Adha many shops close as shop owners join their families on these important days of celebration.

Archaeological sites and nature reserves tend to be very crowded on Fridays and public holidays.

New Year's Day 1 January
Good Friday March/April
Labour Day 1 May
Independence Day 25 May
Army Day & Anniversary of the Great Arab Revolt 10 June
Christmas Day 25 December

The main Islamic holidays are listed below. See the Table of Islamic Holidays, above, for equivalent dates in the Western calendar.

Islamic New Year First Day of Muharram.
Prophet's Birthday Celebrated on 12 Rabi' al-Awal.
Eid al-Isra Wal Mi'raj Celebrates the nocturnal visit of the Prophet Mohammed to heaven.
Ramadan Ninth month of the Muslim Calendar.
Eid al-Fitr Starts at the beginning of Shawwal to mark the end of fasting in the preceding month of Ramadan.
Eid al-Adha Commemoration of Allah sparing Ibrahim (Abraham in the Bible) from sacrificing his son, Isaac. It also marks the end of the haj.

Ramadan

During the holy month of Ramadan Muslims refrain from eating, drinking, having sex and smoking during daylight hours in accordance with the fourth pillar of Islam (see the boxed text, p60). Even gum-chewing is considered *haram* (forbidden).

Although many Muslims in Jordan do not follow the injunctions to the letter, most conform to some extent. Foreigners are not expected to follow suit, but it's bad form to eat, drink or smoke in public during this period (see Celebrations, p79).

Business hours during Ramadan are erratic and tempers tend to flare towards the end of the month. After 6.30pm many villages turn into ghost towns as people go home to break their fast. Tourist attractions and hotel restaurants remain open and public transport generally functions normally, but the serving of alcohol may be restricted to room service or simply be unavailable.

INSURANCE

Travel insurance that covers theft, loss and medical problems is essential. The policy should cover ambulance fees and emergency flights home.

Some policies specifically exclude 'dangerous activities', which can include scuba diving, motorcycling and even trekking. You must have insurance if you plan to dive in Aqaba – decompression-chamber treatment is an expensive business!

You may prefer a policy that pays doctors or hospitals directly. Alternatively, if you submit a claim after the event, ensure you keep all documentation. Some policies ask you to call back (reverse charges) to a centre in your home country where an immediate assessment of your problem is made. See also Insurance, p324.

INTERNET ACCESS

Jordan is part of the cyber community, and boasts numerous Internet Service Providers (ISPs), including **Cyberia** (www.cyberia.jo).

Almost every town in Jordan has at least one public internet centre. The most competitive rates, and the highest number of internet centres, are found outside major universities such as Yarmouk University

(Irbid) and the University of Jordan in northern Amman. Costs range from about 750 fils to JD3 per hour.

If you have a laptop it's possible to connect to the internet from top-end and a few midrange hotels that have direct-dial phones. Check with the hotel desk for local dial-up numbers.

The easiest way to collect mail through internet centres is to open a web-based account such as **Hotmail** (www.hotmail.com) or **Yahoo! Mail** (mail.yahoo.com). Most places are also set up for various online chat services, such as MSN Messenger.

LEGAL MATTERS

The Jordanian legal system has evolved from distinct traditions. Civil and commercial law is largely based on British-style common law, while religious and family matters are generally covered by Islamic Sharia courts, or ecclesiastic equivalents for non-Muslims.

Travellers, naturally, are expected to respect the law. Penalties for drug use of any kind are stiff, and criticising the king can bring a jail term of up to three years. Traffic police generally treat foreign drivers with a degree of good-natured indulgence, as long as no major traffic laws have been broken. However, excessive speeding, drunk driving and seat belt avoidance are not tolerated. If you break the law, your embassy can only contact your relatives and recommend local lawyers.

MAPS

The Jordan Tourism Board's free *Map of Jordan* is a handy driving map. The Royal Geographic Centre of Jordan also publishes good maps, including a hiking map of Petra.

Several detailed maps are available outside Jordan: ITMB's 1:700,000 map *Jordan* is probably the easiest map to find, *Jordan* by Kümmerly and Frey is the best driving map, and the latest edition of GEO Project's *Jordan* (1:730,000) has an excellent map of Amman.

MONEY

Known as the *jay-dee* among hip young locals, the currency in Jordan is the dinar (JD) and it is made up of 1000 fils. You will sometimes hear the terms *piastre* or *qirsh*: this refers to 10 fils (10 qirsh equals 100 fils). Often when a price is quoted the unit will be omitted, so if you're told that something is 25, it's a matter of working out whether it's 25 fils, 25 piastre or 25 dinars! Although it sounds confusing, most Jordanians wouldn't dream of ripping off a foreigner, with the possible exception of taxi drivers (see p294).

Coins come in denominations of 10, 25, 50, 100, 250 and 500 fils, and one dinar. Notes come in denominations of JD1, 5, 10, 20 and 50. Try to change larger notes as often as possible – when paying for petrol, for example, or for your hotel bill – as it can be hard to pay with large notes in small establishments.

Changing money is very easy in Jordan, and most major currencies are accepted in cash and travellers cheques. Until recently, US dollars were the most readily accepted; at the time of writing, with the dollar still weak against other major currencies, UK pounds and euros are the flavour of the month; you'll get nowhere with Australian or New Zealand dollars.

There are no restrictions on bringing dinars into Jordan. It's possible to change dinars back into some foreign currencies in Jordan, but you'll need to show receipts to prove that you changed your currency into dinars at a bank in Jordan.

Syrian, Lebanese, Egyptian, Israeli and Iraqi currency can all be changed in Amman. Egyptian and Israeli currency are also easily changed in Aqaba. Banks and moneychangers charge about the same for exchanging cash, but large hotels charge more. There are small branches of major banks at the borders and airports.

If you are a collector of notes and coins, you may be interested in old Iraqi money, bearing the portrait of Saddam Hussein, for sale on street corners in downtown Amman. Even if they're fake, they're good as a conversational gambit with the Iraqi refugees who are selling them.

ATMs

It is possible to travel in Jordan almost entirely on plastic. ATMs giving cash advances abound in all but the smaller towns –just don't forget your PIN!

There are no local charges on credit-card cash advances, but the maximum daily withdrawal amount is around JD500,

DIRECTORY

depending on your particular card. All banks have large signs (in English) indicating which credit cards they accept.

Visa is the most widely accepted card at ATMs and for cash advances, followed by MasterCard. Other cards, such as Cirrus and Plus, are also accepted by many ATMs (eg Jordan National Bank and HSBC). If an ATM swallows your card, call ☎ 06-5669123 (Amman).

Credit Cards

Most major credit cards are accepted at top-end hotels and restaurants, travel agencies, larger souvenir shops and bookshops. Commissions of up to 5% may be added to the bill, so it may be better to get a cash advance and pay with the paper stuff.

The following are emergency numbers to contact in Amman if you lose your credit card:

American Express (☎ 06-5607014)
Diners Club (☎ 06-5675850)
MasterCard (☎ 06-4655863)
Visa (☎ 06-5680554)

International Transfers

Some major banks (such as Arab Bank and Jordan National Bank) can arrange the international transfer of money. Cairo-Amman Bank is part of the international service offered by **Western Union** (www.westernunion.com). **MoneyGram** (www.moneygram.com) has agreements with several banks. Fees are high with both, so obtaining a cash advance with a credit card is a better bet.

Moneychangers

In theory, moneychangers do not charge commission on travellers cheques, but in practice many do, so shop around. It's advisable to check the rates at banks or in the English-language newspapers before changing money.

Tax

Jordan has a sales tax of 16%, but this is generally only added to the bill in midrange and top-end restaurants. Midrange and top-end restaurants and hotels may also add on an additional 10% service charge. The Aqaba special economic zone has a sales tax of only 5% and many Jordanians head there on shopping sprees to take advantage of the lower consumer prices.

See Duty-Free, opposite, for information on tax rebates for tourists.

Tipping

Tips of 10% are generally expected in better restaurants. Elsewhere, rounding up the bill to the nearest 250 fils or giving back the loose change is appreciated, especially by petrol attendants and taxi drivers.

Travellers Cheques

Most types of travellers cheques are accepted, with the most recognised being American Express (Amex). Check the commission before changing them.

PHOTOGRAPHY & VIDEO
Airport Security

All airports in Jordan have X-ray machines for checking luggage. Digital images are not affected when scanned by this equipment, but if you have print film keep it in a zip-lock bag ready for manual inspection. Don't keep your film in your checked-in luggage.

Equipment

Digital accessories and memory cards are widely available; a 1GB memory card costs around JD20. Many camera shops can burn photos onto a CD and print digital pictures.

Photographing People

Some Jordanians, particularly women and the elderly, object to being photographed, so ask first. Persisting in taking a photograph against someone's wishes can lead to ugly scenes, so exercise courtesy and common sense. Children generally line up to be photographed.

Jordanians are very proud of their country and can be offended if you take pictures of anything 'negative' or suggestive of poverty and squalor; this may include the activity of a marketplace.

Restrictions

Photography in military zones and 'strategic areas' like bridges and public buildings is forbidden. Take particular care in the Eastern Desert as there are several sensitive military sites not far from the desert castles. You also need to be careful along the Dead Sea Highway where there are numerous checkpoints protecting the sensitive border with Israel and the Palestinian Territories.

Technical Tips

The single biggest factor to take into account is light. Taking pictures in the middle of the day will almost guarantee a washed-out shot, as the strong contrasts of light and shade are hard for a camera to deal with. Where possible, try to exploit the softer light of the early morning and late afternoon, which enhances subtleties in colour and eliminates problems of glare. If you do need to take shots in bright light, use a lens filter and keep the sun behind you.

If you want your camera to continue working for your next trip, don't get sand in it! A large zip-lock plastic bag and a lens brush will help keep your camera clean. Bear in mind, too, that a lens filter is cheaper to replace than the lens itself.

POST
Postal Rates

Amman is the best place from which to send parcels – see p93. For more detailed postal information, **Jordan Post** (www.jordanpost .com.jo) has an informative website.

Sending Mail

Stamps are available from souvenir shops where postcards are sold and there are post-boxes around towns. Letters posted from Jordan take up to two weeks to reach Australia and the USA, but often as little as three or four days to the UK and Europe. Every town has a post office, but parcels are best sent from Amman or Aqaba.

Reliable courier companies include **FedEx** (www.fedex.com.jo), which has an office in Amman, and **DHL** (www.dhl.com), which has offices in Amman and Aqaba. Half a kilo costs around JD50 to most countries, although the per-kilo rate decreases dramatically the more you send.

SHOPPING

Jordan, with its strong tradition of handicraft production, is a fun place to shop. If you are after goods of a high quality, it pays to visit specialised craft centres as opposed to one-stop shopping in souvenir shops. For a full description of the kinds of craft that Jordan is famous for, please see p65.

Bargaining

Bargaining, especially when souvenir-hunting, is essential, but shopkeepers are less likely than their Syrian and Egyptian counterparts to shift far from their original asking prices. See the boxed text, p300.

Duty Free

There are duty-free shops at Queen Alia International Airport and next to the Century Park Hotel in Amman, plus small outlets at the border crossings with Israel and the Palestinian Territories.

Most upmarket shops offer tax rebates. If you spend over JD350, keep your receipts, fill out a tax rebate form and leave the country within 90 days, you can get the 16% tax refunded to your credit card at a booth at the airport, just before check-in.

Export Restrictions

Exporting anything more than 100 years old is illegal, so don't buy any souvenir (including 'ancient' coins or oil lamps) that is deemed by the salesman to be 'antique' – if only because it probably isn't. If you're unsure about an item's provenance, contact the **Customs Department** (☎ 06-4623186; www.cus toms.gov.jo) in Amman.

Handicrafts

Several outlets around Jordan sell high-quality items handmade by Jordanian women. Profits from the sale of all items go to local NGOs aiming to develop the status of women, provide income generation for

POSTAL RATES FROM JORDAN				
Type	Middle East	UK/Europe	USA/Canada	Australia
Letter/postcard	325 fils	475 fils	625 fils	625 fils
1kg parcel	JD4.200	JD14.300	JD14.600	JD13.600
Extra 1kg	JD3.600	JD4	JD8.100	JD7.100

GETTING A GOOD DEAL

In common with neighbouring countries, Jordan has a tradition of bargaining for goods. This means that items do not have a value per se: their value is governed by what you are willing to pay balanced against the sum the vendor is happy to sell the goods for. This subtle exchange is dependent on many changeable factors, such as how many other sales the vendor has made that day, whether you look like a person who can afford an extra dinar or two, and even whether the vendor had a row with their spouse in the morning. Equally, it is your chance to decide what you are willing to pay for an item and then use your interpersonal skills to see if you can persuade the vendor to match it.

Bargaining, or haggling, is a highly sociable activity, often conducted over a cup of tea or even, for large purchases, lunch with the family. As with all social interaction, there's an unwritten code of conduct that keeps such negotiations sweet. Avoid paying the first price quoted: this is often considered arrogant and bad manners. Start below the price you wish to buy at so you have room to compromise when the vendor quotes a higher price than he or she wishes to sell at – but don't quote too low or the vendor may be insulted. Never lose your temper: if negotiations aren't going to plan, simply smile and say goodbye. You'll be surprised how often the word *ma'a salaama* (goodbye) brings the price down.

Resist comparing prices with other travellers. If they were happy with what they paid for something, they certainly won't be if you tell them you bought the same thing for less. And besides, as shopping is one of the most memorable and sociable parts of travelling in Jordan, a 'good deal' generally means a good deal more than just the exchange of money.

---

marginalised families, nurture young artists and/or protect the local environment.

For more information on these local cottage industries, see the boxed text on p22 and p197. Also consult the GreenDex on p358 to see if a shop gets the green 'thumbs up' from our authors.

Products from these small-scale initiatives include silver jewellery from Wadi Musa; handmade paper products from Iraq al-Amir, Aqaba and Jerash; ceramics from Salt; painted ostrich eggs from Shaumari; weavings from Iraq al-Amir; and traditional clothing from across Jordan. Stylish home decor items aimed at the foreign market, including cushions, tablecloths and wall hangings, are also available.

Unfortunately, some shop owners have jumped on the cooperative bandwagon and claim to be part of charitable foundations when they are not. Check that the sign above the shop exactly matches the shop you are looking for!

Other Souvenirs

If you can carry it hand-luggage, a Jordanian water pipe makes a good souvenir; buy a supply of charcoal if you intend to use it when you get home. Easier to carry around is the traditional Arab headcloth, or *keffiyeh,* and *agal* (the black cord used to keep it on your head), so characteristic of the region. The elegant flowing ankle-length Bedouin robe known as a *jalabiyya* is available at shops all over Jordan. Mind you, while you may think you look pretty hip in this attire, the locals may not agree.

A few music shops in downtown Amman sell either ouds (Arabic lutes) or *darbukkas,* the standard Middle Eastern–style drums. The ones you'll see for sale in tourist shops, however, are more for display than to play.

Other souvenirs include olive oil, modern mosaics from Madaba and Hebron-style glass from Naur (outside Amman). Jordan's capital of kitsch is Wadi Musa, where Nabataean T-shirts, Petra reproductions and bottles of coloured sand, skilfully created through tiny funnels, are sold throughout town.

Woodwork items, generally imported from Syria, include walnut jewellery boxes and chess sets inlaid with mother-of-pearl. Inspect the joints and inlay carefully if your purchase is to survive the journey home.

SMOKING

The tide of anti-smoking sentiment sweeping across many parts of the world has yet to reach Jordan. There are no laws in place banning smoking in public and the occasional no-smoking signs (such as those at the airport) are blithely ignored. Top-end hotels in Amman, the Dead Sea and Aqaba reserve a few non-smoking rooms for their guests and the occasional quality restaurant enforces a non-smoking policy at selected tables, but in all other public places, including buses and taxis, smoking is still considered de rigueur.

SOLO TRAVELLERS
Jordan is an excellent destination for travelling alone. The country is friendly, safe, compact and easy to travel in with plenty of opportunities to meet Jordanians and mix with fellow travellers (particularly in Amman, Madaba and Wadi Musa).

During any bus ride (as one traveller, Fernando Perego, writes), 'local people extend the hand of friendship' and, as often or not, the journey will end in an invitation to share tea or meet the family. Dr Perego was even invited to visit the local clinic. Another traveller, Nathalie Ollier, found that her planned itinerary of a morning trip to Mukawir turned into an all-day tea-tasting event as she was taken from one interested shop owner, bus driver or village resident to another. People will be surprised you are alone, but on the whole will leave you be if you're after a bit of peace and quiet.

For advice for women travelling alone, see p304.

TELEPHONE
The telephone system in Jordan is privatised, so visitors can make a call from a private telephone agency, call from a hotel or shop, or buy a telephone card from one of the 1000 or more pay phones throughout Jordan.

Local calls cost around 150 fils for three minutes. The easiest place to make a call is at your hotel, where local calls are often free. Otherwise, most shopkeepers and private telephone agencies will lend you their telephone if you have a prepaid Ma'alak card (available in various denominations from grocery stores). The cost of overseas calls from Jordan varies widely: one to 10 minutes costs from around JD3.

Overseas calls can be made at any card pay phone or from hotels, but are substantially more expensive. Reverse-charge telephone calls are normally not possible.

Mobile Phones
Mobile phones in Jordan use the GSM system. Two main service providers are **Fastlink** (☎ 06-5823111; www.fastlink.com.jo) and **Jordan Telecom Group** (☎ 06-4606666; www.jordantelecomgroup.com), both of which offer a full range of plans and pre-paid SIM cards. Rates for signing up start at JD10, including 175 minutes of talk time.

Per-minute mobile charges are around 350 fils to Europe and Australia and 700 fils to the USA.

Telephone Codes
To make a call from a landline, you must precede the six- or seven-digit number with a two-digit area code. See Quick Reference, inside the front cover, for details.

TIME
Jordan is two hours ahead of GMT/UTC in winter and three hours ahead between 1 April and 1 October, when daylight-saving time is introduced. Note that Jordan's daylight-saving time is slightly out of sync with summer clock changes in Europe. There are no time differences within Jordan. Jordan is on the same time zone as Israel and the Palestinian Territories, Syria and Egypt.

TOILETS
Most hotels and restaurants, except those in the budget category, now have Western-style toilets. In most others you'll be using squat toilets with a hose for ablutions and a water bucket provided for flushing.

Toilet paper (the use of which is considered an unsanitary practice in most Middle Eastern countries) is seldom available, except in the midrange and top-end hotels and restaurants. Local people prefer to use the hose and then deposit any toilet paper (used for drying purposes) in the basket by the side of the toilet bowl; these baskets should be used to avoid blockages as the sewerage system is not designed for paper. For those who can't do without it, toilet paper can be bought in most grocery shops throughout Jordan.

If caught short in the desert or hillsides of Jordan, it is imperative you choose a spot well away from water courses and bury the outcome in as deep a pit as possible to avoid creating new 'Kleenex trails'.

TOURIST INFORMATION

Jordan has a good network of tourist offices and visitor centres. The main tourist office in Amman is located on the ground floor of the **Ministry of Tourism & Antiquities** (www .tourism.jo) in Jebel Amman (see p95).

The comprehensive website of the **Jordan Tourism Board** (JTB; www.visitjordan.com) has regularly updated information. JTB also publishes some excellent brochures in several languages available from its offices in Jordan and abroad. Contact the following offices for a brochure and map package:

France (☎ 01-55609446; gsv@articleonze.com; 122 rue Paris, 92100 Boulogne-Billancourt, Paris)
Germany (☎ 069-92318870; jordan@adam-partner.de; Weser Strasse 4 60329 Frankfurt)
UK (☎ 0207-3716496; info@jordantourismboard.co.uk; 115 Hammersmith Rd, London, W14 0QH)
USA (☎ 1877-7335673, 703-2437404; www.seejordan .org; Suite 102, 6867 Elm St, McLean, VA 22101)

TRAVELLERS WITH DISABILITIES

In late 2000 Jordan celebrated its first-ever Olympic gold medal, won by the female athlete Maha Barghouthi in the Sydney Paralympics. Jordanians are very proud of this achievement and it threw a spotlight on people with disabilities. The benefits of this are taking a long time to filter through and for now Jordan is still not a great place for travellers with disabilities. Although Jordanians are happy to help, cities are crowded and the traffic is chaotic, and visiting tourist attractions – such as the vast archaeological sites of Petra and Jerash – involves long traverses over uneven ground.

There is some good news, however. The Jordanian government has legislated that wheelchair access must be added to all new public buildings. Horse-drawn carriages are provided at Petra for visitors with disabilities to help with access to the main sites. The Royal Diving Club is a member of the **Access to Marine Conservation for All** (AMCA; www .amca-international.org), an initiative to enable people with disabilities to enjoy diving.

VISAS

Visas are required by all foreigners entering Jordan (JD10). Visas can be obtained on arrival either at the airport or at most of Jordan's land borders. Tourist visas are valid for three months (that is, you must enter the country within three months of

the date of issue) and allow stays of up to one month from the date of entry.

At the Airport

Visas are issued on arrival at the airport in Amman from the visa desk opposite the immigration counters. Payment must be made in Jordanian dinars. There are moneychangers adjacent to the counters, but ATMs are only available after immigration. After getting your visa, you don't need to line up in the immigration queues: simply show your stamp to an immigration official and you'll be waved through.

At Land Borders

Visas for Jordan are issued with a minimum of fuss at any of Jordan's land borders, with the exception of King Hussein Bridge. If you intend to enter Jordan using this crossing from Israel and the Palestinian Territories, then you need to obtain a single/multiple entry visa (cost JD10/20) from one of Jordan's embassies or consulates abroad. This only applies, however, if you're entering Jordan through this crossing for the first time. If you are re-entering Jordan (you may have decided, for example, to take a detour to Jerusalem for a few days while staying in Amman), you do not need to reapply for a Jordanian visa at King Hussein Bridge, providing you return within the validity of your Jordanian visa or its extension. Remember to keep the stamped exit slip and present it on returning. Note that you also must return through the same border – this option does not apply at any of Jordan's other border crossings.

See p309 for details regarding border crossings.

Via the Aqaba Economic Zone

If you arrive in Jordan's southern city of Aqaba, by air on an international flight, sea from Nuweiba in Egypt or by land from Eilat, you are entitled to a free visa as part of the free-trade agreement with the Aqaba Special Economic Zone Area (ASEZA). If you stay in Jordan for more than 15 days, you must register with the **ASEZA office** (☎ 03-2035757; www.aqabazone.com) in Aqaba.

Multiple Entry Visa

Multiple entry visas (JD20) must be obtained in advance from Jordanian consulates

GETTING VISAS FOR OTHER MIDDLE EAST COUNTRIES IN JORDAN

Travelling between Jordan and neighbouring countries is possible by obtaining the relevant visas. Bear in mind that you will be refused entry to Syria, Iraq and Saudi Arabia if there is any indication in your passport of entry to Israel and the Palestinian Territories (see the boxed text, p312).

For details regarding border crossings, see p309. For addresses of embassies and consulates, see p294.

Egypt

Most nationalities are issued a visa (US$15, payable in dollars) on arrival in Egypt.

If you're travelling by boat from Jordan to Nuweiba and you only intend to visit the Sinai Peninsula, you can get a free 'Sinai Entry Stamp' on arrival, valid for 15 days. Similarly, if you're travelling overland via Israel and the Palestinian Territories, these stamps are available at the Taba border.

If you wish to travel further than Sharm el-Sheikh, then you need to request a full visa for Egypt on arrival (not available at Taba). Single/multiple entry visas (JD12/15) can be obtained in advance from the Egyptian consulate at Aqaba. One passport photo is required and the visa is usually processed within two hours. The relatively chaotic Egyptian embassy in Amman charges a little more (JD15/19), but also issues visas the same day (after 3pm).

Iraq

Travel to Iraq is not advised at present. It takes two to three weeks to get approval for visa applications from the Ministry of Interior in Baghdad.

Israel & the Palestinian Territories

Staff at the heavily fortified Israeli embassy in Amman actively discourage visa applications, as visas are available at the three border crossings currently open to foreigners – Jordan Bridge (known as Sheikh Hussein Bridge in Jordan), Allenby Bridge (King Hussein Bridge) and Yitzhak Rabin (Wadi Araba) – and many nationalities do not require one.

Visas of one month's duration are available at Jordan Bridge and Yitzhak Rabin border crossings. Three-month Israeli visas are available at Allenby Bridge border crossing.

Lebanon

Lebanese visas are readily available at Lebanese entry points, but not at the Lebanon Embassy in Amman. As such, if you are travelling to Lebanon via Syria you will need to obtain your Syrian visa *before* you arrive in Jordan.

Saudi Arabia

It is not possible to visit Saudi Arabia as a casual traveller. You must either have a Saudi resident's visa to enter the country or, if you are travelling from Jordan to Kuwait or to Yemen and you can prove there is no other way of getting to your destination (ie you are travelling in your own car), you may be granted a three- or seven-day transit visa. This must be applied for well in advance from your country of normal residence and is subject to many additional stipulations. Check with the Saudi Arabian embassy in your own country before attempting this process.

Syria

If you intend to travel to Syria, you must obtain a visa for Syria *before* you arrive in Jordan. Only foreign residents in Jordan (ie expatriate workers and diplomats) and residents of a country without Syrian representation can be issued a Syrian visa at the embassy in Amman. Some readers have received a Syrian visa after obtaining a letter of recommendation (in Arabic) from their embassy in Amman, but this is definitely more the exception than the rule and should not be counted on.

Visas are theoretically available at the Syria–Jordan border, providing there is no Syrian representation in your country of residence. Some travellers have even reported getting a visa at the border regardless of this rule. If visiting Syria is an important part of your trip, however, you may not want to leave this to the good humour of the border guard.

It's important to remember that you cannot enter Syria from Jordan if you have a visa stamp in your passport from Israel and the Palestinian Territories – see the boxed text, p312.

or embassies outside the country. In the Middle East, you can find Jordanian embassies in all the neighbouring states, including Israel and the Palestinian Territories. You may want to avoid getting a Jordanian multiple-entry visa from the latter, however, if you intend to travel elsewhere in the region. This is because many Arab countries refuse entry to those who have Israeli stamps or documentation in their passports (see the boxed text, p312).

Visa Extensions

From Amman and Aqaba visas can easily be extended, at no extra charge, for stays of up to three months. After assembling the necessary paperwork (see p95) it takes about 30 minutes to complete the registration process at a police station. You may be required to have an HIV test (JD20), which usually takes 24 hours to process. The maximum stay allowed on an extended tourist visa is six months. Failure to register results in a fine for every day you have overstayed.

For longer-term residency, or to sort out any problems with your visa, you may be asked to go to the **Directorate of Residency & Borders** (Map p99; ☎ 06-5623348; Majed al-Idwans St, Shmeisani, Amman; ☒ 8am-3pm Sun-Thu, to 1pm Sat). Take service taxi 6 or 7 to Shmeisani from downtown, from where it's a 15-minute walk. The office is next to the Shmeisani central police station (*markaz mudiret ash-shurta*; مركز مديرية الشرطة).

WOMEN TRAVELLERS

As a woman travelling alone around Jordan for three weeks, I have found the people only helpful, hospitable and friendly.

K Millar, UK

Attitudes Towards Women

Attitudes of Jordanian men towards foreign women in Jordan can be trying to say the least. The reasons for this are complex and variable. By contemporary Western standards, Jordan's largely Muslim society is generally conservative and most men have little or no contact with women or sex before marriage. Some men formulate their stereotype of a Western woman based on Western films and TV, and are thereby convinced that all foreign women are promiscuous and will jump into bed at the drop of a hat.

The fact that some women choose to do just that contributes to this impression.

Precautions

There will probably be times when you will have male company that you'd rather do without. This may involve nothing more than irritating banter, proposals of marriage and declarations of undying love. Harassment, however, can also take the form of leering, sometimes followed by minor physical misdemeanours – a grope in a bus for example. Serious harassment and rape is rare in Jordan.

Where possible, it's best to ignore such behaviour or pass it off as part of the experience or you'll end up letting a few sad individuals spoil your whole trip. Plenty of women travel through Jordan, often alone (this author included), and never encounter serious problems.

To minimise harassment, it's imperative to respect Muslim sensibilities regarding clothing, especially in small towns and rural areas, which tend to be more conservative than Amman. In the trendy districts of Amman such as Abdoun and Shmeisani, in large hotels and resorts or even in the middle of Petra (where tour group parties generally wear whatever they feel like) you'll feel comfortable dressing as you would at home. Outside those areas, aim for knee-length dresses or loose trousers, and cover your shoulders and upper arms.

On public beaches at the Dead Sea and in Aqaba, wear a swimsuit (and preferably a T-shirt and shorts) when swimming and save the bikinis for top-end resorts and dive centres. Never go topless – especially in the wadis where skinny dipping in freshwater pools is never as unseen as you might imagine.

Some foreign women go to the extent of covering their head, but this is inappropriate for non-Muslims in Jordan and can be misconstrued – particularly by the women of Jordan's Christian communities who do not wear headscarves.

Some behaviour may well warrant a good public scene, emphasising the shame and dishonour involved. You'll be surprised how quickly bystanders will take matters into hand if they feel someone has overstepped the mark. If you have to say something to ward off an advance, *imshi* (clear off) should do the trick, but try not to swear or lose your temper or you will lose public sympathy into the bargain. In theory, the chances of getting harassed are greater in budget hotels where there are fewer controls on who comes and goes.

Lastly, some advice for single female travellers from single female readers:

- Don't go to a bar unaccompanied.
- Avoid eye contact with any man you don't know – wearing dark glasses can help.
- A wedding ring will add to your respectability in Arab eyes, even if you're not married; a photo of your children/ husband (real or fake) will clinch it.
- Don't sit in the front seat of a chartered private or service taxi.
- On public transport, sit next to a woman if possible.
- Don't go outside with wet hair, as this apparently implies that you've had sex recently!
- Be cautious when venturing alone to remote regions of large archaeological sites such as Petra – including Siq Al-Barid (Little Petra) – and Jerash.
- Check for peep holes in rooms and bathrooms (particularly cigarette holes in curtains).
- Pay a little more for a better hotel.
- Place a chair against your locked hotel room door in case of 'accidental' late-night intrusions.
- Be particularly circumspect about declarations of undying love from Jordanian guides, even (and especially) the handsome ones!

If you suffer serious harassment go to a police station or tourist-police booth; the latter can be found at most tourist sites. The tourist police in Jordan take reports seriously. Should the need arise, do not hesitate to call the nationwide **Halla Line/tourism complaints number** (☎ 80022228) especially for tourists; it is staffed by English-speaking police officers.

Most toiletries are easily found in Jordan, though tampons are not always readily available. You should bring your own contraceptives and any special medications.

Restaurants, Bars & Coffeehouses

Some places such as coffeehouses are usually seen as a male preserve. Although it's quite permissible for Western women to enter, in some places the stares may make you feel uncomfortable.

A few restaurants have a 'family section' where local and foreign women, unaccompanied by men, can eat in peace. In some of the local bars and coffeehouses there is only one toilet, so try to avoid using these (same advice goes for male travellers!). Midrange bars and cafés in Amman almost always welcome women (see p111). For an idea of the difficulties of eating in restaurants as a solo woman, see the boxed text, p81.

WORK

There is not much in the way of casual work in Jordan as all such jobs are in hot demand from Palestinian and Iraqi refugees. If you are interested in staying longer in the country and have a specific skill or qualification then it's best to apply for work before leaving home. That way, your employer will be responsible for paying for your air ticket and will sponsor your work permit.

Diving

Qualified dive instructors or divemasters may be able to get work at one of the diving centres in Aqaba, particularly during peak season (September to March). Keep in mind, however, that positions are hotly contested by locals.

Language Teaching

English-teaching opportunities are open to those with TOEFL qualifications. The **British Council** (☎ 06-4636147; www.britishcouncil .org.jo) recruits teachers from the UK with a RSA Preparatory Certificate (the Diploma is preferred) or equivalent and at least two years' work experience. For details contact the British Council **information centre** (☎ UK 0161-9577755; www.britishcouncil.org) before arriving in Jordan. Casual vacancies within Jordan occasionally arise: address your CV to the Teaching Centre Manager.

The **American Language Center** (☎ 06-5523901; www.alc.edu.jo) runs the other top language school. Like the British Council, teachers are mostly recruited before arrival in Jordan.

If you are keen to stay in Jordan for a whole year, Father Innocent at the **St George's Church Pilgrim House** (☎ 5523901; diodoros@ wanadoo.jo) in Madaba invites volunteers to teach English in his school in return for board and keep, private Arabic lessons, participation in evening lessons run by the British Council and 'pocket money'. For further details see p189.

Volunteer Work

If you are keen to learn more about Jordan's ecological projects, there are limited opportunities to work within some of the country's nature reserves on a three-month voluntary program. Board and lodging are generally offered in return for a variety of services such as working in the visitor centres. For more information, contact the **RSCN** (www.rscn.org.jo).

These posts are best filled by local Jordanian people, but if you have a specialist skill in management or conservation, you may strike it lucky.

Those hoping to work with Palestinian refugees should contact the public information office of the **UN Relief & Works Agency** (UNRWA; Map p99; ☎ 06-5609100, ext 165; jorpio@unrwa.org; Al-Zubeid Bldg, Mustapha bin Abdullah St, Shmeisani, Amman). There is no organised volunteer program, but if you are in Jordan for a few months (they prefer longer-term commitments, rather than just a few weeks) and have a particular professional skill in education, relief or health, you may be able to arrange something. Contact them at least three months in advance.

For more volunteer opportunities, see www.volunteerabroad.com/jordan.cfm.

Transport

CONTENTS

GETTING THERE & AWAY

Ever since Burckhardt rediscovered Petra for the Western world in the 19th century, tourists have been finding ways of visiting this part of the Middle East. For the modern-day visitor, this means that there are plenty of well-established and efficient ways of both getting to Jordan (often on direct flights) and visiting the main sights of interest while there.

As Jordan is a relatively small country, some people choose to combine their trip with visits to neighbouring countries. This is possible by flying from Amman to regional capitals; by crossing Jordan's land borders with Syria and Israel and the Palestinian Territories; or by taking a boat across the Red Sea to Nuweiba in Egypt. As Amman is well connected with other Arab countries, it's also possible to combine a trip with Dubai (an increasingly important world destination) in the UAE, and other Gulf capitals.

Please note that prices in this chapter are likely to change due to the rapid fluctuations in fuel costs at the time of writing.

ENTERING THE COUNTRY

Entering Jordan is straightforward whether by air, land or sea, with visas (see p302) and money-exchange facilities available at all borders.

Passport

Your passport should be valid for at least six months after you arrive in Jordan. Always carry your passport with you when travelling around sensitive areas such as near the border of Israel and the Palestinian Territories, along the Dead Sea Highway and roads linking the Dead Sea Highway to interior towns. Checkpoints and passport checks are common in all these areas.

AIR
Airports & Airlines

Queen Alia International Airport (☎ 06-4453187; www.qaia.gov.jo), about 35km south of Amman, is the country's main gateway. A sign reads: 'No one likes to wait, we know, but there are great things ahead.' This is heartening because the airport is pretty uninspiring at present. There are two terminals: Terminal 1 is used for most Royal Jordanian flights and Terminal 2 is used by other airlines. The terminals are within easy walking distance, on opposite sides of the airport road. Both terminals have ATMs, foreign exchange counters, a post office and left-luggage counter. The departure lounge has a reasonable café; there is also a good range of gift items, books, Arabic sweets and Dead Sea products for sale in the duty-free section.

Alia Hotel (☎ 06-451000; www.aliahoteljordan .com; s/d JD70/85), the only airport hotel, is 2km from the airport terminal.

The only other international airport is at Aqaba where some international carriers

---

THINGS CHANGE...

The information in this chapter is particularly vulnerable to change. Check directly with the airline or a travel agent to make sure you understand how a fare (and ticket you may buy) works and be aware of the security requirements for international travel. Shop carefully. The details given in this chapter should be regarded as pointers and are not a substitute for your own careful, up-to-date research.

stop en route to Amman. Flights to Sharm el-Sheikh in Egypt are handled from here and occasional charter flights from Europe stop here, too.

The national airline, **Royal Jordanian** (Map p87; ☎ 06-5678321; www.rja.com.jo; 9th fl, Housing Bank Centre, Shmeisani, Amman), is a well-established airline with a good safety record. It has direct flights to most major cities in Europe and all Middle East capitals. **Royal Wings** (www .royalwings.com.jo), a subsidiary of Royal Jordanian, has smaller planes for short flights from Amman to Aqaba (twice daily).

The following airlines fly to Jordan and have offices in Amman:

Air France (airline code AF; Map p99; ☎ 06-666055; www.airfrance.com; hub Charles de Gaulle, Paris)
British Airways (airline code BA; Map p87; ☎ 828801; www.ba.com; hub Heathrow, London)
Emirates (airline code EK; Map p90; ☎ 06-643341; www.emirates.com; hub Dubai)
Gulf Air (airline code GF; Map p90; ☎ 06-653613; www .gulfairco.com; hub Bahrain)
KLM (airline code KL; Map p94; ☎ 06-655267; www .klm.com; hub Amsterdam)
Kuwait Airways (airline code KU; Map p99; ☎ 06-690144; www.kuwait-airways.com; hub Kuwait City)
Lufthansa Airlines (airline code LH; Map p99; ☎ 06-601744; www.lufthansa.com; hub Frankfurt)
Qatar Airways (airline code QR; Map p99; ☎ 06-684526; www.qatarairways.com; hub Doha)

Turkish Airlines (airline code TK; Map p90; ☎ 06-659102; www.turkishairlines.com; hub İstanbul)

Tickets

Jordan is not a cheap destination to fly into, but special offers are often available on the internet during non-peak seasons (November to February and mid-May to end of August). Some airlines offer 'open-jaw' tickets that allow you to fly into Amman, but out of Beirut (Lebanon) or Damascus (Syria).

A few airlines, notably Gulf Air, still require reconfirmation of onward or return international flights at least 72 hours before departure.

ONLINE BOOKING AGENCIES

It is often cheaper to buy an air ticket to Jordan through online agencies. The following agencies provide a variety of e-ticketing, hotel-booking and car-hire services:
Cheap Tickets (www.cheaptickets.com)
Expedia (www.expedia.com)
Orbitz (www.orbitz.com)
Travelocity (www.travelocity.com)
Last Minute (www.lastminute.com)

Readers have also recommended www .connections.be and www.airstop.be for discounted online tickets from Europe to Jordan; www.cheaptickets.co.uk is another

---

CLIMATE CHANGE & TRAVEL

Climate change is a serious threat to the ecosystems that humans rely upon, and air travel is the fastest-growing contributor to the problem. Lonely Planet regards travel, overall, as a global benefit, but believes we all have a responsibility to limit our personal impact on global warming.

Flying & Climate Change

Pretty much every form of motor travel generates CO_2 (the main cause of human-induced climate change) but planes are far and away the worst offenders, not just because of the sheer distances they allow us to travel, but because they release greenhouse gases high into the atmosphere. The statistics are frightening: two people taking a return flight between Europe and the US will contribute as much to climate change as an average household's gas and electricity consumption over a whole year.

Carbon Offset Schemes

Climatecare.org and other websites use 'carbon calculators' that allow jetsetters to offset the greenhouse gases they are responsible for with contributions to energy-saving projects and other climate-friendly initiatives in the developing world – including projects in India, Honduras, Kazakhstan and Uganda.

Lonely Planet, together with Rough Guides and other concerned partners in the travel industry, supports the carbon-offset scheme run by climatecare.org. Lonely Planet offsets all of its staff and author travel.

For more information check out our website: lonelyplanet.com.

reliable agency specialising in airfares from UK to Jordan.

Australia & New Zealand

There are no direct flights between Australasia and Jordan. Most flights travel via Southeast Asian capitals or through hubs in the Middle East.

Gulf Air and Emirates fly from Sydney and Melbourne and sometimes offer openjaw tickets to other Middle East destinations. Recommended agencies in Australia for discount fares:

Flight Centre (☎ 133 133; www.flightcentre.com.au)

STA Travel (☎ 134 782; www.statravel.com.au)

Trailfinders (☎ 1300 780 212; www.trailfinders.com.au)

Recommended agencies in New Zealand for discount fares:

Flight Centre (☎ 800 243 544; www.flightcentre .co.nz)

STA Travel (☎ 508 782 872; www.statravel.co.nz)

Middle East

There are regular flights from Amman to other regional capitals. Flights are not particularly cheap, however, but specials over the Thursday/Friday Islamic weekend are sometimes available.

In Amman, the best places to start looking for air tickets are the agencies along Al-Malek Al-Hussein St, near the flyover.

In Tel Aviv, try the **Israel Student Travel Association** (ISSTA; ☎ 03-7777316; www.issta.com; 128 Ben Yehuda St). There's also a branch in Jerusalem (☎ 02-6252799; 1 HaNevi'im St).

In İstanbul there are lots of travel agencies on the northern side of Divan Yolu in Sultanahmet, all of them specialising in budget air tickets. **Orion-Tour** (☎ 212-2326300; www.oriontour.com; Halaskargazi Caddesi 284/3, Marmara Apartimani, Sisli 80220) is recommended.

The area around Midan Tahrir in Cairo is teeming with travel agencies. One of the best is **Egypt Panorama Tours** (☎ 02-359 0200; www.eptours .com) just outside Al-Ma'adi metro station.

It is important to remember that you cannot enter Syria (and some other Middle

Eastern countries) from Jordan if you have a visa stamp in your passport from Israel and the Palestinian Territories – see boxed text, p312.

UK & Continental Europe

National carriers and other regional airlines (such as BMI in the UK) offer direct flights to Amman from London, Paris, Amsterdam and Frankfurt – the major hubs for discounted fares in continental Europe. Direct flights are also available from other European capital and regional cities.

Recommended agencies in Europe for discount fares:

CTS Viaggi (☎ 06-441111; www.cts.it) A student and youth specialist in Italy.

Nouvelles Frontières (☎ 08-25000747; www .nouvelles-frontieres.fr) Branches across France.

STA Travel (www.statravel.com) Branches across Europe.

Trailfinders (☎ 0207-9383366; www.trailfinders.com) A popular agency in the UK.

Voyages Jules Vernes (☎ 0207-6161000; www .vjv.co.uk) UK-based agency, operating charter flights to Aqaba; they may sell extra seats to the public.

Voyageurs du Monde (☎ 08-92235656; www.vdm .com) Branches across France.

USA & Canada

Royal Jordanian has direct flights between Amman and New York, Chicago and Detroit, with onward code-share flights with America West. Most flights, however, require a change of aircraft in Europe (London for British Airways, Paris for Delta/Air France and Amsterdam for Northwest/KLM). Alternatively, connections can be made through Gulf cities, such as Dubai (UAE), Manama (Bahrain) or Doha (Qatar).

Air Canada and Royal Jordanian offer flights, via London or Frankfurt, from Canada to Amman.

Recommended agencies in the USA and Canada:

STA Travel (☎ 800-7814040; www.statravel.com) Has offices throughout USA.

Travel CUTS (☎ 1866-2469762; www.travelcuts.com) Canada's national student travel agency with offices in all major cities.

LAND

It's easy to reach Jordan by land from Syria or from Israel and the Palestinian Territories. Foreign residents of Saudi Arabia (and transit passengers who can show they have no

TRANSPORT

other way of reaching Jordan – see the boxed text, p303) are also able to enter Jordan by land. For information regarding visas on arrival from these countries, see Visas, p302.

Most travellers arrive in Jordan by bus or service taxi, although there is no problem in bringing your own car or motorcycle (see p318).

Leaving Jordan by land requires a little more planning on account of certain visa stipulations: if you're intending to visit Syria, in particular, read the information about obtaining visas for other Middle Eastern countries in the boxed text, p303.

Egypt

Most people travel between Jordan and Egypt by boat (p314). It's quicker and cheaper, however, to travel overland via Israel and the Palestinian Territories (but read the boxed text, p312, regarding the Israeli border-stamp stigma before making a decision).

If you choose this route, taxis run between Aqaba and the Wadi Araba border crossing (known as Yitzhak Rabin on the Israeli and Palestinian Territories side) and between Yitzhak Rabin and Taba on the Egyptian border. Alternatively, you can take a taxi from Yitzhak Rabin or Taba to Eilat bus station and take a bus to either border from there. The whole trip takes about 1½ hours. If using this route, see the boxed text, p303.

Iraq

Travel to Iraq is not recommended at present. Occasional service taxis run the gauntlet between Baghdad and Abdali bus station in Amman. They use the al-Karama–Tarbil border post, 330km from Amman. This is currently an extremely dangerous journey, however, through the notorious 'Sunni triangle'.

Israel & the Palestinian Territories

Since the historic 1994 peace treaty between Jordan and Israel and the Palestinian Territories, three border crossings have opened to foreigners – Sheikh Hussein Bridge in the north, King Hussein Bridge near Amman, and Wadi Araba in the south. These border crossings are known respectively as Jordan Bridge, Allenby Bridge and Yitzhak Rabin in Israel and the Palestinian Territories; you should refer to them as such only when travelling on that side of the border.

BORDER CROSSINGS

It's worth reading about each of the border crossings before deciding which one to use. This is because the most frequented border, King Hussein Bridge, is not the quick nip between Amman and Jerusalem that it may suggest on the map.

On both sides of all three borders there are moneychanging facilities (not recommended for large sums as commissions are inflated), places to eat and drink, and duty-free shops. On the Jordanian side of all three borders there's a post office and a **tourist information counter** (✆ 8am-2pm, closed Fri).

Borders are closed on the Jewish holiday of Yom Kippur and the Islamic holiday of Eid al-Fitr (see p295).

If you're departing from Jordan on a Friday or Saturday, arrive at the border early as public transport in Israel and the Palestinian Territories doesn't run during the Jewish Shabbat (between sunset Friday and sunset Saturday).

King Hussein Bridge Crossing (Allenby Bridge)

Known in Arabic as 'Jisr al-Malek Hussein', this **border crossing** (✆ 8am-6pm Sun-Thu, to noon Fri & Sat) is only 40km from Amman and 30km from Jerusalem. As such, it offers travellers the most direct route between the two cities, providing they have the right paperwork (see p302 for visa considerations at this border). A further issue when using this border in either direction is that the crossing can take up to three hours, depending on Israeli security measures; avoid 11am to 3pm when delays are more common.

To reach this border from Amman, take a service taxi from Amman's Abdali (or Wahadat) bus station to King Hussein Bridge (JD4, 45 minutes) or there's a single daily JETT bus (JD8) at 6.30am.

Buses (JD2) go between the two borders and although the ride to the Israeli and Palestinian Territories side is short, it lasts an eternity with repeated stops for passport and bag checks. It's not possible to walk, hitch or take a private car across this border.

To get to Jerusalem from the border, take a *sherut* (Israeli shared taxi; around US$40 for the car) to Jerusalem's Damascus Gate. Alternatively, take a bus to Jerusalem or, if that's not running, a bus to Jericho and then a *sherut* to Damascus Gate.

A DAY OUT AT THE BORDER CROSSING *Kerryn Burgess*

Travelling from Jordan to Israel via the King Hussein Bridge border crossing (known as the Allenby Bridge crossing in Israel) is time consuming. Allow at least three hours from the time you arrive at the cluster of buildings on the Jordan side until the time you're into a waiting *sherut* (Israeli shared taxi) on the Israel and Palestinian Territories side. On the Jordan side, things are relatively straightforward. You may have to wait for up to an hour for the bus that takes you across the border itself. The distance is short, but the bus will be stopped and searched several times. At least once, you'll be asked to leave the bus and stand in a 'holding pen' while the bus is searched and your passport is checked yet again. On the Israeli side, expect to negotiate large crowds, chaotic queues and lack of signage about where to go next. If in doubt, ask someone from the queue who's done the crossing before; don't expect anyone official to be available or helpful. You'll be separated from your luggage, which must be X-rayed. Expect to be questioned at length by immigration officials about your reasons for visiting Israel. It happens to everyone. If you know any Israelis in Israel, have their telephone number handy to provide to immigration officials. They won't necessarily make contact, but it can help smooth the way for you anyway. Be sure to read the boxed text, p312.

Travelling in the other direction (from Israel and the Palestinian Territories into Jordan) is usually quicker. Nevertheless, we suggest you think twice before deciding to make a 'day trip' to Jerusalem or elsewhere on the other side of the border, unless you don't mind spending a good portion of the day at the crossing.

Kerryn Burgess is the commissioning editor for the Middle East at Lonely Planet.

If travelling in the other direction, an Israeli exit tax of 127NIS (around US$29, compared to around 70NIS at other borders) is payable. If you intend to return to Israel, keep the Jordanian entrance form safe – you will have to present it on exiting the border.

Sheikh Hussein Bridge Crossing (Jordan Bridge)

Known in Arabic as 'Jisr Sheikh Hussein', this **border crossing** (6.30am-10pm Sun-Thu, 8am-8pm Fri & Sat) links northern Jordan with Beit She'an in Galilee, 6km away.

To reach this border from Irbid, regular service taxis leave the West bus station for the border (JD1, 45 minutes). From the bridge it's a 2km walk (or hitch) to the Israeli side, from where you have to take a taxi to the Beit She'an bus station for onward connections inside Israel and the Palestinian Territories.

If travelling in the other direction, take a bus to Tiberias, and change at Beit She'an (6km from the border). From there, take another bus to the Israeli border (arrive early because there are few buses). After passport formalities and payment of Israeli exit tax (70NIS), a compulsory bus takes you to the Jordanian side.

From the Jordanian side, either wait for the bridge or take a minibus or shared taxi to Irbid (from where

there are regular connections to Amman), go to Shuneh ash-Shamaliyyeh (North Shuna) by private or service taxi, or walk (3km) to the main road and flag down a minibus or service taxi.

Wadi Araba Crossing (Yitzhak Rabin – formerly known as Arava)

This handy **border crossing** (6.30am-10pm Sun-Thu, 8am-8pm Fri & Sat) in the south of the country links Aqaba to Eilat. To reach there from Aqaba, take a taxi (JD5, 15 minutes). Once at the border you can walk across. From the border, buses run to central Eilat, only 2km away. All in all, Aqaba to Eilat takes about an hour.

In the other direction, if you're travelling from Jerusalem and you want to skip Eilat, ask the driver to let you out at the turn-off for the border, a short walk away. The exit tax is 68NIS here. At the Jordanian border take a taxi into Aqaba (JD5, 15 minutes) or negotiate a taxi fare direct to Petra (around JD40, two hours) or to Wadi Rum (around JD18, one hour).

BUS

Several cities in Jordan are now regularly linked to cities in Israel and the Palestinian Territories. Travelling by bus directly between Amman and Tel Aviv saves the hassle

TRANSPORT

ISRAELI BORDER-STAMP STIGMA

Our mailbags are full of questions about the infamous 'Israeli stamp stigma'. Here are a few frequently asked questions.

I've never heard of this Israeli stamp business – what's it all about? Given the tensions between Arab countries and the Jewish state of Israel, any evidence of a visit to Israel in your passport (such as an entry or exit stamp from a border crossing) will bar you from entering a number of countries in the region, including Syria.

So what can I do if I plan to combine my visit to Jordan with a trip to Israel and Syria? When you enter or leave Israel, you can ask immigration officials to stamp a separate piece of paper instead of your passport.

So there's no problem then? That depends on where you go next. If you have, say, an exit stamp from one border and an entry stamp dated a week later from a different border in Jordan, it will be obvious to the Syrian authorities, for example, that you must have been in Israel and the Palestinian Territories in the meantime. Indeed, travellers have been turned away from Syria's border with Jordan for having unexplained periods of time in their passport, such as six weeks in Jordan without any evidence of a Jordanian visa extension.

So how do I get round that problem? You can fly into and out of Ben-Gurion airport; enter and depart through King Hussein Bridge border crossing with a multiple entry visa and ask the Jordanian officials to stamp a piece of paper instead of your passport; or plan to visit Israel and the Palestinian Territories at the end of your trip.

Is an Israeli stamp a problem when trying to enter most Arab countries? No, it's not a problem when entering Jordan, Egypt, Turkey, Tunisia and Morocco. Officially, Bahrain, Qatar, the UAE and Oman will refuse you entry if you have evidence of a visit to Israel in your passport, but in reality they don't usually look for an offending stamp.

For which countries in the Middle East is it a problem?

Syria, Lebanon, Iran, Saudi Arabia, Libya and Yemen. If you get an Israeli or Jordanian exit or entry stamp in your passport, there's little you can do. If you report that your passport is 'lost' to your embassy in any country in the Middle East, it may be met with cynicism and even rejection. The bottom line is that the restrictions that some Arab countries make are in place for a purpose and if you try to sidestep those rules, you can expect your intentions to be misinterpreted at some point.

---

of getting to/from the borders on your own, but it's more expensive than crossing independently, and you'll have to wait for all passengers to clear customs and immigration.

From Amman, **Trust International Transport** (Map p87; ☎ 06-5813427) has buses from its office at 7th Circle (p116) to Tel Aviv (JD25, six hours), Haifa (JD20, seven hours) and Nazareth (JD20, seven hours), departing daily except Saturday at 8.30am. Buses cross the border at Sheikh Hussein Bridge. Bus schedules change frequently, so check departure times and book (and collect) tickets in advance from the bus station. There is one **Jordan Express Tourist Transport** (JETT; Map p99; ☎ 06-5854679; www.jett.com.jo) bus to King Hussein Bridge (JD8, one hour, 6.30am).

CAR & MOTORCYCLE
If you're driving from Israel and the Palestinian Territories, you must use the border crossings at Sheikh Hussein Bridge or Wadi Araba.

Saudi Arabia
Getting a visa, even a transit visa, to Saudi Arabia is a very difficult feat – see the boxed text, p303, for details.

If you are eligible for a visa, then the main land route for public transport is at Al-Umari, south of Azraq. The other two crossing points are Ad-Durra, south of Aqaba, and further east at Al-Mudawwara. Several companies run services to and from Jeddah and Riyadh from Amman's Abdali bus station.

Syria
It's relatively simple to travel between Jordan and Syria, but if you travel directly between Amman and Damascus it's quicker and cheaper to take a direct bus or service

taxi rather than negotiate local transport and border crossing formalities on your own.

If you're heading to Syria from Jordan, make sure you get a Syrian visa before arriving in Jordan (see the boxed text, p303), either in your home country or in Istanbul, Ankara or Cairo.

BORDER CROSSINGS

There are border crossings with Syria at Ramtha and Jabir. They are known respectively as Der'a and Nasib in Syria, but you should refer to them as such only when travelling on the Syrian side of the border.

Both border crossings are efficient and are open 24 hours. If you intend to drive between Jordan and Syria, the better border to cross is at Der'a–Ramtha.

On the Jordanian sides of both borders, there is a post office and **tourist office** (8am-5pm Sat-Thu, to 2pm Fri), places to eat and drink, and moneychangers (open most of the time) where Jordanian dinars and Syrian pounds can be changed.

Jabir (Nasib)

Most service taxis between Amman and Damascus now use this crossing. If you're coming from Syria and plan to visit eastern Jordan (eg Azraq), this border is useful for connections to Zarqa or Mafraq.

Ramtha (Der'a)

Ramtha is the border most commonly used by travellers visiting sights in northern Jordan (eg Jerash and Umm Qais) and in southern Syria (eg Ezra'a and Bosra ash-Sham). There are buses to Ramtha from Amman's Abdali station (JD1, two hours) and Irbid (JD1). From Ramtha, service taxis and minibuses run regularly to the border. If hitching, ask the immigration office on the Jordanian side to flag down a vehicle for a lift to the Syrian border.

You can also get direct transport between Irbid or Amman and Damascus, without stopping in Ramtha.

BUS

The air-conditioned **Jordan Express Tourist Transport** (JETT; Map p99; 06-5854679; www.jett .com.jo; Al-Malek al-Hussein St, Shmeisani) bus travels between Amman and Damascus (JD7, seven hours) twice daily in either direction. JETT also has a daily bus to Aleppo (JD10,

eight hours). JETT's international terminal is close to the Abdali bus station in Amman. The bus schedule changes frequently so check times of departure and book (and preferably collect tickets) in advance from the bus station.

The Palace Hotel in Amman (p106) offers a minibus tour to Damascus, with stops in Jerash, Bosra and Shaba. You'll need a minimum of four passengers (which can be hard to assemble given the necessity of arranging visas in advance); the price is around JD20 per person.

SERVICE TAXI

The enormous yellow *servees* (shared taxis) to Damascus leave regularly throughout the day and are faster than the buses, although you'll have to wait longer in the evening for one to fill up. Service taxis take less time to cross the border than trains or buses because there are fewer passengers to process, and the drivers are experienced in helping passengers with immigration and customs formalities.

From Amman, service taxis for Damascus ('ash-Sham' in Arabic) leave from the eastern or lower end of Abdali bus station (Map p90); from Damascus, they leave from Baramke Garage. The trip costs around JD10 from Amman and takes about three hours. Service taxis also travel between Damascus and Irbid's south bus station (JD5, 2½ hours).

TRAIN

A biweekly train service still leaves Amman for Damascus (JD3) along the **Hejaz Railway** (www.jhr.gov.jo) on Monday and Thursday at 8am, but few travellers go this way as the dawdling service takes all day, with a change of trains at the border. The quaint old station is on King Abdullah I St, about 2.5km east of Raghadan bus station in Amman. The **ticket office** (06-4895413) is only open from 7am on the morning of departure, although you may find someone around at other times. To reach the station, take a service taxi from Raghadan bus station, or a private taxi (around JD1).

Elsewhere in the Middle East

For other destinations in the Middle East, travellers need time, patience and, most importantly, the necessary visas. Most trips involve long, hot journeys with frustrating delays so most people end up flying.

JETT has occasional through-services to Beirut (JD20) and Cairo (US$65), departing from the international bus office in Amman. The fare to Cairo must be paid in US dollars, and includes the Aqaba–Nuweiba ferry ticket. Check with the JETT office ahead of your departure as schedules and prices change frequently.

SEA

Visiting Egypt is both a popular side trip from Aqaba or feasible as part of your onward journey. As Jordan has no land borders with Egypt, the journey involves a short boat ride. At most times of the year this is a matter of turning up and buying your ticket. During haj, however, when Aqaba is abuzz with thousands of excitable Egyptian pilgrims returning home from Mecca, you may find the journey becomes something more epic. Most nationalities can obtain Egyptian tourist visas either on the boat or on arrival at Nuweiba – see the boxed text, p303, for details before making your plans.

There are two main boat services to Nuweiba in Egypt, which leave from the passenger terminal just south of Aqaba. Departure times are often subject to change so call the **passenger terminal** (☎ 03-2013891; www.abmaritime.com.jo/english) before travelling.

The fast boat (one hour) leaves daily at noon (except Saturday) and costs US$70. Children under 12 pay US$55. Departure tax (JD5) is not included in the ticket price. The return ferry leaves Nuweiba at 3.30pm.

There is also a slower (three hours or more) car ferry service that officially leaves at midnight. Some days it doesn't leave at all. Tickets cost US$60 (children under 12 US$50).

Note that fares from Nuweiba must be paid for in US dollars. The service leaves Nuweiba at around 2pm but expect delays.

You need to show your passport to buy tickets. It's not possible to buy return tickets. There are money-exchange facilities at the terminals at Aqaba and Nuweiba. The Jordanian side offers a decent exchange rate but avoid travellers cheques, which attract a huge commission.

Passports are collected on the boat in both directions and handed back on arrival at immigration. Bear in mind, if you are travelling from Egypt you will arrive in Aqaba too late for public transport to Petra or Wadi Rum, so you'll have to overnight in Aqaba or arrange a taxi.

TOURS

Organised tours from abroad are generally divided into cultural/historical tours, overland adventures that combine several Middle Eastern countries, and activity-based holidays that involve some hiking and camel riding.

See p323 for details of companies inside Jordan that can organise individual tours and itineraries.

Australia

Adventure World (☎ 02-89130755; www.adventure world.com.au)
Peregrine Adventures (☎ 03-86014444; www.peregrineadventures.com)

Israel & the Palestinian Territories

Desert Eco Tours (☎ 972-52276575; www.desert ecotours.com) Specialises in camel, hiking and 4WD tours; based in Eilat.

UK

Abercrombie and Kent (☎ 0845-6182200; www.abercrombiekent.co.uk)
Alternative Travel Group (☎ 0186-5315678; www.atg-oxford.co.uk; 69-71 Banbury Rd, Oxford OX2 6PJ) Activities in Dana, Wadi Rum and Aqaba.
Cox & Kings (☎ 0207-8735000; www.coxandkings.co.uk)
Exodus (☎ 0208-6755550; www.exodus.co.uk)
Explore (☎ 0845-0131537; www.explore.co.uk)
High Places (☎ 0114-2757500; www.highplaces.co.uk) Ten-day hiking and scrambling trip in Wadi Rum.
Imaginative Traveller (☎ 0845-0778802; www.imaginative-traveller.com)
Martin Randall Travel (☎ 0208-7423355; www.martinrandall.com)
Tribes (☎ 017-28685971; www.tribes.co.uk)

USA

Archaeological Tours (☎ 1866-7405130; www.archaeologicaltrs.com; 271 Madison Ave, suite 904, NY, NY 10016) A 14-day historical tour with archaeologists.
Jordan Tourism Board North America (☎ 1877-7335673; www.visitjordan.com) Professionally organised assorted tours.

GETTING AROUND

Jordan is a relatively small country, making it possible to drive the 430km from the Syrian border in the north to the Saudi border in the south in just over five hours – but of course size isn't everything. Most of Jordan's attractions lie not along the main arteries (such as the Desert Highway) but along the spectacular switchbacked mountain roads of the north or the historical, ambling and rural King's Highway. As such, if you want to make the most of your trip to Jordan, you need to factor in a little more time for your journey than the distance on the map may indicate.

There is only one domestic flight (Amman to Aqaba) and no internal public train service, so public transport in Jordan comprises a combination of buses/minibuses, service taxis and private taxis.

Chartering a service taxi (white) or private taxi (yellow) is another alternative and often the driver adds untold value to the trip by giving you local information and cultural insights. Where public transport is limited or nonexistent, hitching is another way of getting around.

AIR

There is only one domestic air route, operated by Royal Jordanian twice daily between Amman and Aqaba (JD35 one way, one hour).

Royal Wings (www.royalwings.com.jo), a subsidiary of Royal Jordanian, flies daily between Aqaba and Amman. You can buy tickets for either airline at any travel agency or Royal Jordanian office. See p259 for details.

BICYCLE

Cycling can be fun or sheer folly depending on the time of year. From March to May and September to November are the best times to get on your bike – you won't have to battle with the stifling summer heat or the bitter winter winds.

It ought to be said that cycling in Jordan wouldn't be a first choice for everybody: there are few places to stop along the highways; the traffic is unpredictable; drivers are not used to cyclists; many of the cities and main towns, such as Amman and Karak, are sprinkled over steep hills; and spare parts are hard come by because so few locals ride bikes. If that isn't enough to put you off, then the stone throwing might be:

> There is no way to cycle along the King's Highway without getting stoned. We read it in your guidebook before leaving, but thought that kids would not stone three male adults with beards and long trousers who are looking angry. We were wrong. And it's not only *some* groups of kids who try to stone you, but basically it's becoming a major hobby for all male children between three and 20… Cycle in the morning when children are at school.
>
> Bernhard Gerber, Switzerland

If you are still undeterred, then there is some good news. Roads are generally smooth and tourist attractions are well signposted in English. With some preparation, and an occasional lift in a bus, cyclists can average about 40km a day. Most major sights are conveniently placed less than a day's ride apart, heading south from the Syrian border, ie Irbid–Amman–Madaba–Karak–Dana–Petra–Ma'an–Wadi Rum–Aqaba. All these places have accommodation of some kind and restaurants, so there's no need to carry tents, sleeping bags and cooking equipment. Most other attractions can be easily visited on day trips, by bike or public transport.

The King's Highway is the most scenic route, but also the most physically demanding, especially as strong prevailing north–south winds take their toll. In fact, you may want to take public transport across the extremely wide and steep Wadi Mujib valley between Madaba and Karak, and between the turn-off to Wadi Rum and Aqaba, which is very steep, has appalling traffic and plenty of treacherous turns.

Other scenic routes are from the eastern plateau in the north down into the Jordan Valley – but don't forget the climbs back up again are unremittingly long and tough on the calf muscles. It's probably best to avoid the dull and busy Desert Highway, together with the Safi to Aqaba stretch of the Dead Sea Highway, which is always hot and has very few facilities.

TRANSPORT

TRANSPORT

PUBLIC TRANSPORT IN A HURRY

Wondering if you can get from Jerusalem to Petra in one day or vice versa? Check the following summary of transport to find out exactly how far you can get in a single day on public transport. Note that names in brackets refer to the name of the border crossing on the other side of the relevant border.

Between	Summary of Transport	Approx. Time	More Information
Petra & Jerusalem via Amman & the West Band Taking this route means you may be able to avoid evidence of a visit to Israel in your passport. Beware of long delays at the border. Note that you can't take your own car through this crossing.	**From Petra**		
	Bus to Amman's Wahadat bus station	3 hours	Transport p217
	Share-taxi or bus to King Hussein Bridge (Allenby Bridge)	1 hour	Visas p303 Border Crossings p310
	Bus across the border (border closed by noon Fri & Sat)	3 hour delay	
	Share-taxi or bus to Jerusalem's Damascus Gate	30 mins	
	From Jerusalem		
	Share-taxi or bus to Allenby Bridge (King Hussein Bridge)	30 mins	Transport p115 Visas p302
	Bus across the border (border closed by noon Fri & Sat)	3 hour delay	Border Crossings p310
	Share-taxi or bus from the Jordanian side of the border to Amman (Wahadat bus station)	1 hour	
	Change buses for final leg to Petra	3 hours	
Petra & Jerusalem via Aqaba & Eilat You can travel with your own vehicle this way. If arriving in Jordan, you may be exempt from paying for a Jordanian visa as you'll be entering via Aqaba free-trade zone. There are less border delays involved on this route.	**From Petra**		
	Bus to Aqaba (main bus station)	2½ hours	Transport p217
	Share-taxi or bus to Wadi Araba (Yitzhak Rabin) border	15 mins	Visas p303 Border Crossings p311
	Walk across the border (open every day)	30 mins	
	Share-taxi or bus to Eilat	15 mins	
	Bus to Jerusalem's Damascus Gate	5 hours	
	From Jerusalem		
	Bus to Eilat's bus station	5 hours	Transport p259
	Share-taxi or bus to Yitzhak Rabin (Wadi Araba) border	15 mins	Visas p302 Border Crossing p311
	Walk across the border (open every day)	30 mins	
	Share-taxi to Aqaba	15 mins	
	Share-taxi or bus to Petra	2½ hours	
Petra & Damascus via Amman This trip requires an early start in either direction. As romantic as it may seem, if you want to get to Petra from Damascus in the same day, you can forget using the Hejaz Railway.	**From Petra**		
	JETT bus to JETT bus station in Amman (or bus to Wahadat bus station)	3 hours	Transport p115 Visas p303
	JETT bus to Damascus (the bus waits for you to cross the border as part of the service)	4 hours	Border Crossing p313
	From Damascus		
	JETT bus to JETT bus station in Amman (the bus waits for you to cross the border as part of the service)	4 hours	Transport p115 Visas p302 Border Crossing p313
	JETT bus to Petra	3 hours	

Between	Summary of Transport	Approx. Time	More Information
Petra & Sharm El-Sheikh via Aqaba & Nuweiba Note that from Sharm El-Sheikh or Nuweiba to Wadi Rum or Petra requires an overnight stop in Aqaba.	**From Petra (by boat)**		
	Bus to Aqaba (main bus station)	2½ hours	Transport p259
	Share-taxi or bus to ferry terminal	30 mins	Visas p303
	Boat at noon to Nuweiba	1 hour	Border Crossing p314
	Bus to Sharm El-Sheikh	2½ hours	
	From Nuweiba (by boat)		
	Not possible in a day		
Petra & St Catherine's Mount via Aqaba You can only get a visa for the Sinai Peninsula at the Taba crossing so if you want to travel further than Sharm El-Sheikh, this trip needs some careful planning.	**From Petra (by land)**		
	Bus to Aqaba (main bus station)	2½ hours	Transport p259
	Share-taxi to Wadi Araba (Yitzhak Rabin) border	15 mins	Visas p303 Border Crossing p311
	Walk across border	30 mins	
	Share-taxi or bus to Taba	15 mins	
	Share-taxi to St Catherine's Mount	3 hours	
	From St Catherine's Mount (by land)		
	Not possible in a day		

Spare parts are not common in Jordan, so carry a spare tyre, extra chain links, spokes, two inner tubes, repair kit and tool kit with spanner set. Also bring a low-gear set for the hills and a couple of water containers; confine your panniers to a maximum of 15kg. It may be an idea to contact the **Cycling Association** (www.cycling-jordan.com) for tips before departure.

BUS

Public minibuses are the most common form of transport for locals and visitors. They normally only leave when full, so waiting times of an hour or more are inevitable, especially in rural areas. Tickets are normally bought on the bus. Standing is not usually allowed and some seat-shuffling often takes place to ensure that unaccompanied foreign men or women do not sit next to members of the opposite sex. Locals signify that they want to get off by rapping a coin on a side window. Overcharging tourists on these buses is rare except on routes to and from Wadi Musa (for Petra), where drivers will probably try to charge you extra for 'luggage'.

The larger air-con buses offer a more speedy and reliable service because they generally depart according to a fixed schedule and they don't stop en route to pick up passengers. Tickets should ideally be bought a day in advance from an office at the departure point.

The national bus company **JETT** (Map p99; ☎ 06-5854679; www.jett.com.jo; Al-Malek al-Hussein St, Shmeisani, Amman) operates the most comfortable bus service from Amman to Aqaba. It also has services to King Hussein Bridge border crossing, Petra and Hammamat Ma'in.

Other reliable companies with regular services from Amman include **Trust International Transport** (Map p87; ☎ 06-5813427) to Aqaba, and **Hijazi** (Map p90; ☎ 06-638110) to Irbid.

CAR & MOTORCYCLE

Jordan is a great place to drive and there are some spectacular routes linking the high ground with the Jordan Valley, lying below sea level (see the boxed text, p170). Indeed, there aren't many countries where you can claim to be driving uphill to the sea, but if you're on the Dead Sea Highway heading for the Red Sea, then Jordan is one of them!

Strictly speaking you don't need an International Driving Permit (IDP) to drive in Jordan unless you plan on crossing any borders, but it may help if you meet with an accident.

Bringing Your Own Vehicle

If you are bringing your own vehicle, then you will need the vehicle's registration papers and liability insurance. You also need a *Carnet de passage en douane,* which is effectively a passport for the vehicle and acts as a temporary waiver of import duty. The carnet will also need to specify any expensive spare parts that you're planning to carry with you, such as a gearbox. This is designed to prevent car-import rackets. Contact your local automobile association for details about all documentation.

At the borders with Jordan (and the ferry terminal in Nuweiba, Egypt) you'll be obliged to take out local insurance of JD35 (valid for one month), plus a nominal 'customs fee' of JD5 for 'foreign car registration'.

Finally, bring a good set of spare parts and some mechanical knowledge, as you will not always be able to get the help you may need. This is especially the case for motorcycles: there are precious few mechanics in Jordan able to deal with the average modern motorcycle and its problems.

The **Royal Automobile Club of Jordan** (☎ 06-5850626, for carnets 4622467; www.racj.com) can arrange a carnet if you are bringing your own car.

Checkpoints

You may pass through checkpoints in Jordan, particularly when driving along the Dead Sea Highway near the sensitive border with Israel and the Palestinian Territories, or on the roads that climb out of the Jordan Valley. Always stop at checkpoints. Foreigners are generally waved through without any fuss, though you may have to show your passport. As such, always keep your passport, driving licence, hire agreement and registration papers handy.

Fuel & Spare Parts

The volatility of petrol prices in Jordan is forcing up inflation and causing a knock-on effect for all prices, even the cost of hay (which has to be collected by vehicle). At the time of writing, *benzin 'adi* (regular) petrol costs around 540 fils per litre, and the slightly less frequently available *mumtaz* (super) costs 620 fils. These prices are

ROAD DISTANCES (KM)

	Ajloun	Amman	Aqaba	Azraq	Bethany	Irbid	Jerash	Karak	King Hussein Bridge	Ma'an	Madaba	Ramtha	Safi	Tafila	Umm Qais	Wadi Musa (Petra)
Amman	73															
Aqaba	396	328														
Azraq	155	103	415													
Bethany	83	40	290	135												
Irbid	32	89	408	143	115											
Jerash	22	51	370	132	85	38										
Karak	182	118	252	205	235	202	164									
King Hussein Bridge	78	56	367	152	30	109	89	151								
Ma'an	279	212	116	289	245	294	255	154	252							
Madaba	95	32	325	119	35	115	77	86	64	210						
Ramtha	57	94	410	141	135	28	40	205	430	296	118					
Safi	170	135	180	385	105	198	189	50	105	130	85	240				
Tafila	242	180	189	266	140	267	229	63	215	90	151	296	40			
Umm Qais	55	115	425	160	145	25	70	215	130	325	145	40	225	265		
Wadi Musa (Petra)	297	230	97	317	220	313	275	142	268	45	228	316	140	81	305	
Wadi Rum	368	290	40	370	320	380	335	257	355	95	315	370	245	180	405	100

almost certain to have risen since the publication of this book. Remember to check
with your car-hire company as to which
petrol your car requires; most take super.
Unleaded petrol (*khal min ar-rasas)* is only
reliably available in Amman and even then
at only a few stations. Diesel is available at
about 320 fils per litre.

Petrol stations are run by the state-
monopoly Jordan Petroleum Refinery
Company. Stations can mostly be found on
the outskirts of major towns, and at some
junctions. Along the Desert Highway there
are plenty of stations. There are fewer along
the King's Highway, and *very* few along the
Dead Sea Highway.

Garages with handy mechanics can be
found in the outskirts of most towns. They
can handle most repairs, at negotiable
prices, but if it's not your car, always check
with your car-hire company before getting
anything done.

4WDs

Four-wheel drives are only necessary if
you're going to remote parts of the desert,
such as Burqu. You are highly advised to
have prior experience of off-road driving
before hiring a 4WD: driving in soft sand
in 45°C heat, for example, is a recipe for
disaster if you don't know what you're
doing.

Four-wheel-drive vehicles can be hired
from reputable agencies in Aqaba (p259)
and Amman (p116); they are far more expensive than normal sedans, costing at least
JD75 per day. Also, companies only offer
100 to 200 free kilometres; you then pay
extra for each kilometre.

To get around Wadi Rum, you'll need
to charter a 4WD jeep: these almost always
come with a local driver. You can, however,
drive your own 4WD in the area if you are
an experienced off-road driver (see p273).

Hire

Hiring a car is a great way of getting the
most out of Jordan and for exploring off-
the-beaten-track.

There's no great need to hire a car to
travel to places like Petra and Jerash, which
are well served by public transport and
which need a day or more to be explored
properly on foot; or to Wadi Rum, where a
4WD invariably comes with a local driver.

Hiring a car to travel along the King's Highway, however, which is not well served by
public transport, makes good sense and
opens up lots of possible side trips almost
unthinkable if relying on the bus.

There are many car-hire agencies in
Amman, a few in Aqaba and one or two
irregularly staffed offices at Queen Alia
airport and the King Hussein border with
Israel and the Palestinian Territories. Most
car-hire agencies outside these areas usually
consist of an office with one guy, one desk,
one telephone and one car for hire (usually
his!). The best deals are in Amman (see
p116), where competition among agencies
is fierce.

The following are some of the more reliable agencies. Charges, conditions, drop-
off fees, insurance costs and waiver fees in
case of accident vary considerably so shop
around. Daily rates run at around JD25 to
JD30, and weekly rates at JD140 to JD200.
This doesn't include tax or petrol, but usually includes free unlimited kilometres. You
can normally drop off the rental car in another city (eg Aqaba), for a fee of around
JD25.

Always read your contract carefully before signing; remember that many places
require a minimum three days' hire and all
require a deposit of up to JD400 payable
upon pick-up (usually by credit card) and
refunded upon the return of the car.

Avis (Map p87; ☎ 06-5699420, 24hr 777-397405; www
.avis.com.jo; King Abdullah Gardens, Amman) Offices
at King Hussein Bridge and Aqaba, and branches at the
airport, Le Royal Hotel & Jordan InterContinental Hotel.
The biggest car-hire company in Jordan.

Budget (Map p87; ☎ 06-5698131; www.budget.com;
125 Abdul Hameed Sharaf St, Amman)

Europcar (Map p87; ☎ 06-5655581, 800-22270; www
.europcar.middleeast.com; Isam Al-Ajlouni St, Amman)
Branches at Radisson SAS, King Abdullah Gardens and in
Aqaba (Map p248).

Hertz (Map p87; ☎ 06-5624191, 24hr line at airport
06-4711771; www.hertz.com; King Abdullah Gardens,
Amman) Offices at the airport, Grand Hyatt Amman,
Sheraton & in Aqaba (Map p248).

Reliable Rent-a-Car (Map p87; ☎ 06-5929676, 079-
5521358; www.rentareliablecar.com; 19 Fawzi al-Qawegli
St, Amman) Cars JD20 to JD25. Offers free drop-off and
pick-up in Madaba or the airport, will deliver the car to you
anywhere in Amman and will even drive you to the edge
of town if you are nervous about Amman traffic. Contact
Mohammed Hallak.

TRANSPORT

To ensure that you don't break down in the middle of nowhere, you should always hire a car less than three years old – most reputable companies won't offer anything else. Most hire cars have air-con and a heater, which is a godsend in summer or winter. Cars with automatic transmission are more expensive, but these are a boon to anyone not used to driving in mountain terrain or on the right-hand side of the road. Road maps are not provided by car-hire agencies, but child-restraining seats are generally available for an extra fee.

Some agencies are closed on Friday and public holidays. If so, prearrange collection and delivery to avoid longer hire periods. Check the car over with a staff member for bumps, scratches and obvious defects, and check brakes, tyres etc before driving off.

Most agencies only hire to drivers over 21 years old; some stipulate that drivers must be at least 26 years. It's not possible to drive a hire car from Jordan into neighbouring countries.

Insurance

Most car-hire rates come with basic insurance that involves a deductible of up to JD400 (ie in case of an accident you pay a maximum of JD400). Most agencies offer additional Collision Damage Waiver (CDW) insurance for an extra JD7 to JD10 per day, which will absolve you of all accident costs (in some cases a maximum of JD100 excess).

Insurance offered by major companies often includes Personal Accident Insurance and Theft Protection, which may be covered by your travel insurance policy from home. Always read the conditions of the contract carefully before signing – an English translation should always be provided.

If you're driving into Jordan in a private vehicle, compulsory third-party insurance must be purchased at the border for about JD35 (valid for one month). You also pay a nominal customs fee of JD5 for 'foreign car registration'.

Road Conditions

The condition of the roads varies; unsigned speed humps are common, as are shallow ditches across the road, usually at the entrance to a town.

If you're driving around Jordan, read the following carefully:

- Signposting is erratic – generally enough to get you on your way but not enough to get you all the way to the destination.
- Many road signs are in English, but they are sometimes badly transliterated (eg 'Om Qeis' for Umm Qais or, our favourite, 'AT TA NOURAN I QUI ES SI' for the At-Tannour Antiquities Site!). Brown signs denote tourist attractions, blue signs are for road names and green signs are for anything Islamic, such as a mosque.
- Take care when it's raining: water and sand (and sometimes oil) make a lethal combination on the roads.
- The Jordanian road system makes more use of U-turns than flyovers.
- One-way streets are often not signposted and can be fiendish in Karak and Irbid.
- Always watch out for obstacles: pedestrians who walk along the road; cars darting out of side roads; and herds of goats and camels, even on the major highways.
- Roundabouts are often large, and all drivers (local and foreign) find them totally confusing.
- Petrol stations are not that common, so fill up as often as you can.
- Parking in major towns, especially Amman, is a problem, but it's easy to find (and normally free) at major attractions like Jerash, Petra and Madaba.
- Most roads (and even the highways) are dangerous at night because white lines are not common, obstacles (eg herds of camels) are still roaming about, and some cars have no headlights or, worse, use only high beam.
- Jordanians are extremely reluctant to commit to a single lane, so there's a lot of straddling of two lanes and overtaking using the slow lane.

Road Hazards

Despite the small population, and relatively well-maintained roads, accidents are alarmingly frequent. In 2007 there was one death every 9.4 hours from road accidents.

The roads where accidents are more common are those frequented by long-distance trucks; eg the short stretch of Hwy 65 (south of Aqaba to the Saudi border) and Hwys 10 and 40 east of Amman.

In the case of an accident in a hire car, don't move the vehicle. Get a policeman from the local station to attend the scene immediately, get a police report (Arabic is OK) and contact the car-hire company. Not obtaining a police report will normally invalidate your insurance. Depending on where you are, most companies will send someone to the scene within hours. If there's any serious injury to you or someone else, contact your travel insurance company at home as well as your embassy/consulate in Amman.

If your own private car is involved in an accident, your driving licence and passport will be held by the police until the case has been finalised in a local court – which may take weeks.

Drivers are always considered guilty if they hit a pedestrian, regardless of the circumstances.

Telephone numbers for local police stations are mentioned throughout the book, but two numbers (☎ 191 and ☎ 192) are valid for police emergencies anywhere in Jordan, and should be answered by English-speaking staff.

Road Rules

Visitors from any country where road rules are rigorously obeyed may be shocked by the traffic in Jordan, especially in Amman. Indicators are seldom used, the ubiquitous horn is preferred over slowing down and pedestrians must take their chances. But anyone who has driven elsewhere in the Middle East may find the traffic comparatively well behaved. Provided that you can keep driving in Amman down to a minimum and plan how to get to your destination, you're unlikely to encounter too many difficulties if you take reasonable care.

Vehicles drive on the right-hand side of the road in Jordan. The general speed limit inside built-up areas is 50km/h or 70km/h on multilane highways in Amman, and 90km/h to 110km/h on the national highways.

Wearing a seat belt is now compulsory, though many Jordanians are reluctant to use them. Traffic police are positioned at intervals along the highways. Police tend to be fairly indulgent towards foreigners, as long as they do nothing serious.

TRANSPORT

HITCHING A RIDE WITH THE POLICE *Jenny Walker*

It was 20 years ago and springtime had brought to the hillsides of Northern Amman abundant bouquets of wildflowers. There were pastel-shaded anemones, bright yellow rock roses and occasional splashes of blood red poppies. But where, I wanted to know, was the elusive black iris, the national flower of Jordan?

After several days searching for this magnificent velvet-petalled king of the flower world, I finally gave up and began to make my way along the King's Highway.

It had been a long wait by the dusty roadside. The occasional rambling Peugeot spluttered by on cheap petrol. A languid hand draped from a half-opened window indicated that it would be quicker for me to walk than to hazard a ride in such an assembly of spare parts. I resigned myself to another long hike. At that moment, a police car rounded the corner, and to my consternation, pulled in front of me. Three policemen viewed me suspiciously and asked what I was doing alone and unchaperoned. I must have seemed harmless enough because they invited to take me to the next town.

A while later, I looked out of the car window at the very place in which a large clump of iris was growing lustily by the side of the road. 'Stop!' I shouted excitedly. 'Look, the iris!' The police dutifully backed up and we all hopped out to see. Before I could whip my camera from the bag, one of the policemen had an iris round the throat while the other two were grappling with its roots. 'No!' I cried. 'I don't' want to take it. I just want a photo!' Somewhat bemused, they reverently patted the startled iris back into its roadside bed, let me take my photo, and delivered me to the next town as promised.

I've just returned to the same spot on the highway. Remarkably, the only other car on the road was a police car whose driver honked the horn good-naturedly and left me alone to root around under the olive trees. And there they were: not just one clump, but three: perhaps they are evidence of a new national pride in the environment I didn't witness two decades ago. Or perhaps, as I'd rather like to think, they multiplied in thanks for a good deed.

TRANSPORT

HITCHING
Getting a Ride

Hitching is never entirely safe in any country in the world. Travellers who choose to hitch should understand that they are taking a small but potentially serious risk. People who choose to hitch will be safer if they travel in pairs and let someone know where they are planning to go.

Despite this general advice, hitching is quite feasible in Jordan, especially in areas where public transport is limited or nonexistent, such as parts of the King's Highway and to the desert castles east of Amman.

Always start hitching early, and avoid 1pm to 4pm when it's often too hot and traffic is reduced while many locals enjoy a siesta. Somewhat surprisingly, police stationed at major junctions and checkpoints are often happy to wave down drivers and cajole them into giving you a lift. You may even be given a ride by the police themselves (see the boxed text, p321).

To indicate that you're looking for a lift, simply raise your index finger in the direction you're heading. On a large truck, you may be asked for a fare; in a private vehicle, you should ask if payment is expected and, if so, how much the driver wants. Otherwise, just offer a small amount when you get out – it will often be refused.

Finally, a few general tips. Make sure you carry a hat and lots of water; don't look too scruffy; don't hitch in groups of more than two; take extra care if you are a woman; and avoid riding in trucks on steep and windy roads (eg between the Wadi Rum turn-off and Aqaba) as they can be painfully slow.

Picking up Hitchhikers

Although there's no obligation to give anyone a ride, if you're driving a private or hired car, it's hard not to feel a twinge of guilt as you fly past weary-looking locals. On remote stretches like the Wadi Mujib stretch of the King's Highway, where public transport is limited or nonexistent, it's courteous to give a ride or two. Besides, it's a great way to meet Jordanian people. You should never charge a local for these lifts. They will assume, probably fairly, that any foreigner driving a private or hired car doesn't need the extra money.

LOCAL TRANSPORT
Bus

The two largest cities, Amman and Irbid, have efficient and cheap public bus networks. That said, few buses have destination signs in English (although some have 'English' numbers), there are no schedules or timetables available and local bus stations are often chaotic. Service taxis are much more useful and still inexpensive.

Taxi

There are two main types of taxis in Jordan. Yellow private taxis work like ordinary taxis. White service (servees) taxis run along set routes within and between many towns, as well as between Jordan and neighbouring countries.

Both service taxis and private taxis can be chartered. Hiring a service taxi for a day is usually cheaper than hiring your own car. To charter a service taxi along a set route (eg Aqaba to Ma'an), find out the standard fare per person and then pay for all the seats in a car (normally four). A long-distance trip in a private taxi costs more, but drivers are more amenable to stops and side trips.

If the taxi driver doesn't speak English, use the Arabic script in this guidebook or ask a local who does speak English to write down the destination(s) in Arabic.

PRIVATE TAXI

Yellow private taxis are very common in major towns like Amman, Irbid, Jerash, Ma'an, Madaba, Wadi Musa (Petra) and Aqaba, as well as around important transport junctions like Shuneh al-Janubiyyeh (South Shuna) and Tafila. There is no pricing standard among taxis. Taxis in Amman are metered and most drivers will use the meter; in Wadi Musa there is a standard fare of JD1 anywhere in town; elsewhere you'll just have to negotiate a reasonable fare.

Taxis are not expensive in Jordan and, after climbing up and down the *jebels* (hills) of Amman, or staggering around in the infernal summer heat of Aqaba, you'll be glad to fork out the equivalent of less than US$2 for a comfortable air-con ride across town.

Note that metered fares are displayed in fils not dinars and if you proffer the fare in dinars by mistake, the driver is unlikely to correct you.

SERVICE TAXI

Service taxis are usually battered Peugeot 504 or 505 station wagons with seven seats, or Mercedes sedans with five seats. They are always white, and usually have writing and numbers (in Arabic) indicating their route.

Because of the limited number of seats, it usually doesn't take long for one to fill up. They cost up to twice as much as a minibus, and about 50% more than a public bus, but are quicker because they stop less often along the way to pick up passengers. However, they're not always that much more comfortable than a bus or minibus, unless you get the prized front seat. To avoid waiting for passengers, or to give yourself extra room, you can always pay for an extra seat.

Lone female travellers should always ask to sit in the front seat if the back is jammed with men, otherwise it's worth paying for an extra seat. If chartering a taxi, single females should always sit in the back.

Major cities, such as Amman and Irbid, are well served by service taxis that run along set routes within each city, and often go to (or past) places of interest to visitors. As with intercity service taxis, the route is listed in Arabic on the driver's door and drivers wait until they are full before departing.

TOURS

An alternative to a pricey group tour organised from abroad is to arrange your own private mini-tour with a Jordanian travel agency. Many of these can arrange hiking or archaeological itineraries and provide a car and driver.

For hiking and activities in Jordan's nature reserves you are best off contacting the tourism department of the **Royal Society for the Conservation of Nature** (RSCN; www.rscn.org.jo), which can arrange short activity breaks or entire itineraries (see p72). For an extended trip to Wadi Rum it's best to contact a local Bedouin agency such as **Wadi Rum Mountain Guides** (www.bedouinroads.com).

If you're travelling independently, and on a tight budget, jumping on a budget-priced organised tour from Amman to a remote place like the desert castles of eastern Jordan is far easier, and often cheaper, than doing it yourself. See p105.

The following local agencies are reliable:

Alia Tours (☎ 06-5620501; www.aliatours.com.jo) Standard tours.

Atlas Travel & Tourist Agency (☎ 06-4642034; www.atlastours.net) Also offers side trips to Israel and the Palestinian Territories, Syria and Lebanon.

Desert Guides Company (☎ 06-5527230, 079-5532915; www.desertguidescompany.com) Trekking, mountain-bike and adventure trips.

Golden Crown Tours (☎ 06-5511200; www.goldencrowntours.com) Offers archaeological, religious and adventure tours.

Jordan Beauty Tours (☎ 079-5581644, 077-7773978; www.jordanbeauty.com; Petra)

Jordan Direct (☎ 06-5938238; www.jdtours.com; Boumedien St, Amman) Located in Amin Marie Complex.

Jordan Inspiration Tours (☎ 03-2157317, 079-5554677; www.jitours.com; Petra)

Jordan Select Tours (☎ 06-5930588; www.select.jo) High-end tours.

La Beduina (☎ 03-2157099; www.labeduinatours.com)

Petra Moon (☎ 0302156665; www.petramoon.com; Wadi Musa) A professional agency that also offers an interesting range of treks in remote areas of Petra and Dana.

Royal Tours (☎ 06-5857154; www.royaltours.com.jo) Part of Royal Jordanian, and good for stopover packages.

Zaman Tours & Travel (☎ 03-2157723; www.zamantours.com; Wadi Musa) Adventure tours, camping, camel treks and hiking.

TRANSPORT

Health

CONTENTS

Prevention is the key to staying healthy when travelling in the Middle East. Infectious diseases can and do occur in Jordan, but these can be avoided with a few precautions. The most common reason for travellers needing medical help is as a result of traffic accidents. Medical facilities in Jordan are generally very good, particularly in Amman.

BEFORE YOU GO

A little planning before departure, particularly for pre-existing illnesses, will save you a lot of trouble later. See your dentist before a long trip; carry a spare pair of contact lenses and glasses (and take your optical prescription with you); and carry a first-aid kit with you.

It's tempting to leave it all to the last minute – don't! Many vaccines don't ensure immunity for two weeks, so visit a doctor four to eight weeks before departure.

Bring medications in their original, clearly labelled, containers. A signed and dated letter from your physician describing your medical conditions and medications, including generic names, is also a good idea. If carrying syringes or needles, be sure to have a physician's letter documenting their medical necessity.

INSURANCE

Find out in advance if your insurance plan will make payments directly to providers or reimburse you later for overseas health expenditures; it's also worth ensuring your travel insurance will cover repatriation home or transport to better medical facilities elsewhere. Your insurance company may be able to locate the nearest source of medical help, or you can ask at your hotel. In case

---

REQUIRED & RECOMMENDED VACCINATIONS

The following vaccinations are recommended for most travellers to Jordan, though you should check with your local health provider:

- diphtheria & tetanus – single booster recommended if you've had none in the previous 10 years
- hepatitis A – a single dose at least two to four weeks before departure gives protection for up to a year; a booster 12 months later gives another 10 years or more of protection
- hepatitis B – now considered routine for most travellers
- measles, mumps and rubella – two doses of MMR recommended unless you have previously had the diseases. Young adults may require a booster.
- polio – generally given in childhood and should be boosted every 10 years
- typhoid – recommended if you're travelling for more than a couple of weeks
- yellow fever – vaccination is required for entry into Jordan for all travellers over one year of age if coming from infected areas such as sub-Saharan Africa, and parts of South America

For more information on these diseases and vaccinations, see Infectious Diseases, p326.

of an emergency, contact your embassy or consulate. Your travel insurance will not usually cover you for anything other than emergency dental treatment. Not all insurance covers emergency aeromedical evacuation home or to a hospital in a major city, which may be the only way to get medical attention for a serious emergency.

See p296 for more information on insurance.

RECOMMENDED VACCINATIONS

Plan ahead for getting your vaccinations: some of them require more than one injection, while some vaccinations should not be given together. Note that some vaccinations should not be given during pregnancy or to people with allergies – discuss this with your doctor.

MEDICAL CHECKLIST

Following is a list of other items you should consider packing in your medical kit.
- acetaminophen/paracetamol (Tylenol) or aspirin
- adhesive or paper tape
- antibacterial ointment (eg Bactroban) for cuts and abrasions
- antibiotics (if travelling off-the-beaten-track)
- antidiarrhoeal drugs (eg loperamide)
- antihistamines (for hay fever and allergic reactions)
- anti-inflammatory drugs (eg ibuprofen)
- bandages, gauze, gauze rolls
- insect repellent containing DEET (for the body)
- insect spray containing Permethrin (for clothing, tents and bed nets)
- iodine tablets or other water-purification tablets
- oral rehydration salts
- scissors, safety pins, tweezers
- steroid cream or cortisone (for allergic rashes)
- sunblock
- thermometer

INTERNET RESOURCES

There is a wealth of travel-health advice on the internet. For further information, the Lonely Planet website (www.lonelyplanet .com) is a good place to start. The World Health Organization (www.who.int/ith) publishes a superb book, *International*

Travel and Health, which is revised annually and is available online at no cost.

Another website of general interest is MD Travel Health (www.mdtravelhealth.com), which provides complete travel-health recommendations for every country, updated daily, also at no cost.

The Center for Disease Control (www.cdc.gov) offers a useful overview of the health issues facing travellers to Jordan and neighbouring countries.

The US embassy in Amman has a list of recommended doctors in Jordan at http://us embassy-amman.org.jo/cons/doctors.doc.

FURTHER READING

Lonely Planet's *Healthy Travel – Asia & India* is packed with useful information including pre-trip planning, emergency first aid, immunisation and disease information and what to do if you get sick on the road. Other recommended references include *Traveller's Health* by Dr Richard Dawood, *International Travel Health Guide* by Stuart R Rose, MD and *The Travellers' Good Health Guide* by Ted Lankester, an especially useful health guide for volunteers and long-term expatriates working in the Middle East.

IN TRANSIT

DEEP VEIN THROMBOSIS (DVT)

Deep vein thrombosis occurs when blood clots form in the legs during plane flights, chiefly because of a prolonged immobility. The longer the flight is, the greater the risk. Though most clots are reabsorbed uneventfully, some may break off and travel through the blood vessels to the lungs, where they may cause life-threatening complications.

The chief symptom of DVT is swelling or pain of the foot, ankle or calf, usually but not always on just one side. When a blood

HEALTH

clot travels to the lungs, it may cause chest pain and difficulty in breathing. Travellers with any of these symptoms should immediately seek medical attention.

To prevent the development of DVT on long flights you should walk about the cabin, perform isometric compressions of the leg muscles (ie contract the leg muscles while sitting), drink plenty of fluids, and avoid alcohol and tobacco.

JET LAG & MOTION SICKNESS

Jet lag is common when crossing more than five time zones; it results in insomnia, fatigue, malaise or nausea. To avoid jet lag, drink plenty of fluids (non-alcoholic) and eat light meals. Upon arrival, seek exposure to natural sunlight and readjust your schedule (for meals, sleep etc) as soon as possible.

Antihistamines such as dimenhydrinate (Dramamine) and meclizine (Antivert, Bonine) are usually the first choice for treating motion sickness. Their main side-effect is drowsiness. A herbal alternative is ginger, which works like a charm for some people.

IN JORDAN

AVAILABILITY & COST OF HEALTH CARE

There are modern, well-equipped public hospitals in Amman, Irbid, Aqaba and Karak; smaller hospitals in Madaba, Ramtha and Zarqa; and basic health centres in most other towns. Jordan also has over 50 private hospitals, which cater primarily to patients from neighbouring countries, particularly the Gulf States, who are attracted by lower medical costs. Emergency treatment not requiring hospitalisation is free in Jordan.

Most towns have well-stocked pharmacies, but check the expiry date of medicine you buy in Jordan. It is better to bring any unusual or important medical items with you from home, together with a copy of a prescription. The telephone numbers for pharmacies (including those open at night) in Amman and Irbid, and for hospitals in Amman, Zarqa, Irbid and Aqaba, are listed in the English-language newspapers. All doctors (and most pharmacists) who have studied in Jordan speak English because medicine is taught in English at Jordanian universities, and many have studied abroad. Dental surgeries are also fairly modern and well-equipped.

For minor illnesses such as diarrhoea, pharmacists can often provide valuable advice, and sell over-the-counter medication.

For an ambulance in Jordan call ☎ 193.

INFECTIOUS DISEASES
Diphtheria & Tetanus

Diphtheria is spread through close respiratory contact. It causes a high temperature and severe sore throat. Sometimes a membrane forms across the throat requiring a tracheostomy to prevent suffocation. Vaccination is recommended for those likely to be in close contact with the local population in infected areas. The vaccine is given as an injection alone, or with tetanus (you may well have had this combined injection as a child), and lasts 10 years.

Hepatitis A

Hepatitis A is spread through contaminated food (particularly shellfish) and water. It causes jaundice and, although it is rarely fatal, can cause prolonged lethargy and delayed recovery. Symptoms include dark urine, a yellow colour to the whites of the eyes, fever and abdominal pain. Hepatitis A vaccine (Avaxim, VAQTA, Havrix) is given as an injection; hepatitis A and typhoid vaccines can also be given as a single-dose vaccine, hepatyrix or viatim.

Hepatitis B

Infected blood, contaminated needles and sexual intercourse can all transmit hepatitis B. It can cause jaundice, and affects the liver, occasionally causing liver failure. All travellers should make this a routine vaccination. (Many countries now give hepatitis B vaccination as part of routine childhood vaccination.) The US Center for Disease Control says the level of hepatitis B is high in Jordan. The vaccine is given singly, or at the same time as the hepatitis A vaccine (hepatyrix). A course will give protection for at least five years. It can be given over four weeks, or six months.

HIV

This is spread via infected blood and blood products, sexual intercourse with an infected partner and from an infected mother to her newborn child. It can be spread through 'blood to blood' contacts such as contaminated instruments during medical and dental procedures, acupuncture, body-piercing and sharing used intravenous needles.

Reliable figures aren't available about the number of people in Jordan with HIV or AIDS, but given the strict taboos in Jordanian society about drugs, homosexuality and promiscuity, the disease is relatively rare. Contracting HIV through a blood transfusion is about as unlikely as in most Western countries, and anyone needing serious surgery will probably be sent home anyway.

You may need to supply a negative HIV test in order to get a second visa extension for a stay of longer than three months.

Polio

Generally spread through either contaminated food or water, polio is one of the vaccines given in childhood and should be boosted every 10 years, either orally (a drop on the tongue), or as an injection. Polio may be carried asymptomatically, although it can cause a transient fever and, in rare cases, potentially permanent muscle weakness or paralysis. Polio is not currently present in Jordan but is prevalent in neighbouring countries.

Rabies

Spread through bites or licks on broken skin from an infected animal, rabies is fatal. Animal handlers should be vaccinated, as should those travelling to remote areas where a reliable source of post-bite vaccine is not available within 24 hours. Three injections are needed over a month. If you've come into physical contact with an infected animal and haven't been vaccinated you'll need a course of five injections starting within 24 hours or as soon as possible after the injury. Vaccination does not provide you with immunity, it merely buys you more time to seek appropriate medical help.

Tuberculosis

Tuberculosis (TB) is spread through close respiratory contact and occasionally through infected milk or milk products. BCG vaccine is recommended for those likely to be mixing closely with the local popula-

tion. It is more important for those visiting family or planning on a long stay, and those employed as teachers and health-care workers. TB can be asymptomatic, although symptoms can include cough, weight loss or fever, months or even years after exposure. An X-ray is the best way to confirm if you have TB. BCG gives a moderate degree of protection against TB. It causes a small permanent scar at the site of injection, and is usually only given in specialised chest clinics. As it's a live vaccine it should not be given to pregnant women or immunocompromised individuals. The BCG vaccine is not available in all countries.

Typhoid

This is spread through food or water that has been contaminated by infected human faeces. The first symptom is usually fever or a pink rash on the abdomen. Septicaemia (blood poisoning) may also occur. Typhoid vaccine (typhim Vi, typherix) will give protection for three years. In some countries, the oral vaccine Vivotif is also available.

Yellow Fever

Yellow-fever vaccination is not required for Jordan but you *do* need a yellow-fever certificate, from a designated clinic, if arriving from an infected area, or if you've been in an infected area in the two weeks prior to arrival in Jordan.

TRAVELLER'S DIARRHOEA

Becoming sick from unhygienic food preparation in Jordan is slim, especially if you follow this advice:

- Avoid tap water unless it has been boiled, filtered or chemically disinfected (iodine tablets)
- Beware of ice cream that may have melted and then been refrozen (eg a power cut in the last day or two)
- Be careful of shellfish such as mussels, oysters and clams, particularly outside of Aqaba, as well as the raw-meat dishes available in Lebanese restaurants
- Eat meals only at busy restaurants and be cautious of buffets that may have been standing for more than a day.

If you do develop diarrhoea, be sure to drink plenty of fluids, preferably an oral-rehydration solution containing salt and

HEALTH

sugar (weak black tea with a little sugar, soda water, or soft drinks allowed to go flat and diluted 50% with clean water are also good). In an emergency you can make up a solution of six teaspoons of sugar and half a teaspoon of salt to a litre of boiled or bottled water.

A few loose stools don't require treatment but if you start having more than four or five stools a day, you should start taking an antibiotic (usually a quinolone drug) and an antidiarrhoeal agent (such as loperamide). If diarrhoea is bloody, persists for more than 72 hours, is accompanied by fever, shaking chills or severe abdominal pain, you should seek medical attention.

Where this is not possible the recommended drugs for bacterial diarrhoea (the most likely cause of severe diarrhoea in travellers) are norfloxacin 400mg twice daily for three days or ciprofloxacin 500mg twice daily for five days. These drugs are not recommended for children or pregnant women. The drug for children is cotrimoxazole, with dosage dependent on weight. A five-day course is given. Ampicillin or amoxycillin may be given to pregnant women, but medical care is necessary.

ENVIRONMENTAL HAZARDS

Jordan is not a dangerous place to visit but it does have a few hazards unique to desert environments. While heat-related problems are the most common, don't forget that the desert can be bitterly cold in winter: there is a real risk of hypothermia if camping between December and February without adequate bedding. For hazards connected with swimming, diving or snorkelling, see p283.

Heat Illness

Read this section carefully, especially if you are travelling to Jordan between May and September. Despite the warnings, some visitors get themselves into trouble hiking through the desert in the heat of the day, especially around Wadi Rum.

Heat exhaustion occurs following heavy sweating and excessive fluid loss with inadequate replacement of fluids and salt. This is particularly common in hot climates when taking unaccustomed exercise before full acclimatisation. Symptoms include headache,

dizziness and tiredness. Dehydration already occurs by the time you feel thirsty – aim to drink sufficient water to produce pale, diluted urine. The treatment of heat exhaustion consists of fluid replacement with water or fruit juice or both, and cooling by cold water and fans. The treatment of the salt-loss component consists of salty fluids as in soup or broth, and adding a little more table salt to foods than usual.

Heat stroke is much more serious. This occurs when the body's heat-regulating mechanism breaks down. Excessive rise in body temperature leads to sweating ceasing, irrational and hyperactive behaviour and eventually loss of consciousness and death. Rapid cooling by spraying the body with water and fanning is an ideal treatment. Emergency fluid and electrolyte replacement by intravenous drip is usually also required.

Insect Bites & Stings

Mosquitoes may not carry malaria but can cause irritation and infected bites. Using DEET-based insect repellents will prevent bites. Mosquitos also spread dengue fever.

Bees and wasps only cause real problems to those with a severe allergy (anaphylaxis). If you have a severe allergy to bee or wasp stings you should carry an adrenaline injection or similar. For general bug bites, calamine lotion or a sting-relief spray will give relief and ice packs will reduce the pain and swelling.

Scorpion stings are notoriously painful and in Jordan can sometimes be fatal, especially for young children. Scorpions often shelter in shoes or clothing so check your shoes in the morning, particularly if you are camping in the vicinity of Little Petra.

Bed bugs are often found in hostels and cheap hotels. They lead to very itchy lumpy bites. Spraying the mattress with an appropriate insect killer will get rid of them; better still, find a better hotel!

Scabies are also frequently found in cheap accommodation. These tiny mites live in the skin, particularly between the fingers. They cause an intensely itchy rash. Scabies is easily treated with lotion available from pharmacies; people who you come into contact with also need treating to avoid spreading scabies between asymptomatic carriers.

Snakebite

To minimise your chances of being bitten always wear boots, socks and long trousers when walking through undergrowth where snakes may be present. Don't put your hands into holes and crevices, and be careful when collecting firewood.

Half of those bitten by venomous snakes are not actually injected with poison (envenomed). If bitten by a snake, do not panic. Immobilise the bitten limb with a splint (eg a stick) and apply a bandage over the site, with firm pressure, similar to bandaging a sprain. Do not apply a tourniquet, or cut or suck the bite. Get the victim to medical help as soon as possible so that antivenin can be given if necessary.

Water

Tap water in Jordan is generally safe to drink, but for a short trip it's better to stick to bottled water; alternatively boil water for 10 minutes, use water purification tablets or a filter. In the Jordan Valley, amoebic dysentery can be a problem. The tap water in southern Jordan, particularly Wadi Rum, comes from natural springs at Diseh and so is extremely pure.

TRAVELLING WITH CHILDREN

All travellers with children should know how to treat minor ailments and when to seek medical treatment. Make sure the children are up to date with routine vaccinations, bearing in mind some vaccines are not suitable for children under one year old.

In hot, humid climates any wound or break in the skin may lead to infection. The area should be cleaned and then kept dry and clean. Remember to avoid contaminated food and water. If your child is vomiting or experiencing diarrhoea, lost fluid and salts must be replaced. It may be helpful to take rehydration powders for reconstituting with boiled water. Ask your doctor about this.

Children should be encouraged to avoid dogs or other mammals because of the risk of rabies and other diseases. Any bite, scratch or lick from a warm-blooded, furry animal should be thoroughly cleaned. If there is any possibility that the animal is infected with rabies, immediate medical assistance should be sought.

Travel with Children from Lonely Planet includes advice on travel health for younger children.

WOMEN'S HEALTH

Emotional stress, exhaustion and travelling through different time zones can all contribute to an upset in the menstrual pattern. If using oral contraceptives, remember that some antibiotics, diarrhoea and vomiting can stop the pill from working and lead to the risk of pregnancy – remember to take condoms with you just in case. Condoms should be kept in a cool, dry place or they may crack and perish.

Emergency contraception is most effective if taken within 24 hours after unprotected sex. The International Planned Parent Federation (www.ippf.org) can advise about the availability of contraception in different countries. Tampons and sanitary towels are easily available in Amman but not necessarily in smaller towns.

Travelling during pregnancy is potentially risky during the first 12 weeks, when miscarriage is most likely, and after 30 weeks, when complications such as high blood pressure and premature delivery can occur. Most airlines will not accept a traveller after 28 to 32 weeks of pregnancy. Antenatal facilities are good in Jordan and medical staff speaks English. Taking written records of the pregnancy, including details of your blood group, is helpful if you need medical attention while away. Ensure your insurance policy covers pregnancy delivery and postnatal care.

HEALTH

Language

CONTENTS

Arabic is Jordan's official language. English is also widely spoken but any effort to communicate with the locals in their own language will be well rewarded. No matter how far off the mark your pronunciation or grammar might be, you'll often get the response (usually with a big smile): 'Ah, you speak Arabic very well!'.

Learning a few basics for day-to-day travelling doesn't take long at all, but to master the complexities of Arabic would take years of consistent study. The whole issue is complicated by the differences between Classical Arabic (*fus-ha*), its modern descendant MSA (Modern Standard Arabic) and regional dialects. The classical tongue is the language of the Quran and Arabic poetry of centuries past. For a long time it remained static, but in order to survive it had to adapt to change, and the result is more or less MSA, the common language of the press, radio and educated discourse. It is as close to a *lingua franca* (common language) as the Arab world comes, and is generally understood – if not always well spoken – across the Arab world.

Fortunately, the spoken dialects of Jordan are not too distant from MSA. For outsiders trying to learn Arabic, the most frustrating element nevertheless remains understanding the spoken language. There is virtually no written material to refer to for back-up, and acquisition of MSA in the first place is itself a long-term investment. An esoteric argument flows back and forth about the relative merits of learning MSA first (and so perhaps having to wait some time before being able to communicate adequately with people in the street) or focusing your efforts on a dialect. If all this gives you a headache, you'll have some idea as to why so few non-Arabs, or non-Muslims, embark on a study of the language.

PRONUNCIATION

Pronunciation of Arabic in any of its guises can be tongue-tying for someone unfamiliar with the intonation and combination of sounds. Pronounce the transliterated words slowly and clearly.

This language guide should help, but bear in mind that the myriad rules governing pronunciation and vowel use are too extensive to be covered here.

Vowels

Technically, there are three long and three short vowels in Arabic. The reality is a little different, with local dialect and varying consonant combinations affecting their pronunciation (this is the case throughout the Arabic-speaking world). More like five short and five long vowels can be identified; in this guide we use all but the long 'o' (as in 'or').

a	as in 'had'
aa	as the 'a' in 'father'
e	short, as in 'bet'; long, as in 'there'
i	as in 'hit'
ee	as in 'beer', only softer
o	as in 'hot'
u	as in 'put'
oo	as in 'food'

Consonants

Pronunciation for all Arabic consonants is covered in the alphabet table, right. Note that when double consonants occur in the

THE STANDARD ARABIC ALPHABET

Final	Medial	Initial	Alone	Transliteration	Pronunciation
ﺎ			ﺍ	aa	as in 'father'
ﺐ	ﺒ	ﺑ	ﺏ	b	as in 'bet'
ﺖ	ﺘ	ﺗ	ﺕ	t	as in 'ten'
ﺚ	ﺜ	ﺛ	ﺙ	th	as in 'thin'
ﺞ	ﺠ	ﺟ	ﺝ	j	as in 'jet'
ﺢ	ﺤ	ﺣ	ﺡ	H	a strongly whispered 'h', like a sigh of relief
ﺦ	ﺨ	ﺧ	ﺥ	kh	as the 'ch' in Scottish *loch*
ﺪ			ﺩ	d	as in 'dim'
ﺬ			ﺫ	dh	as the 'th' in 'this'
ﺮ			ﺭ	r	a rolled 'r', as in the Spanish word *caro*
ﺰ			ﺯ	z	as in 'zip'
ﺲ	ﺴ	ﺳ	ﺱ	s	as in 'so', never as in 'wisdom'
ﺶ	ﺸ	ﺷ	ﺵ	sh	as in 'ship'
ﺺ	ﺼ	ﺻ	ﺹ	ṣ	emphatic 's'
ﺾ	ﻀ	ﺿ	ﺽ	ḍ	emphatic 'd'
ﻂ	ﻄ	ﻃ	ﻁ	ṭ	emphatic 't'
ﻆ	ﻈ	ﻇ	ﻅ	ẓ	emphatic 'z'
ﻊ	ﻌ	ﻋ	ﻉ	'	the Arabic letter *'ayn*; pronounce as a glottal stop – like the closing of the throat before saying 'Oh-oh!' (see Tricky Sounds, p332)
ﻎ	ﻐ	ﻏ	ﻍ	gh	a guttural sound like Parisian 'r'
ﻒ	ﻔ	ﻓ	ﻑ	f	as in 'far'
ﻖ	ﻘ	ﻗ	ﻕ	q	a strongly guttural 'k' sound; also often pronounced as a glottal stop
ﻚ	ﻜ	ﻛ	ﻙ	k	as in 'king'
ﻞ	ﻠ	ﻟ	ﻝ	l	as in 'lamb'
ﻢ	ﻤ	ﻣ	ﻡ	m	as in 'me'
ﻦ	ﻨ	ﻧ	ﻥ	n	as in 'name'
ﻪ	ﻬ	ﻫ	ﻩ	h	as in 'ham'
ﻮ			ﻭ	w	as in 'wet'
				oo	long, as in 'food'
				ow	as in 'how'
ﻲ	ﻴ	ﻳ	ﻱ	y	as in 'yes'
				ee	as in 'beer', only softer
				ai/ay	as in 'aisle'/as the 'ay' in 'day'

Vowels Not all Arabic vowel sounds are represented in the alphabet. For more information on the vowel sounds used in this language guide, see Vowels (left).

Emphatic Consonants To simplify the transliteration system used in this book, the emphatic consonants have not been included.

transliterations, both are pronounced. For example, the word *al-hammam* (toilet), is pronounced 'al-ham-mam'.

TRICKY SOUNDS

Arabic has two sounds that are very tricky for non-Arabs to produce: the 'ayn and the glottal stop. The letter 'ayn represents a sound with no English equivalent that comes even close. It is similar to the glottal stop (which is not actually represented in the alphabet), but the muscles at the back of the throat are gagged more forcefully and air is released – it has been described as the sound of someone being strangled. In many transliteration systems 'ayn is represented by an opening quotation mark, and the glottal stop by a closing quotation mark. To make the transliterations in this language guide (and throughout the rest of the book) easier to use, we have not distinguished between the glottal stop and the 'ayn, using the closing quotation mark to represent both sounds. You should find that Arabic speakers will still understand you.

TRANSLITERATION

It's worth noting here that transliteration from the Arabic script into English – or any other language for that matter – is at best an approximate science.

The presence of sounds unknown in European languages and the fact that the script is 'incomplete' (most vowels are not written) combine to make it nearly impossible to settle on one universally accepted method of transliteration. A wide variety of spellings is therefore possible for words when they appear in Latin script – and that goes for places and people's names as well.

The whole thing is further complicated by the wide variety of dialects and the imaginative ideas Arabs themselves often have on appropriate spelling in, say, English (words spelt one way in Jordan may look very different again in Syria and Lebanon, with strong French influences); not even the most venerable of Western Arabists have been able to come up with a satisfactory solution.

While striving to reflect the language as closely as possible and aiming at consistency, this book generally anglicises place, street and hotel names (and the like) as the

locals have done. Don't be surprised if you come across several versions of the same thing.

ACCOMMODATION

I'd like to book a ...	*biddee ehjuz ...*
Do you have a ...?	*fi ...?*
(cheap) room	*ghurfa (rkheesa)*
single room	*ghurfa mufrada*
double room	*ghurfa bi sareerayn*
for one night	*li layli waHde*
for two nights	*layltayn*
May I see it?	*mumkin shoofa?*
It's very noisy/dirty.	*kteer dajeh/wuskha*
How much is it per person?	*'addaysh li kul waHid?*
How much is it per night?	*'addaysh bel layli?*
Where is the bathroom?	*wayn al-Hammam?*
We're leaving today.	*niHna musafireen al-youm*
address	*al-'anwaan*
air-conditioning	*kondishon/mookayif*
blanket	*al-bataaniyya/al-Hrem*
camp site	*mukhayam*
electricity	*kahraba*
hotel	*funduq/otel*
hot water	*mai saakhina*
key	*al-miftaH*
manager	*al-mudeer*
shower	*doosh*
soap	*saboon*
toilet	*twalet/bet al-mai*

CONVERSATION & ESSENTIALS

Arabs place great importance on civility and it's rare to see any interaction between people that doesn't begin with profuse greetings, enquiries into the other's health and other niceties.

Arabic greetings are more formal than in English and there is a reciprocal response to each. These sometimes vary slightly, depending on whether you're addressing a man or a woman. A simple encounter can become a drawn-out affair, with neither side wanting to be the one to put a halt to the stream of greetings and well-wishing. As an *ajnabi* (foreigner), you're not expected to know all the ins and outs, but if you come up with the right expression at the appropriate moment the locals will love it.

The most common greeting is *salaam alaykum* (peace be upon you), to which the correct reply is *wa alaykum as-salaam* (and upon you be peace). If you get invited to a birthday celebration or are around for any of the big holidays, the common greeting is *kul sana wa intum bikher* (I wish you well for the coming year).

After having a bath or shower, you will often hear people say to you *na'iman*, which roughly means 'heavenly' and boils down to an observation along the lines of 'nice and clean now, eh'.

Arrival in one piece is always something to be grateful for. Passengers will often be greeted with *il-Hamdu lillah al as-salaama* (thank God for your safe arrival).

Hi.	*marHaba*
Hi. (response)	*marHabtain*
Hello.	*ahlan wa sahlan* or just *ahlan* (Welcome)
Hello. (response)	*ahlan beek/i* (m/f)

It's an important custom in Jordan to ask after a person's or their family's health when greeting, eg *kayf es-saHa?* (How is your health?), *kayf il'ayli?* (How is the family?). The response is usually *bikher il-Hamdu lillah* (Fine, thank you).

Goodbye.	*ma'a salaama/Allah ma'ak*
Good morning.	*sabaH al-khayr*
Good morning. (response)	*sabaH 'an-noor*
Good evening.	*masa' al-khayr*
Good evening. (response)	*masa 'an-noor*
Good night.	*tisbaH 'ala khayr*
Good night. (response)	*wa inta min ahlu*

Yes.	*aiwa/na'am*
Yeah.	*ay*
No.	*la*
Please. (request)	*min fadlak/fadleek* (m/f)
Please. (polite)	*law samaHt/samaHti* (m/f)
Please. (come in)	*tafaddal/tafaddali* (m/f)/ *tafaddaloo* (pl)
Thank you.	*shukran*
Thank you very much.	*shukran kteer/ shukran jazeelan*
You're welcome.	*'afwan* or *tikram/tikrami* (m/f)
One moment, please.	*lahza min fadlak/i* (m/f)
Pardon/Excuse me.	*'afwan*

Sorry!	*aasif/aasifa!* (m/f)
No problem.	*mafi mushkili/moo mushkila*
Never mind.	*ma'alesh*
Just a moment.	*laHza*
Congratulations!	*mabrouk!*

Questions like 'Is the bus coming?' or 'Will the bank be open later?' generally elicit the response: *in sha' Allah* (God willing), an expression you'll hear over and over again. Another common one is *ma sha' Allah* (God's will be done), sometimes a useful answer to probing questions about why you're not married yet.

How are you?	*kayf Haalak/Haalik?* (m/f)
How're you doing?	*kayfak/kayfik?* (m/f)
Fine thank you.	*bikher il-Hamdu lillah*
What's your name?	*shu-ismak/shu-ismik?* (m/f)
My name is ...	*ismi ...*
Pleased to meet you. (when departing)	*fursa sa'ida*
Nice to meet you. (lit: you honour us)	*tasharrafna*
Where are you from?	*min wayn inta/inti?* (m/f)
I'm from ...	*ana min ...*
Do you like ...?	*inta/inti bitHeb ...?* (m/f)
I like ...	*ana bHeb ...*
I don't like ...	*ana ma bHeb ...*

I	*ana*
you	*inta/inti* (m/f)
he	*huwa*
she	*hiyya*
we	*niHna*
you	*into*
they	*homm*

DIRECTIONS

How do I get to ...?	*keef boosal ala ...?*
Can you show me (on the map)?	*mumkin tfarjeeni ('ala al-khareeta)?*
How many kilometres?	*kam kilometre?*
What street is this?	*shoo Hal shanki had?*
on the left	*'ala yasaar/shimaal*
on the right	*'ala yameen*
opposite	*muqaabil*
straight ahead	*dughri*
at the next corner	*tanee mafraq*
this way	*min hon*
here/there	*hon/honeek*
in front of	*amaam/iddaam*

SIGNS

Entrance	مدخل
Exit	خروج
Open	مفتوح
Closed	مغلق
Prohibited	ممنوع
Information	معلومات
Hospital	مستشفي
Police	شرطة
Men's Toilet	حمام للرجال
Women's Toilet	حمام للنساء

near	qareeb
far	ba'eed
north	shimaal
south	janub
east	sharq
west	gharb

EMERGENCIES

Help me!	saa'idoonee!
I'm sick.	ana mareed/mareeda (m/f)
Call the police!	ittusil bil shurta!
doctor	duktoor/tabeeb
hospital	al-mustash-fa
police	ash-shurta
Go away!	imshee!/rouh min hoon!
Shame (on you)!	aayb!
(said by woman)	

HEALTH

I'm ill.	ana maareed/mareeda (m/f)
My friend is ill.	sadeeqi maareed (m)/
	sadeeqati maareeda (f)
It hurts here.	beeyujani hon

I'm ...	andee ...
asthmatic	azmitrabo
diabetic	sukkari
epileptic	saraa/alsaa'a

I'm allergic ...	andee Hasasiyya ...
to antibiotics	min al-mudad alHayawi
to aspirin	min al-aspireen
to penicillin	min al-binisileen
to bees	min al-naHl
to nuts	min al-mukassarat

antiseptic	mutahhi
aspirin	aspireen/aspro (brand name)
Band-Aids	plaster

chemist/pharmacy	as-sayidiliyya
condoms	kaboot
contraceptive	waseela lee mana' al-Ham
diarrhoea	is-haal
fever	Harara
headache	wajaa-ras
hospital	mustashfa
medicine	dawa
pregnant	Hamel
prescription	wasfa/rashetta
sanitary napkins	fuwat saHiyya
stomach ache	wajaa fil battu
sunblock cream	krem waki min ashilt al-shams
tampons	kotex (brand name)

LANGUAGE DIFFICULTIES

Do you speak English?	bitiHki ingleezi?
I understand.	ana afham
I don't understand.	ana ma bifham

I speak ...	ana baHki ...
English	ingleezi
French	faransi
German	almaani

I speak a little Arabic.	ana baHki arabi shway
I don't speak Arabic.	ana ma beHki arabi
I want an interpreter.	biddee mutarjem
Could you write it down, please?	mumkin tiktabhu, min fadlak?
How do you say ... in Arabic?	kayf t'ul ... bil'arabi?

NUMBERS

0	sifr	٠
1	waHid	١
2	itnayn/tintayn	٢
3	talaata	٣
4	arba'a	٤
5	khamsa	٥
6	sitta	٦
7	saba'a	٧
8	tamanya	٨
9	tis'a	٩
10	'ashara	١٠
11	yeeda'sh	١١
12	yeetnaa'sh	١٢
13	talaatash	١٣
14	arbatash	١٤
15	khamastash	١٥
16	sittash	١٦
17	sabatash	١٧
18	tamantash	١٨
19	tasatash	١٩

LANGUAGE

20	'ashreen	٢٠
21	wHid wa 'ashreen	٢١
22	itnayn wa 'ashreen	٢٢
30	talaateen	٣٠
40	arba'een	٤٠
50	khamseen	٥٠
60	sitteen	٦٠
70	saba'een	٧٠
80	tamaneen	٨٠
90	tis'een	٩٠
100	miyya (meet before a noun)	١٠٠
200	miyyatayn	٢٠٠
1000	'alf	١٠٠٠
2000	'alfayn	٢٠٠٠
3000	talaat-alaf	٣٠٠٠

PAPERWORK

date of birth	tareekh al-meelad/-wilaada
name	al-ism
nationality	al-jenseeya
passport	jawaz al-safar (or paspor)
permit	tasriH
place of birth	makan al-meelad/-wilaada
visa	visa/ta'shira

SHOPPING & SERVICES

| I'm looking for ... | ana abHath ... aa'n |
| Where is the ...? | wayn/fayn ...? |

bank	al-bank
beach	ash-shaati'/al-plaaj/al-baHr
chemist/pharmacy	as-sayidiliyya
city/town	al-medeena
city centre	markaz al-medeena
customs	al-jumruk
entrance	al-dukhool/al-madkhal
exchange office	al-masref/al-saraf
exit	al-khurooj
hotel	al-funduq/al-otel
information desk	isti'laamaat
laundry	al ghaseel
market	al-sooq
mosque	al-jaami'/al-masjid
museum	al-matHaf
newsagents	al-maktaba
old city	al-medeena al-qadeema/ al-medeena l'ateeqa
passport & immigration office	maktab al-jawazaat wa al-hijra
police	ash-shurta
post office	maktab al-bareed
restaurant	al-mata'am
telephone office	maktab at-telefon/ maktab al-haalef

| temple | al-ma'abad |
| tourist office | maktab al-siyaHa |

I want to change ...	baddee sarref ...
money	masaari
travellers cheques	sheeket siyaHiyya

What time does it open?	emta byeftaH?
What time does it close?	emta bi sakkir?
I'd like to make a telephone call.	mumkin talfen min fadlak

Where can I buy ...?	wayn/fayn feeni eshtiree ...?
What is this?	shu hada?
How much?	addaysh/bikam?
How many?	kim waHid?
How much is it?	bi addaysh?
That's too expensive.	hada ghalee kheteer
Is there ...?	fee ...?
There isn't (any).	ma fee
May I look at it?	mumkin shoof?

big/bigger	kbeer/akbar
cheap/cheaper	rkhees/arkhas
closed	msakkar
expensive	ghaali
money	al-fuloos/al-masaari
open	maftuH
small/smaller	sagheer/asghar

TIME & DATES

What's the time?	addaysh essa'aa?
When?	emta?
now	halla'
after	b'adayn
on time	al waket
early	bakkeer
late	ma'qar
daily	kil youm
today	al-youm
tomorrow	bukra
day after tomorrow	ba'ad bukra
yesterday	imbaarih
minute	daqeeqa
hour	saa'a
day	youm
week	usboo'
month	shahr
year	sana
morning	soubeH
afternoon	ba'ad deher
evening	massa
night	layl

LANGUAGE

Monday	al-tenayn
Tuesday	at-talaata
Wednesday	al-arba'a
Thursday	al-khamees
Friday	al-jum'a
Saturday	as-sabt
Sunday	al-aHad

The Western Calendar Months

The Islamic year has 12 lunar months and is 11 days shorter than the Western calendar, so important Muslim dates will occur 11 days earlier each (Western) year.

There are two Western calendars in use in the Arab world. In Egypt and westwards, the months have virtually the same names as in English (January is *yanaayir*, October is *octobir* and so on), but in Lebanon and eastwards, the names are quite different. Talking about, say, June as 'month six' is the easiest solution, but for the sake of completeness, the months from January are:

January	kanoon ath-thani
February	shubaat
March	azaar
April	nisaan
May	ayyaar
June	Huzayraan
July	tammooz
August	'aab
September	aylool
October	tishreen al-awal
November	tishreen ath-thani
December	kaanoon al-awal

The Hejira Calendar Months

1st	MoHarram
2nd	Safar
3rd	Rabi' al-Awal
4th	Rabay ath-Thaani
5th	Jumaada al-Awal
6th	Jumaada al-Akhira
7th	Rajab
8th	Shaban
9th	Ramadan
10th	Shawwal
11th	Zuul-Qeda
12th	Zuul-Hijja

TRANSPORT
Public Transport

Where is the ...?	wayn/fayn ...?
airport	al-mataar
bus station	maHattat al-baas/ maHattat al-karaj

ticket office	maktab at-tazaakar
train station	maHattat al-qitaar

What time does the ... leave/arrive?	ay saa'a biyitla'/biyusal ...?
boat/ferry	al-markib/as-safeena
(small) boat	ash-shakhtura
bus	al-baas
plane	al-teeyara
train	al-qitaar

Which bus goes to ...?	aya baas biyruH 'ala ...?
I want to go to ...	ana badeh ruH ala ...
Does this bus go to ...?	hal-baas biyruH 'ala ...?
How many buses per day go to ...?	kam baas biyruH ben nahar ...?
How long does the trip take?	kam sa'a ar-riHla?
Please tell me when we get to ...	'umal ma'aroof illee lamma noosal la ...
Stop here, please.	wa'if hoon 'umal ma'aroof
Please wait for me.	'umal ma'aroof istanna
May I sit here?	mumkin a'ood hoon?
May we sit here?	mumkin ni'ood hoon?

1st class	daraja oola
2nd class	daraja taaniya
ticket	at-tazaakar
to/from	ila/min

Private Transport

I'd like to hire a ...	biddee esta'jer ...
Where can I hire a ...?	wayn/fayn feeni esta'jer ...?
bicycle	bisklet
camel	jamal
car	sayyaara
donkey	Hmaar
4WD	jeep
horse	Hsaan
motorcycle	motosikl
tour guide	al-dalee as-siyaaHi/ al-murshid as-siyaaHi

Is this the road to ...?
Hal Haza al-tareeq eela ...?
Where's a service station?
wayn/fayn maHaltet al-benzeen?
Please fill it up.
min fadlak (emla/abee) Ha
I'd like (30) litres.
biddee talaateen leeter

diesel	deezel
petrol	benzeen

(How long) can I park here?
  (kam sa'a) mumkin aas-f hon?
Where do I pay?
  fayn/wayn mumkin an addf'aa?
I need a mechanic.
  bidee mekaneesyan
The car/motorbike has broken down (at ...).
  al-sayyaara/-mutusikl it'atlit ('an ...)
The car/motorbike won't start.
  al-sayyaara/-mutusikl ma bit door
I have a flat tyre.
  nzel al-doolab
I've run out of petrol.
  mafi benzeen or *al-benzeen khalas*
I've had an accident.
  aamalt hads

TRAVEL WITH CHILDREN

Is there a/an ...?	*fee ...?*
I need a/an ...	*biddee ...*
car baby seat	*kursee sayyaara leel bebe'*
disposable nappies	*pamperz* (brand name)
nappies (diapers)	*Ha fa daat*
formula (baby's milk)	*Haleeb bebe'*
highchair	*kursee atfaal*
potty	*muneeyai*
stroller	*arabeyet atfaal*

Do you mind if I breastfeed here?
  mumkin aradda hon?
Are children allowed?
  Hal yousmah leel atfaal?

Also available from Lonely Planet:
Middle East Phrasebook

Glossary

This glossary lists terms used in this book that may be unfamiliar to those living outside Jordan. Most are Arabic words commonly used in Jordan but some abbreviations are also included. See the boxed text (opposite) for architectural terminology, which may come in handy when visiting the sights of Petra and Jerash.

abu – father of...
agal – black headrope used to hold a keffiyeh in place
ain (ayoun) – spring or well
amir – see *emir*
arak – alcoholic spirit
ASEZA – Aqaba Special Economic Zone Authority
Ayyubid dynasty – the dynasty founded by *Saladin* (Salah ad-Din) in Egypt in 1169

bab (abwab) – gate
Badia – stony desert
Bedouin (pl Bedu) – nomadic desert dweller
beit – house
beit ash-sha'ar – goat-hair Bedouin tent
bin – son of...; also *ibn*

caliph – Islamic ruler
caravanserai – large inn enclosing a courtyard, providing accommodation and a marketplace for caravans
Circassians – Muslims from the Caucasus who emigrated to Jordan in the 19th century

Decapolis (Latin) – literally '10 cities'; this term refers to a number of ancient cities in the Roman Empire, including Amman and Jerash
deir – monastery

eid – Islamic feast
Eid al-Adha – Feast of Sacrifice marking the pilgrimage to Mecca
Eid al-Fitr – Festival of Breaking the Fast, celebrated throughout the Islamic world at the end of Ramadan
emir – Islamic ruler, leader, military commander or governor; literally 'prince'

haj – the pilgrimage to Mecca
hammam(at) – natural hot springs; also a Turkish steam bath
haram – forbidden area
hejab – woman's headscarf

ibn – son of...; also *bin*
il-balad – downtown; the centre of town
imam – religious leader

jebel – hill or mountain
JETT – Jordan Express Travel & Tourism, the major private bus company in Jordan
JTB – Jordan Tourism Board

keffiyeh – checked scarf worn by Arab men
kilim – flat, woven mat
Koran – see *Quran*
Kufic – a type of highly stylised old Arabic script

maidan – town or city square
malek – king
malekah – queen
Mamluk dynasty – literally 'slaves'; Muslim dynasty named for a former slave and soldier class
medina – old walled centre of any Islamic city
mezze – starters, appetisers
mihrab – niche in the wall of a mosque that indicates the direction of Mecca
minaret – tower on top of a mosque
muezzin – mosque official who calls the faithful to prayer, often from the *minaret*

Nabataean – ancient trading civilisation based around Petra
nargileh – water pipe used to smoke tobacco (used mainly by men)

oud – Arabic lute

PLO – Palestine Liberation Organisation

qala'at – castle or fort
qasr – castle or palace
qibla – direction of Mecca
Quran – holy book of Islam
qusayr – small castle or palace

Ramadan – Muslim month of fasting
RSCN – Royal Society for the Conservation of Nature

Saladin – (Salah ad-Din in Arabic) Kurdish warlord who re-took Jerusalem from the Crusaders; founder of the *Ayyubid dynasty*
servees – service taxi
sheesha – see nargileh

AND A TRICLINIUM IS…?

Reading a guidebook to some of Jordan's most famous sights can seem like an exercise in linguistics – including Latin, Nabataean, Greek, Arabic and the languages of geography and classical architecture. Listen to any tour guide, especially at Petra, and you'll assume they're expert in all of them. But you don't have to be a polyglot to make the most of Jordan's wonders. Have a quick *shoofti* (Arabic word meaning 'you (female) looked') at the glossary of architectural terms below and you'll soon know your pediments from your porticos.

agora – open meeting space for commerce
baetyls – divine stones
capitals – carved tops of columns
cardo maximus – Roman main street, running north-south
colonnade – row of columns
Corinthian – look for fluted columns with leafy capitals
decumanus – Roman main street, from east to west
Doric – look for unfluted columns with plain capitals
high place – sacred site on mountain-top
loculi – grave
necropolis – cemetery
nymphaeum – literally 'temple of the Nymphs'; public baths, fountains and pools
pediment – triangular crowning feature on front of building
portico – structure supported by columns
propylaeum – gateway or grand entrance
stele – commemorative stone or column with inscriptions
temenos – sacred courtyard
tetrapylon – an archway with four entrances
triclinium – Roman dining room

sheikh – venerated religious scholar, dignitary or venerable old man
siq – gorge or canyon (usually created by tectonic forces rather than by wind or water)
souq – market

tell – ancient mound created by centuries of urban rebuilding
Trans-Jordan – Jordan's original name

Umayyad dynasty – first great dynasty of Arab Muslim rulers
umm – mother of…
UNRWA – UN Relief & Works Agency

wadi – valley or river bed formed by watercourse, dry except after heavy rainfall (plural: widyan)

zerb – Bedouin oven, buried in the sand

The Authors

JENNY WALKER
Coordinating Author

Jenny Walker's first involvement with Jordan was as a student, while conducting research for a dissertation on Doughty and Lawrence (BA, University of Stirling). This experience, together with many other firsthand encounters with the Middle East, led to a subsequent thesis entitled *Perception of the Arabic Orient* for a postgraduate research degree at the University of Oxford. Jenny has written extensively on the Middle East for Lonely Planet and with her husband authored *Off-Road in the Sultanate of Oman*, a country they've lived and worked in for more than a decade. Jenny has travelled in over 95 countries – from Panama to Mongolia – on diverse assignments.

For this edition, Jenny wrote the Destination; Getting Started; Itineraries; History; The Culture; Environment; Food & Drink; Dead Sea Highway; King's Highway; Petra; Aqaba, Wadi Rum & the Desert Highway; Directory; and Transport chapters.

MATTHEW D FIRESTONE

Matthew is a trained biological anthropologist and epidemiologist, though he abandoned a promising academic career in favour of spending his youth living out of a backpack. With his best explorer's hat and hiking boots in hand, Matthew blazed a trail across Jordan in the footsteps of Indiana Jones. Although an excursion to Petra failed to reveal the final location of the Holy Grail, Matthew's travels took him from the depths of the Red Sea to the western border of Iraq. He may not have found eternal life, but at least he found a bit of adventure – and a whole lot of sand.

For this edition, Matthew wrote the Amman, Jerash & the North, The Desert Castles, and Diving & Snorkelling chapters.

LONELY PLANET AUTHORS

Why is our travel information the best in the world? It's simple: our authors are passionate, dedicated travellers. They don't take freebies in exchange for positive coverage so you can be sure the advice you're given is impartial. They travel widely to all the popular spots, and off the beaten track. They don't research using just the internet or phone. They discover new places not included in any other guidebook. They personally visit thousands of hotels, restaurants, palaces, trails, galleries, temples and more. They speak with dozens of locals every day to make sure you get the kind of insider knowledge only a local could tell you. They take pride in getting all the details right, and in telling it how it is. Think you can do it? Find out how at **lonelyplanet.com**.

CONTRIBUTING AUTHORS

Ethan Gelber wrote The Community-Based Travel Trail, p22. Ethan has been a responsible sojourner, and writing about it, since he first hefted his backpack 25 years ago. His passion for bicycle touring, communication and community development in travel has led to him guiding bicycle tours, founding an educational, nonprofit, internet adventure (www.bikeabout.org), creating responsible travel resources for Sri Lanka (www.localternative.com), media wrangling for a global network of sustainable travel booking websites (www.whl.travel) and authoring three Lonely Planet cycling guides.

Dr Alon Tal wrote The Dead Sea is Dying, p173. He founded the Israel Union for Environmental Defense and the Arava Institute for Environmental Studies, and has served as chair of Life and Environment, Israel's umbrella group for green organisations. Professor of the Desert Ecology Department at Ben-Gurion University, he heads the Jewish National Fund's sustainable development committee and still finds time to hike and bike around Israel with his wife and daughters.

Hassan Ansah wrote Empowering Palestinian Refugees, p144. Hassan is a freelance writer and journalist who has taught at the Western International University in Phoenix, Arizona, USA, and at the American University in Cairo (AUC), Egypt.

Behind the Scenes

THIS BOOK

This 7th edition of Jordan was researched and written by Jenny Walker (coordinating author) and Matthew D Firestone. For details of who wrote which chapter, see p340. Other authors made special contributions: Hassan Ansah wrote Empowering Palestinian Refugees (p144), Kerryn Burgess wrote A Day Out at the Border Crossing (p311), Ethan Gelber wrote The Community- Based Travel Trail (p22) and Dr Alon Tal wrote The Dead Sea is Dying (p173). The Health chapter was adapted from material written by Dr Caroline Evans. The 6th edition of Jordan was researched and written by Bradley Mayhew, the 5th edition by Anthony Ham, and earlier editions by Paul Greenway and Damien Simonis. This guidebook was commissioned in Lonely Planet's Melbourne office and produced by the following:

Commissioning Editors Kerryn Burgess, Emma Gilmour
Coordinating Editor Dianne Schallmeiner
Coordinating Cartographer Alex Leung
Coordinating Layout Designer Margaret Jung
Managing Editor Geoff Howard
Managing Cartographers Adrian Persoglia, Amanda Sierp
Managing Layout Designer Laura Jane
Assisting Editors Jackey Coyle, Peter Cruttenden

Assisting Cartographers Ross Butler, Mick Garrett, Csanad Csutoros
Cover Designer James Hardy
Colour Designer Carlos Solarte
Project Manager Eoin Dunlevy
Language Content Coordinator Quentin Frayne

Thanks to Shahara Ahmed, Sasha Baskett, Melanie Dankel, Sally Darmody, Mark Germanchis, Lisa Knights, Wibowo Rusli

THANKS
JENNY WALKER

It has been a great pleasure meeting the people of Jordan for this project and I was quickly reminded why Jordan is such a wonderful country. I'd like to extend special thanks to Chris Johnson (Director, RSCN) and other RSCN officials for their generous time. The legendary Ruth of Jordan Jubilee; Marguerite van Geldermalsen; Tyler Norris (executive director), Daniel Adamson and Mahmoud Twaisi of Abraham Path Initiative; Charl, owner of Mariam Hotel; Suzie and Tahseen of Beit Ali; Mayzoon X, Agnes Quadros and Xavier Hay also deserve a special mention. Many thanks to my fellow author, Matthew Firestone, who has persuaded me that the light blues (from Cambridge) can be trusted after

---

THE LONELY PLANET STORY

Fresh from an epic journey across Europe, Asia and Australia in 1972, Tony and Maureen Wheeler sat at their kitchen table stapling together notes. The first Lonely Planet guidebook, *Across Asia on the Cheap*, was born.

Travellers snapped up the guides. Inspired by their success, the Wheelers began publishing books to Southeast Asia, India and beyond. Demand was prodigious, and the Wheelers expanded the business rapidly to keep up. Over the years, Lonely Planet extended its coverage to every country and into the virtual world via lonelyplanet.com and the Thorn Tree message board.

As Lonely Planet became a globally loved brand, Tony and Maureen received several offers for the company. But it wasn't until 2007 that they found a partner whom they trusted to remain true to the company's principles of travelling widely, treading lightly and giving sustainably. In October of that year, BBC Worldwide acquired a 75% share in the company, pledging to uphold Lonely Planet's commitment to independent travel, trustworthy advice and editorial independence.

Today, Lonely Planet has offices in Melbourne, London and Oakland, with over 500 staff members and 300 authors. Tony and Maureen are still actively involved with Lonely Planet. They're travelling more often than ever, and they're devoting their spare time to charitable projects. And the company is still driven by the philosophy of *Across Asia on the Cheap*: 'All you've got to do is decide to go and the hardest part is over. So go!'

all. Thanks also to our expert contributors, Ethan Gelber and Dr Alon Tal. I reserve an especially large thank you for the commissioning editor, Kerryn Burgess, whose contribution to this book extends well beyond the brief and whose professional input I both cherish and enjoy. As ever, I'm hugely grateful to my beloved husband, Sam Owen, for his unwavering endeavours in this project. We enjoyed exceptional times over the course of our three research trips to Jordan and I think it shows!

MATTHEW D FIRESTONE

As I do in all of my books, I'd like to thank first and foremost my family for their unwavering support despite my increasing love for exotic (and at times) dangerous travel. To my mom and dad, thanks for continuing to approve of my Lonely Planet lifestyle, even though I keep turning down assignments in Western Europe for ones in the Middle East and Africa. To my millionaire sister, thanks for continually reminding me how sketchy I am, even though this time around I wasn't permitted to cross the Iraqi border! Second, I'd like to thank Kerryn for giving me the opportunity to return to the Middle East, and to once again follow in the footsteps of my lifelong hero, Dr Indiana Jones. And of course, I'd like to give a shout out to my coordinating author Jenny, who did a fine job of convincing me that not all people from Oxford are that bad (go Cambridge!!). Finally, I can't forget my roommate, hermano and all-around partner in crime, Tac, for keeping me sane throughout the writing process.

OUR READERS

Many thanks to the travellers who used the last edition and wrote to us with helpful hints, useful advice and interesting anecdotes:

Karin Amna, Edward Archer, Sara Bassam, Rene Bendt, Rein Berkers, Mark Brechtl, Rachel Carlin, Richard Cassem, Henry

Cheape, Nina Collins, Conny De Waal, Sandra Dietze, Nawaf Fageir, Lia Genovese, Laura Griffith, Helen Haworth, Yvonne Hermkens, Luisa Houck, Tony Howard, Fedor Hrnciar, Yiannis Kompatsiaris, Roberta Lima, David Locke, Robert Marcus, Peter Marsh, Erinn Maury, Tala Momani, Amit Morali, Margarete Neuwirth, Funda Ozan, Yen Phung, Jeremy Polmear, Adrian Schmidt, Ulrike Schneider, Sabina Schreck, Paul Smith, Emanuela Tasinato, Stephan Tenhaef, Denise Turcinov, Aodeh Zlabeh

ACKNOWLEDGMENTS
Many thanks to the following for the use of their content:

Globe on title page ©Mountain High Maps 1993 Digital Wisdom, Inc.

Index

GreenDex

GOING GREEN

Want your travels in Jordan to make a difference? Want to feel that your hard-earned cash is going to help preserve and protect Jordan's cultural and natural heritage?

You can do just that by spending your money in places where it will have a positive social, cultural or environmental effect. All you need to do is consult the GreenDex listing below before making a hotel reservation or choosing where to shop, to see whether Lonely Planet authors have given it the green thumbs-up. All the listings have been chosen for their support of local and traditional communities, their nonprofit-making status, their sound environmental practices, or because they demonstrate an active sustainable-tourism policy.

If you would like to contribute to this list for future editions, we'd love to hear from you. Email us at www.lonelyplanet.com/contact. For more about sustainable tourism and Lonely Planet, see www.lonelyplanet.com/responsibletravel.

MAP LEGEND

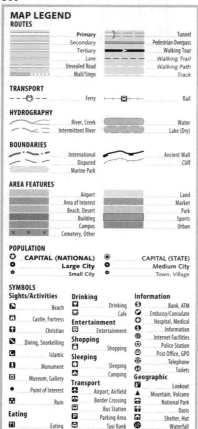

ROUTES

Primary
Secondary
Tertiary
Lane
Unsealed Road
Mall/Steps
Tunnel
Pedestrian Overpass
Walking Tour
Walking Trail
Walking Path
Track

TRANSPORT

Ferry
Rail

HYDROGRAPHY

River, Creek
Intermittent River
Water
Lake (Dry)

BOUNDARIES

International
Disputed
Marine Park
Ancient Wall
Cliff

AREA FEATURES

Airport
Area of Interest
Beach, Desert
Building
Campus
Cemetery, Other
Land
Market
Park
Sports
Urban

POPULATION

○ **CAPITAL (NATIONAL)**
● **Large City**
● Small City
◉ **CAPITAL (STATE)**
● **Medium City**
○ Town, Village

SYMBOLS

Sights/Activities
Beach
Castle, Fortress
Christian
Diving, Snorkelling
Islamic
Monument
Museum, Gallery
Point of Interest
Ruin

Eating
Eating

Drinking
Drinking
Cafe

Entertainment
Entertainment

Shopping
Shopping

Sleeping
Sleeping
Camping

Transport
Airport, Airfield
Border Crossing
Bus Station
Parking Area
Taxi Rank

Information
Bank, ATM
Embassy/Consulate
Hospital, Medical
Information
Internet Facilities
Police Station
Post Office, GPO
Telephone
Toilets

Geographic
Lookout
Mountain, Volcano
National Park
Oasis
Shelter, Hut
Waterfall

LONELY PLANET OFFICES

Australia
Head Office
Locked Bag 1, Footscray, Victoria 3011
☎ 03 8379 8000, fax 03 8379 8111
talk2us@lonelyplanet.com.au

USA
150 Linden St, Oakland, CA 94607
☎ 510 250 6400, toll free 800 275 8555
fax 510 893 8572
info@lonelyplanet.com

UK
2nd fl, 186 City Rd,
London EC1V 2NT
☎ 020 7106 2100, fax 020 7106 2101
go@lonelyplanet.co.uk

Published by Lonely Planet Publications Pty Ltd
ABN 36 005 607 983

Mixed Sources
Product group from well-managed forests and other controlled sources
www.fsc.org Cert no. SGS-COC-005002
© 1996 Forest Stewardship Council